CASES IN CRIMINAL PROCEDURE, *Continued*

MW00806101

RANK / CASE	HOLDING	VOTE AND MAJORITY OPINION WRITER	CHAPTER IN THE BOOK	PAGE
8.* *Apprendi v. New Jersey,* 530 U.S. 466 (2000)	Judges may not alone determine a finding of fact that increased the level of punishment for the defendant beyond the prescribed statutory maximum. Any fact, other than the fact of prior conviction, must be submitted to a jury and proved beyond a reasonable doubt. A finding of fact cannot be made by the judge alone based on a lower degree of certainty.	5 to 4 Justice Stevens	Not applicable	
9. *Batson v. Kentucky,* 476 U.S. 79 (1986)	A prosecutor's use of peremptory challenges to exclude members of the defendant's race from a jury solely on racial grounds violates the equal protection rights of both the defendant and the excluded jurors.	7 to 2 Justice Powell	12	373
10. *Chimel v. California,* 395 U.S. 752 (1969)	Once a lawful arrest has been made, the police may search any area within the suspect's "immediate control," meaning the area from which the suspect may grab a weapon or destroy evidence.	6 to 2 Justice Stewart	7	205
11. *Spinelli v. United States,* 393 U.S. 410 (1969)	"Innocent-seeming activity and data" and a "bald and unilluminating assertion of suspicion" in an affidavit are not to be given weight in a magistrate's determination of probable cause. An officer may use credible hearsay to establish probable cause, but an affidavit based on an informant's tip must satisfy the two-pronged *Aguilar* test.	5 to 3 Justice Harlan	3	76
12. *United States v. Ross,* 456 U.S. 798 (1982)	If the police legitimately stop a car and have probable cause to believe that it contains contraband, they can conduct a warrantless search of the car. The search can be as thorough as a search authorized by a warrant issued by a magistrate. Therefore, every part of the vehicle in which the contraband might be stored may be inspected, including the trunk and all receptacles and packages that could possibly contain the object of the search.	6 to 3 Justice Stevens	8	247
13. *Payton v. New York,* 445 U.S. 573 (1980)	In the absence of exigent circumstances or consent, the police may not enter a private home to make a routine warrantless arrest.	6 to 3 Justice Stevens	6	161
14. *Oliver v. United States,* 466 U.S. 170 (1984)	A place that is posted with a "No Trespassing" sign, has a locked gate (with a footpath around it), and is located more than a mile from the owner's house has no reasonable expectation of privacy and is considered an open field, unprotected by the Fourth Amendment.	6 to 3 Justice Powell	9	276

Criminal Procedure
LAW AND PRACTICE

Criminal Procedure
LAW AND PRACTICE

TENTH EDITION

Rolando V. del Carmen
Sam Houston State University

Craig Hemmens
Washington State University

CENGAGE
Learning®

Australia • Brazil • Mexico • Singapore • United Kingdom • United States

CENGAGE
Learning®

Criminal Procedure: Law and Practice,
Tenth Edition
Rolando V. del Carmen and Craig Hemmens

Product Director: Marta Lee-Perriard

Senior Product Manager: Carolyn Henderson Meier

Content Developer and Content Project Manager: Christy Frame

Product Assistant: Valerie Kraus

Senior Marketing Manager: Kara Kindstrom

Managing Art Director: Andrei Pasternak

Senior Manufacturing Planner: Judy Inouye

Production Service: Lumina Datamatics Inc.

Text and Cover Designer: Diane Beasley

Cover Images: police officer: ftwitty/ iStockphoto; columns: DHuss/ Getty Images; prison cell: MoreISO/ iStockphoto; law library: SNEHIT/ Shutterstock

For product information and technology assistance, contact us at
Cengage Learning Customer & Sales Support, 1-800-354-9706.

For permission to use material from this text or product,
submit all requests online at **www.cengage.com/permissions**.
Further permissions questions can be e-mailed to
permissionrequest@cengage.com.

Library of Congress Control Number: 2015948337

Student Edition:
ISBN: 978-1-305-57736-7

Loose-leaf Edition:
ISBN: 978-1-305-66018-2

Cengage Learning
20 Channel Center Street
Boston, MA 02210
USA

Cengage Learning is a leading provider of customized learning solutions with employees residing in nearly 40 different countries and sales in more than 125 countries around the world. Find your local representative at **www.cengage.com**.

Cengage Learning products are represented in Canada by Nelson Education, Ltd.

To learn more about Cengage Learning Solutions, visit **www.cengage.com**.

Purchase any of our products at your local college store or at our preferred online store **www.cengagebrain.com**.

Printed in the United States of America
Print Number: 03   Print Year: 2017

This book is dedicated to the many graduate and undergraduate students and law enforcement personnel I have had over the years from whom I have learned so much.

—**Rolando V. del Carmen**

This book is dedicated to my wife and colleague, Mary K. Stohr, and to the many students I have had who have taught me so much.

—**Craig Hemmens**

About the Author

Rolando V. del Carmen is Distinguished Professor of Criminal Justice (Law) in the College of Criminal Justice, Sam Houston State University. In August 2007, he was made a Regents Professor, a rare honor given by the Board of Regents of the Texas State University System. He received his B.A. and LL.B. (the equivalent of a J.D.) degrees from Silliman University in the Philippines, a Master of Comparative Law (M.C.L.) from Southern Methodist University, a Master of Laws (LL.M.) from the University of California, Berkeley, and a Doctor of the Science of Law (J.S.D.) from the University of Illinois in Champaign-Urbana. He has authored numerous books and articles on law and criminal justice and has lectured nationally and internationally on various law-related topics. A recipient of many national and state awards, he has the distinction of having received all three major awards given by the Academy of Criminal Justice Sciences (ACJS): the Academy Fellow Award (1990), the Bruce Smith Award (1997), and the Founder's Award (2005). He has taught numerous graduate and undergraduate classes in law and has been a mentor and friend to many of his students.

Craig Hemmens is Chair and Professor in the Department of Criminal Justice & Criminology at Washington State University. He holds a J.D. from North Carolina Central University School of Law and a Ph.D. in Criminal Justice from Sam Houston State University. He previously served as Department Head and Professor in the Department of Criminology and Criminal Justice at Missouri State University, and as Academic Director of the Paralegal Studies Program, Chair of the Department of Criminal Justice, and Director of the Honors College at Boise State University. Professor Hemmens has published 20 books and more than 200 articles and other writings. His primary research interest is criminal procedure. He has served as the editor of the *Journal of Criminal Justice Education* and on the editorial board of the *Journal of Criminal Justice Education*, *Criminal Justice Review*, the *Prison Journal*, *Criminal Justice Policy Review*, and *Criminal Justice Studies*. His publications have appeared in *Justice Quarterly*, the *Journal of Criminal Justice*, *Crime and Delinquency*, the *Criminal Law Bulletin*, and the *Prison Journal*.

Brief Contents

Contents

CHAPTER 9
Plain View, Open Fields, Abandonment, and Border Searches   262

CHAPTER 10
Lineups and Other Means of Pretrial Identification   289

Preface to the Tenth Edition

THIS BOOK WAS written in an effort to demystify the law and court decisions so they can more effectively guide the conduct of law enforcement officials and in the process properly protect the rights of their constituency. Policing a free society is difficult because it sometimes involves a highly charged situation between the police and a member of the public. That encounter can be nasty and, sometimes, deadly. In a few seconds, the officer may be faced with a life-or-death situation for her or him and the person being confronted. A decision, wrong in hindsight but blurred at that moment, can lead to serious consequences for both parties. In a few instances, there is no margin for error. Police officers must know and understand the law so they become more fully aware of what they can do legally in the course of their high-risk and sometimes dangerous work. Mistakes cannot be eliminated, but are easier for the public to accept when made by the officer in good faith. Students of criminal justice, and all citizens, must understand how the law governs police-citizen encounters.

ORGANIZATION AND CHANGES TO THE TENTH EDITION

The tenth edition retains the format and chapter sequence of the ninth edition. A decision was made early on, after comments were received from the reviewers, that the book's structure and sequence be preserved. Thus, there are no major changes in structure and content in this edition. Reviewers indicated they liked the chapter sequencing and that there were no major topical areas missing. Thus, there are no major changes in structure and content in this edition. There are no chapters added or deleted. One minor change to the organization is the addition of sections: the fifteen chapters are divided into six sections, each containing two to four chapters. We thought this might assist instructors in organizing their presentation of the material and give them a clearer sense of how much time should be spent on each section.

The majority of changes to this edition are designed to update case coverage and related procedural issues. We have also spent considerable effort adding or enhancing coverage of cutting-edge issues such as bail, the use of force, special needs searches, voir dire, stop and frisk, racial profiling, seizures of text and e-mail messages, the use of technology in law enforcement, and much more—all of which we hope results in a more relevant, current, and engaging textbook. We discuss all the recent Supreme Court cases through the most recent (2014–2015) term of the U.S. Supreme Court.

In addition to updating the content in each chapter, we have updated the pedagogical material, including the Chapter Outline, Key Terms, and Top 5 Cases at the beginning of each chapter, and added a new feature, Learning Objectives; the Review Questions, Test Your Understanding, and Recommended Reading at the end of each chapter; and the In Action and Highlight boxes, as well as the margin notes and term definitions. We have also updated Figures and Tables throughout as needed.

Below we note the content changes/updates in each chapter:

Chapter 1 discusses the court system, court cases, and sources of rights. Knowledge of criminal procedure starts with understanding how state and federal courts are structured and work. The student at this early stage must be familiar with the U.S. Constitution and other sources of rights that set boundaries in policing. We have clarified the discussion of incorporation and jurisdiction.

Chapter 2 presents an overview of the criminal justice process, which familiarizes the reader with the entire criminal justice process, from initial contact with the police to the imposition of sanctions after conviction. It is the foundation of understanding subsequent chapters that deal with the specifics of how criminal procedure works. We have added a discussion of recent cases dealing with jury selection and appeals.

Chapters 3 and 4 discuss probable cause, reasonable suspicion, and the exclusionary rule, important terms/concepts in criminal procedure which reoccur throughout the subsequent chapters. We have added a discussion of recent Supreme Court cases dealing with probable cause and reasonable suspicion, and clarified some of the discussion of probable cause.

Chapter 5 discusses stop and frisk and stationhouse detention. Chapter 6 deals with arrests and the use of force during an arrest. These two chapters probe the extent and boundaries of the power of the police when dealing with people, as opposed to things. We have added recent Supreme Court cases on stop and frisk and reasonable suspicion.

Chapters 7, 8, and 9 address searches and seizures of things. This is an important part of policing, but not as crucial as the previous two chapters on searches and seizures of persons. Unless properly organized and separately discussed, this aspect of the Fourth Amendment can be confusing. Some textbooks discuss arrests of persons and searches and seizures of things together—we think this is a major mistake, and something that sets our textbook apart from the competition. Confusion also results if searches and seizures of things, covered in Chapter 7, are discussed together with seizures of motor vehicles, discussed in Chapter 8. These two types of searches (of things and of motor vehicles) are both covered by the Fourth Amendment, but have different rules and are best addressed separately. A discussion of searches and seizures that are not fully protected by the Fourth Amendment, covered in Chapter 9, closes this topic area. These types of searches are best discussed in this section, but deserve a separate chapter because they do not come under the full umbrella of Fourth Amendment protection and are governed by different rules. This chapter includes a discussion of related topics, such as eyewitness testimony and DNA identification that recently have been the subjects of increased discussion and debate. We have added recent Supreme Court cases in these areas, and updated some of the material on arrest, use of force, and third-party searches.

Chapter 10 covers lineups and other means of pretrial identification, and Chapter 11 covers confessions and admissions and *Miranda v. Arizona*. These go together because they are closely related (although their sequence can be interchanged; confessions and admissions can precede pretrial identifications). *Miranda v. Arizona* is arguably the most recognizable case ever decided by the U.S. Supreme Court in any field of law, not just in criminal procedure. It forms the core of any discussion on the admissibility of confessions and admissions and virtually defines day-to-day police work, particularly out in the field. Chapter 11 analyzes that case and cases subsequently decided that refine the various aspects of admissions and confessions. We have added a discussion of recent Supreme Court cases dealing with interrogations and confessions, and clarified some of the discussion of the post-*Miranda* decisions.

Chapter 12 covers five major constitutional rights of the defendant at trial. We have added material on voir dire and jury selection.

Chapter 13 covers sentencing, the death penalty, and other forms of punishment. Although clearly not a part of day-to-day police work, sentencing and punishment give the reader a complete picture of the criminal justice process and represent the ultimate formal result of police work. We have updated the chapter with recent Supreme Court cases dealing with the death penalty, in particular the restrictions on to whom it can be applied.

Chapter 14 covers legal liabilities of public officers and merits a separate chapter because it affects the totality of the police experience and presents a downside in policing. Lawsuits filed against law enforcement agents and agencies have influenced modern-day policing and have led to changes in law enforcement policies and practices. We have added a discussion of recent Supreme Court cases dealing with law enforcement officer liability.

Chapter 15 covers electronic surveillance and the war on terror. Electronic surveillance has been a part of policing for a long time, but what can be done or cannot be done has undergone changes in recent due to legislation and Court refinement of constitutional rules. We have updated this chapter with a discussion of the recent Supreme Court cases dealing with electronic surveillance, as well as current issues in the area. Electronic surveillance and the war on terror are discussed in the last chapter because some courses in criminal procedure include them, whereas others do not.

ANCILLARIES

For the Instructor

MindTap for Criminal Justice from Cengage Learning represents a new approach to a highly personalized, online learning platform. A fully online learning solution, Mind-Tap combines all of a student's learning tools—readings, multimedia, activities, and assessments into a singular Learning Path that guides the student through the curriculum. Instructors personalize the experience by customizing the presentation of these learning tools for their students, allowing instructors to seamlessly introduce their own content into the Learning path via "apps" that integrated into the MindTap platform. Additionally MindTap provides interoperability with major Learning Management Systems (LMS) via support for industry standards and fosters partnerships with third-party educational application providers to provide a highly collaborative, engaging, and personalized learning experience.

Online Instructor's Resource Manual includes learning objectives, key terms, a detailed chapter outline, a chapter summary, lesson plans, discussion topics, student activities, "What If" scenarios, media tools, a sample syllabus, and an expanded test bank with 30 percent more questions than the prior edition. The learning objectives are correlated with the discussion topics, student activities, and media tools.

Online Test Bank Each chapter of the test bank contains questions in multiple-choice, true/false, completion, essay, and new critical thinking formats, with a full answer key. The test bank is coded to the learning objectives that appear in the main text, and includes the section in the main text where the answers can be found. Finally, each question in the test bank has been carefully reviewed by experienced criminal justice instructors for quality, accuracy, and content coverage so instructors can be sure they are working with an assessment and grading resource of the highest caliber.

Cengage Learning Testing Powered by Cognero This assessment software is a flexible, online system that allows you to import, edit, and manipulate test bank content from the *Criminal Procedure* test bank or elsewhere, including your own favorite test questions; create multiple test versions in an instant; and deliver tests from your LMS, your classroom, or wherever you want.

Online PowerPoint® Lectures Helping you make your lectures more engaging while effectively reaching your visually oriented students, these handy Microsoft Power-Point slides outline the chapters of the main text in a classroom-ready presentation. The PowerPoint slides are updated to reflect the content and organization of the new edition of the text, are tagged by chapter learning objective, and feature some additional examples and real-world cases for application and discussion.

For the Student

MindTap for Criminal Justice from Cengage Learning represents a new approach to a highly personalized, online learning platform. A fully online learning solution, MindTap combines all of your learning tools—readings, multimedia, activities, and assessments into a singular Learning Path that guides you through the course.

ACKNOWLEDGMENTS

Changes in the tenth edition reflect written comments and suggestions by the reviewers and editors of the ninth edition. These reviewers are:

Paul McElvein, Erie Community College
James Kellogg, Missouri Baptist University
Greg Plumb, Park University
Gary L. Neumeyer, Arizona Western College

To these colleagues we express thanks for all they have done for this book. They have improved this book in ways too many to list.

All of the reviewers of the tenth and previous editions are highly respected colleagues who teach or have taught courses in criminal procedure. The reviewers of the eighth and other previous editions include Kelly D. Ambrose, Marshall University; Kevin Behr, Coastal Bend College; Beth Bjerregaard, University of North Carolina at Charlotte; Don Bradel, Bemidji State University; Jerry Burnette, New River Community College; William Castleberry, University of Tennessee at Martin; Susan Coleman, West Texas A&M University; Edward Donovan, Metropolitan State College of Denver; Robert Drowns, Metropolitan State University; Catherine Eloranto, Clinton Community College; Jack Enter, Georgia State University, Atlanta; Lorie Fridell, Florida State University; James Hague, Virginia Commonwealth University; Robert Hardgrave, Jr., University of Texas at Austin; William Head, Texas Christian University; Thomas Hickey, Castleton State College; Louis Holscher, San Jose State University; Tom Hughes, University of Louisville; Martrice Hurrah, Shelby State Community College; William D. Hyatt, Western Carolina University; W. Richard Janikowski, University of Memphis; Judith Kaci, California State University at Long Beach; Raymond Kessler, Sul Ross State University; Dave Kramer, Bergen Community College; James Miller, Columbia College; Pamela Moore, University of Texas at Arlington; Patrick Mueller, Stephen F. Austin State University; Gary Neumeyer, Arizona Western College; Robert Pagnani, Columbia-Greene Community College; Robert Peetz, Midland College; Robert Reinertsen, Western Illinois University; Ray Richards, San Jacinto College; Steve Rittenmeyer, Western Illinois University at Macomb; Clifford Roberson, California State University at Fresno; Leo Rowe, Troy University; Lore Rutz-Burri, Southern Oregon University; Joseph Schuster, Eastern Washington State College at Cheney; Pamella Seay, Edison Community College; Caryl Lynn Segal, University of Texas at Arlington; Mark Stevens, North Carolina Wesleyan College; Eric Stewart, Community College of Aurora; Greg Talley, Broome Community College; Roger Turner, Shelby State Community College; Segrest N. Wailes, Jackson State University; Frank Ziegler, Northeastern State University; and Alvin Zumbrun, Catonsville Community College. Their suggestions have guided the revision of this book and have doubtless shaped this book's format and content. We want these esteemed colleagues to know we are deeply and truly grateful.

This tenth and the previous editions would not have been possible without the help of friends and colleagues. Thanks are due to the following for their contributions: Mary K. Stohr of Washington State University, Michael S. Vaughn, Jerry Dowling, and Phillip Lyons of Sam Houston State University; John Scott Bonien, senior assistant attorney general of the state of Washington; Jeffery Walker of the University of Alabama-Birmingham; David Carter of Michigan State University; Tom Hickey of Castleton State University; and Judge James W. Bachman of Bowling Green State University.

The hundreds of undergraduate and graduate students we have had the pleasure of teaching over the years inspired the writing of this book. From them we learned so much about how legal material can best be learned by students and colleagues in the criminal justice field. There are too many to list, but we want them to know how much I value their contributions.

Some of the case briefs in this book are taken, with modification, from the book *Briefs of Leading Cases in Law Enforcement*, by Rolando V. del Carmen and Jeffery T. Walker, which is now in its seventh edition. I thank the publishers of that book for allowing the use of those briefed cases.

Special and sincere thanks to the personnel at Cengage Publishing Company, all tested and highly experienced professionals. They improved this book beyond measure, in both content and format. They are: Carolyn Henderson Meier, Christy Frame, Valerie Kraus, Kara Kindstrom, Andrei Pasternak, Judy Inouye, and Brittani Morgan.

Some features are taken from various sources, mostly from government publications. The authors deeply appreciate the permission given for their inclusion in this text.

This book derives its strength from the efforts of many people, but the authors stand alone in accepting blame for its shortcomings. Continuous and critical feedback from readers is always welcome and deeply appreciated. As previous editions have shown (and as is true of all written work), feedback from readers ensures better future editions. To all who have provided solicited or unsolicited feedback for the ninth and past editions, thank you for your help.

A TEXT FOR A NATIONAL AUDIENCE

This text is written for a national audience, not just for readers in a few states. Policing in the United States is mainly a state and local concern; thus it is not enough for police officers to know the content of this text. Knowledge of specific state law, court decisions, or agency policy is a must in law enforcement in the United States. In case of doubt and where an actual case is involved, users of this text are strongly advised to read their own state laws or consult a knowledgeable lawyer for authoritative guidance.

TOWARD A DEMYSTIFICATION OF THE LAW

This text aims to help demystify law and court decisions so they can more effectively guide the conduct of the police and in the process protect citizens' constitutional rights even more effectively. It is hoped that this book contributes in some small way to achieving that goal—in the interest of society and for the benefit of law enforcement officers who risk their lives daily so the rest of us can enjoy safety and peace.

Rolando V. del Carmen
Distinguished Professor of Criminal Justice (Law) and Regents Professor
College of Criminal Justice
Sam Houston State University

Craig Hemmens
Department of Criminal Justice and Criminology
Washington State University

CHAPTER 1

The Court System, Sources of Rights, and Fundamental Principles

LEARNING OBJECTIVES

1. Differentiate between the federal and court systems.
2. Explain the dual court system.
3. Explain the effect of a court's decision upon territorial jurisdiction.
4. Distinguish which criminal acts can be prosecuted in both federal and state courts.
5. Contrast the legal concepts of jurisdiction and venue.
6. Describe the sources of legal rights within the United States.
7. Define the legal concept of judicial review.
8. Describe the concept of "Rule of Law."
9. Identify the components of a case brief.
10. Construct a case brief when given a case.

KEY TERMS

Bill of Rights
case-by-case
  incorporation
case citation
case law
common law
double jeopardy
dual court system
dual sovereignty
due process clause
en banc
incorporation
  controversy
judicial precedent
judicial review
jurisdiction
original jurisdiction
rule of four
rule of law
selective incorporation
stare decisis
statutory law
total incorporation
total incorporation plus
venue

dual court system
the United States has two
court systems: one for
federal cases and another
for state cases.

IN THIS CHAPTER, we first focus on the structure of federal and state court systems in the United States.

Criminal cases in the United States may be tried in federal and state courts if the act constitutes violation of the laws of both jurisdictions. However, most criminal cases are tried in state courts, because maintaining peace and order is primarily the responsibility of state and local governments. Important topics covered in this chapter include the territorial effect of judicial decisions, the principle of judicial precedent based on stare decisis, the extent of federal and state jurisdiction, the principle of dual sovereignty, the legal concepts of jurisdiction and venue, and the various sources of individual rights. The chapter discusses the incorporation controversy—how it developed and what role it plays in determining which constitutional rights now also extend to an accused in state prosecutions. It ends with a discussion of the rule of law.

THE U.S. COURT SYSTEM

The United States has a **dual court system**, meaning that there is one system for federal cases and another for state cases (see Figure 1.1). The term *dual court system* is, however, misleading. In reality, the United States has fifty-two separate judicial systems, representing the court systems in the fifty states, the federal system, and the courts of Washington, D.C. But because these systems have much in common, they justify a general grouping into two: federal and state.

FIGURE 1.1 The Dual Court System

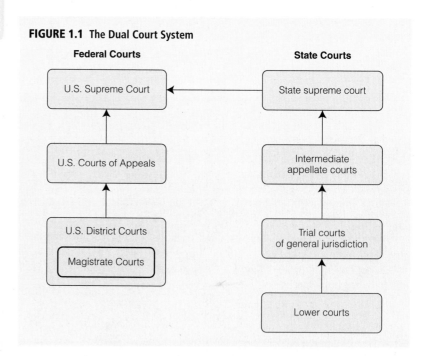

The Federal Court System

Article III, Section 1 of the U.S. Constitution provides that

> The judicial Power of the United States shall be vested in one supreme Court, and in such inferior Courts as the Congress may from time to time ordain and establish. The Judges, both of the supreme and inferior Courts, shall hold their Offices during good Behavior, and shall, at stated Times, receive for their Services a Compensation, which shall not be diminished during their continuance in office.

The highest court in the federal court system is the U.S. Supreme Court (see Figure 1.1). (*Note:* Whenever the word *Court* is used with a capital *C* in this text, the reference is to the U.S. Supreme Court. The word *court* with a lowercase *c* refers to all other courts on the federal or state level.) It is composed of a chief justice and eight associate justices, all of whom are nominated and appointed by the president of the United States with the advice and consent of the Senate (see Figure 1.2).

A federal law passed in 1869 fixed the number of U.S. Supreme Court justices at nine, but this number can be changed by law. Supreme Court justices enjoy life tenure and may be removed only by impeachment, which very rarely occurs. The

FIGURE 1.2 The Federal Court System

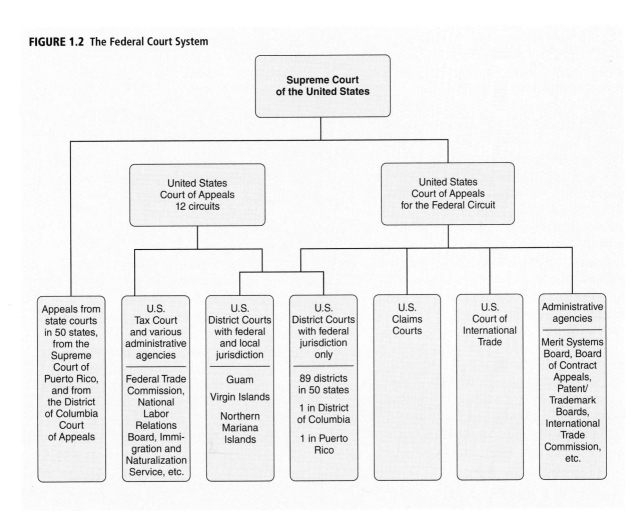

Court is located in Washington, D.C., and always decides cases **en banc** (*as one body*), never in division (small groups or panels). The votes of five justices are needed to win a case. The Court meets to hear arguments and decide cases beginning on the first Monday in October and continues sessions usually through the end of June of the following year. Court cases are argued and decisions are announced during this time, although the Court holds office throughout the year. Members of the U.S. Supreme Court are called justices. All others, from the U.S. Court of Appeals down to the lower courts, are called judges.

Exhibit 1.1   A Brief Overview of the Supreme Court

The Supreme Court of the United States

The Supreme Court consists of the chief justice of the United States and such number of associate justices as may be fixed by Congress. The number of associate justices is currently fixed at eight (28 U.S.C. §1). Power to nominate the justices is vested in the president of the United States, and appointments are made with the advice and consent of the Senate. Article III, §1, of the Constitution further provides that "[t]he Judges, both of the supreme and inferior Courts, shall hold their Offices during good behaviour, and shall, at stated Times, receive for their Services, a Compensation, which shall not be diminished during their Continuance in Office."

Court officers assist the Court in the performance of its functions. They include the administrative assistant to the chief justice, the clerk, the reporter of decisions, the librarian, the marshal, the court counsel, the curator, the director of data systems, and the public information officer. The administrative assistant is appointed by the chief justice. The clerk, reporter of decisions, librarian, and marshal are appointed by the Court. All other Court officers are appointed by the chief justice in consultation with the Court.

Constitutional Origin. Article III, §1, of the Constitution provides that "[t]he judicial Power of the United States, shall be vested in one supreme Court, and in such inferior Courts as the Congress may from time to time ordain and establish." The Supreme Court of the United States was created in accordance with this provision and by authority of the Judiciary Act of September 24, 1789 (1 Stat. 73). It was organized on February 2, 1790.

Jurisdiction. According to the Constitution (Art. III, §2):

"The judicial Power shall extend to all Cases, in Law and Equity, arising under this Constitution, the Laws of the United States, and Treaties made, or which shall be made, under their Authority;—to all Cases affecting Ambassadors, other public Ministers and Consuls;—to all Cases of admiralty and maritime Jurisdiction;—to Controversies to which the United States shall be a Party;—to Controversies between two or more States;—between a State and Citizens of another State;—between Citizens of different States;—between Citizens of the same State claiming Lands under Grants of different States, and between a State, or the Citizens thereof, and foreign States, Citizens or Subjects.

"In all Cases affecting Ambassadors, other public ministers and Consuls, and those in which a State shall be Party, the supreme Court shall have original Jurisdiction. In all the other Cases before mentioned, the supreme Court shall have appellate jurisdiction, both as to Law and Fact, with such Exceptions, and under such Regulations as the Congress shall make."

Appellate jurisdiction has been conferred upon the Supreme Court by various statutes, under the authority given Congress by the Constitution. The basic statute effective at this time in conferring and controlling jurisdiction of the Supreme Court may be found in 28 U.S.C. §1251 et seq., and various special statutes.

Rule-Making Power. Congress has from time to time conferred upon the Supreme Court power to prescribe rules of procedure to be followed by the lower courts of the United States. See 28 U.S.C. §2071 et seq.

The Building. The Supreme Court is open to the public from 9 A.M. to 4:30 P.M., Monday through Friday. It is closed Saturdays, Sundays, and the federal legal holidays listed in 5 U.S.C. §6103. Unless the Court or the chief justice orders otherwise, the clerk's office is open from 9 a.m. to 5 p.m., Monday through Friday, except on those holidays. The library is open to members of the bar of the Court, attorneys for the various federal departments and agencies, and members of Congress.

The Term. The term of the Court begins, by law, on the first Monday in October and lasts until the first Monday in October of the next year. Approximately 8,000 petitions are filed with the Court in the course of a term. In addition, some 1,200 applications of various kinds are filed each year that can be acted upon by a single justice.

Source: The Supreme Court of the United States, "About the Supreme Court," *http://www.supremecourtus.gov/about/briefoverview.pdf*. Modified by the author.

The Court has **original jurisdiction**, meaning the case is brought to the Court directly instead of on appeal, over certain cases as specified in the Constitution. The vast majority of cases, however, reach the Court either on *appeal* or on a *writ of certiorari*. A third way—by certification—is rarely used; and a fourth method—through a writ of error—was discontinued in 1928.[1] The Court reviews cases on appeal because it must. In reality, however, the Court does not have to consider a case on appeal on its merits, because it can avoid full consideration by saying that the case "lacks substantial federal question" to deserve full consideration by the Court.

The Court generally has discretion to decide what cases it wants to hear. Most cases (about 85 percent) get to the Supreme Court from the lower courts on a *writ of certiorari*, which is defined as "an order by the appellate court which is used when the court has discretion on whether or not to hear an appeal."[2] In writ of certiorari cases, the **rule of four** applies, meaning that at least four justices must agree for the Court to consider a case on its merits. If the case fails to obtain four votes for inclusion in the Court docket, the decision of the court where the case originated (usually a federal court of appeals or a state supreme court) prevails.

About 10,000 cases reach the Supreme Court each year from various federal and state courts, but the Court renders written decisions on only a limited number (75 cases during the 2011 term, 78 cases during the 2012 term, and 72 cases during the 2013 term). The rest are dismissed *per curiam*, meaning that the decision of the immediate lower court in which the case originated (whether it was a state supreme court, a federal court of appeals, or any other court) is left undisturbed.

Not accepting a case does not mean that the Supreme Court agrees with the decision of the lower court. It simply means that the case could not get the votes of at least four justices to give it further attention and consider it on its merits. The public perception that only the most important cases are accepted and decided by the Supreme Court is not necessarily true. Cases generally get on the Supreme Court docket because at least four justices voted to include the case. The standard used for inclusion is left to individual justices to decide.

The Federal Courts of Appeals Next to the Supreme Court in the federal judicial hierarchy are the U.S. courts of appeals, officially referred to as the U.S. Court of Appeals

original jurisdiction
the case is brought to the court directly instead of on appeal.

rule of four
at least four justices must agree for the court to consider the case on its merits.

MYTH vs. REALITY

MYTH Anyone can appeal their case to the Supreme Court.

FACT The Supreme Court only accepts cases that involve a federal statute or a "significant federal question." Many lawsuits do not involve these subjects and so are not eligible for review by the Supreme Court.

Table 1.1 The Justices of the U.S. Supreme Court

Name	Born	Age at appt.	Appt. by	Senate conf. vote	First day/ Length of service	Previous positions
John Roberts (Chief Justice)	January 27, 1955 (age 57) in Buffalo, New York	50	George W. Bush	78–22	September 29, 2005/6 years, 4 months	Circuit Judge, Court of Appeals for the D.C. Circuit (2003–2005); Private practice (1993–2003); Professor, Georgetown University Law Center (1992–2005); Principal Deputy Solicitor General (1989–1993); Private practice (1986–1989); Associate Counsel to the President (1982–1986); Special Assistant to the Attorney General (1981–1982)
Antonin Scalia	March 11, 1936 (age 75) in Trenton, New Jersey	50	Ronald Reagan	98–0	September 26, 1986/25 years, 4 months	Circuit Judge, Court of Appeals for the D.C. Circuit (1982–1986); Professor, University of Chicago Law School (1977–1982); Assistant Attorney General (1974–1977); Professor, University of Virginia School of Law (1967–1974); Private practice (1961–1967)
Anthony Kennedy	July 23, 1936 (age 75) in Sacramento, California	51	Ronald Reagan	97–0	February 18, 1988/23 years	Circuit Judge, Court of Appeals for the Ninth Circuit (1975–1988); Professor, McGeorge School of Law, University of the Pacific (1965–1988); Private practice (1963–1975)
Clarence Thomas	June 23, 1948 (age 63) in Pin Point, Georgia	43	George H. W. Bush	52–48	October 23, 1991/20 years, 3 months	Circuit Judge, Court of Appeals for the D.C. Circuit (1990–1991); Chairman, Equal Employment Opportunity Commission (1982–1990); legislative assistant for Missouri Senator John Danforth (1979–1981); employed by Monsanto Company Inc. (1977–1979); Assistant Attorney General in Missouri under State Attorney General John Danforth (1974–1977)
Ruth Bader Ginsburg	March 15, 1933 (age 78) in New York City	60	Bill Clinton	96–3	August 10, 1993/18 years, 5 months	Circuit Judge, Court of Appeals for the D.C. Circuit (1980–1993); General Counsel, American Civil Liberties Union (1973–1980); Professor, Columbia Law School (1972–1980); Professor, Rutgers University School of Law (1963–1972)
Stephen Breyer	August 15, 1938 (age 73) in San Francisco, California	56	Bill Clinton	87–9	August 3, 1994/17 years, 5 months	Chief Judge, Court of Appeals for the First Circuit (1990–1994); Circuit Judge, Court of Appeals for the First Circuit (1980–1990); Professor, Harvard Law School (1967–1980)
Samuel Alito	April 1, 1950 (age 61) in Trenton, New Jersey	55	George W. Bush	58–42	January 31, 2006/6 years	Circuit Judge, Court of Appeals for the Third Circuit (1990–2006); Professor, Seton Hall University School of Law (1999–2004); U.S. Attorney for the District of New Jersey (1987–1990); Deputy Assistant Attorney General (1985–1987); Assistant to the Solicitor General (1981–1985); Assistant U.S. Attorney for the District of New Jersey (1977–1981)
Sonia Sotomayor	June 25, 1954 (age 57) in New York City	55	Barack Obama	68–31	August 8, 2009/2 years, 5 months	Circuit Judge, Court of Appeals for the Second Circuit (1998–2009); District Judge, District Court for the Southern District of New York (1992–1998); Private practice (1984–1991); Assistant District Attorney, New York County, New York (1979–1984)
Elena Kagan	April 28, 1960 (age 51) in New York City	50	Barack Obama	63–37	August 7, 2010/1 year, 5 months	Solicitor General of the United States (2009–2010); Dean of Harvard Law School (2003–2009); Professor, Harvard Law School (2001–2003); Visiting Professor, Harvard Law School (1999–2001); Associate White House Counsel (1995–1999); Deputy Director of the Domestic Policy Council (1995–1999); Professor, University of Chicago Law School (1995); Associate Professor, University of Chicago Law School (1991–1995)

Source: Biographies of Current Justices of the Supreme Court, http://www.supremecourt.gov/about/biographies.aspx

for a particular circuit (see Figure 1.3). These courts have 179 judgeships located in thirteen judicial "circuits." Of these thirteen circuits, twelve are identified by region, including one solely for the District of Columbia. The Thirteenth Circuit is the Court of Appeals for the Federal Circuit, which has jurisdiction throughout the country on certain types of cases based on subject matter. Each circuit (other than that for the District of Columbia and the Federal Circuit) covers three or more states and hears cases from these states. For example, the Fifth Circuit covers the states of Texas,

Mississippi, and Louisiana, whereas the Tenth Circuit includes the states of Utah, Wyoming, Colorado, Kansas, New Mexico, and Oklahoma.

Each court has six or more judges, depending on the circuit's caseload. The First Circuit has six judges, whereas the Ninth Circuit has twenty-nine. Judges of the courts of appeals are nominated and appointed by the president of the United States for life, with the advice and consent of the Senate, by a majority vote, and can be removed only by impeachment. Unlike the Supreme Court, courts of appeals may hear cases as one body (en banc) or in groups (in divisions) of three or five judges.

The Federal District Courts Occupying the lowest level in the hierarchy of federal courts are the district courts, the trial courts for federal cases. The federal government has 677 federal judgeships located in ninety-four judicial districts in the United States, Guam, Puerto Rico, and the Virgin Islands. Each state has at least one judicial district, but some states have as many as four. Judges are nominated and appointed by the president of the United States for life, with the advice and consent of the Senate, and can be removed only by impeachment. In practice, the senior U.S. senator from the state makes the recommendation for the appointment if he or she belongs to the president's political party.

FIGURE 1.3 Geographical Boundaries of the U.S. Courts of Appeal and District Courts

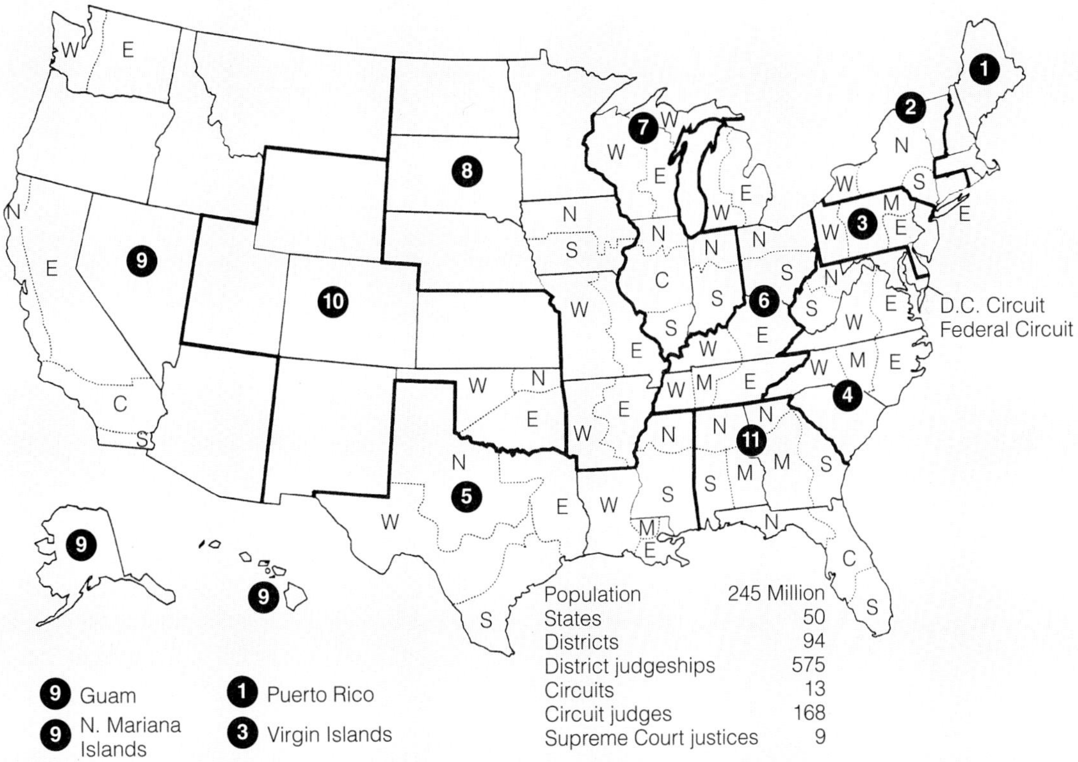

Population	245 Million
States	50
Districts	94
District judgeships	575
Circuits	13
Circuit judges	168
Supreme Court justices	9

9 Guam
9 N. Mariana Islands
1 Puerto Rico
3 Virgin Islands

Source: *Russell Wheeler and Cynthia Harrison*, Creating the Federal Judicial System, 2nd ed. (*Washington, D.C.: Federal Judicial Center, 1996*), p. 26.

The Federal Magistrate Courts Also under the federal system are the U.S. magistrate courts, established primarily to relieve district court judges of heavy caseloads. They are presided over by U.S. magistrates and have limited authority, such as trying minor offenses and misdemeanor cases in which the possible penalty is incarceration for one year or less. They are also empowered to hold bail hearings, issue warrants, review habeas corpus petitions, and hold pretrial conferences in civil and criminal cases. Unlike other federal court judges, whose offices are created by Article III (the judiciary article) of the Constitution, the offices of federal magistrates were created by the Congress of the United States. Magistrates are appointed by federal court judges in that district and are not guaranteed life tenure. As of 2014, there were 551 magistrate judge positions. U.S. magistrate courts do not constitute a separate court in the federal courts system. Instead, they are part of the federal district court system.

The Federal Courts and the Public

With certain very limited exceptions, each step of the federal judicial process is open to the public. Federal courthouses are designed to inspire in the public a respect for the tradition and purpose of the American judicial process, and many courthouses are historic buildings.

A citizen who wishes to observe a court in session may go to a federal courthouse, check the court calendar, which is posted on a bulletin board or television monitor, and watch any proceeding. Anyone may review the file and papers in a case by going to the clerk of court's office and asking to review or copy the appropriate case file. Increasingly, court schedules, dockets, judgments, opinions, and pleadings are being made available to the public in electronic format through the Internet. Unlike most of the state courts, however, the federal courts do not permit television or radio coverage of trial court proceedings.

The right of public access to court proceedings is partly derived from the Constitution and partly from court and common law tradition. By conducting their judicial work in public view, judges enhance public confidence in the courts, and they allow citizens to learn firsthand how our judicial system works.

In a few, limited situations the public may not have full access to court records and court proceedings. In a high-profile trial, for example, there may not be enough space in the courtroom to accommodate everyone who would like to observe. Access to the courtroom also may be restricted for security or privacy reasons, such as the protection of a juvenile or a confidential informant. Finally, certain documents may be placed under seal by the judge, meaning that they are not available to the public. Examples of sealed information include certain types of confidential business records, certain law enforcement reports, juvenile records, and cases involving national security issues.

Source: *The Federal Court System in the United States: An Introduction for Judges and Judicial Administrators in Other Countries*, 3rd ed, p. 11.

The State Court System

The structure of the state court system varies from state to state. In general, however, state courts follow the federal pattern. This means that most states have one state supreme court, which makes final decisions on cases involving state laws and provisions of the state constitution. Texas and Oklahoma, however, have two highest courts—one for civil cases and the other for criminal cases (see Figure 1.4a and Figure 1.4b). State courts decide nearly every type of case but are limited by the provisions of the U.S. Constitution, their own state constitution, and state law.

Below the state supreme court in the state judicial hierarchy are the intermediate appellate courts. Only thirty-five of the fifty states have intermediate appellate courts.

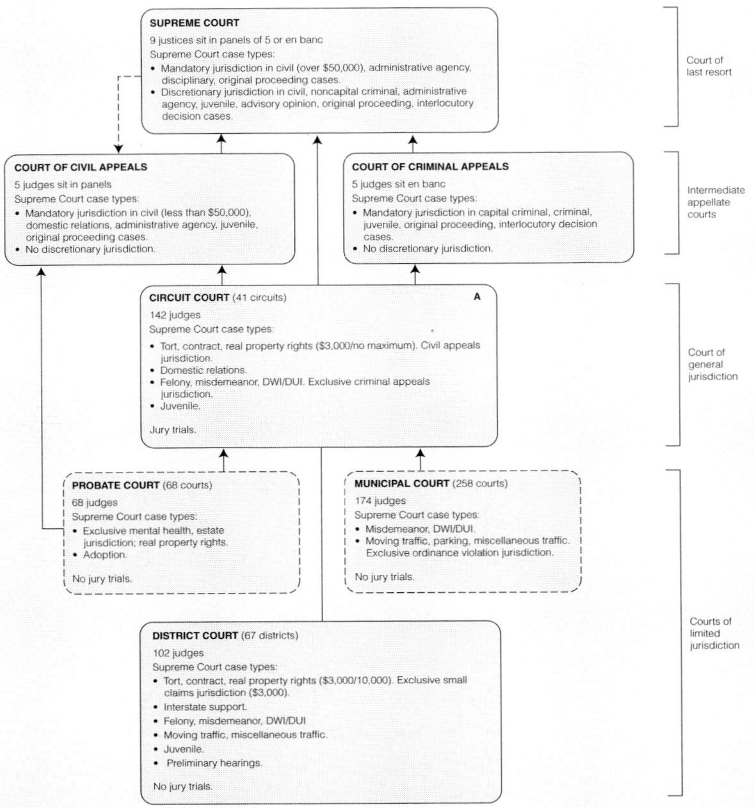

FIGURE 1.4B Oklahoma Court Structure

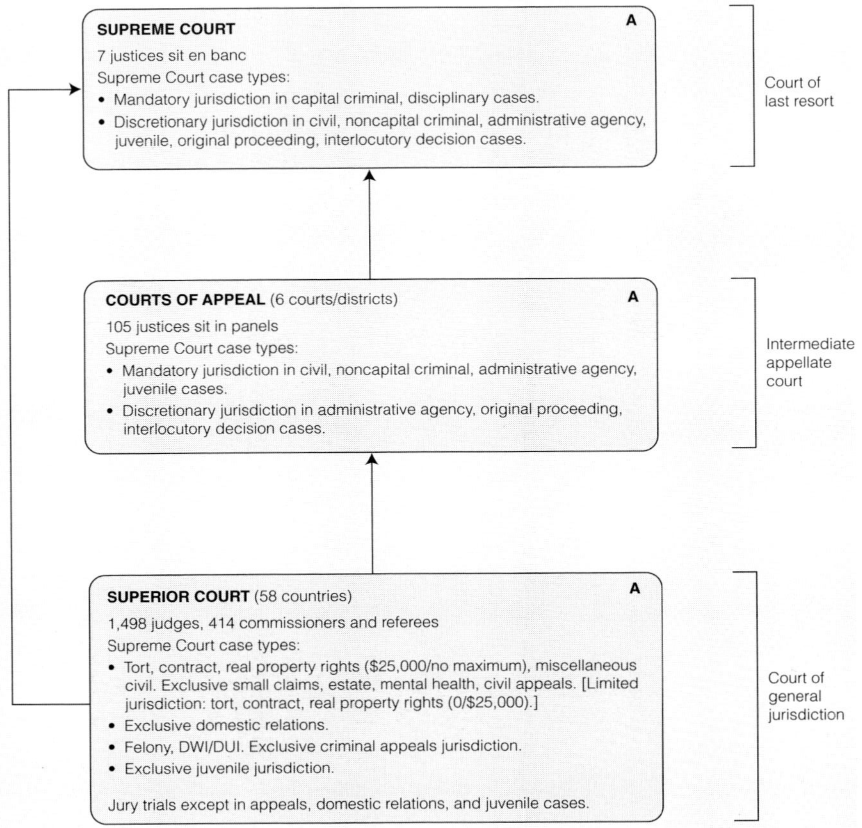

Court of last resort

SUPREME COURT

7 justices sit en banc

Supreme Court case types:
- Mandatory jurisdiction in capital criminal, disciplinary cases.
- Discretionary jurisdiction in civil, noncapital criminal, administrative agency, juvenile, original proceeding, interlocutory decision cases.

A

Intermediate appellate court

COURTS OF APPEAL (6 courts/districts)

105 justices sit in panels

Supreme Court case types:
- Mandatory jurisdiction in civil, noncapital criminal, administrative agency, juvenile cases.
- Discretionary jurisdiction in administrative agency, original proceeding, interlocutory decision cases.

A

Court of general jurisdiction

SUPERIOR COURT (58 countries)

1,498 judges, 414 commissioners and referees

Supreme Court case types:
- Tort, contract, real property rights ($25,000/no maximum), miscellaneous civil. Exclusive small claims, estate, mental health, civil appeals. [Limited jurisdiction: tort, contract, real property rights (0/$25,000).]
- Exclusive domestic relations.
- Felony, DWI/DUI. Exclusive criminal appeals jurisdiction.
- Exclusive juvenile jurisdiction.

Jury trials except in appeals, domestic relations, and juvenile cases.

A

FIGURE 1.4A Texas Court Structure

Court of last resort

Intermediate appellate courts

Court of general jurisdiction

Courts of limited jurisdiction

SUPREME COURT

9 justices sit in panels of 5 or en banc

Supreme Court case types:
- Mandatory jurisdiction in civil (over $50,000), administrative agency, discretionary, original proceeding cases.
- Discretionary jurisdiction in civil, noncapital criminal, administrative agency, juvenile, advisory opinion, original proceeding, interlocutory decision cases.

COURT OF CRIMINAL APPEALS

5 judges sit en banc

Supreme Court case types:
- Mandatory jurisdiction in capital criminal, criminal, juvenile, original proceeding, interlocutory decision cases.
- No discretionary jurisdiction.

COURT OF CIVIL APPEALS

5 judges sit in panels

Supreme Court case types:
- Mandatory jurisdiction in civil (less than $50,000), domestic relations, administrative agency, juvenile, original proceeding cases.
- No discretionary jurisdiction.

A

CIRCUIT COURT (41 circuits)

142 judges

Supreme Court case types:
- Tort, contract, real property rights ($3,000/no maximum). Civil appeals jurisdiction.
- Felony, misdemeanor, DWI/DUI. Exclusive criminal appeals jurisdiction.
- Juvenile.

Jury trials.

MUNICIPAL COURT (258 courts)

174 judges

Supreme Court case types:
- Misdemeanor, DWI/DUI.
- Moving traffic, parking, miscellaneous traffic. Exclusive ordinance violation jurisdiction.

No jury trials.

PROBATE COURT (68 courts)

68 judges

Supreme Court case types:
- Exclusive mental health, estate jurisdiction, real property rights.
- Adoption.

No jury trials.

DISTRICT COURT (67 districts)

102 judges

Supreme Court case types:
- Tort, contract, real property rights ($3,000/10,000). Exclusive small claims jurisdiction ($3,000).
- Interstate support.
- Felony, misdemeanor, DWI/DUI
- Moving traffic, miscellaneous traffic.
- Juvenile.
- Preliminary hearings.

No jury trials.

The Court System, Sources of Rights, and Fundamental Principles   **9**

Where such courts do not exist, cases appealed from the trial courts go directly to the state supreme court. Each state has trial courts with general jurisdiction, meaning that they try civil and criminal cases. They go by various names, such as circuit court, district court, or court of common pleas. New York's court of general jurisdiction is called the supreme court. Although these courts are of general jurisdiction, some states divide them according to specialty areas, such as probate, juvenile, and domestic relations.

At the base of the state judicial hierarchy are courts of limited jurisdiction, such as county courts, justice of the peace courts, and municipal courts. They have limited jurisdiction in both civil and criminal cases and also decide cases involving local ordinances passed by county or city governments. Unlike federal court judges, who are appointed by the president with the advice and consent of the Senate, a great majority of state court judges are elected.

WHERE JUDICIAL DECISIONS APPLY

The power of every U.S. court to try and decide cases is limited in some way. One type of limitation is territorial or geographic. A judicial decision is authoritative and has value as precedent for future cases only within the geographic limits of the area in which the deciding court has jurisdiction. Consequently, U.S. Supreme Court decisions on questions of federal law and the Constitution are binding on all U.S. courts because the whole country is under its jurisdiction. Decisions of a federal court of appeals are the last word within that circuit if there is no Supreme Court action. The First Circuit Court of Appeals, for example, settles federal issues for Maine, Massachusetts, New Hampshire, Rhode Island, and Puerto Rico, the areas within its jurisdiction. When a district court encompasses an entire state, as is the case in Maine or Alaska, its decision on a federal law produces a uniform rule within the state. However, in a state such as California, where there are multiple districts, there can be divergent and even conflicting decisions even on the district court level.

The same process operates in the state court systems, but in one regard, state supreme court decisions are recognized as extending beyond state borders. Because the Constitution declares the sovereignty of the states within the area reserved for state control, the court of last resort in each state is the final arbiter of issues of purely state and local law. For example, the Idaho Supreme Court's interpretation of a state statute or municipal ordinance will be respected as authoritative even by the U.S. Supreme Court—unless it involves a constitutional question, in which case the U.S. Supreme Court becomes the final arbiter.

The existence of a dual court system and the limited jurisdictional reach of the vast majority of courts make it highly probable that courts will render conflicting decisions on a legal issue. The appellate process provides a forum for resolving these conflicts if the cases are appealed. If no appeal is made, the conflict remains. For example, a federal district court in the Western District of North Carolina may rule that jail detainees are entitled to contact visits, while another federal district court in the Eastern District of North Carolina, in a different case, may rule otherwise. However, this inconsistency will be resolved only if the federal appellate court for North Carolina (the Fourth Circuit) decides the issue in an appealed case.

Despite the territorial or geographic limitations of court decisions, there are important reasons why decisions from other jurisdictions should not be ignored. First, there

Frank Roberts is a 32-year-old grocery store clerk living in Pullman, Washington. His former girlfriend Pamela Perkins (they broke up several months ago) lives about ten miles away, across the state line in Moscow, Idaho. On the evening of February 14, 2015, Frank goes to visit Pamela at her home in Moscow to ask her if they can renew their relationship; when she declines, he becomes angry and strikes her with his fist, knocking her down. He then picks her up and forces her to go outside and get in his car. She protests, asking him to leave her alone, but he ignores her pleas. He then drives back to his home in Pullman. When he arrives, Pamela jumps out of the car and tries to escape, but he catches up to her and pushes her to the ground. A neighbor walking his dog asks what is going on, and Frank punches him in the face. Fortunately, a police officer happens by at this moment, and is able to arrest Frank without further incident.

You are a college student in a criminal procedure class, and your professor has assigned you to review this matter and identify the following:

1. *What possible charges does Frank Roberts face?*
2. *What court(s) may have jurisdiction and venue over Frank Roberts?*

---

may be no settled law on an issue in a given area. When the issue has not been decided previously by a local court (known as a *case of first impression*), the local federal or state court will probably decide it on the basis of the dominant, or "better," rule that is being applied elsewhere. The second reason is that law is evolving, not stagnant. Over time, trends develop. When a particular court senses that its prior decisions on an issue are no longer in the mainstream, it may consider revising its holding, especially if the issue has not been settled by the U.S. Supreme Court. The decisions in other jurisdictions may enable lawyers to detect a trend and anticipate what local courts might do in the future.

STARE DECISIS AND JUDICIAL PRECEDENT

Stare decisis is a Latin term that means "to abide by, or adhere to, decided cases." Courts generally adhere to stare decisis: When a court has laid down a principle of law as applicable to a certain set of facts, it will follow that principle and apply it to all future cases with similar facts and circumstances. The judicial practice of stare decisis leads to **judicial precedent**, meaning that decisions of courts have value as precedent for future cases with similar fact patterns. These terms are often used interchangeably because they vary only slightly in meaning. The principle of stare decisis ensures predictability of court decisions, whereas judicial precedent is a process courts follow as a result of stare decisis. Judicial precedent is made possible by stare decisis.

A decision is precedent only for cases that come within that court's jurisdiction. For example, the decisions of the Fifth Circuit Court of Appeals are valued as precedent only in the states (Texas, Louisiana, and Mississippi) within the territorial jurisdiction of the court. By the same token, the decisions of the Florida Supreme Court are precedent only in cases decided by Florida courts. U.S. Supreme Court decisions are precedent for cases anywhere in the United States. For example, the case of *Miranda v. Arizona* is precedent for cases involving custodial interrogation, so all cases decided in the United States on that issue must be decided in accordance with *Miranda*. Variations

stare decisis
to abide by, or adhere to, decided cases.

judicial precedent
decisions of courts have value as precedent for future cases similarly circumstanced.

do occur, however, because the facts of cases differ. Therefore, the Court can refine, modify, or expand the *Miranda* doctrine. Moreover, judicial precedent can be discarded at any time by the court that decided it. *Miranda* has been modified and refined by the Court a number of times in subsequent cases (see Chapter 11, "Confessions and Admissions"). Although it is unlikely, the Court could also abandon the *Miranda* doctrine at any time or prescribe a different rule, depending on what the Court determines is required by the Constitution. All that is needed to overturn a judicial precedent are the votes of at least five justices of the Court.

The most binding kind of precedent is that set by cases decided by the U.S. Supreme Court. The decision of any court, however, can set a precedent. Sometimes, lower courts do not follow a precedent set by a higher court. In these cases, the appellate court can reverse the lower court decision on appeal.

FEDERAL VERSUS STATE CRIMINAL TRIALS

The rule that determines whether a criminal case should be filed and tried in federal or state court is this: If an act is a violation of federal law, the trial will be held in a federal court; if an act is a violation of state law, the trial will be held in a state court. A crime that violates both federal and state laws (such as kidnapping, transportation of narcotics, counterfeiting, or robbery of a federally insured bank) may be tried in both federal and state courts if the prosecutors so desire. For example, if X robs the Miami National Bank, X can be prosecuted for the crime of robbery under Florida law and also for robbery of a federally insured bank under federal law. The prosecutions are for the same act but involve two different laws and two different jurisdictions. There is no double jeopardy because of the concept of **dual sovereignty**, which means that federal and state governments are each considered sovereign in their own right.

The Oklahoma City bombing cases provide relevant examples. The two defendants in that crime were convicted in federal court. Timothy McVeigh was given the death penalty and subsequently executed. The other defendant, Terry Nichols, was also convicted in federal court and given life imprisonment with no possibility of parole. He was later tried in an Oklahoma state court, convicted of 161 state murder charges, and sentenced to life times 161. This did not constitute double jeopardy because of dual sovereignty.

Defendants can also be tried in two different states for essentially the same crime, if the crime or an element thereof was committed in those states. For instance, if someone kidnaps a person in Pullman, Washington, and drives him or her eight miles across the border to Moscow, Idaho, that person has committed the crime of kidnapping in Washington and in Idaho. Whether a state will try a defendant who has already been convicted in another state again depends on state law and the discretion of the prosecutor. The government that first obtains custody of the suspect is usually allowed to try him or her first.

Note, however, that although successive prosecutions by separate sovereignties are constitutional, they may be prohibited by state law or internal agency policy. Moreover, a prosecutor may not want to file the case, even if he or she can, because of the expense involved or if "justice has been served," perhaps because the defendant has been sufficiently punished. In high-profile cases, however, prosecutors from other jurisdictions may want to try the defendant regardless of the verdict and punishment

dual sovereignty
federal and state governments are both considered sovereign.

MYTH vs. REALITY

MYTH Double jeopardy prevents someone from being punished twice for the same act.

FACT Double jeopardy only prevents multiple punishments for the same act by the same sovereign, or government. If someone does something that is a both a federal crime and a state crime, that person could be punished twice—by the federal government and the state government where the act occurred.

in other jurisdictions. For example, although Terry Nichols was sentenced to life in prison by the federal government in the Oklahoma City bombing case, Oklahoma tried him again under state law so he could be given the death penalty. He did not get the death penalty but was sentenced to life times 161 by the Oklahoma state court.

JURISDICTION VERSUS VENUE

The terms *jurisdiction* and *venue* can be confusing. Sometimes used interchangeably, they nevertheless represent very different concepts. **Jurisdiction** refers to the power of a court to try a case. A court's jurisdiction is determined by the law that created the court and defined its powers. The parties to a litigation cannot vest the court with jurisdiction it does not possess; only legislation can do that.

jurisdiction
the power of a court to try a case.

To render a valid judgment against a person, a court must also have jurisdiction over that person. The fact that a defendant has been brought to court against his or her wishes and by questionable methods does not invalidate the jurisdiction of the court. In *Frisbie v. Collins*, 342 U.S. 519 (1952), the Supreme Court ruled that an invalid arrest is not a defense against being convicted of the offense charged. In that case, while living in Illinois, the accused was forcibly seized, blackjacked, handcuffed, and then taken back to Michigan by law enforcement officers. The Court ruled that the power of a court to try a person for a crime is not impaired by the fact that the person has been brought within the court's jurisdiction through forcible abduction. The Court said, "It matters not how a defendant is brought before the court; what matters is that the defendant is before the court and can therefore be tried."

Frisbie v. Collins (1952)

Another case involved former Panamanian dictator General Manuel Noriega. In December 1989, the U.S. government sent troops to Panama, who arrested Noriega and flew him to Florida to face narcotics trafficking charges. Noriega protested, claiming that U.S. courts had no jurisdiction over him because the Panama invasion, which led to his arrest, violated international law. The U.S. courts ruled, however, that the method of arrest did not deprive the courts of jurisdiction. Noriega was tried in the United States, convicted, and sentenced to 40 years in prison.[3]

The term **venue** is place-oriented. The general rule is that cases must be tried in the place where the crime was committed. Legislation establishes mandatory venue for some types of cases and preferred venue for others. In criminal cases, the trial is usually held in the place where the crime was committed, but the venue may be changed

venue
the place where a case is to be tried.

and the trial held in another place for causes specified by law. This change is made to ensure the accused a fair and impartial trial in cases that have had such massive pretrial publicity or strong community prejudice as to make it difficult to select an impartial jury. The motion for a change of venue is usually filed by the defendant. The decision of a trial judge to grant or deny the motion is seldom reversed on appeal.

Jurisdiction	Venue
Power to try a case	Place where a case is tried
Determined by law	Determined by where the crime was committed
Cannot be changed, except by law	Can be changed, usually due to massive pretrial publicity

THE ADVERSARY SYSTEM

The litigation process in United States courts is referred to as an "adversary" system because it relies on the litigants to present their dispute before a neutral fact finder. According to American legal tradition, inherited from the English common law, the clash of adversaries before the court is thought most likely to allow the jury or judge to determine the truth and resolve the dispute. In some other legal systems, judges or magistrates conduct investigations to find relevant evidence or obtain testimony from witnesses. In the United States, however, the work of collecting evidence and preparing to present it to the court is accomplished by the litigants and their attorneys, normally without assistance from the court. The essential role of the judge is to structure and regulate the development of issues by the adversaries and to make sure that the law is followed and that fairness is achieved.

Source: *The Federal Court System in the United States: An Introduction for Judges and Judicial Administrators in Other Countries*, 3rd ed, p. 22.

SOURCES OF RIGHTS

The rules governing criminal proceedings in the United States come from four basic sources: (1) constitutions (federal and state), (2) statutes, (3) case law, and (4) court rules.

Constitutions

Both the federal and state constitutions are sources of rules that protect the rights of individuals.

The Federal Constitution The U.S. Constitution is primarily concerned with establishing the powers and limits of the federal government. The first three articles of the Constitution set forth the powers and duties of the executive, Congress, and the Supreme Court. The only individual rights mentioned in the original Constitution are the right to seek a writ of habeas corpus (a document challenging the legality of a person's detention), the prohibition on bills of attainder (legislation imposing punishment without trial), and the prohibition on ex post facto laws (legislation making prior conduct criminal).

When the Constitution was submitted to the states for ratification, several states were reluctant to ratify it without a more specific enumeration of individual rights. In response to these concerns, the **Bill of Rights** was added. The Bill of Rights contains the most important rights available to an accused in a criminal prosecution. The constitutional rights set forth in the Bill of Rights are the minimum rights of individuals facing criminal prosecution. They can be expanded, and an accused can be given more rights by state constitutions and by federal and state law. The constitutions of the various

Bill of Rights
the first ten amendments to the U.S. Constitution.

states also contain provisions designed to protect the rights of individuals in state criminal proceedings. These rights are similar to those enumerated in the Bill of Rights, but they apply only to a particular state. For example, most state constitutions guarantee the right to counsel and cross-examination and prohibit self-incrimination.

Listed below are the rights guaranteed in the Bill of Rights and how they might be violated in law enforcement.

◆ **Amendment 1:**

Freedom of religion
Freedom of speech
Freedom of the press
Freedom of assembly
Freedom to petition the government for redress of grievances

Police actions that might violate the First Amendment include: dispersal of groups practicing religion in public places; limitations on the use of public places by speakers to protest government policies; limiting access by the press to evidence of crime or to ongoing police investigations; enforcing juvenile curfew ordinances; and prohibiting public gatherings, parades, or meetings without a valid permit.

◆ **Amendment 2:**

The right to keep and bear arms. This has become more controversial in recent years as local governments and states have passed rules limiting the availability of weapons. Passage of these laws, which inevitably rely on the police for enforcement, have led to legal challenges.

◆ **Amendment 3:**

This amendment provides that "no Soldier shall, in time of peace be quartered In any house, without the consent of the Owner, nor In time of war, but in a manner to be prescribed by law." This is a relic of history and has no relevance to current law enforcement.

◆ **Amendment 4:**

Freedom from unreasonable searches and seizures

This is the most important constitutional right in policing because it involves detentions, stops, arrests, and searches of people, motor vehicles, and places. Several chapters in this book address issues stemming from the constitutional prohibition of unreasonable searches and seizures. Violations of this right can lead to criminal or civil liability for the police.

◆ **Amendment 5:**

Right to a grand jury indictment for a capital or other serious crime
Protection against **double jeopardy** (being punished more than once for the same offense)
Protection against self-incrimination
Prohibits the taking of life, liberty, or property without due process of law
Violation of the privilege not to incriminate oneself is the biggest issue for law enforcement under the Fifth Amendment.

double jeopardy
being punished more than once for the same offense.

- **Amendment 6:**

  Right to a speedy and public trial
  Right to an impartial jury
  Right to be informed of the nature and cause of the accusation
  Right to confront witnesses
  Right to summon witnesses
  Right to the assistance of counsel

    The constitutional rights guaranteed under the Sixth Amendment are primarily limitations on what the courts can do during trial. Police issues, however, may arise in connection with the right to counsel—as when the police question a suspect without counsel or do not provide counsel during a police lineup.

- **Amendment 7:**

    This amendment provides that "in Suits at common law, where the value in controversy shall exceed twenty dollars, the right of trial by jury shall be preserved, and no fact tried by a jury, shall be otherwise re-examined in any Court of the United States, than according to the rules of common law." This does not apply to law enforcement and is a largely irrelevant amendment.

- **Amendment 8:**

  Protection against excessive bail
  Protection against cruel and unusual punishment

    The rights under the Eighth Amendment usually do not involve the police. The prohibition against excessive bail involves the court, and the prohibition against cruel and unusual punishment usually applies during sentencing and when a defendant is in prison. The beating of suspects by the police and the use of brutal methods to obtain confessions are punished under criminal law or sanctioned as violations of the constitutional right to due process and equal protection but not under the prohibition against cruel and unusual punishment.

- **Amendment 9**

    This amendment states that "the enumeration in the Constitution, of certain rights, shall not be construed to deny or disparage others retained by the people." This amendment is not relevant in law enforcement cases.

- **Amendment 10:**

    This amendment says that "the powers not delegated to the United States by the Constitution, not prohibited by it to the States, are reserved to the States respectively, or to the people." This has little relevance to law enforcement and is not used in criminal cases.

The Bill of Rights refers to the first ten amendments to the U.S. Constitution. In addition to the Bill of Rights, however, Amendment 14 to the Constitution is also a source of rights in criminal cases in both federal and state courts.

- **Amendment 14:**

  Right to due process
  Right to equal protection

What does due process mean? It is difficult to come up with a definition that applies alike to all law enforcement situations. This is because the meaning of due process varies based on the circumstances of "people, time, and place." In essence, however, due process means fundamental fairness. This denotes that whenever there is fundamental unfairness by the police, a potential claim to a violation of due process by a member of the public arises. For example, an officer beats up a suspect without justification or uses excessive force during arrest. This can be a violation of due process because both are fundamentally unfair. There are instances, however, when the use of force is justified. In these cases, allegations of a violation of the due process clause of Fourteenth Amendment fail. It all depends on the circumstances. Ultimately, whether a person's due process right is violated or not is mainly determined by the jury or judge during trial and based on specific circumstances.

The right to equal protection requires that people be treated the same unless there is justification for treating them differently. These justifications are defined by legislation or court decisions, not by individual police officers or departments. For example, applying different policing standards to neighborhoods inhabited by different racial and ethnic groups can be a violation of the right to equal protection, as can treating suspects differently based on race or national origin. Racial profiling can be a violation of equal protection right, as might different responses by the police to complaints based on religion.

State Constitutions In addition to the federal Constitution, all fifty states have their own constitutions. Many state constitutions have their own bills of rights and guarantees of protection against deprivation of rights by state government. The provisions of these constitutions must be consistent with the provisions of the federal Constitution or they may be declared unconstitutional if challenged in court. The provisions of state constitutions or state law sometimes give defendants more rights and protection than provided under the federal Constitution. The general rule is that if a state constitution or a state law gives a defendant *less* protection than the U.S. Constitution provides, that limitation is unconstitutional and the U.S. Constitution prevails. But if provisions of the state constitution or state law give a defendant *more* protection than the U.S. Constitution provides, that grant of protection by the state prevails. For example, assume that a state constitution, for some unlikely reason, requires a defendant to testify even when the result is self-incrimination. This provision would be declared unconstitutional because it contravenes the provisions of the Fifth Amendment.

By contrast, the U.S. Supreme Court has ruled that trustworthy statements obtained in violation of the *Miranda* rule may be used to impeach (challenge) the credibility of a defendant who takes the witness stand (*Harris v. New York*, 401 U.S. 222 [1971]). However, if a state's constitution (as interpreted by state courts) or state law prohibits the use of such statements to impeach the credibility of a witness, they cannot be used in that state.

Harris v. New York (1971)

Statutory Law

Statutory law is law passed by the Congress of the United States or by state legislatures. Federal and state laws may cover the same rights mentioned in the U.S. Constitution but in more detail. For example, an accused's right to counsel during trial is guaranteed by the U.S. Constitution, but it may also be given by federal or state law and is just as binding in court proceedings. Moreover, the right to counsel given by law in a state

statutory law
law passed by legislatures.

may exceed that guaranteed in the federal Constitution. The right to a lawyer during probation revocation hearings, for instance, is not constitutionally required, but many state laws give probationers this right. The right to a jury trial is not constitutionally required in juvenile cases, but it may be given by state law.

State law often determines the procedures the police must follow and available remedies if these procedures are breached. For example, state law may provide that the police cannot stop motor vehicles unless they have probable cause (U.S. Supreme Court decisions allow the stopping of motor vehicles based on reasonable suspicion, a lower degree of certainty than probable cause). Or state law may bar police pursuits of motor vehicles except in rural areas and only when the suspect is likely to have committed a serious crime and poses an imminent danger to the public. If this is the state law, the police are bound by that limitation on their authority even though the U.S. Supreme Court considers the prohibited practice constitutional.

Case Law versus Common Law

case law
law promulgated in cases decided by the courts.

Case law is law created in cases decided by the courts, and explained in opinions written by the judges explaining the decision. When deciding cases, the courts gradually develop legal principles that become law. This law is called *unwritten* or *judge-made* law, as distinguished from laws passed by legislative bodies. Written laws often represent the codification of case law that has become accepted and is practiced in a particular state.

common law
law generally derived from ancient usages and customs or from judgments and decrees of courts recognizing, affirming, and enforcing them.

Case law is sometimes confused with common law. The two are similar in that neither kind of law is a product of legislative enactment but has evolved primarily through judicial decisions. They differ in that **common law** originated from the ancient and unwritten laws of England. Although later applied in the United States, common law is generally derived from ancient usages and customs or from the judgments and decrees of the courts recognizing, affirming, and enforcing those usages and customs. Although common law and case law both result from court decisions, common law usually does not have value as precedent in state criminal prosecutions, except if specified by state law. By contrast, case law has value as precedent within the territorial jurisdiction of the court that issued the opinion.

These differences may be summarized as discussed in the table:

Case Law	Common Law
Sources are U.S. court decisions	Sources are the ancient, unwritten laws of England
Court decisions may be recent or old	Court decisions are ancient
Authoritative, but only within the territorial jurisdiction of that court	May or may not be authoritative in a certain jurisdiction, usually depending on provisions of state law
May evolve or change with a new decision	Does not change

Court Rules

Various rules have developed as a result of the supervisory power of courts over the administration of criminal justice. Federal courts have supervisory power over federal criminal cases, and state courts have similar power over state criminal cases. The rules promulgated by supervisory agencies (such as some states' supreme courts) have the force and effect of law and therefore must be followed. For example, the highest court of Missouri may promulgate regulations that supplement the provisions of Missouri laws on pleading and procedure. They cover details that may not be included in a state's codes of criminal procedure.

THE JUDICIAL REVIEW DOCTRINE

Courts in the United States exercise **judicial review**, which is defined as "the power of any court to hold unconstitutional and hence unenforceable any law, any official action based on a law, or any other action by a public official that it deems to be in conflict with the Constitution."[4] The doctrine of judicial review is not expressly provided for in the Constitution but was first enunciated by the Court in the case of *Marbury v. Madison*, 5 U.S. 137 (1803), considered by legal scholars to be the most important case ever decided by the Court.

judicial review
the power of courts to declare law or acts unconstitutional.

Marbury v. Madison (1803)

The facts of *Marbury* and the politics involved are complex, but they focused on the issue whether the Congress of the United States could add to the original jurisdiction given to the Court in Article III the Constitution. In a unanimous opinion written by Chief Justice John Marshall, the Court held that "an act repugnant to the Constitution is void," adding, "It is emphatically the province and duty of the judicial department to say what the law is. Those who apply the rule to particular cases, must of necessity expound and interpret that rule. . . . A law repugnant to the Constitution is void; . . . courts as well as other departments are bound by that instrument."[5]

In sum, without the power being expressly provided for by the Constitution, the Court held that courts in general could declare unconstitutional any act of Congress or any act of any public official that is not in accordance with or contravenes the Constitution.

The judicial review doctrine applies to the following: laws passed by Congress, laws passed by state legislatures, ordinances passed by municipalities, and acts of public officials. Thus it is clearly a significant and pervasive doctrine. It means that laws passed by legislatures can and will be reviewed by the courts, if a proper case is brought before it, and declared unenforceable if found to violate the Constitution. For the executive department, it means that officials of the executive branch of government, from the president of the United States to government clerks must act in accordance with the Constitution, else what they do will be declared unconstitutional. For law enforcement officers, it means that whatever they do can be challenged in court and declared unconstitutional. If held to have violated constitutional rights, the act can result in civil liabilities or the imposition of criminal sanctions.

THE RULE OF LAW

The concept of the rule of law goes back to the days of ancient Greece and has different meanings to different people.[6] Since the tragic events of September 11, 2001, the concept of the rule of law has generated more interest and has been the subject of debate about its proper meaning. In the words of philosopher writer George Fletcher,

> Of all the dreams that drive men and women into the streets, from Buenos Aires to Budapest, the "rule of law" is the most puzzling. We have a pretty good idea what we mean by "free market" and "democratic elections." But legality and the "rule of law" are ideals that present themselves as opaque even to legal philosophers.[7]

One writer maintains that, at one end of the spectrum, the concept is associated with adherence to laws that have been passed by legislatures, regardless of how just or unjust they may be. At the other end, it is associated with the concept of justice and derives its validity from the "morality of the laws that rule." Under this interpretation, mere passage of laws by the legislature does not constitute compliance with the concept of rule of law. An additional requirement is that the law passed must be just.[8] Some people equate the rule of law with the "supremacy of the law," whereas others associate it with "obedience to the law." A legalistic view, meaning adherence to court decisions, is reflected in former Vice President Al Gore's reaction when he lost the *Bush v. Gore* case involving the 2000 presidential election. He said, "I strongly disagree with the Supreme Court decision and the way in which they interpreted and applied the law. But I respect the rule of law, so it is what it is."[9]

rule of law
no person is above the law.

Among its many meanings, perhaps the best-known meaning of the **rule of law** is this: No person is above the law; every person, from the most powerful public official down to the least powerful individual, is subject to the law and can be held accountable in court for his or her actions. In the words of David Hume, a British philosopher, the phrase means "a government of laws and not of men."[10] That phrase also highlights one of the main distinctions between a democratic and a totalitarian society. In a democratic society, even the most powerful public official or private person can be held accountable under the law for what he or she does; in a totalitarian society, the ruler (and, by extension, those authorized to carry out the ruler's commands) enjoys boundless power and can do whatever he or she pleases without accountability in any court of law while in office or even after leaving office.

The rule of law is important in today's climate of law enforcement for two reasons. First, the events of 9/11 and the continuing concern about terror attacks have led to the passage of laws curtailing the rights and liberties of citizens and noncitizens. Should the Constitution be interpreted to accommodate the immediate needs of a changing time? In other words, should laws passed by legislatures that seek to protect the public from external threats be allowed to limit individual rights that have traditionally been protected by the Constitution? These are questions the Supreme Court has already considered and will continue to consider as cases are brought before it as further events unfold.

Second, police accountability in the United States is closely tied to the concept of the rule of law. In many countries, the police are immensely powerful, with little or no accountability for their actions. In the United States, however, criminal and civil liabilities (discussed in Chapter 14) are an ever-present reality in policing and represent the apex of police accountability. Law enforcement officers, from the police chief to a newly hired recruit, can be and are held criminally and civilly liable for what they do. The public considers this accountability a classic illustration of the concept that no person in this country, not even one wearing a badge of authority, is above the law. This is the most notable difference between policing a free society and law enforcement in a totalitarian country.

Rule of law, therefore, is a concept that law enforcement officers in the United States must be fully aware of and understand if they are to perform their tasks properly, constitutionally, and with minimum fear of liability.

THE INCORPORATION CONTROVERSY

The **incorporation controversy** refers to the debate over whether the Bill of Rights in the U.S. Constitution (referring to Amendments 1–10) protects against violations of rights by the federal government only or whether it also limits acts by state and local government officials. In short, does the Bill of Rights apply to the states? For example, the Fourth Amendment states, in part, "The right of the people to be secure in their persons, houses, papers, and effects, against unreasonable searches and seizures, shall not be violated." Does this limitation apply only to federal officials (such as FBI agents, who are thereby prohibited from making unreasonable searches or seizures), or does it also apply to state and local officials (such as police officers)?

incorporation controversy
issue of whether the Bill of Rights protects the public only against violations of rights by federal officials or whether it also protects against violations of rights by state officials.

Background

The most important safeguards available to an accused in the United States are found in the Bill of Rights. These ten amendments were ratified as a group and made part of the U.S. Constitution in 1791, two years after the Constitution itself was ratified by the original thirteen states. Initially, the Bill of Rights was viewed as limiting only the acts of federal officers, because the Constitution itself at the time of its passage limited only the powers of the federal government, not the states. State and local officers originally were limited only by provisions of their own state constitutions, state laws, or local ordinances.

In 1868, however, the Fourteenth Amendment was passed. Section 1 of that amendment states, in part, "No State shall make or enforce any law which shall abridge the privileges or immunities of citizens of the United States; nor shall any State deprive any person of life, liberty, or property, without due process of law; nor deny to any person within its jurisdiction the equal protection of the laws." This provision clearly applies to the states (*"No State* shall make or enforce. . . .") and has two main clauses: the due process clause and the equal protection clause.

The **due process clause** of the Fourteenth Amendment has been interpreted over the years by the U.S. Supreme Court as "incorporating" most of the provisions of the Bill of Rights, giving rise to the incorporation controversy. Therefore, although the fundamental rights granted by the Bill of Rights were originally meant to cover only violations by federal officers, the wording of the Fourteenth Amendment (specifically, the due process clause) has been interpreted by the Court, in various cases over the years, to prohibit violations of rights by *either* federal *or* state officers. In other words, those rights that are incorporated under the Fourteenth Amendment apply to state as well as federal criminal proceedings.

Approaches to Incorporation

The question of what constitutional rights are to be incorporated into the due process clause of the Fourteenth Amendment (and therefore held applicable to the states) is an issue decided by the U.S. Supreme Court over a period of years, on a case-by-case (and right-by-right) basis. Different justices have taken differing approaches to the incorporation controversy. These approaches can be classified into four "positions":

An Example of How the Supreme Court Incorporates a Right

Facts: Duncan was convicted in a Louisiana court of simple battery (a misdemeanor punishable under Louisiana law by a maximum sentence of two years in prison and a $300 fine). Duncan requested a jury trial, but the request was denied because under Louisiana law, jury trials were allowed only when "hard labor" or capital punishment could be imposed. Duncan was convicted and given sixty days in jail and fined $150. He appealed to the U.S. Supreme Court, claiming that the state's refusal to give him a jury trial for a crime punishable by two or more years of imprisonment violated his constitutional right to a jury trial.

Issue: *Was the state's refusal to give the defendant a jury trial for a crime that carried a two-year imprisonment as the maximum sentence a violation of the constitutional right to a jury trial specified in the Sixth Amendment as incorporated through the due process clause of the Fourteenth? Yes.*

Decision: The decision of the Louisiana Supreme Court was remanded for further proceedings.

Holding: A crime punishable by two years in prison, although classified under Louisiana law as a misdemeanor, is a serious crime, and therefore the defendant is entitled to a jury trial.

Case Significance: The *Duncan* case made the right to trial by jury applicable to the states in cases in which the maximum penalty is two years imprisonment, regardless of how state law classifies the offense. Although *Duncan* did not clearly state the minimum sentence, a subsequent case (*Baldwin v. New York*, 399 U.S. 66 [1972]) later held

that any offense that carries a *potential* sentence of more than six months is a serious offense, so a jury trial must be afforded on demand. This requirement applies even if the sentence *actually* imposed is less than six months.

Excerpts from the Opinion: The test for determining whether a right extended by the Fifth and Sixth Amendments with respect to federal criminal proceedings is also protected against state action by the Fourteenth Amendment has been phrased in a variety of ways in the opinions of this Court. The question has been asked whether a right is among those "fundamental principles of liberty and justice which lie at the base of all our civil and political institutions," whether it is "basic in our system of jurisprudence," and whether it is "a fundamental right, essential to a fair trial." The claim before us is that the right to trial by jury guaranteed by the Sixth Amendment meets these tests. The position of Louisiana, on the other hand, is that the Constitution imposes upon the States no duty to give a jury trial in any criminal case, regardless of the seriousness of the crime or the size of the punishment which may be imposed.

Because we believe that trial by jury in criminal cases is fundamental to the American scheme of justice, we hold that the Fourteenth Amendment guarantees a right of jury trial in all criminal cases which—were they tried in federal court—would come within the Sixth Amendment's guarantee. Since we consider the appeal before us to be such a case, we hold that the Constitution was violated when appellant's demand for jury trial was refused.

---

selective incorporation, total incorporation, total incorporation plus, and the case-by-case approach. (Read the *Duncan v. Louisiana* case brief to see an example of how the U.S. Supreme Court incorporates a right.)

Since the mid-1920s, most U.S. Supreme Court justices have taken the **selective incorporation** approach. This approach asserts that only those rights considered "fundamental" should be incorporated under the due process clause of the Fourteenth Amendment and held applicable to state criminal proceedings. Other criteria used by the Court in deciding whether to incorporate a right are: (1) whether a right is among those "fundamental principles of liberty and justice which lie at the base of our civil and political institutions," (2) whether it is "basic in our system of jurisprudence," and (3) whether it is a "fundamental right essential to a fair trial." Regardless of the

selective incorporation only those rights considered fundamental should be applied to the states.

phrase used, advocates of selective incorporation claim that the due process clause of the Fourteenth Amendment requires only fundamental fairness in state proceedings, not the automatic absolute, all-inclusive application of all provisions of the Bill of Rights. Selective incorporation has been the predominant approach since the Court began hearing incorporation cases.

Justices who, over the years, have taken the second approach—**total incorporation**—argue that the Fourteenth Amendment's due process clause should be interpreted as incorporating all the rights given in the first ten amendments to the U.S. Constitution, and no others. This position was enunciated by Justice Hugo Black, who wrote in a concurring opinion in 1968, "I believe as strongly as ever that the Fourteenth Amendment was intended to make the Bill of Rights applicable to the states" (*Duncan v. Louisiana*, 391 U.S. 145 [1968]). His is a blanket and uncomplicated approach: it proposes to incorporate "lock, stock, and barrel" all the provisions in the Bill of Rights.

The third approach—**total incorporation plus**—is an extension of total incorporation. It proposes that, in addition to extending all the provisions of the Bill of Rights to the states, other rights ought to be added, such as the right to clean air, clean water, and a clean environment. Justice William O. Douglas, an activist jurist, was the main advocate of this approach, but over the years it has failed to gain many converts in the Court.

The fourth approach—**case-by-case incorporation**—advocates an examination of the facts of a specific case to determine whether there is an injustice so serious as to justify extending the provisions of the Bill of Rights to that particular case. It is otherwise known as the "fair trial" approach, because the standard used is whether the accused obtained a fair trial. It differs from the selective incorporation approach in that selective incorporation focuses on whether a specific right (such as the right to counsel) should apply to the states. By contrast, the case-by-case approach more narrowly focuses on the facts of a specific case to decide whether *that particular case*, given its peculiar facts, should come under the due process clause.

The problem with the case-by-case approach is that the application of the Bill of Rights becomes unpredictable and totally dependent on the facts, so a particular case has little or no value as precedent.

total incorporation
all the rights in the Bill of Rights should be held as applying to the States.

Duncan v. Louisiana (1968)

total incorporation plus
in addition to applying all the provisions of the Bill of Rights to the States, other rights ought to be added, such as the right to clean air, clean water, and a clean environment.

case-by-case incorporation
examines the facts of a specific case to determine whether there is an injustice so serious as to justify extending the provisions of the Bill of Rights to this particular case.

A Summary of the Four Approaches to Incorporation

The four approaches to incorporation are summarized as follows:

1. **Selective Incorporation**: Only those rights in the Bill of Rights that are considered fundamental should be applied to the States.
2. **Total Incorporation**: Every one of the provisions of the Bill of Rights should be applied to the States.
3. **Total Incorporation Plus**: All the provisions of the Bill of Rights should be applied to the States, plus other unspecified rights.
4. **Case-by-Case Incorporation**: Examines the facts of a specific case to determine whether there is an injustice so serious as to justify extending the provisions of the Bill of Rights to that case and to that case only.

Case-by-case differs from selective incorporation in that the case-by-case approach looks at the facts of a particular case to determine if the violation is so bad that the

Bill of Rights should apply to that case. In contrast, selective incorporation looks at whether a particular right is so fundamental that it should apply to all cases involving that right. It is not concerned with a particular case.

Fundamental Right as the Test for Selective Incorporation

Palko v. Connecticut (1937)

The Court has defined *fundamental rights* as those "of the very essence of a scheme of ordered liberty" and "principles of justice so rooted in the traditions and conscience of our people as to be ranked as fundamental" (*Palko v. Connecticut*, 302 U.S. 319 [1937]). These vague though lofty phrases mean that the Court will determine on a case-by-case basis whether a particular right should be incorporated.

As noted previously, selective incorporation is the approach used by the Supreme Court over the years. In specific cases, the Court (using the selective incorporation approach) has held that the following provisions of the Bill of Rights apply in both federal and state proceedings:

◆ First Amendment provisions for freedom of religion, speech, assembly, and petition for redress of grievances (*Fiske v. Kansas*, 274 U.S. 380 [1927])
◆ Fourth Amendment protections against unreasonable arrest, search, and seizure (*Wolf v. Colorado*, 338 U.S. 25 [1949]; *Mapp v. Ohio*, 367 U.S. 643 [1961])
◆ Fifth Amendment protection against self-incrimination (*Malloy v. Hogan*, 378 U.S. 1 [1964])
◆ Fifth Amendment prohibition against double jeopardy (*Benton v. Maryland*, 395 U.S. 784 [1969])
◆ Sixth Amendment right to counsel (*Gideon v. Wainwright*, 372 U.S. 335 [1963])
◆ Sixth Amendment right to a speedy trial (*Klopfer v. North Carolina*, 386 U.S. 21 [1967])
◆ Sixth Amendment right to a public trial (*In re Oliver*, 333 U.S. 257 [1948])
◆ Sixth Amendment right to confrontation of opposing witnesses (*Pointer v. Texas*, 380 U.S. 400 [1965])
◆ Sixth Amendment right to an impartial jury (*Duncan v. Louisiana*, 391 U.S. 145 [1968])
◆ Sixth Amendment right to a compulsory process for obtaining witnesses (*Washington v. Texas*, 388 U.S. 14 [1967])
◆ Eighth Amendment prohibition against cruel and unusual punishment (*Robinson v. California*, 370 U.S. 660 [1962])

In incorporating a right, the Supreme Court expressly states that a provision of the Bill of Rights is made applicable to the states through the due process clause of the Fourteenth Amendment. For example, in *Duncan v. Louisiana*, 391 U.S. 145 (1968), the Supreme Court ruled that the right to trial by jury, guaranteed to defendants in federal trials under the Sixth Amendment, must also be given to defendants in state courts because of the due process clause of the Fourteenth Amendment. Hence, that right is deemed guaranteed.

Rights Not Incorporated

Although the following rights are required in federal proceedings, the states do not have to grant an accused these rights unless they are required by the state constitution or state law.[11]

- The Fifth Amendment right to indictment by grand jury
- The prohibition against excessive bail and fines

The Result of the Incorporation Controversy: "Nationalization" of the Bill of Rights

Through a process of selective incorporation, using the Fourteenth Amendment's due process clause, people facing federal or state criminal charges now have the same rights, except the rights to grand jury indictment and to protection against excessive bail and fines. In effect, through a process of selective incorporation the Bill of Rights has been nationalized. It makes no difference whether an accused is tried in New York, North Dakota, Nevada, or any other state or by the federal government, the rights are now the same because of incorporation. As a result, in no other field of law are the rights of individuals in the United States as similar as they are in the processing of an accused. Since the United States has a federal form of government, laws differ in various states. Criminal law, tort law, juvenile law, and civil law vary from state to state. However, the basic rights of suspects and defendants in all the fifty states and the federal government are the same due to incorporation.

COURT CASES

Court cases, particularly those decided by the U.S. Supreme Court, are important because they constitute case law and set precedents for cases decided by lower courts throughout the country. The full text of Court decisions can be found in law publications, often available in libraries, and on the Internet. To use these sources, you must know the basics of case citations, which provide the road map for where to find original court decisions as printed in various publications.

Case Citation

Case citation indicates where a case may be found in the vast firmament of legal publications. For example, if a reader wants to read the U.S. Supreme Court decision in the case of *Mapp v. Ohio*, he or she needs the official case citation, which is 367 U.S. 643 (1961). This means that *Mapp v. Ohio* is found in volume 367 of the *United States Reports*, starting on page 643, and that it was decided in 1961. If a reader wants to read the California Supreme Court decision in the case of *Peterson v. City of Long Beach*, he or she needs the citation, which is 155 Cal Rptr 360 (1979). The reader can then go to volume 155 of the *California Reporter* and start reading the case on page 360. The case was decided in 1979. The citation does not indicate the number of pages the case covers, only the page where the case starts.

Court cases may be published by official government sources or by private publishers. The better practice is to use the official government source for citation purposes, although private publications' citations may also be used when the official government source is unavailable or if there is no official government publication. For example, *Mapp v. Ohio* is also found in 81 S.Ct. 1684 (the *Supreme Court Reporter* is not a government publication) and 6 L.Ed.2d 1081 (the *Lawyers' Edition* is not a government publication). However, the better practice is to use 367 U.S. 643 (1961) because it is the official case citation.

case citation
indicates where a case may be found in legal publications.

Mapp v. Ohio (1961)
Peterson v. City of Long Beach (1979)

Here are examples of case citations, some government and others private, and what they mean:

◆ U.S. (*United States Reports*)—The official source of U.S. Supreme Court decisions; published by the U.S. government; reports only U.S. Supreme Court cases
◆ S.Ct. (*Supreme Court Reporter*)—Reports U.S. Supreme Court decisions; published by West Publishing Company, a private publisher

Exhibit 1.2   How to Find Cases on the Internet

In addition to printed sources, law cases are now also available on the Internet. Here are some of the free Internet sources:

◆ For U.S. Supreme Court decisions: Type the case title (for example, *Miranda v. Arizona*) into an Internet search engine such as Google. Or go to *http://www.findlaw.com/casecode/supreme.html*, and then click on Supreme Court Decisions "by year." Click the year the case was decided. You will then see court decisions alphabetically arranged. Note, however, that these means of Internet access may change.*

◆ For U.S. Courts of Appeals decisions:

Decisions of the First Circuit: *http://www.ca1 .uscourts.gov*

Decisions of the Second Circuit: *http://www.ca2 .uscourts.gov*

Decisions of the Third Circuit: *http://www.ca3 .uscourts.gov*

Decisions of the Fourth Circuit: *http://www.ca4 .uscourts.gov*

Decisions of the Fifth Circuit: *http://www.ca5 .uscourts.gov*

Decisions of the Sixth Circuit: *http://www.ca6 .uscourts.gov*

Decisions of the Seventh Circuit: *http://www.ca7 .uscourts.gov*

Decisions of the Eighth Circuit: *http://www.ca8 .uscourts.gov*

Decisions of the Ninth Circuit: *http://www.ca9 .uscourts.gov*

Decisions of the Tenth Circuit: *http://www.ca10 .uscourts.gov*

Decisions of the Eleventh Circuit: *http://www .ca11.uscourts.gov*

Decisions of the D.C. Circuit: *http://www.cadc .uscourts.gov*

Decisions of the Federal Circuit: *http://www .cafc.uscourts.gov*

◆ For decisions of federal district courts: Some federal district courts have their own websites. If you do not have a federal district court's website, you can go to *http://www.law.cornell.edu* (Cornell Legal Information Institute) or to *http:// www.uscourts.gov/courtlinks/* (Federal Judiciary website).†

◆ If you are a student, your institution may have access to Academic Universe, an excellent source of federal and state cases on all levels. Instructions for accessing Academic Universe vary from one institution to another.

◆ Other legal sources are available on the Internet for a fee. The most popular are VersusLaw, Westlaw, and LexisNexis. VersusLaw is recommended for non-lawyers as the best legal site for a fee because it is simple, inexpensive, and has no specific minimum period of time. It contains federal and state court opinions on various levels. At some universities, Westlaw and LexisNexis are available to students and are excellent sources of material for legal research.

*See *World's Leading Law Internet Sites* (Rockville, MD: Surfless Publications), p. 12.
†Stephen Elias and Susan Levinkind, *Legal Research: How to Find & Understand the Law*, 9th ed. (Berkeley, CA: Nolo Press, 2001), ch. 9, p. 20.

- L.W. (*United States Law Week*)—Reports U.S. Supreme Court decisions; published by the Bureau of National Affairs, Inc.
- F.2d (*Federal Reports, Second Series*)—Reports decisions of the federal courts of appeals (thirteen circuits); published by West
- F.Supp (*Federal Supplement*)—Reports most decisions of federal district courts throughout the United States; publishes only a small percentage of cases decided by federal district courts (most federal district court cases are not published at all); published by West
- P.2d (*Pacific Reporter, Second Series*)—Reports state court decisions in the Pacific states; one of seven regional reporters that publish state court cases; the other six are *Atlantic Reporter* (A), *Northeastern Reporter* (N.E.), *North Western Reporter* (N.W.), *Southeastern Reporter* (S.E.), *Southern Reporter* (S), and *South Western Reporter* (S.W.); all published by West
- Cal Rptr (*California Reporter*)—Publishes California state court appellate-level cases; the various states have similar series

HOW TO BRIEF A CASE

Case briefs help readers understand court cases better and are used extensively as a learning tool in law schools and in the practice of law. In case briefs, students read a case, break it into segments, and then reassemble it in a more concise and organized form to facilitate learning.

To familiarize readers with the basics of case briefing, a sample case brief is presented in this section. There is no agreement among scholars on how a case should be briefed for instructional purposes. The elements of a brief ultimately depend on the preferences of the instructor or student doing the briefing. The sample brief given here is as simple as it gets. Some briefs are more complex; they include dissenting and concurring opinions (if any), comments, case excerpts, and other elements an instructor or student might deem necessary.

The basic elements of a simple case brief are as follows:

1. Case title
2. Citation
3. Year decided
4. Facts
5. Issue or issues
6. Court decision
7. Holding
8. Case significance

The case of *Minnesota v. Dickerson* could be briefed in the following way. (For comparison, read the original version of this case on the Internet by searching on "Minnesota v. Dickerson.")

1. **Case title:** *Minnesota v. Dickerson*
2. **Citation:** 508 U.S. 366
3. **Year decided:** 1993

Note: In your brief, the above elements go in this order: *Minnesota v. Dickerson*, 508 U.S. 366 (1993). This means that the case of *Minnesota v. Dickerson* is found in volume 508 of the *United States Reports*, starting on page 366, and was decided in 1993.

4. **Facts:** During routine patrol, two police officers spotted Dickerson leaving an apartment building that one of the officers knew was a crack house. Dickerson began walking toward the police but, upon making eye contact with them, reversed direction and walked into an alley. Because of his evasive actions, the police became suspicious and decided to investigate. They pulled their vehicle into the alley and ordered Dickerson to stop and submit to a pat-down search. The search revealed no weapons, but one officer felt a small lump in Dickerson's pocket, thoroughly examined it with his fingers, and subsequently determined that it felt like a lump of cocaine in cellophane. The officer then reached into Dickerson's pocket and pulled out the lump, which turned out to be a small plastic bag containing crack cocaine. Dickerson was arrested and charged with possession of a controlled substance.

Note: The facts section can be too detailed or too sketchy, both of which can be misleading. In general, be guided by this question: Which minimum facts must be included in your brief so that somebody who has not read the whole case (as you have) will nonetheless understand it? The amount of detail required is for you to decide— you must determine the facts that are important or unimportant. Keep the important; weed out the unimportant.

5. **Issue or issues:** Was the seizure of the crack cocaine valid under stop and frisk? No.

Note: The issue statement should always be in question form, as it is here. The issue statement should not be so broad as to apply to every case even remotely similar in facts, nor so narrow as to apply only to the particular facts of that case. Here are some examples: Are police seizures without probable cause valid? (*Too broad.*) Is police seizure of something that feels like a lump in a suspect's pocket valid? (*Too narrow.*) Was the seizure of the crack cocaine valid under stop and frisk? (*Just right.*) Some cases have more than one issue. If these issues cannot be merged, they must be stated as separate issues.

6. **Court decision:** The U.S. Supreme Court affirmed the decision of the Minnesota Supreme Court that held the seizure to be invalid.

Note: The Supreme Court decision answers two questions: (1) Did the Court affirm, reverse, or modify the decision of the immediate lower court (in this case, the Minnesota Supreme Court); and (2) what happened to the case? Sometimes students confuse the Court decision with the holding (see item 7). The difference is that the Court decision is a brief statement that tells you what happened to the case on appeal and what the Court said is to be done with it. In this briefed case, the case ends because the lower court decision was affirmed. It would have been different had the Court ordered that the case be "reversed and remanded." The case would then have gone back to the lower court for reconsideration in light of the Supreme Court's ruling.

7. **Holding**: A frisk that goes beyond the scope allowed in *Terry v. Ohio* in stop and frisk cases is not valid. In this case, the search went beyond the pat-down search allowed by *Terry* because the officer "squeezed, slid, and otherwise manipulated the packet's content" before determining it was cocaine. The evidence obtained is not admissible in court.

Note: State in brief, exact, clear language what the Court said. In some cases, the holding may be taken verbatim from the case itself, usually toward the end. The holding is the most important element of the case because it states the rule announced by the Court. The holding becomes precedent, which means the same rule is applicable to future similar cases to be decided by the courts.

8. **Case significance**: This case is important because it sets the limits of how the police can frisk in stop and frisk cases. Here the officer went beyond merely patting down the suspect for a weapon. Instead, the officer squeeze, slid, and manipulated the item after feeling it. Only then did he realize it could be drugs. Doing that without probable cause went beyond what is allowed by as part of a frisk.

Note: This part of a case brief can be optional and is written primarily for the benefit of the student so he or she can evaluate the importance of the case. Some professors, however, require it as part of the case brief. Case significance generally indicates whether the case is important or not in the context of a topic. Some cases, such as *Miranda v. Arizona*, 384 U.S. 436 (1966), and *Mapp v. Ohio*, 367 U.S. 643 (1961), are obviously important in that their impact is widespread and immediate. Others, however, are not as obvious in importance and thus are left to the judgment of the case brief writer. Some might consider a case significant, others may not.

Miranda v. Arizona (1966)

SUMMARY

The United States has a dual court system, meaning it has two levels of courts—federal and state.

Where a criminal case is to be tried is determined by this rule: If an act violates federal law, it is tried in federal court; if it violates state law, it is tried in state court. If an act violates both federal and state laws, it can be tried in both courts.

Judicial precedent means that decisions of courts have value as precedent for future cases similarly circumstanced.

Jurisdiction is the power of a court to try a case; *venue* is the place where the case is tried.

Judicial review is "the power of any court to hold unconstitutional and hence unenforceable any law, any official action based on a law, or any

other action by a public official that it deems to be in conflict with the Constitution."

Rule of law generally means that no person is above the law, and that every person, from the most powerful public official down to the least powerful individual, is subject to the law and can be held accountable in court for what he or she does.

The *incorporation controversy* is about whether the Bill of Rights protects against violations of rights by the federal government only or also limits actions of state and local government officials. The four approaches to incorporation are selective incorporation, total incorporation, total incorporation plus, and the case-by-case approach.

REVIEW QUESTIONS

1. "The United States has a dual court system." Explain what this means, and provide examples.
2. "The general rule is that a case is accepted by the U.S. Supreme Court for decision only if that case has nationwide significance." Is this statement true or false? Defend your answer.
3. "A court decision is effective only within a limited jurisdiction." What does this mean? Give an example.
4. "Every criminal act can be prosecuted in both federal and state courts." Is this statement true or false? Explain your answer.
5. Distinguish between judicial review and judicial precedent.
6. How does jurisdiction differ from venue?
7. What does this case citation mean: *Duncan v. Louisiana*, 391 U.S. 145 (1968)?
8. How can you find the U.S. Supreme Court decision in *Miranda v. Arizona*, 384 U.S. 436 (1966) on the Internet?
9. What is the rule of law? What are its implications for police officers?
10. What is the incorporation controversy? How did it originate?
11. Distinguish between selective incorporation and case-by-case incorporation.

TEST YOUR UNDERSTANDING

1. Assume you are a lawyer arguing a case in the Fifth Circuit Court of Appeals in New Orleans on the issue of whether or not prisoners can be required to cut their hair short and to have a haircut every month. Your client, an inmate in prison in Louisiana, wants the right to wear his hair long. The Fifth Circuit has not decided a case on the same issue, but your legal research shows that the Ninth Circuit Court of Appeals (for Washington and other states in that circuit) has already decided this issue, saying that prison inmates have a right to have long hair. Will the decision of the Ninth Circuit be of any use to you when arguing your case before the Fifth Circuit? Justify your answer.

2. Despite airport security precautions, X hijacked an airplane in Chicago and forced the pilot, crew, and passengers to fly to New York. Upon reaching New York, X shot the pilot before giving up and surrendering to the New York City police. X was later prosecuted for various crimes stemming from the hijacking. Cases were filed against X in Chicago, the New York state court, and the New York federal court. X claims that he could be tried only in a state court in Illinois. Will X's claim succeed? State the reasons for your answer.

3. Y, an undocumented alien, was caught speeding in Phoenix. When the police stopped Y for this moving violation, they found five pounds of cocaine in his car, located in the passenger side of the car and open to view by the police. Y was arrested and brought before a local magistrate, who set his bail at half a million dollars. Y appealed. You are the appellate court judge. Will you uphold Y's contention that his bail is excessive? Give reasons for your answer.

RECOMMENDED READINGS

"U.S. Court System" [a comprehensive description], *http://www2.maxwell.syr.edu/plegal/scales/court.html.*

"Judicial Review: The Issue: Does the Constitution Give the Supreme Court the Power to Invalidate the Actions of Other Branches of Government?" *http://www.law.umkc.edu/faculty/projects/ftrials/conlaw/judicialrev.htm.*

Susan N. Herman and Lawrence M. Solan. *Jury in the twenty-first century: An interdisciplinary symposium.* 66 Brooklyn Law Review 1–19 (2001).

Joseph L. Hoffman. *Plea bargaining in the shadow of death.* Fordham Law Review 2313–2391 (2001).

"Incorporation Debate: The Issue: Does the Fourteenth Amendment Incorporate the Protections of the Bill of Rights and Make Them Enforceable against the States?" *http://law2.umkc.edu/faculty/projects/ftrials/conlaw/incorp.htm*

NOTES

1. Henry J. Abraham, *The Judicial Process,* 7th ed. (New York: Oxford University Press, 1998), p. 198.
2. Henry C. Black, *Black's Law Dictionary,* 5th ed. (St. Paul, MN: West, 1979), p. 1443.
3. *Time Magazine,* December 14, 1998, p. 44.
4. Supra note 1, p. 300.
5. Ibid., pp. 342–343.
6. Ronald A. Cass, *The Rule of Law in America* (Baltimore, MD: The Johns Hopkins University Press, 2001), p. 1.
7. As quoted in Cass, p. 1.
8. Supra note 7, p. 2.
9. Houston Chronicle, November 16, 2002, p. 24A.
10. As quoted in Cass, supra note 7, p. 2.
11. J. W. Peltason, Edwin Corwin, and Sue Davis, *Understanding the Constitution,* 15th ed. (Fort Worth, TX: Harcourt College Publishers, 2000), p. 214.

CHAPTER 2

Overview of the Criminal Justice Process

LEARNING OBJECTIVES

1. Identify the three basic stages of procedures for processing the defendant through the criminal justice system
2. Create a flow chart of the procedures prior to and during the trial process.
3. Describe the process that occurs during a criminal trial.
4. Explain the criminal justice procedures that begin after conviction of the defendant.
5. Describe the process for accessing the court while imprisoned in either a jail or a prison.
6. Compare and contrast criminal procedures between different jurisdictions.
7. Describe the jury selection process including types of juror challenges.
8. Contrast the different types of verdicts in a trial.
9. Describe the three types of pleas for a defendant.
10. List the different processes for charging a defendant.

KEY TERMS

affirmation
Alford plea
arraignment
arrest
bail
bench warrant
bifurcated procedure
bill of indictment
booking
capias
challenge for cause
citation
complaint
criminal procedure
discovery
exculpatory evidence
felony
grand jury
habeas corpus
hung jury
indictment
information
jury nullification
Miranda warnings
misdemeanor
motion
motion for a directed verdict of acquittal
motion for a mistrial
nolle prosequi motion
nolo contendere plea
peremptory challenge
plea
plea bargain
preliminary hearing
preventive detention
prima facie case
rebuttal evidence
release on recognizance (ROR)
reversal
reverse-and-remand decision
sequestration
standing mute
summons
venire
verdict
voir dire

THE TOP 5 IMPORTANT CASES

in Overview of the Criminal Justice Process

■ **DUNCAN V. LOUISIANA (1968)** The function of a jury is to "guard against the exercise of arbitrary power."

■ **BOYKIN V. ALABAMA (1969)** When a defendant pleads guilty, the record must show affirmatively that the plea was voluntary and that the accused had a full understanding of its consequences. Otherwise, the plea is invalid.

■ **SANTOBELLO V. NEW YORK (1971)** Once the trial court accepts a guilty plea entered in accordance with a plea bargain, the defendant has a right to have the plea bargain enforced. Therefore, the judge must decide either to enforce the agreement or to allow the defendant to withdraw the guilty plea.

■ **NORTH CAROLINA V. ALFORD (1979)** A guilty plea is not invalid simply because the defendant does not admit guilt or even continues to assert innocence, provided that there is some basis in the record for the plea. All that is required for a valid guilty plea is a knowing waiver of the rights involved, not an admission of guilt.

■ **COUNTY OF RIVERSIDE V. MCLAUGHLIN (1991)** Detention of a suspect for forty-eight hours without a probable cause hearing is presumptively reasonable. If the time to the hearing is longer than that, the burden of proof shifts to the police to prove reasonableness. But if the time to the hearing is shorter, the burden of proof to establish unreasonable delay rests on the person detained.

CRIMINAL PROCEDURE can be defined as the process followed by the police and the courts in the apprehension and punishment of criminals—from the filing of a complaint by a member of the public or the arrest of a suspect by the police, up to the time the defendant is punished, if convicted. Criminal procedure highlights the sometimes difficult conflict between the constitutional rights of a suspect or defendant and the power of government to maintain peace and order and ensure public safety.

criminal procedure
the process followed by the police and the courts in the apprehension and punishment of criminals.

That conflict must be resolved through prescribed rules; criminal procedure is those rules. Although sometimes offered as one course in law schools, criminal procedure and criminal law differ in that criminal procedure prescribes the process whereby a suspect or defendant is eventually found guilty or not guilty, while criminal law defines the acts that are punishable by the federal government or the states. One involves *process*; the other involves *substance*.

Criminal laws differ in detail and terminology from one state to another, but criminal procedure is very similar from one jurisdiction to another. This is because criminal procedure is mostly a product of U.S. Supreme Court decisions. The main source of rights in criminal procedure is the Bill of Rights (the first ten amendments to the Constitution). Through a process of incorporation, the rights enumerated in the Bill of Rights have been made applicable to criminal proceedings anywhere in the country; hence, the application of basic criminal procedure is uniform nationwide.

In addition to the Bill of Rights, there are other sources of rights for the defendant, including state constitutions, federal and state laws, case law, court rules, and rules prescribed by agencies. This often results in variations from one jurisdiction to another. Whatever the differences, the general rule is that states can give more rights to a suspect by limiting the actions of the police or the courts. These additional sources of rights cannot deprive a suspect of any right given by the Bill of Rights; they can only add to them. For example, the U.S. Supreme Court has held that it is constitutional for police to stop motor vehicles based on reasonable suspicion. State law, however, may prohibit such stops unless there is probable cause, thus expanding the rights of suspects. Another example is that the Constitution does not require confessions by suspects to be in writing to be admissible in evidence. State law, however, may exclude oral confessions unless they are also in writing or supported by other evidence.

This chapter presents an overview of the criminal justice process from a legal perspective. The procedure is divided into three time frames: (1) before trial, (2) during trial, and (3) after trial. In most cases, an arrest triggers criminal justice procedures against the accused. In some cases, however, the procedure is initiated through the filing of a complaint that leads to the issuance of a warrant by a judge or magistrate. Procedure during trial starts with the selection of jurors and ends with a jury verdict. If the accused is found guilty, the sentencing phase follows, after which the defendant may appeal the conviction and sentence.

THE PROCEDURE BEFORE TRIAL

Criminal procedure before trial begins with the filing of a complaint by a member of the public followed by an arrest or the arrest of a suspect by police, booking, first appearance, setting of bail, preliminary examination, decision to charge, grand jury indictment or information, arraignment, plea, and plea bargaining. This section describes what happens at each stage; see Figure 2.1 for a summary of before trial and trial progressions.

Filing of Complaint

complaint
a charge made before a law enforcement or judicial officer alleging the commission of a criminal offense.

A **complaint** is a charge made before a law enforcement or judicial officer alleging the commission of a criminal offense. It may be filed by the victim or by a police officer who has obtained information about or witnessed the criminal act, although some states restrict the filing of a complaint to the prosecutor. The complaint serves as a basis for issuing an arrest warrant. If the accused has been arrested without a warrant, the complaint is prepared and filed at the defendant's initial appearance before the magistrate, usually by the arresting officer. See Figure 2.2 for an example of a complaint form.

FIGURE 2.1 A Summary of the Pretrial and Trial Stages

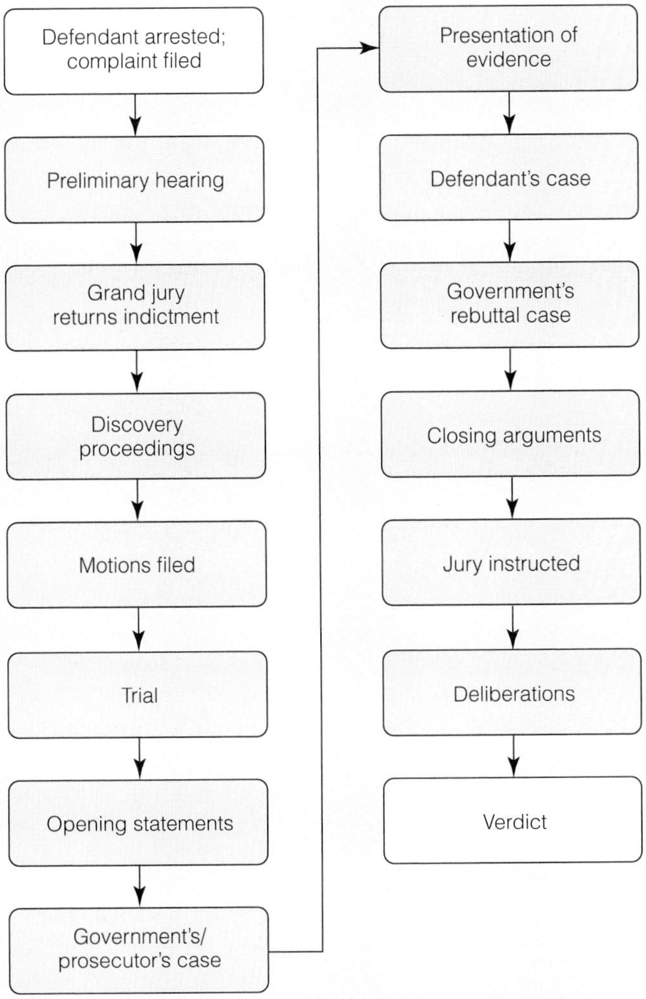

```
Defendant arrested;          ──→    Presentation of
complaint filed                      evidence
      │                                   │
      ▼                                   ▼
Preliminary hearing                 Defendant's case
      │                                   │
      ▼                                   ▼
Grand jury                          Government's
returns indictment                  rebuttal case
      │                                   │
      ▼                                   ▼
Discovery                           Closing arguments
proceedings                               │
      │                                   ▼
      ▼                             Jury instructed
Motions filed                             │
      │                                   ▼
      ▼                             Deliberations
Trial                                     │
      │                                   ▼
      ▼                             Verdict
Opening statements
      │
      ▼
Government's/
prosecutor's case ──────────────────┘
```

Source: "U.S. Courts," http://www.uscourts.gov.

The Arrest

An **arrest** is the taking of a person into custody for the purpose of criminal prosecution or interrogation. There are two kinds of arrest: arrest with a warrant and arrest without a warrant. In *arrest with a warrant*, a complaint has been filed and presented to a judge, who has read it and found probable cause (as defined in Chapter 3) to justify the issuance of an arrest warrant (see Figure 2.3). In contrast, *arrest without a warrant* usually happens when a crime is committed in the presence of a police officer or, in some jurisdictions, by a citizen's arrest for certain offenses. As many as 95 percent of all arrests are made without a warrant. An officer must be convinced of the existence of probable cause before making an arrest. This belief is later established in a sworn complaint or testimony at a preliminary hearing.

Statutes in many states authorize the use of a citation or summons rather than an arrest for less serious offenses. A **citation** is an order issued by a court or law

arrest
the taking of a person into custody for the purpose of criminal prosecution or interrogation.

citation
an order issued by a court or law enforcement officer requiring a person to appear in court at a specified date to answer certain charges.

FIGURE 2.2 Complaint Form, State of Missouri

<pre>
STATE OF MISSOURI   )
) ss.
COUNTY OF CLINTON   )

        IN THE ASSOCIATE CIRCUIT COURT OF CLINTON COUNTY, MISSOURI

STATE OF MISSOURI,   )
                    Plaintiff   )
)
        -vs-   )   Case No.
)
)
                    Defendant   )
</pre>

C O M P L A I N T

_____, being duly sworn, deposes and states that in

the County of Clinton, State of Missouri, heretofore, to-wit: on or about

_____, one _____, in violation

of Section 570.120, RSMo, committed the Class A misdemeanor of passing bad checks

punishable upon conviction under Sections 558.011.1(5) and 560.016, RSMo, in that the

defendant, with purpose to defraud, issued a check in the amount of $_____,

drawn upon the _____, dated _____,

payable to _____, knowing that such check would not

be paid.

    Affiant further states that he has actual personal knowledge of the facts, matters and
things above set out and is a competent witness thereto.

                                                      _____
                                                       Plaintiff

Subscribed and sworn to before me this _____ day of _____, 20 ____.

                                                   _____
                                            Clerk of the Associate Circuit Court

Source: Complaint form for Clinton County, State of Missouri.

summons
a writ directed to the sheriff or other officer requiring the officer to notify a person that he or she must appear in court on a day named and answer the complaint.

bench warrant
a process issued by the court for the attachment or arrest of a person.

enforcement officer requiring a person to whom the citation is issued to appear in court on a specified date to answer certain charges. A **summons** is a writ directed to the sheriff or other proper officer requiring the officer to notify the person named that he or she must appear in court on a specified date and answer the complaint stated in the summons. Citations and summonses have the advantage of keeping a person out of jail pending the hearing. They also save the police officer the time and paperwork that go with arrest and booking. In either case, if the person fails or refuses to appear in court as scheduled, a bench warrant may be issued. A **bench warrant** is defined as a "process issued by the court itself, or 'from the bench,' for the attachment or arrest of a person; either in case of contempt, or where an indictment has been found, to bring in a witness who fails to obey a subpoena."[1]

FIGURE 2.3 Warrant for Arrest Form, State of New Mexico

9-210A
[For use with District Court Criminal Rule 5-210]

STATE OF NEW MEXICO
COUNTY OF _____
JUDICIAL DISTRICT

STATE OF NEW MEXICO

v.   No. _____

_____ , Defendant

Warrant No. _____
Judge _____

WARRANT FOR ARREST

THE STATE OF NEW MEXICO TO ANY OFFICER AUTHORIZED TO EXECUTE THIS WARRANT:

BASED ON A FINDING OF PROBABLE CAUSE, YOU ARE COMMANDED to arrest the above-named defendant and bring the defendant without unnecessary delay before this court to answer the charge of (*here state common name and description of offense charged*):

_____

_____

_____

contrary to Section(s) _____ NMSA 1978.

Bond provisions:

Bond is set in the amount of $_____ ☐ cash bond 10% of bond ☐ surety ☐ property bond.

Date: _____

_____
                Judge

Description of defendant:
Name _____
Alias _____
Date of birth _____
Social Security No. _____
Address _____
Sex ☐ male   ☐ female   Height _____ Weight _____
Hair color _____   Eyes _____
Scars, marks, and tattoos: _____

Vehicle (*make, model, year, and color, if known*)
_____

Extradition information:

The State will extradite the defendant: (*check and complete*)
☐ from any contiguous state
☐ from anywhere in the continental United States
☐ from any other State
☐ from anywhere

Prosecuting attorney: _____
By: _____
Date: _____
Originating officer: _____
Originating agency: _____

RETURN WHERE DEFENDANT IS FOUND

I arrested the above-named defendant on the _____ day of _____ , _____, and served a copy of this warrant on the _____ day of _____ , _____ and caused this warrant to be removed from the warrant information system identified in this warrant.

_____
Signature

_____
Title

Source: "Forms from the New Mexico Supreme Court," http://www.supremecourt.nm.org/supctforms/dc-criminal/VIEW/9-210.html.

The *Miranda* warnings (discussed in Chapter 11) need not be given every time an officer makes an arrest. The warnings do not have to be given by the officer after an arrest unless the arrested person is asked questions by the officer that tend to incriminate. In many cases, however, the officer simply makes the arrest and does not ask questions, particularly when the arrest is made with a warrant. The officer in these cases does not have to ask questions; all he or she does is take the suspect to a lockup or jail for detention. In many jurisdictions, the *Miranda* warnings are routinely given when the suspect appears before a judge or magistrate even if no questions are asked.

Booking at the Police Station

Booking consists of making an entry in the police blotter indicating the suspect's name, the time of arrest, and the offense involved. Prior to this, the arrestee is searched for weapons or any evidence that might be related to a crime, and his or her belongings are inventoried. If the offense is serious, the suspect may also be photographed and fingerprinted. Before or after booking, the suspect in major cities is usually placed in a lockup, which is a place of detention run by the police department, or in jail in smaller cities or communities where no lockups are available. In most jurisdictions, the arrestee is allowed a telephone call, usually to a lawyer or a family member. In some jurisdictions, the arrestee is allowed to post a predetermined amount of bail for minor offenses on a promise that he or she will appear in court at a particular time. If bail is not posted or is denied, the person is kept in detention until such time as he or she can be brought before a magistrate.

Initial Appearance before a Magistrate

In some states, the initial appearance before a magistrate is known as *presentment*, or *arraignment on the warrant*. Most states require that an arrested person be brought before a judge, magistrate, or commissioner "without unnecessary delay." What this means varies from state to state, depending on state law or court decisions. In federal and most state proceedings, a delay of more than six hours in bringing the suspect before the magistrate is one factor to be considered in determining whether any incriminating statements made by the accused were in fact voluntary. Other jurisdictions do not specify the number of hours but look at the surrounding circumstances and decide on a case-by-case basis whether the delay was unnecessary. See Figure 2.4, which shows the procedure for a criminal case in Wisconsin.

Once before a magistrate, the arrestee is informed of his or her rights. This procedure may include giving the ***Miranda* warnings**, which have five parts. The parts are:

1. You have a right to remain silent.
2. Anything you say can be used against you in a court of law.
3. You have a right to the presence of an attorney.
4. If you cannot afford an attorney, one will be appointed for you prior to questioning.
5. You have the right to terminate this interview at any time.

The *Miranda* warnings are not required by the Constitution at this stage of the proceedings since they need to be given only if there is "custodial interrogation," which usually does not take place at this stage. Some states by law or practice, however, require the giving of the *Miranda* during initial appearance, although without

FIGURE 2.4 A Criminal Case in the Wisconsin Court System

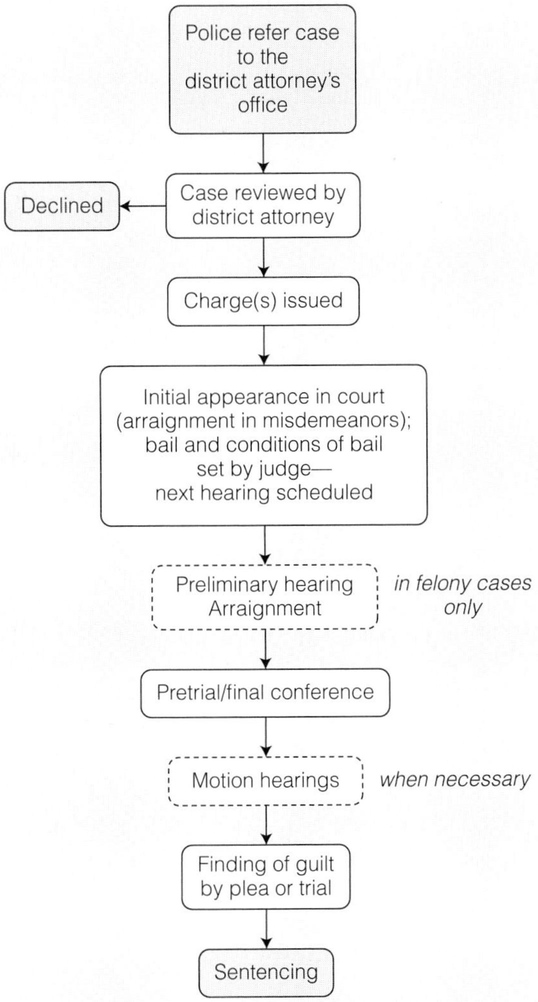

Source: Dane County, Wisconsin, "The Criminal Court Process," http://countyofdane.com/daoffice/process.htm.

warning number 5, "You have the right to terminate this interview at any time." It is given primarily to inform the accused of the right against self-incrimination and the right to counsel.

The suspect is also informed during the initial hearing of any other rights that may be given by state law. These vary from state to state and may include the right to a preliminary hearing, confrontation, and a speedy trial; the right not to incriminate oneself; and the exclusion in court of illegally obtained evidence.

Many jurisdictions require magistrates to give the *Miranda* warnings when the suspect is brought in, but the warnings must also be given by the arresting officer if he or she questions the suspect prior to the appearance before a magistrate. Failure to issue the warnings makes the suspect's statements inadmissible in court. Conversely, if the officer does not need to ask the suspect any questions (as would usually be the case in arrests with a warrant), the *Miranda* warnings need not be

Rothgery v. Gillespie County, Texas (2008)

given. The officer arrests the person named in the warrant and brings him or her before a magistrate or judge.

If the charge is a misdemeanor, the arrestee may be arraigned while appearing before the magistrate and required to plead to the pending charge. Many misdemeanor cases are disposed of at this stage, through a guilty plea or some other procedure. If the charge is a felony, the arrestee ordinarily is not required to plead to the charge at this time. Rather, he or she is held for preliminary examination on the felony charge.

The Court has held that "a criminal defendant's initial appearance before a magistrate judge, where he learns the charge against him and his liberty is subject to restriction, marks the initiation of adversary judicial proceedings that trigger attachment of the Sixth Amendment right to counsel (*Rothgery v. Gillespie County, Texas*, 544 U.S. 191 [2008]). In *Rothgery*, the police arrested the suspect and brought him before a magistrate judge for an initial hearing. In this hearing and based on state law, probable cause was established, bail was set, and the suspect was formally notified of the charges. After the hearing, the suspect was committed to jail but was released after posting bond. Claiming indigency and while free, he asked several times for an appointed lawyer, but his requests went unheeded. Rothgery was subsequently indicted and rearrested for the same offense. At this time, he was kept in jail because he could not post the increased bail. The case against him was later dismissed when he was assigned a lawyer who looked into the facts of his case and moved for its dismissal. Rothgery sued for damages against the county, claiming that had he been provided a lawyer after the initial hearing, he would not have been indicted, rearrested, or subsequently detained. On appeal, the Court upheld his claim of a violation of the constitutional right to counsel, saying that Rothgery's initial appearance before a judge, where he learned the charge and his liberty was subject to restriction, marked the beginning of an adversary process that triggered the right to counsel. This case reiterates the importance of the initial hearing and affirms that in these types of proceedings the right to court appointed counsel for indigents applies.

Setting Bail

bail
the security required by the court and given by the accused to ensure the accused's attendance in court at a specified time.

preventive detention
detaining a person in jail without bail with the purpose of preventing them from committing additional crimes.

United States v. Salerno (1987)

Bail is defined as the security required by the court and given by the accused to ensure that the accused appears in court at a scheduled time and place to answer the charges brought against him or her. In theory, the only function of bail is to ensure the appearance of the defendant at the time set for trial. In practice, bail has also been used as a form of **preventive detention** to prevent the release of an accused who might otherwise be dangerous to society or whom the judge might not want to release. The Court has upheld as constitutional a provision of the Federal Bail Reform Act of 1984 that permits federal judges to deny pretrial release to persons charged with certain serious felonies, based on a finding that no combination of release conditions can reasonably ensure the community of safety from such individuals (*United States v. Salerno*, 481 U.S. 739 [1987]).

Bail comes in various forms. One is a cash bail bond, where, according to *Black's Law Dictionary*, "a sum of money . . . is posted by a defendant or by another person on his behalf with a court . . . upon condition that such money will be forfeited if the defendant does not comply with the directions of a court requiring his attendance at the criminal action" at a designated time.[2] By statute in a number of states, the magistrate or judge before whom the proceedings are pending may free the accused through

release on recognizance (ROR), meaning, without monetary bail. This usually happens when the accused has strong ties to the community and seems likely to appear for trial. Usually, the judge sets an amount for the bail, but this is not paid unless the defendant does not appear at the designated date, at which time the amount will be paid and forfeited. If he or she fails to do so, an arrest warrant may be issued. Some jurisdictions use a citation release (also be known as a *cite out*), wherein no monetary amount is either pledged or given to the court, but the arrested person must appear in court at an appointed date. Failure to appear means that a certain amount, usually determined later, will be forfeited. Another bail variation is the posting of a property bond, which involves the defendant or anybody pledging real property up to at least the amount of the bail. Should the defendant fail to appear in court, the pledged property can be confiscated by the state and sold, so the state can recover the amount of bail.[3]

release on recognizance (ROR)
the release of a person without monetary bail.

The Preliminary Hearing

An accused charged with a felony is usually entitled to a **preliminary hearing** (sometimes called a *preliminary examination* or *examining trial*), to be held before a magistrate within a reasonable period of time after arrest. Preliminary hearings closely resemble trials, but their purpose is more limited, and the hearing magistrate is generally not the judge who will preside over the actual trial in the case. Representation by defense counsel and cross-examination of witnesses are allowed. The preliminary hearing

preliminary hearing
a hearing held before a judge or magistrate within a reasonably short time after arrest.

HIGHLIGHT ›   The Bail Bond Agent: Only in America

An interesting and controversial practice in the United States is the participation of bail bond agents. Bail bond agents are private people or agencies that charge a fee (usually 10 to 15 percent of the total amount of the bail) that is required for the release of a defendant. This fee is nonrefundable even if defendant shows up in court. The bail bondsperson, however, becomes liable for the total amount of bail if the defendant does not appear in court on the designated date. Bail bond agents usually require that the defendant (or anybody willing to do so for the defendant) pledge their house or any other property as a form of security for confiscation by the bondsperson should the defendant skip bail and the bondsperson forfeits. Having bail bond agents has led to the existence of so-called bounty hunters, individuals who are either employed by or perform jobs on contract for bail bond agents. Bounty hunters work for private persons or agencies, not for the government. If the defendant does not appear in court at the designated date or flees the jurisdiction, the bounty hunter tracks down the defendant and takes him or her into custody so the defendant can be brought to court. To avoid this controversial practice, some jurisdictions use the system of accepting a percentage of the bond amount (for example,

accepting $2,500 cash for a $25,000 bond) and returning the amount to the defendant if the conditions of release are followed and the defendant appears in court at the designated time. This has the advantage of the defendant getting back the posted amount and is an incentive for court appearance.

The Vera Institute of Justice has sponsored studies and programs leading to reforms in the bail system. Notable among these is the Manhattan Bail Project, which has led to reforms in national and international courts. These reforms involve a careful interview of defendants, ascertaining their community ties, and then making recommendations for release without the posting of bail. Its effect has been significant on both the defendant (release without having to pay) and the government (fewer detainees in jail).

Bail bonding by private persons it is almost exclusively an American practice. Some places and countries prohibit the posting of bail by bondspersons or the taking of defendants into detention by bounty hunters. The belief is that this is a function of government and should be performed exclusively by government agents and not by private individuals who profit from it.[4]

---

is usually the first chance for the defense to know the evidence that the prosecution has and the strength of the case against the accused. Because guilt beyond reasonable doubt is not required during the preliminary hearing, the prosecution does not have to present all the evidence it has. On the other hand, the defense does not have to present anything if it so chooses because, regardless of what it does, the judge may set the case for trial if probable cause is established.

Preliminary hearings are usually held for three reasons:

1. *Determination of probable cause.* The primary purpose of the preliminary hearing is to ascertain whether there is probable cause to support the charges against the accused. If not, the charges are dismissed. This process keeps unsupported charges of grave offenses from coming to trial and thereby protects people from harassment, needless expenditure, and damage to their reputation.

   What is the maximum time an arrested person can be detained without a probable cause determination? A 1991 Supreme Court decision is instructive because it sets a tentative limit. The Court held that detention of a suspect for up to forty-eight hours without a probable cause hearing is presumptively reasonable. If the time to a hearing is longer than that, the burden of proof is on the police to prove reasonableness. But if the time to a hearing is shorter, the burden of proof to establish unreasonable delay shifts to the detainee (*County of Riverside v. McLaughlin*, 500 U.S. 44 [1991]). A subsequent case held *McLaughlin* applicable to all cases that had not been decided at the time of the *McLaughlin* decision (*Powell v. Nevada*, 511 U.S. 79 [1992]).

2. *Discovery.* **Discovery** is a procedure used by either party in a case to obtain necessary or helpful information that is in the possession of the other party. It is initiated by one side through a motion filed in court seeking discovery of specific evidence the other side might have, such as recorded statements, the results of physical examinations or scientific tests, experiments, and other physical evidence. The items subject to discovery are generally specified by law, court rules, or court decisions. The purpose of discovery is to take the element of surprise out of the trial by ensuring that each side is aware of the strengths and weaknesses of the other, so realistic decisions can be made.

   > Although used extensively in civil cases, the scope of discovery in criminal cases is one-sided in favor of the defense because the accused can invoke the guarantee against self-incrimination and refuse to turn over relevant evidence to the prosecution. For example, the prosecutor has a constitutional obligation to disclose **exculpatory** (that which tends to establish innocence) **evidence** to the defense, while the defense attorney does not have any obligation to disclose *incriminatory* (that which tends to establish guilt) evidence to the prosecution, because such is a right given to the accused by the Fifth Amendment to the Constitution.

3. *Decision on binding over.* Some states use the preliminary hearing to determine if the accused will be "bound over" for a grand jury hearing. In these states, there must be a finding of cause at the preliminary examination before a grand jury hearing will be held. Other states use the preliminary examination to determine whether the accused should be bound over for trial, bypassing grand jury proceedings altogether.

County of Riverside v. McLaughlin (1991)

Powell v. Nevada (1992)

discovery
the procedure used in a case to obtain information from the other party.

exculpatory evidence
which tends to establish the defendant did not commit the crime charged.

In some cases, a preliminary examination is not required. These include:

1. *When an indictment has been handed down prior to the preliminary hearing.*
2. *If the grand jury has previously returned an indictment (usually because the case was referred to it before arrest).* The grand jury proceedings constitute a determination that there is probable cause and thus that the accused should stand trial.
3. *When a misdemeanor is involved.* In most jurisdictions, preliminary hearings are not required in misdemeanor cases, because only lesser penalties are involved. The accused goes directly to trial on the complaint or information filed by the district attorney.
4. *When there is a waiver of the preliminary hearing.* The accused may voluntarily give up the right to a preliminary examination. For example, a plea of guilty to the charge generally operates as a waiver of the preliminary examination. The accused is bound over for sentencing to the court that has jurisdiction over the crime.
5. *As a result of any of three actions in federal cases.* In federal cases, a preliminary hearing is required unless the defendant waives it or is instead indicted, if the federal prosecutor charges the defendant with a felony or a misdemeanor and prefers to use an information (to be discussed), or if the defendant is accused of a misdemeanor and consents to hold a trial before the magistrate judge.[5]

In sum, there are exceptions in both state and federal jurisdictions to the holding of a preliminary hearing.

After the preliminary hearing, the magistrate may take any of the following actions:

1. *Hold the defendant to answer.* If the magistrate finds probable cause, naming facts that would lead a person of ordinary caution or prudence to entertain a strong suspicion of the guilt of the accused, the accused is "held to answer" and bound over for trial in a court having jurisdiction over the offense charged.
2. *Discharge the defendant.* If the magistrate does not find probable cause, the defendant is discharged.
3. *Reduce the charge.* Most states allow the magistrate to reduce a felony charge to a misdemeanor on the basis of the results of the preliminary hearing. This enables grand juries and higher courts to avoid being swamped with cases that really belong in the lower courts.

The Decision to Charge

Discretion abounds in criminal justice, but particularly in policing and prosecution. After a suspect is taken into custody, the police usually have discretion to charge or not to charge him or her with an offense. As the seriousness of the offense increases, the discretion of the police decreases. For example, the police have almost no discretion to charge or not charge the suspect with an offense in homicide cases but may dispose of minor traffic offenses at the scene of the incident. The prosecutor also exercises immense discretion.

In most states, the prosecutor is not under the control of any superior other than the electorate. This discretion is most evident in the prosecutor's decision to charge or not to charge. In the words of former attorney general and U.S. Supreme Court

Justice Robert Jackson, "The prosecutor has more control over life, liberty, and reputation than any other person in America."[6] In most cases, the prosecutor has the final say about whether a suspect should be prosecuted. If the prosecutor decides to charge even though the evidence is weak, a suspect can do little else but go to trial and hope for an acquittal. In words attributed in 1985 to Sol Wachtler, a well-known judge (who was himself indicted in 2014), "A prosecutor can indict a ham sandwich." Conversely, if the evidence is strong but the prosecutor declines to charge, there is little anyone can do legally to persuade the prosecutor to charge. Even after a suspect has been charged, the prosecutor may file a **nolle prosequi motion**, which seeks a dismissal of the charges. Such a motion is almost always granted by the court.

Indictment versus an Information

A criminal prosecution is initiated by the filing of an accusatory pleading in the court having jurisdiction. Prior to the filing, the accused will have appeared before a magistrate to be informed of his or her rights and to post bail. The accused also will have had a preliminary examination to determine whether there is probable cause for him or her to be bound over for trial. However, the prosecution formally commences when the government files an indictment or information. An **indictment** is a written accusation of a crime filed by the grand jury and signed by the grand jury foreperson, while an **information** is a criminal charge filed by the prosecutor without the intervention of a grand jury. The Court has long held that indictment by a grand jury is not a constitutional requirement (*Hurtado v. California*, 110 U.S. 516 [1884]). This is one of the few rights in the Bill of Rights that has not been incorporated by the Supreme Court. In states using the grand jury system, an indictment is usually required in felony offenses, but an information is sufficient in misdemeanors.

A **grand jury** hearing, in which a decision is made whether to charge a suspect with an offense, is not a right guaranteed under the U.S. Constitution in all criminal prosecutions. Amendment 5 of the Bill of Rights simply provides that "no person shall be held to answer for a capital or otherwise infamous crime, unless on a presentment or indictment of a Grand Jury. . . ." Many states today use it (some on an optional basis), but it is required in all federal felony prosecutions and in nineteen states. The grand jury is a peculiar institution in that "it belongs to no branch of the institutional government" (the executive, the legislative, or the judiciary) and is intended to "serve as a buffer or referee between the government and the people who are charged with crimes" (*United States v. Williams*, 504 U.S. 36 [1992]).

The grand jury proceedings start when a **bill of indictment**, defined as a written accusation of a crime, is submitted to the grand jury by the prosecutor. Hearings are then held before the grand jury, and the prosecutor presents evidence to prove the accusation. Traditionally, grand jury hearings are secret because the charges may not be proved and therefore it would be unfair to allow their publication. For the same reason, unauthorized persons are excluded, and disclosure of the proceedings is generally prohibited. The accused has no right to present evidence in a grand jury proceeding; however, the accused may be given an opportunity to do so at the discretion of the grand jury. A person appearing before the grand jury does not have a right to counsel—even if he or she is also the suspect—because the grand jury proceeding is an investigation, not a trial. Clearly, the rights of a suspect are minimal during a grand jury proceeding, despite the fact that he or she has a lot at stake. In the words of one former prosecutor, "Technically, an indictment

nolle prosequi motion
a motion seeking dismissal of charges.

indictment
a written accusation of a crime filed by the grand jury.

information
a criminal charge filed by the prosecutor without the intervention of a grand jury.

grand jury
a jury that usually determines whether a person should be charged with an offense.

United States v. Williams (1992)

bill of indictment
a written accusation of a crime submitted to the grand jury by the prosecutor.

Art. 19.01. Appointment of jury commissioners; selection without jury commission.

(a) The district judge, at or during any term of court, shall appoint not less than three, not more than five persons to perform the duties of jury commissioners, and shall cause the sheriff to notify them of their appointment, and when and where they are to appear. The district judge shall in the order appointing such commissioners, designate whether such commissioners shall serve during the term at which selected or for the next succeeding term. Such commissioners shall receive as compensation for each day or part thereof they may serve the sum of ten dollars and they shall possess the following qualifications:

1. Be intelligent citizens of the county and able to read and write the English language;
2. Be qualified jurors in the county;
3. Have no suit in said court which requires intervention of a jury;
4. Be residents of different portions of the county; and
5. The same person shall not act as jury commissioner more than once in any 12-month period.

(b) In lieu of the selection of prospective jurors by means of a jury commission, the district judge may direct that 20 to 75 prospective grand jurors be selected and summoned, with return on summons, in the same manner as for the selection and summons of panels for the trial of civil cases in the district courts. The judge shall try the qualifications for and excuses from service as a grand juror and impanel the completed grand jury in the same manner as provided for grand jurors selected by a jury commission.

Source: *Texas Criminal and Traffic Manual*, LexisNexis Publisher, 2009–2010.

is a written accusation, a piece of paper stating that the grand jury has accused a person of certain crimes. But on a more immediate level, the filing of an indictment in court informs a defendant and the rest of the world that the state thinks it has enough evidence to convict the person at trial. It is an act that ruins careers and reputations."[7]

If the required number of grand jurors (usually a majority, or twelve out of twenty-three) believes that the evidence warrants conviction for the crime charged, the bill of indictment is endorsed as a "true bill" and filed with the court having jurisdiction. The bill itself constitutes the formal accusation. If the jury does not find probable cause, the bill of indictment is ignored and a "no bill" results. In some states, witnesses (as opposed to the prospective defendant) who testify before the grand jury receive complete immunity from criminal charges arising out of the case. In federal court, however, a witness receives grand jury immunity only if immunity is given beforehand by the government.

An information is a written accusation of a crime prepared by the prosecuting attorney on behalf of the state. The information is not presented to a grand jury. In most states, prosecutors have the option to use an information in all cases instead of a grand jury indictment. Five states require an indictment only in death penalty or life imprisonment cases.[8] To safeguard against possible abuse, most states provide that a prosecution by information may be commenced only after a preliminary examination and determination of probable cause by a magistrate or after a waiver of the preliminary examination by the accused.

The information filed by the prosecutor must reasonably inform the accused of the charges against him or her, giving the accused an opportunity to prepare and present a defense. The essential nature of the offense must be stated, although the charges may follow the language of the penal code that defines the offense.

The Arraignment

arraignment
the appearance of an accused in court where he or she is informed of the charges and asked to plead.

At a scheduled time and after prior notice, the accused is called into court for an **arraignment**, in which he or she is informed of the charges and asked to plead. The accused's presence during arraignment is generally required, except in minor offenses. If the accused has not been arrested, or if he or she is free on bail and does not appear, a bench warrant, or **capias**—a warrant issued by the court for an officer to take a named defendant into custody—will be issued to compel his or her appearance. An exception in many states provides that an accused charged with a misdemeanor may appear through a lawyer at the arraignment. In some jurisdictions, the arraignment is also the first time an accused is asked whether or not he or she is guilty of the offense charged.

capias
a warrant issued by the court for an officer to take a defendant into custody.

In federal courts, the arraignment consists of: "(1) ensuring that the defendant has a copy of the indictment or information; (2) reading the indictment or information to the defendant or stating to the defendant the substance of the charge; and then (3) asking the defendant to plead to the indictment or information."[9]

The Plea by the Defendant

plea
an accused's response in court to the indictment or information.

A **plea** is an accused's response in court to the indictment or information that is read in court. There are generally three kinds of pleas in modern criminal justice practice: nolo contendere, not guilty, and guilty. Some states add a fourth plea: not guilty by reason of insanity. In federal courts and some states, defendants may enter a conditional plea. In federal cases, this means "a defendant may enter a conditional plea of guilty or nolo contendere, reserving in writing the right to have an appellate court review an adverse determination of a specified pretrial motion. A defendant who prevails on appeal may then withdraw the plea."[10]

nolo contendere plea
a plea of "no contest."

A Nolo Contendere Plea A **nolo contendere plea** literally means "no contest." The defendant accepts the penalty without admitting guilt. The effect of this plea is the same as that of a guilty plea, but the defendant may benefit because the plea cannot be used as an admission in any subsequent civil proceeding arising out of the same offense. For example, suppose Bob pleads nolo contendere to a criminal charge of driving while intoxicated. This plea cannot be used as an admission of guilt in a subsequent civil case brought against Bob by the injured party to recover damages. The injured party must independently prove Bob's liability and not simply rely on the nolo contendere plea.

By contrast, had Bob pleaded guilty to the charge of driving while intoxicated, the plea could have been used by the injured party in a civil case. The guilty plea automatically establishes Bob's civil liability, relieving the plaintiff of the burden of proving it. This is because the burden of proof in a civil case is by a preponderance of the evidence, which is a much lower burden than the burden of proof in a criminal case. Nolo contendere pleas are permitted in federal courts and in the courts of about half the states, usually for misdemeanor offenses and at the discretion of the judge.

Even where such pleas are permitted, however, the accused generally does not have an absolute right to make the plea. It can be made only with the consent of the prosecution or with the approval of the court. It is also generally used only for misdemeanor offenses, although some states allow its use even for felonies.

A Plea of Not Guilty If the defendant pleads not guilty, the trial is usually scheduled to take place within a month. The delay is designed to give both the prosecution and the defense time to prepare their cases. When the defendant refuses to plead, or when the court is not sure of the defendant's plea, the court will enter a not guilty plea. Refusing to enter a plea is known as **standing mute**. Between the filing of the not guilty plea and the start of the trial, the defense lawyer often files a number of written motions with the court. One of the most common is a *motion to suppress* evidence that allegedly was illegally seized. The motion requires a hearing at which the police officer who made the search testifies to the facts surrounding the seizure of the evidence and the court determines whether the evidence was, in fact, illegally obtained. Another common motion is a *motion for a change of venue*, which is often made when there has been prejudicial pretrial publicity against the accused.

A Plea of Guilty When a defendant pleads guilty, the record must show that the plea was voluntary and that the accused had a full understanding of its consequences; otherwise, the plea is invalid (*Boykin v. Alabama*, 395 U.S. 238 [1969]). By pleading guilty, the defendant waives several important constitutional rights, such as the right to a trial by jury, the right to confront witnesses, and the protection against self-incrimination. Therefore, it is necessary to make sure that the accused knows exactly what he or she is doing and was not coerced into making the plea. In many states, the judge is required by law to inform the defendant that a guilty plea means he or she is waiving the rights associated with a trial, including the right to be convicted based on guilt proven beyond a reasonable doubt. Other states go further and require that the prosecutor present evidence in court of the defendant's guilt and have it entered into the record.

Boykin v. Alabama (1969)

An **Alford plea** is a guilty plea in which the defendant claims innocence yet pleads guilty for other reasons. For example, say Joe, a defendant, has been in jail for six weeks pending trial because he cannot afford to post bail. Joe is charged with a misdemeanor, which carries a penalty of one month in jail. Although Joe claims innocence, he pleads guilty knowing that if credited with the time he has already served in jail he will immediately be set free. The Court has ruled that an Alford plea is valid because all that is required for a valid guilty plea is a knowing waiver of the rights involved, not an admission of guilt (*North Carolina v. Alford*, 400 U.S. 25 [1970]). In this case the Supreme Court also ruled that a judge may refuse to accept a guilty plea from a defendant if that defendant continues to maintain his or her innocence. The judge, therefore, has the option to accept or reject an Alford plea. A plea of guilty that represents an intelligent and informed choice among alternatives available to the defendant is valid even if it is entered in the hope of avoiding the death penalty (*Brady v. United States*, 397 U.S. 742 [1970]).

Alford plea
a plea in which the defendant claims innocence yet pleads guilty for other reasons.

North Carolina v. Alford (1970)

Brady v. United States (1970)

Most jurisdictions allow the withdrawal of a guilty or nolo contendere plea if valid reasons exist. For example, federal courts allow a defendant to withdraw a guilty or nolo contendere plea in two situations: "(1) before the court accepts the plea, for any reason or no reason; or (2) after the court accepts the plea, but before it imposes sentence if the court rejects a plea agreement, or the defendant can show a fair or just reason for requesting the withdrawal."[11]

The Supreme Court has ruled that a waiver by the accused of the right to counsel at the plea state is considered "knowing and intelligent," and therefore valid, if the trial court informs the accused of the nature of the charges, the right to have counsel regarding the plea, and the possible punishments that come with such a plea (*Iowa v. Tovar*, 541 U.S. 77 [2004]).

Iowa v. Tovar (2004)

Plea Bargains

plea bargain
defendant agrees to plead guilty in exchange for a lower charge, a lower sentence, or other considerations.

A **plea bargain** is the name given to the process in which a defendant agrees to plead guilty to an offense in exchange for a lower charge, a lower sentence, or other considerations. This section examines how plea bargains work and the legal issues involved.

How Plea Bargains Work   Noted authors LaFave, Israel, and King identify three forms of plea bargaining: (1) an arrangement whereby the defendant and prosecutor agree that the defendant should be permitted to plead guilty to a charge less serious than is supported by the evidence; (2) an agreement whereby the defendant pleads "on the nose," that is, to the original charge, in exchange for some kind of a promise from the prosecutor concerning the sentence to be imposed; and (3) an arrangement whereby the defendant pleads guilty "to one charge in exchange for the prosecutor's promise to drop or not to file other charges."[12]

Not all guilty pleas are the result of plea bargaining. Many people plead guilty for other reasons, without bargaining with the prosecutor. Conversely, not all plea bargain negotiations result in a guilty plea; the terms may be unacceptable to either side or to the judge. Some forms of inducement may be inherently unfair or coercive; a plea obtained by such means is involuntary and therefore invalid. For example, a threat to prosecute the accused's spouse as a codefendant despite a lack of evidence would invalidate the plea because of improper pressure.

Plea bargains take many forms and are struck just about anywhere, mostly in informal settings—the hallway of a courthouse, out on the street, or in the office of the prosecutor or judge. It most cases, plea bargaining takes place between the prosecutor and the defense lawyer sometimes without the accused being present. In some cases, it occurs in the presence of a judge, but in others the judge does not want to know what is taking place until the results are presented in court. The following scenario, described by a former New York City prosecutor, portrays a disturbing, yet often realistic, backdrop for plea bargaining.

> Prison for a trial that might easily be six months. The message was loud and clear: take my reasonable offer of five days or you're going to rot in Riker's [a detention center in New York] fighting the issues. The defendant's eyes bug out; half-heartedly he pleads guilty. Strong-arming defendants into a plea was rough justice, but it kept the number of dispositions up, the number of "bodies in the system" down, and sped cases along to a conviction.[13]

Plea bargains are controversial. In the words of a former prosecutor, "The general public tends to regard plea bargaining as too lenient. The defense bar and others of like mind think it too coercive."[14] Despite imperfections and persistent criticisms, plea bargaining is here to stay and is considered a necessity for the criminal justice system. Without it, prosecutions become more lengthy and expensive. The American Bar Association says that plea bargaining exists because of four "practical" reasons that follow:[15]

1. Defendants can avoid the time and cost of defending themselves at trial, the risk of harsher punishment, and the publicity a trial could involve.
2. The prosecution saves the time and expense of a lengthy trial.
3. Both sides are spared the uncertainty of going to trial.
4. The court system is saved the burden of conducting a trial on every crime.

Legal Issues in Plea Bargains Plea bargains raise legal issues that include the following:

1. *Should a prosecutor's promise to a defendant to induce a guilty plea be kept?* If a plea is based to any significant degree upon the prosecutor's promise, that promise must be fulfilled. If it is not fulfilled, either the promise is enforced or the plea may be withdrawn.

   In *Santobello v. New York*, 404 U.S. 257 (1971), the state of New York indicted Santobello on two felony counts. After negotiations, the prosecutor in charge of the case agreed to permit Santobello to plead guilty to a lesser offense and agreed not to make any recommendation about the sentence to be imposed. Santobello then pleaded guilty, but during sentencing a few months later, a new prosecutor asked for the maximum sentence to be imposed. The judge imposed the maximum, but he later maintained that the prosecutor's request was not the reason the maximum sentence was imposed and that he was not influenced by it. The defendant moved to withdraw his guilty plea, but the request was denied by the judge.

   Santobello v. New York (1971)

   On appeal, the Supreme Court ruled that, once the trial court accepts a guilty plea entered in accordance with a plea bargain, the defendant has a right to have the bargain enforced. Therefore, the judge must decide either to enforce the agreement or to allow the defendant to withdraw the guilty plea (see the *Santobello* Case Brief).

   To avoid the undesirable result of the *Santobello* case, most prosecutors tell the accused what they will or will not recommend for a possible sentence in exchange for a guilty plea, but they stipulate that the judge is not legally obligated to honor that recommendation. In many states, the judge is required to ask the parties in open court about the terms of the plea bargain. If the terms are unacceptable, the judge enters a not guilty plea for the defendant and the case goes to trial. One study found that about 30 percent of the time judges asked the defendant if promises other than the plea bargaining agreement had been made. The same study showed that in 65 percent of the cases judges asked defendants if any threats or pressures had caused them to plead guilty. Judges rejected only 2 percent of the guilty pleas encountered in the study.[16]

2. *Is the defendant entitled to a lawyer during the plea bargaining process?* Under the Sixth Amendment, the defendant is entitled to a lawyer at all "critical stages" of the criminal justice process. Clearly, plea bargaining is a critical stage of the criminal justice process; therefore, defendants are entitled to counsel if they want it. LaFave, Israel, and King, however, raise the issue of the role of the defense lawyer as the process goes on, saying: "What if, for example, the prosecutor improperly meets with defendant in the absence of defense counsel and engages in plea bargaining with him but the plea of guilty subsequently entered by the defendant is pursuant to a bargain which defendant's counsel was aware of and had discussed with defendant prior to the entry of his plea?"[17] Is the plea bargain valid? Court decisions on that issue are unclear.

3. *How much evidence should the prosecutor disclose in plea bargaining?* The answer is that the government does not have to disclose everything for the agreement to be valid. For instance, the Supreme Court has held that there is no constitutional requirement that the prosecutor disclose material impeachment evidence prior to entering a plea agreement with a criminal defendant, and that "the Constitution, in respect to a defendant's awareness of relevant circumstances, does not

require complete knowledge, but permits a court to accept a guilty plea, with its accompanying waiver of various constitutional rights, despite various forms of misapprehension under which a defendant might labor" (*United States v. Ruiz*, 536 U.S. 622 [2002]).

CASE BRIEF

Santobello v. New York, 404 U.S. 257 (1971)

The Leading Case on Plea Bargains

Facts: The state of New York indicted Santobello on two felony counts. After negotiations, the assistant district attorney in charge of the case agreed to permit Santobello to plead guilty to a lesser offense and agreed not to make any recommendation regarding the sentence. Santobello then pleaded guilty, but during sentencing a few months later, a new assistant district attorney asked for the maximum sentence to be imposed. The judge imposed the maximum but later maintained that the request was not the reason the maximum was imposed and that he was not influenced by it. The defendant moved to withdraw his guilty plea, but the request was denied. Santobello appealed, but the appellate court held that New York's failure to keep a commitment concerning the sentence recommendation on a guilty plea did not require a new trial. The defendant appealed to the Supreme Court.

Issue or Issues: *May a plea be withdrawn if the prosecution fails to fulfill all its promises, even if the result would have been the same if the prosecution had kept its promise?* Yes.

Decision: The Court vacated and remanded the decision of the New York court.

Holding: Once the court has accepted a guilty plea entered in accordance with a plea bargain, the defendant has a right to have the bargain enforced. If the prosecution does not keep the bargain, a court should decide whether the circumstances require enforcement of the plea bargain or whether the defendant should be granted an opportunity to withdraw the guilty plea. In this case, the prosecutor's broken promise to make no sentencing recommendation pursuant to a guilty plea, even though it was not maliciously broken, is sufficient to vacate the judgment and remand the case back to the trial court.

Case Significance: *Santobello* gives reliability to the bargaining process in that a defendant can rely on the promise of the prosecutor. If the defendant relied on that promise as an incentive for pleading guilty and the promise is not kept, the guilty plea can be withdrawn.

Excerpts from the Opinion: Disposition of charges after plea discussions is not only an essential part of the process but a highly desirable part for many reasons. It leads to prompt and largely final disposition of most criminal cases; it avoids much of the corrosive impact of enforced idleness during pretrial confinement for those who are denied release pending trial; it protects the public from those accused persons who are prone to continue criminal conduct even while on pretrial release; and, by shortening the time between charge and disposition, it enhances whatever may be the rehabilitative prospects of the guilty when they are ultimately imprisoned.

However, all of these considerations presuppose fairness in securing agreement between an accused and a prosecutor. It is now clear, for example, that the accused pleading guilty must be counseled, absent a waiver. Fed. Rule Crim. Proc. 11, governing pleas in federal courts, now makes clear that the sentencing judge must develop, on the record, the factual basis for the plea, as, for example, by having the accused describe the conduct that gave rise to the charge. The plea must, of course, be voluntary and knowing and if it was induced by promises, the essence of those promises must in some way be made known. There is, of course, no absolute right to have a guilty plea accepted. A court may reject a plea in exercise of sound judicial discretion.

This phase of the process of criminal justice, and the adjudicative element inherent in accepting a plea of guilty, must be attended by safeguards to insure the defendant what is reasonably due in the circumstances. Those circumstances will vary, but a constant factor is that when a plea rests in any significant degree on a promise or agreement of the prosecutor, so that it can be said to be part of the inducement or consideration, such promise must be fulfilled.

On this record, the petitioner bargained and negotiated for a particular plea in order to secure dismissal of more serious charges, but also on the condition that no sentence recommendation would be made by the prosecutor. It is now conceded that the promise to abstain from a recommendation was made, and at this stage the prosecution is not in a good position to argue that its inadvertent breach of agreement is immaterial.

4. *What constitutes an involuntary plea?* An involuntary plea violates a defendant's constitutional rights; therefore, it may be withdrawn at any time. However, what constitutes an involuntary plea is a difficult issue and must be determined by the courts on a case-by-case basis. Federal procedure permits a voluntary guilty plea to be withdrawn only before sentence is imposed—except that the court may permit a withdrawal after sentencing "to correct manifest injustice." Some states follow the federal procedure; others simply do not allow the withdrawal of voluntary pleas at any time.

5. *Should plea bargaining be prohibited by law?* Plea bargaining is controversial; nonetheless, only a few jurisdictions have abolished it. Among them are Alaska and some counties in Louisiana, Texas, Iowa, Arizona, Michigan, and Oregon. Plea bargains may be prohibited by state law or by agency policy prescribed by chief prosecutors or judges. The predominant view is that, because they reduce the number of cases that come to trial, plea bargains are an essential and necessary part of the criminal justice process. Most authors agree that around 90 percent of cases that reach the courts are eventually resolved through guilty pleas. It is assumed that "the system can function only if a high percentage of cases are disposed of by guilty pleas and this will happen only if concessions are granted to induce pleas." It is further assumed that "a reduction from 90 percent to 80 percent in guilty pleas requires the assignment of twice the judicial manpower and facilities—judges, court reporters, bailiffs, clerks, jurors, and courtrooms."[18]

In sum, despite its negatives, plea bargaining generally benefits the state, the defendant, and the criminal justice system. Its results may not achieve ideal justice (whatever that means), but the practice is here to stay.

THE PROCEDURE DURING TRIAL

During the trial, several procedures take place. The jury is selected; the prosecutor and defense counsel make opening statements; the prosecution and defense present their cases; rebuttal evidence is presented; the two sides make closing arguments; the defense motions for acquittal prior to the verdict; the judge instructs the jury; and the jury deliberates and returns with a verdict. This section looks at what happens during each of these stages of the trial.

The Selection of Jurors

A **venire** is a group of prospective jurors assembled according to procedures established by state law. Twenty-three of the fifty states use the voter registration list as the sole source of names for jury duty. Ten states and the District of Columbia use a merged list of voters and holders of driver's licenses.[19] The jury commissioner then sends letters to the prospective jurors with instructions to report at a specific time and place for possible jury duty. Most states have statutory exemptions from jury duty, the most common of which are undue hardship, bad health, and status as an officer of the court. Many states by law also exempt people in specific occupations, such as doctors, dentists, members of the clergy, elected officials, police officers, firefighters, teachers, and sole proprietors of businesses.[20]

venire
a group of prospective jurors assembled according to procedures established by law.

The types of jurors lawyers choose for trials has become an issue in itself. Ideally, jurors in any trial must be impartial, meaning they are not prone to either convict or acquit. In reality, however, neither side wants impartial jurors. Both the prosecutor and the defense attorney want jurors who are sympathetic to their side. The use of consultants by both sides has become common in high-profile criminal cases. There is nothing unconstitutional about this practice and, unless prohibited by state law, "loading up the jury" will continue—at least in cases in which either or both sides can afford to hire jury consultants. Jurors' names are usually made public, but some states allow the use of anonymous jurors in cases where the chance of possible retaliation against them is high.

Prospective jurors may be questioned to determine whether there are grounds for challenge. This process is known as **voir dire**, meaning *to tell the truth.* In federal courts, the trial judge usually asks the questions, although the judge may permit counsel to conduct the examination or submit questions for the judge to ask the jury. In most state courts, the lawyers ask the questions. Some judges conduct a multiple voir dire, a practice whereby a judge selects several juries at one time for future trials. There are two types of challenges to prospective jury members: challenge for cause and peremptory challenge.

voir dire
a process in which prospective jurors are questioned to determine whether there are grounds for challenge.

Challenge for Cause A **challenge for cause** is a dismissal of a potential juror for causes specified by law. Each cause is something that renders the potential juror ineligible, or is likely to cause the juror to be unable to be impartial. Some typical challenges for cause include:

challenge for cause
a challenge for the dismissal of a juror based on causes specified by law.

1. The person is not a qualified voter in the state or county.
2. The person is under indictment for or has been convicted of a felony.
3. The person is insane.
4. The person is a prospective witness for either party in the case.
5. The person served on the grand jury that handed down the indictment.
6. The person has already formed an opinion on the case.
7. The person is biased for or against the defendant.

peremptory challenge
the dismissal of a prospective juror for reasons that need not be stated.

Peremptory Challenge A **peremptory challenge** is a dismissal of a potential juror for reasons that do not need to be stated. Such challenges are made entirely at the discretion of each party. The number of peremptory challenges allowed varies from one state to another and may also depend on the seriousness of the offense. The more serious the offense, the more peremptory challenges may be allowed. For example, the prosecution and the defense may be allowed six peremptory challenges each in misdemeanor cases and twelve in felony cases. For capital offenses, the number may go as high as sixteen or twenty. Peremptory challenges have been identified as a reason that minorities are underrepresented in trial juries. Recent Supreme Court decisions hold that peremptory challenges based on race or gender are unconstitutional, if such challenges are, in fact, admitted by the lawyer (which is unlikely) or proved by the opposing party.

As noted earlier, there are two types of juries: grand juries and trial (also known as petit) juries. Think of it like this—grand juries are larger (or grande, to those of you who like their coffee served in big cups) and trial juries are smaller (or petite). This section discusses trial juries, but Table 2.1 compares the two types to enhance your understanding of grand juries and trial juries.

Jim Thigpen is a fifty-four-year-old white male who was arrested and charged with possession of child pornography. Information from an informant (a photo clerk who developed the defendant's film) led local police to investigate and ultimately arrest Thigpen. He was arrested in his home, where police recovered pornographic material containing images of unclothed minor children. Police reports indicate that many of the photos contain images of Thigpen, unclothed and in the company of minor children. Police also confiscated three personal computers that were found to contain child pornography (video files and still photographs). Thigpen has been an elementary school teacher in the Freehold School District for the past ten years. He is currently suspended with pay.

Thigpen is awaiting trial on four felony charges related to child pornography. The trial is expected to begin immediately following jury selection. The prosecution and defense have selected and agreed upon nine jurors; tomorrow they will select the remaining four jurors (to form a panel of twelve and one alternate). Based on juror questionnaires, the remaining potential jurors include the following:

- Jane, a sixty-four-year-old retired elementary school teacher, who is married with two children.
- Leon, a fifty-year-old white male building contractor, who is married with three children.
- Rita, a thirty-year-old homemaker, married with no children, who reportedly made loud negative comments about male pedophiles at a party.
- Bill, a twenty-nine-year-old musician, who has been previously convicted of a felony.
- Clint, a seventy-year-old retired police officer, who spent a large part of his career investigating sex crimes.
- Paul, a thirty-four-year-old carpenter, who is also an immigrant from Ecuador and may be residing in the United States illegally.
- Reuben, a forty-eight-year-old gay rights activist.
- Cynthia, a thirty-two-year-old emergency room nurse, who has worked on an outspoken child advocacy campaign.
- José, a thirty-four-year-old factory worker, who has recently been treated for exhaustion and whose medical history includes a nervous breakdown.
- Francine, a sixty-five-year-old hotel housekeeper, who resides on the same block as the defendant. Francine states that she has never met the defendant but did see small children in and around his home.
- Maria, a fifty-seven-year-old accountant, who lives alone.

1. *You have been hired as a jury consultant for the defense. Which of the remaining potential jurors would you recommend be impaneled on the jury, and why? Which potential jurors would you excuse? For each of those you would excuse, which type of challenge (challenge for cause or peremptory challenge) would you use?*

2. *You have been hired as a jury consultant for the prosecution. Which of the remaining prospective jurors would you recommend be impaneled on the jury, and why? Which prospective jurors would you excuse? For each of those you would excuse, which type of challenge (challenge for cause or peremptory challenge) would you use?*

Opening Statement by the Prosecution

The prosecutor's opening statement acquaints the jury with the nature of the charge against the accused and describes the evidence that will be offered to sustain the charge. Opinions, conclusions, references to the character of the accused, argumentative statements, and references to matters on which evidence will not be offered are not allowed, and the defense may object to them. The prosecution goes first because the state has the burden of proof, and hence the burden of production.

Opening Statement by the Defense

The defense may make an opening statement after the prosecution. Opinions differ about the tactical value of having the defense make an opening statement. Some argue

Table 2.1 Grand Juries and Trial (Petit) Juries Compared

Grand Jury	Trial Jury (also known as Petit Jury)
Usually composed of sixteen to twenty-three members, with twelve votes required for an indictment	Usually consists of twelve members, with a unanimous vote required for conviction (but not in all states)
Choice usually determined by state law, with jury of peers not a consideration	Usually chosen from voter registration list and driver's license rolls, with jury of peers a consideration
Does not determine guilt; function is to return indictments or conduct investigations of reported criminality	Decides guilt and, in some states, determines punishment
Retains the same membership for a month, six months, or one year, depending on the state; may return several indictments during that period	A different jury for every case
Hands down indictments based on probable cause	Convicts on the basis of proof of guilt beyond a reasonable doubt
May initiate investigations of misconduct	Cannot initiate investigations of misconduct

that, in making an opening statement, the defense risks assuming the burden of proving something in the minds of the jury. Others note that failure to make a statement may imply a weak or nonexistent defense. It is generally considered best for the defense to make its opening statement after the prosecution has presented its entire case; in some jurisdictions, it can be made only at that time.

Presentation for the Prosecution

After opening the case, the prosecutor offers evidence in support of the charge. Although the prosecutor may introduce physical evidence, most evidence takes the form of the testimony of witnesses. Witnesses are examined in the following order.

◆ Direct examination (by the prosecutor)
◆ Cross-examination (by the defense lawyer)
◆ Redirect examination (by the prosecutor)
◆ Recross-examination (by the defense lawyer)

Theoretically, this cycle can continue, but the judge usually puts a stop to the examination of witnesses at this stage. The general rule is that lawyers for the prosecution or the defense cannot ask leading questions of witnesses they present, but they are allowed to ask leading questions during cross-examination of the opposing lawyer's witness. A *leading question* is one that suggests to the witness the desired answer. For example:

> Leading question for the prosecution witness on direct examination: "You saw the accused stab the victim, didn't you?"

> Leading question for the defense witness on direct examination: "The accused never stabbed the victim, did he?"

Prosecutors present evidence in an effort to prove their cases beyond a reasonable doubt. Evidence can be classified into two types: direct and circumstantial. *Direct evidence* is evidence based on actual personal knowledge or observation by a witness. An example is testimony by a witness that he saw the defendant shoot the victim. *Circumstantial evidence*, by contrast, is evidence that results from deductions and inferences drawn from certain facts. Examples are that the accused's fingerprints were found at the scene of the crime or that the gun used to kill the victim belongs to the accused. The public perception is that direct evidence is stronger than circumstantial evidence, but this is not always true. For example, incriminating DNA evidence in rape cases, which is circumstantial evidence, is compelling and difficult for the defense to overcome. Conversely, some studies show that eyewitness testimony, a form of direct evidence, can be highly unreliable.

Presentation for the Defense

When the prosecution has rested, the defendant's lawyer opens the defense and offers supporting evidence. Witnesses are examined in the order noted earlier, with the defense lawyer conducting the direct examination and the prosecutor cross-examining the witness.

The defense may choose not to present any evidence if it believes that the prosecution failed to establish its case beyond a reasonable doubt. The rule in criminal cases is that the prosecution must establish its case on its own and cannot rely on a weak defense. If the prosecution fails to establish guilt beyond a reasonable doubt, the defense does not have to do anything to win an acquittal. The problem, however, is that guilt beyond a reasonable doubt is subjective, meaning that what may not amount to guilt beyond a reasonable doubt in the mind of the defense lawyer may in fact have established guilt beyond a reasonable doubt in the minds of jurors. Most defense attorneys take the safer course and present evidence on behalf of the accused. After presenting all the evidence, the defense rests its case.

Rebuttal Evidence

After both sides have presented their main case, each has an opportunity to present **rebuttal evidence**, which is evidence to destroy the credibility of witnesses or any evidence relied on by the defense—and vice versa. Cross-examination seeks to destroy the credibility of witnesses, but direct contrary evidence is often more effective. It is particularly so when the defense has an alibi, meaning that the accused maintains that he or she was not at the scene of the crime at the time it was committed.

rebuttal evidence
evidence presented to destroy the credibility of witnesses or any evidence presented by the other side in a case.

Closing Arguments

In most jurisdictions, the prosecution presents its closing argument first; the defense replies; then the prosecution offers a final argument to rebut the defense. The prosecution is given two presentations because it bears the heavy burden of proving guilt beyond a reasonable doubt. In some jurisdictions, the defense presents its closing argument first and then the prosecution presents its closing argument. The prosecution gets to go last, because the state has the burden of proof. Closing arguments are limited to evidence or issues brought out during the trial.

The Prosecution's Argument The prosecution summarizes the evidence and presents theories on how the jury should view the evidence to establish the defendant's guilt. The prosecutor is given a lot of discretion regarding what he or she says during the summation. However, the comments cannot include improper remarks, to which the defense may object and which (if serious enough) may even lead to a mistrial, new trial, or reversal on appeal. For example, suppose that during the summation, the

MYTH vs. REALITY

MYTH The defense gets to make the last closing argument, like in the movies.

FACT The prosecution gets to make the last closing argument, on the ground that the state has the burden of proof and therefore gets the last word.

prosecutor suggests that the defendant's failure to testify is evidence of his guilt. This is prosecutorial misconduct that is strong grounds for a mistrial because it violates the defendant's right against self-incrimination.

The Defense's Argument The closing argument by the defense is an important matter of tactics and strategy. Generally, the defense emphasizes the heavy burden of proof placed on the prosecution—namely, proof of the defendant's guilt beyond a reasonable doubt on all elements of the crime charged. The defense then stresses that this obligation has not been met, so the defendant must be acquitted. Neither the prosecutor nor the defense counsel is permitted to express a personal opinion about the defendant's innocence or guilt. It is improper, for example, for a defense lawyer to tell the jury, "I am personally convinced that my client did not commit the crime." The facts as presented must speak for themselves without the lawyer's interjecting his or her own beliefs.

Defense Motions before the Verdict

motion
a request made orally or in writing, asking the judge for a legal ruling on a something related to a case.

The defense can file various motions prior to jury deliberations and verdict. A **motion** is a request made orally or in writing, asking the judge for a legal ruling on a matter related to a case. The most common are motions for acquittal, a directed verdict of acquittal, and a mistrial.

A Motion for Acquittal In most cases, the defense moves for a judgment of acquittal at the close of the prosecution's case on grounds of failure to establish a **prima facie case**, meaning that the prosecution failed to establish its case by sufficient evidence; hence, a reasonable person could not conclude that the defendant is guilty. A prima facie case can be overthrown by evidence presented by the defense, but if a prima facie case has not been established, then the defendant must be acquitted without the defense having to present its case. For example, after the prosecution completes its case, the lawyer for the defendant, who is charged with murder, presents a motion for acquittal alleging that the prosecution failed to introduce sufficient evidence to convince a reasonable person that a murder occurred. If the motion is denied by the judge (as it usually is), the defense proceeds with its case and the defendant can renew the motion to acquit at the close of the case.

prima facie case
a case that is strong enough to prevail if it is not contradicted by the opposing party.

motion for a directed verdict of acquittal
a motion filed by the defense seeking acquittal of the accused before the prosecution failed to introduce sufficient evidence to convict the defendant.

A Motion for a Directed Verdict of Acquittal At the close of the presentation of evidence in a jury trial, the defendant may make a **motion for a directed verdict of acquittal**—again on the grounds that the prosecution failed to introduce sufficient evidence concerning the offense charged. A few states do not permit a motion for a directed verdict, on the theory that the right to a jury trial belongs to the prosecution as well as to the accused, so the judge cannot take the case away from the jury. However, most states allow the judge to direct a verdict of acquittal as part of the court's inherent power to prevent a miscarriage of justice through conviction on insufficient evidence.

Motions for acquittal or for a directed verdict of acquittal are based on the legal principal that in a criminal case all elements of the offense—and not just the issue of guilt or innocence—must be proved by the prosecution beyond a reasonable doubt. If the prosecution fails to do this (for example, fails to establish beyond a reasonable doubt that the defendant was present at the scene of the crime), the defense does not have to present its own evidence in order to win an acquittal.

A Motion for a Mistrial Improper conduct at trial constitutes grounds for a mistrial, in which the trial is declared invalid before it is completed. If granted, the defendant can be tried again. A **motion for a mistrial** is usually filed by the defense and is made prior to jury deliberations. Grounds for a mistrial include such errors as the introduction of inflammatory evidence and prejudicial remarks by the judge or the prosecution.

motion for a mistrial
a motion filed seeking for the trial to be declared invalid before it is completed alleging improper conduct.

Instructions to the Jury

The trial judge must instruct the jury properly on all general principles of law relevant to the charge and the issues raised by the evidence. In some states, judges do this after the closing arguments; other states give judges the option of doing so before or after the closing arguments.

Included in these instructions are the elements of the particular offense and the requirement that each element and the defendant's guilt must be proved beyond a reasonable doubt. Most states empower the trial judge to comment on the evidence, but some states forbid such comment—leaving the assessment of the nature and credibility of the evidence to the jury. In most criminal cases, the parties—especially defense counsel—will ask the court that certain instructions be used. The court must decide whether to give, refuse, or modify the instructions proposed by the parties; decide which additional instructions it will give; and advise counsel of its decision. Often the judge holds a conference on instructions with the prosecutor and defense counsel, but the decision on which instructions to give rests with the judge. Any error in the instructions can be challenged on appeal.

Jury Deliberation

The foreperson of the jury is usually elected by the jury members immediately after the jury has been instructed by the judge and has left the courtroom and moved to the jury room to start its deliberations. The foreperson presides over the deliberations and gives the verdict to the court once a decision has been reached.

Jury deliberations are conducted in secret, and jurors are not subject to subsequent legal inquiry, regardless of their decision. However, nothing prevents a juror from later voluntarily discussing the details of the deliberation with the attorneys, the media, or anyone else. Jurisdictions differ about whether the jury—during the trial and/or during deliberations—should be sequestered (kept together and not allowed to return to their respective homes at night or on weekends). **Sequestration** is most often imposed in sensational, high-profile cases, in which the risk of jury tampering or misbehavior is high. Most states permit the trial judge to order sequestration at his or her discretion.

sequestration
an order by the court keeping the jurors together during trial or deliberation and not allowing them to go home at night or weekends.

The Verdict

A jury or judge's **verdict** is the determination of the defendant's guilt—either "guilty" or "not guilty." The jury does not deliver an "innocent" verdict, as their job is not to determine if the defendant is innocent but rather if the prosecutor proved the defendants guilty beyond a reasonable doubt—a different question in some instances. In some states, a third verdict is "not guilty because insane" or "guilty but mentally ill." The difference in these two verdicts is that in "not guilty because insane" findings the accused does not suffer the civil effects of a conviction and, after treatment and if

verdict
the pronouncement of defendant's guilt or innocence. A third pronouncement relating to mental health can occur in some states.

HIGHLIGHT ⟩ What Is a Death-Qualified Jury?

The question: Assume you are opposed to the death penalty. Can you be disqualified from being a juror in a death penalty case?

The answer: That depends on how strongly you oppose the imposition of the death penalty. In *Witherspoon v. Illinois*, 391 U.S. 510 (1968), the U.S. Supreme Court held that jurors cannot be removed, even if by state law, merely because of general scruples against capital punishment. Doing that denies the accused of the right to an impartial jury. However, the Court added that a juror may be excluded "for cause" if it is "unmistakably clear" that he or she would automatically vote against the death penalty if sought by the prosecutor or if the

juror could not be impartial in the determination of the defendant's guilt.

In *Lockhart v. McCree*, 476 U.S. 162 (1986), the Court affirmed its ruling in *Witherspoon* when it held that removal for cause of jurors whose attitudes toward the death penalty would "prevent or substantially impair the performance of their duties at the punishment phase" is constitutional and does not violate the Sixth Amendment right of the accused to an impartial jury.

The result of these two cases is a *death-qualified jury*, meaning a jury that may be more conviction-prone because those unalterably opposed to the death penalty are removed "for cause."

---

restored to sanity, may be released. In contrast, in a "guilty but mentally ill" verdict the accused is found guilty and usually undergoes treatment. If restored to sanity, the accused then serves time like other convicted defendants.

In federal and most state trials, the jury vote for conviction or acquittal must be unanimous. This section looks at what happens when there is a hung jury, a less-than-unanimous vote, acquittal, and a guilty verdict. It also examines the phenomenon of jury nullification.

hung jury
a jury that cannot agree to convict or acquit an accused.

Hung Juries Failure to reach a unanimous vote for either way results in a **hung jury** and a mistrial. The length of time a jury must deliberate before a hung jury is declared is determined by the judge. If the judge dismisses the jury because it cannot agree on the result, the case may be tried again before another jury. There is no double jeopardy, because the first jury did not agree on a verdict. There is no constitutional limit on the number of times a defendant can be tried again if the trial results in a hung jury, but prosecutors usually take into consideration whether a conviction can realistically be obtained and the expense of retrying the case.

Apodaca v. Oregon (1972)

Johnson v. Louisiana (1972)

Burch v. Louisiana (1979)

Ballew v. Georgia (1978)

Williams v. Florida (1970)

Less-than-Unanimous Votes In *Apodaca v. Oregon*, 406 U.S. 404 (1972), the U.S. Supreme Court held that state laws providing for a less-than-unanimous vote for conviction are constitutional and will be upheld—at least in the case of a required ten-to-two vote. In *Johnson v. Louisiana*, 406 U.S. 356 (1972), it held that a law providing for a nine-to-three jury vote for conviction is also constitutional.

The U.S. Supreme Court has decided that a state law providing for a six-member jury in all criminal cases except those involving the death penalty is valid. Unlike those of twelve-member juries, the verdicts of six-member juries must be unanimous (*Burch v. Louisiana*, 441 U.S. 130 [1979]). The Court has also decided that five-person juries are unconstitutional because they would not permit effective group discussion, would diminish the chances of drawing from a fair, representative cross-section of the community, and might impair the accuracy of fact finding (*Ballew v. Georgia*, 435 U.S. 223 [1978]). Most states, however, still provide for twelve-member juries in felony trials (*Williams v. Florida*, 399 U.S. 78 [1970]).

Acquittal A verdict of acquittal ("not guilty") terminates the case immediately and sets the defendant free. A not guilty verdict does not necessarily mean that the defendant did not commit the offense; it can simply mean that the defendant may have committed the offense but the prosecutor did not prove it beyond a reasonable doubt.

Guilty After the jury has announced a guilty verdict, the defendant has a right to have the jury polled. The jury must then express its vote in open court, either as a group or individually. After a guilty verdict, the defendant also may file a motion for a new trial. This motion asks the trial court to set aside the verdict and give the defendant another trial. This usually happens under a variety of circumstances when subsequent events or newly discovered evidence requires that the defendant be given a new trial "in the interest of justice." States have laws governing the granting of new trials. In federal courts, the rules provide that any motion for a new trial must be based on newly discovered evidence and be filed within three years after the verdict or finding of guilty. A habeas corpus motion is essentially a motion for a new trial. It alleges that a prisoner's constitutional rights were violated during the trial but that those violations were not discovered then and could not have been included in the appeal. The similarities and differences between a motion for a mistrial and a motion for a new trial can be summarized as shown in the table.

Motion for a Mistrial	Motion for a New Trial
Filed by the defense	Filed by the defense
If granted, the accused can be tried again	If granted, the accused can be tried again
Usually alleges violations of the defendant's rights during the trial	Usually alleges violations of the defendant's rights before or during the Trial
Filed before the judge or jury renders a verdict	Filed after a judge or jury renders a guilty verdict
Usually filed during the trial	May be filed months or years after the trial
Filed before the defendant starts serving the sentence	May be filed while defendant is serving the sentence

Jury Nullification **Jury nullification** occurs when a jury decides a case contrary to the weight of the evidence presented during the trial. This means that the jury acquits the defendant or convicts the defendant of a lesser offense despite the evidence presented; in essence, the evidence and the verdict point in opposite or different directions. Jury nullification usually occurs when the jury believes that applying the law would result in an injustice. Jury nullification has long been a part of the American criminal justice process and is traditionally seen as a shield against prosecutorial excesses by the government. Only a handful of states, however, allow the defense attorney to inform the jury that it can engage in jury nullification if it sees fit. Thus, nullification is something of a "hidden" right.

An observer points out that jury nullification usually takes place in two instances: (1) when the jury sympathizes with a guilty defendant (an example is a husband who killed his wife, who suffered from a painful and terminal disease), or (2) when the law is controversial or morally debatable (examples are prostitution laws or marijuana possession, regardless of the circumstances).[21] The Court held in *United States v. Powell*, 469 U.S. 57 (1984), that juries have the power to engage in jury nullification. In *Duncan v. Louisiana*, 391 U.S. 145 (1968), the Court wrote that the function of a jury is to "guard against the exercise of arbitrary power." Jury nullification is difficult to prove or disprove

jury nullification
when a jury decides a case contrary to the weight of the evidence presented during trial.

United States v. Powell (1984)

Duncan v. Louisiana (1968)

because of subjectivity in interpreting whatever evidence may be presented. Concerns about possible jury nullification arise primarily as a result of controversial verdicts in high-profile cases, such as the O. J. Simpson trial. Some members of the American public believed that the evidence in this established Simpson's guilt beyond a reasonable doubt, and therefore he had to be convicted. However, others—including the jury— believed that guilt beyond reasonable doubt had not been established, and therefore Simpson deserved to be acquitted. It is hard to say that one side is right and the other is wrong, because guilt beyond reasonable doubt is a difficult burden to meet and the public is not present during the entire trial and able to see and hear all the evidence.

If a jury decides to acquit a defendant regardless of the evidence presented, charges based on the same offense cannot be brought again, because of the prohibition against double jeopardy. Jury nullification, abhorrent though the results may be to some people, is a final act to which there is no legal recourse.

THE PROCEDURE AFTER TRIAL

After the trial, if the defendant is convicted, sentencing, appeals, and habeas corpus petitions take place. This section looks at what happens during each of these actions.

Imposition of Sentence

Sentencing is the formal pronouncement of judgment by the court or judge on the defendant after conviction in a criminal prosecution, imposing the punishment to be inflicted.[22] Sentences can take various forms, depending upon state law. They can be in the form of a fine, community-based sanctions, probation, jail time (usually for misdemeanors), prison time (usually for felonies), and the ultimate punishment—death. Except for death, these sentences are not mutually exclusive, meaning they can be imposed concurrently or consecutively. For example, an offender can be given prison time and then later released on parole.

The sentence to be imposed is set by law, but judges or juries are given discretion to impose minimum or maximum terms. Sentences can be classified as fixed, determinate, or indeterminate. *Fixed sentences* refer to a specific type and length of sentence imposed by law. For example, state law may provide that public intoxication is punishable by a fixed term of three days in jail. Or, the sentence can be *determinate*, meaning that there is a minimum and a maximum time imposed, but the range is narrow. An example is a state law providing that a person found guilty of Class A misdemeanor can be sentenced to between ten and thirty days in jail. In contrast, an indeterminate sentence has a minimum and a maximum, but the gap is huge. For example, in Texas a first-degree felony offender can be sentenced to from five to ninety-nine years in prison, mostly depending on the discretion of the judge. In fact, under certain circumstances, the first-degree felony offender can be given probation if some circumstances are present. (Sentencing is discussed in greater detail in Chapter 13.)

In states where juries may impose the sentence at the option of the accused, juries usually determine guilt and (if the verdict is guilty) decide on the sentence at the same time. Some states, however, have a **bifurcated procedure**, in which the guilt-determinations stage and the sentencing stage are separate. In those states, after a defendant is found guilty, the jury receives evidence from the prosecution and the defense

bifurcated procedure
a trial procedure where the guilt–innocence stage and the sentencing stage are separate.

concerning the penalty to be imposed. The rules of evidence are relaxed at this stage, so evidence not admitted during the trial (such as the previous record of the accused and his or her inclination to violence) may be introduced. The jury then deliberates a second time to determine the penalty.

Most states give the sentencing power to the judge, even when the case is tried before a jury. After receiving a guilty verdict from the jury, the judge usually postpones sentencing for a few weeks. The delay enables him or her to hear post-trial motions (such as a motion for a new trial or a directed verdict) and to order a probation officer to conduct a presentence investigation. The judge has the option to use the presentence investigation report (PSIR) in any manner, including accepting or disregarding it completely. Most states allow the defense lawyer or the accused to see the PSIR, thus affording an opportunity to rebut any false or unfair information it may contain.

Appeal

After the sentence is imposed, there is usually a period of time (such as thirty days) during which the defendant may appeal the conviction and sentence to a higher court. There is no constitutional right to appeal, but all states grant defendants that right by law or court procedure. In some states, death penalty appeals go straight from the trial court to the state supreme court, bypassing state courts of appeals. In other states, appeals in death penalty cases are automatic and need not be filed by the defendant.

Theoretically, any criminal case may go as high as the U.S. Supreme Court on appeal, as long as either federal law or constitutional issues are involved. In reality, however, the right is generally limited by the *rule of four*—the Court's practice of accepting an appealed case only if four out of the nine Court members vote to do so. Out of the more than ten thousand cases brought to the Court each year, fewer than one hundred are actually heard by the Court.

The appeals court may affirm, reverse, or reverse and remand the decision of the lower court. **Affirmation** means that the decision of the lower court where the case came from is upheld. **Reversal** means that the decision of the lower court where the case came from is overthrown, vacated, or set aside by the appellate court. A **reverse-and-remand decision** is less final than an outright reversal of the lower court decision in that the lower court's decision is reversed but the lower court has an opportunity to hear further arguments and give another decision in the case.

Habeas Corpus

If the convicted defendant is still incarcerated and the appellate process has been exhausted, he or she can file a writ of habeas corpus alleging that the incarceration is unconstitutional. **Habeas corpus** (a Latin term that literally means *you have the body*) is a writ directed to any person detaining another (usually a sheriff or a prison warden), commanding that person to produce the body of the prisoner in court and to explain why detention is justified and should be continued. It is a remedy against any type of illegal incarceration by the government and is frequently called the Great Writ of Liberty. Habeas corpus is always available to anyone deprived of their freedom, although successful filings are rare. It is usually filed in the court where the defendant was tried. This helps explain why habeas cases seldom succeed. Table 2.2 highlights the main differences between an appeal and habeas corpus petitions.

affirmation
the decision of the lower court is upheld on appeal.

reversal
the decision of the lower court is overthrown on appeal.

reverse-and-remand decision
the lower court's decision is reversed but the lower court can hear further arguments and give another decision in the case.

habeas corpus
a writ directed to a person detaining another commanding that person to produce the body of a person who is imprisoned or detained in court and explain why detention should be continued.

Table 2.2 Appeal and Habeas Corpus Compared

Appeal	Writ of Habeas Corpus
A direct attack upon the conviction	A collateral attack, meaning a separate case from the criminal conviction
Part of the criminal proceeding	A civil proceeding
Purpose is to reverse conviction	Purpose is to secure release from prison
Filed only after conviction	May be filed any time a person is deprived illegally of freedom by a public officer, before or after conviction, with some exceptions
Accused has been convicted but may be free on bail	Person is serving time or is detained illegally; cannot be filed if person is free
Based on any type of error made during the trial	Based on a violation of a constitutional right, usually during the trial
Must be undertaken within a certain period of time after conviction; otherwise the right of action lapses	Right of action does not lapse; may be filed even while person is serving time in prison
All issues raised must be from the trial record	New testimony may be presented

PROCEDURAL DIFFERENCES IN JURISDICTIONS

This chapter summarizes the criminal justice process in general; the procedures described are the most typical in various jurisdictions. The procedures discussed so far refer primarily to criminal cases involving *felonies*, which are serious offenses. *Misdemeanors* are sometimes processed informally and expeditiously.

This next section looks at exceptions in which the procedures discussed in this chapter may not apply. These are in misdemeanors, when there are variations among state laws, when there are variations within state laws, and when there are differences between theory and reality.

Application to Felony Cases

Misdemeanors and petty offenses are usually processed in a simpler and more expeditious way than felonies. Whether a crime is classified as a felony or a misdemeanor depends on the law of the state and so may vary from one state to another. Generally, a **felony** is a crime punishable by death or imprisonment in a state prison (as opposed to imprisonment in a local jail), or a crime for which the punishment is imprisonment for more than one year. Examples include murder, rape, robbery, and burglary. All other criminal offenses are generally considered **misdemeanors.** Examples of misdemeanors are traffic violations, theft of small amounts, or parking violations.

felony
a crime usually punishable by death or imprisonment in a prison for more than one year.

misdemeanor
a crime usually punishable with jail time or other non-prison penalties.

Variation among States

The distinctions between felony and misdemeanor procedures apply in federal court and in most state courts. However, there are differences from state to state, and the terms used may vary. For example, some states use the grand jury for charging a person with a serious crime; others do not use a grand jury at all. Some states allow a jury trial for all offenses; others impose restrictions. As long as a particular procedure is not required by the U.S. Constitution, states do not have to use it. Although criminal procedure has largely been nationalized, discretion still abounds, so long as the procedure it is not considered a violation of fundamental rights.

Variation Within a State

Likewise, there may be variations in procedure among different courts in a given state even though all are governed by a single state code of criminal procedure. Thus, the procedures used in, say, the courts of San Francisco to process felony or misdemeanor offenses may not be exactly the same as those of Los Angeles. Differences exist because of the idiosyncrasies and preferences of judicial personnel or long-standing practices peculiar to a jurisdiction. For example, some jurisdictions hold preliminary hearings in all cases, whereas others hardly ever hold preliminary hearings. Some jurisdictions refer misdemeanor cases to a grand jury; others do not. Certain cities may hold a suspect for a maximum of forty-eight hours without a hearing; other cities hold night court to ensure that detainees are given a hearing almost immediately. Variations in procedure are tolerated by the courts as long as they are not violations of the law or of basic constitutional rights such as the right to due process.

Ideal versus Reality

The procedures just outlined, as well as those found in state codes, are the prescribed procedures. But there may be differences between the ideal (prescribed) procedures and reality (the procedures actually used by local criminal justice agencies). Many agencies have their own traditional ways of doing things, which may be at odds with procedures prescribed by law or court decisions. Nevertheless, these procedures continue to be used, either because of ignorance or because they have not been challenged. In some cases, courts tolerate certain practices as long as they do not grossly compromise the constitutional and statutory rights of the accused.

SUMMARY

The criminal justice process may be divided into three stages.

Stage 1: The Procedure before Trial

◆ *Filing of complaint.* By the victim or a police officer

◆ *Arrest.* With or without a warrant; sometimes a citation or summons is used instead of an arrest

◆ *Booking.* Recording the suspect's name, time of arrest, and offense; inventorying belongings; photographing and fingerprinting

◆ *Appearance before a magistrate without unnecessary delay.* Accused is made aware of his or her rights

◆ *Bail.* Set by the magistrate, or the defendant is released on his or her own recognizance

◆ *Preliminary examination.* Usually held for determination of probable cause, discovery purposes, or determination to bind over

◆ *Decision to charge.* Prosecutor has the discretion to charge or not to charge

◆ *Indictment or information.* Indictment is a charge made by the grand jury; information is a charge filed by the prosecutor; an indictment is required in most states for serious offenses

- *Arraignment.* Accused appears before a judge, is informed of the charges, and is asked for a plea
- *Plea.* Nolo contendere (or no contest), not guilty, or guilty

Stage 2: The Procedure during Trial

- *Selection of jurors.* Use of voir dire; types of challenges are for cause and peremptory
- *Opening statements.* By prosecution and defense, both summarizing the evidence they will present and their version of the case
- *Presentation by prosecution.* Offers evidence supporting the charge
- *Presentation by defense.* Offers evidence for the accused
- *Rebuttal evidence.* Evidence presented by either side to destroy the credibility of witnesses or evidence presented by the other side
- *Closing arguments.* By the prosecution and then by the defense
- *Judge's instructions to jury.* Includes the elements of the offense charged and the caution that each element must be proved beyond a reasonable doubt
- *Jury deliberation.* Jurors may be sequestered at the option of the judge
- *Verdict.* Pronouncement of guilt or innocence

Stage 3: The Procedure after Trial

- *Sentencing.* Punishment handed down by judge or jury
- *Appeal.* Allowed within a certain period of time, usually thirty days
- *Habeas corpus.* May be filed any time during incarceration; the petitioner seeks release from incarceration, alleging that the incarceration is illegal or unconstitutional

REVIEW QUESTIONS

1. Define criminal procedure. Distinguish it from criminal law. Why do we have both?
2. Distinguish between a grand jury and a trial jury. If you had a choice, would you prefer to serve as a grand juror or a trial juror? Why?

3. How does an indictment differ from an information? When is one used and not the other?
4. Ed is charged with sexual assault. Assume you are a defense lawyer for Ed. Will you ask for a preliminary examination for your client or not? Explain your answer.
5. What is a plea bargain? Are you in favor of or against plea bargaining? Support your position.
6. Distinguish between the two types of jury challenges. Which type is more likely to lead to racial and gender discrimination against jurors, and why?
7. "Every error in a criminal trial causes a reversal of a defendant's conviction on appeal." Is this statement true or false? Explain your answer.
8. Identify five differences between an appeal and a writ of habeas corpus.
9. Criminal procedure is governed by U.S. Supreme Court decisions, yet variations exist from one jurisdiction to another. Why, and are these variations valid?
10. What is jury nullification? Are you for or against it? Justify your answer.

TEST YOUR UNDERSTANDING

1. X, a student, was charged with speeding and reckless negligence. The incident caused a lot of damage to another car, owned by a faculty member. X is given a choice by the local judge to plead either nolo contendere or guilty. You are X's lawyer. Which plea would you recommend for X, and why?
2. Y pleaded guilty to burglary after having been promised by the prosecutor that he would get probation. The judge sentenced Y instead to a year in jail. Can Y withdraw his guilty plea? State reasons for your answer.
3. Z was accused of murder, convicted, given the death penalty, and sent to death row. Z appealed his conviction and sentence to the state supreme court. Ten months later, the state's highest court turned down Z's appeal. A year later, Z's lawyer obtained reliable information and proof that the main witness against Z gave false testimony

during the trial. What remedy, if any, does Z have? Why are other remedies not available?

4. Assume you are a judge. A defendant brought before you pleads guilty, saying: "I swear before God and my family that I did not commit the burglary with which am charged. But I am pleading guilty because I cannot post bail and have been in jail for a month now. I am informed by a lawyer-friend that if I plead guilty, I can be free immediately because the maximum penalty for my offense is thirty days in jail". Three questions for you as a judge:

(a) Will you accept the plea under these circumstances?

(b) What procedure will you follow, whether you accept the plea or reject it?

(c) Assuming you accept the plea or reject it, is your action valid?

RECOMMENDED READINGS

Joseph L. Hoffman. *Plea bargaining in the shadow of death.* Fordham Law Review 2313–2391 (2001).

Candace McCoy. *Plea bargaining as coercion: The trial penalty and plea bargaining reform.* The Criminal Law Quarterly 67–107 (April 2005).

Ric Simmons. *Re-examining the grand jury: Is there room for democracy in the criminal justice system?* Cleveland State Law Review 829–862 (2000).

Justin J. Wert and Kan Lawrence. *Habeas corpus in America: The politics of individual rights.* University Press of Kansas, 2011.

Gregory M. Gilchrist. *Plea bargains, convictions, and legitimacy.* American Criminal Law Review, vol. 48, January 1, 2011, p. 143.

NOTES

1. *Black's Law Dictionary*, 6th ed., abridged (St. Paul, MN: West, 1991), p. 128.
2. Ibid., p. 107.
3. "Bail Bondsman," *http://en.wikipedia.org/wiki/Bail_bondsman*, as modified by the author.
4. Supra note 1, at p. 120.
5. Cornell Law School, Legal Information Institute, "Federal Rules of Criminal Procedure," *http://www.law.cornell.edu/rules/frcrmp/Rule5_1.htm*.
6. Robert H. Jackson, "The Federal Prosecutor," *http://www.roberthjackson.org/Man/theman2-7-6-1/*.
7. David Heilbroner, *Rough Justice* (New York: Pantheon Books, 1990), p. 197.
8. Steven L. Emanuel, *Emanuel Law Outlines: Criminal Procedure,* 22nd ed. (New York: Aspen Law & Business, 2001), p. 348.
9. Cornell Law School, Legal Information Institute, "Federal Rules of Criminal Procedure," *http://www.law.cornell.edu/rules/frcrmp/Rule10.htm*.
10. Cornell Law School, Legal Information Institute, "Federal Rules of Criminal Procedure," *http://www.law.cornell.edu/rules/frcrmp/Rule11.htm*.
11. Ibid.
12. Wayne R. LaFave, Jerold H. Israel, and Nancy J. King, *Criminal Procedure,* 3rd ed. (St. Paul, MN: West, 2000), p. 956.
13. Supra note 7, p. 147.
14. George Fisher, former prosecutor, in "Plea Bargain," by Dirk Olin, *New York Times Magazine*, September 9, 2002, p. 29.
15. American Bar Association, Division for Public Education, "How Courts Work: Steps in a Trial," *http://www.abanet.org/publiced/courts/pleabargaining.html*.
16. Bureau of Justice Statistics, *Report to the Nation on Crime and Justice.* (Washington, D.C.: U.S. Government Printing Office, 1983), p. 65.
17. Supra note 11, pp. 983–984.
18. Ibid., p. 957.
19. Supra note 16, p. 67.
20. Ibid.
21. Comments from Reviewer 6 of the seventh edition of this book. The authors thank this anonymous manuscript reviewer for these observations.
22. Supra note 1, p. 1528.

CHAPTER 3

Probable Cause and Reasonable Suspicion

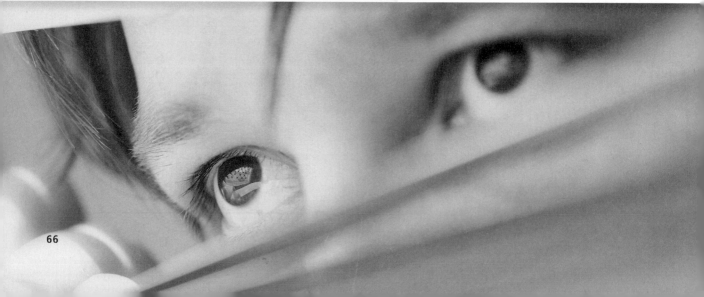

THE TOP 5 IMPORTANT CASES

in Probable Cause and Reasonable Suspicion

◾ *BRINEGAR V. UNITED STATES* (1949) Probable cause is more than bare suspicion; it exists when the facts and circumstances within the officers' knowledge and of which they had reasonably trustworthy information are sufficient in themselves to justify a "man of reasonable caution" in the belief that an offense has been or is being committed.

◾ *SPINELLI V. UNITED STATES* (1969) "Innocent-seeming activity" and a "bald and unilluminating assertion of suspicion" in an affidavit are not to be given weight in a magistrate's determination of probable cause. An officer may use credible hearsay to establish probable cause, but an affidavit based on an informant's tip must satisfy the two-pronged *Aguilar* test.

◾ *MICHIGAN V. SUMMERS* (1981) The general rule is that every arrest, as well as every seizure having the essential attribute of a formal arrest, is unreasonable unless supported by probable cause.

◾ *ALABAMA V. WHITE* (1990) Reasonable suspicion is a less demanding standard than probable cause. It can be established with information different in quantity or content from that required to establish probable cause.

◾ *MARYLAND V. PRINGLE* (2003) In determining probable cause, the term "man of reasonable caution" is best interpreted using the standard of an "objectively reasonable police officer."

THE ONE LEGAL TERM that police officers must be thoroughly familiar is *probable cause*. This term is used extensively in police work and often provide standard for determining whether the police acted lawfully. If the police acted lawfully, the arrest is valid and the evidence obtained is admissible in court. Without probable cause, however, the evidence will be thrown out of court. In *Michigan v. Summers*, 452 U.S. 692 (1981), the Supreme Court stated, "The general rule is that every arrest, and every seizure having the essential attributes of a formal arrest, is unreasonable unless it is supported by probable cause."

Michigan v. Summers (1981)

The probable cause requirement in police work is based on the Fourth Amendment to the U.S. Constitution, which states, "The right of the people to be secure in their persons, houses, papers, and effects, against unreasonable searches and seizures, shall not be violated, and no Warrants shall issue, but upon probable cause. . . ."

Another important legal term used in policing, and immediately below probable cause in the level of certainty, is *reasonable suspicion*. With reasonable suspicion, police can stop and frisk a suspect, but reasonable suspicion alone cannot be the basis for a valid arrest. Although we know that reasonable suspicion has a lower degree of certainty than probable cause, the two terms are sometimes difficult to distinguish because both can be subjective, meaning that what is probable cause or reasonable suspicion to one police officer or judge may not be that to another. Although higher in degree of certainty, probable cause is discussed first in this chapter because it is the more important and popular term in policing and is more often used in day-to-day policing.

Determinations of probable cause and reasonable suspicion during trial are made by the trial court, but these decisions can be reviewed by appellate courts if the case is appealed. Most determinations, however, are initially made by law enforcement officers at the scene of the crime or when they make a warrantless arrest.

Not all contacts or encounters with the police require probable cause or reasonable suspicion. These are needed only when the contacts involve a search or seizure. Police do not need probable cause or reasonable suspicion to ask questions of witnesses to a crime, speak to person on the street, or to set up roadblocks to detect drunk driving because these are not considered a search or seizure. Subsequent chapters in this text discuss more extensively when contacts or encounters with the police require probable cause or reasonable suspicion and when they do not.

PROBABLE CAUSE

Probable cause has both legal and practical meanings. This section examines the variety of ways probable cause is defined, determined, and established.

Probable Cause Defined (The Legal Definition)

probable cause
more than bare suspicion; it exists when the "facts and circumstances within the officers' knowledge and of which they had reasonably trustworthy information are sufficient in themselves to warrant a man of reasonable caution in the belief that an offense has been or is being committed."

Brinegar v. United States (1949)

Probable cause has been defined by the Supreme Court as more than bare suspicion; it exists when "the facts and circumstances within the officers' knowledge and of which they had reasonably trustworthy information are sufficient in themselves to warrant a man of reasonable caution in the belief that an offense has been or is being committed." The Court added, "The substance of all the definitions of probable cause is a reasonable ground for belief of guilt. . . ." (*Brinegar v. United States*, 338 U.S. 160 [1949]). The Court measures probable cause by the test of *reasonableness*, a necessarily subjective standard that falls between mere suspicion and certainty. Facts and circumstances leading to an arrest or seizure must be sufficient to persuade a reasonable person that an illegal act has been or is being committed. Always, the test involves the consideration of a particular suspicion and a specific set of facts. Hunches or generalized suspicions are not reasonable grounds for concluding that probable cause exists.

A "Man of Reasonable Caution"

man of reasonable caution
refers to the average man or woman on the street. It does not refer to a person with training in the law.

The original term **man of reasonable caution** (some courts use "reasonable man" or "ordinarily prudent and cautious man") does not refer to a person with training in the law, such as a magistrate or a lawyer. Instead, it refers to the average "man (or woman) on the street" (for instance, a plumber, butcher, or teacher) who, under the same circumstances, would believe that the person being arrested had committed the offense or that items to be seized would be found in a particular place.

Despite this, however, the experience of the police officer must be considered in determining whether probable cause existed in a specific situation. In *United States v. Ortiz*, 422 U.S. 891 (1975), the Court ruled that "officers are entitled to draw reasonable inferences from these facts in light of their knowledge of the area and their prior experience with aliens and smugglers." Given their work experience, training, and background, police officers are better qualified than the average person to evaluate certain facts and circumstances. Thus, what may not amount to probable cause to an untrained person may be sufficient for probable cause in the estimation of a police officer because of his or her training and experience. This is particularly true in drug cases, in which what may look like an innocent activity to an untrained eye may indicate to a police officer that a criminal act is taking place.

United States v. Ortiz (1975)

MYTH vs. REALITY

MYTH Police officers cannot use their experience and training in part to create probable cause.

FACT The Supreme Court has repeatedly stated that a police officer's training and experience can be part (but not the only) of the basis for probable cause.

The concept of a "man of reasonable caution" was reaffirmed by the Court in *Maryland v. Pringle*, 540 U.S. 366 (2003), when the Court said: "To determine whether an officer had probable cause to arrest an individual, we examine the events leading up to the arrest, and then decide 'whether these historical facts, viewed from the standpoint of an objectively reasonable police officer amount to' probable cause." Therefore, the term "man of reasonable caution" is best interpreted using the standard of an "objectively reasonable police officer." This is the most precise phrase the Court has provided in the many cases in which it has interpreted the meaning of "man of reasonable caution."

Maryland v. Pringle (2003)

The Practical Definition of Probable Cause

For practical purposes, probable cause exists when an officer has trustworthy evidence sufficient to make "a reasonable person" think it more likely than not that the proposed arrest or search is justified. In mathematical terms, this implies that the officer (in cases of arrest or search without a warrant) or the magistrate (in cases of arrest or search with a warrant) is slightly more than 50 percent certain that the suspect has committed the offense or that the items can be found in a certain place. Despite the degree of certainty that the phrase "more than 50 percent" conveys, the Court itself has repeatedly cautioned against quantification (using numbers) when determining probable cause. In *Maryland v. Pringle*, 540 U.S. 366 (2003), the Court said:

> The probable-cause standard is incapable of precise definition or quantification into percentages because it deals with probabilities and depends on the totality of circumstances. We have stated, however, that "[t]he substance of all the definitions of probable cause is a reasonable ground for belief of guilt, and that the belief of guilt must be particularized with respect to the person to be searched or seized."

HIGHLIGHT ▸ The Legal versus the Practical Definition of Probable Cause

Legal definition: Probable cause is more than bare suspicion. It exists when "the facts and circumstances within the officers' knowledge and of which they had reasonably trustworthy information are sufficient in themselves to warrant a man of reasonable caution in the belief that an offense has been or is being committed."

Practical definition: Probable cause exists when it is more likely than not (more than 50 percent certainty) that the suspect committed an offense or that the items sought can be found in a certain place.

The Court then added that "on many occasions, we have reiterated that the probable-cause standard is a 'practical non-technical conception' that deals with 'the factual and practical considerations of everyday life on which reasonable and prudent men, not legal technicians, act.'" Therefore, it must be stressed that although the phrase "more than 50 percent" is convenient and, to many, extremely helpful in determining probable cause, the Court itself does not use it. It is therefore a layperson's term rather than a precise legal concept that courts use.

Same Definition of Probable Cause in the Many Areas of Police Work

Probable cause is required in four important areas of police work:

- Arrests with a warrant
- Arrests without a warrant
- Searches and seizures of property with a warrant
- Searches and seizures of property without a warrant

An arrest is, of course, a form of seizure—but a seizure of a person, not of property. For practical purposes, other aspects of the criminal justice process, such as grand jury proceedings or preliminary hearing determinations, may have their own interpretation of probable cause, but police work uses the same definition as the Court.

Both the legal and the practical definitions of probable cause are the same in all phases of police work—whether it involves arrests with or without a warrant or searches and seizures of property with or without a warrant. It is also the same definition whether the search involves persons, property, or motor vehicles. But there are important differences in focus, as discussed later.

Arrest of Persons versus Search and Seizure of Property

In cases of *arrest of persons*, the probable cause concerns are: (1) whether an offense has been committed and (2) whether the suspect did, in fact, commit the offense. In contrast, in cases of *search and seizure of property*, the concerns are: (1) whether the items to be seized are connected with criminal activity and (2) whether they can be found in the place to be searched. It follows, therefore, that what constitutes probable cause for arrest may not constitute probable cause for search and seizure—not because of different definitions but because the officer is looking at different things. For example, suppose a suspect is being arrested in her apartment for robbery, but the police have reason to believe that the stolen goods are in her car, which is parked in the driveway. In this case, there is probable cause for arrest but not for a search of the apartment, except for a search that is incidental to the arrest.

HIGHLIGHT > **Probable Cause Is Difficult to Quantify**

"Probable cause is a fluid concept—turning on the assessment of probabilities in particular factual contexts—not readily, or even usefully, reduced to a neat set of legal rules. . . . While an effort to fix some general numerical precise degree of certainty corresponding to 'probable cause' may not be helpful, it is clear that 'only the probability, and not a prima facie showing, of criminal activity is the standard of probable cause.'"

Source: *Illinois v. Gates*, 462 U.S. 213 (1983).

With a Warrant versus without a Warrant

In arrests and seizures with a warrant, the determination of probable cause is made by the magistrate to whom the complaint or affidavit is presented by the police. In this case, the officer does not have to worry about establishing probable cause. However, such a finding of probable cause by the magistrate is not final. It may be reviewed by the judge during the trial, and if probable cause did not, in fact, exist, the evidence obtained is not admissible in court. In some jurisdictions, the absence of probable cause in a warrant must be established by the defendant through clear and convincing evidence—a difficult level of proof for the defendant to establish and certainly higher than probable cause.

By contrast, in arrests and searches and seizures without a warrant, the police officer makes the initial determination of probable cause, usually on the spot and with little time to think. This determination is subject to review by the court if challenged at a later time, usually in a *motion to suppress* evidence before or during the trial. Moreover, a trial court's determination of probable cause can be reviewed by an appellate court if the case is appealed. The important function of the courts in making the final determination whether probable cause exists is best summarized in a statement written by Justice Frankfurter in an earlier decision, *McNabb v. United States*, 318 U.S. 332 (1943), which says:

McNabb v. United States (1943)

> A democratic society, in which respect for the dignity of all men is central, naturally guards against the misuse of the law enforcement process. Zeal in tracking down crime is not in itself an assurance of soberness of judgment. Disinterestedness in law enforcement does not alone prevent disregard of cherished liberties. Experience has therefore counseled that safeguards must be provided against the dangers of the overzealous as well as the despotic. The awful instruments of the criminal law cannot be entrusted to a single functionary. The complicated process of criminal justice is therefore divided into different parts, responsibility for which is separately vested in the various participants upon whom the criminal law relies for its vindication.

Two consequences arise from the absence of probable cause in search and seizure cases. First, the evidence obtained cannot be admitted in court during the trial, hence likely weakening the case for the prosecution. Second, the police officer may be sued in a civil case for damages or, in extreme cases, subjected to criminal prosecution.

The Supreme Court has expressed a strong preference for the use of a warrant in police work. Because the affidavit has been reviewed by a neutral and detached magistrate, the issuance of a warrant ensures a more orderly procedure and is a better guarantee that probable cause is, in fact, present. In reality, however, the vast majority of arrests and searches are made without a warrant, under the numerous exceptions to the warrant requirement (these are discussed in subsequent chapters).

Why Obtain a Warrant?

Police officers are advised to obtain a warrant whenever possible for two reasons. First, there is a presumption of probable cause because the affidavit or complaint has been reviewed by a magistrate who found probable cause to justify issuing a warrant. The arrest or search and seizure is therefore presumed valid unless the accused proves otherwise in court. It is difficult for the accused to overcome the presumption that the warrant is valid. If the finding of probable cause is reviewed during the trial, the court's remaining task is simply to determine if there was a substantial basis for the issuing magistrate's finding of probable cause, not to look at specific factual allegations (*Illinois v. Gates*, 462 U.S. 213 [1983]).

Illinois v. Gates (1983)

Second, having a warrant is a strong defense in civil cases for damages brought against the police officer for alleged violation of a defendant's constitutional rights. For example, suppose a police officer is sued for damages by a person who alleges that she was arrested without probable cause. If the arrest was made by virtue of a warrant, the officer will likely not be held liable (with some exceptions) even if it is later determined in the trial or on appeal that the magistrate erred in thinking that probable cause existed. Magistrates and judges who err in the issuance of warrants are not civilly liable for damages because they have judicial immunity. The only exception to a warrant's being a valid defense in civil cases for damages is when an officer serves a warrant that is clearly invalid due to obvious mistakes that he or she should have discovered, such as a failure to specify the place or person subject to the warrant.

Who Determines Probable Cause?

In searches and seizures without a warrant, probable cause initially is determined by the officer. In searches and seizures with a warrant, the initial determination is made by the magistrate who issues the warrant. Both determinations are reviewable by the trial court or by an appellate court if the case is later appealed.

Because probable cause, if later challenged in court, must be established by police testimony in warrantless arrests or searches, it is important that the police officer be able to clearly articulate the facts and circumstances establishing that probable cause existed at the time he or she acted. For example, if an officer arrests a person seen coming out of a building at midnight, the officer must be able to explain, in court, the factors that led him or her to make the arrest—such as the furtive behavior of the suspect, nervousness when being questioned, and possession of what appeared to be stolen items.

Establishing Probable Cause after an Officer's Illegal Act

If no probable cause existed at the time the officer conducted a search or made an arrest, the fact that probable cause is later established does not make the act legal; the evidence obtained cannot be used in court. For example, suppose an officer arrests a suspicious-looking person and a body search reveals that the person had several vials of cocaine in his pocket. Under the exclusionary rule (discussed in Chapter 4), the evidence obtained cannot be used in court because there was no probable cause to make the arrest, making the arrest unlawful.

When officers seek to obtain a warrant from a magistrate, it is important that the affidavit establish probable cause. This is because probable cause must be based solely on what is contained in the affidavit. Information not included in the affidavit cannot be used to determine probable cause even if the officer knew about that information at the time the affidavit was submitted. For example, suppose Officer Hill states in the affidavit that her information came from an informant. If this is insufficient to establish probable cause, the fact that Officer Hill had a second informant who added more information cannot save the warrant from being invalid if that fact is not included in the affidavit (*Whiteley v. Warden*, 401 U.S. 560 [1971]). In short, what is not in the affidavit does not count toward establishing probable cause. Probable cause is never established by what turns up after the initial illegal act.

Whiteley v. Warden (1971)

Officer Joe Roberts of the Perrineville Police Department drug task force is close to completing a six-month-long drug investigation; he has just completed a search warrant affidavit in the hope of securing additional evidence in the case. Officer Roberts has a 2 p.m. appointment with Judge Canterbury, who will review the affidavit and decide whether or not to approve Officer Roberts' request for a search warrant. Officer Roberts intends to execute the search warrant immediately following the approval of Judge Canterbury. Here is Officer Roberts' search warrant affidavit:

Date of affidavit: October 13, 2015.

Location to be searched: The residence located at 405 South Street

The affidavit: In June 2015, several residents of South Street contacted the Perrineville Police Department to complain of suspected drug activity. Their complaint included excessive noise and steady vehicular traffic at the residence of 405 South Street. On numerous occasions some neighbors also reported finding empty syringes and glass pipes on the front lawn and driveway of the home.

The affiant conducted a surveillance of the location on nine separate occasions between August 4 and September 12. On four separate surveillances, officers from Perrineville PD conducted traffic stops on vehicles that left the South Street location. On September 12, 2015, a single traffic stop resulted in four arrests for drug possession. On September 13, 2015, these defendants were interviewed by the affiant (Officer Roberts), and they informed the affiant that they had purchased two ounces of heroin from this location on three separate occasions. The most recent purchase was made on the evening of September 12. They identified "Larry Owen," a 26-year-old white male, as the person from whom they had purchased the heroin. The deed and municipal tax records to the South Street residence list Larry Owen as the owner. The defendants stated that they observed Owen remove the heroin from a rear bedroom dresser drawer. The heroin was located inside a large metal container. Owen removed the container, then measured out two ounces and repackaged the heroin into a small clear baggie. Owen then sold the baggie containing heroin to the defendants for $300 cash. The heroin was subsequently seized by Perrineville officers during the traffic stop. Preliminary drug analysis confirmed that the seized substance contained heroin.

Assume you are Judge Canterbury, and answer the following questions:

1. *Has the affiant (Officer Roberts) established probable cause to search?*
2. *Are there any identifiable problems with the affidavit? If so, identify and explain the problem(s).*

Suspicion alone (a lower degree of certainty than probable cause) is never sufficient for an arrest. However, what starts off as mere suspicion can develop into probable cause sufficient to make an arrest. For example, suppose a police officer asks questions of a motorist who failed to stop at a stop sign. The officer suspects that the driver may be drunk. If the initial questions indicate that the driver is, in fact, drunk, then the officer may make a valid arrest for drunk driving. Also, any evidence obtained as a result of that arrest is admissible in court.

An officer may have probable cause to arrest without having personally observed the commission of the crime. For example, suppose that, while out on patrol, an officer is told by a motorist that a robbery is taking place in a store down the block. The officer proceeds to the store and sees a man running toward a car with goods in his hands. The man sees the police car, drops the items, gets into the car, and tries to drive away. In this case, probable cause to believe a crime has occurred is present, so an arrest would be valid.

The Supreme Court recognizes that affidavits or complaints are often prepared hastily in the midst of a criminal investigation. Therefore, the policy is to interpret the allegations in a commonsense rather than an overly technical manner and to consider the affidavit sufficient in close cases (*United States v. Ventresca*, 380 U.S. 102 [1965]).

Any Trustworthy Information Can Establish Probable Cause

In establishing probable cause, the officer may use any trustworthy information, even if the rules of evidence prohibit its admission during the trial. For example, hearsay information and a suspect's prior criminal record (both inadmissible in a trial) may be taken into consideration when determining probable cause. In cases of hearsay information, trustworthiness depends on the reliability of the source and the information given. Reliance on prior criminal record requires other types of evidence. The key point is that, in determining whether probable cause exists, the magistrate may consider any evidence, regardless of its source.

The Three Ways Whereby Probable Cause Is Established

Probable cause is established in three ways:

1. Through an officer's own knowledge of particular facts and circumstances
2. Through information given by a reliable third person (an informant)
3. Through information plus corroboration by the officer

All three ways rely upon the officer to establish probable cause. If the officer seeks the issuance of an arrest or a search and seizure warrant from a magistrate or judge, probable cause is established through an affidavit. If the officer acts without a warrant, probable cause is established by oral testimony in court during the trial. It is therefore important for the officer to be able to state clearly, whether in an affidavit or in court later, why he or she felt that probable cause was present. In some states, in addition to the evidence contained in the affidavit, the police officer may present oral evidence to the judge.

In one case, the Court ruled that a suspect's reputation for criminal activity may be considered by the magistrate issuing the warrant when determining probable cause (*United States v. Harris*, 403 U.S. 573 [1971]). In that case, the officer's affidavit submitted to the magistrate to support a request for a search warrant stated that the suspect "had a reputation with me for over four years as being a trafficker of non-tax-paid distilled spirits, and over this period I have received numerous information from all types of persons as to his activities." The affidavit further stated that another officer had located illicit whiskey in an abandoned house under the suspect's control and that an informant had purchased illegal whiskey from the suspect. Although a suspect's reputation for criminal activity is never by itself sufficient to establish probable cause, reputation combined with factual statements about the suspect's activity may be considered by the magistrate issuing the warrant.

An Officer's Own Knowledge of Facts and Circumstances The officer's own knowledge means that he or she has personally obtained the information, using any of the five senses. These are the: (1) sense of sight (Officer Smith sees Joe stab Bob), (2) hearing (Officer Smith hears a shotgun blast), (3) smell (Officer Smith smells marijuana while in an apartment), (4) touch (Officer Smith frisks a suspect and touches something that feels like a gun), and (5) taste (Officer Smith tastes something alcoholic). This contrasts with knowledge obtained from another person. Factors that a police officer may take into account in establishing belief that probable cause exists include, but are not limited to, the following:

◆ The prior criminal record of the suspect
◆ The suspect's flight from the scene of the crime when approached by the officer
◆ Highly suspicious conduct on the part of the suspect
◆ Admissions by the suspect
◆ The presence of incriminating evidence
◆ The unusual hour
◆ The resemblance of the suspect to the description of the perpetrator
◆ Failure to answer questions satisfactorily
◆ Physical clues, such as footprints or fingerprints, linked to a particular person
◆ The suspect's presence in a high-crime area
◆ The suspect's reputation for criminal activity

This list is not exhaustive; courts have taken other factors into account.

It is hard to say to the extent to which some or any of the preceding factors contribute to establishing probable cause, as that would depend on the type of event, the strength of the relationship, and the intensity of the suspicion. One factor may be sufficient to establish probable cause in some instances; in others, several factors may be required. In *United States v. Cortez*, 449 U.S. 411 (1981), the Court said that probable cause "does not deal with hard certainty, but with probabilities."

United States v. Cortez (1981)

This statement illustrates how difficult it is to set highly specific rules about what can or cannot be taken into account in determining probable cause. One thing is certain, however: The more facts that are included, the higher the likelihood that probable cause will be established.

MYTH vs. REALITY

MYTH An anonymous tip cannot serve as the primary basis for probable cause.

FACT An anonymous tip can, if sufficiently corroborated by the police, serve as the primary basis for probable cause.

Information Given by an Informant This section looks at how the Court evaluates information given by informants, both those who are engaged in criminal activity and those who are not. The Court evaluates both the quality of the information and the credibility of the informant. The major decisions reflecting the Court's evolving views on the subject are discussed. The section also examines the role the informant's identity plays in determining the value of his or her information in establishing probable cause.

Information Given by an Informant Engaged in Criminal Activity: In *Aguilar v. Texas*, 378 U.S. 108 (1964), the Court established a two-pronged test for determining probable cause on the basis of information obtained from an informant engaged in criminal activity (who therefore has low credibility with the courts):

Aguilar v. Texas (1964)

◆ *Prong 1: Reliability of the informant.* The affidavit must describe the underlying circumstances from which a neutral and detached magistrate can find that the informant is reliable. For example, "Affiant [a person who makes or subscribes to an affidavit] received information this morning from a trustworthy informant who has supplied information to the police during the past five years and whose information has proved reliable, resulting in numerous drug convictions."
◆ *Prong 2: Reliability of the informant's information.* The affidavit must describe the underlying circumstances from which the magistrate can find that the informant's information is reliable and not the result of mere speculation or

suspicion. For example, "My informant told me that he personally saw Henry Banks, a former convict, sell heroin worth $500 to a buyer named Skippy Smith, at 10 o'clock last night in Banks's apartment located at 1300 Shady Lane, Apt. 10, and that Banks has been selling and continues to sell drugs from this location."

Spinelli v. United States (1969)

The *Aguilar* test was reiterated five years later in *Spinelli v. United States*, 393 U.S. 410 (1969). (Read more about *Spinelli* in the Case Brief.) However, the *Aguilar* and *Spinelli* decisions have now been modified by *Illinois v. Gates*:

◆ *The original interpretation of Aguilar:* Court decisions interpreted the two prongs in *Aguilar* as separate and independent of each other. This meant that the reliability of each—informant and information—had to stand on its own and be established separately before probable cause could be established. For example, the fact that an informant is absolutely reliable (Prong 1) cannot make up for the lack of a description of how the informant obtained his or her information (Prong 2).

◆ *The new interpretation of Aguilar: Illinois v. Gates*: The "separate and independent" interpretation of the two prongs in *Aguilar* was overruled by the Supreme Court in *Illinois v. Gates*, 462 U.S. 213 (1983). In *Gates*, the Court abandoned the requirement of two independent tests as too rigid, holding instead that the two prongs should be treated merely as relevant considerations in the *totality of circumstances*. Therefore, the "totality of circumstances" has replaced "separate and independent" as the standard for probable cause in the *Aguilar* test. The Court wrote:

> The task of the issuing magistrate is simply to make a practical, commonsense decision whether, given all the circumstances set forth in the affidavit before him. . . . There is a fair probability that contraband or evidence of a crime will be found in a particular place.

The appropriate test, therefore, is this: If a neutral and detached magistrate determines that, based on an informant's information and all other available facts, there is probable cause to believe that an arrest or a search is justified, then the warrant may be issued.

Under the *Gates* ruling, if an informer has been very reliable in the past, then his or her tip may say little about how he or she obtained the information. Conversely, if the informant gives a lot of detail and says that he or she personally observed the event, then doubts about the informant's reliability may be overlooked. Corroboration by the police of the informant's story and/or all other available facts may be taken into account in determining probable cause based on the totality of circumstances.

Information Given by an Informant Not Engaged in Criminal Activity: The preceding discussion focused on informants who are themselves engaged in criminal activity and who therefore suffer from low credibility. If the information comes from noncriminal sources, the courts tend to look more favorably on the informant's reliability.

The Importance of the Identity of the Informant: The Constitution does not require an officer to reveal the identity of an informant either to the magistrate when seeking the issuance of a warrant or during the trial. As long as the magistrate is convinced that the police officer is truthfully describing what the informant told him or her, the informant need not be produced nor his or her identity revealed. For example, based on an informant's tip, police arrested a suspect without a warrant and searched him

The Leading Case on the Sufficiency of Allegations for Probable Cause

Facts: Spinelli was convicted by a federal court of interstate travel in aid of racketeering. The evidence used against him was obtained with a search warrant issued by a magistrate, authorizing the search of his apartment. The warrant was issued on the basis of an affidavit from an FBI agent that stated the following:

1. That the FBI had kept track of Spinelli's movements on five days during the month of August 1965. On four of those five occasions, Spinelli was seen crossing one of two bridges leading from Illinois into St. Louis, Missouri, between 11 a.m. and 12:15 p.m.
2. That an FBI check with the telephone company revealed that an apartment house near a parking lot that Spinelli frequented had two telephones listed under the name of Grace P. Hagen.
3. That Spinelli was known to the affiant and to federal law enforcement agents and local police "as a bookmaker, an associate of bookmakers, a gambler, and an associate of gamblers."
4. That the FBI "has been informed by a confidential informant that William Spinelli is operating a handbook and accepting wagers and disseminating wagering information by means of the telephones" listed under the name of Grace P. Hagen.

Spinelli was convicted of traveling across the state line from Illinois to Missouri with the intention of conducting gambling activities prohibited by Missouri law. The United States Court of Appeals for the Eighth Circuit rejected his contention that the search warrant that led to incriminating evidence against him was not supported by probable cause and affirmed his conviction. The Court granted certiorari.

Decision: The Court reversed and remanded the decision of the Court of Appeals for the Eighth Circuit.

Issue or Issues: *Did the above affidavit contain probable cause sufficient for the issuance of a search warrant?* No.

Holding: Allegations one and two in the affidavit reflect only innocent-seeming activity and data: "Spinelli's travels to and from the apartment building and his entry into a particular apartment on one occasion could hardly be taken as bespeaking gambling activity; and there is nothing unusual about an apartment containing two separate telephones." Allegation three is "but a bald and unilluminating assertion

of suspicion that is entitled to no weight in appraising the magistrate's decision." Allegation 4 must be measured against the two-pronged *Aguilar* test. Here, the reliability of the informant was not established; neither did the affidavit prove the reliability of the informant's information. The affidavit therefore failed to establish probable cause, so the conviction was reversed and remanded.

Case Significance: The *Spinelli* case illustrates the types of allegations that are insufficient to establish probable cause. It restates the two-pronged *Aguilar* test for probable cause if the information comes from an informant. However, note that the *Aguilar* test, though still valid, has been substantially modified by *Illinois v. Gates*.

Excerpts from the Opinion: In the present case the informant's tip—even when corroborated to the extent indicated—was not sufficient to provide the basis for a finding of probable cause. This is not to say that the tip was so insubstantial that it could not properly have counted in the magistrate's determination. Rather, it needed some further support. When we look to the other parts of the application, however, we find nothing alleged which would permit the suspicions engendered by the informant's report to ripen into a judgment that a crime was probably being committed. As we have already seen, the allegations detailing the FBI's surveillance of Spinelli and its investigation of the telephone company records contain no suggestion of criminal conduct when taken by themselves—and they are not endowed with an aura of suspicion by virtue of the informer's tip. Nor do we find that the FBI's reports take on a sinister color when read in light of common knowledge that bookmaking is often carried on over the telephone and from premises ostensibly used by others for perfectly normal purposes. Such an argument would carry weight in a situation in which the premises contain an unusual number of telephones or abnormal activity is observed, but it does not fit this case where neither of these factors is present. All that remains to be considered is the flat statement that Spinelli was "known" to the FBI and others as a gambler. But just as a simple assertion of police suspicion is not itself a sufficient basis for a magistrate's finding of probable cause, we do not believe it may be used to give additional weight to allegations that would otherwise be insufficient.

The affidavit, then, falls short of the standards set forth in *Aguilar*, *Draper*, and our other decisions that give content to the notion of probable cause.

in conjunction with the arrest. Heroin was found on his person. During the trial, the police officer refused to reveal the name of the informant, claiming that the informant was reliable because the information he had given in the past had led to arrests. After being convicted, the defendant appealed. The Court held that a warrantless arrest, search, and seizure may be valid even if the police officer does not reveal the identity of the informant, because other evidence at the trial proved that the officer did rely on credible information supplied by a reliable informant. The Court added that the issue in this case was whether probable cause existed, not the defendant's guilt or innocence (*McCray v. Illinois*, 386 U.S. 300 [1967]).

McCray v. Illinois (1967)

An Exception: An exception to the preceding identity rule is that, when the informant's identity is material to the issue of guilt or innocence, identity must be revealed. Under what circumstances the informant's identity is material to the issue of guilt is a matter to be determined by the judge. In *McCray*, the Court said that the determination of whether the informant's name should be revealed "rests entirely with the judge who hears the motion to suppress to decide whether he needs such disclosure as to the informant in order to decide whether the officer is a believable witness." If the judge decides that the informant's name should be disclosed because the information is "material" (although the Court has never defined what that really means) to the issue of guilt, then the police must either drop the case to preserve the informant's anonymity or disclose the name and thereby blow his or her cover. An alternative to disclosing the informant's name in court is to hold an *in camera* (private) hearing, producing the informant only before the judge so he or she can interview the informant in private.

Information Given by an Ordinary Citizen: Most courts have ruled that the ordinary citizen who is either a victim of a crime or an eyewitness to a crime is a reliable informant, even though his or her reliability has not been established by previous incidents. For example, suppose a woman tells an officer that she has personally witnessed a particular individual selling narcotics in the adjoining apartment, gives a detailed description of the alleged seller, and describes the way sales are made. There is probable cause to obtain a warrant or, in exigent (meaning *emergency*) circumstances, to make a warrantless arrest.

Information Given by Another Police Officer: Information given by a police officer is considered reliable by the courts. In one case, the Court noted, "Observations of fellow officers of the government engaged in a common investigation are plainly a reliable basis for a warrant applied for by one of their number" (*United States v. Ventresca*, 380 U.S. 102 [1965]). Sometimes the police officer makes an affidavit in response to statements made by other police officers, as in cases of inside information from a detective or orders from a superior. The Court has implied that under these circumstances the arrest or search is valid only if the officer who passed on the information acted with probable cause.

"Stale" Information: In search and seizure cases, problems may arise concerning whether the information provided has become "stale" after a period of time. The problem occurs in search and seizure cases because in these cases the issue is always whether evidence of a crime may be found at that time in a certain place. In one case, the Court held that there was no probable cause to search for illegal sale of alcohol in a hotel where the affidavit alleged that a purchase of beer had occurred more than three weeks earlier (*Sgro v. United States*, 287 U.S. 206 [1932]).

Sgro v. United States (1932)

A more recent case involved an informant's claim that he had witnessed a drug sale at the suspect's residence approximately five months earlier and had observed a shoe box containing a large amount of cash that belonged to the suspect. The Court said that this was stale information that could not be used to establish probable cause (*United States v. Leon*, 468 U.S. 897 [1984]). However, the Court has not specified how much time may elapse between the informant's observation and the issuing of a warrant, stating instead that the issue "must be determined by the circumstances of each case."

United States v. Leon (1984)

Information Plus Corroboration by an Officer If probable cause cannot be established using information provided by the informant alone, the police officer can remedy the deficiency by conducting his or her own corroborative investigation. Together, the two may establish probable cause even if the informant's information or the officer's corroborative findings alone would not have been sufficient. For example, suppose an informant tells a police officer that she heard that Fred is selling drugs and that the sales are usually made at night in the apartment of Fred's girlfriend. That information alone would not establish probable cause. However, if the officer, acting on the information, places the apartment under surveillance, sees people going in and out, and is actually told by a buyer that he has just purchased drugs from Fred inside the apartment, there is a strong basis for probable cause either to arrest Fred without a warrant (if exigent circumstances exist) or to obtain a warrant from a magistrate.

A leading case on information plus corroboration is *Draper v. United States*, 358 U.S. 307 (1959). In this case, a narcotics agent received information from an informant that Draper had gone to Chicago to bring three ounces of heroin back to Denver by train. The informant also gave a detailed description of Draper. Given this information, police officers set up surveillance of trains coming from Chicago on the mornings of September 8 and 9, the dates the informant had indicated. On seeing a man who fit the informant's description, the police moved in and arrested him. Heroin and a syringe were seized in a *search incident to the arrest* (meaning a search that takes place right after the arrest). During trial, Draper sought exclusion of the evidence, claiming that the information given to the police failed to establish probable cause. Ultimately, the Supreme Court disagreed, saying that information received from an informant that is corroborated by an officer may be sufficient to provide probable cause for an arrest, even though such information was hearsay and would not otherwise have been admissible in a criminal trial.

Draper v. United States (1959)

Probable Cause and Motor Vehicle Passengers

In *Maryland v. Pringle*, 540 U.S. 366 (2003), the Court decided an important issue police officers face daily: Can the police arrest the passenger of a motor vehicle if they have probable cause to arrest the driver? In this case, a police officer stopped a car for speeding. The officer searched the car and seized $763 from the glove compartment and cocaine from behind the backseat armrest. The three occupants denied ownership of the drugs and money. Pringle, who was the passenger in the front seat, was later convicted of drug possession with intent to distribute and was given ten years in prison without the possibility of parole. He appealed, arguing that finding of cocaine in the back armrest, when he was a passenger in the front seat of the car being driven by its owner, was insufficient to establish probable cause for an arrest for drug possession.

The Court disagreed, holding instead that the officer had probable cause to arrest Pringle because it was reasonable to infer that any (or all) of the occupants of the car "had knowledge of, and exercised dominion and control over," the drugs in the car. Pringle had asserted that this was a case of "guilt by association," and cited *Ybarra v. Illinois*, 444 U.S. 85 (1979), in which the Court held that a search of a bartender for possession of a controlled substance, based on a warrant, "did not permit body searches of all the tavern's patrons and that the police could not pat down the patrons for weapons, absent individualized suspicion." The Court rejected this analogy, saying that Pringle and the other passengers were "in a relatively small automobile, not a public tavern," and that in this case "it was reasonable for the officer to infer a common enterprise among the three men."

Ybarra v. Illinois (1979)

It is important to note that *Pringle* does not automatically authorize the arrest of all car passengers if probable cause exists that a crime (such as drugs being found, as in the *Pringle* case) has been committed in the car. Instead, the test is "whether or not there is probable cause to believe that the passengers committed the crime solely or jointly." In the *Pringle* case, such inference was reasonable from the facts of that particular case. Under other circumstances, the inference might not be reasonable. Ultimately, whether the inference is reasonable or unreasonable is for the courts to decide on a case-by-case basis.

Is an Arrest Based on Probable Cause for a Different Offense Valid?

The Supreme Court has held that the Fourth Amendment does not require the offense establishing probable cause to be "closely related" to the same conduct as the offense initially identified by the officer (*Devenpeck v. Alford*, 543 U.S. 146 [2004]). In this case Alford pulled behind a disabled vehicle and activated wig-wag headlights, which are usually used only by the police and other emergency vehicles. A patrol car going in the opposite direction turned around to assist. Alford saw this, hurriedly returned to his vehicle, and drove away. The officer radioed his supervisor (Devenpeck), pursued Alford's vehicle, and pulled it over. The officer observed that Alford was listening to a police scanner and had handcuffs in his car. The officer informed his supervisor that he was concerned the suspect could be a police impersonator. When Devenpeck arrived, he questioned Alford and received evasive answers. He saw a tape recorder in the vehicle seat with the record button activated. Devenpeck confirmed that Alford was recording their conversation. The officers arrested Alford, not for impersonating a police officer (the original reason he was a suspect), but for violating the Washington State Privacy Act, which prohibited such recordings without the consent of all the parties to the communication. Tried and convicted, Alford appealed, saying that his arrest was unlawful because the probable cause for which there was reason to arrest (impersonating a police officer) was not "closely related" to or "based on" the offense for which he was arrested (violation of the state privacy act). The Court disagreed, saying that for an arrest to be constitutional, there is no requirement under the Fourth Amendment that the offense establishing probable cause for an arrest be "closely related" to or "based on" the same conduct as the offense for which the defendant was initially suspected.

Devenpeck v. Alford (2004)

The Court's decision in this case was based on three factors that are significant in police work. First, an officer who has probable cause may arrest under one provision of the law, and then, upon further investigation, may decide that the suspect's actions are more appropriately punishable under a different offense. Second, the Court stressed that the officer's state of mind is not a factor in establishing probable cause. What is important is that probable cause is present. Third, the Court recognized that while it is good practice to inform a person of the reason for an arrest, there is no constitutional requirement to do so, and therefore failure to do so does not invalidate what is otherwise a valid arrest.

REASONABLE SUSPICION

Another important term in law enforcement is *reasonable suspicion*, a level of proof required by the courts in stop-and-frisk cases. A **level of proof** is the degree of certainty required by the law for an act by government agents to be legal. As a level of proof, reasonable suspicion ranks below probable cause but above suspicion in its degree of certainty. (See Table 3.1 for rankings of levels of proof and their applications in legal proceedings.) This section looks at the definition of reasonable suspicion and how the totality of circumstances affects reasonable suspicion.

level of proof
the degree of certainty required by the law for an act by government agents to be legal.

Reasonable Suspicion Defined

Black's Law Dictionary defines **reasonable suspicion** as that "quantum of knowledge sufficient to induce an ordinarily prudent and cautious man under similar circumstances to believe criminal activity is at hand. It must be based on specific and articulable facts, which, taken together with rational inferences from those facts, reasonably warrant intrusion."[1]

The Court has not clearly defined reasonable suspicion. However, in *Alabama v. White*, 496 U.S. 325 (1990), the Court said: "Reasonable suspicion is a less demanding standard than probable cause not only in the sense that reasonable suspicion can be established with information that is different in quantity or content than that required to establish probable cause, but also in the sense that reasonable suspicion can arise from information that is less reliable than that required to show probable cause." The Case Brief gives more insight into *Alabama v. White*, which is the leading case on reasonable suspicion.

reasonable suspicion
the quantum of knowledge sufficient to induce an ordinarily prudent and cautious person in similar circumstances to believe criminal activity is occurring.

Alabama v. White (1990)

The Totality of Circumstances

In *United States v. Arvizu*, 534 U.S. 266 (2002), the Court said that reasonable suspicion is to be determined based on the totality of the circumstances, and that the police officer

United States v. Arvizu (2002)

Table 3.1 Levels of Proof in Law and Their Applications in Legal Proceedings

Level of Proof	Degree of Certainty	Type of Proceeding
1. No information	0% certainty	Not sufficient in any legal proceeding
2. Hunch		Not sufficient in any legal proceeding
3. Suspicion		Start a police or grand jury investigation
4. Reasonable suspicion		Stop and frisk by police
5. Probable cause	51% certainty	Issuance of warrant; search, seizure, and arrest without warrant; filing of an indictment
6. Preponderance of the evidence	51% certainty	Winning a civil case, affirmative criminal defense
7. Clear and convincing evidence		Denial of bail in some states and insanity defense in some states
8. Guilt beyond a reasonable doubt		Convict an accused; prove every element of a criminal act
9. Absolute certainty	100% certainty	Not required in any legal proceeding

CASE BRIEF

Alabama v. White, 496 U.S. 325 (1990)

The Leading Case on Reasonable Suspicion

Facts: Police responded to an anonymous telephone call that conveyed the following information: White would be leaving her apartment at a particular time in a brown Plymouth station wagon with the right taillight lens broken; she was in the process of going to Dobey's Motel; and she would be in possession of about an ounce of cocaine hidden inside a brown attaché case. The police saw White leave her apartment without an attaché case, but she got into a car matching the description given in the telephone call. When the car reached the area where the motel was located, a patrol unit stopped the car and told White she was suspected of carrying cocaine. After obtaining her permission to search the car, the police found the brown attaché case. Upon request, White provided the combination to the lock; the officers found marijuana and arrested her. At the station, the officers also found cocaine in her purse. White was charged with and convicted of possession of marijuana and cocaine. She appealed her conviction, saying that the police did not have reasonable suspicion required under *Terry v. Ohio*, 392 U.S. 1 (1968), to make a valid stop and that the evidence obtained therefore should be suppressed.

The Court of Criminal Appeals of Alabama held that officers did not have the reasonable suspicion necessary to justify an investigatory stop of respondent's car and that the marijuana and cocaine that the officers seized were fruits of respondent's unconstitutional detention. The U.S. Supreme Court granted review.

Issue or Issues: *Did the anonymous tip, corroborated by independent police work, constitute reasonable suspicion to justify a stop?* Yes.

Decision: The Court reversed and remanded the decision of the Court of Criminal Appeals of Alabama.

Holding: The stop made by the police was based on reasonable suspicion, and so the evidence obtained was admissible in court.

Case Significance: This case categorically states that reasonable suspicion is not as demanding a standard as probable cause and that it can be established with information that is different in quality and quantity from that required for probable cause. The information here from the anonymous telephone call would likely not, in by itself, have established reasonable suspicion. The Court said: "[A]lthough it is a close question, the totality of the circumstances demonstrates that significant aspects of the informant's story were sufficiently corroborated by the police to furnish reasonable suspicion." What established reasonable suspicion in this case was therefore a combination of an anonymous telephone tip and corroboration by the police.

Excerpts from the Opinion: Reasonable suspicion is a less demanding standard than probable cause not only in the sense that reasonable suspicion can be established with information that is different in quantity or content than that required to establish probable cause, but also in the sense that reasonable suspicion can arise from information that is less reliable than that required to show probable cause. Reasonable suspicion, like probable cause, is dependent upon both the content of information possessed by police and its degree of reliability. Both factors—quantity and quality—are considered in the "totality of the circumstances—the whole picture," that must be taken into account when evaluating whether there is reasonable suspicion. Thus, if a tip has a relatively low degree of reliability, more information will be required to establish the requisite quantum of suspicion than would be required if the tip were more reliable. The *Gates* Court applied its totality-of-the-circumstances approach in this manner, taking into account the facts known to the officers from personal observation, and giving the anonymous tip the weight it deserved in light of its indicia of reliability as established through independent police work. The same approach applies in the reasonable-suspicion context, the only difference being the level of suspicion that must be established. We conclude that when the officers stopped respondent, the anonymous tip had been sufficiently corroborated to furnish reasonable suspicion that respondent was engaged in criminal activity and that the investigative stop therefore did not violate the Fourth Amendment.

The Court's opinion in *Gates* gave credit to the proposition that because an informant is shown to be right about some things, he is probably right about other facts that he has alleged, including the claim that the object of the tip is engaged in criminal activity. Thus, it is not unreasonable to conclude in this case that the independent corroboration by the police of significant aspects of the informer's predictions imparted some degree of reliability to the other allegations made by the caller.

We think it also important that, as in *Gates*, "the anonymous [tip] contained a range of details relating not just to easily obtained facts and conditions existing at the time of the tip, but to future actions of third parties ordinarily not easily predicted." The fact that the officers found a car precisely matching the caller's description in front of the 235 building is an example of the former. Anyone could have "predicted" that fact because it was a condition presumably existing at the time of the call. What was important was the caller's ability to predict respondent's future behavior, because it demonstrated inside information—a special familiarity with respondent's affairs. The general public would have had no way of knowing that respondent would shortly leave the building, get in the described car, and drive the most direct route to Dobey's Motel.

Because only a small number of people are generally privy to an individual's itinerary, it is reasonable for police to believe that a person with access to such information is likely to also have access to reliable information about that individual's illegal activities. When significant aspects of the caller's predictions were verified, there was reason to believe not only that the caller was honest but also that he was well informed, at least well enough to justify the stop.

Although it is a close case, we conclude that under the totality of the circumstances the anonymous tip, as corroborated, exhibited sufficient indicia of reliability to justify the investigatory stop of respondent's car.

must have "a particularized and objective basis for suspecting wrongdoing." In this case, the U.S. Border Patrol installed sensors in several border areas in Arizona. The sensors detected a vehicle; the officers followed it for several miles, and then stopped the vehicle.

The stop was based on the following observations: the roads taken by the vehicle were remote and not well suited for the vehicle type, the time the vehicle was on the road coincided with a shift change for roving patrols in the area, the vehicle slowed dramatically upon first observing the officer, the driver of the vehicle would not look at the officer when passing, the children in the vehicle seemed to have their feet propped up on some cargo, the children waved mechanically at the officer as if being instructed to do so, and the vehicle made turns that would allow it to completely avoid the checkpoint.

After the stop and having obtained consent from Arvizu, the officer searched the vehicle and found drugs. Arvizu later claimed that the search was illegal because there was no reasonable suspicion for the stop, because each of the indicators noted was an innocent activity and therefore "carried little or no weight in the reasonable-suspicion calculus." The Court disagreed, saying that "in making reasonable-suspicion determinations, reviewing courts must look at the 'totality of the circumstances' of each case to see whether the detaining officer has a 'particularized and objective basis' for suspecting legal wrongdoing." The Court added that "this process allows officers to draw on their own experiences and specialized training to make inferences from and deductions about the cumulative information available." The Court then concluded that, although each of the factors used by the officer in this case is "susceptible to

HIGHLIGHT > Reasonable Suspicion Is Not Clearly Defined

Reasonable suspicion has not been defined with precision by the Supreme Court. In one case, however, the Court stated: "Reasonable suspicion is a less demanding standard than probable cause not only in the sense that reasonable suspicion can be established with information that is different in quantity or content than that required to establish probable cause, but also in the sense that reasonable suspicion can arise from information that is less reliable than that required to show probable cause."

Source: *Alabama v. White*, 496 U.S. 325 (1990).

innocent explanation," taken together, they constituted a sufficient and objective basis for legally stopping the vehicle.

PROBABLE CAUSE COMPARED WITH REASONABLE SUSPICION

Probable Cause	Reasonable Suspicion
Legal definition: Stated by the Court in *Brinegar v. United States*, 338 U.S. 160 (1949)	No good legal definition given by the Court
Practical definition: "More likely than not"	Practical definition: "Less certain than probable cause, but more than mere suspicion"
Sufficient for arrest	Sufficient for stop and frisk, but not for arrest
After arrest, officer may search arrested person and immediate vicinity	After valid stop, officer may frisk suspect if there is fear for officer's safety
Sufficient for issuance of warrant	Not sufficient for issuance of warrant
Overall, higher degree of certainty than reasonable suspicion	Overall, lower degree of certainty than probable cause

Clearly, as noted in this chapter, probable cause and reasonable suspicion are fluid concepts that cannot be defined with precision. It is, however, important to remember the following:

◆ Probable cause requires a higher degree of certainty than reasonable suspicion.
◆ Both terms are subjective, meaning that what is probable cause or reasonable suspicion to one officer, judge, or juror may not be to another.
◆ If information such as a tip has a low degree of reliability (quality), more information (quantity) will be required to establish probable cause or reasonable suspicion than if the information were more reliable.
◆ Both terms are additive, meaning that the more facts an officer can articulate, the greater the likelihood that probable cause or reasonable suspicion will be established.
◆ Both terms are determined based on the totality of circumstances.

DETERMINING PROBABLE CAUSE OR REASONABLE SUSPICION ON APPEAL

Probable cause is initially determined by a police officer (in arrests or searches without a warrant) or by a judge or magistrate (in arrests or searches with a warrant). Reasonable suspicion is always initially determined by the officer in stop-and-frisk cases. However, these determinations are not binding; they can always be, and often are, challenged during trial. Should the challenge be made, usually in a defendant's motion to suppress the evidence obtained, the trial judge then determines whether probable cause or reasonable suspicion did, in fact, exist.

The trial court's determination of probable cause or reasonable suspicion is not final and can be reviewed on appeal. In one case, the defendants had pleaded guilty to possession of cocaine with intent to distribute, but they reserved the right to appeal the federal district court's denial of their motion to suppress the evidence of cocaine found in their car. The court had ruled that the officer had reasonable suspicion to stop and question the petitioners as they entered their car, as well as probable cause to remove one of the car's panels, which concealed two kilos of cocaine. The issue raised on appeal was whether a trial court's findings of reasonable suspicion and probable cause are final or whether they can be reviewed by an appellate court on appeal. In response, the Court held that the ultimate question of reasonable suspicion to stop and the presence of probable cause to make a warrantless arrest "should be reviewed *de novo*" (meaning anew, afresh, or a second time) on appeal (*Ornelas et al. v. United States*, 517 U.S. 690 [1996]). The Court stressed that "we have never, when reviewing a probable-cause or reasonable-suspicion determination ourselves, expressly deferred to the trial court's determination." The Court added that "independent review is therefore necessary if appellate courts are to maintain control of and to clarify the legal principles." The Court cautioned, however, that "a reviewing court should take care both to review findings of historical fact only for clear error and to give due weight to inferences drawn from those facts by resident judges and local law enforcement officers."

Ornelas et al. v. United States (1996)

In sum, on appeal, the appellate court determines for itself whether reasonable suspicion or probable cause is present based on the facts of the case. This is different from other issues on appeal where the appellate court seldom, if ever, reviews questions of facts. That issue is left to the trial court. Instead, the appellate court focuses on questions of law. But while trial court findings of probable cause and reasonable suspicion are reviewable on appeal, such reviews are to be based on clear error and the appellate court must give due weight to whatever inferences and conclusions may have been drawn by the trial judge and law enforcement officers.

SUMMARY

◆ Probable cause has both legal and practical meanings:

Legal definition: Probable cause exists when "the facts and circumstances within the officers' knowledge and of which they had reasonably trustworthy information are sufficient in themselves to warrant a man of reasonable caution in the belief that an offense has been or is being committed."

Practical definition: Probable cause exists when it is *more likely than not* (more than 50 percent certainty) that the suspect committed an offense or that the items sought can be found in a certain place.

◆ In the absence of probable cause, the search or arrest is illegal, and the evidence obtained must be excluded by the court.

◆ Probable cause cannot be established by what is found after an illegal search or arrest.

◆ *Probable cause is established in three ways*: It is established through the officer's own knowledge, information given by an informant, or information plus corroboration.

◆ *Obtaining a warrant offers two clear advantages*: Probable cause is presumed present, and it is a good defense in civil cases for damages.

◆ *Probable cause compared to other levels of proof*: Probable cause is lower in certainty than clear and convincing evidence but higher than reasonable suspicion.

◆ Another important term in law enforcement is *reasonable suspicion*, a level of proof required by the courts in stop and frisk cases.

◆ Reasonable suspicion has both legal and practical meanings:

Legal definition: "That quantum of knowledge sufficient to induce an ordinarily prudent and cautious man under similar circumstances to believe criminal activity is at hand."

Practical definition: It is lower in certainty than probable cause but higher than mere suspicion.

◆ Determination of reasonable suspicion must be based on the totality of the circumstances, taking into account an officer's knowledge and experience.

◆ Reasonable suspicion is required during stop-and-frisk cases but is not sufficient for arrest.

◆ Reasonable suspicion is initially determined by the officer but is reviewable by a magistrate, trial judge, and appellate court judge.

◆ *Reasonable suspicion compared to other levels of proof*: Reasonable suspicion is lower in certainty than probable cause but higher than mere suspicion.

REVIEW QUESTIONS

1. What is the U.S. Supreme Court's definition of *probable cause*? For practical purposes, when does probable cause exist?

2. The Court says that probable cause is to be determined using the standard of an "objectively reasonable police officer." What does this mean? Give your own example of an incident where an "objectively reasonable police officer" would have concluded that he or she had probable cause to make an arrest.

3. What are the advantages of obtaining a warrant in an arrest and in search and seizure cases?

4. How has the case of *Illinois v. Gates* changed the interpretation of the two-pronged test established in *Aguilar v. Texas*?

5. What did the U.S. Supreme Court say in *Spinelli v. United States*? Was there probable cause in that case or not? Justify your answer.

6. What are the three ways whereby probable cause is established? How does one differ from the other?

7. Give an example of how probable cause is established through information plus corroboration.

8. Define *reasonable suspicion*. How has the Supreme Court defined it? For what purpose can it be used in law enforcement?

9. "Reasonable suspicion determinations must be based on the totality of the circumstances." Explain what this means.

10. "A police officer's determination of probable cause or reasonable suspicion is final." Is this statement true or false? Discuss.

TEST YOUR UNDERSTANDING

1. Officer Makin, a university police officer, received information that a student living in a campus dormitory was selling drugs. This information was conveyed to Officer Makin by an anonymous caller to the officer's cell phone. Officer Makin knew the suspect in question and had similar suspicions. Officer Makin immediately went to the dormitory and stopped the student as he was leaving the building. Officer Makin arrested him, searched his pockets, and found drugs. Were these actions valid? Justify your answer.

2. Officer Klein was told by criminal informant Albert that while out drinking with Bob the night before, Bob said he had cocaine in his dormitory room. Acting on this information, Officer Klein went to a magistrate and asked for a warrant to search Bob's dormitory room. You are the magistrate. Will you issue the warrant? Why or why not?

3. While on patrol, Officer Jenkins was told by a neighbor of Aaron that Aaron was selling drugs. Asked how he knew this, the informant said that during the past few evenings he saw people come in and out of that house and that "those people are seedy and suspicious, and always look like they are high on drugs, particularly after they come out of Aaron house." The neighbor said further that he was in the driveway of the house one evening last week and smelled marijuana coming from Aaron's house. The informant added that Aaron had moved into the house about a year ago, did not have children, seemed to have no work, and yet appeared to live well; that Aaron and his wife refused to associate with anybody in the neighborhood; and that "they are simply weird." You are the judge whom Officer Jenkins has asked for a warrant based on the information from this citizen informant. Will you issue the warrant? Justify your response.

4. Officer Johnson was told by an informant that the informant had suspicions that Robin, in the apartment next door, was selling drugs from her (Robin's) apartment. During the next three nights, Officer Johnson observed Robin's apartment and saw a number of people going in and out. Officer Johnson stopped one of them, who immediately threw away what she had in her hand. The discarded object turned out to be crack cocaine. After retrieving it, Officer Johnson entered the apartment without a warrant and found more cocaine on the living room table. Officer Johnson seized the drugs. Was there anything invalid about what Officer Johnson did? State your reasons.

RECOMMENDED READINGS

Gabriel M. Helmer. Note. *Strip search and the felony detainee: A case for reasonable suspicion.* 81 Boston University Law Review 1: 239, 288 (2001).

Marvin Zalman. *Fleeing from the Fourth Amendment.* 36 Criminal Law Bulletin 129 (2000).

Kit Kinports. *Diminishing probable cause and minimalist searches.* The Ohio State Journal of Criminal Law, vol. 6, April 2009, p. 649.

Wesley McNeil Oliver. *The modern history of probable cause.* Tennessee Law Review, Winter 2011, vol. 78, issue 2, pp. 377–429.

NOTE

1. Henry C. Black, *Black's Law Dictionary*, 6th ed., abridged (St. Paul, MN: West, 1991), p. 875.

CHAPTER 4

The Exclusionary Rule

LEARNING OBJECTIVES

1. Describe the purpose of the exclusionary rule.
2. Explain the role of the exclusionary rule as to the admissibility of evidence.
3. Discuss the legal development of the exclusionary rule.
4. Compare and contrast the legal concepts of fruit of the poisonous tree and the exclusionary rule in regards to the admissibility of evidence.
5. Discuss the effect of *Mapp v. Ohio* upon the criminal justice system.
6. Identify which of the following apply to a scenario: the exclusionary rule, fruit of the poisonous tree, or evidence is lawful.
7. Explain the exceptions to the exclusionary rule and the court decisions that created them.
8. Create arguments for and against the use of the exclusionary rule.
9. Discuss the circumstances as to when the exclusionary rule can and cannot be invoked.
10. When given a scenario, you will determine whether the fruit of the poisonous tree is applicable and why.
11. Explain the importance of having probable cause.

KEY TERMS

exclusionary rule

judge-made rule

fruit of the poisonous tree doctrine

good faith exception

harmless error

inevitable discovery exception

independent source exception

purged taint exception

silver platter doctrine

standing

iStockphoto.com/Vasko

THE TOP 5 IMPORTANT CASES

in the Exclusionary Rule

▶ **SILVERTHORNE LUMBER CO. V. UNITED STATES (1920)**
Once the primary evidence (the "tree") is shown to have been unlawfully obtained, any secondary evidence (the "fruit") derived from it is also inadmissible. This case enunciated the fruit of the poisonous tree doctrine.

▶ **ELKINS V. UNITED STATES (1960)** The Fourth Amendment prohibits the use of illegally obtained evidence in federal prosecutions, whether the evidence is obtained by federal or state officers. This case eliminated the silver platter doctrine.

▶ **MAPP V. OHIO (1961)** The exclusionary rule, which prohibits the use of evidence obtained as a result of unreasonable search and seizure, is applicable to state criminal proceedings.

▶ **UNITED STATES V. LEON (1984)** The Fourth Amendment's exclusionary rule should not be applied to bar the prosecution from using evidence that has been obtained by officers acting in reasonable reliance on a search warrant that is issued by a detached and neutral magistrate but is ultimately found to be invalid.

▶ **HERRING V. UNITED STATES (2009)** Evidence obtained by the police from unlawful searches is admissible as long as the police mistakes that led to unlawful search are merely the result of isolated negligence and not the product of systematic error or reckless disregard of constitutional rights.

THE EXCLUSIONARY RULE is a controversial rule in criminal procedure that has generated debate among criminal justice professionals at all levels. No other rule of evidence has had as much impact on police procedures. The rule is applied by the courts and has a direct impact on day-to-day law enforcement. It continues to undergo modification and refinement in Supreme Court decisions. Every law enforcement officer should be thoroughly familiar with the exclusionary rule because the success or failure of criminal prosecutions sometimes depends on it.

This section looks at the definition of the exclusionary rule, its purpose, the role of the judiciary in forming the rule, how the rule developed in federal and state courts, and when it does or does not apply.

THE EXCLUSIONARY RULE DEFINED

exclusionary rule
states that evidence obtained by the government in violation of the Fourth Amendment guarantee against unreasonable search and seizure is not admissible in a criminal prosecution to prove guilt.

The **exclusionary rule** provides that any evidence obtained by the government in violation of the Fourth Amendment guarantee against unreasonable search and seizure is not admissible in a criminal prosecution to prove guilt. U.S. Supreme Court decisions strongly suggest that the exclusionary rule applies only to Fourth Amendment search-and-seizure cases. But what happens if the constitutional right violated is a Fifth, Sixth, or Fourteenth Amendment right? For example, suppose Jane is charged with an offense and retains a lawyer to represent her. However, the police interrogate Jane in the absence of her lawyer—a violation of her Sixth Amendment right to counsel. Or suppose Jane is interrogated by the police while in custody without having been given the *Miranda* warnings—a violation of her Fifth Amendment right to protection against self-incrimination. In both instances, the evidence obtained is inadmissible, but will it be suppressed under the exclusionary rule?

United States v. Leon (1984)

The Court has repeatedly stated that only the fruits, including any evidence obtained, of a violation of the Fourth Amendment guarantee of protection against unreasonable search and seizure will be suppressed under the exclusionary rule. In *United States v. Leon*, 468 U.S. 897 (1984), the Court said that the exclusionary rule is a "judicially created remedy designed to safeguard *Fourth Amendment* rights." Therefore, not every violation of a constitutional right comes under the exclusionary rule.

Evidence obtained in violation of any of the other constitutional rights is also excludable in a criminal trial—but not under the exclusionary rule. For example, suppose a confession is obtained without giving the suspect his or her *Miranda* warnings. *Miranda* is primarily a Fifth Amendment right to protection against self-incrimination, so it is the suspect's Fifth Amendment rights that are violated in this example. The evidence is excludable anyway, usually as a due process violation under the Fifth or Fourteenth Amendment. In *United States v. Patane*, 542 U.S. 630 (2004), involving an alleged violation of the *Miranda* warnings, the Court said that "the Self-Incrimination clause contains its own exclusionary rule," thus adding strength to the argument that the exclusionary rule does not apply to Fifth Amendment violations.

United States v. Patane (2004)

If the evidence was erroneously admitted by the judge during the trial, the defendant's conviction will overturned on appeal unless the error is proved by the prosecutor to be harmless. Appellate court judges determine what is a harmless error on a case-by-case basis from the facts and record of the case.

THE PURPOSE OF THE RULE IS TO DETER POLICE MISCONDUCT

United States v. Janis (1976)

The Court has repeatedly stated that the primary purpose of the exclusionary rule is to *deter police misconduct*. In *United States v. Janis*, 428 U.S. 433 (1976), the Court said that where "the exclusionary rule does not result in appreciable deterrence, then, clearly, its use . . . is unwarranted." The assumption is that if the evidence obtained illegally is not admitted in court, police misconduct in search-and-seizure cases will cease or at least reduced. (For arguments in opposition to this assumption, see Exhibit 4.1.) The rule now applies to federal and state cases. This means that evidence illegally seized by state or federal officers cannot be used in any state or federal prosecution.

A JUDGE-MADE RULE

Is the exclusionary rule a constitutional or a **judge-made rule**? If the rule is mandated by the Constitution, then the Supreme Court cannot eliminate it, and neither can Congress change it. If it is judge-made, however, the Court may eliminate it at any time, or, arguably, it can be modified by Congress. Some writers maintain that this rule of evidence is judge-made—that it cannot be found in the Constitution; instead, it has been established by case law. Its proponents disagree, claiming that the rule is of constitutional origin and therefore beyond the reach of Congress, even if Congress should want to limit it. These proponents point to a statement of the Court, in *Mapp v. Ohio*, 367 U.S. 643 (1961), that "the exclusionary rule is an essential part of both the Fourth and Fourteenth Amendments." However, the Court has more recently suggested that the exclusionary rule is a judge-made rule of evidence. In *Arizona v. Evans*, 514 U.S. 1 (1995), the Court stated, "The exclusionary rule operates as a judicially created remedy designed to safeguard against future violations of Fourth Amendment rights through the rule's general deterrent effect."

judge-made rule
a rule crafted by judges, not provided for in the Constitution.

Mapp v. Ohio (1961)

Arizona v. Evans (1995)

HISTORICAL DEVELOPMENT

This section looks at how the exclusionary rule developed in both the federal and state courts.

In Federal Courts The exclusionary rule is of American origin. It did not exist in English common law or prior to the American Revolution. The first exclusionary rule case involving searches and seizures was decided by the Court in 1886, when it held that the forced disclosure of papers amounting to evidence of a crime violated

Exhibit 4.1 · Reasons Why the Exclusionary Rule May Not Deter Officer Misconduct

The Court has long assumed that the exclusionary rule deters police misconduct. This may not be true, however, for a number of reasons, among which are:

◆ The officer may truly believe his or her actions were valid. Only later and after a hearing are they declared invalid by the court during trial.

◆ The officer may lack proper training in Fourth Amendment cases and may not know, in close cases, what is a valid action and what is not.

◆ Most searches and seizures do not result in prosecution; therefore, the exclusionary rule often cannot be invoked because it applies only if the case goes to trial.

◆ A great majority of criminal cases, particularly misdemeanors, result in a plea bargain. There is no actual trial, so the exclusionary rule is not invoked.

◆ Filing a case against a suspect may not be the main reason for police seizure. In some cases, the police may simply want to confiscate contraband or keep suspects locked up and off the streets for a few hours but not actually prosecute them.

◆ The contraband obtained by the police is seldom, if ever, returned to the suspect even if the police obtained it illegally (nor would the suspect want it returned to him or her because of the risk of immediate rearrest).

◆ Except in highly publicized cases, the erring officer is seldom disciplined, particularly if the seizure results in a conviction despite the exclusion of the illegally seized evidence.

silver platter doctrine permitted federal courts to admit evidence illegally seized by state law enforcement officer and handed over to federal officers for use in federal cases.

MYTH vs. REALITY

MYTH The only purpose served by the exclusionary rule is the deterrence of police misconduct.

FACT The Supreme Court originally listed two reasons for the exclusionary rule: (1) deterrence of police misconduct and (2) promotion of judicial integrity. The Court in recent years has not focused on judicial integrity, however.

the constitutional right of the suspect to protection against unreasonable search and seizure, so such items were inadmissible in court proceedings (*Boyd v. United States*, 116 U.S. 616 [1886]). It is worth noting that two years before *Boyd*, the Court, in *Hopt v. The Territory of Utah*, 110 U.S. 574 (1884), addressed the issue of the exclusion of a confession in a murder case. The *Hopt* case, however, involved a confession and was not a search-and-seizure case, to which the exclusionary rule traditionally applies. It was not until 1914 that evidence illegally obtained by federal officers was held to be excluded in all federal criminal prosecutions (*Weeks v. United States*, 232 U.S. 383 [1914]).

From 1914 to 1960, federal courts admitted evidence of a federal crime if the evidence had been illegally obtained by state officers, as long as it had not been obtained by or in connivance with federal officers. This was because the Fourth Amendment did not, at this time, apply to the actions of state officials, only to the actions of federal officials. This questionable practice was known as the **silver platter doctrine**, which permitted federal courts to admit evidence illegally seized by state law enforcement officers and handed over to federal officers for use in federal cases. Under this doctrine, such evidence was admissible because the illegal act was not committed by federal officers. In 1960, the Court put an end to this questionable practice by holding that the Fourth Amendment prohibited the use of illegally obtained evidence in federal prosecutions, whether obtained by federal or by state officers, thereby laying to rest the silver platter doctrine (*Elkins v. United States*, 364 U.S. 206 [1960]).

In State Courts In 1949, the Court held that state courts were not constitutionally required to exclude illegally obtained evidence, so the exclusionary rule did not apply to state prosecutions (*Wolf v. Colorado*, 338 U.S. 25 [1949]). In 1952, the Court modified that position somewhat by ruling that, although the exclusionary rule did not apply to the states, some searches were so "shocking" as to require exclusion of the evidence seized under the due process clause. However, these were limited to cases involving coercion, violence, or brutality (*Rochin v. California*, 342 U.S. 165 [1952]). In *Rochin* the Court determined that evidence obtained in violation of the constitutional right to due process was inadmissible, but not necessarily under the exclusionary rule since the rule is limited to Fourth Amendment violations. The right to due process comes under the Fifth or Fourteenth Amendment. Finally, in *Mapp v. Ohio* (1961), the Court overruled the *Wolf* decision and held that the Fourth Amendment required state courts to exclude evidence obtained by unlawful searches and seizures.

HIGHLIGHT › **The Court's Justification for the Exclusionary Rule**

"The effect of the Fourth Amendment is to put the courts of the United States and Federal officials, in the exercise of their power and authority, under limitations and restraints as to the exercise of such power and authority, and to forever secure the people, their persons, houses, papers, and effects, against unreasonable searches and seizures under the guise of law. This protection reaches all alike. . . . The tendency of those who execute the criminal laws of the country to obtain conviction by means of unlawful seizures and enforced confessions, the latter obtained after subjecting accused persons to unwarranted practices destructive of rights secured by the Federal Constitution, should find no sanction in the judgments of the courts, which are charged at all times with the support of the Constitution, and to which people of all conditions have a right to appeal for maintenance of such fundamental rights."

Source: *Weeks v. United States*, 232 U.S. 383 (1914).

THE RULE NOW APPLIES TO STATE CRIMINAL PROSECUTIONS

The facts in *Mapp v. Ohio*, 367 U.S. 643 (1961), are important because improper police behavior made it relatively easy for the Court to decide to exclude the evidence obtained. In *Mapp*, three Cleveland police officers went to Mapp's residence, knocked on the door, and demanded entrance. After telephoning her attorney, Mapp refused to admit them without a search warrant. The officers again sought entrance three hours later when at least four additional officers had arrived on the scene. When Mapp did not come to the door immediately, the police forced their way in. Meanwhile, Mapp's attorney arrived, but the officers did not permit him to see his client or enter the house. Mapp demanded to see the search warrant, which the officers by then claimed to have. When one of the officers held up a paper and claimed it was a warrant, Mapp grabbed the paper and placed it in her bra. A struggle ensued in which the officers handcuffed Mapp because, they claimed, she was belligerent.

In handcuffs, Mapp was forced into her bedroom, where the officers searched a dresser, a chest of drawers, a closet, and some suitcases. The search spread to include the rest of the house, including the basement and a trunk found in it. Obscene materials were discovered in this trunk. At the trial, no search warrant was produced by the prosecution, nor was the absence of a warrant explained. The seized materials were admitted into evidence during trial and Mapp was convicted of possession of obscene materials. On appeal, the Court excluded the evidence, holding that the exclusionary rule prohibiting the use of evidence in federal courts if illegally obtained was now applicable to state criminal proceedings.

Mapp is significant because, since 1961, the exclusionary rule has been applied to federal and state criminal prosecutions (read the Case Brief to learn more about *Mapp*). Arguably its importance ranks second only to *Miranda* in terms of impact on day-to-day policing. Before *Mapp*, the use of the exclusionary rule was left to the discretion of the states; some used it, whereas others did not. It is perhaps the second most important law enforcement case ever decided by the Court (the first is *Miranda v. Arizona*, which is discussed in Chapter 11).

What caused the Court to change its mind about the exclusionary rule, when twelve years earlier, in *Wolf v. Colorado*, 338 U.S. 25 (1949), it had ruled the exclusionary rule was not applicable in state prosecutions? The Court noted that, when *Wolf* was decided, almost two-thirds of the states were opposed to the exclusionary rule.

HIGHLIGHT ❯ The Origin of the Exclusionary Rule

"Under the exclusionary rule, evidence obtained in violation of the Fourth Amendment cannot be used in a criminal trial against the victim of the illegal search and seizure. The Constitution does not require this remedy; it is a doctrine of judicial design. Excluded evidence is oftentimes quite reliable and the 'most probative information bearing on the guilt or innocence of the defendant.' Nevertheless, the rule's prohibition applies to such direct evidence, as well as to the 'fruit of the poisonous tree'—secondary evidence derived from the illegally seized evidence itself."

Source: *United States v. Houltin*, 566 F.2d 1027 (5th Cir. 1978).

However, since then more than half of those states, by legislation or judicial decision, had adopted the *Weeks* rule excluding illegally obtained evidence in their own criminal prosecutions.

The Court further noted that *Wolf* was partially based on the assumption that "other means of protection" against officer misconduct made the exclusionary rule unnecessary. The Court considered that a mistake, finding instead that the experience of California and other states had established that "such other remedies have been worthless and futile." The Court therefore decided to abandon what it deemed the "obvious futility of relegating the Fourth Amendment to the protection of other remedies." Clearly, the Court realized the need to apply the exclusionary rule to all criminal prosecutions in order to protect Fourth Amendment rights.

CASE BRIEF

Mapp v. Ohio, 367 U.S. 643 (1961)

The Leading Case on the Extension of the Exclusionary Rule to the States

Facts: Mapp was convicted of possession of lewd and lascivious books, pictures, and photographs, in violation of Ohio law. Three Cleveland police officers went to Mapp's residence pursuant to information that a person who was wanted in connection with a recent bombing was hiding out in her home (this person was Don King, who later gained national notoriety as a boxing promoter). The officers knocked on the door and demanded entrance, but Mapp, telephoning her attorney, refused to admit them without a warrant. The officers again sought entrance three hours later, after the arrival of more police officers. When Mapp did not respond, the officers broke the door open. Mapp's attorney arrived but was denied access to his client. Mapp demanded to see the search warrant the police claimed they had. When one of the officers held up a paper and claimed it was the warrant, Mapp grabbed the paper and placed it in her bra. A struggle ensued, and the paper was recovered after Mapp was handcuffed, ostensibly for being belligerent. A search of the house turned up a trunk that contained obscene materials. The materials were admitted into evidence at the trial, and Mapp was convicted of possession of obscene materials.

Mapp appealed from a judgment of the Supreme Court of Ohio, which affirmed her conviction for possessing obscene literature in violation of Ohio law. She contended that the evidence seized during a search and introduced at the trial was prohibited under the Fourth Amendment.

Issue or Issues: *Is evidence obtained in violation of the Fourth Amendment guarantee against unreasonable search and seizure admissible in state court? No.*

Decision: The decision of the Supreme Court of Ohio was reversed.

Holding: The exclusionary rule that prohibits the use of evidence obtained as a result of unreasonable search and seizure is applicable to state criminal proceedings.

Case Significance: The *Mapp* case is significant because the Court held that the exclusionary rule was henceforth to be applied nationally, thus forbidding both state and federal courts from admitting evidence obtained illegally in violation of constitutional protection against unreasonable search and seizure. The facts in *Mapp* illustrate what can happen if police conduct is not restricted. *Mapp v. Ohio* is arguably second only to *Miranda v. Arizona* as the most important case in criminal procedure.

Excerpts from the Opinion: [O]ur holding that the exclusionary rule is an essential part of both the Fourth and Fourteenth Amendments is not only the logical dictate of prior cases, but it also makes very good sense. There is no war between the Constitution and common sense. Presently, a federal prosecutor may make no use of evidence illegally seized, but a State's attorney across the street may, although he supposedly is operating under the enforceable prohibitions of the same Amendment. Thus the State, by admitting evidence unlawfully seized, serves to encourage disobedience to the Federal Constitution which it is bound to uphold. In non-exclusionary States, federal officers, being human, were by it invited to and did, as our cases indicate, step across the street to the State's attorney with their unconstitutionally seized evidence. Prosecution on the basis of that evidence was then had in a state court in utter disregard of the enforceable Fourth Amendment. If the fruits of an unconstitutional search had been inadmissible in both state and federal courts, this inducement to evasion would have been sooner eliminated.

There are those who say, as did Justice (then Judge) Cardozo, that under our constitutional exclusionary doctrine "[t]he criminal is to go free because the constable has blundered." In some cases this will undoubtedly be the result. But, as was said in *Elkins*, "there is another consideration—the imperative of judicial integrity." The criminal goes free, if he must, but it is the law that sets him free. Nothing can destroy a government more quickly than its failure to observe its own laws, or worse, its disregard of the charter of its own existence. As Mr. Justice Brandeis, dissenting, said in *Olmstead v. United States*, "Our Government is the potent, the omnipresent teacher. For good or for ill, it teaches the whole people by its example. . . . If the Government becomes a lawbreaker, it breeds contempt for law; it invites every man to become a law unto himself; it invites anarchy." Nor can it lightly be assumed that, as a practical matter, adoption of the exclusionary rule fetters law enforcement. Only last year this Court expressly considered that contention and found that "pragmatic evidence of a sort" to the contrary was not wanting. The Court noted that

The federal courts themselves have operated under the exclusionary rule of *Weeks* for almost half a century [367 U.S. 643, 660]; yet it has not been suggested either that the Federal Bureau of Investigation has thereby been rendered ineffective, or that the administration of criminal justice in the federal courts has thereby been disrupted. Moreover, the experience of the states is impressive. . . . The movement towards the rule of exclusion has been halting but seemingly inexorable. Id., at 218–219.

The ignoble shortcut to conviction left open to the State tends to destroy the entire system of constitutional restraints on which the liberties of the people rest. Having once recognized that the right to privacy embodied in the Fourth Amendment is enforceable against the States, and that the right to be secure against rude invasions of privacy by state officers is, therefore, constitutional in origin, we can no longer permit that right to remain an empty promise. Because it is enforceable in the same manner and to like effect as other basic rights secured by the Due Process Clause, we can no longer permit it to be revocable at the whim of any police officer who, in the name of law enforcement itself, chooses to suspend its enjoyment. Our decision, founded on reason and truth, gives to the individual no more than that which the Constitution guarantees him, to the police officer no less than that to which honest law enforcement is entitled, and, to the courts, that judicial integrity so necessary in the true administration of justice.

INVOKING THE RULE

The exclusionary rule may be raised by the defendant at just about any stage of the criminal justice proceeding and even when the defendant is serving a sentence after a conviction. Indeed, opportunities to invoke the exclusionary rule in a criminal case are virtually unending—from the trial up to habeas corpus proceedings. This almost perpetual availability points to the importance of the exclusionary rule as a vehicle to remedy violations of the Fourth Amendment right.

In Pretrial Motions

The basic procedure for excluding evidence on a claim of illegal search and seizure is a *pretrial motion to suppress* the evidence. If this fails, the motion can be filed again during the trial when the evidence is introduced. The burden of proof in a motion to suppress the evidence depends on whether the search or seizure in question was made with or without a warrant. If the search or seizure was pursuant to a warrant, there is a presumption of validity. The burden is therefore on the accused to show that the warrant was issued without probable cause. This is a heavy burden for the accused to bear, because it usually takes clear and convincing evidence (a higher degree of certainty than probable cause) to prove that probable cause did not, in fact, exist.

In contrast, if the search was made without a warrant, the prosecution has the burden of establishing probable cause or, in its absence, of proving that the search was an exception to the warrant requirement.

On Appeal

If the evidence is admitted by the trial judge, the trial proceeds, and the prosecution uses the evidence. If the accused is convicted, the defense may appeal to the appellate court the allegedly erroneous decision to admit the evidence. If the trial judge decides to exclude the evidence, most jurisdictions allow the prosecution to appeal that decision immediately, via an interlocutory appeal; otherwise, the effect of the allegedly wrongful decision might be the acquittal of the defendant. If the defendant is acquitted, there can be no appeal at all, which would thus deprive the prosecution of any opportunity to challenge the judge's decision to suppress. The appeal by the prosecutor, however, will likely cause a delay in the trial if it takes a long time for the appellate court to resolve the issue. The prosecutor might decide not to appeal the exclusion if he or she believes there is sufficient other evidence to convict.

If a motion to exclude was made in a timely manner, it is an error for the court to admit evidence obtained by an illegal search or seizure. On appeal, such mistakes automatically lead to the reversal of any conviction, unless the admission of the evidence is found by the appellate court to be a harmless error. To prove **harmless error**, the prosecution must show beyond a reasonable doubt that the evidence erroneously admitted did not contribute to the conviction. To establish harmless error, it is not enough for the prosecution to show that there was other evidence sufficient to support the verdict. Rather, it must show that there is no reasonable possibility that a different result would have been reached without the tainted evidence (*Chapman v. California*, 386 U.S. 18 [1967]).

harmless error
the evidence erroneously admitted by the trial court did not contribute to the conviction and there is other evidence to support the verdict.

Chapman v. California (1967)

In Habeas Corpus Proceedings

If the motion to exclude the evidence fails during appeal, the defendant must serve the sentence imposed. The defendant may still invoke the exclusionary rule at this late stage through a *habeas corpus proceeding* (a proceeding that seeks the defendant's release from jail or prison because his or her constitutional rights were allegedly violated before or during trial). Suppose, for example, Alan is convicted of murder based on evidence illegally seized by the police. Alan's motions to exclude were denied during pretrial and at trial. Alan was convicted and is now serving time in prison. While in prison, Alan obtains reliable and compelling evidence, not available to him during trial, that the police illegally seized the gun used in the murder. The time to appeal the conviction is past, but Alan may file a habeas corpus case asking the court to set him free because his constitutional rights were violated and therefore his imprisonment is unconstitutional. Strict limitations set by federal law limit what prisoners can do in habeas cases, but exceptions are made if a defendant can establish a strong case for the violation of a constitutional right and such evidence was not available to him or her during trial.

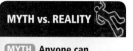

MYTH vs. REALITY

MYTH Anyone can claim the benefits of the exclusionary rule if the prosecution seeks to use illegally seized evidence against them in court.

FACT Only defendants with "standing" can claim the benefits of the exclusionary rule.

Standing and Illegally Seized Evidence

Standing is a legal concept that generally determines whether a person can legally file a lawsuit. It therefore determines whether a person can be a proper party in a case and can seek certain remedies. The general rule on standing is that the exclusionary rule may be used only by the person whose Fourth Amendment rights have been violated, meaning the person whose reasonable expectation of privacy was breached by the police. In *Minnesota v. Carter*, 525 U.S. 83 (1998), the Court said:

> "The Fourth Amendment protects people, not places." But the extent to which the Fourth Amendment protects people may depend upon where those people are. We have held that "capacity to claim the protection of the Fourth Amendment depends . . . upon whether the person who claims the protection of the Amendment has a legitimate expectation of privacy in the invaded place."

standing
a legal concept that determines whether a person can legally file a lawsuit or submit a petition to the court.

Minnesota v. Carter (1998)

Not everybody who was at the scene of the violation by the police can use the rule. The Court has held that an overnight guest, staying at a residence while the owner was away, has legal grounds to cite the exclusionary rule (*Minnesota v. Olson*, 495 U.S. 91 [1990]) because that guest has a reasonable expectation of privacy. In another case, however, the Court decided that defendants who were on a short-term visit and who, together with the lessee, used an apartment to package drugs rather than as a residence, had no legitimate expectation of privacy in the apartment. Therefore, the action by a police officer of looking in an apartment window through a gap in the closed blinds and observing the defendants and the apartment's lessee bagging cocaine did not violate the defendants' legitimate expectation of privacy (*Minnesota v. Carter*, 525 U.S. 83 [1998]).

Minnesota v. Olson (1990)

Why did an overnight guest in *Olson* have standing, whereas defendants on a short-term visit and who used the apartment, together with the lessee, for a business purpose—to package drugs—in *Carter* did not? The Court reasoned that in *Carter*, the "purely commercial nature of the transaction . . ., the relatively short period of time on the premises, and the lack of any previous connection between respondents and the householder, all lead us to conclude that respondents' situation is closer to that of one simply permitted on the premises," and not that of an overnight guest, and therefore had no reasonable expectation of privacy.

DETERMINING WHAT IS NOT ADMISSIBLE

Neither the illegally seized evidence nor the fruit of the poisonous tree is admissible at trial. There is a difference, however, between these two legal concepts. Some scholars consider it a "distinction without a difference," yet it is worthy of notice. It is true, however, that in the end it may not really matter because in either case the illegally obtained evidence is not admissible to prove defendant's guilt.

Illegally Seized Evidence (The Primary Evidence)

If seized illegally, evidence including contraband, fruits of the crime (for example, stolen goods), instruments of the crime (such as burglary tools), or "mere evidence" (shoes, a shirt, or similar items connecting a person to the crime), or a confession given without the *Miranda* warnings (where needed) is not admissible at a trial to establish defendant's guilt.

Fruit of the Poisonous Tree (The Secondary Evidence)

fruit of the poisonous tree doctrine
once the primary evidence is shown to have been unlawfully obtained, any secondary evidence derived from it is also inadmissible.

Silverthorne Lumber Co. v. United States (1920)

The **fruit of the poisonous tree doctrine** states that once the primary evidence (the "tree") is shown to have been unlawfully obtained, any secondary evidence (the "fruit") derived from it is also inadmissible (*Silverthorne Lumber Co. v. United States*, 251 U.S. 385 [1920]). Considered an extension of the exclusionary rule, this doctrine is based on the principle that evidence illegally obtained should not be used to gain other evidence, because the original illegally obtained evidence taints all evidence subsequently obtained. The tainted secondary evidence (some courts prefer to call it "derivative evidence" or "secondary evidence") can take various forms:

◆ *Example 1.* The police conduct an illegal search of a house and find a map that shows the location of the stolen goods. Using the map, the police recover the goods in an abandoned warehouse. Both the map and the goods are inadmissible as evidence but for different reasons. The map is not admissible because it is illegally seized evidence; the goods (physical evidence) are not admissible because they are fruit of the poisonous tree.

◆ *Example 2.* Police officers make an illegal search of Fred's house and find heroin. They confront Fred with the evidence, and she confesses to possession of an illicit drug. Fred's confession is the fruit of the illegal search (verbal evidence) and must be excluded.

◆ *Example 3.* The police enter a suspect's house without probable cause or consent and discover the suspect's diary, an entry of which contains the details of a murder and the location of the murder weapon. The police go to the location and find the weapon. The diary is not admissible as evidence in court because it is illegally seized evidence; the murder weapon is not admissible because it is fruit of the poisonous tree.

In sum, these two types of inadmissible evidence may be distinguished as follows: Illegally seized evidence is obtained as a direct result of the illegal act (the search), whereas the fruit of the poisonous tree is the indirect result of the same illegal act. The fruit of the poisonous tree is thus at least one step removed from the illegally seized evidence, but it is equally inadmissible (see Figure 4.1).

FIGURE 4.1 Illegally Obtained Evidence Distinguished from Fruit of the Poisonous Tree

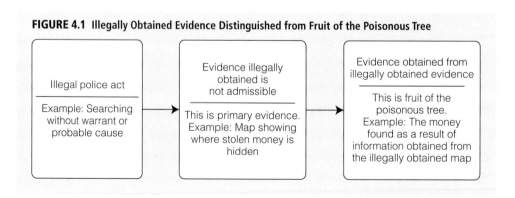

EXCEPTIONS TO THE RULE

Court decisions have identified situations in which the evidence obtained is admissible in court even though something may have been wrong with either the conduct of the police or the court that issued the warrant. These exceptions fall into four categories:

- The good faith exception and its many variations
- The inevitable discovery exception
- The purged taint exception
- The independent source exception

It must be noted, however, that some states have rules that exclude these types of evidence even if constitutionally these are admissible. The more narrow rules, if any, prevail because they in effect give more rights to the accused than the Constitution allows, something the states can do.

Category 1: The Good Faith Exception and Its Many Variations

Over the years, the Court has carved out a **good faith exception** to the exclusionary rule. Under this exception, the evidence obtained by the police is admissible in court even if there was an error or mistake, as long as the error or mistake was not committed by the police, or, if committed by the police, the error or mistake was honest and reasonable. It must be emphasized that not all claims of good faith result in the evidence being admissible. What is needed instead is an honest and "objectively reasonable belief" by the officer (as determined by the trial judge or jury) that the act was valid.

Thus far the Court has identified seven situations, based on actual cases, that constitute exceptions under the good faith exception:

1. When the error was committed by the judge or magistrate, not by the police (*Massachusetts v. Sheppard*, 468 U.S. 981 [1984])
2. When the error was committed by a court employee (*Arizona v. Evans*, 514 U.S. 1 [1995])
3. When the police erroneously, but reasonably and honestly, believed that the information they gave to the magistrate when obtaining the warrant was accurate (*Maryland v. Garrison*, 480 U.S. 79 [1987])
4. When the police reasonably believed the person who gave them permission to enter the premises had the authority to do so (*Illinois v. Rodriguez*, 497 U.S. 117 [1990])
5. When the police action was based on a law that was later declared unconstitutional (*Illinois v. Krull*, 480 U.S. 340 [1987])
6. When the evidence was obtained police officers who relied on mistakes by other officers, as long as these errors were merely negligent and isolated and not systemic, recurring, or deliberate (*Herring v. United States*, 555 U.S. 135 [2009])
7. When the police conduct a search in good faith based on established legal precedent, even if the search is later found to be unconstitutional (*Davis v. United States* 564 U.S. --- [2011]).

Each of these good faith exception cases is discussed next.

good faith exception
evidence obtained by the police is admissible even if there was an error or mistake, as long as the error or mistake was not committed by the police, or, if committed by the police, it was honest and reasonable.

When the error was committed by the judge or magistrate: The first good faith exception to the exclusionary rule applies when the error was committed by the judge or magistrate and not by the police. The Court held in *Massachusetts v. Sheppard*, 468 U.S. 981 (1984), that evidence obtained by the police acting in good faith on a search warrant that was issued by a neutral and detached magistrate, but that is ultimately found to be invalid, may be admitted and used at the trial.

In the *Sheppard* case, a police detective executed an affidavit for an arrest and search warrant authorizing the search of Sheppard's residence. The affidavit stated that the police wanted to search for certain described items, including clothing of the victim and a blunt instrument that might have been used to murder the victim. The affidavit was reviewed and approved by the district attorney. Because it was a Sunday, the local court was closed, and the police had a difficult time finding a warrant application form. The detective finally found a warrant form previously used in another district in the Boston area to search for controlled substances. After making some changes to the form, the detective presented it and the affidavit to the judge at his residence, informing him that the warrant form might need further revisions.

The judge concluded that the affidavit established probable cause to search the residence and told the detective that the necessary changes in the warrant form would be made. The judge made some changes, but he did not change the substantive portion, which continued to authorize a search for controlled substances, nor did he alter the form to incorporate the affidavit. The judge then signed the warrant and returned it and the affidavit to the detective, informing him that the warrant was of sufficient authority in form and content to authorize the search.

The ensuing search of Sheppard's residence was limited to the items listed in the affidavit, and several incriminating pieces of evidence were discovered. The defendant was convicted of first-degree murder in a trial at which the evidence obtained under the warrant was used. On appeal, the Court ruled that the evidence obtained was admissible in court because the officer conducting the search had acted in good faith, relying on a search warrant that had been issued by a magistrate but that was subsequently declared invalid.

In a companion case decided that same day, *United States v. Leon*, 468 U.S. 897 (1984), the Court made the same decision on a different set of facts. Acting on information from a confidential informant, officers of the Burbank, California, police department had initiated a drug-trafficking investigation that involved surveillance of Leon's activities. On the basis of an affidavit summarizing the officer's observations, the police prepared an application for a warrant to search three residences and Leon's automobiles for an extensive list of items. The application was reviewed by several deputy district attorneys, and a state court judge issued a warrant that was apparently valid. When Leon was later indicted for federal drug offenses, he filed motions to suppress the evidence seized. The trial court excluded the evidence on the grounds that no probable cause had existed for issuing the warrant, because the reliability of the informant had not been established and the information obtained from the informant was stale.

The government took the case to the Supreme Court solely on the issue of whether a good faith exception to the exclusionary rule should be recognized. The Court ruled that the Fourth Amendment's exclusionary rule should not be applied to bar the use of evidence in the prosecution's case that has been obtained by officers acting in reasonable reliance on a search warrant issued by a detached and neutral magistrate but ultimately found to be invalid because probable cause was lacking.

The *Sheppard* and *Leon* cases are arguably the most important cases decided on the exclusionary rule since *Mapp v. Ohio.* They represent a significant, although narrow, exception to the exclusionary rule. In these cases, the Court said that there were objectively reasonable grounds for the police's mistaken belief that the warrants authorized the searches. The officers took every step that could reasonably have been taken to ensure that the warrants were valid. The difference between these two cases is that in *Sheppard* the issue was the improper use of a form (a technical error) by the judge, whereas in *Leon* it was the use of a questionable informant and stale information by the judge to determine probable cause. The cases are similar, however, in that the mistakes were made by the judges, not the police. When the warrants were given to the officers, it was reasonable for them to conclude that each authorized a valid search. Suppression of the evidence in instances such as these would not serve the deterrent function of the exclusionary rule, as there was no police misconduct to deter. In sum, the Court reasoned that the evidence was admissible because the judge, and not the police, erred; therefore, the exclusionary rule did not apply, because it is designed to control the conduct of the police, not of judges.

When the error was committed by a court employee: Another good faith exception to the exclusionary rule was carved out by the Court in *Arizona v. Evans*, 514 U.S. 1 (1995). In this case, Evans was arrested by the Phoenix, Arizona, police during a routine traffic stop when a patrol car computer indicated there was an outstanding misdemeanor warrant for his arrest. A subsequent search of Evans's car revealed a bag of marijuana. He was charged with possession of marijuana. Evans moved to suppress the evidence under the exclusionary rule, arguing that the marijuana was illegally obtained because the misdemeanor warrant, which was the basis of the stop, was dismissed seventeen days before the arrest but was not entered in the computer due to court employee error. Evans was convicted and appealed, claiming that the evidence obtained should have been held inadmissible under the exclusionary rule. The Court rejected Evans's claim and admitted the evidence.

In admitting the evidence, the Court stressed the following: (1) The exclusionary rule historically has been designed to deter police misconduct, not to deter mistakes committed by court employees; (2) Evans offered no evidence that court employees are inclined to ignore or subvert the Fourth Amendment or that lawlessness by court employees required the extreme Court action of exclusion of the evidence; and (3) there was no basis to believe that the application of the exclusionary rule would have a significant effect on the behavior of court employees responsible for informing the police that the warrant had been dismissed. (Read the Case Brief to learn more about *Arizona v. Evans*.)

When the police erred accidentally: In *Maryland v. Garrison*, 480 U.S. 79 (1987), police officers obtained a warrant to search "the premises known as 2036 Park Avenue, third-floor apartment" for drugs and drug paraphernalia that allegedly belonged to a person named McWebb. The police honestly believed that there was only one apartment at the location. In fact, however, there were two apartments on the third floor, one belonging to McWebb and the other belonging to Garrison. Before the officers became aware that they were in Garrison's apartment instead of McWebb's, they discovered contraband that led to Garrison's conviction for violating provisions of Maryland's Controlled Substance Act. Garrison appealed his conviction, claiming

Maryland v. Garrison (1987)

that the evidence obtained by police was inadmissible based on the exclusionary rule. The Court disagreed, stating that "the validity of a warrant must be judged in light of the information available to officers when the warrant is sought." The Court added: "Plainly, if the officers had known, or even if they should have known, that there were two separate dwelling units on the third floor . . . they would have been obligated to exclude respondent's apartment from the scope of the requested warrant. But we must judge the constitutionality of their conduct in light of the information available to them at the time they acted . . . The validity of the warrant must be assessed on the basis of the information that the officers disclosed, or had a duty to discover and to disclose, to the issuing magistrate."

In the *Garrison* case, the officers had a warrant when they searched the apartment. The issue in that case, therefore, was whether the warrant itself was valid in light of the erroneous information given by the police that helped them obtain the warrant. A slightly different situation is a scenario in which the police have a valid warrant but act outside the scope of the warrant. In such cases, the good faith exception does not apply because although the warrant was valid, the extent of the search was invalid. For example, the police have a valid warrant to seize a 42-inch flat-panel plasma TV set, but while searching for it, the police open cabinet drawers and find drugs. The good faith exception does not apply because the police clearly acted outside the scope of the warrant (it is unreasonable to search cabinet drawers when looking for a 42-inch TV set, as it could not be located in them); therefore, the drugs are not admissible as evidence.

When the police reasonably believed that authority to enter was valid: A good faith exception has been fashioned by the Court under the "apparent authority" principle regarding consent. In *Illinois v. Rodriguez*, 497 U.S. 117 (1990), the suspect, Rodriguez, was arrested in his apartment and charged with possession of illegal drugs that the police said were in plain view when they entered his apartment. The police gained entry into Rodriguez's apartment with the assistance of a woman named Fischer, who told police that the apartment was "ours" and that she had clothes and furniture there. She unlocked the door with her key and gave the officers permission to enter. In reality, Fischer had moved out of the apartment and therefore no longer had any common authority over it. The Court held that the consent given by Fischer was nonetheless valid because the police reasonably and honestly believed, given the circumstances, that she had authority to give consent, thus establishing the apparent authority principle as one of the good faith exceptions to the exclusionary rule.

Illinois v. Rodriguez (1990)

When police action was based on a law later declared unconstitutional: In *Illinois v. Krull*, 480 U.S. 340 (1987), police officers entered the wrecking yard belonging to Krull without a warrant and found evidence of stolen vehicles. Such warrantless entry was authorized by a state statute. The next day, however, a federal court declared the statute unconstitutional, saying that it permitted police officers too much discretion and therefore violated the Fourth Amendment. On appeal, the Court did not dispute the constitutionality of the statute, saying instead that the evidence obtained was admissible under the good faith exception to the exclusionary rule. The Court agreed, holding that suppression is inappropriate when the fault lies not with the police, but with the legislature.

Illinois v. Krull (1987)

The Leading Case on the Good Faith Exception to the Exclusionary Rule

Facts: Officers saw Evans going the wrong way on a one-way street in front of the police station. Evans was stopped, and officers determined that his driver's license had been suspended. When Evans's name was entered into a computer data terminal, it indicated that there was an outstanding misdemeanor warrant for his arrest. While being handcuffed, Evans dropped a hand-rolled cigarette that turned out to be marijuana. A search of Evans's car revealed more marijuana under the passenger's seat. At trial, Evans moved to suppress the evidence as the fruit of an unlawful arrest because the arrest warrant for the misdemeanor had been quashed seventeen days prior to his arrest but had not been entered into the computer due to a clerical error by a court employee. This was, in fact, true. The motion was denied, and Evans was convicted. On appeal, the Supreme Court of Arizona agreed with Evans and held that the exclusionary rule required suppression of evidence due to erroneous information that resulted from an error committed by an employee of the court. The Arizona police appealed to the U.S. Supreme Court.

Issue or Issues: *Does the exclusionary rule require suppression of the evidence of marijuana obtained from Evans?* No.

Decision: The decision of the Supreme Court of Arizona was reversed and remanded.

Holding: The exclusionary rule does not require suppression of evidence seized in violation of the Fourth Amendment where the erroneous information resulted from clerical errors of court employees.

Case Significance: This case adds another exception to the exclusionary rule: when the error is committed by court employees instead of by the police. The exclusionary rule was fashioned to deter police misconduct, so the Court has refused to apply it to cases where the misconduct was not by the police. The theme in this and prior cases is that, if the error is not committed by the police, then the exclusionary rule should not apply because it was meant to control the behavior of the police. *Evans* is therefore consistent with the Court's holding in previous cases.

Excerpts from the Opinion: In *Leon*, we applied these principles to the context of a police search in which the officers had acted in objectively reasonable reliance on a search warrant, issued by a neutral and detached magistrate, that later was determined to be invalid. On the basis of three factors, we determined that there was no sound reason to apply the exclusionary rule as a means of deterring misconduct on the part of judicial officers who are responsible for issuing warrants. First, we noted that the exclusionary rule was historically designed "to deter police misconduct rather than to punish the errors of judges and magistrates." Second, there was "no evidence suggesting that judges and magistrates are inclined to ignore or subvert the Fourth Amendment or that lawlessness among these actors requires the application of the extreme sanction of exclusion." Third, and of greatest importance, there was no basis for believing that exclusion of evidence seized pursuant to a warrant would have a significant deterrent effect on the issuing judge or magistrate.

Applying the reasoning of *Leon* to the facts of this case, we conclude that the decision of the Arizona Supreme Court must be reversed. The Arizona Supreme Court determined that it could not "support the distinction drawn . . . between clerical errors committed by law enforcement personnel and similar mistakes by court employees," and that "even assuming . . . that responsibility for the error rested with the justice court, it does not follow that the exclusionary rule should be inapplicable to these facts."

Finally, and most important, there is no basis for believing that application of the exclusionary rule in these circumstances will have a significant effect on court employees responsible for informing the police that a warrant has been quashed. Because court clerks are not adjuncts to the law enforcement team engaged in the often competitive enterprise of ferreting out crime, they have no stake in the outcome of particular criminal prosecutions. The threat of exclusion of evidence could not be expected to deter such individuals from failing to inform police officials that a warrant had been quashed.

If it were indeed a court clerk who was responsible for the erroneous entry on the police computer, application of the exclusionary rule also could not be expected to alter the behavior of the arresting officer. As the trial court in this case stated: "I think the police officer [was] bound to arrest. I think he would [have been] derelict in his duty if he failed to arrest . . . Excluding the evidence can in no way affect [the officer's] future conduct unless it is to make him less willing to do his duty."

When the police obtain the evidence based on mistakes of other police officers as long as these errors are merely isolated, negligent, and not the result of a systemic, recurring, or deliberate acts: In *Herring v. United States*, 555 U.S. 135 (2009), officers from the Coffee County, Alabama, Sheriff's Department arrested Herring on an outstanding warrant from Dale County, Alabama. They then searched him and his motor vehicle. They recovered drugs in his pocket and a gun under the seat of his truck. The arrest, however, was discovered, a few minutes later, to be based on an arrest warrant (for failure to appear on a felony charge) that had been issued by nearby Dale County, but which had been recalled five months earlier. However, someone erred and failed to remove it from the computer system. All this took place within about ten to fifteen minutes. Meanwhile, Herring had been arrested and the drugs and a gun (which he could not possess because he was a convicted felon) had been recovered. Despite his objections based on the illegality of the search due to a recalled warrant, the evidence was admitted during trial. Herring was convicted and sentenced to twenty-seven months in prison. On appeal, the Court held that "a criminal defendant's Fourth Amendment rights are not violated when police mistakes that led to unlawful searches are merely the result of isolated negligence" and do not constitute systemic errors or a reckless disregard of constitutional requirements.

Herring is significant because the mistake was by a clerk from a neighboring county involved in law enforcement. The evidence was admitted because, the Court said, there was no proof that the practice was systemic, recurring, or deliberate. In short, mere isolated negligence and nonsystemic errors by the police are in the category of good faith and do not lead to the exclusion of the evidence seized. Where courts are to draw the line between the various types of police negligence is hard to tell.

Herring v. United States (2009) [margin note]

When officers conduct a search based on previously decided cases, even if the search is later found to be invalid based on a subsequent court decision In *Davis v. United States*, 564 U.S. — (2011), the car where Davis was a passenger was pulled over by the police in a routine traffic stop. Both Davis and the driver were eventually arrested, Davis for supplying the police with a false name and the driver for driving while intoxicated. They were handcuffed and placed in the backseat of squad cars. The police then searched the vehicle and found a gun in Davis's jacket, which was in the vehicle. He was charged and convicted of being a felon in possession of a firearm. Davis admitted that the police search of the vehicle where he was riding was valid based on *New York v. Belton*, 453 U.S. 454 (1981) in which the Court held that the search of a motor vehicle after a lawful custodial arrest was valid. However, he asserted that the *Belton* rule was later modified in *Arizona v. Gant*, 556 U.S. 332 (2009), which held that *Belton* did not apply to cases where the arrestee had been removed from the vehicle (as was Davis) and no longer constituted a threat to the officer, neither was he in a position to destroy evidence. The Court disagreed and refused to apply the *Gant* case, saying that searches made in objectively reasonable reliance on binding appellate precedent at that time (as the police did in this case, relying on *Belton*) are not subject to the exclusionary rule.

Davis v. United States (2011) [margin note]

New York v. Belton (1981) [margin note]

Arizona v. Gant (2009) [margin note]

Davis is interesting because in this case the Court subjects the exclusionary rule to a cost-benefit analysis and articulates what many people believe is a high price society pays for the rule. Said the Court:

Exclusion exacts a heavy toll on both the judicial system and society at large. It almost always requires courts to ignore reliable, trustworthy evidence bearing on guilt or innocence. And its bottom-line effect, in many cases, is to suppress the truth and set the criminal loose in the community without punishment. Our cases hold that society must swallow this bitter pill when necessary, but only as a "last resort." For exclusion to be appropriate, the deterrence benefits of suppression must outweigh its heavy costs.

The preceding paragraphs discuss the many good faith exceptions to the exclusionary rule. Their facts vary, but in all these cases the police acted in good faith and their actions were deemed reasonable. Let us now look at the three other categories of exception to the exclusionary rule.

Category 2: The Inevitable Discovery Exception

The second category of exceptions to the exclusionary rule is the **inevitable discovery exception**. This says that evidence is admissible if the police can prove that they would "inevitably" have discovered it anyway by lawful means, regardless of their illegal action. The exception usually applies to instances when the evidence obtained is a weapon or a body. For example, while the police were taking a suspect back to Des Moines from Davenport, Iowa, where he surrendered, they induced him to tell them the location of the body of the girl they believed he had murdered by appealing to the suspect (whom the police addressed as "Reverend"), saying that it would be nice to give the deceased a Christian burial. The police did not directly question the suspect but instead asked him to "think it over." The suspect then led the police to the body of the murdered girl. Before the departure from Davenport, the suspect's lawyer had requested that no questioning take place during that drive. While conceding that the police violated the defendant's right to counsel by encouraging him to discuss the location of the body, the Court nevertheless admitted the evidence on the grounds that the police would have discovered it anyway. At the time that the suspect was leading police to the body, searchers were approaching the actual location, so the body would inevitably have been found (*Nix v. Williams*, 467 U.S. 431 [1984]).

It is important to note that the inevitable discovery exception only applies where evidence would inevitably been discovered—it is not sufficient that the evidence "could have" or "might have" been discovered. The inevitable discovery claim by the police is strengthened if the department has a policy about such searches that, if followed, would have led to the inevitable discovery of what was seized—as long as the policy is constitutional.

inevitable discovery exception
evidence is admissible if the police can prove that they would inevitably have discovered the evidence anyway by lawful means.

Nix v. Williams (1984)

Category 3: The Purged Taint Exception

A third category of exceptions is based on the concept of purged taint. The **purged taint exception** applies if the defendant's subsequent voluntary act dissipates the taint of the initial illegality. A defendant's intervening act of free will is sufficient to break the causal chain between the tainted evidence and the illegal police conduct, so the evidence becomes admissible. For example, in one case, the police broke into a suspect's house illegally and obtained a confession from him, but the suspect refused to sign it. The suspect was released on his own recognizance. A few days later, he voluntarily went back to the police station and signed the confession. The Court said that the suspect's act indicated free will and therefore purged the tainted evidence of illegality (*Wong Sun v. United States*, 371 U.S. 471 [1963]).

purged taint exception
evidence obtained is admissible if the defendant's subsequent voluntary act dissipates the taint of the initial illegality.

Wong Sun v. United States (1963)

Brown v. Illinois (1975)

In a subsequent case, the Court clarified what it meant by the purged taint exception it created in *Wong Sun*, in effect saying it is not that simple. In *Brown v. Illinois*, 422 U.S. 590 (1975), the police arrested Brown without probable cause or a warrant. After receiving the *Miranda* warnings, he made two incriminating statements while in custody. During his trial, he moved to suppress these statements, but the motions were rejected by the trial court and Brown was convicted. The Illinois Supreme Court later held that although the arrest was unlawful, the statements were admissible because the *Miranda* warnings broke the causal connection between the illegal arrest and the giving of the statements. On appeal, the U.S. Supreme Court disagreed and held the statement inadmissible, saying that, circumstances in the case considered, the confession had not been purged of the taint of the illegal arrest without probable cause.

To break the causal connection between an illegal arrest and a confession that is the fruit of the illegal arrest, the intervening event must be meaningful. For example, in another case, after an unlawful arrest, a suspect confessed to the commission of a robbery. Even though the suspect received three sets of *Miranda* warnings and met briefly at the police station with friends prior to the confession, the Court said that these events were not meaningful and that the evidence obtained was therefore not admissible during the trial (*Taylor v. Alabama*, 457 U.S. 687 [1982]).

Taylor v. Alabama (1982)

Key to understanding the purged taint exception to the exclusionary rule is whether the defendant's subsequent voluntary act dissipated or negated the initial illegal act of the police. This is a subjective determination made by the court on a case-by-case basis and does not lend itself to specific rules. For example, in the *Wong Sun* case, the Court held that the suspect's subsequent act of going back to the police station and signing the confession was sufficient to rid the confession of its initial illegality. But what if Wong Sun had come back an hour or a few hours later, instead of a few days later? Or, suppose it had been one day instead of a few days later—would his act have been considered one of free will sufficient to break the illegality?

By contrast, the Court held in the *Taylor* case that the intervening events (Taylor having been given three sets of *Miranda* warnings and meeting briefly with friends at the police station) between the unlawful arrest and the confession were not meaningful enough to purge the taint of the initial illegal act of the police. What if the meeting with friends had lasted for hours or days instead of just briefly? Would the purged taint exception have applied? In sum, whether the initial taint has been sufficiently purged is a subjective judgment that may differ from one judge to another; there are no easy answers as to when the purged taint exception may apply.

HIGHLIGHT ⟩ It Is Difficult to Know What "Purged Taint" Means

"The question whether a confession is the product of a free will under *Wong Sun* must be answered on the facts of each case. No single fact is dispositive. The workings of the human mind are too complex, and the possibilities of misconduct too diverse, to permit protection of the Fourth Amendment to turn on such a talismanic test. The *Miranda* warnings are an important factor, to be sure, in determining whether the confession is obtained by exploitation of an illegal arrest. But they are not the only factor to be considered. The proximity of the arrest and the confession, the presence of intervening circumstances, and, particularly, the purpose and flagrancy of the official misconduct are all relevant."

Source: The majority opinion in *Brown v. Illinois*, 422 U.S. 590 (1975).

Category 4: The Independent Source Exception

A fourth category of exceptions to the exclusionary rule is independent source. The **independent source exception** holds that evidence is admissible if the police can prove that it was obtained from an independent source not connected with the illegal search or seizure (*United States v. Crews*, 445 U.S. 463 [1980]). In the *Crews* case, the Court said that the initial illegality (illegal detention of the suspect) could not deprive the prosecutors of the opportunity to prove the defendant's guilt through the introduction of evidence wholly untainted by police misconduct.

For example, in another case, a 14-year-old girl was found in the defendant's apartment during an illegal search. The girl's testimony that the defendant had sexual relations with her was admissible because she was an independent source that predated the search of the apartment. Prior to the search, the girl's parents had reported her missing, and a police informant had already located her in the defendant's apartment (*State v. O'Bremski*, 423 P.2d 530 [1967]).

There are differences between the independent source and the purged taint exceptions. Under the independent source exception, the evidence was obtained from a source not connected with the illegal search or seizure. Thus, although the evidence might be viewed as suspect, it is admissible because no illegality was involved (as when evidence was legally obtained before the police committed an illegal act). By contrast, under the purged taint exception, the evidence was obtained as a result of an illegal act, but the defendant's subsequent voluntary act removes the taint of the initial illegal act (as in the *Wong Sun* case, in which the suspect went back to the police station and voluntarily signed the confession). The subsequent voluntary act, in effect, purges the evidence of its initial illegality.

independent source exception
evidence obtained is admissible if the police can prove that it was obtained from an independent source not connected with the illegal search or seizure.

United States v. Crews (1980)

State v. O'Bremski (1967)

WHEN THE RULE DOES NOT APPLY

The exclusionary rule is not applicable in all Fourth Amendment proceedings. There are eight situations or types of proceedings in which the rule does not apply, according to court decisions. In these situations or proceedings, the evidence obtained is admissible in court:

◆ Police violations of the knock-and-announce rule
◆ In searches by private persons
◆ Grand jury investigations
◆ As part of the sentencing determination
◆ Arrests based on probable cause that violate state law
◆ Violations of agency rules
◆ Noncriminal proceedings
◆ Parole revocation hearings

This section looks at each of the preceding exceptions.

In Violations of the Knock-and-Announce Rule

The Court has held that violation of the knock-and-announce rule does not require exclusion of the evidence seized (*Hudson v. Michigan*, 547 U.S. 586 [2006]). In *Hudson*,

Hudson v. Michigan (2006)

the police obtained a warrant to search for drugs and firearms in Hudson's home. The police went there and announced their presence, but waited only 3–5 seconds (the usual wait is 20–30 seconds) before opening the door and entering. Hudson sought to have the evidence suppressed, saying that the premature entry by the police violated his Fourth Amendment rights. His motion was denied and he was convicted. On appeal, the Court rejected Hudson's argument, asserting that violation of the knock-and-announce rule does only prevents the destruction of evidence and reduces the likelihood of armed resistance by suspects, dangers which allow for the suspension of the knock-and-announce rule anyway. The Court added that there are other remedies available to defendants for violations of the knock-and-announce rule, such as civil lawsuits and seeking the discipline of erring officers.

In Searches by Private Persons

The Fourth Amendment's prohibition against unreasonable searches and seizures applies only to the actions of government officials, so prosecutors may use evidence illegally obtained by private citizens (by methods such as illegal wiretap or trespass) as long as the police did not encourage, assist, or participate in the illegal private search. In one case, the Court said that the Fourth Amendment's "origin and history clearly show that it was intended as a restraint upon the activities of sovereign authority, and was not intended to be a limitation upon other than governmental agencies" (*Burdeau v. McDowell*, 256 U.S. 465 [1921]).

Burdeau v. McDowell (1921)

In Grand Jury Investigations

A person being questioned by the grand jury cannot refuse to answer questions on the grounds that the questions are based on illegally obtained evidence (such as information from an illegal wiretap). The reason is that the application of the exclusionary rule in such proceedings would unduly interfere with the grand jury's investigative function (*United States v. Calandra*, 414 U.S. 338 [1974]).

United States v. Calandra (1974)

In Sentencing

Some lower courts have permitted the trial judge to consider illegally obtained evidence in determining sentences after conviction, even when the same evidence had been excluded during the trial because it was illegally obtained. During sentencing, they reason, a trial judge should consider any reliable evidence. The fact that it was obtained illegally does not necessarily affect its reliability. The evidence is not admissible, however, if state law prohibits its admission.

When an Arrest Based on Probable Cause Violates State Law

The Court has held that evidence seized after the police made an arrest that violated state law but was based on probable cause does not violate the exclusionary rule and is admissible at trial (*Virginia v. Moore*, 553 U.S. 164 [2008]). In this case, the Virginia state police received information that Moore was driving on a suspended license. Virginia state law specifically provides that for these types of minor offenses no arrest is to

Virginia v. Moore (2008)

be made by the police; instead, the suspect is to be issued a citation and summons to appear in court at a later time. However, the police arrested Moore after the stop and obtained his consent to search his hotel room. The search yielded sixteen grams of crack cocaine. Moore was later charged with possession of cocaine and convicted. On appeal he claimed that the crack cocaine was not admissible as evidence during his trial because the seizure violated his Fourth Amendment right since it violated state law. The Court disagreed, saying that although the arrest was against state law, such a violation did not constitute a violation of the Fourth Amendment because it was based on probable cause. Since it did not violate the Fourth Amendment, the evidence seized could be used during prosecution.

This case clarifies the extent of the exclusionary rule and adheres to the principle that not all police mistakes or illegal actions constitute a violation of the Fourth Amendment that would lead to the exclusion of the evidence seized. There was no question that what the police did violated state law, but such violation did not mean Moore's Fourth Amendment constitutional right was violated because the police had probable cause to make the arrest. Since the exclusionary rule applies only to violations of the Fourth Amendment, the evidence obtained was admissible. This does not mean that there are no consequences of police misbehavior when they violate state law. There could be punishment imposed by state law or agency policy for such violations, but the evidence seized is nonetheless admissible.

When Only Agency Rules Are Violated

The evidence is admissible if the search violates an agency rule but not the Constitution (*South Dakota v. Neville*, 459 U.S. 553 [1983]). For example, suppose police department policy prohibits home searches without written consent. If an officer obtains evidence in the course of a home search conducted without written consent but with verbal consent, the exclusionary rule does not apply because written consent is not required under the Constitution for the search to be valid. The evidence is admissible unless it is excludable under state statute or court decisions.

South Dakota v. Neville (1983)

In Noncriminal Proceedings

The exclusionary rule applies only to criminal proceedings, not to proceedings such as civil or administrative hearings. Illegally obtained evidence may be admissible against another party in a civil tax proceeding or in a deportation hearing. It may also be admissible in administrative proceedings, as when an employee is being disciplined. For example, illegally obtained evidence may be admissible in cases in which a police officer is being investigated by the internal affairs division for violation of departmental rules.

However, court decisions have established that even in administrative cases, there are instances when illegally obtained evidence may not be admitted. One is if state law or agency policy prohibits the admission of such evidence. Another is if the evidence was obtained in bad faith, as when evidence against a police officer under investigation is obtained illegally and for the purpose of establishing grounds for disciplinary action.

In Parole Revocation Hearings

Pennsylvania Board of Probation and Parole v. Scott (1998)

The Court has held that the exclusionary rule does not apply in state parole revocation proceedings (*Pennsylvania Board of Probation and Parole v. Scott*, 524 U.S. 357 [1998]). In *Scott*, parole officers conducted what was later determined to be an invalid search because of the absence of reasonable suspicion to believe that a parole violation had, in fact, occurred. The Court held that the exclusionary rule does not apply to parole revocation proceedings primarily because the rule does not apply "to proceedings other than criminal trials" and because application of the rule "would both hinder the functioning of state parole systems and alter the traditionally flexible, administrative nature of parole revocation proceedings." Although *Scott* involved parole revocation, there is good reason to believe that the exclusionary rule does not apply to probation revocation proceedings either, given the similar goals and functions of parole and probation.

IN ACTION   *THE EXCLUSIONARY RULE*

Officers of the Ashford Police Department stepped up patrols in the Echo Heights neighborhood in response to special requests from residents. The home-owners became concerned over the recent rash of burglaries in their well-preserved neighborhood of historic homes.

Late in the evening of May 16, while patrolling in Echo Heights, Officer Jenkins observed a white male emerge from behind a hedge and proceed to crawl in the eastward window of the residential home at 666 Reagan Court. Officer Jenkins called for backup and advised the dispatcher that he would be investigating. Officer Jenkins continued to watch the Reagan Court home. He observed the same male subject exit the home through a side door. Officer Jenkins watched the suspect approach a green sedan parked in front of the home. Officer Jenkins confronted the suspect and placed him under arrest for burglary. Officer Jenkins searched the suspect and recovered two marijuana cigarettes, a gold watch, and a car key from the suspect's coat pockets. During this period the suspect tried to convince Officer Jenkins that he lived at the residence and had been forced to climb through a window because he had forgotten his house key. Officer Jenkins ignored the suspect's explanation.

Officer Jenkins notified the dispatcher that he had a suspect in custody for burglary and possession of marijuana. Officer Jenkins then turned his attention to the green sedan. He used the recovered key to open the sedan's trunk. Upon opening the trunk, he immediately smelled fresh marijuana and saw a large number of plastic bags containing a green leafy substance he believed to be marijuana. Officer Jenkins seized the marijuana and impounded the vehicle.

As a criminal justice student, evaluate the preceding scenario from the following two vantage points:

1. *Assume that the residence was broken into and that Officer Jenkins established probable cause to believe that the suspect committed the crime.*

   ◆ *Is Officer Jenkins's arrest of the suspect lawful?*
   ◆ *Is Officer Jenkins's subsequent search of the suspect lawful, and is the evidence recovered from the suspect's coat admissible in court?*
   ◆ *Is Officer Jenkins's search of the sedan lawful, and is the evidence recovered from the sedan's trunk admissible in court?*

2. *Assume that the suspect actually resides at the residence and that on this particular night he forgot his house key, which is why Officer Jenkins observed him climbing through a window.*

   ◆ *Is Officer Jenkins's arrest of the suspect lawful?*
   ◆ *Is Officer Jenkins's subsequent search of the suspect lawful, and is the evidence recovered from the suspect's coat admissible in court?*
   ◆ *Is Officer Jenkins's search of the sedan lawful, and is the evidence recovered from the sedan's trunk admissible in court?*

ARGUMENTS FOR THE EXCLUSIONARY RULE

Proponents make the following arguments in support of the exclusionary rule.[1]

1. It deters violations of constitutional rights by police and prosecutors. A number of studies and testimonies by police officers support this contention.
2. It manifests society's refusal to convict lawbreakers by relying on official lawlessness—a clear demonstration of our commitment to the rule of law, which states that no person, not even a law enforcement official, is above the law.
3. It results in the freeing of the guilty in only a relatively small proportion of cases. A 1978 study by the General Accounting Office found that, of 2,804 cases in which defendants were likely to file a motion to suppress evidence, exclusion succeeded in only 1.3 percent of those cases. Moreover, the same study reported that, of the cases presented to federal prosecutors for prosecution, only 0.4 percent were declined by the prosecutors because of Fourth Amendment search-and-seizure problems.[2] In 1983, another study found that "only between 0.6 and 2.35 percent of all felony arrests are 'lost' at any stage in the arrest disposition process (including trials and appeals) because of the operation of the exclusionary rule."[3]
4. It has led to more professionalism among the police and increased attention to training programs. Fear that evidence will be excluded has forced the police to develop greater expertise in their work.
5. It preserves the integrity of the judicial system, because the admission of illegally seized evidence would make the court a party to violations of constitutional rights.
6. It prevents the government, whose agents have violated the Constitution, from profiting from its wrongdoing. Somebody has to pay for the mistake—better it be the government than the suspect who has already been wronged.
7. It protects the constitutional right to privacy.

ARGUMENTS AGAINST THE EXCLUSIONARY RULE

A number of scholars, judges, and some justices of the Supreme Court have opposed the exclusionary rule. Among their arguments are the following:

1. In the words of Justice Benjamin Cardozo, "The criminal goes free because the constable has blundered." It is wrong to make society pay for an officer's mistake—punish the officer, not society.
2. It excludes the most credible, probative kinds of evidence—fingerprints, guns, narcotics, dead bodies—and thereby impedes the truth-finding function of the courts.[4]
3. It discourages internal disciplinary efforts by law enforcement agencies. If police are disciplined when the evidence will be excluded anyway, they suffer a double setback.
4. It encourages police to perjure themselves in an effort to get the evidence admitted. Particularly in major cases, the police might feel that the end justifies the means—in other words, it is better to lie than to let a presumably guilty person go free.
5. It diminishes respect for the judicial process and generates disrespect for the law and the administration of justice.[5]

6. There is no proof that the exclusionary rule deters police misconduct. In the words of Chief Justice Warren Burger, "There is no empirical evidence to support the claim that the rule actually deters illegal conduct of law enforcement officials."

7. Only the United States uses the exclusionary rule; other countries do not. Justice Scalia says, "[It] has been 'universally rejected' by other countries."

8. It has no effect on those large areas of police activity that do not result in criminal prosecutions. If the police make an arrest or search without any thought of subsequent prosecution (such as when they simply want to remove a person from the streets overnight or when they confiscate contraband to eliminate the supply), they do not have to worry about the exclusionary rule, because it takes effect only if the case goes to trial and the evidence is used.

9. The rule is not based on the Constitution; it is only an invention of the Court.

10. It does not punish the individual police officer whose illegal conduct led to the exclusion of the evidence.

ALTERNATIVES TO THE EXCLUSIONARY RULE

The continuing debate about the exclusionary rule has produced several proposals to admit the evidence obtained and then to deal with the wrongdoing of the police separately. Among these proposals are the following:

◆ *An independent review board in the executive branch.* This proposal envisions a review board composed of non-police personnel to review allegations of violations of constitutional rights by the police. The problem with this alternative is that police oppose it because it singles them out among public officials for differential treatment. Moreover, they view outsiders as unlikely to be able to understand the difficulties and dangers inherent in police work.

◆ *A civil tort action against the government.* This would mean filing an action seeking damages from the government for acts by its officers. It poses real difficulty for the plaintiff, who would have to shoulder the financial cost of the litigation. Most defendants do not have the resources to finance a civil case, particularly after

HIGHLIGHT ＞ **Justice Scalia Says the Exclusionary Rule Is Not Used in Other Countries**

"The Court-pronounced exclusionary rule . . . is distinctly American. When we adopted that rule in *Mapp v. Ohio*, 367 U.S. 643 (1961), it was 'unique to American Jurisprudence.' Since then, a categorical exclusionary rule has been 'universally rejected' by other countries, including those with rules prohibiting illegal searches and police misconduct, despite the fact that none of those countries 'appears to have any alternative form of discipline for police that is effective in preventing search violations.' England, for example, rarely excludes evidence found during an illegal search or seizure and has only recently begun excluding evidence from illegally obtained confessions. Canada rarely excludes evidence and will only do so if admission will 'bring the administration of justice into disrepute.' The European Court of Human Rights has held that introduction of illegally seized evidence does not violate the 'fair trial' requirement in Article 6, Section 1 of the European Convention on Human Rights."

Source: Dissenting opinion by Justice Antonin Scalia in *Roper v. Simmons*, 543 U.S. 551 (2005).

a criminal trial. Moreover, low damages awards against police officers usually discourage the filing of civil tort actions except in egregious cases.

◆ *A hearing separate from the main criminal trial but before the same judge or jury.* The purpose of the hearing is to determine if, in fact, the officer behaved illegally in obtaining the evidence used during the trial and, if so, to impose the necessary sanctions on the officer. Although this is the least expensive and most expedient alternative, its effectiveness is questionable. If the violation is slight, the judge or jury will not look with favor on what may be considered an unnecessary extension of the original trial. Furthermore, if the criminal trial ends in a conviction, the chances of the officer being punished for what he or she did become remote.

◆ *Adoption of an expanded good faith exception.* The final report of the Attorney General's Task Force on Violent Crime in the late 1980s proposed a good faith exception different from and broader than that allowed by the Court in the *Sheppard* and *Leon* cases. The proposed good faith exception covers all cases in which the police would claim and can prove that they acted in good faith (not just when the magistrate issues an invalid warrant). It is based on two conditions: (1) The officer must allege that he or she had probable cause for the action in question, and (2) the officer's apparent belief that he or she was acting legally must be a reasonable one. These are questions of fact that would be determined by the judge or jury. Opponents fear that this proposal would lead to more violations of rights using good faith as a convenient excuse.

Good faith is a vague concept that is best determined on a case-by-case basis; it can vary from one judge or jury to another. Opponents also maintain that this exception discourages training and rewards lack of knowledge. (The theory is that the more untrained and uninformed the police officer, the greater the claim to good faith his or her ignorance would permit.) The case of *Herring v. United States*, 555 U.S. 135 (2009), discussed previously, comes close to the Court adopting this recommendation. Some scholars maintain that it opens a much wider opportunity for the courts to admit evidence seized by the police as long as they are acting in good faith and the violations are not recurring or systemic. Where and how the courts will draw the boundary to these types of violations will determine whether *Herring* will in effect extend the good faith exception to virtually all acts of good faith by the police.

◆ *Adoption of the British system.* Under the British system, the illegally obtained evidence is admitted in court, but the erring officer is subject to internal departmental sanctions. The problem is that this system is not effective even in England, where the police system is highly centralized and generally has attained a higher level of professionalism. Internal discipline by peers has been and is a problem in American policing; the public will most likely view this as an ineffective means of control.

THE FUTURE OF THE EXCLUSIONARY RULE

The debate on the exclusionary rule continues. Proponents and opponents of the exclusionary rule range across a spectrum, from the purists to the accommodationists. Proponents want the rule to remain intact and to be applied strictly, the way it was applied in the two decades after *Mapp v. Ohio.* Any concession is interpreted as widening the door that will eventually lead to the doctrine's demise. Others are not so unbending, conceding instead "logical" and "reasonable" exceptions. Some opponents are not satisfied with such victories as the *Sheppard, Leon, Herring,* and *Davis* cases. They want to scrap the rule completely and admit the evidence without reservation or subsequent sanctions. Still others feel that the exclusionary rule should be modified, but there is no consensus about what that modification should be.

What, then, of the future? The controversy surrounding the exclusionary rule has abated, but the debate will not completely fade away, particularly in view of the *Herring* and *Davis* decisions that have narrowed the exclusionary rule. In view of the several exceptions carved out by the Court, the exclusionary rule is no longer as controversial as it once was, nor is it as much a controlling force in law enforcement as when it was first used.

During his time on the Supreme Court, Chief Justice Burger called for the rule's abolition, calling it "conceptually sterile and practically ineffective." Other justices have publicly expressed dissatisfaction with the rule and want it to be abolished or modified. They have made major inroads, particularly through the use of the good faith exception, but chances of complete abolition appear remote. To paraphrase Mark Twain, reports concerning the demise of the exclusionary rule are greatly exaggerated. It is here to stay.

SUMMARY

- The exclusionary rule states that evidence obtained by the police in violation of the Fourth Amendment right against unreasonable searches and seizures is not admissible in court.
- The purpose of the exclusionary rule is to deter police misconduct.
- It is a judge-made rule designed to protect the Fourth Amendment right against unreasonable searches and seizures.
- It excludes two kinds of evidence: that which is illegally seized and fruit of the poisonous tree.
- *Mapp v. Ohio* (1961) applied the exclusionary rule to state criminal cases.
- There are four categories of exceptions to the exclusionary rule: good faith, inevitable discovery, purged taint, and independent source.
- The exclusionary rule does not apply in the following situations or types of proceedings: violations of the knock-and-announce rule, private searches, grand jury investigations,

sentencing, arrests based on probable cause that violate state law, when only agency rules are violated, noncriminal proceedings, and parole revocation hearings.
- Despite continuing debate, the exclusionary rule is here to stay.

REVIEW QUESTIONS

1. What is the exclusionary rule? Does it apply only to violations of Fourth Amendment rights or also to violations of any constitutional right in the Bill of Rights?
2. The purpose of the exclusionary rule is to deter police misconduct. Critics, however, say the exclusionary rule has failed to achieve that purpose. Do you agree? Why or why not?
3. Is the exclusionary rule a constitutional or a judge-made rule? Can it be modified by the U.S. Congress through legislation?

4. What is the silver platter doctrine? Is it in use today?

5. "*Mapp v. Ohio* is the most significant case decided by the Court on the exclusionary rule." Is this statement true or false? Defend your answer.

6. Distinguish between illegally seized evidence and the fruit of the poisonous tree. Give examples.

7. "The exclusionary rule does not apply if the police seize evidence illegally but in good faith." Is this statement true or false? Explain your answer.

8. What does *Arizona v. Evans* say? Why is this case important?

9. What did the Court hold in *Herring v. United States*? Is this case significant or not? Defend your answer.

10. Name at least four situations or types of proceedings in which the exclusionary rule does not apply. Discuss each.

11. What is the inevitable discovery exception to the exclusionary rule? Give an illustration.

12. What is the purged taint exception to the exclusionary rule? Why is it difficult to apply?

13. Are you in favor of or against the exclusionary rule? Justify your answer.

TEST YOUR UNDERSTANDING

1. Officer P searched the house of Citizen Q based on a warrant. He found five pounds of cocaine. Officer P then asked Q if there were other drugs in his residence. Q replied, "I have other drugs in my car in the garage, but they belong to my girlfriend." P then went to the garage, searched the car, and found a pound of heroin and three illegal weapons. P seized all these. All seized evidence was later introduced in the trial of Q and his girlfriend. Questions: (a) What is admissible in court? All, some, or none of the evidence? and (b) If any evidence is to be excluded, is the exclusion based on evidence illegally seized or fruit of the poisonous tree? Give reasons for your answers.

2. Officer X was sent by a radio dispatcher to Apartment B in a dilapidated building at 44 Magnolia Avenue based on an urgent 911 call from there that said somebody had just been shot.

Officer X went to Apartment B at that address and heard somebody moaning and groaning inside. Officer X identified himself, demanded to be admitted, was admitted, and saw illegal drugs all over the place. Officer X seized the illegal drugs. It turned out later that Officer X had gone to the wrong apartment. The 911 call came from Apartment D, at the same street address, but the 911 dispatcher misheard the caller and sent the police to Apartment B by mistake. You are the judge during the trial. Will you admit or exclude the drugs seized? State your reasons.

3. Bob and Clara, who for years were live-in lovers, had a big fight one night. Clara hastily moved out of the apartment they shared. Three days later, Clara went to the police and told them that Bob was dealing drugs from his apartment. Clara said she no longer lived there but had a key to the apartment, that she had gone back there a couple of times, and that she and Bob were in the process of reconciling—none of which was true. Clara led the police to the apartment and opened it with her key. The police saw marijuana, amphetamines, and other illegal drugs in the apartment. They seized all these and introduced them later in court as evidence against Bob. You are the judge. Will you admit or exclude the evidence? Support your decision.

4. Officer Watt of the local county sheriff's department late one evening went to the apartment of Alex because of a report he received from another officer that this second officer had just received reliable information from an informant that Watt had just unloaded pounds of illegal drugs from her car and was bringing them upstairs for distribution and sale. Officer Watt had dealt with the same informant several times before and found the information given on previous occasions to be reliable. Officer Watt went to the apartment and asked to be allowed to enter. The search did not yield any drugs, but instead Watt found stolen things from nearby apartments that had been reported stolen earlier. You are the judge at trial. Will you admit the evidence obtained by Officer Watt against Alex, based on the good faith exception? Support your answer.

RECOMMENDED READINGS

"Exclusionary Rule—Origins and Development of the Rule, the Policy Debate, Other Constitutional Exclusionary Rules, Proposals for Reform," *http://law.jrank.org/pages/1111/Exclusionary-Rule.html*.

Tonja Jacobi. *The law and economics of the exclusionary rule*. Notre Dame Law Review 2011/12/01, vol. 87, p. 585.

Orin S. Kerr. *Good faith, new law, and the scope of the exclusionary rule*. Georgetown Law Journal 2011/04/01, vol. 99, p. 1077.

Lisa A. Mattern. *Knock-and-announce violations and the purposeful enforcement of the exclusionary rule*. Florida Law Review 2007/04/01, vol. 59, p. 465.

NOTES

1. For an excellent discussion of the arguments for and against the exclusionary rule, see Yale Kamisar, Stephen H. Sach, Malcolm R. Wilkey, and Frank G. Carrington, "Symposium on the Exclusionary Rule," 1 *Criminal Justice Ethics*, pp. 4ff (1982). Some arguments for and against the exclusionary rule in these lists are taken from that source.

2. *Houston Chronicle,* July 8, 1979, sec. 4, p. 2.

3. A study by Thomas Davies, as cited in Kermit L. Hall (ed.), *The Oxford Companion to the Supreme Court of the United States* (New York: Oxford University Press, 1992), p. 266.

4. Id. note 3, p. 118.

5. Steven Schlesinger, "Criminal Procedure in the Courtroom," in James Q. Wilson (ed.), *Crime and Public Policy* (San Francisco: ICS Press, 1983), p. 195.

CHAPTER 5

Stop and Frisk and Stationhouse Detention

LEARNING OBJECTIVES

1. Explain the legal requirements for a lawful stop and for a lawful frisk.

2. When given a scenario, you will explain if the legal requirements for the following are present: stop, and search.

3. Compare and contrast the legal requirements for a lawful arrest and stationhouse detention.

4. Discuss the purpose for a lawful stop and frisk.

5. Contrast the differences between a lawful frisk with a lawful search.

6. Describe the circumstances of *Terry v. Ohio* and its effect upon law enforcement.

7. Compare and contrast the differences between a lawful stop and frisk with a lawful arrest.

8. Using court decisions, you will evaluate whether race can be used as a criteria for a lawful stop.

9. Explain how the doctrine of stop and frisk can be applied to the following: motor vehicles and residences.

10. Discuss the legal development of stop and frisk.

KEY TERMS

drug courier profile

fishing expedition

frisk

plain touch doctrine

racial profiling

reasonable suspicion

stationhouse detention

stop

Lisa F. Young/Shutterstock.com

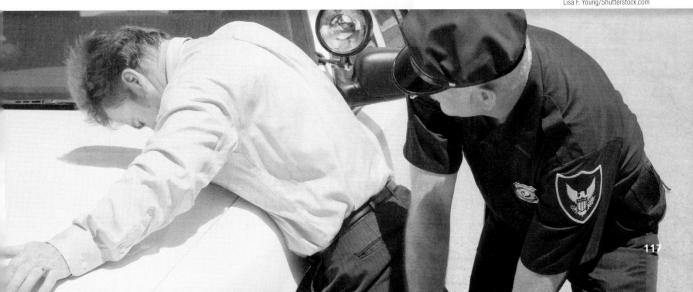

117

THE  IMPORTANT CASES

in Stop and Frisk and Stationhouse Detention

■ *TERRY V. OHIO* (1968) The police have the authority to stop a person without probable cause, so long as there is reasonable suspicion to believe that the person has committed a crime or is about to commit a crime. The person may be frisked if there is reasonable concern for officer safety.

■ *FLORIDA V. ROYER* (1983) Although the initial stop and questioning of a suspect who fit a drug courier profile was valid, the subsequent conduct of the police was more intrusive than necessary to carry out the limited investigation permitted under stop and frisk.

■ *MINNESOTA V. DICKERSON* (1993) A frisk that goes beyond that allowed in *Terry v. Ohio* in stop and frisk cases is invalid. In this case, the search went beyond the pat-down search allowed by *Terry* because the officer "squeezed, slid, and otherwise manipulated the packet's content" before knowing it was cocaine.

■ *PENNSYLVANIA V. MIMMS* (1997) A police officer may order the driver of a vehicle to exit the vehicle after a routine stop even if the officer has no reasonable suspicion that the driver poses a threat to the officer's safety.

■ *ILLINOIS V. WARDLOW* (2000) Presence in a high-crime area, combined with unprovoked flight upon observing police officers, gives officers sufficient grounds to investigate to further determine if criminal activity is about to take place.

IN THIS CHAPTER, we deal with stop and frisk and stationhouse detention as forms of intrusion upon a person's freedom. In these cases, no arrest can be made, because probable cause has not been established. However, what begins as a stop and frisk can quickly turn into an arrest if subsequent developments lead the police to conclude that probable cause has been established. Stops, frisks, and stationhouse detentions come under the Fourth Amendment but are not subject to the same constitutional requirements as arrests, searches, or seizures and follow different rules. Another form of intrusion are stationhouse detentions. They are more intimidating than stops and frisks and are best considered arrests from a legal perspective even though they are less intrusive than arrests.

STOP AND FRISK

Terry v. Ohio (1968)

This section studies the issue and origin of stop and frisk law; *Terry v. Ohio* (1968), the leading case on the law; the guidelines police officers must follow to make a legally valid stop and frisk; and the role of reasonable suspicion in valid stop and frisk cases.

Issue and Origin

One recurring legal issue in policing is whether a police officer may stop a person in a public place (or in an automobile), question the person about his or her identity and activities, and frisk the person for dangerous (and perhaps illegally possessed) weapons. A *stop* and a *frisk* are forms of searches and seizures and therefore come under the Fourth Amendment. But because they are less intrusive than arrests, searches, or seizures, all the police need to conduct them is *reasonable suspicion* rather than *probable cause*. Recall from Chapter 3 that reasonable suspicion is a lower burden of proof than probable cause.

HIGHLIGHT › **New York and Florida Laws on Stop and Frisk**

New York Criminal Procedure, Article 140, § 140.50 Temporary Questioning of Persons in Public Places; Search for Weapons

1. In addition to the authority provided by this article for making an arrest without a warrant, a police officer may stop a person in a public place located within the geographical area of such officer's employment when he reasonably suspects that such person is committing, has committed, or is about to commit either (a) a felony or (b) a misdemeanor defined in the penal law, and may demand of him his name, address and an explanation of his conduct.

2. Any person who is a peace officer and who provides security services for any court of the unified court system may stop a person in or about the courthouse to which he is assigned when he reasonably suspects that such person is committing, has committed, or is about to commit either (a) a felony or (b) a misdemeanor defined in the penal law, and may demand of him his name, address and an explanation of his conduct.

3. When upon stopping a person under circumstances prescribed in subdivisions one and two a police officer or court officer, as the case may be, reasonably suspects that he is in danger of physical injury, he may search such person for a deadly weapon or any instrument, article, or substance readily capable of causing serious physical injury and of a sort not ordinarily carried in public places by law-abiding persons. If he finds such a weapon or instrument, or any other property possession of which he reasonably believes may constitute the commission of a crime, he may take it and keep it until the completion of the questioning, at which time he shall either return it, if lawfully possessed, or arrest such person.

Florida Statutes 856.021 Loitering or Prowling; Penalty

1. It is unlawful for any person to loiter or prowl in a place, at a time, or in a manner not usual for law-abiding individuals, under circumstances that warrant a justifiable and reasonable alarm or immediate concern for the safety of persons or property in the vicinity.

2. Among the circumstances which may be considered in determining whether such alarm or immediate concern is warranted is the fact that the person takes flight upon appearance of a law enforcement officer, refuses to identify himself or herself, or manifestly endeavors to conceal himself or herself or any object. Unless flight by the person or other circumstance makes it impracticable, a law enforcement officer shall, prior to any arrest for an offense under this section, afford the person an opportunity to dispel any alarm or immediate concern which would otherwise be warranted by requesting the person to identify himself or herself and explain his or her presence and conduct. No person shall be convicted of an offense under this section if the law enforcement officer did not comply with this procedure or if it appears at trial that the explanation given by the person is true and, if believed by the officer at the time, would have dispelled the alarm or immediate concern.

3. Any person violating the provisions of this section shall be guilty of a misdemeanor of the second degree, punishable as provided in § 775.082 or § 775.083.

Several states have passed stop and frisk laws that allow an officer, based on reasonable suspicion rather than probable cause, to stop a person in a public place, ask questions to determine if the person has committed or is about to commit an offense, and frisk the person for weapons if the officer has reasonable concern for his or her safety. These stop and frisk laws vary from state to state. Other states and some federal courts have upheld such practices in judicial decisions even without statutory authorization.

Both statutory and judicial approval of stop and frisk are justified on the ground that this practice does not constitute an arrest (although it comes under the Fourth Amendment) and therefore can be justified on less than probable cause. The practice is pervasive, particularly in major metropolitan places. The *Wall Street Journal* has been cited as saying that in 2011 "New York City police officers stopped and questioned 684,330 persons, a record number since the department started producing yearly tallies of the tactic." Of the people who were stopped, 12 percent were arrested or received summons, while others were simply allowed to leave. Moreover, "males made up 92 percent of the stops, 87 percent of the total were either black or Hispanic and whites were 9 percent."[1]

The Leading Case

One of the most important cases in law enforcement, and the landmark case that declared stop and frisk constitutional, is *Terry v. Ohio*, 392 U.S. 1 (1968). On October 31, 1963, Detective Martin McFadden, an officer with thirty-nine years of experience as a police officer and an expert on pickpocket cases, observed two men on a street in downtown Cleveland at about 2:30 P.M. It appeared to Detective McFadden that the two men were "casing" a store in preparation for robbing it. Each man walked back and forth, peering into the store window, and then both returned to the corner to confer. At one point, a third person joined them but left quickly. The detective observed the two men rejoin the third man a couple of blocks away. The detective then approached them, told them who he was, and asked for some identification. After receiving a mumbled response, the detective frisked the three men. Terry and one of the other men were carrying handguns. They were tried and convicted of carrying concealed weapons.

On appeal, the Supreme Court held that the police have the authority to detain a person briefly for questioning even without probable cause to believe that the person has committed a crime. Such an investigatory stop does not constitute an arrest and is permissible when prompted by both: (1) the observation of unusual conduct leading to a reasonable suspicion that criminal activity is about to take place, and (2) the ability to point to specific and articulable facts to justify that suspicion. In addition to the stop, the officer may frisk the person if the officer reasonably suspects personal danger to himself or herself or to other persons. (Read the Case Brief to learn more details about this case.)

The last paragraph of the majority opinion in *Terry v. Ohio* sets the foundation and rules for stop and frisk:

> We . . . hold today that where a police officer observes unusual conduct which leads him reasonably to conclude in light of his experience that criminal activity may be afoot and that the person with whom he is dealing may be armed and presently dangerous, where in the course of investigating this behavior he identifies himself as a policeman

and makes reasonable inquiries, and where nothing in the initial stages of the encounter serves to dispel his reasonable fear for his own or others' safety, he is entitled for the protection of himself and others in the area to conduct a carefully limited search of the outer clothing of such persons in an attempt to discover weapons which might be used to assault him. Such a search is a reasonable search under the Fourth Amendment, and any weapons seized may properly be introduced in evidence against the person from whom they are taken.

The Guidelines

Terry v. Ohio set the following guidelines, in sequence, to determine whether a stop and frisk is valid.

The Stop Two requirements must be met to satisfy the guidelines for a valid stop.

◆ *Circumstances.* The police officer must observe unusual conduct that leads him or her reasonably to conclude, in the light of his or her experience, that: (1) criminal activity is about to take place or has just taken place, and (2) the person with whom he or she is dealing may be armed and presently dangerous.
◆ *Initial police action.* In the course of investigating such behavior, the officer must: (1) identify himself or herself as a police officer, and (2) make reasonable inquiries.

The Frisk If the two preceding requirements are satisfied, the officer, for his or her own protection and that of others in the area, may conduct a carefully limited search (called a pat-down) of the outer clothing of the person, in an attempt to discover weapons that might be used to assault the officer. The guidelines given in *Terry v. Ohio* are usually translated into instructions in police manuals regarding the steps officers are to follow in stop and frisk cases:

1. Observe.
2. Approach and identify.
3. Ask questions.

If the answers do not dispel the officers' concern for safety, they then follow this procedure:

1. Conduct a pat-down of the outer clothing.
2. If a weapon is felt, confiscate it and arrest the suspect (optional).
3. Conduct a full body search after the arrest (optional).

If, in the course of a frisk under these circumstances, the officer finds a dangerous weapon, he or she may seize it, and the weapon may be introduced into evidence against the party from whom it was taken.

Suppose an officer observes two men loitering outside a convenience store in the middle of the day. The men confer several times in front of the store, and stare through the store window. Each wears a heavy coat although it is a warm day. One of the suspects goes to a car parked across the street and sits behind the wheel. As the last customer leaves the store, the second suspect puts his hand into the pocket of his coat and starts to head into the store. The officer can then stop the suspect, identify himself or

The Leading Case on Stop and Frisk

Facts: Police detective Martin McFadden, an officer with thirty-nine years of experience in the Cleveland police force, observed two men on a street in downtown Cleveland at approximately 2:30 P.M. on October 31, 1963. It appeared to McFadden that the two men (one of whom was Terry) were casing a store. Each walked back and forth, peering into the store window, and then both returned to the corner to confer. At one point, a third man joined them but left quickly. After McFadden observed the two rejoining the same third man a couple of blocks away, he approached them, told them who he was, and asked them for identification. After receiving a mumbled response, McFadden frisked all three men. Terry and one of the other men were carrying handguns. Both were tried and convicted of carrying concealed weapons. They appealed.

Issue or Issues: *Is stop and frisk valid under the Fourth Amendment?* Yes.

Decision: The decision of the Supreme Court of Ohio was affirmed.

Holding: The police have the authority to detain a person briefly for questioning even without probable cause to believe that the person has committed a crime. Such an investigatory stop does not constitute an arrest and is permissible when prompted by both the observation of unusual conduct leading to a reasonable suspicion that criminal activity may be afoot and the ability to point to specific and articulable facts to justify that suspicion. Subsequently, an officer may frisk a person if the officer reasonably suspects that he or she is in danger.

Case Significance: The *Terry* case made clear that the practice of stop and frisk is valid. Prior to *Terry*, police

departments regularly used stop and frisk either by law or by judicial authorization. But its validity was doubtful because the practice is based on reasonable suspicion instead of probable cause, which is necessary in arrest and search cases. The Court held that stop and frisk is constitutionally permissible despite the lack of probable cause for either a full arrest or a full search and despite the fact that a brief detention not amounting to a full arrest is a seizure, requiring some degree of protection under the Fourth Amendment.

Excerpts from the Opinion: The Fourth Amendment provides that "the right of the people to be secure in their persons, houses, papers, and effects, against unreasonable searches and seizures, shall not be violated." This inestimable right of personal security belongs as much to the citizen on the streets of our cities as to the homeowner closeted in his study to dispose of his secret affairs. . . . We have recently held that "the Fourth Amendment protects people, not places," *Katz v. United States*, 389 U.S. 347, 351 (1967), and wherever an individual may harbor a reasonable "expectation of privacy," id., at 361 (Mr. Justice Harlan, concurring), he is entitled to be free from unreasonable governmental intrusion. Of course, the specific content and incidents of this right must be shaped by the context in which it is asserted. For "what the Constitution forbids is not all searches and seizures, but unreasonable searches and seizures." *Elkins v. United States*, 364 U.S. 206, 222 (1960). Unquestionably, petitioner was entitled to the protection of the Fourth Amendment as he walked down the street in Cleveland. . . . The question is whether in all the circumstances of this on-the-street encounter, his right to personal security was violated by an unreasonable search and seizure.

herself, ask for an explanation of the suspect's conduct, and then frisk the suspect if the answers do not alleviate the officer's suspicions. There is reason, based on the officer's experience, to believe that criminal activity is about to take place, that the suspects are likely to be armed, and that they pose a threat to public safety.

reasonable suspicion
not defined with precision by the Court, but is a less demanding standard than probable cause.

Reasonable Suspicion Is Required, Not Probable Cause

For the stop and frisk to be valid, there must be reasonable suspicion to stop *and* reasonable suspicion to frisk. The term **reasonable suspicion** has not been defined with precision by the Court. In one case, however, the Court said, "Reasonable suspicion is a less demanding standard than probable cause not only in the sense that reasonable suspicion can be established with information that is different in quantity or content from that required to establish probable cause, but also in the sense that reasonable suspicion can arise from information that is less reliable than that required to show probable cause" (*Alabama v. White*, 496 U.S. 325 [1990]). On a scale of certainty, reasonable suspicion ranks lower than probable cause but higher than mere suspicion. Note, however, that reasonable suspicion is what the Constitution requires. States, by legislation, may require a higher degree of certainty, such as probable cause, in stop and frisk cases.

Alabama v. White (1990)

To justify a stop, reasonable suspicion must be grounded on specific, objective facts and logical conclusions based on the officer's experience. Reasonable suspicion cannot be based on a mere hunch (which has 0 percent certainty) or even a suspicion (which may have 10 percent certainty). Specific, objective facts are needed. In *United States v. Arvizu*, 534 U.S. 266 (2002), the Court held that "in making reasonable suspicion determinations, reviewing courts must look at the totality of the circumstances in each case to see whether the detaining officer has particularized an objective basis for suspecting wrongdoing."

United States v. Arvizu (2002)

In *Arvizu*, the defendant argued on appeal that most of the ten factors relied upon by the border patrol agent to establish reasonable suspicion were not in themselves illegal. The Court rejected that argument, saying that the totality of the circumstances, not the legality (or illegality) individual factors, was the test for reasonable suspicion. The Court then added that "this process allows officers to draw on their own experiences and specialized training to make inferences from and deductions about the cumulative information available." In an earlier case, the Court held that an appellate court that reviews, on appeal, the legality of police actions taken without a warrant should conduct a *de novo* (new) review of the trial court's finding on the ultimate issues of reasonable suspicion and probable cause and not simply rely on the trial court's findings (*Ornelas et al. v. United States*, 517 U.S. 690 [1996]).

Ornelas et al. v. United States (1996)

TWO SEPARATE ACTS

Although the term *stop and frisk* implies that the frisk automatically follows the stop, they are actually two separate acts, each having its own legal requirements.

HIGHLIGHT › The Reasonable Suspicion Requirement

In order to stop and detain someone under the Fourth Amendment, the U.S. Constitution requires that a law enforcement officer justify the stop on something more than a mere suspicion or hunch. The stop must be based on an articulable and reasonable suspicion that criminal activity is afoot. In developing and articulating reasonable suspicion, a profile (such as a drug courier profile) can be a useful tool in categorizing and attaching particular significance to otherwise innocent behavior. However, each decision to detain an individual must be judged on the individual facts available to an officer at the time of the stop, viewed in light of the officer's training and experience.

Source: William U. McCormack. "Detaining Suspected Drug Couriers." *FBI Law Enforcement Bulletin* (June 1991), pp. 31–32.

The Stop

A **stop** is justified only if the police officer has reasonable suspicion, in light of his or her experience, that criminal activity is about to take place or has taken place. A stop for anything else (such as to search for evidence) is illegal. For example, one officer stopped a suspect on the grounds that: (1) the suspect was walking in an area that had a high incidence of drug traffic, (2) he "looked suspicious," and (3) he had not been seen in that area previously by the officer. The Court held that these circumstances, although amounting to vague suspicion, did not meet the "reasonable suspicion based on objective facts" test, so the stop was unconstitutional (*Brown v. Texas*, 443 U.S. 47 [1979]).

Brown v. Texas (1979)

Note, however, that what starts as a stop may turn into a valid arrest if probable cause is established during the stop. For example, suppose that, while on patrol late one night in a neighborhood notorious for burglary, Officer Roberts sees a person emerge from an alley carrying something bulky. Officer Roberts asks him to stop, whereupon the person drops the bulky object and takes off running. Officer Roberts would have probable cause to arrest that person because of the combination, or totality, of circumstances.

The next sections examine several issues related to what constitutes a legally valid stop.

MYTH vs. REALITY

MYTH A police may automatically conduct a frisk after he or she makes a stop based on reasonable suspicion.

FACT A frisk does not automatically follow from a valid stop—it is valid only if during the stop the officer has reasonable suspicion to fear for his or her safety or the safety of others.

When Is a Stop a Seizure? The Fourth Amendment forbids unreasonable searches and seizures. Not all contacts with the police, however, constitute a seizure. For example, the mere asking of questions by the police does not constitute a seizure. The important question is: When is contact with the police a "stop" that constitutes a seizure under Fourth Amendment protection (and therefore requires reasonable suspicion), and when is it a "stop" that does not constitute a seizure under the Fourth Amendment? The Court has answered this question, saying: "We conclude that a person has been 'seized' within the meaning of the Fourth Amendment only if, in view of all of the circumstances surrounding the incident, a reasonable person would have believed that he was not free to leave" (*United States v. Mendenhall*, 446 U.S. 544 [1980]).

United States v. Mendenhall (1980)

Here, three phrases stand out: (1) "in view of all of the circumstances," (2) "a reasonable person," and (3) "not free to leave." In *Mendenhall*, federal officers approached a suspect as she was walking through an airport concourse. They identified themselves and asked to see her identification and airline ticket, which she produced and the officers inspected. She later alleged that what the officers did amounted to a seizure (a stop) that was illegal unless supported by reasonable suspicion. On appeal, the Court disagreed, saying that what happened in this case did not constitute a seizure. The Court cited several circumstances in this case, including:

◆ The incident took place in a public concourse.
◆ The agents wore no uniforms and displayed no weapons.
◆ They did not summon the suspect to their presence but instead approached her and identified themselves as federal agents.
◆ They requested, but did not demand to see, her ticket.

In this case, merely approaching the suspect, asking her if she would show them her ticket, and then asking a few questions did not constitute a seizure under the Fourth Amendment.

In the same case, the Court gave examples of conduct by the police that might indicate a seizure, even if the person did not attempt to leave. These included the display of a weapon, some physical contact by the officer, or the use of language or tone of voice indicating that compliance with the officer's request might be compelled. The Court then noted, "In the absence of some such evidence, other inoffensive contact between a member of the public and the police cannot, as a matter of law, amount to a seizure of that person." In sum, circumstances determine whether contact with the police constitutes a seizure.

Are Vehicle Stops Based on Racial Profile Valid? A highly controversial issue in law enforcement is the practice of stopping motorists, particularly on drug-corridor highways, based on racial profiles. The U.S. Department of Justice defines **racial profiling** as any police-initiated action that relies on race, ethnicity, or the national origin of an individual instead of on individual acts or behavior. In some places and among some groups, the perception is pervasive that law enforcement departments disproportionately stop drivers belonging to minority groups, usually blacks and Hispanics. Several studies have demonstrated that racial and ethnic minorities are pulled over for traffic offense at much higher rates than one would expect based on their percentage of the population.

racial profiling
any police-initiated action that relies on race, ethnicity, or the national origin of an individual instead of on individual acts or behavior.

A study done by the Bureau of Justice Statistics of the U.S. Department of Justice in 2007 found that "police are more likely to search Black and Hispanic drivers than White drivers." This study further showed that Black drivers are three times as likely and Hispanic drivers twice as likely to be searched as White drivers.[2] The perception that racial profiling is pervasive has led to the creation of phrases such as Driving while Black (DWB) and Driving while Hispanic (DWH).

Are vehicle stops based on racial profiling valid? Although the Court has not directly addressed this issue, it is safe to say, based on previous Court decisions involving race, that stopping a motorist based on race alone is clearly unconstitutional because it violates the equal protection clause of the Constitution. The more difficult question, however, is whether race can legally be taken into consideration at all when looking at the "totality of circumstances," a phrase the Court often uses in reasonable suspicion and probable cause cases. In short, if race is merely a contributing instead of the sole factor, is its use constitutional? In *United States v. Sokolow*, 490 U.S. 1 (1989), the Court said that stops cannot be based on drug courier profiles alone; instead the facts, taken in totality, must amount to reasonable suspicion that can justify a stop. Although *Sokolow* did not involve race, it would apply even more persuasively if the stop had been made solely on the basis of race. Discrimination based on race is generally prohibited because race is a highly protected category under the Constitution and in various federal and state laws.

United States v. Sokolow (1989)

In *Whren v. United States*, 517 U.S. 806 (1996), the Court said that, although pretextual vehicle stops are constitutional, racially motivated law enforcement could be challenged under the equal protection clause (meaning based on discriminatory treatment) as applied to the Fourth Amendment but not under the due process clause (based on an absence of fundamental fairness). Therefore, based on *Whren*, if a motorist is stopped because of a valid reason (such as running a stop sign), the stop is valid even if the officer would not have stopped the vehicle if the driver had not been Hispanic or another person of color. The Court noted, however, that if something like this situation arises, it could be challenged under the equal protection clause. The Court did not indicate how it would rule on such a case. Saying it can be challenged under the Fourteenth Amendment is different from categorically saying it is unconstitutional.

Whren v. United States (1996)

Are Stops Based on Race Alone Valid? As in the case of racial profiling, the Court has not directly addressed this issue, but it is safe to say that stopping a motorist based on race alone (as distinguished from racial profiling where race or ethnicity is only one of the identifiers, but not the only one) is unconstitutional. It clearly violates the equal protection clause. The more difficult question, however, is whether race can be taken as one factor in the totality of circumstances when determining reasonable suspicion for a stop. Again, the issue has not been addressed by the Court, and courts of appeals differ.

The U.S. Court of Appeals for the Second Circuit has held that "police officers in Oneonta, New York, did not violate the Constitution when they tried to stop every black man in town after a woman said she had been robbed in her home by a young black man." The court questioned the police tactics but ruled it did not constitute discriminatory racial profiling, because the officers were trying to find a suspect in a specific crime based on a description (*Brown v. Oneonta*, 195 F.3d 111 [2nd Cir. 1999]). In an earlier case, the Sixth U.S. Circuit Court of Appeals held that race is a permissible factor to justify reasonable suspicion during airport interdiction, based on facts known to the officer (*United States v. Travis*, 62 F.3d 170 [6th Cir. 1995]).

By contrast, the Ninth U.S. Circuit Court of Appeals has ruled that "in most circumstances, law enforcement officials cannot rely on ethnic appearance as a factor in deciding whether to stop someone suspected of a crime," adding that "because of the growth in the Hispanic population in the region (the San Diego, California, area), ethnicity was an irrelevant criterion for law officers to stop a person, unless there was other very specific information identifying the suspect."[3] The case involved three Mexicans who were stopped near San Diego by border patrol officers, based on a tip. The suspects were found to have bags of marijuana, a handgun, and ammunition. They were convicted and deported but later challenged their conviction, saying it was illegal because the border patrol had cited five factors in the decision to stop the suspects, "including a U-turn just before reaching an immigration checkpoint, other suspicious behavior, and their Hispanic appearance." The court held that the stop was valid because of the presence of other factors but firmly rejected ethnic appearance as an acceptable criterion.

Racial profiling is banned by state law or police department policy in many states. It is also banned in federal law enforcement, except in the case of possible terrorism and national security suspects.

Can Stopped Suspects Be Forced to Answer Questions? A suspect who is stopped cannot be forced by the officer to reply to questions. In one case, the Court implied that, although the police have a right to approach any person and ask questions, the person asked does not have any obligation to respond (*Florida v. Royer*, 460 U.S. 491 [1983]). Said the Court:

> [t]he person approached . . . need not answer any question put to him; . . . he may decline to listen to the questions at all and may go on his way. . . . He may not be detained even momentarily without reasonable, objective grounds for doing so; and his refusal to listen or answer does not, without more, furnish those grounds. . . . If there is no detention—no seizure within the meaning of the Fourth Amendment—then no constitutional rights have been infringed.

Such a refusal, however, may give the officer sufficient justification to frisk because it may fail to dispel suspicions of danger. Such a refusal may also be taken to help establish reasonable suspicion or probable cause, provided other circumstances are present.

Brown v. Oneonta (1999)

United States v. Travis (1995)

Florida v. Royer (1983)

Can a Stopped Person Be Forced to Identify Oneself? Some places have ordinances making it a crime for any person in a public area to refuse to identify himself or herself at the request of a uniformed police officer, if the officer has reason to believe that the public safety requires such identification. Are these ordinances or laws valid? The Court has held that the Fourth Amendment allows officers, pursuant to a stop and frisk, to require a person to provide his or her name, and that the person may be arrested for refusing to comply, but only under certain circumstances (*Hiibel v. Sixth Judicial District Court of Nevada, et al.*, 542 U.S. 177 [2004]).

In *Hiibel*, an officer asked a suspect if he had any identification. The man, apparently intoxicated, refused and began taunting the officer by putting his hands behind his back and daring the officer to arrest him. The officer arrested the suspect based on a Nevada law authorizing such arrests. The suspect later challenged the law, arguing it violated his Fourth Amendment right against unreasonable searches and seizures and his Fifth Amendment right against self-incrimination. The Court rejected both challenges, saying that such laws in themselves are not unconstitutional as long as they are not vague or overly broad. (Read the Case Brief to learn more about the *Hiibel* case.)

Hiibel v. Sixth Judicial District Court of Nevada, et al. (2004)

Does Unprovoked Flight Constitute Reasonable Suspicion? The Court has held that unprovoked flight upon observing police officers may constitute reasonable suspicion sufficient to justify a stop (*Illinois v. Wardlow*, 528 U.S. 119 [2000]). In *Wardlow*, the respondent had fled upon seeing a caravan of police motor vehicles converge in an area in Chicago known for heavy narcotics trafficking. A police officer stopped him and then conducted a frisk for weapons because, in the officer's experience, weapons were involved in the sale of narcotics in that area. The officer found a handgun and arrested Wardlow.

Illinois v. Wardlow (2000)

On appeal of his conviction for unlawful possession of a weapon by a felon, Wardlow maintained that the stop was invalid because his unprovoked flight upon seeing the police did not in itself constitute reasonable suspicion. The Court disagreed, holding that the action by the officer was valid because the flight constituted reasonable suspicion and therefore justified the stop. (The frisk itself was not an issue in the case, the assumption being that the subsequent frisk was valid.)

The unprovoked flight in *Wardlow* took place in an urban area of heavy narcotics trafficking. Would the Court have decided differently had the unprovoked flight occurred in an affluent suburb or in any other place not known for drug trafficking? The Court decision is unclear on this issue. Instead, the Court said: "Headlong flight—wherever it occurs—is the consummate act of evasion: it is not necessarily indicative of wrongdoing, but it is certainly suggestive of such." The Court then added that "the determination of reasonable suspicion must be based on commonsense judgments and inferences about human behavior." Responding to the argument by Wardlow that the flight from the police was in itself an innocent act, the Court said: "Even in *Terry*, the conduct justifying the stop was ambiguous and susceptible of an innocent explanation." Thus the Court placed great emphasis on the unprovoked flight itself but then also mentioned the locale, saying: "In this case, moreover, it was not merely respondent's presence in an area of heavy narcotics trafficking that aroused the officers' suspicion but his unprovoked flight upon noticing the police." Given this language and the Court's lack of a categorical statement, lower courts have rendered conflicting decisions on the issue of whether or not unprovoked flight alone, in the absence of other circumstances, constitutes reasonable suspicion. That issue may have to be clarified by the Court.

Are Stops Based on Hearsay Information Valid? An investigative stop based on secondhand or hearsay information is valid. For example, in one case a police officer on patrol in a high-crime area received a tip from a person known to the officer that a suspect was carrying narcotics and had a gun. The officer approached the suspect's parked automobile and ordered him to step out. When the suspect responded by rolling down his window, the officer reached into the car and removed a loaded pistol from the suspect's waistband. The suspect was then arrested, and a subsequent search of the car led to the recovery of additional weapons and a substantial quantity of heroin. The Court rejected the defendant's contention that a stop and frisk cannot be based on secondhand information, saying that the information from the known informant "carried enough indicia of reliability to justify" the forcible stop of the suspect (*Adams v. Williams*, 407 U.S. 143 [1972]).

Adams v. Williams (1972)

Are Stops Based on Anonymous Tips Valid? The preceding case, *Adams v. Williams*, involved information obtained by the police from a known informant. But what if the tip is anonymous? The Court has ruled that an anonymous tip, corroborated by independent police work, may provide reasonable suspicion to make an investigatory stop if it carries sufficient indicia of reliability (*Alabama v. White*, 496 U.S. 325 [1990]). In this case, the police received an anonymous telephone tip that a woman named White would leave a certain apartment at 3:00 P.M. in a brown Plymouth station wagon with a broken tail light, that she would be going to Dobey's Motel, and that she would have cocaine in a brown attaché case. The police immediately proceeded to the apartment building, where they saw a vehicle matching the anonymous caller's description. They then observed White leaving the building and driving the vehicle. The police followed her to Dobey's Motel, where she consented to a search of her vehicle, which revealed marijuana. White was then arrested; a subsequent search found cocaine in her purse. She was tried and convicted.

On appeal, she sought suppression of the evidence, alleging that the search was illegal because the stop was not based on reasonable suspicion. The Court disagreed, saying that "standing alone, the tip here is completely lacking in the necessary indicia of reliability, since it provides virtually nothing from which one might conclude that the caller is honest or his information reliable and gave no indication of the basis for his predictions regarding White's criminal activities." However, "although it is a close question, the totality of the circumstances demonstrates that significant aspects of the informant's story were sufficiently corroborated by the police to furnish reasonable suspicion."

HIGHLIGHT > Reasonable Suspicion as a Requirement in Policing

"Reasonable suspicion is a less demanding standard than probable cause not only in the sense that reasonable suspicion can be established with information that is different in quantity or content than that required to establish probable cause, but also in the sense that reasonable suspicion can arise from information that is less reliable than that required to show probable cause. . . . Reasonable suspicion, like probable cause, is dependent upon both the content of information possessed by police and its degree of reliability. Both factors—quantity and quality—are considered in the 'totality of the circumstances—the whole picture.'"

Source: *Alabama v. White*, 496 U.S. 325 (1990).

In a subsequent case, however, the Court held that an anonymous tip lacking indicia of reliability does not justify a stop and frisk (*Florida v. J. L.*, 529 U.S. 266 [1999]). In this case, the police responded to an anonymous tip that a young black male, wearing a plaid shirt and carrying a gun, was standing with two companions at a bus stop. The officers went to the place, conducted a frisk, and found a gun in the pocket of the suspect's pants. The defendant was convicted and appealed his conviction, saying that the search was illegal. In a unanimous decision, the Court excluded the gun from evidence, holding that an anonymous tip that a person is carrying a gun is not enough to justify a stop and frisk. More information is needed to establish reasonable suspicion.

Florida v. J. L. (1999)

In distinguishing this case from *Alabama v. White*, 496 U.S. 325 (1990), the Court noted that the officers' suspicion that J. L. had a weapon was based entirely on the anonymous tip, and that tip provided no "predictive information" that would allow the police to test the informant's knowledge or credibility.

Note that in this case the state of Florida and the federal government wanted *Terry* to be modified to create a firearm exception to the reasonable suspicion requirement. Under this exception, a tip alleging that the suspect had an illegal gun would have justified a stop and frisk even if reasonable suspicion did not exist. The Court refused to adopt this exception.

In a recent case the Court suggested that an anonymous tip that indicated a motorist might be driving under the influence did justify a traffic stop to investigate. In *Navarette v. California* (--- U.S. --- (2014), a distressed motorist placed a 911 call claiming to have been forced off the road by a reckless driver. Two California Highway Patrol officers responded and performed a traffic stop on a pickup truck with a license plate matching the one reported during the 911 call. While speaking with the driver of the truck, Lorenzo Navarette, and the passenger, his brother Jose Navarette, the officers smelled marijuana inside the vehicle. The officers then initiated a search of the vehicle and discovered thirty pounds of marijuana in the truck bed. The Navarette brothers were arrested and convicted of drug possession. The Supreme Court affirmed the convictions. The officers who arrested the Navarette brothers acknowledged that they had not witnessed any corroborating signs of reckless driving. Therefore, the stop was based upon nothing but an anonymous tip. However, the Court determined that the totality of the circumstances created reasonable suspicion of driving while intoxicated. First, the anonymous tip had been highly detailed, suggesting it was based in fact. Second, 911 technology now allows police to determine who was calling in, even if they did not give their name, thus decreasing the likelihood of false tips, since those giving false tips could be prosecuted. Third, he highlighted the necessity of apprehending reckless drivers before they caused harm to other motorists or themselves, and since reckless drivers might well be drunk drivers, and drunk driving presents an immediate, significant public concern, the stop was justified.

Navarette v. California (2014)

Is Information Based on a Flyer from Another Jurisdiction Enough for a Stop? The Court has decided that the police may stop a suspect on the basis of reasonable suspicion that the person is wanted for investigation in another jurisdiction (*United States v. Hensley*, 469 U.S. 221 [1985]). In this case, Hensley was wanted for questioning in connection with an armed robbery in St. Bernard, Ohio. The police circulated a "wanted" flyer to neighboring police departments. The police in nearby Covington, Kentucky, saw Hensley's car a week later and, knowing that he was wanted for questioning, stopped him and discovered firearms in the car. He was later convicted in

United States v. Hensley (1985)

federal court of illegal possession of firearms. He appealed the conviction, claiming that the stop was illegal because there was no probable cause, so the evidence obtained should have been excluded.

In a unanimous opinion, the Court held that the police may act without a warrant to stop and briefly detain a person they know is wanted for investigation by a police department in another city. If the police have a reasonable suspicion, grounded in specific and articulable facts, that a person they encounter was involved in or is wanted for questioning in connection with a completed felony, then a *Terry*-type stop is permissible. Any evidence legally obtained as a result of that stop is admissible in court.

drug courier profile
a set of identifiers developed by law enforcement agencies describing the types of individuals who are likely to transport drugs.

Are Stops Based on a Drug Courier Profile Alone Valid? A **drug courier profile** (as distinguished from a racial profile) is a set of identifiers developed by law enforcement agencies describing the types of individuals who are likely to transport drugs. May a person who fits such a profile be stopped by the police on that basis alone? The Court has said that profiles are helpful in identifying people who are likely to commit crimes, but a drug courier profile alone does not justify a *Terry*-type stop. The facts, taken in totality, must amount to a reasonable suspicion (*United States v. Sokolow*, 490 U.S. 1 [1989]).

The emphasis is on the totality of circumstances. In this case, Sokolow purchased two round-trip tickets for a flight from Honolulu to Miami. The facts surrounding that purchase, known to Drug Enforcement Administration (DEA) agents, were as follows: (1) Sokolow paid $2,100 for two round-trip tickets from a roll of $20 bills; (2) he traveled under an assumed name that did not match his listed telephone number; (3) his original destination was Miami, a place known for illicit drugs; (4) he stayed in Miami for only forty-eight hours, although the flight from Honolulu to Miami and back took twenty hours; (5) he appeared nervous during his trip; and (6) he had luggage, but none was checked.

Because of these facts, which fit a drug courier profile developed by the DEA, Sokolow and his companion were stopped and taken to the DEA office at the airport, where their luggage was sniffed by a trained dog, which alerted, indicating drugs were inside. Cocaine was found, and Sokolow was convicted of possession with intent to distribute. On appeal, the Supreme Court said that there was nothing wrong with the use of a drug courier profile in this case because the facts, taken together, amounted to reasonable suspicion that criminal conduct was taking place. The Court noted that whether the facts in this case fit a profile was less significant than the fact that, taken together, they established a reasonable suspicion that justified a stop; therefore, the stop was valid.

Sokolow indicates that, although a drug courier profile is helpful, the totality of circumstances is more important in establishing reasonable suspicion. The Court noted that the activities of Sokolow, taken in isolation and individually, were consistent with innocent travel, but taken together, they amounted to reasonable suspicion. There is nothing wrong with using drug courier profiles for a stop if the facts in a particular case, taken together, amount to reasonable suspicion. But the practice of using drug courier profiles alone to stop people, whether they are in airports or motor vehicles, is unconstitutional.

Are Stops of Parolees without Suspicion Valid? Although stop and frisk requires reasonable suspicion, the Court has held that stops and searches without suspicion of parolees are valid (*Samson v. California*, 547 U.S. 843 [2006]). In Samson, a police officer

Samson v. California (2006)

stopped and searched a parolee on the street in San Bruno, California. The officer had no warrant and later admitted that the only reason for the stop was that he knew Samson was on parole. The subsequent search found methamphetamine. Samson was arrested and charged with drug possession. He moved to exclude the evidence, saying that the search violated his Fourth Amendment right against unreasonable searches and seizures because the officer admitted he did not have any justification for the stop and subsequent search other than that Samson was on parole. The Court disagreed, saying that a parolee does not have a reasonable expectation of privacy. Convicted criminals who are out of prison on parole are still in the legal custody of the Department of Corrections until the conclusion of their sentence. Moreover, a condition of his parole was that he consent to a suspicionless search of his person at any time. His status as a parolee and his written consent prior to release made the stop and subsequent search valid.

What Are the Reasonable Scope and Duration of a Stop? An investigatory stop must be temporary and not last any longer than necessary under the circumstances to achieve its purpose. Officers cannot detain a person for as much time as is convenient. This has been decided by the Court in a number of cases.

In one case, the Court held that a ninety-minute detention of an air traveler's luggage was excessive. In that case, the suspect's luggage was detained long enough to enable a trained dog to sniff for marijuana. The Court decided that while the initial seizure was justified, the ninety-minute delay exceeded the permissible limits of an investigative stop.

In another case, the Court held that the removal of a detainee without his consent from the public area in an airport to the police room in the airport converted the stop to an arrest. In this case, airport narcotics police stopped the suspect because he fit a drug courier profile. When the agents asked for and examined his ticket and driver's license, they discovered that he was traveling under an assumed name. They then

HIGHLIGHT Operation Cease-Fire

According to an article in the *New York Times*, police authorities in Oakland, California, "are taking a page from juvenile hall that has become increasingly popular nationwide: They have decided to call in the bad guys and tell them to knock it off. Or else." The news item goes on to say that Oakland police "have drawn up a kind of criminal hit parade that includes the top 100 'persons of interest' in the city, primarily ex-convicts, who the authorities believe are causing trouble and contributing to a climate of lawlessness." The plan involves the police calling these persons into court and informing them "they must behave." "We are going to tell them that we know they've been responsible for a number of things" in their neighborhood and that the police have been watching them, adding "we want you to change your life around. And if you don't, you will suffer the consequences."

The plan is called Operation Cease-Fire and is patterned on "an experiment that was first tried a decade ago in Boston, where law enforcement officials credit the straight-talk approach with helping sharply reduce the number of homicides within months." In police circles, it is popularly known as the "Boston Miracle," and caught the attention of police officers nationwide. It was later tried in Chicago, Los Angeles, and San Francisco.

1. *Is Operation Cease-Fire a variation of stop and frisk, or does it go beyond those actions?*
2. *Do the police have reasonable suspicion to justify what they are doing?*
3. *Is this practice constitutional?*

Source: *New York Times*, August 22, 2006, p. 1.

Hiibel v. Sixth Judicial District Court of Nevada, et al., 542 U.S. 177 (2004)

The Leading Case on Whether the Police Can Arrest a Person Who Refuses to Give His or Her Name

Facts: A caller reported to the Humboldt County Sheriff's Office seeing a man assault a woman in a red and silver GMC truck on Grass Valley Road. When an officer arrived at the scene, he found a truck matching the description parked on the side of the road where the caller had described it. The officer observed skid marks in the gravel behind the vehicle, indicating a sudden stop. The officer also observed a man standing by the truck and a woman sitting inside it. The officer approached the man and explained that he was investigating the report of an assault. The man appeared intoxicated. The officer asked if he had any identification, but the man refused to answer. After repeated requests and refusals to identify himself, the man began to taunt the officer by putting his hands behind his back and telling the officer to arrest him. After warning the man that he would be arrested if he refused to comply, the officer placed Hiibel under arrest pursuant to a Nevada law allowing officers to detain a person suspected of committing a crime to ascertain his or her identity. Nevada law states that "any person so detained shall identify himself, but may not be compelled to answer any other inquiry of any peace officer."

Hiibel was convicted of obstructing and delaying a public officer in attempting to discharge his duty because he refused to identify himself. The Supreme Court of Nevada rejected his Fourth Amendment challenge to the conviction. Hiibel appealed to the U.S. Supreme Court, asserting violations of his Fourth and Fifth Amendment rights. Certiorari was granted.

Issue or Issues: *Can a person be arrested for refusal to identify himself or herself to a police officer? Yes, but only under certain circumstances.*

Decision: The decision of the Supreme Court of Nevada was affirmed.

Holding: Requiring a suspect to disclose his or her name in the course of a stop and frisk does not violate the Fourth or the Fifth Amendment.

Case Significance: This case is significant because it resolves an important issue in law enforcement: whether or not the stop-and-identify laws that many jurisdictions have are constitutional. An earlier California law that

required a suspect to furnish an officer "credible and reliable" identification when asked to identify himself or herself was declared unconstitutional because of vagueness or overbreadth. What was at issue in this case was whether the Nevada stop-and-identify law, which is more clearly worded, is constitutional. The Nevada law provides as follows:

1. Any peace officer may detain any person whom the officer encounters under circumstances which reasonably indicate that the person has committed, is committing[,] or is about to commit a crime. . . .

2. The officer may detain the person pursuant to this section only to ascertain his identity and the suspicious circumstances surrounding his presence abroad. Any person so detained shall identify himself, but may not be compelled to answer any other inquiry of any peace officer.

Hiibel claimed the law violated his Fourth and Fifth Amendment rights, not that it was vague or overly broad (which would violate his Fourteenth Amendment right to due process). The Court rejected his claims, saying that the Nevada statute "properly balances the intrusion on the individual's interest against the promotion of legitimate government interest." The alleged violation of the Fifth Amendment right against self-incrimination was also rejected by the Court, saying that the "Fifth Amendment prohibits only compelled testimony that is incriminating" In this case, "Hiibel's refusal to disclose was not based on any articulated real and appreciable fear that his name would be used to incriminate him, or that it would furnish evidence needed to prosecute him." He refused to identify himself "because he thought his name was none of the officer's business," and not because he feared subsequent prosecution; therefore, the Fifth Amendment right against self-incrimination could not be successfully invoked.

Excerpts from the Opinion: The Nevada statute is consistent with Fourth Amendment prohibitions against unreasonable searches and seizures because it properly balances the intrusion on the individual's interests against the promotion of legitimate government interest. Hiibel's contention that his conviction violates the Fifth

Amendment's prohibition on self-incrimination fails because disclosure of his name and identity presented no reasonable danger of incrimination. The Fifth Amendment prohibits only compelled testimony that is incriminating, and protects only against disclosures that the witness reasonably believes could be used in a criminal prosecution or could lead to other evidence that might be so reasonably used. In this case, [Hiibel's] refusal to disclose his name was not based on any articulated real and appreciable fear that his name would be used to incriminate him, or that "it would furnish a link in the chain of evidence needed to prosecute" him [internal citations omitted].

identified themselves as narcotics agents and told him that he was suspected of being a drug courier. Without his consent, they took him to a police room about forty feet away from the main concourse. One officer sat with him in the room while another officer retrieved his luggage from the airline and brought it back to the room. The agents then asked the suspect if he would consent to a search of the suitcases. The suspect took out a key and unlocked one of the bags, which contained drugs.

The Court concluded that, although the initial stop and questioning were valid, the subsequent conduct of the officers was "more intrusive than necessary" to carry out the limited investigation permitted under stop and frisk; therefore, it constituted an arrest. Because the police were interested mainly in gaining consent to search the suspect's luggage, there was no need to isolate him to gain that consent (*Florida v. Royer*, 460 U.S. 491 [1983]).

In a third case, *United States v. Sharpe*, 470 U.S. 675 (1985), the Court found it reasonable for the police to detain a truck driver for twenty minutes. The driver was suspected of carrying marijuana in a truck camper. The length of the stop was due in part to the fact that the driver attempted to evade the stop, causing the two officers pursuing him to become separated. The officer who performed the stop therefore had to wait fifteen minutes for his more experienced partner to arrive before conducting the search. Marijuana was found in the camper, and the driver was arrested. The Supreme Court held that, to determine whether a detention is reasonable in length, the court must look at the purpose to be served by the stop and the time reasonably needed to carry it out. It added that courts should refrain from second-guessing police officers' choices, especially when the police are acting in a swiftly developing situation, as in this case. This case indicates that the reasonableness of a stop must take into account not just the length of time involved but the needs of law enforcement as well.

United States v. Sharpe (1985)

In sum, it is difficult to state exactly what the time limit is for a valid stop. What we do know is that the Court uses this test: whether the stop is longer than necessary under the circumstances to achieve its original purpose. If it is, the contact ceases to be a stop (based on reasonable suspicion) and becomes an arrest, which is invalid unless based on probable cause.

Are Airport Stops and Searches Valid? Airplane passengers have for decades been subjected to stops and searches at airports. These have had few legal challenges, and those challenges have been rejected based for a variety of reasons. Stops and searches are presumably made with the consent of the passengers, who want to ensure their own safe air travel. A passenger who refuses is not allowed to board; hence, a self-enforcing process is involved. The procedure is also easily justified based on a compelling state interest, which is ensuring passengers' safe travel. It is difficult to overcome the presumption that airport stops and searches result in passenger safety. These searches are also easily justified based on "special needs" rather than as a law enforcement activity. The Court has held in a number of cases that the Fourth Amendment does not apply rigidly to cases involving special needs. The special need in airport searches is obviously to ensure safety among air travelers. Thus, airport stops and searches are easy to justify and valid, unless the measures used are overly intrusive for the purpose such stops and searches are aimed to achieve. In addition to the special needs justification, it may also be argued that airport searches are a form of administrative search, which has a lower Fourth Amendment protection.

Torbet v. United Airlines, Inc. (2002)

Some cases have addressed specific issues related to airport searches. In *Torbet v. United Airlines, Inc.*, 298 F.3d 1087 (9th Cir. 2002), the Ninth U.S. Circuit Court of Appeals held that airport security guards may conduct a random check of a traveler's carry-on bag, even if the bag has passed through an X-ray scan at an airport without arousing suspicion that it contained weapons or explosives.

United States v. Pulido-Baquerizo (1986)

In *United States v. Pulido-Baquerizo*, 800 F.2d 899 (9th Cir. 1986), the Ninth Circuit also held that airline passengers who put their bags on an X-ray machine's conveyor belt at a secure boarding area implied consent to a visual inspection and limited hand search of the bag if the X-ray scan is inconclusive about whether there are dangerous items in the bag. In effect, this decision says that consent to search by putting the bag on an X-ray machine also constitutes consent to search the bag further.

Since 9/11, airport stops and searches have become more intense and intrusive. There are allegations of racial profiling and suspicions that some passengers are being singled out for "flying while Arab (FWA)." Even if proved to be true, legal challenges to this type of racial profiling may prove difficult because of serious and valid security concerns. As long as terrorism fears continue to be a part of air travel, courts will likely allow practices that do not grossly violate constitutional rights.

What Degree of Intrusion in a Stop Is Permissible? The investigative method used must be the least intrusive and the most reasonably available to verify or dispel the officer's suspicion. Anything more intrusive makes the act invalid. Therefore, the greater the degree of police control over a detainee, the greater the likelihood that reviewing courts will impose the higher standard of probable cause. In the absence of some justification, the display of weapons by the police when making an investigative stop might turn a stop into an arrest. But the display of weapons in itself does not automatically convert a stop into an arrest.

Lower courts tend to look at the display of weapons on a case-by-case basis to determine if the stop has been converted into an arrest because of such a display of force. The Supreme Court has not clarified the amount of force, if any, that can be used by the police in stop and frisk cases.

A Case Study: Stops and Race in the New York City Police Department

One of the most extensive studies on the relationship between stops and race was done by the College of Criminal Justice of John Jay University in New York City "Stop, Questions & Frisk: Policing Practices in New York City—A Primer," reached several conclusions, including:

1. That "police officers are stopping people in New York City in increasing numbers. There were nearly 36,000 more stops in 2009 compared with 2008, and the number of stops annually has more than tripled since 2003."
2. That "on average, for every 100 people officers stopped in 2008, they found contraband of some kind (including guns, knives, other weapons, and illegal drugs) on approximately three people."
3. That the "stops tend to be concentrated in a handful of police precincts and that the vast majority of people stopped are blacks or Hispanics."
4. That "even though blacks and Hispanics combined are stopped in far greater numbers than whites, the outcomes of the stops proportionally for the two groups are roughly the same."

The *New York Times* reports that in 2011, according to the New York Police Department, "96 percent of shooting victims . . . and 90 percent of murder victims were minorities." It further stated: "The Police Department has said that it conducted a record 684,330 stops [in 2011] and that 87 percent of those stopped were Black or Hispanic. About 10 percent of the stops led to arrests or summonses and 1 percent to the recovery of a weapon." The New York Police Department defends the practice saying that it recovered 8,000 weapons, 800 of them handguns, via stops. Moreover, "over the last decade, the number of murders has dropped by 50 percent, 'in part because of stop, question and frisk,'" according to the police department spokesperson.[4]

The Frisk

A **frisk** is a pat-down for weapons. It can follow a stop, but only if there is nothing in the initial stages of the encounter that would dispel fears based on reasonable suspicion about the safety of the police officer or others. A frisk has only one purpose: the protection of the officer or others. In *Terry*, the Court said:

frisk
a pat-down for weapons.

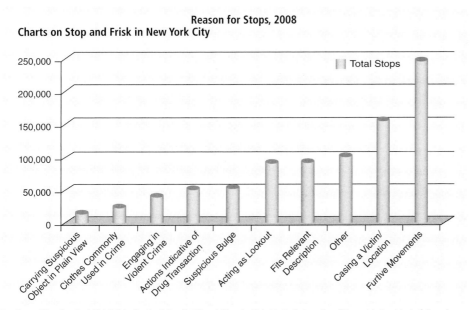

Reason for Stops, 2008
Charts on Stop and Frisk in New York City

Data Source: "Stop, Question & Frisk: Policing Practices in New York City—A Primer," published by the Center on Race, Crime and Justice, John Jay College of Criminal Justice (March 2010), p. 8.

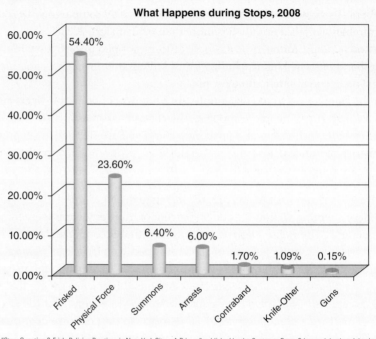

What Happens during Stops, 2008

Data Source: "Stop, Question & Frisk: Policing Practices in New York City—A Primer," published by the Center on Race, Crime and Justice, John Jay College of Criminal Justice (March 2010), p. 10.

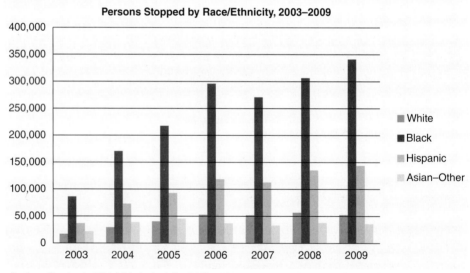

Persons Stopped by Race/Ethnicity, 2003–2009

Data Source: "Stop, Question & Frisk: Policing Practices in New York City—A Primer," published by the Center on Race, Crime, and Justice, John Jay College of Criminal Justice (March 2010), p. 15.

> When an officer is justified in believing that the individual whose suspicious behavior he is investigating at close range is armed and presently dangerous to the officer or to others, it would appear to be clearly unreasonable to deny the officer the power to take necessary measures to determine whether the person is in fact carrying a weapon and to neutralize the threat of physical harm.

A frisk should take place after a stop only if justified by concerns of safety for the officer or others. It is not an automatic consequence of a valid stop. For example, suppose Fred is stopped by a police officer late one night on a dimly lighted street corner on reasonable suspicion that Fred is about to commit an offense. The officer asks Fred questions to which Fred gives evasive answers, appearing uneasy and nervous. The officer may go ahead and frisk, because nothing in the initial encounter has dispelled his reasonable concern for his or others' safety.

By contrast, suppose that after the stop and initial questioning, the officer becomes convinced that Fred in fact lives in a nearby apartment and is returning home from a trip to a nearby store to buy cigarettes. Then, the officer has no justification to conduct a frisk.

The Court has stated that the totality of the circumstances must be taken into account when determining the legality of a frisk. The detaining officers must have a specific, objective basis for suspecting the stopped person of criminal activity

The legal requirement that an officer must have reasonable suspicion that his or her safety may be in jeopardy before frisking someone applies only to a frisk, not to a stop. This means that an officer does not need to have reasonable suspicion that a person is armed and dangerous before stopping a person. All the officer needs for a valid stop is reasonable suspicion that criminal activity is about to take place or has taken place.

This section looks at some of the other issues surrounding legally valid frisks.

What Is the Extent of the Frisk? A frisk must be limited initially to a pat-down of a person's outer clothing, and only an object that feels like a weapon may properly be seized. The object may turn out not to be a weapon, but if it feels like one, the frisk is justified. Conversely, if the object does not feel like a weapon, it cannot be seized. For example, suppose that after a valid stop based on reasonable suspicion, a police officer has a reasonable fear that the suspect may be armed. She then frisks the suspect and in the process feels something soft that cannot possibly be considered a weapon. She cannot legitimately seize the object in question. If seized, the object is not admissible as evidence in court, regardless of how incriminating it might be.

Confusion has arisen over the extent of a frisk after a stop because of the decision in *United States v. Robinson*, 414 U.S. 218 (1973). In the *Robinson* case, the Supreme Court held that a body search after an authorized arrest for driving without a permit is valid even when the officer admits that there was no possible danger to himself or herself and therefore no reason to look for a weapon. However, *Robinson* involved an arrest, not a stop and frisk, so arrest laws applied. Once the stop and frisk turns into an arrest based on probable cause, then the *Robinson* decision applies, and a body search may then be conducted. However, a frisk alone does not justify a body search, because its sole purpose is to protect the officer or others. Additionally, use of force beyond a pat-down for weapons is likely to cause reviewing courts to treat the contact as an arrest instead of a frisk.

United States v. Robinson (1973)

What Is Allowed during a Frisk? *Minnesota v. Dickerson*, 508 U.S. 366 (1993), clarified the limits of what the police can or cannot do in the course of a frisk. In *Dickerson*, police officers in Minnesota, noticing a suspect's evasive actions when they approached, coupled with the fact that he had just left a building known for cocaine traffic, decided to investigate further. They ordered the suspect to submit to a frisk. The frisk revealed no weapons, but the officer conducting it testified that he felt a small lump in the suspect's jacket pocket. Upon manipulating the lump with his fingers, the officer

Minnesota v. Dickerson (1993)

concluded it was crack cocaine. He then reached into the suspect's pocket and retrieved what indeed turned out to be a small bag of crack cocaine. The suspect was convicted of possession of a controlled substance.

On appeal, Dickerson argued that the evidence should have been suppressed, because its seizure was illegal in that it went beyond a pat-down search for a weapon. The Supreme Court held that objects that police detect in the course of a valid protective frisk may be seized without a warrant, but only if the officer's sense of touch makes it *immediately apparent* that the object, although nonthreatening, is contraband, so that probable cause is present. In this case, however, the officer went beyond the lawful scope of *Terry* when, having concluded that the object he felt inside the suspect's jacket was not a dangerous weapon, he proceeded to "squeeze, slide, and manipulate it" in an effort to determine if it was contraband. Given the circumstances under which the evidence was obtained, the Court determined the evidence was inadmissible.

Dickerson is significant because it clarifies what an officer may validly confiscate in the course of a frisk and under what circumstances. The Court held that what the officer did in this case was illegal because, even though he felt no danger to his person during the frisk, he went ahead anyway and conducted a further search when he manipulated the object with his fingers. Officers during a frisk have only one justification for confiscating anything: they felt something that might reasonably be considered a weapon.

A valid frisk can turn in an instant into a valid search if, in the course of the frisk, the officer has probable cause to think that the object is seizable. For example, suppose Officer Roberts frisks a suspect because she has reasonable grounds to believe that the

IN ACTION — *STOP AND FRISK*

Officer Young has been on the Providence police force for approximately six months. The past year has been a busy one for Officer Young: He completed the police academy, graduating second in his class; he completed an intense field-training program; and, although just a rookie, he is currently leading his department in arrests. Last month the chief of police recognized Officer Young's hard work by presenting him with an award for making a drug arrest in which he seized crack cocaine and marijuana from a suspect in Providence's growing downtown business district.

The Providence Police Department has been deploying foot patrols in the downtown area to curb drug activity that has recently begun to plague the area. Business owners have started attending town meetings to voice concerns about the increased crime. Tonight, while on foot patrol, Officer Young arrested a suspect for drug possession and recovered a stolen handgun from the same suspect.

According to Officer Young's police report, he observed a lone male subject walking on the sidewalk approximately one block from where he made his previous arrest (the one

that earned him his achievement award). The subject was wearing all dark clothing. Officer Young confronted the lone subject and engaged him in conversation. The subject was evasive and refused to say why he was walking along the street. Officer Young asked the subject to submit to a pat-down frisk for officer safety, but the subject did not respond to this request. Officer Young conducted the pat-down frisk, during which he recovered a loaded handgun and five rocks of crack cocaine. The subject was placed under arrest and booked into jail pending felony criminal charges.

You are the on-duty sergeant tonight, and your responsibilities include reading and approving police reports. You have just finished reading Officer Young's arrest report.

1. *Do you have any questions for Officer Young?*
2. *Was the pat-down frisk legal?*
3. *Did Officer Young have probable cause to place the subject under arrest?*
4. *Will the seized evidence be admissible in court?*
5. *Do you approve the report?*

suspect is carrying a weapon. While frisking, she feels something under the suspect's clothing, and although it does not feel like a weapon, the reasonable conclusion is that it is contraband—based on her experience as an officer in that area. Officer Roberts may seize the item based on probable cause. In this case, the seizable nature of the object must be "immediately apparent" to the officer for the seizure to be valid.

What Constitutes Plain Touch? *Minnesota v. Dickerson* is considered by many scholars to officially recognize the use of the **plain touch** (also known as *plain feel*) **doctrine**. For a long time, the Supreme Court has recognized the plain view doctrine (discussed in Chapter 9), which holds that items in plain view are subject to seizure by officers because they are not protected by the Fourth Amendment. Although using the sense of touch has long been accepted by the courts as a way of establishing probable cause through the use of the five senses (sight, hearing, smell, taste, and touch), the *Dickerson* case reiterated the Supreme Court's recognition of this variant of the plain view doctrine, which is based on "sight." The plain touch doctrine states that if an officer, while conducting a frisk for weapons, feels what he or she has probable cause to believe is a weapon or contraband, the officer may seize the object.

> **plain touch doctrine**
> if an officer feels what he or she believes is a weapon, contraband, or evidence, the officer may expand the search or seize the object.

It is worth noting that in *Minnesota v. Dickerson*, the search would probably have been considered valid if the officer had testified that, although what he touched did not feel like a weapon, it was immediately apparent to him, given his experience and the totality of circumstances, that the object was contraband.

Are "Fishing Expeditions" Allowed? The frisk cannot be used as a **fishing expedition** to see if some type of usable evidence can be found on the suspect. The frisk's only purpose is to protect the police officer and others in the area from possible harm. A frisk for any other reason is illegal and leads to the exclusion of any evidence obtained, regardless of how incriminating the evidence may be.

> **fishing expedition**
> an act to see if some type of usable evidence can be found on the suspect.

Because the sole purpose of a frisk is police safety, anything felt in the course of the frisk that does not feel like a weapon cannot legally be seized unless the incriminating character of the object is "immediately apparent" to the officer, as discussed previously. For example, suppose Officer Roberts frisks a person because she suspects, after a valid stop, that the person is dangerous. In the course of the pat-down, Officer Roberts feels a soft object in the person's pocket that she thinks might be cocaine. If the object is confiscated based on that suspicion alone, the evidence is not admissible in court, because Officer Roberts did not think that what she felt was a weapon, nor was it "immediately apparent" to her that what she felt was cocaine, so she did not have probable cause to conduct a search. Suppose, however, that during that frisk Officer Roberts also comes across something that feels like a weapon. That weapon can be confiscated and the suspect arrested and then searched. If the cocaine is found in his pocket in the course of that search, that evidence is admissible because the frisk, which led to the arrest and subsequent search, is valid, even if no weapon is found.

Is Consent to Frisk Based on Submission to Police Authority Valid? Consent to frisk that is not voluntary and intelligent is invalid. As in all search and seizure cases, consent must be obtained without coercion or intimidation. For example, suppose Officer Phillips, after a valid stop but without fearing for his life, tells a suspect in an authoritative tone that he would like to conduct a frisk—to which the suspect accedes. Such a frisk is not valid because consent, if it was given at all, was likely an act of submission

Although using the sense of touch has long been accepted by the courts as a way of establishing probable cause, the *Dickerson* case reiterated the Supreme Court's recognition of this variant of the plain view doctrine. The plain touch doctrine states that "if the officer, while staying within the narrow limits of a frisk for weapons, feels what he has probable cause to believe is a weapon, contraband, or evidence, the officer may expand the search or seize the object." It differs from plain view in that what is used to determine probable cause is the sense of touch.

Source: *Minnesota v. Dickerson*, 508 U.S. 366 (1993).

to police authority and therefore not voluntary or intelligent. Validity would depend on how that alleged consent was obtained. The burden of proving that the consent was invalid lies with the person who gave the consent.

Can an Officer Frisk after a Stop without Asking Questions? In *Terry v. Ohio*, the Court stated:

> Where in the course of investigating this behavior he identifies himself as a policeman and makes *reasonable inquiries*, and where nothing in the initial stages of the encounter serves to dispel his reasonable fear for his own or others' safety, he is entitled for the protection of himself and others in the area to conduct a carefully limited search of the outer clothing of such persons in an attempt to discover weapons which might be used to assault him. [emphasis added]

This can be interpreted to mean that *reasonable inquiries* are required before a frisk. There may be instances, however, when a frisk is justified without the officer having to ask questions right after the stop. This is likely to occur in cases where the officer has reasonable suspicion, even before questions are asked, that the person stopped poses a danger to him or her or others. The Court in *Terry* also said that a frisk is justified if a "reasonably prudent man in the circumstances would be warranted in the belief that his safety or that of others was in danger." The only possible exception is if state law requires the officer to make reasonable inquiries before conducting a frisk.

Does a Frisk Include Things Carried? Assume that Alex has been stopped and subsequently frisked. Is the frisk limited to patting down Alex for a weapon, or can luggage carried by Alex also be frisked? The Court has not directly addressed this issue, but there are reasons to believe that frisks of belongings (backpacks and other containers from which weapons may be easily retrieved and which are in the immediate possession of the suspect) are likely justifiable. The burden, however, is on the officer to establish that the extended frisk was necessary for officer safety, meaning that the belonging was situated such that it constituted an immediate danger to the officer. Like other forms of searches, the frisk cannot be used as a fishing expedition for evidence.

STOP AND FRISK AND ARREST COMPARED

The concepts of stop and frisk and arrest can be confusing. Both involve a restriction of an individual's freedom by the police, and both can lead to a similar result—the individual's being charged with a crime. The distinctions between these two concepts need to be clearly understood; they are summarized in Table 5.1.

HIGHLIGHT › Was It a Case of Racial Profiling? the Fatal Shooting of Trayvon Martin

On February 26, 2012, Trayvon Martin, a 17-year-old, was fatally shot by neighborhood watch volunteer George Zimmerman, in Sanford, Florida. Martin reportedly "had just come from a convenience store with some Skittles and an iced tea. He was walking in the Retreat at Twin Lakes, a gated community in the Orlando suburb of Sanford that had seen a recent rash of burglaries and thefts. He had on a hoodie and was heading for the home of his father's girlfriend." Martin was seen by Zimmerman, who was not a police officer but was captain of a neighborhood watch group in that area. Zimmerman called 911 from his SUV and told the dispatcher, "This guy looks like he's up to no good or he's on drugs or something." He said he was following the guy, which the dispatcher told him not to do. It is still unclear how the shooting started. Zimmerman claimed that Martin had attacked him and that the shooting was in self-defense and justified under Florida's stand-your-ground law. The Sanford Police Department investigated the case and decided not to file charges against Zimmerman.

Almost a month after the incident, as a result of intense pressure from national activists and mass media publicity, the police chief, who stood by his department's initial investigation, removed himself temporarily from his position. So did the local prosecutor, saying that his temporary stepping down was aimed at "toning down the rhetoric and preserving the integrity of the investigation." Meantime, the shooting and death had generated national publicity and focused further attention on an already volatile issue of racial profiling. In an editorial, *USA Today* asked: "Would Zimmerman have thought a white teen in a hoodie looked like he 'was up to no good'? And, most pointedly, if Zimmerman were black and had shot a white, unarmed 17-year-old, would the police have let him go?" Zimmerman was eventually tried for shooting Martin, but he was acquitted, based on his claim of self-defense.

Source: *USA Today*, March 23, 2012, pp. 3A, 10A.

Table 5.1 Distinctions between Stop and Frisk and Arrest

	Stop and Frisk	Arrest
Degree of certainty needed	Reasonable suspicion	Probable cause
Extent of intrusion	Pat-down for weapons	Full body search
Purpose	Stop: To prevent criminal activity; Frisk: To ensure officer safety	To take the person into custody or to determine if a crime has taken place
Warrant	Not needed	Required, unless arrest falls under one of the exceptions
Duration	No longer than necessary to achieve the purpose	In custody until legally released
Force allowed	Stop: None	Reasonable
	Frisk: Pat-down	

OTHER STOP AND FRISK APPLICATIONS

Stop and frisk law has been applied to cases involving motor vehicles, weapons in a car, and residences. This section looks at what Court decisions have said about these applications.

Application to Motor Vehicles

Motorists are subject to stop and frisk under the same circumstances as pedestrians. This means that motorists can be stopped only if there is reasonable or articulable suspicion of possible involvement in an unlawful activity and may be frisked only if there is fear for the officer's safety. The Court has decided important cases related to stop and frisk as applied to motor vehicles, including the following.

Pennsylvania v. Mimms (1977)

After a vehicle is stopped, may a police officer automatically order the driver to step out of the car even if the officer has no reasonable suspicion that the driver poses a threat to the officer's safety? The answer is yes (*Pennsylvania v. Mimms*, 434 U.S. 106 [1977]). In *Mimms*, two police officers on routine patrol observed Mimms driving an automobile with an expired license plate. The officers stopped the vehicle for the purpose of issuing a traffic summons. One of the officers approached and asked Mimms to step out of the car and produce his owner's card and operator license. When Mimms stepped out, the officers noticed a large bulge under his sports jacket. Fearing that it might be a weapon, one officer frisked Mimms and discovered in his waistband a loaded revolver. Mimms sought to exclude the evidence during trial, claiming that it was obtained illegally because he was asked to step out for no justifiable reason.

On appeal, the Court rejected Mimms's contention, saying that once a police officer has lawfully stopped a vehicle for a traffic violation, he or she may order the driver to get out even without suspecting any other criminal activity or threat to the officer's safety. Such an intrusion upon the driver is minimal. After the driver has stepped out, if the officer then reasonably believes that the driver may be armed and dangerous, the officer may conduct a frisk. Note, however, that although the authority of an officer to ask a driver to step out of the car is automatic after a valid stop, a frisk after the driver gets out of the car is not automatic. It can be undertaken only if there is reasonable suspicion of a threat to the officer's safety.

After a valid stop, an officer may look around and into the passenger compartment the vehicle and confiscate seizable items in plain view under the plain view doctrine. Items that are not in plain view cannot be seized without probable cause. A search of the car may also be conducted after a valid consent. (Vehicle stops and searches are discussed more extensively in Chapter 8.)

Arizona v. Johnson (2009)

Can a passenger in a car be asked to exit the vehicle and then be frisked even if the car was stopped only for a traffic violation? In a unanimous decision, the Court answered yes, saying that the officers were justified in conducting the frisk (*Arizona v. Johnson*, 555 U.S. 323 [2009]). In this case, Johnson was a passenger in a car that was stopped by the Arizona State Police gang investigators unit for failure to carry vehicle insurance. Johnson was seated in the back seat. The police asked the car occupants questions about recent gang activity in the area. Johnson had a handheld police scanner in his pocket and was wearing clothes that signified membership in the Crip gang. Johnson admitted being from a town known as the home of a Crip gang and that he had been to prison. He was then ordered to exit the vehicle. The officer patted him down and felt the butt of a pistol. Johnson begun to struggle with the officer and was handcuffed and the pistol was confiscated. He was later charged and convicted of illegal possession of a weapon. On appeal, he claimed that the seizure was illegal because the officers had no probable cause to believe he was involved in criminal activity or to search him. The Court disagreed, saying that a driver or passenger of a vehicle that has been stopped for a minor traffic violation can be asked to exit the vehicle and frisked if the officers have reasonable suspicion that the passenger may be armed and dangerous. The fact that the police believed Johnson was a member of a street gang that had a reputation for violence constituted reasonable suspicion that justified the frisk. The Court said that the "legitimate and weighty" interest in officer safety outweighs the additional intrusion on the driver or passenger.

Application to Weapons in a Car

Stop and frisk as applied to weapons in motor vehicles also has come under Court scrutiny.

Can the stop of a car based on reasonable Suspicion Justify a Search of the Vehicle?
The answer is yes, the police may also conduct a brief search of the vehicle after a stop if the officer has a reasonable suspicion that the motorist is dangerous and that there might be a weapon in the vehicle to which the motorist may have quick access. If an officer has reasonable suspicion that a motorist who has been stopped is dangerous and may be able to gain control of a weapon in the vehicle, the officer may conduct a brief search of the passenger compartment even if the motorist is no longer inside the car. Such a search should be limited, however, to areas in the passenger compartment where a weapon might be found or hidden.

Application to Residences

A variation of stop and frisk concerns police checking rooms of a residence other than the one where an arrest has taken place.

Can the police conduct a protective sweep of a residence after an in-house arrest of a suspect? The answer is yes. The Court has authorized the police practice of limited "protective sweeps" without a warrant while officers are conducting an in-house arrest of a suspect (*Maryland v. Buie*, 494 U.S. 325 [1990]). This practice allows officers to go to other rooms in the house when making an arrest. Some observers consider this practice similar to a "frisk of a house." In *Buie*, the Court held that protective sweeps are allowed under the following conditions: (1) there must be "a reasonable belief based on specific and articulable facts that the area to be swept harbors an individual posing a danger to those on the arrest scene"; (2) the sweep must extend only to a "cursory inspection of those spaces where a person may be found"; and (3) the sweep must last "no longer than it takes to complete the arrest and depart the premises." In sum, the requirements for the protective sweep of a house during arrest are similar to the requirements for the frisk of a person after a valid stop.

Maryland v. Buie (1990)

STATIONHOUSE DETENTION

stationhouse detention
detention takes place at the police station and is used for obtaining fingerprints, photographs, conducting police lineups, or securing identification or other types of evidence.

From stop and frisk, we move on to stationhouse detention. Like stop and frisk, **stationhouse detention** is a lesser limitation of freedom than arrest—but it is a greater limitation than the on-the-street detention in a stop and frisk. As the term suggests, stationhouse detention takes place in a police station, while stop and frisk usually takes place in the street or a public place. In contrast, the purpose of stationhouse detention can be many and varied. For example, stationhouse detention is used in many jurisdictions for obtaining fingerprints or photographs, ordering police lineups, administering polygraph examinations, and securing other identification or physical evidence. This section looks at whether stationhouse detention can be used to obtain fingerprints and for interrogations (see Table 5.2).

For Fingerprinting

Davis v. Mississippi (1969)

In *Davis v. Mississippi*, 394 U.S. 721 (1969), a case involving twenty-five youths who were detained for questioning and fingerprinting when the only leads in a rape investigation were a general description and a set of fingerprints, the Supreme Court excluded the evidence obtained from the fingerprints. But the Court also implied that detention for fingerprinting might be permissible even without probable cause to arrest. However, the Court made it clear that "narrowly circumscribed procedures" were required, including at least some objective basis for suspecting the person of a crime, a legitimate investigatory purpose for the detention (such as fingerprinting), detention at a time not inconvenient for the subject, and a court order stating that adequate evidence existed to justify the detention.

Hayes v. Florida (1985)

In *Hayes v. Florida*, 470 U.S. 811 (1985), however, the Court held that reasonable suspicion alone does not permit the police to detain a suspect at the police station to obtain fingerprints. Therefore, when the police transported a suspect to the stationhouse for fingerprinting without his consent, probable cause, or prior judicial authorization, the detention violated the Fourth Amendment. The Court noted that the police must have probable cause or an arrest warrant (based on probable cause) to forcibly transport someone to the police station for investigative purposes.

Note, however, that in the *Hayes* case, the suspect was transported without his consent to a stationhouse for fingerprinting. Therefore, in cases where consent is obtained, probable cause is not necessary. The problem is that courts consider the confines of a stationhouse generally intimidating; therefore, obtaining voluntary and intelligent

Table 5.2 Stop and Frisk and Stationhouse Detention Compared

Similarities
Both are lesser limitations of freedom than an arrest.
Both require reasonable suspicion instead of probable cause.
Both are protected by the Fourth Amendment, but to a lesser degree.
Both are practices used by law enforcement officers to prevent or solve crimes.

Differences
Stop and frisk are two separate acts; stationhouse detention is one continuous act.
Stop and frisk usually last only briefly; stationhouse detention can last for a longer time.
Stop and frisk take place outside the police station; stationhouse detention takes place in the police station.

consent may later be a problem if the existence of probable cause is challenged. Should the officer rely on consent, it is best to make it clear to the suspect that he or she is not under arrest, that he or she can leave at any time, and that the fingerprinting is purely voluntary. Moreover, the suspect's signature on a waiver form, duly witnessed, strengthens the officer's claim of voluntary and intelligent consent.

In the same case, however, the Court said that field detention (as opposed to stationhouse detention) for purposes of fingerprinting a suspect does not require probable cause as long as: (1) there is reasonable suspicion that the suspect has committed a criminal act, (2) there is reasonable belief that the fingerprinting will either negate or establish the suspect's guilt, and (3) the procedure is conducted quickly.

For Interrogation

The Court has held that probable cause is necessary for a stationhouse detention accompanied by interrogation (as opposed to just fingerprinting) even if no arrest is made. In *Dunaway v. New York*, 442 U.S. 200 (1979), the defendant was asked to come to police headquarters, where he received his *Miranda* warnings, was questioned, and ultimately confessed. There was no probable cause to arrest him, but there was some reason for the police to suspect him in connection with the crime being investigated. The Court held that the defendant was in fact arrested and not simply stopped on the street, so probable cause was required to take him to the police station. Because probable cause was lacking, the confession obtained was not admissible. The Court added that the detention of Dunaway in this case was indistinguishable from a traditional arrest because he was not questioned briefly where he was found but instead was transported to a police station and would have been physically restrained if he had refused to accompany the officers or had tried to escape from their custody.

Dunaway v. New York (1979)

SUMMARY

- A stop is a police practice whereby a person is stopped in public and questioned.
- A frisk is a pat-down for weapons.
- Although often viewed as a single action, stop and frisk are best understood as two separate acts; each must be based on reasonable suspicion.
- Stop and frisk are authorized by law or court decision.
- The purpose of a stop is to prevent criminal activity or to respond if criminal activity has just taken place.
- A frisk has one purpose—to protect officers (or others). A frisk for any other purpose is illegal.

- Reasonable suspicion is less certain than probable cause but more certain than mere suspicion; it must be based on specific, objective facts.
- There are two limitations on a stop: (1) it must be temporary and no longer than necessary to achieve its purpose; and (2) it must be the least intrusive action available to the officer.
- There are two limitations on a frisk: (1) officers cannot squeeze, slide, or manipulate felt objects during a pat-down; and (2) it cannot be used as a fishing expedition for evidence.
- Motor vehicles can be stopped only if there is reasonable suspicion of the occupants' possible

involvement in an unlawful activity. The driver and passengers may then be asked to get out of the car. But they may be frisked only if there is fear for the officer's safety.

◆ Stationhouse detention for fingerprinting or interrogation should be considered an arrest and subject to Fourth Amendment protection.

REVIEW QUESTIONS

1. When is a stop valid? What is its purpose?
2. When is a frisk valid? What is its purpose?
3. "An officer who makes a valid stop can automatically conduct a valid frisk." Is this statement true or false? Explain your answer.
4. What is reasonable suspicion? How does it differ from probable cause?
5. Assume you are stopped by the police for valid reasons. Can you be forced to answer questions? Can you be forced to identify yourself? What may happen if you refuse? Explain your answer.
6. What did the Supreme Court say in *Terry v. Ohio*, and why is it important?
7. Are stops based on race alone valid? Are stops that consider race as merely one of the factors in the stop valid? Explain your answer.
8. Distinguish between stop and frisk and an arrest.
9. What does *Minnesota v. Dickerson* say about the scope and extent of what an officer can do during a frisk?
10. "A police officer who validly stops a motor vehicle can automatically ask the driver to get out of the vehicle and then frisk the driver." Is this statement true or false? Justify your answer.
11. An officer has "invited" a suspect to come to the stationhouse for questioning in connection with a report received from a confidential informant that said the suspect may have been involved in a burglary. During the questioning, is that suspect under arrest or not? What are the implications either way?

TEST YOUR UNDERSTANDING

1. One night around midnight, while driving home from a birthday celebration at one of the downtown bars in Huntsville, you noticed that you were being followed by a police car for several blocks. Worried that you might have had a little too much to drink, you made a quick turn and tried to separate yourself from the police car. Based on this fact alone, the officer driving the police car immediately sped after you, turned on his flashing lights and siren, and pulled you over. From your reading of *Illinois v. Wardlow*, was the stop valid? Defend your answer.
2. Sean, a student, was stopped by the police, based on reasonable suspicion, after midnight in the suburbs of Los Angeles and detained for one hour. Was his detention valid? Give reasons for your answer.
3. John was stopped by the police at dawn in a Miami, Florida, suburb because he looked suspicious. John was wearing heavy clothing although it had been a warm night, looked lost in the neighborhood, and acted nervous upon seeing the police. Was the stop valid? Analyze each of the reasons specified above and determine if, in and of themselves, they justify the stop. Would your answer be different or the same if all of these circumstances were taken together? Explain.
4. You are a rookie university police officer who has been on the job for a few weeks. While patrolling the campus one evening, you see a man emerge from a dark alley near one of the dormitories. The man appears shabby and unkempt. You tell him to stop and ask him questions. The man is nervous and somewhat incoherent but says he is a janitor in the building and has just gotten off work. You frisk him and recover bundles of crack cocaine from his pockets. Is this evidence admissible in court under stop and frisk? Explain why.
5. Officer Jones invited Frank, a suspect in a robbery case, to come to the police station "to answer a few questions." Suspect Frank willingly accepted this invitation. Frank was kept at the station for four hours, during which time he was fingerprinted. Were Frank's fingerprints legally obtained by the police? Support your answer.

6. Officer Jordan was patrolling an area in Chicago late one night where there had been reports of robberies and burglaries. He saw somebody who looked Hispanic who was walking alone with hands in his pockets. Officer Jordan stopped the man and asked him questions about where he lived. The man said he lived "around here," but refused to give the exact address. Officer Jordan then frisked him and felt something "bulging" around his waistline. He immediately confiscated this, which turned out to be a tool for breaking into homes. You are the judge in the case that was filed against the suspect. Will you admit or exclude the evidence? State reasons for your decision based on whether the stop and the subsequent frisks were both valid.

RECOMMENDED READINGS

Beverly Rice. "When Can the Police Stop and Frisk You on the Street?" *http://www.legalzoom.com/legal-articles/when-police-frisk-you%20.html.*

"Stop and Frisk Law: A Guide to Doctrines, Tests, and Special Circumstances," *http://www.apsu.edu/oconnort/ 3000/3000lect03.htm.*

Bennett L. Gershman. *Use of race in "stop-and-frisk"; stereotypical beliefs linger, but how far can the police go?* 72 Journal (New York State Bar Association) 42, 45 (2000).

Fred E. Inbau. *Stop and frisk: The power and obligation of the police.* 89 Journal of Criminal Law and Criminology 1445, 1448 (1999).

Jesper Ryberg. *Racial profiling and criminal justice.* Journal of Ethics, vol. 15, March 2011.

NOTES

1. "Stop-and-Frisks Hit Record in 2011," http://online.wsj.com/article/SB.html.
2. *USA Today*, April 30, 2007, p. 3A.
3. *Houston Chronicle*, April 13, 2000, p. 10A.
4. "Taking On Police Tactic, Critics Hit Racial Divide," *New York Times*, March 22, 2012, http://www.nytimes.com

CHAPTER 6

Arrests and Use of Force

LEARNING OBJECTIVES

1. Define what an arrest is.
2. Describe the four elements of a lawful arrest.
3. Compare and contrast the two types of seizure (actual and constructive).
4. Describe the circumstances surrounding *Tennessee v. Garner* and the effect of the decision on the use of force by law enforcement.
5. Construct a continuum of force in response to a situation with legal justification.
6. Compare and contrast the legal requirements for an arrest with and without a warrant.
7. Explain when an officer may make an arrest without a warrant.
8. Describe the circumstances when knock and announce is required, as well as when it is not.
9. Explain the legal requirements of an arrest warrant.
10. Describe what actions an officer may or may not perform after an arrest.

KEY TERMS

actual seizure

arrest

arrest warrant

bench warrants

blanket exceptions

capias

citation

citizen's arrest

constructive seizure

deadly force

exigent circumstances

John Doe warrants

neutral and detached magistrate

nondeadly force

posse comitatus

protective sweeps

punitive force

reasonable force

seizure

telephonic warrants

use-of-force continuums

iStockphoto.com/Darren Mower

THE TOP 5 IMPORTANT CASES

in Arrests and Use of Force

■ *PAYTON V. NEW YORK (1980)* In the absence of exigent circumstances or consent, the police may not enter a private home to make a routine warrantless arrest.

■ *TENNESSEE V. GARNER (1985)* It is constitutionally reasonable for a police officer to use deadly force only when the officer has probable cause to believe that the suspect poses a threat of serious physical harm to the officer or others.

■ *WILSON V. ARKANSAS (1995)* The knock-and-announce rule is part of the Fourth Amendment's requirement that searches and seizures be reasonable, but that rule is not rigid and is subject to exceptions based on law enforcement interests.

■ *ATWATER V. CITY OF LAGO VISTA (2001)* An arrest for an offense not punishable with jail or prison time is constitutional.

■ *BRIGHAM CITY, UTAH V. STUART (2006)* Police may enter a home and make an arrest without a warrant if they have objectively reasonable basis for believing that an occupant is seriously injured or immediately threatened with such injury.

THE FOURTH AMENDMENT to the U.S. Constitution provides that "the right of the people to be secure in their persons, houses, papers, and effects, against unreasonable searches and seizures, shall not be violated, and no Warrants shall issue, but upon probable cause, supported by Oath or affirmation, and particularly describing the place to be searched, and the persons or things to be seized." An arrest constitutes a "seizure" of a person, so the restrictions of the Fourth Amendment apply. Police officers must be well informed about the law of arrest, because successful prosecution usually depends on the legality of the arrest. If the arrest is legal, then searches of the arrestee and the area within his or her control are also legal; conversely, if the arrest is illegal, any evidence obtained thereafter is not admissible in court.

The validity of an arrest is determined primarily by federal constitutional standards, particularly the requirement of probable cause. An arrest, with or without a warrant, is not valid unless there is probable cause—as determined by federal constitutional standards as expressed by the U.S. Supreme Court. In arrests (seizures of persons, as distinguished from searches and seizures of things), probable cause "exists if the facts and circumstances known to the officer warrant a prudent man in believing that the offense has been committed" and that the person being arrested committed it.

State laws that are not consistent with constitutional standards are invalid, but state laws that give more rights to suspects or defendants than are required by the Fourth Amendment are valid. For example, traffic offenders may be constitutionally arrested if there is probable cause, but state law may prohibit the police from making an arrest and provide instead for the issuance of a citation for the offender to appear in court on a specified date. In sum, state laws can give more rights to suspects and defendants but cannot take away basic constitutional rights.

THE BROAD PICTURE: ARRESTS ARE SEIZURES OF PERSONS

What happens when persons are seized (arrested) by the police? This section addresses what the Fourth Amendment says about the seizure of persons as opposed to the seizure of things (discussed in Chapter 7). Both come under the Fourth Amendment, but the rules differ slightly.

Arrests and the Fourth Amendment

When analyzing the constitutionality of seizures under the Fourth Amendment, the first question should be whether in fact a seizure under the Fourth Amendment has occurred. If no such seizure has occurred, then the provisions of the Fourth Amendment do not apply, because those provisions apply only to "unreasonable searches and seizures." If a seizure did in fact occur, the question then becomes what kind of seizure was it, and what kind of protection is given by the courts in that type of seizure?

Some contacts with the police are not considered seizures under the Fourth Amendment, because the degree of intrusiveness is slight or minimal. For example, the following contacts do not come under the Fourth Amendment because they are not deemed seizures:

◆ The police asking questions of people on the street to gather general information.
◆ The police asking a driver to get out of a car during a routine traffic stop (*Pennsylvania v. Mimms*, 434 U.S. 106 [1977]).
◆ The police boarding a bus and asking questions of the passengers that a person is free to refuse to answer (*Florida v. Bostick*, 501 U.S. 429 [1991]).
◆ The police driving alongside a person "to see where he was going" (*Michigan v. Chesternut*, 486 U.S. 657 [1988]) and asking questions of witnesses to a crime.

Arrest Is Just One Form of Seizure

Seizures of persons are usually associated with arrest, *but arrest is only one form of seizure*—although one of the most intrusive. There are other intrusions into a person's freedom that do not constitute arrest but nonetheless come under the protection of the Fourth Amendment. For example, stop and frisk, border searches, and roadblocks are seizures that come under the Fourth Amendment, but the constitutional requirements for these types of police actions differ from those for an arrest because they are lesser forms of intrusion. The term **seizure** under the Fourth Amendment is therefore broader than the term *arrest*. Every arrest is a seizure, but not every seizure is an arrest.

In *Brower v. Inyo County*, 489 U.S. 593 (1989), the Court said that seizure "requires an intentional acquisition of physical control," adding that a seizure for purposes of the Fourth Amendment "does not occur whenever there is a governmentally caused termination of an individual's freedom of movement . . . but *only when there is governmental termination of freedom of movement through means intentionally applied*" [emphasis added].

seizure
the taking of a person into custody.

Brower v. Inyo County (1989)

The Top Ten Intrusive Searches and Seizures of Persons

This top ten list is presented to illustrate the degrees of intrusiveness in search and seizure cases. As gathered from Court decisions, the intrusiveness of searches and seizures of persons under the Fourth Amendment can be ranked as follows (with 1 being the most intrusive and 10 the least intrusive):

1. Surgery to remove a bullet from a suspect's chest (*Winston v. Lee*, 470 U.S. 753 [1985]).
2. Removal of heroin capsule using stomach pump (*Rochin v. California*, 342 U.S. 752 [1969]).
3. Anal and cavity searches (*Kennedy v. Los Angeles Police Department*, 887 F.2d 920 [9th Cir. 1989]).
4. Arrest (*United States v. Santana*, 427 U.S. 38 [1975]).
5. Removal of blood in a hospital (*Schmerber v. California*, 384 U.S. 457 [1966]).
6. Stationhouse detention (*Hayes v. Florida*, 470 U.S. 811 [1985]).
7. Stop and frisk (*Terry v. Ohio*, 392 U.S. 1 [1968]).

Winston v. Lee (1985)

Rochin v. California (1969)

Kennedy v. Los Angeles Police Department (1989)

United States v. Santana (1975)

Schmerber v. California (1966)

Hayes v. Florida (1985)

Terry v. Ohio (1968)

HIGHLIGHT ▶ There Is No Bright-Line Rule as to When a Person Has Been Seized

No bright-line rule applicable to all investigatory pursuits can be fashioned. Rather, the appropriate test is whether a reasonable person, viewing the particular police conduct as a whole and within the setting of all the surrounding circumstances, would have concluded that the police had in some way restrained his or her liberty so that he or she was not free to leave. As the Court stated: "The test is necessarily imprecise because it is designed to assess the coercive effect of police conduct, taken as a whole, rather than to focus on particular details of that conduct in isolation. Moreover, what constitutes a restraint on liberty prompting a person to conclude that he is not free to 'leave' will vary, not only with the particular police conduct at issue, but also with the setting in which the conduct occurs."

Source: *Michigan v. Chesternut*, 486 U.S. 567 (1988).

Au Yi Lau v. United States
Immigration and Natural-
ization Service (1971)

Carroll v. United States
(1925)

United States v. Martinez-
Fuerte (1976)

8. Immigration and border searches (*Au Yi Lau v. United States Immigration and Naturalization Service*, 445 F.2d 217 [9th Cir. 1971]).
9. Routine traffic stop of a vehicle (*Carroll v. United States*, 267 U.S. 132 [1925]).
10. Roadblocks to control the flow of illegal aliens (*United States v. Martinez-Fuerte*, 428 U.S. 543 [1976]).

This list is illustrative and admittedly subjective. Individual perceptions (including those of professors and students) differ about which type of search and seizure is more intrusive. Its significance, however, lies in that the list shows how, over the years, Court decisions have established a sliding scale of intrusion as well as a sliding scale of constitutional protection. The general rule is this: *The more severe the intrusion, the greater is the protection given by the courts.* For example, in *Winston v. Lee*, 470 U.S. 753 (1985), the Court held that surgery (number 1 on the list) under general anesthetic to remove a bullet from a suspect's chest for use as evidence cannot be undertaken *even with probable cause and a judicial order* (the highest possible form of protection in Fourth Amendment cases) unless there are compelling reasons. This is because such a procedure is highly intrusive (could have put a life at risk from the operation to remove a bullet lodged in the suspect's chest) and violates the Fourth Amendment. In contrast, persons subjected to roadblocks to control the flow of illegal aliens (number 10 on the list) do not need much protection under the Fourth Amendment, because roadblocks are not highly intrusive and there is a strong governmental interest involved (*United States v. Martinez-Fuerte*, 428 U.S. 543 [1976]).

What Is the Legal Test to Determine Whether a Seizure Has Occurred?

Whose perception determines whether a person has in fact been seized? This question is important because the perception of the police may be different from that of a suspect. For example, arrest may not be in an officer's mind when detaining a suspect, but the suspect may feel that he or she is under arrest. Whose perception determines whether a person has been seized—that of the police or that of the person detained? The answer is: neither. In the leading case on this issue, the Court held that the appropriate test to determine if a seizure has occurred is *whether a reasonable person, viewing the particular police conduct as a whole and within the setting of all the surrounding circumstances, would have concluded that the police had in some way restrained a person's liberty so that he or she was not free to leave* (*Michigan v. Chesternut*, 486 U.S. 567 [1988]). In sum, it is the perception of a reasonable person based on a totality of circumstances.

The Court in *Chesternut* said that there can be no single, clear rule applicable to all investigatory pursuits. In this case, after observing the approach of a police car, Chesternut began to run. Officers followed him "to see where he was going." As the officers drove alongside Chesternut, they observed him pull a number of packets from his pocket and throw them to the ground. The officers stopped and seized the packets, concluding that they might be contraband (they were illegal narcotics). Chesternut was arrested, and a subsequent body search revealed more illegal narcotics.

Chesternut was charged with felony narcotics possession and convicted. On appeal, he sought exclusion of the evidence, alleging that the officers' investigatory pursuit "to see where he was going" constituted a seizure under the Fourth Amendment. The Supreme Court rejected this contention, noting that Chesternut was not seized before he discarded the drug packets and that the activity of the officers in following him to see where he was going did not violate the Fourth Amendment.

In another case, *Florida v. Bostick*, 501 U.S. 429 (1991), without any suspicion and with the intention of catching drug smugglers, two uniformed law enforcement officers boarded a bus in Fort Lauderdale, Florida, that was en route from Miami to Atlanta. The officers approached Bostick and asked to see some identification and his bus ticket. The officers also asked Bostick for consent to search his bag and told him he could refuse consent. Bostick consented to the search of his bag, and cocaine was found. In court, he sought to suppress the evidence, alleging it was improperly seized. The Florida Supreme Court agreed with Bostick, adopting an inflexible rule stating that the officers' practice of "working the buses" was per se unconstitutional.

Florida v. Bostick (1991)

On appeal, the U.S. Supreme Court rejected the Florida rule, holding that the result of such a rule was that the police in Florida (as elsewhere) could approach persons at random in most places, ask them questions, and seek consent to search, but they could not engage in the same behavior on a bus. Rather, the Court said, "[T]he appropriate test is whether, taking into account all of the circumstances surrounding the encounter, a reasonable passenger would feel free to decline the officers' requests or otherwise terminate the encounter." This was reemphasized by the Court in a later decision when it said that a seizure by the police of the person within the meaning of the Fourth Amendment occurs only when, "taking into account all of the circumstances surrounding the encounter, the police conduct would have communicated to a reasonable person that he was not at liberty to ignore the police presence and go about his business" (*Kaupp v. Texas*, 583 U.S.626 [2003]).

Kaupp v. Texas (2003)

Who decides what is a "reasonable person" under this standard? The answer: the jury or judge that tries the case. The standard they use is subjective and can vary from one jury or judge to another. In *United States v. Mendenhall*, 446 U.S. 544 (1980), the Court suggested the following circumstances could cause a reasonable person to believe they were not free to leave:

United States v. Mendenhall (1980)

1. the threatening presence of several officers,
2. the display of a weapon by an officer,
3. some physical touching of the person, and
4. the use of language or tone of voice indicating that compliance with the officer's request was required.

ARREST DEFINED

An **arrest** is defined as the taking of a person into custody against his or her will for the purpose of criminal prosecution or interrogation (*Dunaway v. New York*, 442 U.S. 200 [1979]). It occurs "only when there is governmental termination of freedom of movement through means intentionally applied" (*Brower v. County of Inyo*, 489 U.S.

arrest
the taking of a person into custody against his or her will for the purpose of criminal prosecution or interrogation.

Dunaway v. New York
(1979)

Brower v. County of Inyo
(1989)

593 [1989]). An arrest deprives a person of liberty by legal authority. Mere words alone do not normally constitute an arrest; there must be some kind of restraint. A person's liberty must be restricted by law enforcement officers to the extent that the person is not free to leave of his or her own volition. It does not matter whether the act is termed an "arrest" or a mere "stop" or "detention" under state law. The totality of circumstances (judged by the standard of a reasonable person) determines whether or not an arrest has taken place.

This section looks at which actions constitute arrest and how long a person can be detained before a temporary detention becomes an arrest.

Forced Detention and Arrest

When a person is taken into custody against his or her will for purposes of criminal prosecution or interrogation, it is an arrest under the Fourth Amendment, regardless of what state law says. For example, suppose state law provides that a police officer may "detain" a suspect for four hours in the police station for questioning without having "arrested" that person. If the suspect is detained in the police station against his or her will, that person has been arrested under the Constitution, regardless of how state law calls it, and is therefore entitled to rights given to suspects who have been arrested.

Conversely, no arrest or seizure occurs when an officer simply approaches a person in a public place and asks if he or she is willing to answer questions—so long as the person is not involuntarily detained. A voluntary encounter between a police officer and a member of the public is not an arrest or a seizure. For example, there is no seizure if an officer approaches a person who is not suspected of anything and, without show of force or intimidation, asks questions of the person—who may or may not respond.

IN ACTION   WHAT THE POLICE MAY DO AFTER AN ARREST

Officer Lewis makes a traffic stop after observing a driver fail to stop at a stop sign. Officer Lewis identifies the driver (Frank Roberts) through his driver's license, vehicle registration, and insurance paperwork. Officer Lewis notices marijuana in the ashtray of the vehicle and asks Roberts if he has been smoking marijuana. Roberts admits that he has. Officer Lewis places Roberts under arrest, handcuffs him, and places him in the backseat of his police vehicle. Having placed Thomas under arrest, Officer Lewis conducts a search of the vehicle. During the vehicle search, Officer Lewis discovers a handgun in the unlocked glove compartment and a baggie of marijuana under the front passenger seat.

Officer Lewis then transports Roberts to the police station to be booked into jail on the warrant and weapon and drug possession charges.

1. Is the discovery of the marijuana in the vehicle's ashtray lawful? Explain.
2. Is the search of Thomas's vehicle after his arrest lawful? Explain.
3. Is the seizure of the drug evidence from the vehicle lawful? Explain.
4. In your opinion, will the drug and weapon evidence be admissible in court?

The Length of Detention and Arrest

An important question concerns how long the suspect can be detained and how intrusive the investigation must be before the stop becomes an arrest requiring probable cause. The answer depends on the reasonableness of the detention and the intrusion. The detention must not be longer than that required by the circumstances, and it must take place by the "least intrusive means," meaning that it must not be more than that needed to verify or dispel the officer's suspicions. In the words of the Court in *United States v. Sharpe*, 470 U.S. 675 (1985): "In assessing whether a detention is too long to be justified as an investigative stop, we consider it appropriate to examine whether the police diligently pursued a means of investigation that was likely to confirm or dispel their suspicions quickly, during which time it was necessary to detain the defendant." Detention for a longer period of time than is necessary converts a stop into an arrest.

United States v. Sharpe (1985)

In sum, *a person has been seized if, under the totality of circumstances, a reasonable person would not have felt free to leave.* This rule applies to seizures of persons in general, such as in stop and frisk, not just in arrest cases.

THE FOUR ELEMENTS OF AN ARREST

Four elements must be present for an arrest to take place:

◆ Seizure and detention
◆ Intention to arrest
◆ Arrest authority
◆ The understanding of the individual that he or she is being arrested

Seizure and Detention

This first element of an arrest may be either actual or constructive. **Actual seizure** is accomplished by taking the person into custody with the use of hands or firearms (denoting use of force without touching the individual) or by merely touching the individual without the use of force. In contrast, **constructive seizure** is accomplished without any physical touching, grabbing, holding, or use of force; it occurs when the individual peacefully submits to the officer's will and control. See an example of the state of Missouri's Uniform Complaint and Summons in Figure 6.1.

actual seizure
the taking of a person into custody with the use of hands, force, or firearms.

Mere words alone do not constitute an arrest. The fact that a police officer tells a person, "You are under arrest," is not sufficient. The required restraint must be accompanied by actual seizure or peaceful submission to the officer's will and control. Furthermore, mere authority to arrest alone does not constitute an arrest. There must be either an actual or a constructive seizure. When neither takes place, no arrest takes place.

constructive seizure
occurs without any physical touching, grabbing, holding, or use of force when the individual peacefully submits to the officer's will and control.

The case of *California v. Hodari*, 499 U.S. 621 (1991), illustrates the element of seizure and detention in an arrest situation. In this case, two police officers were patrolling a high-crime area of Oakland, California, late one night. They saw several youths huddled around a small red car parked at the curb. When the youths saw the police

California v. Hodari (1991)

car approaching, they fled. Officer Pertoso, who was wearing a jacket with the word "POLICE" embossed on its front, left the car to give chase. Pertoso did not directly follow the youth who turned out to be Hodari; instead, Pertoso took another route that brought him to Hodari on a parallel street. Hodari was looking behind himself as he ran and did not turn to see Pertoso until they were right in front of each other—whereupon Hodari tossed away what looked like a small rock. The officer then tackled Hodari and recovered the rock, which turned out to be crack cocaine.

The issue on appeal was whether Hodari had been seized within the meaning of the Fourth Amendment, thus necessitating a warrant, when he dropped the crack cocaine. The Court said no and admitted the evidence, saying:

> To constitute a seizure of the person . . . there must be either the application of physical force, however slight, or where that is absent, submission to the officer's "show of authority" to restrain the subject's liberty. No physical force was applied in this case, since Hodari was untouched by [Officer] Pertoso before he dropped the drugs. Moreover, assuming that Pertoso's pursuit constituted a "show of authority" enjoining Hodari to halt, Hodari did not comply with that injunction and therefore was not seized until he was tackled. Thus, the cocaine abandoned while he was running was not the fruit of a seizure . . . and his motion to exclude evidence of it was properly denied.

To summarize, there was no seizure because no physical force (actual seizure) had been applied prior to the suspect's tossing away the crack cocaine, nor had the suspect voluntarily submitted to the authority of the officer (constructive seizure).

The Intention to Arrest

The second element is intention to arrest. An arrest has taken place when a police officer indicates, by words or deeds, that he or she intends to take the suspect into custody. In this case, the intention to arrest is clear because it is either expressed or clearly implied in the officer's action.

Without the requisite intent, there is no arrest even if a person is temporarily stopped or inconvenienced. For example, no arrest occurs when an officer pulls over a motorist to issue a ticket, asks a motorist to step out of his or her car, stops a motorist to check his or her driver's license, or stops a person to warn of possible danger. In these cases, there may be a temporary deprivation of liberty and a certain amount of inconvenience, but there is no intent by the police officer to take the person into custody; therefore, there is no arrest.

The requirement of intention to arrest is hard to prove because it exists only in the mind of the police officer. There are cases, however, in which actions clearly indicated that the officer intended to take the person into custody, even though intent to arrest was later denied by the officer. For example, when an officer places handcuffs on a suspect, the intent to arrest likely exists even if the officer denies such intent. In short, "actions speak louder than words."

When it is not clear from the officer's actions whether there was an intent to arrest, the Supreme Court has said that "a policeman's unarticulated plan has no bearing on the question whether a suspect was 'in custody' at a particular time" (*Berkemer v. McCarty*, 468 U.S. 420 [1984]). The test is the interpretation of a reasonable person, regardless of what the officer had or did not have in mind. For example, Officer Phillips invites a suspect to the police station for interrogation about a murder. The officer does not inform the suspect that she is free to leave; neither does the officer allow the

Berkemer v. McCarty (1984)

FIGURE 6.1 Missouri Uniform Complaint and Summons

MISSOURI UNIFORM COMPLAINT AND SUMMONS
ABSTRACT OF COURT RECORD

ORI NO. MO0510000
JOHNSON CO. SHERIFF'S DEPT.
STATE OF MISSOURI
IN THE CIRCUIT COURT OF JOHNSON
JOHNSON COUNTY ASSOC. CIRCUIT DIV.

N⁰ 851402263

THE UNDERSIGNED POLICE OFFICER STATES THAT:

on or about (DATE)	upon/at or near (LOCATION/LOG PT.)	at (TIME)	☐ AM ☐ PM

WITHIN COUNTY AND STATE AFORESAID

Name (LAST, FIRST, MIDDLE)

Street Address

City	State	Zip Code

Date of Birth	Age	Race	Sex	Height	Weight

Driver's License No.	☐ OP ☐ CH ☐ MC QUAL	State

Dept. of Revenue use only — Do not write in this space.

Disobeyed Signal (when light turned red)	☐ Past Middle of Intersection ☐ Middle of Intersection	☐ Not Reached Intersection
Disobeyed Stop Sign	☐ Stopped Wrong Place	☐ Walk Speed ☐ Faster
Improper Turn ☐ Left ☐ Right ☐ "U"	☐ No Signal ☐ Into Wrong Lane ☐ Cut Corner	☐ From Wrong Lane ☐ Prohibited
☐ Improper Passing ☐ Improper Lane Use	☐ At Intersection ☐ Between Traf. ☐ Cut In ☐ On Right ☐ On Hill ☐ Wrong Side of Pavement	☐ Lane Straddling ☐ Wrong Lane ☐ On Curve

DID UNLAWFULLY	V E H	Year	Make	Model	Style	Color
☐ OPERATE ☐ PARK	L I C	Number		State		Year

AND THEN AND THERE COMMITTED THE FOLLOWING OFFENSE.

Describe Violation

Driving ____ MPH when limited to ____ MPH	Detection Method ☐ STA RADAR ☐ MOV RADAR	☐ WATCH (AIR) ☐ WATCH (GRND)	☐ PACE ☐ OTHER
In violation of ☐ RSMO ☐ ORD	Missouri Charge Code	☐ IN ACCIDENT ☐ DWI/BAC	

THE ABOVE COMPLAINT IS TRUE AS I VERILY BELIEVE.

Officer	Badge No.

SWORN TO BEFORE ME THIS DATE.

Name & Title	Date

I promise to dispose of the charges of which I am accused through court appearance or prepayment of fine and court costs.	Court Date	Court Time	☐ AM ☐ PM
	Street Address COUNTY COURTHOUSE		
Signature X	City WARRENSBURG, MO 64093		

ON INFORMATION UNDERSIGNED PROSECUTOR COMPLAINS AND IN-FORMS COURT THAT ABOVE FACTS ARE TRUE AS HE VERILY BELIEVES.

Prosecutor's Signature	Date

FORM 37.1162A   G. A. THOMPSON, P. O. BOX 64681, DALLAS, TEXAS 75206   FORM MO17-5R

Source: Official form of the state of Missouri.

suspect, upon her request, to leave prior to the end of the interrogation. The officer later testifies that he had no intention to arrest the suspect and that he merely wanted to "ask a few questions." Under the Fourth Amendment, however, that suspect had been arrested because a reasonable person under the same circumstances would likely conclude that an arrest had been made.

Arrest Authority

The third element of arrest, authority to restrain, distinguishes arrest from deprivations of liberty (such as kidnapping or illegal detention) by private individuals. When there is proper authorization, the arrest is valid; conversely, when proper authorization is lacking, the arrest is invalid. Invalid arrest can arise in the following cases: (1) when the police officer mistakenly thinks he or she has authority to arrest and (2) when the officer knows that he or she is not authorized to make the arrest but does so anyway. Whether a police officer has arrest authority when off duty varies from state to state. Some states authorize police officers (by law, court decision, or agency policy) to make an arrest any time they witness a criminal act. In these states, the officer is, in effect, on duty twenty-four hours a day, seven days a week, for purposes of making an arrest, whether in uniform or not. Other states authorize police officers to make an arrest only when they are on duty. This policy minimizes possible department liability for acts done by police officers when they are not on duty.

Understanding by the Arrestee

The fourth element of an arrest, the understanding that he or she is being arrested, may be conveyed to the arrestee through words, actions, or both. In most cases, the police officer says, "You are under arrest," thereby conveying intention through words. Similarly, some actions strongly imply that a person is being taken into custody even though the police officer makes no statement. Examples of actions that strongly imply arrest include a suspected burglar being subdued by police and taken to a squad car and a person being handcuffed and then taken to the police station even though no words are spoken. The element of understanding is not required for an arrest in the following three instances: (1) when the suspect is drunk or under the influence of drugs and does not understand what is going on, (2) when the suspect is insane, and (3) when the suspect is unconscious.

ARRESTS WITH A WARRANT

Black's Law Dictionary defines an **arrest warrant** as "a writ or precept issued by a magistrate, justice, or other competent authority, addressed to a sheriff, constable, or other officer, requiring him to arrest the body of a person therein named, and bring him before the magistrate or court to answer, or to be examined, concerning some offense which he is charged with having committed."[1] There are different types of arrest warrants. Among these are **bench warrants**, issued when a person does not appear for a hearing; **telephonic warrants**, issued after a telephone communication between the issuing judge and the officer applying for it; and **John Doe warrants**, issued when the person to be arrested is well described in the warrant but not identified by name.

Warrant forms vary from state to state and even from one city to another, but they typically include the following: which court is issuing it, the name of the person to be arrested, the offense charged and some specifics of the offense, an order for the officer to bring the arrested person before the issuing court, the date the warrant was issued,

arrest warrant
a writ issued by a duly authorized person that instructs a law enforcement officer to bring the person to a magistrate or judge in connection with an offense with which he or she has been charged.

bench warrants
issued when a person does not appear for a hearing.

telephonic warrants
issued after a telephonic communication between the issuing judge and the officer.

John Doe warrants
issued when the person to be arrested is well described in the warrant, but not identified by name.

FIGURE 6.2 Arrest Warrant

GENERAL SESSIONS COURT OF
_____ **COUNTY,**
TENNESSEE

STATE OF TENNESSEE

vs.

_____
Defendant

State Control # _____

Case # _____

INFORMATION ABOUT THE DEFENDANT

Name: _____
Address: _____
DOB: _____ Sex: _____
Race: _____ Ht.: _____
Wt.: _____ Hair: _____ Eyes: _____
Phone: _____ DL#: _____
Place of Employment: _____

May Be Found at: _____

Other: _____

_____

WITNESSES

Summon as witnesses on the part of the State:

_____
_____

Date: _____

Summon as witnesses on the part of the Defendant:

_____
_____

ARREST WARRANT

TO THE DEFENDANT

☐ Based on the affidavit of complaint filed in this case, there is probable cause to believe that you have committed the offense(s) of violation(s) of T.C.A. §
_____
_____

☐ Defendant has failed to appear in court or to report to jail when required to do so.

☐ _____
_____

TO ANY LAWFUL OFFICER

You are therefore commanded in the name of the State of Tennessee to immediately **ARREST** the defendant named above and bring the defendant to this court to answer the charges.

Bail is set at $ _____

Conditions of Bond: _____

_____

Date: _____

_____
Judge/Clerk/Judicial Commissioner

The warrant must include a copy of the affidavit of complaint. T.C.A. § 40-6-208.

OFFICER'S RETURN

☐ Warrant served by arresting defendant today or on _____

_____
_____

☐ _____

Officer's Signature: _____

Officer's Name (Printed): _____

Officer's Agency (Printed): _____

Date: _____

Legal Authority: TRCRP 4

Source: Official form of the state of Tennessee.

FIGURE 6.3 Arrest Custody Report

STATE OF VERMONT
ARREST / CUSTODY REPORT

CAUTION
Y | N

DATE OF ARREST
MO | DAY | YR

AGENCY COMPLAINT NO.

ARRESTING AGENCY _____

IDENTIFICATION:

| LAST NAME | FIRST NAME | MIDDLE NAME | DOB | | AGE | SEX | RACE* | ETHNIC* |

STREET

| EMPLOYED | UNEMPLOYED | STUDENT | REFUSED TO ANSWER |

PLACE OF BIRTH (CITY / STATE)

CITY / TOWN

| STATE | ZIP CODE | SOC. SEC. NO. | ID NUMBER |

EMPLOYER / SCHOOL

ADDRESS

ALIAS   LAST NAME   FIRST NAME   MIDDLE NAME

SCARS / MARKS

| 1 SING | 2 MAR | 3 SEP | 4 DIV | 5 WID | 6 COHAB |
MARITAL STATUS

HEIGHT   WEIGHT lb.

| 1 BLA | 2 BRO | 3 BLD | 4 RED | 5 GREY | 6 BALD | 7 WHI |
HAIR COLOR

| 1 BRO | 2 BLU | 3 HAZ | 4 OTH |
EYE COLOR   SPECIFY

D.M.V. INFORMATION:

D.M.V. CASE NO. _____

OPERATOR LICENSE NO.   STATE   EXPIRATION DATE

| INJURY | FATAL | PROP. DAMAGE |
ACCIDENT

| REFUSED | NO | YES | RESULT | % |
TEST

REGISTRATION NO.   STATE   EXPIRATION DATE   VEHICLE MAKE   TYPE   YEAR

ARREST DATA:

TIME   PLACE   GRID / COUNTY-TOWN   OFFENSE GRID

V.S.A.

OFFENSE   TITLE   SECTION   SUB-SECTION   OFFENSE DATE

FINGERPRINTS   PHOTOGRAPH
Y | N   Y | N

| RELEASED TO GUARDIAN | ARRAIGNED | CITED | LODGED | BAIL |
IMMEDIATE DISPOSITION

OFFENSE CODE   ATTACH TO A/C - 3   COMMENTS

COMPANION CASE NO.

FINGERPRINT OFFICER

ARRESTING OFFICER SIGNATURE   ID. NO.

PHOTOGRAPH OFFICER

APPROVING OFFICER SIGNATURE   ID. NO.

OFFENSE: (STATE'S ATTORNEY USE)

DOCKET # _____

V.S.A.

COUNT: ____ OF ____

CHARGED   TITLE   SECTION   SUB-SECTION

| NO PROSECUTION | DIVERSION | FORWARDED TO COURT | RETURNED |
COMMENT: _____

*RACE CODE: W-WHITE, B-BLACK, I-INDIAN, A-ASIAN, U-UNKNOWN
*ETHNIC CODE: 1-HISPANIC, 2-NON HISPANIC   **A/C - 1 AGENCY**   VT 453 7/83

Source: Official form of the state of Vermont.

and the judge's or magistrate's signature. (Figure 6.2 shows an example of an arrest warrant from the state of Tennessee.)

This section looks at when a warrant is needed, what happens when one is issued, the contents of a warrant, what happens when a warrant is served, the time of day arrests can be made, the possession and expiration of a warrant, and legal authorizations other than a warrant.

When Is a Warrant Needed?

Most arrests are made without a warrant. Nonetheless, there are specific instances when a warrant is needed, including the following:

1. *A warrant is needed if the crime is not committed in the officer's presence.* When crimes are not committed in the presence of an officer, the victim reports the crime to the police and then the police investigate. Examples include the following:

   ◆ Report by a victim of a robbery.
   ◆ Report by a victim of a sexual assault.
   ◆ Report by a wife of her husband's murder.

   After investigation, the police present an affidavit to the judge or magistrate and ask for an arrest warrant to be issued. If the judge or magistrate concludes probable cause exists, the warrant is issued and then executed by the police. This sequence, however, is subject to exceptions, particularly in cases where exigent (emergency) circumstances make it necessary for the police to take prompt action to prevent the suspect's escape.

2. *A warrant is needed if the suspect is in a private residence and there is no reason for an immediate arrest.* The police may not enter a private home to make a routine warrantless arrest (*Payton v. New York*, 445 U.S. 573 [1980]). In this case, after two days of intensive investigation, detectives assembled sufficient evidence to establish probable cause to believe that Payton had murdered the manager of a gas station. They went to Payton's apartment to arrest him without a warrant. The warrantless entry and arrest were authorized by New York law. They knocked on the metal door, and when there was no response, they summoned emergency assistance and then used crowbars to open the door and enter the apartment. No one was there, but in plain view was a .30-caliber shell casing that was seized and later admitted into evidence at Payton's murder trial.

   Payton v. New York (1980)

   Payton was convicted; he appealed, alleging that the Fourth Amendment requires police officers to obtain a warrant if making a felony arrest in a private residence when there is time to obtain a warrant. The Supreme Court agreed, saying that a warrant is needed in these types of cases (routine arrests in the absence of consent) and that state laws authorizing warrantless arrests in routine felony cases are unconstitutional. (See the Case Brief for more details on this case.)

3. *A warrant is needed in home entries for minor offenses.* In the case of a minor offense, a warrantless entry into a home to make an arrest is seldom justified. For example, suppose an officer suspects a person of driving while intoxicated, a nonjailable offense in the particular state. The officer goes to the suspect's home to make an arrest before the alcohol can dissipate from the suspect's body. The officer cannot enter the home without a warrant or consent. Given the state's relatively tolerant view of this offense, an interest in preserving the evidence cannot overcome the strong presumption against the warrantless invasion of homes. Thus, in determining whether there are exigent circumstances, a court must consider the seriousness of the offense (*Welsh v. Wisconsin*, 466 U.S. 740 [1984]). However, home entry in felony or misdemeanor cases is justified if there is valid consent or if state law or state court decisions allow it.

   Welsh v. Wisconsin (1984)

The Issuance of a Warrant

To secure the issuance of a warrant, a complaint (by the victim or a police officer) must be filed before a magistrate or judge showing probable cause for arrest of the accused. It must set forth facts showing that an offense has been committed and that the accused is responsible for it. If it appears to the magistrate from the complaint and accompanying documents or testimony that probable cause exists for the charges made against the accused, the magistrate issues an arrest warrant.

In most states, the issuance of arrest warrants is strictly a judicial function and must therefore be performed by a judge or judicial officer. The issuing party must also be "neutral and detached." However, some states hold that, because the requirement of probable cause is designed to be applied by laypeople (as when a police officer arrests a suspect without a warrant based on probable cause), a non-judicial officer such as a court clerk may properly issue warrants if empowered to do so by statute and if otherwise "neutral and detached." For example, the Court has decided that a municipal court clerk can issue an arrest warrant for municipal ordinance violations as long as such an issuance is authorized by state law (*Shadwick v. City of Tampa*, 407 U.S. 345 [1972]).

Shadwick v. City of Tampa (1972)

CASE BRIEF

Payton v. New York, 445 U.S. 573 (1980)

The Leading Case on Home Arrests

Facts: After two days of intensive investigation, New York City detectives had assembled sufficient evidence to establish probable cause to believe that Payton had murdered the manager of a gas station. Early the following day, six officers went to Payton's apartment intending to arrest him. They had not obtained a warrant. Although light and music emanated from the apartment, there was no response to their knock on the metal door. They summoned emergency assistance and, about thirty minutes later, used crowbars to break open the door and enter the apartment. No one was there. In plain view was a .30-caliber shell casing that was seized and later admitted into evidence at Payton's murder trial. Payton was convicted, and he appealed.

Issue or Issues: *Does the Fourth Amendment prohibit the police from making a nonconsensual entry into a suspect's home to make a routine felony arrest without a warrant? Yes.*

Decision: The case was remanded to the New York Court of Appeals for further proceeding not inconsistent with the Court's decision.

Holding: In the absence of consent, the police may not enter a suspect's home to make a routine felony arrest without a warrant.

Case Significance: The *Payton* case settled the issue of whether the police can enter a suspect's home and make a warrantless arrest in a routine felony case, meaning cases in which there is time to obtain a warrant. The practice was authorized by the state of New York and twenty-three other states at the time *Payton* was decided. These authorizations are now unconstitutional, and officers must obtain a warrant before entering a suspect's home to make a routine felony arrest.

Excerpts from the Opinion: Unreasonable searches or seizures conducted without any warrant at all are condemned by the plain language of the first clause of the Amendment. Almost a century ago, the Court stated in resounding terms that the principles reflected in the Amendment "reached farther than the concrete form" of the specific cases that gave it birth, and "apply to all invasions on the part of the government and its employees of the sanctity of a man's home and the privacies of life." Without pausing to consider whether that broad language may require some qualification, it is sufficient to note that the warrantless arrest of a person is a species of seizure required by the Amendment to be reasonable.

The simple language of the Amendment applies equally to seizures of persons and to seizures of property. Our analysis in this case may therefore properly commence with rules that have been well established in Fourth Amendment litigation involving tangible items. As the Court reiterated just a few years ago, the "physical entry of the home is the chief evil against which the wording of the Fourth Amendment is directed." And we have long adhered to the view that the warrant procedure minimizes the danger of needless intrusions of that sort.

It is a "basic principle of Fourth Amendment law" that searches and seizures inside a home without a warrant are presumptively unreasonable. Yet it is also well settled that objects such as weapons or contraband found in a public place may be seized by the police without a warrant. The seizure of property in plain view involves no invasion of privacy and is presumptively reasonable, assuming that there is probable cause to associate the property with criminal activity.

The term **neutral and detached magistrate** means that the issuing officer is not unalterably aligned with the police or prosecutor's position in the case. Several cases illustrate the meaning of this term:

neutral and detached magistrate
an issuing officer who is not unalterably aligned with the police or prosecutor's position in the case.

◆ A magistrate who receives a fee when issuing a warrant but not when denying one is not neutral and detached (*Connally v. Georgia*, 429 U.S. 245 [1977]).

◆ A magistrate who participates in the search to determine its scope lacks the requisite neutrality and detachment (*Lo-Ji Sales, Inc. v. New York*, 442 U.S. 319 [1979]).

◆ A state's chief investigator and prosecutor (state attorney general) is not neutral and detached, so any warrant issued by him or her is invalid (*Coolidge v. New Hampshire*, 403 U.S. 443 [1971]).

Connally v. Georgia (1977)

Lo-Ji Sales, Inc. v. New York (1979)

Coolidge v. New Hampshire (1971)

The warrant requirement assumes that the complaint or affidavit has been reviewed by a magistrate before it is issued. Therefore, pre-signed warrants, which are used in some jurisdictions, are of doubtful validity. Nonetheless, they continue to be used, primarily because their use has not been challenged in court.

The Contents of a Warrant

The contents of a warrant vary from state to state and are usually specified in that state's criminal procedure code. For example, California provides that the arrest warrant contain the following: the name of the person to be arrested, the crime allegedly committed, the time and date of the issuance of the warrant, provisions for bail, the jurisdiction where the warrant is issued, the duty of the officer to bring the person arrested before a magistrate, the signature of the judge, and the court that issued the warrant.[2] In contrast, for misdemeanor charges, Michigan requires that the warrant: be

HIGHLIGHT ▶ A Home Is a Person's Castle

"And the law of England has so particular and tender a regard to the immunity of a man's house, that it stiles it his castle, and will never suffer it to be violated with immunity. . . . For this reason no doors can in general be broken open to execute any civil process;

though, in criminal causes, the public safety supersedes the private."

Source: William Blackstone, *Commentaries on the Laws of England*.

directed to a law enforcement officer, order the officer to immediately arrest the accused and take the person, without unnecessary delay, before a magistrate of the judicial district in which the offense is charged to have been committed, and that the warrant, along with a proper return noted on the warrant, be delivered to the magistrate before whom the arrested person is taken.[3]

Laws in all the states obviously require that the defendant or suspect be named in the warrant. In cases, however, where the name is unknown to the police, state laws provide that the person be identified with reasonable certainty. A *John Doe warrant*— one in which only the name John Doe appears because the real name of the suspect is unknown to the police—is valid only if the requirement of being identified "with reasonable certainty" is present. Some jurisdictions allow the issuance of a John Doe warrant based on DNA identification even though the name of the suspect has not been ascertained. This practice enables the prosecutor to prevent the statute of limitations from running out on an offense.

The Service of a Warrant

An arrest warrant is directed to, and may be executed by, any peace officer in the jurisdiction. In some states, a properly designated private citizen can also serve a warrant. The rules for serving warrants within and outside of a state differ.

1. *Service within a state.* Inside the state of issuance, a warrant issued in one county or judicial district may be served by peace officers of any other county or district in which the accused is found. Some states, such as Texas and California, have statutes giving local police officers statewide power of arrest—thereby allowing the police officers of the county or district where the warrant was issued to make the arrest anywhere in the state. Even if statewide power of arrest is given, it is better, whenever possible, to inform local police agencies of activity within their jurisdiction as a matter of courtesy and to avoid jurisdictional misunderstanding.

2. *Service outside the state.* A warrant generally does not carry any authority beyond the territorial limits of the state in which it is issued. For example, an arrest cannot be made in Washington on the basis of a warrant issued in Missouri. There are exceptions, perhaps the most important of which is the hot (or fresh) pursuit exception, which authorizes peace officers from one state who enter another state in hot pursuit to arrest the suspect for a felony committed in the first state. Most states have adopted a uniform act authorizing hot pursuit service of a warrant. Another exception occurs when an in-state officer makes an arrest based on a "hit," which refers to the officer's finding, through a search of a national computerized database, that a warrant has been issued in another state for a person presently in the officer's state.

The Time of the Arrest

In general, felony arrests may be made at any time, day or night, but misdemeanor arrests are usually made during daylight hours. In some states, an arrest for any crime—felony or misdemeanor—can be made at any hour of the day or night.

The Possession and Expiration of a Warrant

The arresting officer does not need to have the arrest warrant in his or her possession at the time of the arrest as long as it is shown to the accused after the arrest if so requested. An arrest warrant should be executed without unreasonable delay. But unlike a search warrant, which must be served within a limited period of time, an arrest warrant does not expire until it is executed or withdrawn.

Other Legal Authorizations

The use of an arrest warrant is one way in which a person is taken into custody or held accountable by the courts. Other ways are the following:

- *Citation.* A **citation** is a writ from a court ordering a person to appear in court at a specified time. Statutes in many states authorize the use of a citation for less serious offenses, such as traffic violations. A citation means the offender does not have to be taken into custody for that offense at that time. In the event of the person's failure to appear at the time and date indicated, however, an arrest warrant may be issued.

- *Capias.* **Capias** is the general name for several types of writs that require an officer to take a defendant into custody. A capias is more generic than a bench warrant in that it is used to bring a person before the court for a variety of reasons, some of which are not necessarily related to a criminal case (as in cases of protecting a witness or a hearing judgment). It may also be issued when a defendant skips bail or is indicted by a grand jury if the defendant is not already in custody. In contrast, a bench warrant is more specific; it is usually issued to effect an arrest when a person has been found in contempt, when an indictment has been handed down, or when a witness disobeys a subpoena.

citation
a writ from a court ordering a person to appear in court at a specified time.

capias
the general name for several types of writs that require an officer to take a defendant into custody.

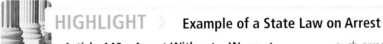

HIGHLIGHT > **Example of a State Law on Arrest**

Article 140—Arrest Without a Warrant

§ 140.05 Arrest Without a Warrant; in General.

A person who has committed or is believed to have committed an offense and who is at liberty within the state may, under circumstances prescribed in this article, be arrested for such offense although no warrant of arrest therefore has been issued and although no criminal action therefore has yet been commenced in any criminal court.

§140.15 Arrest Without a Warrant; When and How Made by Police Officer.

1. A police officer may arrest a person for an offense, pursuant to section 140.10, at any hour of any day or night.
2. The arresting police officer must inform such person of his authority and purpose and of the reason for

such arrest unless he encounters physical resistance, flight or other factors rendering such procedure impractical.

3. In order to effect such an arrest, such police officer may use such physical force as is justifiable pursuant to section 35.30 of the penal law.
4. In order to effect such an arrest, a police officer may enter premises in which he reasonably believes such person to be present, under the same circumstances and in the same manner as would be authorized, by the provisions of subdivisions four and five of section 120.80, if he were attempting to make such arrest pursuant to a warrant of arrest.

Source: New York State criminal procedure law.

ARRESTS WITHOUT A WARRANT

Although arrest warrants are preferred by the courts and desirable for purposes of protecting police from liability lawsuits, they are, in fact, seldom used in police work. About 95 percent of all arrests are made without a warrant. Police officers have a general power to arrest without a warrant in five situations:

◆ Felonies committed in the presence of officers.
◆ Misdemeanors committed in the presence of officers.
◆ Crimes committed in public places.
◆ When exigent (emergency) circumstances are present.
◆ When there is danger to the arresting officer.

Felonies Committed in the Presence of Officers

The authority to arrest for felonies committed in the presence of officers is generally based on old common law principles, which have since been enacted into law in various states. For example, suppose that an officer on patrol sees a robbery being committed. She can make the arrest without a warrant. (See Figure 6.3.) The term *in the presence of a police officer* refers to knowledge gained firsthand by the officer through any of his or her five senses—sight, hearing, smell, touch, or taste. Therefore, the police may make a warrantless arrest if probable cause is established by any of these means:

◆ *Sight.* The officer sees Fred stab Jim or Steve breaking into a residence.
◆ *Hearing.* The officer hears a shot or a cry for help from inside an apartment.
◆ *Smell.* The officer smells gasoline, gunpowder, gas fumes, or marijuana.
◆ *Touch.* The officer examines doors or windows in the dark or touches a car muffler or engine hood to determine if a motor vehicle has just been used.
◆ *Taste.* The officer tastes a white powder to identify it as sugar, salt, or something else. Taste is the least used of the five senses—and the least reliable.

Misdemeanors Committed in the Presence of Officers

The rule in most states is that misdemeanors committed in the presence of officers also give the police authority to make an arrest. Under the old common law, however, the police could not make an arrest if the misdemeanor was merely reported to them by a third party. In states that still observe this common law rule, the officer must obtain an arrest warrant or have the complaining party file a complaint, which can then lead to the issuance of a warrant or summons. However, this common law rule requiring a warrant for these types of cases is now subject to so many exceptions that police authority to arrest even for misdemeanors not committed in the presence of police officers has become the rule rather than the exception.

Crimes Committed in Public Places

United States v. Watson (1976)

The police are not required to obtain an arrest warrant before arresting a person in a public place, even if there is time and opportunity to do so, as long as the police are duly authorized to make the arrest by statute (*United States v. Watson,* 423 U.S. 411 [1976]).

This applies in both felonies and misdemeanors. In the *Watson* case, the Court noted that such authorization is given by federal law and "in almost all of the States in the form of express statutory authorization." The warrantless arrest is valid because a person in a public place has minimum protection under the Fourth Amendment.

When Exigent (Emergency) Circumstances Are Present

The term **exigent circumstances** has many meanings, as the following examples illustrate.

◆ *Example 1: Possibility of disappearance.* An officer is told by a reliable informant that he has just bought cocaine from a stranger in Apartment 23 at the corner of Main and Commerce and that the seller was getting ready to leave. Given the possibility of the suspect's disappearance, the officer can make the arrest without a warrant.

◆ *Example 2: Hot pursuit.* In cases of hot pursuit, when a suspect enters his or her own or another person's dwelling, an officer can follow and make the arrest without a warrant. In one case, police officers, acting without a search or arrest warrant, entered a house to arrest an armed robbery suspect who had been seen entering the place just minutes before. The Supreme Court upheld the warrantless entry and search as reasonable because to delay the entry would have allowed the suspect time to escape (*Warden v. Hayden*, 387 U.S. 294 [1967]).

> **exigent circumstances**
> emergency circumstances that make obtaining a warrant impractical, useless, dangerous, or unnecessary, and that justify warrantless arrests or entries into homes or premises.

The term *hot pursuit* denotes some kind of chase, but it need not be a lengthy one. The fact that the pursuit ended almost as soon as it began does not render it any less a hot pursuit sufficient to justify an entry without warrant into a suspect's house. The following factors are relevant in a fleeing-suspect case: (1) the seriousness of the offense committed, (2) the officer's belief that the suspect was armed, and (3) the likelihood that the suspect might escape if police did not act quickly (*United States v. Williams*, 612 F.2d 735 [3rd Cir. 1979]).

United States v. Williams (1979)

In sum, exigent circumstances are those emergency circumstances that make obtaining a warrant impractical, useless, dangerous, or unnecessary, and that justify warrantless arrests or entries into homes or premises.

When There Is Danger to the Officer

In *Warden v. Hayden*, 387 U.S. 294 (1967), the Court said, "The Fourth Amendment does not require officers to delay in the course of an investigation if to do so would gravely endanger their lives or the lives of others." This safety consideration has been extended by lower courts to include the safety of informants and the public.

Warden v. Hayden (1967)

Be aware, however, that the rules on arrests without a warrant are generally based on common law and court decisions. They can be, and often are, superseded by laws enacted by state legislatures that either limit or expand the power of the officer to make an arrest without a warrant. The state laws govern the conduct of the police in that particular jurisdiction—unless they are declared unconstitutional by the courts.

Entering a Home Without a Warrant

The situations described in the preceding sections all involved arrests made without a warrant. An issue related to arrest is: May an officer enter a home without a warrant?

The Court says yes, in some situations. In one case, the Court held that police may enter a home without a warrant when "they have an objectively reasonable basis for believing that an occupant is seriously injured or imminently threatened with such injury" (*Brigham City, Utah v. Stuart*, 547 U.S. 47 [2006]). In this case, officers responded to a call about a loud party at a residence. Upon arrival, they heard shouting from inside the residence. They also saw two juveniles drinking beer in the backyard. They went to the backyard and saw, through a screen door and window, a fight taking place in the kitchen involving four adults and a juvenile. The officers opened the screen door, announced their presence, and entered the kitchen. They arrested the adults involved in the fight and subsequently charged them with contributing to the delinquency of a minor, disorderly conduct, and intoxication. The defendants claimed that police entry was illegal because they did not have a warrant. The Court disagreed, saying that "law enforcement officers may enter a home without a warrant to render emergency assistance to an injured occupant or to protect an occupant from imminent injury."

Brigham City, Utah v. Stuart (2006)

WHAT THE POLICE CAN DO AFTER AN ARREST

Arrest is a significant part of the criminal justice process—for both the suspect and the police officer. For the suspect, the arrest signifies the start of a deprivation of freedom that can last (if the suspect is convicted) until the sentence has been served. For the police, it sets in motion certain procedures that must be followed for the arrestee to be processed properly. Some of the things an officer can do after an arrest, according to court decisions, include the following:

- ◆ Police can search the arrestee, including a strip search, upon admittance to a detention facility.
- ◆ Police can search the area of immediate control.
- ◆ Police can search the passenger compartment of a motor vehicle.
- ◆ Police can use handcuffs.
- ◆ Police can monitor the arrestee's movements.
- ◆ Police can search the arrestee at the place of detention.
- ◆ Police can collect a DNA sample from the arrestee

All of the preceding situations are discussed next.

Police Can Search the Arrestee, Including a Strip Search

After an arrest, the police may automatically search the arrested person regardless of the offense for which the person has been arrested (*United States v. Robinson*, 414 U.S. 218 [1973]). In *Robinson*, the Court said that a "custodial arrest of a suspect based on probable cause is a reasonable intrusion under the Fourth Amendment; that intrusion being lawful, a search incident to the arrest requires no additional justification."

United States v. Robinson (1973)

The "full body search" rule in *Robinson* applies to all kinds of arrests—whether the suspect is arrested for a brutal murder or for shoplifting. The rule is designed to protect the police and prevent the destruction of evidence. For a long time, however, authorization to body search did not authorize the more intrusive strip or body-cavity searches when the suspect is placed in jail or a detention facility. Courts were split on this issue, but in general strip searches were valid only if there was something to justify it, such as if the police have reasonable suspicion that the suspect may have hidden drugs in his or her cavities. This changed, however, with the Court's recent 5-to-4 decision in *Florence v. Board of Chosen Freeholders of the County of Burlington* (566 U.S. --- [2012]).

Florence v. Board of Chosen Freeholders of the County of Burlington (2012)

In *Florence*, the Court held that strip searches are constitutional for any type of arrest and detention in jails or other detention facilities. In this case, Albert Florence was arrested in New Jersey in 2005, after his wife was pulled over for speeding. He was a passenger in the car which was driven by his wife. A records search revealed that Florence had an outstanding warrant for an unpaid fine. That information, however, was incorrect as the fine had, in fact, been paid. Florence was held for six days in two jails in New Jersey where he was strip-searched in each jail. He later challenged the validity of the strip searches, saying there was no justification for them. The Court disagreed, holding that every detainee who will be admitted to the general population may be required to undergo a strip search, to allow jails to discover weapons or contraband that might be smuggled into the jail.

This decision alters the landscape of what can happen after an arrest of suspects. About 13 million people are admitted each year to the nation's jails. Prior to the decision, strip searches and other more invasive forms of search were prohibited in some states, and courts were divided on the constitutionality of strip searches in the absence of reasonable suspicion that such searches would yield contraband. In sum, officers may now conduct a strip search before placing a person in jail, prison, or other detention facility even if there is no reasonable suspicion that the strip search might yield drugs or other contraband.

Police Can Search the Area of Immediate Control

Once a lawful arrest has been made, the police may search the area within the suspect's immediate control (sometimes known in police lingo as the "grab" or "lunge" area), meaning the area within which the suspect may grab a weapon or destroy evidence (*Chimel v. California*, 395 U.S. 752 [1969]). How far from the suspect does the "area within immediate control" extend? The Court has not set clear limits. In *Chimel*, the Court defined the allowable area of search as follows:

Chimel v. California (1969)

> When an arrest is made, it is reasonable for the arresting officer to search the person arrested in order to remove any weapons that the latter might seek to use in order to resist arrest or effect his escape. . . . In addition, it is entirely reasonable for the arresting officer to search for and seize any evidence on the arrestee's person in order to prevent its concealment or destruction. And the area into which an arrestee might reach in order to grab a weapon or evidentiary items must, of course, be governed by a like rule.

The most limited (and most accurate) interpretation of the phrase *area into which an arrestee might reach* is that the search is limited to the person's wingspan, meaning the area covered by the spread of the suspect's arms and hands. However, a number of courts have permitted the police to search areas in a residence that are beyond a defendant's reach even without a warrant if: (1) there is some type of emergency requiring immediate action that cannot await the preparation of a search warrant (such as possible destruction of evidence), and (2) the search is focused on a predetermined target (such as narcotics in a particular dresser drawer), rather than being a general exploratory search. In one case, an accused was sitting on a bed at the time of her arrest; the area underneath her bed was deemed to be within her reach. In another case, the search of a kitchen shelf six feet away from the arrestee was considered by the court as a search incident to an arrest, although an officer stood between the arrestee (who was being arrested for forgery) and the shelf while the arrest was being made. In sum, the "grab" area is defined on a case-by-case basis.

The Court has also held that a search incident to arrest is valid only if it is "substantially contemporaneous with the arrest and is confined to the immediate vicinity of the arrest" (*Vale v. Louisiana*, 399 U.S. 30 [1970]). If the search goes beyond the area of immediate control, the officer must obtain a search warrant.

Police Can Search the Passenger Compartment of a Motor Vehicle

New York v. Belton (1981)

The Court has held that, when the police have made a lawful custodial arrest of the occupant of a car, they may, incident to that arrest, search the car's entire passenger compartment (front and back seats) and open any containers found therein (*New York v. Belton*, 453 U.S. 454 [1981]). However, the Court has recently limited searches of the passenger compartment incident to arrest in *Arizona v. Gant* (556 U.S. 332 [2009]). (This case is discussed in detail in Chapter 7.)

Police Can Use Handcuffs

The use of handcuffs in arrests is either governed by departmental written policy or unwritten departmental practice. For example, the General Order of the Houston Police Department has this policy: "All persons under arrest will be properly handcuffed behind the back prior to being thoroughly searched and will remain handcuffed while being transported in any police vehicle."[4] The Court has not provided guidance on this issue, and there are no authoritative court decisions prohibiting or requiring it. The matter is left to agency policy or practice. Police training, however, either requires or strongly encourages its use. Officer safety, public safety, and making escape difficult are the main justifications for police departments requiring the use of handcuffs.

Police Can Monitor the Arrestee's Movement

The police may accompany an arrested person into his or her residence after a lawful arrest if they allow the arrestee to go there before being transported to the police station. For example, suppose Frank is arrested by virtue of an arrest warrant. After the arrest, Frank asks permission to go to his apartment to inform his wife and pick up some things he will need in jail. The officer may allow Frank to do that, but the movements of the arrestee can be monitored. In one case, the Supreme Court said, "It is not unreasonable under the Fourth Amendment for a police officer, as a matter of routine, to monitor the movements of an arrested person, as his judgment dictates, following an arrest. The officer's need to ensure his own safety—as well as the integrity of the arrest—is compelling" (*Washington v. Chrisman*, 455 U.S. 1 [1982]). The Court held that the officer is allowed to remain with the arrestee at all times after the arrest.

Washington v. Chrisman (1982)

Police Can Search the Arrestee at the Place of Detention

Once brought to the place of detention (usually either a jail or a police lockup), the arrestee may be subjected to a complete search of his or her person if this was not done during the arrest. This procedure is valid even in the absence of probable cause to search. The justification for the search of an arrestee's person on arrival at the station is that it is simply an inventory incidental to being booked in jail.

The inventory, which is a search under the Fourth Amendment, has these legitimate objectives: (1) to protect the arrestee's property while he or she is in jail, (2) to protect the police from groundless claims that they have not adequately safeguarded the defendant's property, (3) to safeguard the detention facility by preventing the introduction of weapons or contraband, and (4) to ascertain or verify the identity of the person arrested. Such searches may include the individual's wallet or other personal property. This rule that a routine inventory search is lawful applies only when the prisoner is to be jailed. If the suspect is brought in merely to be booked and then released, an inventory search is not appropriate.

Police Can Collect a DNA Sample

Police officers may collect a DNA sample from an arrestee. In *Maryland v. King*, 560 U.S. --- (2013), the Court recently held that it is constitutional to take DNA samples from felony arrestees who are booked on serious charges, because the collection and analysis of DNA serves a legitimate government interest, that of accurately identifying arrestees, and the insertion of a swab inside the arrestee's mouth is a minimal intrusion. So long as such DNA collection and analysis is performed solely for identification purpose and does not provide any other private medical information about the individual, it is considered a routine booking procedure

Maryland v. King (2013)

WHAT THE POLICE CANNOT DO DURING AN ARREST

There are many actions the police cannot take during an arrest, including the following:

◆ Police cannot enter a third-party residence, except in exigent circumstances
◆ Police cannot conduct a warrantless sweep
◆ Police cannot invite the media to ride along

Let us look at each of these prohibitions in turn.

Police Cannot Enter Third-Party Residences

In the absence of exigent circumstances, police officers executing an arrest warrant may not search for the person named in the warrant in the home of a third party without first obtaining a separate search warrant to enter the home. For example, in *Steagald v. United States*, 451 U.S. 204 (1981), federal agents learned from an informant that a federal fugitive could probably be found at a certain address. They procured a warrant for his arrest, but the warrant did not mention the address. Armed with the arrest warrant, the agents went to the address, which was the residence of a third party. The Court held that the arrest warrant could not be used as a legal authority to enter the home of a person other than the person named in the warrant.

Steagald v. United States (1981)

In *Minnesota v. Olson*, 495 U.S. 91 (1990), the Court said that a warrantless, nonconsensual entry of a residence to arrest an overnight guest was not justified by exigent circumstances and therefore violated the Fourth Amendment. In this case, the police

Minnesota v. Olson (1990)

suspected a man named Olson of being the driver of a getaway car used in a robbery and murder. The police arrested the suspected murderer and recovered the murder weapon. They then surrounded the home of two women with whom they believed Olson had been staying. Without seeking permission and with weapons drawn, they entered the home and found Olson hiding in a closet. They arrested him, and he implicated himself in the crime. On appeal, Olson sought to exclude his statement, saying that there were no exigent circumstances to justify the warrantless entry. The Court agreed, saying that Olson's status as an overnight guest was sufficient to show that he had a reasonable expectation of privacy in the home. The Court further said that there were no exigent circumstances justifying the warrantless entry, so the statement could not be admitted in court.

Police Cannot Conduct a Warrantless Protective Sweep Unless Justified

Maryland v. Buie (1990)

The practice of warrantless **protective sweeps** (where the police look at rooms or places in the house other than where the arrest takes place) was authorized by the Court in *Maryland v. Buie*, 494 U.S. 325 (1990), as long as the sweep is justified. In this case, police officers obtained and executed arrest warrants for Buie and an accomplice in connection with an armed robbery. On reaching Buie's house, the officers went through the first and second floors. One of the officers watched the basement so that no one would surprise the other officers. This officer shouted into the basement and ordered anyone there to come out. Buie emerged from the basement and was placed under arrest. Another officer then entered the basement to see if anyone else was there. Once in the basement, the officer noticed in plain view a red running suit similar to the one worn by one of the suspects in the robbery. The running suit was admitted into evidence at Buie's trial over his objection, and he was convicted of robbery with the use of a deadly weapon.

Buie challenged the legality of the protective sweep (which led to the discovery of the evidence) on appeal. The Court rejected Buie's challenge, saying that "[t]he Fourth Amendment permits a properly limited protective sweep in conjunction with an in-home arrest *when the searching officer possesses a reasonable belief based on specific and articulable facts that the area to be swept harbors an individual posing a danger to those on the arrest scene*" (emphasis added). This means that protective sweeps when making arrests are not always valid; a search is valid only if the searching officer can justify it "based on specific and articulable facts that the area to be swept harbors an individual posing a danger to those on the arrest scene." In the absence of such justification, a protective sweep is invalid.

Police Cannot Invite the Media to "Ride Along"

Wilson v. Layne (1999)

The Court has held that the practice of media ride-alongs violates a suspect's Fourth Amendment rights and is therefore unconstitutional (*Wilson v. Layne*, 526 U.S. 603 [1999]). In this case, federal marshals and local sheriff's deputies invited a newspaper reporter and a photographer to accompany them while executing a warrant to arrest the Wilsons' son in their home. The early-morning entry led to a confrontation with the Wilsons. A protective sweep revealed that the son was not in the house. The reporters (who did not participate in executing the warrant) photographed the incident, but the newspaper never published the photographs.

The Wilsons sued, claiming a violation of their Fourth Amendment rights. Balancing the petitioners' right to privacy and the benefits of a media ride-along, the Court said, "Surely the possibility of good public relations for the police is simply not enough, standing alone, to justify the ride-along into a private home. And even the need for accurate reporting on police issues in general bears no direct relation to the constitutional justification for the police intrusion into a home in order to execute a felony arrest warrant."

KNOCK-AND-ANNOUNCE IS REQUIRED BY THE CONSTITUTION, BUT WITH EXCEPTIONS

The Constitution requires that the police must announce their presence and purpose before breaking into a dwelling. There are exceptions to this requirement, however. This section looks at the general rule and the exceptions.

The General Rule

Federal and state statutes require that an officer making an arrest or executing a search warrant announce his or her presence, purpose and authority before breaking into a dwelling. The idea is to enable voluntary compliance by the suspect and avoid violence. Breaking into the premises without first complying with the knock-and-announce requirement may or may not invalidate the entry and any resulting search, depending on the law or court decisions in the state. Some states invalidate the entry and resulting search; others do not. The Court has addressed the issue of whether the knock-and-announce rule is required by the Constitution. The Court said that the Constitution requires an announcement but not in all cases, and that violation of the rule does not require exclusion of the evidence seized after the unlawful entry.

In *Wilson v. Arkansas*, 514 U.S. 927 (1995), police officers obtained an arrest warrant for the suspect and a search warrant for her home. At Wilson's residence, the officers identified themselves as they entered the home through an unlocked door and stated that they had a warrant. They did not, however, knock-and-announce, because Arkansas law did not require it. The police seized drugs, a gun, and some ammunition. Tried and convicted of violating state drug laws, Wilson moved to suppress the evidence, saying that knock-and-announce was required by the Fourth Amendment in all cases.

Wilson v. Arkansas (1995)

In a unanimous opinion, the Court ruled that the "knock-and-announce common law principle is part of the Fourth Amendment's requirement that searches and seizures be reasonable." It quickly added, however, that this did not mean that every entry must be preceded by an announcement, recognizing that "the common law principle of announcement was never stated as an inflexible rule requiring announcement under all circumstances." In essence, the Court held that, although knock-and-announce is part of the requirement of reasonableness in searches and seizures, it is not a rigid rule and is subject to exceptions based on law enforcement interests. Such "reasonableness" need only be based on reasonable suspicion, not on probable cause.

The Exceptions

The Court in *Wilson* did not enumerate the legally acceptable exceptions to the knock-and-announce rule, leaving that determination for another day. There are cases where, because of exigent circumstances, an announcement is not required or necessary because of officer or third-person safety or to preserve evidence. The usual instances are the following:

◆ When announcing presents a significant threat of danger to the officers—for example, when the police are serving a warrant on a fugitive who is armed and dangerous.

◆ When there is danger that contraband or other property sought might be destroyed. Some states permit a magistrate to issue so-called "no-knock" search warrants, particularly in drug cases. They authorize entry without announcement because otherwise the evidence might be destroyed.

◆ When officers reasonably believe that persons within the premises are in imminent peril of bodily harm, as when the police hear a scream for help from inside a residence. In *Brigham City, Utah v. Stuart,* 547 U.S. 47 (2006), the Court also held that the police may enter a residence without a warrant if they reasonably believe an occupant is, or is about to be, seriously injured.

◆ When people within are reasonably believed to be escaping because they are aware of the presence of the police.

◆ When the person to be arrested is in the process of committing the crime.

Be aware, however, that some states require officers to knock-and-announce without exception. In these states, the above exceptions do not apply.

Exceptions to the announcement requirement are governed by law, court decisions, and agency regulations and so vary from state to state. The Court has ruled, however, that **blanket exceptions**—exceptions that apply to a certain type of case regardless of circumstances—are not allowed in drug-dealing cases even by judicial authorization (*Richards v. Wisconsin,* 520 U.S. 385 [1997]).

In *Richards,* a judge in Wisconsin created a rule that did away with the knock-and-announce requirement in all warrants to search for evidence involving drugs. The justification for the rule was that drug-dealing cases frequently involved threats of physical violence or possible destruction of evidence anyway, so there was no need to knock-and-announce. The Supreme Court disagreed, saying that the Fourth Amendment does not allow a bright-line exception to the knock-and-announce requirement in cases involving drug dealing. They added that even in these cases, exceptions to the requirement must be made on a case-by-case basis, and depend on what the police know at the time they attempt entry. It is safe to say that if the Court is disinclined to allow a blanket exception in drug cases, it is hard to imagine what types of cases would justify a blanket exception.

How Long Must the Police Wait before Entering?

While the Court has ruled that knock-and-announce is constitutionally required, it has not set a length of time that officers must wait before entering. It depends on whether the wait was reasonable under the circumstances of that entry. This principle was set in *United States v. Banks,* 550 U.S. 31 (2003). In this case, police officers had an arrest warrant for Lashawn Banks, a suspected drug dealer. They knocked

blanket exceptions
exceptions that apply to a certain type of case regardless of circumstances

Richards v. Wisconsin (1997)

MYTH vs. REALITY

MYTH Police may enter a dwelling without knocking anytime they suspect drugs are inside.

FACT Police must knock and announce unless they have reasonable suspicion that the drugs inside the house will be destroyed, based on the circumstances when they seek to enter the dwelling.

United States v. Banks (2003)

loudly on his apartment door and waited for about 20 seconds. Banks did not come to the door and so the officers broke the door down and entered. Banks was at that time in the shower. He later testified that he heard nothing until he heard his door crash. The police recovered crack cocaine, weapons, and other evidence of drug dealing. Banks filed a motion to suppress the evidence, claiming the entry to be unlawful because the officers waited "for an unreasonably short time before forcing entry," and therefore violated his Fourth Amendment right. On appeal, the Court, in a unanimous decision, disagreed, saying that the actions of the officers were reasonable. The Court said that, as in cases involving the use of force, "reasonableness must be judged from the perspective of a reasonable officer on the scene, rather than with the 20/20 vision of hindsight." The Court concluded that the 20-second wait was reasonable because a longer wait could have resulted in the destruction of evidence.

It must be noted that the requirement and rules for knock-and-announce are the same in arrests (this chapter) and in searches and seizures of things (Chapter 7). The rules are discussed in detail in this chapter; they are summarized in Chapter 7.

OTHER ARREST ISSUES

There are other arrest issues important for law enforcement officers to know. Among these are:

◆ Can the police detain a suspect while obtaining a warrant?
◆ Can the police arrest for traffic violations or petty offenses?
◆ Are arrests for offenses not punishable by prison or jail time valid?
◆ Are citizen's arrests valid?

These issues are discussed next.

HIGHLIGHT › **How Long Must the Police Wait before Entering?**

"On the record here, what matters is the opportunity to get rid of cocaine, which a prudent dealer will keep near a commode or kitchen sink. The significant circumstances include the arrival of the police during the day, when anyone inside would probably have been up and around, and the sufficiency of 15 to 20 seconds for getting to the bathroom or the kitchen to start flushing cocaine down the drain. That is, when circumstances are exigent because a pusher may be near the point of putting his drugs beyond reach. It is imminent disposal, not travel time to the entrance, that governs when the police may reasonably enter; since the bathroom and kitchen are usually in the interior of a dwelling, not the front hall, there is no reason generally to peg the travel time to the location of the door, and no reliable basis for giving the proprietor of a mansion a longer wait than the resident of a bungalow, or an apartment. . . . And 15 to 20 seconds does not seem an unrealistic guess about the time someone would need to get in a position to rid his quarters or cocaine."

Source: *United States v. Banks*, 540 U.S. 31 (2003).

Can the Police Detain a Suspect while Obtaining a Warrant?

Illinois v. McArthur (2001)

The Court has held that, under exigent circumstances and where there is a need to preserve evidence until a warrant can be obtained, the police may temporarily restrain a suspect's movements without violating his or her Fourth Amendment right (*Illinois v. McArthur*, 531 U.S. 326 [2001]).

In *Illinois v. McArthur*, a woman asked police officers to accompany her to the trailer where she lived with her husband, McArthur, while she removed her belongings. The woman went inside, where McArthur was, while the officers waited outside. When the woman came out, she told the officers that McArthur had drugs in the trailer. This established probable cause. The officers knocked and asked permission to search the trailer, which McArthur denied. One officer then left to obtain a warrant. When McArthur stepped onto his porch, the officer prevented him from reentering his trailer. McArthur did reenter the trailer on three occasions, but the officer stood in the doorway and observed him. When the other officer returned with a warrant, they searched the trailer and found drugs and drug paraphernalia.

On appeal, the Court ruled that, under exigent circumstances and where there is a need to preserve evidence until the police obtain a warrant, they may temporarily restrain a suspect without violating his or her Fourth Amendment rights. The minimal nature of the intrusion and the law enforcement interest involved justified the brief seizure.

Can the Police Arrest for Traffic Violations or Petty Offenses?

Most states classify offenses as either felonies or misdemeanors. Some states have additional categories such as traffic offenses, violations, and petty offenses. City or municipal ordinances may create additional offenses. Penalties vary, as do permissible police actions after detention. In some states, an arrest is required in some traffic offenses; in others, an arrest is left to the officer's discretion. Other jurisdictions do not authorize any arrest at all; issuing citations is the only allowable procedure.

Are Arrests for Offenses Not Punishable by Prison or Jail Time Valid?

For a long time it was not clear whether the police could constitutionally arrest an offender a for minor offense not punishable by prison or jail time. Arrest for minor and nonjailable offenses is currently authorized in all fifty states and the District of Columbia. The issue was settled by the Court, however, in the case of *Atwater v. City of Lago Vista*, 532 U.S. 318 (2001), in which the Court said that such arrests are constitutional.

Atwater v. City of Lago Vista (2001)

In this case Atwater, who was driving her children home from school, was arrested by a police officer for her child not wearing a seat belt. The offense was punishable under Texas law by a fine of not more than $50. Atwater pleaded no contest and paid the $50 fine but later challenged the law, claiming it violated her Fourth Amendment right against unreasonable searches and seizures, and was not authorized under common law. On appeal, the Court held that the Fourth Amendment does not prohibit a warrantless arrest for a minor criminal offense that is punishable only by a fine. (Read the Case Brief to learn more about the *Atwater* case.)

The Leading Case on Whether the Police Can Arrest Suspects on Nonjailable Offenses

Facts: At the time of the incident, Texas law required all front-seat passengers to wear a seat belt, a crime punishable by a fine of not more than $50. The law also authorized a police officer to arrest without a warrant for a violation of the law, although the police may choose to merely issue a citation. Atwater was driving a vehicle with her two young children in the front seat; no one was wearing a seat belt. An officer observed the violation and stopped Atwater—telling her as he approached the vehicle that she was going to jail. Following the release of Atwater's children to a neighbor, the officer handcuffed Atwater, placed her in his police car, and took her to the police station, where she was made to remove her shoes, jewelry, and eyeglasses and empty her pockets. Officers later took her mug shot and placed her in a cell for about an hour. She was then taken before a magistrate and released on bond. She later pleaded no contest and paid a $50 fine. Atwater later sued the City of Lago Vista under 42 U.S.C. § 1983, alleging that the officer violated her Fourth Amendment rights by arresting her for a seat belt violation without a warrant. The United States Court of Appeals for the Fifth Circuit affirmed a grant of summary judgment in favor of the city. Atwater filed a petition for appeal to the U.S. Supreme Court, which was granted.

Issue or Issues: *Does the Fourth Amendment forbid a warrantless arrest for a minor criminal offense punishable only by a fine?* No.

Decision: The decision of the Fifth Circuit Court of Appeals was affirmed.

Holding: The Fourth Amendment does not forbid a warrantless arrest for a minor criminal offense, such as a misdemeanor seat belt violation, punishable only by a fine.

Case Significance: This case settles an issue of concern to the police: whether the police can arrest persons who violate laws or ordinances that are not punishable with prison or jail time. At present, all fifty states and the District of Columbia have laws authorizing such warrantless arrests. Atwater maintained that such arrests were not authorized at common law and that the history and intent of the framers of the Constitution did not allow such arrests.

The Court disagreed, saying that it was unclear whether such arrests were authorized under common law or that the framers of the Fourth Amendment were concerned about warrantless arrests by local constables and other peace officers. The Court then said: "We simply cannot conclude that the Fourth Amendment, as originally understood, forbade peace officers to arrest without warrant for misdemeanors not amounting to or involving breach of the peace." Given these arguments, the Court held that warrantless arrests for nonjailable offenses are constitutional.

Excerpts from the Opinion: "The Court rejects Atwater's request to mint a new rule of constitutional law forbidding custodial arrest, even upon probable cause, when conviction could not ultimately carry any jail time and the government can show no compelling need for immediate detention. She reasons that, when historical practice fails to speak conclusively to a Fourth Amendment claim, courts must strike a current balance between individual and societal interests by subjecting particular contemporary circumstances to traditional standards of reasonableness. Atwater might well prevail under a rule derived exclusively to address the uncontested facts of her case, since her claim to live free of pointless indignity and confinement clearly outweighs anything the City can raise against it specific to her. However, the Court has traditionally recognized that a responsible Fourth Amendment balance is not well served by standards requiring sensitive, case-by-case determinations of government need, lest every discretionary judgment in the field be converted into an occasion for constitutional review. Complications arise the moment consideration is given the possible applications of the several criteria Atwater proposes for drawing a line between minor crimes with limited arrest authority and others not so restricted. The assertion that these difficulties could be alleviated simply by requiring police in doubt not to arrest is unavailing because, first, such a tiebreaker would in practice amount to a constitutionally inappropriate least-restrictive-alternative limitation, and, second, whatever guidance the tiebreaker might give would come at the price of a systematic disincentive to arrest in situations where even Atwater concedes arresting would serve an important societal interest. That warrantless misdemeanor arrests do not demand the constitutional attention Atwater seeks is indicated by a number of factors, including that the law has never jelled the way Atwater would have it; that anyone arrested without formal process is entitled to a magistrate's review of probable cause within 48 hours; that many jurisdictions have chosen to impose more restrictive safeguards through statutes limiting warrantless arrests for minor offenses; that it is in the police's interest to limit such arrests, which carry costs too great to incur without good reason; and that, under current doctrine, the preference for categorical treatment of Fourth Amendment claims gives way to individualized review when a defendant makes a colorable argument that an arrest, with or without a warrant, was conducted in an extraordinary manner, unusually harmful to his privacy or physical interests. The upshot of all these influences, combined with the good sense (and, failing that, the political accountability) of most local lawmakers and peace officers, is a dearth of horribles demanding redress. Thus, the probable cause standard applies to all arrests, without the need to balance the interests and circumstances involved in particular situations. An officer may arrest an individual without violating the Fourth Amendment if there is probable cause to believe that the offender has committed even a very minor criminal offense in the officer's presence.

Are Citizen's Arrests Valid?

citizen's arrest
an arrest made by a citizen or nonlaw enforcement personnel without a warrant

People v. Taylor (1990)

Many state statutes authorize a **citizen's arrest**—an arrest made by a citizen without a warrant. It is a practice that had its beginnings in common law, and which continues to this day. In the words of one court, "There have been citizen arrests for as long as there have been public police—indeed much longer (*People v. Taylor*, 222 Cal.App.3rd 612 [1990]).

At common law, citizen's arrests were limited to situations where the following are present: (1) a felony (or a misdemeanor involving a breach of the peace) has been committed, and (2) the citizen has probable cause to believe that the person arrested committed the crime. This common law rule has been modified by legislation in many states. One problem with the common law authorization of citizen's arrests is that the definition of "breach of the peace" varies from one state to another and is usually unclear even to persons knowledgeable in the law. In essence, at present what is allowed or not allowed in citizen's arrests is governed by state law and court decisions and varies from state to state.

The citizen who makes a citizen's arrest runs three risks (assuming that state's statute is based on common law): (1) the crime committed may not be in the category of a felony; (2) if it is a misdemeanor, that it does not constitute a breach of the peace; and (3) if the arrest turns out to be illegal, the citizen is exposed to civil liability under state tort law for false imprisonment and to criminal liabilities.

In general, the person making a citizen's arrest is allowed to use as much reasonable force as police officers could use making a similar arrest. Should the citizen making the arrest use more force than is allowed, serious legal consequences may result.

posse comitatus
the common law authority of a police officer to compel a person to assist in keeping the peace or arresting a felon.

Some states provide by law that police officers, when making an arrest, may enlist the aid of citizens and that citizens are obliged to respond. This is not a citizen's arrest but an arrest in aid of the police. At common law this was known as the posse comitatus. **Posse comitatus** is the common law authority of a police officer to compel any able-bodied person to assist in keeping the peace or arresting a felon. Arrests by police officers with probable cause outside their territorial jurisdiction are valid but they are in the category of citizen's arrests and are therefore subject to the above limitations.

USE OF FORCE DURING AN ARREST

This section addresses the issues surrounding the use of force during an arrest, including the factors that govern the use of force by police, the difference between nondeadly and deadly force, and the rules surrounding their use.

What Governs Police Use of Force?

The use of force, nondeadly or deadly, is governed by: (1) the Constitution of the United States, particularly the due process clause of the Fourteenth Amendment; (2) state law, usually the Penal Code or Code of Criminal Procedure, which defines when an officer may or may not legally use force; (3) judicial decisions, if any, specifying what type of force can be used and when; and, most important, (4) departmental or agency rules.

Officers must be familiar with all of these sources but particularly with their police department's rules on the use of force. Departmental rules are often more limiting than state law and are binding on the officer, regardless of what state law allows. For example, suppose the law of the state of California provides that deadly force may be used to prevent the escape of a jail inmate. In contrast, assume that the policy of the San Francisco Police Department limits the use of deadly force only to cases of self-defense by the police and therefore precludes the use of deadly force to prevent jail escapes. The departmental policy is binding on San Francisco police officers. Violation of departmental policy makes the act punishable even if the use of force is authorized by the state law.

In contrast, assume that departmental policy allows the officer to use deadly force to prevent escapes, but state law prohibits it. In this case, state law prevails over departmental policy. The general rule on use of force is that the more limiting rule binds the police officer.

What the Court Has Ruled in General about Police Use of Force

Graham v. Conner (1989)

One risk to which an officer is exposed when using force is the possibility of a lawsuit by the person arrested, claiming damages for excessive use of force. *Graham v. Conner* (490 US. 396 [1989]) is the leading case on police civil liability for excessive use of force. In *Graham,* an officer saw the suspect and a friend hastily enter and leave a store. In reality, Graham, a diabetic, had asked Berry, a friend, to drive him to a convenience store to buy orange juice, which he needed to control his condition. Seeing a long line in the store, Graham asked Berry to drive him to a friend's house instead. Based on his suspicion, the officer made an investigative stop and ordered Graham and Berry to wait while he ascertained what happened in the store. Meantime, other officers arrived and an encounter ensued in which Graham sustained multiple injuries. He was released when the officer learned that nothing had happened in the store. Graham sued, claiming his Fourth Amendment right against unreasonable search and seizure was violated.

On appeal, the Court ruled that police officers may be held liable under the Constitution and federal law for using excessive force. Such liability, however must be based on the standard of "objective reasonableness." The Court said that the reasonableness of a particular use of force must be judged from the perspective of "a reasonable officer on the scene," rather than "with the 20/20 vision of hindsight." The Court added, "Not every push or shove, even if it may later seem unnecessary in the peace of a judge's chamber," violates the Fourth Amendment. It concluded by saying, "The calculus of reasonableness must embody allowance for the fact that police officers are often forced to make split-second judgments—in circumstances that are tense, uncertain and rapidly evolving—about the amount of force that is necessary in a particular situation." In sum, reasonableness is the standard by which police use of force is judged.

Nondeadly versus Deadly Force

Despite the preceding rules, or perhaps because of them, the law on the use of force during an arrest can be confusing unless viewed in a proper legal framework. That framework is this: There are two kinds of force in police work—nondeadly force and deadly force. **Nondeadly force** is force that, when used, is not likely to result in serious bodily injury or death. In contrast, **deadly force** is force that, when used, poses a high risk of death or serious injury to its human target, regardless of whether or not death, serious injury, or any harm actually occurs. Examples of deadly force are the use of firearms, knives, and lead pipes. Use of nightsticks and chokeholds are considered by some courts to be deadly force, but much depends on how they are used. It is important to know that these two types of force in policing are governed by very different rules for purposes of legal liabilities.

The Use of Nondeadly Force

The rule is that nondeadly force may be used as long as it is *reasonable force*. One of the largest police departments in the country words its general policy on use of force this way: "All reasonable means may be used to effect an arrest. Officers will use only that amount of force that is necessary to secure the arrest and detention of suspects" (General Order No. 500-01: Houston Police Department, March 12, 2002). **Reasonable force** is force that a prudent and cautious person would use if exposed to similar circumstances. It is limited to the amount of force necessary to accomplish lawful results. Anything beyond that is unreasonable force. For example, the police arrest a suspect who kicks, uses fists, and refuses to be handcuffed. The police may use as much force as is necessary to bring that person under control. However, suppose that after subduing the arrestee, the police administer a few extra blows. Such force is unreasonable, because it is unnecessary to accomplish the lawful purpose of placing the suspect under control. That force becomes punitive.

The problem for police officers, however, is that reasonable force is subjective, meaning it depends on the circumstances in each case and ultimately the perception of the judge or jury that tries the case. What may be reasonable to an officer at the time of arrest may look unreasonable to the judge or jury when the case is being tried weeks or months after the incident took place. The officer must be able to remember the circumstances that led to the use of a certain amount of force and hope that the judge or jury would consider it reasonable. Most states allow the use of nondeadly force in specific circumstances, such as to overcome an offender's resistance to a lawful arrest, to prevent escape, to retake a suspect after escape, to protect people and property from harm, and to protect the officer from bodily injury.

nondeadly force
force that, when used, is not likely to result in serious bodily injury or death.

deadly force
force that, when used, poses a high risk of death or serious injury to its human target.

reasonable force
force that a prudent and cautious person would use if exposed to similar circumstances.

The opposite of reasonable force is unreasonable force. Unfortunately, that contrast does not give the police a clear idea of what is allowed or prohibited, particularly in situations where there is no time to think. Given this, it is best to think of the opposite of reasonable force as **punitive force**, meaning force that is used to punish rather than to accomplish lawful results. This distinction is more instructive because an officer, even in highly emotional situations, generally knows whether the force he or she is using is necessary to control the situation or is being used to punish the person being arrested.

punitive force
force that is used to punish rather than to accomplish lawful results.

The Use of Deadly Force

The rule on the use of deadly force is more specific, narrow, and precise than that on the use of nondeadly force. The rules vary in felony and misdemeanor cases.

HIGHLIGHT Research on Police Use of Force, Tasers, and Other Less-Lethal Weapons

The National Institute of Justice's study, "Police Use of Force, Tasers, and Other Less-Lethal Weapons," reported that when officers used force, injury rates to citizens ranged from 17 to 64 percent, while officer injury rates ranged from 10 to 20 percent. Most injuries involve minor bruises, strains, and abrasions. The study's most significant finding was that, while results were not uniform across all agencies, the use of pepper spray and conducted energy devices (CEDs) "can significantly reduce injuries to suspects and the use of CEDs can decrease injuries to officers."

During the past twenty years, new less-lethal weapons technologies have emerged. Pepper spray was among the first to achieve widespread adoption by police forces, and more recently, CEDs (such as Tasers) have become popular. More than 15,000 law enforcement and military agencies use Tasers. Such use has caused controversy (as did pepper spray) and has been associated with in-custody deaths and allegations of overuse and intentional abuse. Here is how it works: CEDs produce 50,000 volts of electricity when used on people. The electricity stuns and temporarily disables people, making them easier to arrest or subdue. The CEDs cause involuntary muscle contractions that cause people to fall, with some people experiencing serious head injuries or bone breaks from the falls; at least six deaths have occurred because of head injuries suffered during CED-related falls. The study says that more than 200 Americans have died after being shocked by Tasers, but despite the dangers, most CED shocks produce no serious injuries.

The study cites a Police Executive Research Forum survey of more than 500 law enforcement agencies nationwide, noting that most agencies have a use-of-force continuum. Use-of-force continuums are covered in training, where officers learn to use suitable force levels depending on circumstances. The continuum covers various circumstances up to the use of firearms.

The survey also found that most agencies allow only soft tactics against a subject who refuses, without physical force, to comply with commands. However, if the subject tenses and pulls when an officer tries to handcuff him or her, most agencies allow chemical agents and hard empty-hand tactics, such as punching. Many also allow for CED use at this point but about 40 percent do not. Almost 75 percent allow CED use if the suspect flees, and almost all allow it when the subject assumes a boxer's stance. Most agencies do not allow baton use until the subject threatens the officer by assuming the boxer's stance.

The study experts noted that safety margins of CED use on normal healthy adults may not be applicable to small children, those with diseased hearts, the elderly, and other at-risk people. Some 31 percent of surveyed agencies forbid CED use against clearly pregnant women, 25.9 percent against drivers of moving vehicles, 23.3 percent against handcuffed suspects, 23.2 percent against people in elevated areas, and 10 percent against the elderly. However, many agencies, while not forbidding use in these circumstances, do restrict CED use except in necessary, special circumstances.

The study experts concluded that while CED use is not risk free, there is no clear medical evidence that shows a high risk of serious injury or death from its direct effects. The experts concluded that enforcement agencies need not avoid using CEDs, provided they are used in accordance with accepted national guidelines. However, caution is urged in using multiple activations.

Source: National Institute of Justice, "Police Use of Force, Tasers, and Other Less-Lethal Weapons," study released by the Office of Justice Programs of the U.S. Department of Justice, May 2011.

Deadly Force in Felony Cases *Tennessee v. Garner*, 411 U.S. 1 (1985), sets the following guideline on the use of deadly force to arrest a suspect: It is constitutionally reasonable for a police officer to use deadly force if the officer has probable cause to believe that the suspect poses a threat of serious physical harm, either to the officer or to others.

In *Garner*, two Memphis, Tennessee, police officers answered a "prowler inside" call one evening. Upon arriving at the scene, they saw a woman standing on her porch and gesturing toward the adjacent house where, she said, she heard glass shattering and was certain that someone was breaking in. One officer radioed the dispatcher to say they were on the scene, while the other officer went into the yard behind the neighboring house. The officer heard a door slam and saw someone run across the backyard. The suspect, Edward Garner, stopped at a six-foot-high chain-link fence at the edge of the yard. With the aid of a flashlight, the officer saw Garner's face and hands. He saw no sign of a weapon and admitted later that he was reasonably sure Garner was unarmed. While Garner was crouched at the base of the fence, the officer called out, "Police, halt," and took a few steps toward him. Garner then began to climb over the fence. The officer shot him. Garner died; $10 and a purse taken from the house were found on his body.

The Court in *Garner* concluded that the use of deadly force to prevent the escape of an apparently unarmed suspected felon was constitutionally unreasonable. It emphasized that "where the suspect poses no immediate threat to the officer and no threat to others, the harm resulting from failing to apprehend him does not justify the use of deadly force," adding that "a police officer may not seize an unarmed nondangerous suspect by shooting him dead." The *Garner* decision rendered unconstitutional the then-existing "fleeing felon" statutes in nearly half of the states, insofar as those statutes allowed the use by the police of deadly force to prevent the escape of a fleeing felon regardless of the circumstances. Fleeing felon statutes are constitutional only if they comport with the requirements set in *Garner*.

Tennessee v. Garner set the following guideline on the use of deadly force to arrest a suspect: "*It is constitutionally reasonable for a police officer to use deadly force when the officer has probable cause to believe that the suspect poses a threat of serious physical harm, either to the officer or to others*" (emphasis added). But then the Court adds:

> . . . if the suspect threatens the officer with a weapon or there is probable cause to believe that he has committed a crime involving the infliction or threatened infliction of serious physical harm, deadly force may be used if necessary to prevent escape, and if, where feasible, some warning has been given.

The Court in *Garner* also said that the use of deadly force to prevent the escape of an apparently unarmed suspected felon was unconstitutionally unreasonable. It emphasized that "where the suspect poses no immediate threat to the officer and no threat to others, the harm resulting from failing to apprehend him does not justify the use of deadly force," adding that "a police officer may not seize an unarmed nondangerous suspect by shooting him dead."

Tennessee v. Garner was not a criminal prosecution case; the officer who killed the suspect was not being prosecuted for murder or manslaughter. Instead, it was a civil case, in which the plaintiffs sought money damages from the department and the state of Tennessee for Garner's death. Nonetheless, *Garner* is the only case decided by the Court thus far that sets guidelines for the use of deadly force by the police.

MYTH vs. REALITY

MYTH Police may shoot a fleeing felon if it is the only way to prevent the felon from escaping.

FACT Police may use deadly only if he or she has probable cause to believe the suspect poses a serious threat to the officer or others or has committed a serious crime.

Use of Deadly Force in Misdemeanor Cases In misdemeanor cases, the safest rule for the officer to follow is: Never use deadly force, except if absolutely necessary for self-defense or the defense of the life of a third person. The use of deadly force in other circumstances in misdemeanor cases exposes the officer to possible criminal and civil liabilities. It raises questions of disproportionality, because the classification by the penal code of the offense as a misdemeanor signifies that the state does not consider the act so serious as to warrant a more severe penalty. Death is too serious a result to prevent the escape of a misdemeanor offender.

The Use-of-Force Continuum

Most law enforcement agencies have policies that guide their use of force. **Use-of-force continuums** describe an escalating series of actions an officer may take to resolve a situation. A use-of-force continuum generally has many levels, and officers are instructed to respond with a level of force appropriate to the situation at hand, acknowledging that the officer may move from one part of the continuum to another in a matter of seconds.

use-of-force continuums description of an escalating series of actions an officer may appropriately use, from no force to deadly force.

An example of a use-of-force continuum from the National Institute of Justice follows.[5]

◆ Officer presence—No force is used. Considered the best way to resolve a situation.
   ◆ The mere presence of a law enforcement officer works to deter crime or diffuse a situation.
   ◆ Officers' attitudes are professional and nonthreatening.
◆ Verbalization—Force is not physical.
   ◆ Officers issue calm, nonthreatening commands, such as "Let me see your identification and registration."
   ◆ Officers may increase their volume and shorten commands in an attempt to gain compliance. Short commands might include "Stop," or "Don't move."
◆ Empty-hand control—Officers use bodily force to gain control of a situation.
   ◆ Soft technique: Officers use grabs, holds, and joint locks to restrain an individual.
   ◆ Hard technique: Officers use punches and kicks to restrain an individual.
◆ Less-lethal methods—Officers use less-lethal technologies to gain control of a situation.
   ◆ Blunt impact: Officers may use a baton or projectile to immobilize a combative person.
   ◆ Chemical: Officers may use chemical sprays or projectiles embedded with chemicals to restrain an individual (e.g., pepper spray).
   ◆ Conducted energy devices (CEDs): Officers may use CEDs to immobilize an individual. CEDs discharge a high-voltage, low-amperage jolt of electricity at a distance.
◆ Lethal force—Officers use lethal weapons to gain control of a situation. Should only be used if a suspect poses a serious threat to the officer or another individual.
   ◆ Officers use deadly weapons such as firearms to stop an individual's actions.

- The term *seizure* is broader than the term *arrest*. All arrests are seizures, but not all seizures constitute an arrest.
- Some contacts with the police are so minimally intrusive they are not considered seizures.
- Neither the perception of the person detained nor of the officer determines whether a seizure has taken place. Instead, the trial judge or jury determines whether a reasonable person under the same circumstances would consider the situation a seizure.
- Arrests have four elements: seizure and detention, intention to arrest, arrest authority, and understanding by the arrestee.
- There are two types of arrests: with a warrant and without a warrant. Each is governed by a different set of legal rules.
- After an arrest, the police may search the arrestee and the area of immediate control.
- The general rule is that the police must knock-and-announce before making an arrest. This rule, however, is subject to many exceptions.
- The rules for police use of nondeadly and deadly force differ. For nondeadly force, only reasonable force can be used. For deadly force, department policy must be strictly followed.
- The use-of-force continuum, used in many police departments during training, familiarizes officers with the proper use of force.
- *Tennessee v. Garner* holds that it is constitutional to use deadly force when the officer has probable cause to believe that the suspect poses a threat of serious physical harm, either to the officer or to others.

REVIEW QUESTIONS

1. Are the terms *seizure* and *arrest* similar or different? Justify your answer and give examples.

2. What is the proper legal test to determine whether a person has been seized under the Fourth Amendment and therefore is entitled to constitutional protection?

3. Assume you are a police officer who is detaining a suspect. What standard will you use to determine if the detention is still a valid detention or if it has turned into an arrest?

4. Identify the four elements of an arrest, and then give an example of each element.

5. "A police officer may make an arrest any time he or she sees a crime being committed." True or false? Explain.

6. What are *exigent circumstances*? Give examples in police work of exigent circumstances. Why is it important for police officers to know about exigent circumstances?

7. What can the police validly do after an arrest? What can they not validly do after an arrest?

8. What is meant by the "area of immediate control" where the police can search after an arrest? Does that phrase have a fixed meaning in terms of distance from where the arrest took place?

9. Suppose an officer has just arrested a suspect five yards from her car. Can the officer search her car? In other words, is it an "area of immediate control"? Justify your answer.

10. "A citizen can make an arrest any time he or she sees a crime being committed." True or false? Explain your answer.

11. Suppose a campus police officer sees a student park a motor vehicle with expired license plates and without a campus sticker. Can the officer arrest the student?

12. State the rules on police use of nondeadly force in felony and misdemeanor cases.

13. What are the differences in the rules on police use of deadly force in felony and misdemeanor cases?

14. What did *Tennessee v. Garner* say about police use of deadly force?

TEST YOUR UNDERSTANDING

1. Assume you are a police officer and have a warrant to arrest a parolee (who is on parole for robbery) for parole violation and possession of drug paraphernalia. You are now at the parolee's apartment. Do you need a warrant, assuming you have time to obtain one? Should you knock-and-announce before making an arrest? Defend your answer.

2. You are a university police officer. Jim, a student, has just parked his car in a university parking lot. Jim gets out of the car. You recognize Jim from a recently issued campus poster and immediately realize he is wanted for sexual assault. Jim is thirty yards away from his car. You arrest Jim, place handcuffs on him, and then search his car. During the search you recover a pound of marijuana and burglary tools in the car's passenger compartment. Are the marijuana and the burglary tools admissible in court? Explain your answer.

3. Alice was stopped by a patrol officer one night and questioned for twenty minutes. In court during the trial, she said she felt she was under arrest. The officer denied this, saying this was furthest from his mind; he merely wanted to ask Alice questions to determine if she was a resident of the neighborhood. Was Alice arrested or not? Justify your answer using the standard of a reasonable person under the same circumstances.

RECOMMENDED READINGS

"Understanding the Police Use of Force," *http://www.ci.westminster.co.us/res/ps/pd/topics_pdforce.htm*.

Jennifer Cook. *Discretionary warrantless searches and seizures and the Fourth Amendment: A need for clearer guidelines.* South Carolina Law Review, 641–659 (2002).

Elizabeth Forbes. *Warrantless Arrests in Police Standoffs: A Common Sense Approach to the Exigency Exception.* Criminal Law Bulletin 45, 6–23 (2009).

Craig Hemmens. *The Police, the Fourth Amendment, and Unannounced Entry: Wilson v. Arkansas.* The Criminal Law Bulletin 33, 29–58 (1997).

L. Richardson. *Arrest efficiency and the fourth amendment.* Minnesota Law Review, June 2011, vol. 95, issue 6, pp. 2035–2098.

NOTES

1. Henry C. Black, *Black's Law Dictionary*, 4th ed. (St. Paul, MN: West, 1968), p. 147

2. California Penal Code, §816.

3. Michigan Court Rules, 764.1.

4. General Order No. 500-01: Houston Police Department, Subject: Effecting Arrests and Searches, March 12, 2002.

5. National Institute of Justice, http://www.nij.gov/nij/topics/law-enforcement/officer-safety/use-of-force/continuum.htm.

CHAPTER 7

Searches and Seizures of Things

LEARNING OBJECTIVES

1. Define search and seizure.
2. Describe the development of the legal concept of reasonable expectation of privacy to include the landmark case of *Katz v. United States*.
3. Explain the four requirements for a search warrant.
4. Illustrate with examples the types of items that can be searched for and seized by law enforcement.
5. Compare and contrast between an arrest warrant and a search warrant.
6. Explain and provide examples of exceptions to a search with a warrant.
7. Describe the elements of consent to search as well as who has authority to give consent.
8. Compare and contrast the requirements for the search and seizure of a computer with that of a cell phone.
9. Compare the legal requirements between the following: searches by a private person, searches by an off duty officer, and surgery to retrieve evidence.
10. Compare and contrast administrative searches and searches by law enforcement.

KEY TERMS

administrative searches

anticipatory search warrant

apparent authority principle

Chimel rule

contemporaneous search

exigent circumstances

fishing expedition

neutral and detached magistrate

reasonable expectation of privacy

right to privacy

search

search warrant

seizure

special needs exceptions

THE **TOP 5** IMPORTANT CASES

in Searches and Seizures of Things

■ *KATZ V. UNITED STATES (1967)* A search is not limited to homes, offices, buildings, or other enclosed places; rather, it can occur in any place where a person has a reasonable expectation of privacy, even if the place is in a public area.

■ *CHIMEL V. CALIFORNIA (1969)* Once a lawful arrest has been made, the police may search anywhere within the suspect's area of immediate control, meaning the area from which the suspect may grab a weapon or destroy evidence.

■ *MARYLAND V. GARRISON (1987)* The validity of a warrant must be judged in light of the "information available to the officers at the time they obtained the warrant."

■ *GEORGIA V. RANDOLPH (2006)* A police search without a warrant is unconstitutional if one occupant consents to a search and the other refuses to give consent.

■ *SAFFORD UNIFIED SCHOOL DISTRICT V. REDDING (2009)* The warrantless search of a thirteen-year-old student's underwear without reasonable suspicion of school rules violation is unconstitutional.

THE FOURTH AMENDMENT AS APPLIED TO THINGS

This chapter discusses searches and seizures of *things*—as distinguished from seizures of *persons*, which are arrests. It does not deal with searches of motor vehicles, which are discussed in Chapter 8. Both searches and seizures of things (this chapter) and searches and seizures of persons (Chapter 6) are governed by the Fourth Amendment of the U.S. Constitution, which states:

> The right of the people to be secure in their persons, houses, papers, and effects, against unreasonable searches and seizures, shall not be violated, and no Warrants shall issue, but upon probable cause, supported by Oath or affirmation, and particularly describing the place to be searched, and the persons or things to be seized.

In addition, searches and seizures also involve the right to privacy. Consequently, many cases involving the Fourth Amendment also raise claims of possible violation of the right to privacy. This is because searches and seizures often require entry into homes or residences or searches of personal belongings; hence, a person's privacy is inevitably involved. For example, suppose the police illegally enter a home to search for drugs without probable cause. In the process of the search, they enter the couple's bedroom, conduct an extensive search, and recover drugs and child pornography. During the trial, the evidence seized probably will be excluded based on violations of the Fourth Amendment and the right to privacy.

The law on searches and seizures of things is understood best if two basic concepts are clear:

1. There are two types of search and seizure: without a warrant and with a warrant. Each is governed by its own rules and are discussed separately in this chapter.
2. The term *search and seizure* is often misunderstood as a single and continuous act. It is, in fact, two separate acts, each with its own meaning. Both are under the Fourth Amendment and subject to the probable cause requirement. After defining them, however, the discussion in this chapter considers search and seizure together because Fourth Amendment cases do not make clear distinctions between the two acts. Moreover, one usually follows the other or is often the result of the other. This means that a *search can result in a seizure, and seizure is often the result of a search.*

THE RIGHT TO PRIVACY IS A CONSTITUTIONAL RIGHT

right to privacy
the right to be let alone.

The **right to privacy** is a constitutional right but is not specifically mentioned in the Constitution—unlike the prohibition against unreasonable searches and seizures, which is specified in the Fourth Amendment. Instead, it is a *penumbra* (shadow) right that is derived from other rights specifically mentioned in the Constitution, including the Fourth Amendment.

The right to privacy and the right against unreasonable searches and seizures under the Fourth Amendment interface on many occasions because both of them prohibit government intrusion into basic individual rights. Arguably, however, the right to privacy is broader than the right against unreasonable searches and seizures because it protects the individual against certain forms of intrusion that do not constitute searches or seizures. For example, the right to privacy has been invoked to prohibit the government from regulating abortion during the early stage of pregnancy and also forbids the government from criminalizing what people do in the privacy of their own homes, such as sexual acts between consenting adults.

Griswold v. Connecticut (1965)

In a 1965 decision, the Court said that "specific guarantees in the Bill of Rights have penumbras, formed by emanations from those guarantees that help give them life and substance" (*Griswold v. Connecticut*, 381 U.S. 479 [1965]). The Court added that "various guarantees create zones of privacy." These are the First Amendment freedom of association; the Third Amendment prohibition against the quartering of soldiers "in any house"; the Fourth Amendment affirmation of the "right of the people to be secure in their persons, houses, papers, and effects, against unreasonable searches and seizures"; the Fifth Amendment prohibition against self-incrimination; and the Ninth Amendment provision that the "enumeration in the Constitution, of certain rights, shall not be construed to deny or disparage others retained by the people." Since 1965, the right to privacy has been recognized as a constitutional right by the Court.

Despite not being mentioned in the Bill or Rights or the Constitution, the right to privacy is now well established by Court decisions and is one of the most asserted rights. It will continue to be an often-invoked right whose outer limits are yet to be determined by the courts in forthcoming years in a cyberspace age. The protection afforded by the Court to the right to privacy is reflected in these words from the Court's decision in *Griswold:* "We deal with a right of privacy older than the Bill of Rights—older than our political parties, older than our school system." It is a basic and fundamental right. The more popular meaning of the right to privacy is "the right to be let alone by other people" (*Katz v. United States*, 389 U.S. 347 [1967]). This includes being "let alone" by the government and law enforcement agents.

Katz v. United States (1967)

"REASONABLE EXPECTATION OF PRIVACY" DEFINED

Privacy is a broad term that encompasses a myriad of situations. The question is, When does privacy enjoy constitutional protection and when does it not? The Court's response: Privacy enjoys constitutional protection when there is a *reasonable expectation of privacy.* In a concurring opinion in *Katz v. United States*, 389 U.S. 347 (1967), Justice Harlan specified two requirements for a **reasonable expectation of privacy** to exist: (1) the person must have exhibited an actual expectation of privacy, and (2) the expectation must be one that society is prepared to recognize as reasonable. These are the same requirements used by courts in today's decisions. Justice Harlan added:

> Thus a man's home is, for most purposes, a place where he expects privacy, but objects, activities, or statements that he exposes to the "plain view" of outsiders are not "protected" because no intention to keep them to himself has been exhibited. On the other hand, conversations in the open would not be protected against being overheard, for the expectation of privacy under the circumstances would be unreasonable.

reasonable expectation of privacy exists when a person exhibits an actual expectation of privacy, and the expectation is one that society is prepared to recognize as reasonable.

To use a more current example, does a person who talks on a cell phone in a public place have a reasonable expectation of privacy? Applying the two tests, a person who talks on a cell phone loudly and in public does not exhibit an actual expectation of privacy and, even if she does, society probably is not prepared to recognize this expectation as reasonable. By contrast, couples who are in bed in their own home have a reasonable expectation of privacy, which society is prepared to accept as reasonable. What society is prepared to recognize as reasonable evolves over time, particularly as technology, social practices, and morals change. Ultimately, the phrase *reasonable expectation of privacy* is a question of fact that is determined in an actual case by a judge or jury, based on surrounding circumstances. It is therefore subjective.

SEARCH DEFINED

A **search** of things is defined as the exploration or examination of an individual's house, premises, or person to discover things that may be used by the government for evidence in a criminal prosecution. A search is not limited to homes, offices, buildings, or other enclosed places; rather, it can occur in any place where a person has a reasonable expectation of privacy, even if the place is in a public area, meaning a place to which anyone has access (*Katz v. United States*, 389 U.S. 347 [1967]). For example, in one case, police installed a peephole in the ceiling of a public restroom to observe what occurred in the stalls. Officers observed two people engaging in an illegal sexual act in one of the stalls. What the officers did without a warrant was illegal, because the two people involved had a reasonable expectation of privacy—they could reasonably expect that their acts would not be observed by others, even though they were in a public restroom. The evidence obtained was therefore not admissible in court.

SEIZURE DEFINED

A **seizure** of things or items is defined as the exercise of dominion or control by the government over a person or thing because of a violation of law. The distinction between a search and a seizure can be summarized as follows: *Search is looking, whereas a seizure is taking*. In one case, the Supreme Court said that "a seizure occurs when there is some meaningful interference with an individual's possessory interests in the property seized" (*Maryland v. Macon*, 472 U.S. 463 [1985]). If a search succeeds, it may lead to a seizure.

SEARCHES AND SEIZURES: THE GENERAL RULE

The general rule is that searches and seizures can be made only with a warrant. Therefore, warrantless searches and seizures are exceptions to the general rule. According to the Court, the most basic constitutional rule is that searches conducted outside the judicial process, without prior approval by a judge or a magistrate, are per se unreasonable under the Fourth Amendment—subject only to a few specifically established and well-delineated exceptions (*Katz v. United States*, 389 U.S. 347 [1967]).

In reality, most searches and seizures are made without a warrant. Nonetheless, police officers must always be aware of the general rule so that they make warrantless searches only if justified under one of the exceptions. In the words of the Court: "The point of the Fourth Amendment, which often is not grasped by zealous officers, is not that it denies law enforcement the support of the usual inferences that reasonable people draw from evidence. Its protection consists in requiring that those inferences be drawn by a neutral and detached magistrate instead of being judged by the officer engaged in the often competitive enterprise of ferreting out crime" (*Johnson v. United States*, 333 U.S. 10 [1948]).

THINGS SUBJECT TO SEARCH AND SEIZURE

Generally, four types of things can be searched and seized:

◆ *Contraband*, such as illegal drugs, counterfeit money, and gambling paraphernalia. With limited exceptions, these items are illegal for anybody to possess.
◆ *Fruits of the crime*, such as stolen goods and forged checks.
◆ *Instrumentalities of the crime*, such as weapons and burglary tools.
◆ *"Mere evidence" of the crime*, such as a suspect's clothing containing bloodstains of the victim, or a suspect's mask or shoes—provided there is probable cause to believe that the item is related to criminal activity.

These are merely general categories of things officers may search and seize. In many states, the law (usually the code of criminal procedure or the penal code) enumerates in detail the items subject to search and seizure. Whatever the listing, an item listed by state law is likely to fall into one of the four categories listed.

THE SCOPE OF THE SEARCH

The scope and manner of the search must be reasonable based on the object of the search. A wise legal maxim for officers to remember is this: *It is unreasonable for a police officer to look for an elephant in a matchbox.* For example, suppose a search warrant is issued for the recovery of a stolen 60-inch plasma television. In looking for the television, the officer cannot open drawers—unless, of course, the drawer is big enough to contain the television. However, if the search warrant is for heroin, then the officer is justified in opening drawers in the course of the search, as heroin could obviously fit inside a drawer. It therefore follows that the smaller the item sought, the more extensive the scope of the search.

IN ACTION *EXTENDING THE SCOPE OF A SEARCH*

Police officers in Springfield, Missouri, develop probable cause (based on a tip from a reliable informant and their corroboration of the information provided) that Jim Garland is the leader of a motorcycle gang that has been burglarizing residences in the area and stealing computers, televisions, jewelry, and other valuable items. The police have probable cause to believe some of the stolen items are located in a rented storage unit. They obtain a search warrant for the storage unit which authorizes them to look for the various stolen items, including items as large as a 60-inch television and as small as some rings and earrings. They execute the search warrant at the storage unit, but do not find any of the items listed in the search warrant. They do discover several plastic baggies containing marijuana, however. They seize the marijuana, and then drive over to Jim Garland's house and knock on the door. When no one answers, they walk around the house to the garage, open the unlocked door, and look inside. They find a number of stolen items that were listed in the search warrant. They seize these items. Just then, Jim Garland returns home, and they arrest him. He is charged with multiple counts of theft, and with drug possession.

1. *Was the search of the storage unit lawful?*
2. *Was the seizure of the marijuana lawful?*
3. *Was the search of the garage lawful? Why or why not?*

While the search is being conducted, the police may detain persons who are on the premises to search them (*Michigan v. Summers*, 452 U.S. 692 [1981]). However, these people must have been named in the warrant. For example, a search warrant for a bar and the bartender does not authorize body searches of the bar patrons (*Ybarra v. Illinois*, 444 U.S. 85 [1979]). In addition, the *Summers* rule that officers executing a search warrant are permitted to detain the occupants of the premises while a search is conducted is limited to the immediate vicinity of the premises to be searched and does not apply when a recent occupant of the premises was detained at a point outside of the immediate vicinity of the premises—in this case about one mile away (*Bailey v. United States*, —U.S. — [2013]).

Searches of property belonging to persons not suspected of a crime are permissible so long as probable cause exists to suspect that evidence of someone's guilt or other items subject to seizure will be found. For example, in one case, several police officers were hurt at a political demonstration. The police could not identify their attackers, but they knew that a newspaper staff photographer had taken photographs of the demonstration. The police were able to obtain a warrant to search the newspaper's offices because probable cause existed that evidence of someone's guilt would be found (*Zurcher v. Stanford Daily*, 436 U.S. 547 [1978]).

THE TIME ALLOWED FOR A SEARCH

The search cannot last indefinitely, with or without a warrant. Once the item mentioned in the warrant is recovered, the search must cease. Continued search without justification becomes a **fishing expedition** for evidence and is illegal. An illegal search is never made legal by what is subsequently found. For example, suppose the police go to an apartment to execute a search for a shotgun allegedly used in a murder. After the shotgun is recovered, the police continue to search for other evidence in connection with the murder. They open a bedroom closet and find a pair of bloodstained jeans worn by the suspect during the murder. The bloody jeans, if seized and used in evidence, will not be admissible, because they were illegally obtained. Note, however, that items in plain view during the execution of the warrant can be seized by the police because such items are not protected by the Fourth Amendment. The plain view exception is discussed in Chapter 9.

fishing expedition
a search for additional evidence conducted after all the evidence named in the search warrant has been discovered.

THE PROCEDURE AFTER THE SEARCH

After the search, the usual police practice is to give the occupant a list of the items that have been seized. If nobody is on the premises, the list must be left there, in a place where it will be found. In *City of West Covina v. Perkins et al.*, 525 U.S. 234 (1999), the Court held that the police are not required by the Constitution to provide the owner of the seized property with a notice of remedies specified by state law for the property's return and the information necessary to use those procedures. The Court stressed the need to provide notice about what has been taken, but concluded that the other requirements specified by California state law, such as detailed notice of the state procedures for the return of the seized property, are not required by the due process clause of the Constitution.

SEARCH AND ARREST WARRANTS COMPARED

Search warrants and arrest warrants have the following similarities:

◆ Probable cause is needed to issue a search warrant or an arrest warrant.
◆ The definition of probable cause is the same for both.
◆ Probable cause for both is ultimately determined by a judge, not by the officer.
◆ In both, officers need to knock-and-announce, subject to state law exceptions.
◆ Items in plain view may be seized when executing a search warrant or an arrest warrant.

Search warrants and arrest warrants have the following differences:

Search Warrant	Arrest Warrant
The officer looks for items to be used as evidence.	The officer seeks to arrest a suspect for detention.
If not executed, a search warrant usually expires after a period of time specified by law.	An arrest warrant does not expire, unless recalled by the court that issued it.
Some jurisdictions limit the execution of the warrant to reasonable hours during the day.	It may be executed at any time, unless exceptions are specified by law.

SEARCH AND SEIZURE WITH A WARRANT

A **search warrant** is a written order, issued by a magistrate, directing a peace officer to search for property connected with a crime and bring it before the court (see Figure 7.1.) In nearly all states, the police officer seeking a search warrant must state the facts that establish probable cause in a written and signed affidavit. The general rule is that a search or seizure is valid under the Fourth Amendment only if made with a warrant. Searches without a warrant may be valid, but they are the exception rather than the rule.

This section looks at several issues related to search warrants, including the requirements for issuing them; the procedure for serving them; the knock-and-announce rule; the scope of search and seizure; the time allotted to conduct a search; and the procedure after the search. Last, the section compares search and arrest warrants.

search warrant
a written order, issued by a magistrate, directing a peace officer to search for property connected with a crime and bring it before the court.

FOUR REQUIREMENTS

There are four requirements for a valid search warrant:

◆ Probable cause
◆ A supporting oath or affirmation
◆ A description of the place to be searched and the things to be seized
◆ The signature of a magistrate

Probable Cause

The conditions required to establish probable cause are discussed more extensively in Chapter 3. For our purposes here, it is sufficient to restate that probable cause is defined as more than mere suspicion; "it exists when the facts and circumstances within the officers' knowledge and of which they have reasonably trustworthy information are

FIGURE 7.1 Search Warrant

STATE OF NEW MEXICO
[COUNTY OF_____]
[CITY OF_____]
_____ COURT   No. _____

[STATE OF NEW MEXICO]
[COUNTY OF_____]
[CITY OF_____]
v.
_____ , Defendant

SEARCH WARRANT

THE [STATE OF NEW MEXICO] [CITY OF_____]
TO ANY OFFICER AUTHORIZED TO EXECUTE THIS WARRANT.

Proof by Affidavit for Search Warrant, having been submitted to me, I am satisfied that there is probable cause that the person named or property described in the Affidavit is located where alleged in the Affidavit and I find that grounds exist for the issuance of the Search Warrant. A copy of the Affidavit is attached and made a part of this Warrant.

YOU ARE HEREBY COMMANDED to search forthwith the person or place described in the Affidavit between the hours of 6:00 A.M. and 10:00 P.M., unless I have specifically authorized a nighttime search, for the person or property described in the Affidavit, serving this Warrant together with a copy of the Affidavit, and making the search, and if the person or property be found there, to seize the person or the property and hold for safekeeping until further order of the court.

You are further directed to prepare a written inventory of any person or property seized. You are further directed to file the return and written inventory with the Court promptly after its execution.

Date: _____

_____
Judge

AUTHORIZATION FOR NIGHTTIME SEARCH

I further find that reasonable cause has been shown for nighttime execution of this Warrant. I authorize execution of this Warrant at any time of the day or night for the following reasons (set forth reasons why a nighttime search is necessary):
_____
_____ .

_____
Judge

RETURN AND INVENTORY

I received the attached Search Warrant on _____ , _____ , and executed it on the _____ day of _____ , _____ , at _____   ☐ A.M.   ☐ P.M. I searched the person or premises described in the Warrant and I left a copy of the Warrant with _____
(name the person searched or owner at the place of search) together with a copy of the inventory for the items seized. The following is an inventory of property taken pursuant to the warrant (attach separate inventory if necessary):
_____
_____
_____

This inventory was made in the presence of _____ (name of applicant for the search warrant) and _____ (name of owner of premises or property). (If not available, name of other credible person witnessing the inventory.)

This inventory is a true and detailed account of all the property taken pursuant to the Warrant.

_____
Signature of Officer

_____
Signature of Owner of Property or Other Witness

Return made this _____ day of_____ , _____ , at _____   ☐ A.M.   ☐ P.M.

_____
(Judge) (Clerk)

After careful search, I could not find at the place or on the person described, the property described in this warrant.

_____
Officer

_____
Date

Source: Official form of the state of New Mexico

sufficient in themselves to warrant a person of reasonable caution in the belief that an offense has been or is being committed" (*Brinegar v. United States*, 338 U.S. 160 [1949]).

Brinegar v. United States (1949)

This definition is the same for arrests and for searches and seizures of things. The difference is that in arrests the focus is on: (1) whether a crime has been committed and (2) whether the person to be arrested committed the crime. By contrast, in searches and seizures of things, the issue of probable cause focuses on: (1) whether the property to be seized is connected with criminal activity and (2) whether it can be found in the place to be searched.

A Supporting Oath or Affirmation

A search warrant is issued based on a sworn affidavit, establishing grounds for the warrant, that is presented to the magistrate. The magistrate issues the warrant only if he or she is satisfied, based on the affidavit, that probable cause for a warrant exists. The contents of the affidavit must be sufficient to allow an independent evaluation of probable cause by the magistrate. To enable the magistrate to make an independent evaluation, the affidavit must contain more than mere conclusions by the police officer. It must allege facts showing that seizable evidence will be found in the place to be searched. The affidavit may be filed by the police officer or the offended or injured party.

Supporting oaths and affirmations can be based on oral statements. Anticipatory warrants can be issued based on the expectation of the imminent arrival of contraband. However, supporting oaths must be based on recent information that helps establish probable cause before a warrant can be issued. We turn to each of these issues next.

Warrants Based on Oral Statements There is no constitutional requirement that a warrant application must be in writing. In some jurisdictions, a warrant may be issued based on an oral statement either in person or by telephone. The oral statement is usually recorded and becomes the basis for a probable cause determination. If probable cause is found, the judge or magistrate then prepares a search warrant.

Anticipatory Search Warrant An **anticipatory search warrant** is a warrant obtained based on probable cause and on an expectation that seizable items will be found at a certain place at a certain time. If the police probable cause to believe contraband or other evidence of a crime will arrive at a specific location at a particular time (or within a reasonable period of time), they need not wait for the delivery to occur to seek a search warrant. Instead, the police may present their probable cause evidence to a magistrate and obtain an anticipatory search warrant based on probable cause

anticipatory search warrant
a warrant obtained based on probable cause and on an expectation that seizable items will be found at a certain place.

HIGHLIGHT › Definition of Probable Cause

Probable cause "exists when the facts and circumstances within the officers' knowledge and of which they have reasonably trustworthy information are sufficient in themselves to warrant a person of reasonable caution in the belief that an offense has been or is being committed."

This is the same definition for searches and seizures of things and searches and seizures of persons (arrests).

Source: *Brinegar v. United States*, 338 U.S. 160 (1949).

that the evidence will be found at the location to be searched at the time the warrant is executed.

In a 2006 case, *United States v. Grubbs*, 547 U.S. 90 (2006), the Court determined that anticipatory search warrants are valid. In this case, a judge issued an anticipatory search warrant for the Grubb's house based on a federal officer's affidavit, which explained that "the warrant would not be executed until a parcel containing a videotape of child pornography—which Grubbs had ordered from an undercover postal inspector—was received at, and physically taken into, the residence." Grubbs was seized by the officers after the package was delivered. During his trial for receiving child pornography, Grubbs moved to suppress the evidence.

On appeal, the Court rejected his arguments and said that "anticipatory warrants are not categorically unconstitutional under the Fourth Amendment's provision" as long as there is probable cause. The Court added that "when an anticipatory warrant is issued, the fact that the contraband is not presently at the place described is immaterial, so long as there is probable cause to believe it will be there when the warrant is executed." Moreover, the Court added that "the particularity requirement does not necessitate specification of the triggering conditions within the warrant itself."

In an earlier case, the U.S. Court of Appeals for the First Circuit said that in issuing an anticipatory warrant, the conditions set by the magistrate must be "explicit, clear, and narrowly drawn so as to avoid misunderstanding or manipulation by government agents." The court said that the issuing judge must narrow the discretion of government agents in two ways: (1) the event that triggered the warrant must be ascertainable and preordained, and (2) the item sought (in this case, contraband) must be on a sure and irreversible course to its destination (*United States v. Ricciardelli*, 998 F.2d 8 [1st Cir. 1993]).

United States v. Ricciardelli
(1993)

A Need for Fresh Information To be valid, the warrant must be based on fresh information. If the information is "stale," the warrant lacks probable cause and is invalid (*United States v. Leon*, 468 U.S. 897 [1984]). In the *Leon* case, the information contained in the affidavit was given by the police officer to the magistrate in September 1981. It was based partially on information the officer had obtained from a confidential informant in August 1981. The Court ruled that "to the extent that the affidavit set forth facts demonstrating the basis of the informant's knowledge of criminal activity, the information included was fatally stale."

United States v. Leon
(1984)

The reason for the fresh information rule is that conditions can change quickly, and an item found in one place at one time may not be there when the warrant is issued and executed. The Court has not specified exactly how much time must elapse before information becomes stale. It is safe to say, however, that the longer the delay, the greater the chance that the information will be considered stale by a reviewing court.

A Description of the Place to Be Searched and Persons or Things to Be Seized

The affidavit must identify both the place that will be searched and the things that will be seized. This section addresses each of these requirements.

The Place to Be Searched The warrant must remove any doubt or uncertainty about which premises are to be searched. For example, if the location is an apartment in a multiple-unit building, the warrant must specify which apartment is to be searched.

The address of the apartment building is not sufficient. An exact address prevents confusion and avoids intrusions on the privacy of innocent people.

In one case, however, the Court held that the validity of a warrant must be judged in light of the "information available to the officers at the time they obtained the warrant" (*Maryland v. Garrison*, 480 U.S. 79 [1987]). In this case, police officers obtained a warrant to search "the premises known as 2036 Park Avenue, third-floor apartment" for drugs and drug paraphernalia that supposedly belonged to a person named McWebb. The police reasonably believed there was only one apartment at that location. In fact, there were two apartments on the third floor, one belonging to McWebb and the other belonging to Garrison. Before the officers became aware that they were in Garrison's apartment instead of McWebb's, they searched the apartment and discovered drugs that provided the basis for Garrison's subsequent conviction.

Maryland v. Garrison (1987)

Garrison sought exclusion of the evidence, saying that the search warrant was so unnecessarily broad that it allowed the search of the wrong apartment. The Supreme Court admitted the evidence, saying that the validity of a warrant must be judged in light of the information available to the officers when the warrant is sought. There was a reasonable effort on the part of the officers to ascertain and identify the place that was the target of the search; nonetheless, a mistake occurred.

Garrison should not be interpreted as validating all search warrants where there is a mistake made in the description of the place to be searched. The test of the validity of search warrants that are "ambiguous in scope" appears to be "whether the officers' failure to realize the overbreadth of the warrant was objectively understandable and reasonable." Therefore, a warrant that is overly broad in describing the place to be searched is not in violation of the Fourth Amendment *if it was based on a reasonable but mistaken belief* at the time the warrant was issued.

The Things to Be Seized Things to be seized must also be described in detail sufficient to narrow the discretion officers can exercise over what may be seized (see Exhibit 7.1). For example, the warrant cannot simply provide for the seizure of "stolen goods," because this language is too general and can lead to a fishing expedition. An acceptable identification would be "a 60-inch high-definition television." Contraband, however, does not have to be described with as much particularity, because it is in itself seizable. So the words *cocaine* or *heroin* would suffice, as would *drug paraphernalia*.

In *Groh v. Ramirez et al.*, 540 U.S. 551 (2004), the Court held that a search warrant that does not comply with the requirement that the warrant particularly describe the person or things to be seized is unconstitutional. In this case, Groh, an agent of the Bureau of Alcohol, Tobacco, and Firearms (ATF), prepared an application for a search warrant based on information that weapons and explosives were located on Ramirez's farm. The application was supported by a detailed affidavit listing the items to be seized and describing the basis for the agent's belief that the items were concealed on the property. Groh presented these documents, along with a warrant form he also completed, to a magistrate. The magistrate signed the warrant form. Although the application and affidavit described the contraband to be discovered, the form only indicated that the place to be searched was Ramirez's home. It did not incorporate any reference to the itemized list contained in the warrant application or affidavit. The day after the magistrate signed the warrant, officers searched Ramirez's home but found no illegal weapons or explosives. Groh left a copy of the

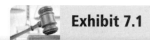

Exhibit 7.1 • An Example of a State Code Listing Specific Items Police Can Search and Seize

Art. 18.02. Ground for issuance.

A search warrant may be issued to search for and seize:

(1) property acquired by theft or in any other manner which makes its acquisition a penal offense;

(2) property specially designed, made, or adapted for or commonly used in the commission of an offense;

(3) arms and munitions kept or prepared for the purposes of insurrection or riot;

(4) weapons prohibited by the Penal Code;

(5) gambling devices or equipment, altered gambling equipment, or gambling paraphernalia;

(6) obscene materials kept or prepared for commercial distribution or exhibition,

subject to the additional rules set forth by law;

(7) drugs kept, prepared, or manufactured in violation of the laws of this state;

(8) any property the possession of which is prohibited by law;

(9) implements or instruments used in the commission of a crime;

(10) property or items, except the personal writings by the accused, constituting evidence of an offense or constituting evidence tending to show that a particular person committed an offense;

(11) persons; or

(12) contraband subject to forfeiture under Chapter 59 of this code.

Source: Texas Code of Criminal Procedure, 2009–2010, LexisNexis Publication.

warrant at the home but did not leave a copy of the warrant application. The following day, in response to a request from Ramirez's attorney, Groh faxed a copy of the application. No charges were filed against Ramirez, but Ramirez later filed suit for damages, claiming his Fourth Amendment rights were violated by the nonspecific warrant.

The Court agreed with Ramirez, saying that a search and seizure warrant that does not contain a particular description of the things to be seized is unconstitutional even if the application for the warrant contains such descriptions. The Court rejected Groh's argument that the search was based on a particular description because it was in the supporting documents. The Court, however, refused to address two other issues involved in the case: (1) whether the warrant would have been valid if it had mentioned that the application clearly listed the items to be seized but that the list was not available during the search, and (2) whether orally describing the items to the defendant during the search complies with the specificity requirement.

The Signature of a Magistrate

neutral and detached magistrate
a magistrate who is not aligned with the government.

As in the cases of arrest warrants, search warrants must be issued only by a **neutral and detached magistrate**, meaning a magistrate that is not aligned with the government. The Court has said, "Inferences must be drawn by a neutral and detached magistrate instead of being judged by the officer engaged in the often competitive enterprise of ferreting out crime" (*Johnson v. United States*, 333 U.S. 10 [1948]). Several examples illustrate this requirement.

◆ A magistrate who receives a fee when issuing a warrant but not when denying one is not neutral and detached (*Connally v. Georgia*, 429 U.S. 245 [1977]).

Connally v. Georgia (1977)

◆ A magistrate who participates in the search to determine its scope lacks the requisite neutrality and detachment (*Lo-Ji Sales, Inc. v. New York*, 442 U.S. 319 [1979]).

Lo-Ji Sales, Inc. v. New York (1979)

◆ The state's chief investigator and prosecutor (state attorney general) is not neutral and detached, so any warrant issued by him or her is invalid (*Coolidge v. New Hampshire*, 403 U.S. 443 [1971]).

Coolidge v. New Hampshire (1971)

THE PROCEDURE FOR SERVING A WARRANT

The search warrant is directed to a law enforcement officer and must state the grounds for issuance and the names of those who gave affidavits in support of it (see Figure 7.2). The execution of a warrant is specified in detail by state law, usually in the state's code of criminal procedure. Failure to execute the warrant in accordance with state or local law generally results in exclusion of the evidence during trial. The warrant usually directs that it be served during the daytime, but if the affidavits are positive that the property is on the person or in the place to be searched, the warrant may direct that it be served at any time. Some states, by law, authorize nighttime searches. The warrant must designate the judge or magistrate to whom the warrant is to be returned. It also must be executed and delivered within a specified number of days from the date of issuance. Some states specify ten days; others allow less time. If the warrant is not served during that time, it expires and can no longer be served.

Note that search warrants differ in this respect from arrest warrants, which are usually valid until served. The officer executing the search warrant must either: (1) give a copy of the warrant and a receipt for any seized property to the person from whom it is taken, or (2) leave a copy and receipt on the premises. A written inventory must be made, and the officer's report, accompanied by the inventory, must be submitted promptly.

SEARCH AND SEIZURE WITHOUT A WARRANT

Searches and seizures without a warrant are discussed here first, before searches and seizures with a warrant, because they are the most common type of search done by police officers. In searches and seizures without a warrant, the burden is on the police to prove in court that probable cause existed at the time of the warrantless search or seizure. It is therefore essential for law enforcement officers to be thoroughly familiar with the law on warrantless searches and seizures. Generally, there are seven exceptions to the rule that searches and seizures must be made with a warrant and with probable cause:

1. The searches with consent exception.
2. The search incident to lawful arrest exception.
3. The exigent circumstances exception.

4. The special needs exception.

5. The administrative searches and inspections exception.

6. The stop and frisk exception.

7. The motor vehicles exception.

Exceptions 1–5 are discussed in sequence in this chapter. The stop and frisk exception is discussed in Chapter 5, and the motor vehicle exception is discussed in Chapter 8. The special needs and administrative searches exceptions are discussed later in this chapter as separate topics because they are not conducted by police officers, although sometimes police officers assist in these searches.

The Searches with Consent Exception

The searches with consent exception is the most common exception to the warrant requirement rule. It states that, if a person gives proper consent, the consent is valid, and anything illegal found and confiscated during the search may be introduced as evidence in court. There are limits to that search, however. The three most important limits are:

◆ The consent must be voluntary.

◆ The search must stay within its allowable scope.

◆ The person must have the authority to give consent.

The Consent Must Be Voluntary Warrantless searches with consent are valid, but the consent must be *voluntary*, meaning it was not obtained by the use of force, duress, or coercion. Whether consent is voluntary is determined by looking at the totality of circumstances. For example, consent given only after the officer demands entry cannot be deemed voluntary. "Open the door" will most likely be interpreted by the courts as a command that must be obeyed, giving the occupant no choice and therefore making the consent involuntary. A request, however, is different from a demand. Requests such as, "Would you mind if I come in and look around?" are more likely to result in voluntary consent than, "I am going to look around."

In *Florida v. Bostick*, 501 U.S. 429 (1991), two officers, with badges and insignia, boarded a bus. They explained their presence as being "on the lookout for illegal drugs." Without any articulable suspicion, they approached Bostick, a passenger, and asked to see some identification and inspect his bus ticket. The officers asked Bostick for consent to search his bag and told him he had the right to refuse consent. Bostick gave consent, and the subsequent search turned up contraband. On appeal of his conviction, the Court held that the consent was valid.

In *United States v. Drayton*, 536 U.S. 194 (2002), the Court went further and said that the Fourth Amendment permits police officers to approach bus passengers, ask questions, and request their consent to search, provided that a reasonable person would understand that he or she is free to refuse. There is no requirement in the Fourth Amendment for officers to advise persons of their right to refuse to cooperate.

Consent need not be spoken, it may be indicated by actions alone. Mere silence or failure to object to a search does not necessarily mean the person is giving consent, however. The consent must be clear. For example, a shrug of the shoulders may signify indifference or resignation rather than consent, but multiple nods strongly imply consent. In *United States v. Shaibu*, 920 F.2d 1423 (9th Cir. 1990), the Ninth Circuit Court of Appeals said that there was no valid consent when the resident opened his door, stepped into the hallway, listened to the officers identify themselves and explain the purpose of their visit, and then retreated wordlessly back into the apartment without closing the door. The government in this case failed to meet its burden of proving consent merely by showing that the defendant left his door open.

There is also no valid consent if permission is given as a result of police misrepresentation or deception, such as saying, "We have a warrant," when none exists (*Bumper v. North Carolina*, 391 U.S. 543 [1968]). Lower courts are divided on the issue of whether consent is valid if the officer does not have a warrant but threatens to obtain one. The issue has not been resolved by the Supreme Court.

Bumper v. North Carolina (1968)

Consent to enter does not necessarily mean consent to search. For example, consent to enter for the purpose of asking questions does not mean consent to search. However, any seizable item in plain view after valid entry may be properly seized because items in plain view are not protected by the Fourth Amendment.

To be valid, the consent to search does not have to be in writing. Oral consent is sufficient. Many police departments, however, require that the officer obtain consent in writing (see Figure 7.2). This is a good policy because the voluntariness of the consent

FIGURE 7.2 Voluntary Consent for Search And Seizure

State of Texas   Date: _____

County of _____   Time: _____

I, _____ , having been informed by the below officers of my constitutional right not to have a search made of the vehicle and/or premises, hereafter mentioned, without a search warrant and of my right to voluntarily consent to such a search, hereby authorize _____ and _____ , Peace Officers of the Houston Police Department, to conduct a complete search of the following:

☐ Vehicle located at: _____

    Vehicle described as: Year: _____ Make: _____ Model: _____

    License #: _____ State: _____ VIN#: _____ ,

    including the containers and contents therein.

☐ Apartment/house located at: _____

☐ Place of business known as: _____

    located at: _____

These officers are authorized by me to seize any and all letters, papers, material and other property which they desire. This consent is being given to the above Peace Officers freely and voluntarily and without threats or promises of any kind and is given with my full and free consent.

_____
Signature

WITNESSES:

_____

_____

_____

Source: Houston Police Department

often becomes an issue of whose word the judge or jury believes. A written consent tilts the scale of voluntariness in favor of the officer, particularly if the consent is signed by witnesses. There are instances, however, when a written consent may be impractical or difficult to obtain. The evidence obtained will nonetheless be admissible as long as voluntariness is established by the police. There is no need for the police to prove in court that the person giving consent knew that he or she actually had a right to refuse consent. The Court has held that ignorance of such a right is only one of the factors to be considered in determining whether the consent given was voluntary.

The Search Must Stay within Its Allowable Scope Warrantless searches with consent are valid, but the search must stay within its allowable scope. The scope of allowable search depends on the type of consent given. For example, the statement, "You may look around," does not authorize the opening of closets, drawers, trunks, and boxes. The consent to search a garage does not imply consent to search an adjoining house, and vice versa. Conversely, consent for police to search a vehicle does extend to closed but unlocked containers found inside the vehicle, as long as it is objectively reasonable for the police to believe that the scope of the suspect's consent permitted them to open that container (*Florida v. Jimeno*, 500 U.S. 248 [1991]). In general, consent to search does not include consent to open a locked (as opposed to closed) container unless the key is voluntarily given to the police.

Consent may be revoked during a search, by the person who gave the consent or by anybody else who possesses authority to do so. However, any evidence obtained before revocation is admissible.

The Person Must Have the Authority to Give Consent The most common situation where consent is given by someone other than the suspect involves occupants of the same residence, such as a spouse or roommate. This type of consent therefore deserves further discussion.

The Supreme Court has held that the warrantless entry of private premises by police officers is valid if based on the **apparent authority principle**. This applies when police obtained the consent of a third party whom they, at the time of entry, reasonably believed to possess common authority over the premise but who, in fact, did not have such authority (*Illinois v. Rodriguez*, 497 U.S. 177 [1990]).

In *Illinois v. Rodriquez*, Rodriguez was arrested in his apartment and charged with possession of illegal drugs that the police said were in plain view when they entered the apartment. The police gained entry to Rodriguez's apartment with the assistance of Fischer, who told the police that the apartment was "ours" and that she had clothes and furniture there. She unlocked the door with her key and gave the officers permission to enter. In reality, Fischer had moved out of the apartment and therefore no longer had any common authority over the apartment. The Court nonetheless held the consent given by Fischer to be valid because the police reasonably believed, given the circumstances, that she had the authority to give consent.

The case of *Georgia v. Randolph*, 547 U.S. 102 (2006), also offers guidance in determining whether consent given by a co-occupant is valid or not. In *Randolph* the Court held the search invalid as to the occupant who specifically refused consent. The majority stated, however, that this ruling does not apply to the following three situations: (1) when "the police must enter a dwelling to protect a resident from domestic violence, so long as they have good reason to believe such a threat exists," (2) in cases where the purpose of the entry is "to give a complaining tenant the opportunity to collect belongings and get out safely, or to determine whether violence (or threat of violence) has just occurred or

Florida v. Jimeno (1991)

apparent authority principle
appears to have authority but, in reality, does not.

Illinois v. Rodriguez (1990)

Georgia v. Randolph (2006)

is about to (soon will) occur, however much a spouse or other co-tenant objected," and (3) in cases where the person giving consent is in a position of authority in a "recognized hierarchy," such as parent and child. See the Case Brief for further details.

The Court provided a clarification of the *Randolph* holding in *Fernandez v. California* (2014). In this case, Los Angeles police officers responding to a gang-related robbery chased a suspect, Fernandez, into an apartment building. The officers entered the building, at which point they heard cries of distress coming from an apartment. A woman, Roxanne Rojas, answered the door when the officers knocked, and the officers asked if anyone else was present. Rojas said no. The officers informed Rojas that they were going to conduct a security sweep of the apartment, as she was bruised and bleeding and appeared to have been recently assaulted. Fernandez then came to the door and denied the officers right of entry. The officers arrested Fernandez on charges of domestic assault and removed him from the scene. The officers returned to the apartment later that day and asked Rojas for permission to search the residence, which she gave. The officers then conducted a warrantless search and turned up several incriminating items related to the armed robbery. Fernandez was convicted on a multitude of charges and appealed the decision on the grounds that the search violated his Fourth Amendment rights due to his prior refusal to grant consent. The California Court of Appeals affirmed the conviction.

Fernandez v. California (2014)

The Court affirmed the conviction. The majority opinion asserted that *Randolph* was a limited exception to the general rule of *Matlock*, and that it applies only when an objecting co-occupant is present. Fernandez's removal from the premises allowed for the police to enter because of the subsequent consent of Rojas. The Court did concede that officers cannot arrest a co-occupant for the sole purpose of removing them physically from the scene to gain consent from the remaining co-occupant.

Who Has the Authority to Give Consent?

Who	Authority?	Explanation
Spouse	Yes	A spouse can give effective consent to search the family home. Exception: In *Georgia v. Randolph* (2006), the Court held that "a physically present co-occupant's stated refusal to permit entry renders warrantless entry and search unreasonable and invalid as to him." In this case, the defendant's estranged wife gave police permission to search their residence for items of drug use after the defendant, who was also present, had unequivocally refused to give consent to the search. The Court ruled that, under the circumstances, the search was unreasonable and invalid.
Former girlfriend or boyfriend	Yes, if he or she has apparent authority	The Supreme Court has held that the warrantless entry of private premises by police officers is valid if based on the apparent authority principle. This applies when police obtained the consent of a third party whom they, at the time of entry, reasonably believed to possess common authority over the premise but who, in fact, did not have such authority (*Illinois v. Rodriguez*, 497 U.S. 177 [1990]).
Roommate	Yes, but . . .	A roommate may give valid consent to search the room. However, that consent cannot extend to areas in which another roommate has a reasonable expectation of privacy, because only he or she uses it. For example, suppose Joe gives consent for the police to search the studio apartment Joe and Fred occupy. That consent is valid with respect to all areas that both Joe and Fred use, such as the bathroom or study table. The consent is not valid for the search of Fred's closet, to which only Fred has access. If Fred lives in another room (as in a multi-room apartment), Joe cannot give consent to search the room used only by Fred.

Who	Authority?	Explanation
Landlord	No	A landlord cannot give valid consent to search property that he or she has rented to another person (*Stoner v. California*, 376 U.S. 483 [1964]).
Lessor	No	Generally, a lessor (the person who leased out the property) cannot give valid consent to search the premises of a property leased to another person.
Apartment manager	Yes	The consent of an apartment manager to the warrantless search of apartment building common areas (such as public hallways and lobbies) is valid as long as the landlord has joint access to or control over those areas.
Driver of a vehicle	Yes	The consent given by the driver of a vehicle for the search of the vehicle, including the trunk, glove compartment, and other areas, is valid even if the driver is not the owner of the vehicle.
College and university administrators	No	Most lower courts hold that college administrators (such as dormitory managers) cannot give consent for the police to search a student's dormitory room. The fact that some resident or dormitory managers may enter a student's room for certain purposes (such as health and safety issues) does not mean that they can give consent for the police to enter a student's room for purposes related to criminal prosecution. This issue, however, has not been authoritatively settled by the Supreme Court.
High school administrators	Yes	Most lower courts hold that high school administrators, under proper circumstances, may give consent for the police to search a student's locker. This is because high school students are considered wards of the school. Therefore, the authority given to high school administrators is greater than that afforded to their college counterparts.

CASE BRIEF

Georgia v. Randolph, 547 U.S. 103 (2006)

The Leading Case on Consent Given by a Co-Occupant of a Shared Dwelling

Facts: Janet Randolph notified police of a domestic dispute and informed them that her husband, Scott Randolph, had just taken their son away. When officers responded, the wife told them her husband was a cocaine user. Shortly after the police arrived at the Randolphs' residence, Scott Randolph returned. He denied using cocaine, saying it was his wife who abused drugs. Later, the wife reaffirmed Randolph's drug use and told police there was "drug evidence" in the house. An officer asked Randolph for permission to search the house, which he unequivocally denied. The officer then asked the wife for consent to search, which she readily gave. She led officers to Randolph's bedroom. The officers found a section of a drinking straw with a powdery residue suspected to be cocaine. Officers then contacted the district attorney's office. The office instructed them to stop the search and apply for a warrant. When the officers returned to the house, the wife withdrew her consent. The police took the straw to the police station, along with the Randolphs. After obtaining a search warrant, officers returned to the house and seized further evidence of drug use. Randolph was indicted for possession of cocaine and convicted in the trial court. He appealed his conviction, saying the evidence against him was illegally seized against his consent.

Issue or Issues: *Is a warrantless search of a shared dwelling valid when one occupant gives consent but another occupant who is present expressly refuses to give consent?* No.

Decision: The judgment of the Supreme Court of Georgia was affirmed.

Holding: A warrantless search of a shared dwelling for evidence over the clear refusal of consent by a physically present resident cannot be justified as reasonable as to him on the basis of consent given to the police by another resident.

Case Significance: Consent is an exception to the Fourth Amendment rule requiring probable cause and a warrant in search and seizure cases. In previous cases, the Court recognized the validity of searches based on voluntary consent of an individual who shares common authority over property to be searched. None of the co-occupant consent-to-search cases, however, included the circumstances of a second occupant physically present and refusing permission to search. This case resolves an issue that was not previously addressed by the Court: whether consent by an occupant of a dwelling over the expressed objection of another occupant authorizes the police to conduct a warrantless search. Previous U.S. Supreme Court cases said one consent sufficed. In previous cases, however, the other occupant was either away or did not expressly refuse consent. In this case, the other occupant (the husband) was present and specifically refused to give consent.

The Court held the search invalid as to the occupant who specifically refused consent. The majority stated, however, that this ruling does not apply to the following three situations: (1) when "the police must enter a dwelling to protect a resident from domestic violence, so long as they have good reason to believe such a threat exists," (2) in cases where the purpose of the entry is "to give a complaining tenant the opportunity to collect belongings and get out safely, or to determine whether violence (or threat of violence) has just occurred or is about to (soon will) occur, however much a spouse or other co-tenant objected," and (3) in cases where the person giving consent is in a position of authority in a "recognized hierarchy," such as parent and child or "barracks housing military personnel of different grades."

Excerpts from the Decision: [It] is fair to say that a caller standing at the door of shared premises would have no confidence that one occupant's invitation was a sufficiently good reason to enter when a fellow tenant stood there saying, "Stay out." Without some very good reason, no sensible person would go inside under those conditions. . . . The visitor's reticence without some such good reason would show not timidity but a realization that when people living together disagree over the use of their common quarters, a resolution must come through voluntary accommodation, not by appeals to authority. . . . Since the co-tenant wishing to open the door to a third party has no recognized authority in law or social practice to prevail over a present and objecting co-tenant, his disputed invitation, without more, gives a police officer no better claim to reasonableness in entering than the officer would have in the absence of any consent at all. . . . So long as there is no evidence that the police have removed the potentially objecting tenant from the entrance for the sake of avoiding a possible objection, there is practical value in the simple clarity of complementary rules, one recognizing the co-tenant's permission when there is no fellow occupant on hand, the other according dispositive weight to the fellow occupant's contrary indication when he expresses it.

The Search Incident to Lawful Arrest Exception

The search incident to lawful arrest exception is widely used in policing. It is used almost every time an officer makes an arrest, with or without a warrant. There are three justifications for warrantless searches incident to arrest: (1) to ensure officer safety, (2) to prevent escape, and (3) to prevent the destruction of evidence. The authorization to search incident to arrest is always available to the officer after an arrest, even if there is no probable cause to believe it is necessary to ensure officer safety, to prevent escape, or to prevent concealment or destruction of evidence. These searches take two forms: body search and search of the area within the person's immediate control. To be legal, searches must be contemporaneous with the arrest.

See the Case Brief of *Chimel v. California*, a leading case on searches after arrest, for a discussion of the **Chimel rule**. The *Chimel* rule states that after a valid arrest, police officers may search the arrestee's "area of immediate control."

Searches incident to a lawful arrest is discussed more extensively in Chapter 6, because it is best and more logically discussed there. The rules, however, are exactly the same as the rules that apply to searches and seizures of things in this chapter, and so the reader is asked to refer to Chapter 6 for a more detailed discussion of this type of search and seizure.

Chimel rule
a rule that allows police officers after an arrest to search the arrestee's "area of immediate control."

CASE BRIEF — *Chimel v. California*, 395 U.S. 752 (1969)

The Leading Case on a Search Incident to an Arrest

Facts: Chimel was suspected of having robbed a coin shop. Armed with an arrest warrant (but not a search warrant), police officers went to Chimel's house and were admitted by his wife. Chimel was not at home but was immediately arrested when he arrived. The police asked Chimel if they could "look around." Chimel denied the request, but the officers searched the entire house anyway and discovered some stolen coins. At the trial, the coins were introduced as evidence over Chimel's objection. Chimel was convicted of robbery. He appealed to the Supreme Court of California, which upheld his conviction. He then took his case to the United States Supreme Court.

Issue or Issues: *In the course of making a lawful arrest, may officers search the immediate area where the person was arrested without a search warrant?* Yes.

Holding: After making an arrest, the police may search the area within the person's immediate control. The purpose of such a search is to discover and remove weapons and to prevent the destruction of evidence.

Case Significance: *Chimel* categorically states that the police may search the area in the arrestee's "immediate control" when making a valid arrest, whether the arrest takes place with or without a warrant. That area of immediate control is defined by the Court as "the area from within which he might gain possession of a weapon or destructible evidence." *Chimel* authoritatively settled an issue over which lower courts had given inconsistent rulings. The current rule is that the police may search without a warrant after a lawful arrest, but the extent of that search is limited to the area of the arrestee's immediate control. The safest, and most limited, interpretation of the term area of immediate control is a person's wingspan, within which it might be possible to grab a weapon or destroy evidence. Some lower courts have given a more liberal interpretation to include such areas as the whole room in which the person is arrested. This interpretation appears to go beyond what the Court had in mind in *Chimel*.

Excerpts from the Opinion: When an arrest is made, it is reasonable for the arresting officer to search the person arrested in order to remove any weapons that the latter might seek to use in order to resist arrest or effect his escape. Otherwise, the officer's safety might well be endangered, and the arrest itself frustrated. In addition, it is entirely reasonable for the arresting officer to search for and seize any evidence on the arrestee's person in order to prevent its concealment or destruction. And the area into which an arrestee might reach in order to grab a weapon or evidentiary items must, of course, be governed by a like rule. . . . There is ample justification, therefore, for a search of the arrestee's person and the area within his immediate control.

The Exigent Circumstances Exception

exigent circumstances
some kind of an emergency that makes getting a search warrant impractical, useless, dangerous, or unnecessary.

The **exigent circumstances** exception is a general catchall category that encompasses a number of diverse situations. What they have in common is some kind of an emergency that makes getting a search warrant impractical, useless, dangerous, or unnecessary. Discussed next are four illustrative situations that fall under exigent circumstances. They are danger of physical harm to the officer or destruction of evidence, searches in hot pursuit of dangerous suspects, danger to a third person, and driving while intoxicated.

Danger of Physical Harm to the Officer or Destruction of Evidence The Court has implied that a warrantless search may be justified if there are reasonable grounds to believe that delaying the search until the warrant is obtained would endanger the physical safety of the officer or would allow the destruction or removal of the evidence (*Vale v. Louisiana*, 399 U.S. 30 [1970]). However, in *Vale*, the Supreme Court did not

Vale v. Louisiana (1970)

allow a warrantless search when there was *merely a possibility* that the evidence would be destroyed. Thus, *Vale* has a narrow interpretation: The threat of danger or destruction must be real or imminent.

Three years later, in *Cupp v. Murphy*, 412 U.S. 291 (1973), the Court held that the taking of fingernail scrapings without consent or formal arrest does not violate the Fourth Amendment protection against unreasonable search and seizure if the evidence is likely to disappear before a warrant can be obtained.

Cupp v. Murphy (1973)

The Court has ruled, however, that the fact that the place searched was the scene of a serious crime (in this case the murder of an undercover officer) did not in itself justify a warrantless search in the absence of any "indication that the evidence would be lost, destroyed, or removed during the time required to obtain a search warrant and there [was] no suggestion that a warrant could not easily and conveniently have been obtained" (*Mincey v. Arizona*, 437 U.S. 385 [1978]).

Mincey v. Arizona (1978)

In *Mincey*, an undercover police officer was shot and killed during a narcotics raid on Mincey's apartment. Shortly thereafter, homicide detectives arrived at the scene of the crime and conducted "an exhaustive four-day warrantless search of the apartment which included the opening of dresser drawers, the ripping up of carpets, and the seizure of 200 to 300 objects." At trial, Mincey sought to suppress the evidence obtained, saying that the warrantless search was invalid. The government justified the warrantless search based on the "murder scene" exception to the warrant requirement created by the Arizona Supreme Court in previous cases. The Court disagreed, saying that the warrantless search in this case could not be justified based on "the ground that a possible homicide inevitably presents an emergency situation, especially since there was no emergency threatening life or limb." The seriousness of the offense cannot of itself create exigent circumstances justifying a warrantless search, when there is no indication that evidence would be lost during the time required to obtain a search warrant.

In *Flippo v. West Virginia*, 528 U.S. 11 (1999), the Court reaffirmed its decision in *Mincey* when it said that there is no crime scene exception to the search warrant requirement, adding that "a warrantless search by the police is invalid unless it falls within one of the narrow and well-delineated exceptions to the warrant requirement." In this case, Flippo's conviction was influenced by photographs removed by the police from a briefcase they found at the crime scene and opened without a warrant. The photographs, admitted at trial, suggested that Flippo was having a homosexual affair with a member of his church and that this provided a motive for him to kill his wife. The Court rejected the murder scene exception to the warrant requirement used by the prosecution, saying that this exception was squarely in conflict with *Mincey.*

Searches in Hot Pursuit of Dangerous Suspects The police may enter a house without a warrant to search for a dangerous suspect who is being pursued and whom they have reason to believe is on the premises. For example, in one case, the police pursued a robbery suspect to a house (which later turned out to be his own). The suspect's wife opened the door to the police, who asked and received permission to search for a "burglar." The police looked for weapons that might have been concealed and found incriminating clothing in a washing machine. The clothing was confiscated and introduced as evidence during the trial. The Court held that the warrantless search was justified by hot pursuit (regardless of the validity of the suspect's wife's consent). Because the police were informed that an armed robbery had taken place and that the suspect had entered a particular house less than five minutes before they got there, they acted reasonably when they entered the house and began to search for the suspect and for weapons that he had allegedly used in the robbery (*Warden v. Hayden*, 387 U.S. 294 [1967]).

Danger to a Third Person An officer may enter a dwelling without a warrant in response to screams for help. In *Warden v. Hayden*, 387 U.S. 294 (1967), the Court said, "The Fourth Amendment does not require police officers to delay in the course of an investigation if to do so would gravely endanger their lives or the lives of others." In a more recent case, the Court held as follows: "Police may enter a home without a warrant when they have an objectively reasonable basis for believing that an occupant is seriously injured or imminently threatened with such injury" (*Brigham City, Utah v. Stuart*, 547 U.S. 47 [2007]). (This case is discussed more extensively in Chapter 6.)

Driving While Intoxicated (DWI) The police may, without a search warrant and by force, if necessary, take a blood sample from a person arrested for drunk driving, as long as the setting and procedures are reasonable (as when the blood is drawn by a doctor in a hospital). Exigent circumstances exist because alcohol in the suspect's bloodstream might disappear in the time required to obtain a warrant (*Schmerber v. California*, 384 U.S. 757 [1966]).

However, in *Welch v. Wisconsin*, 466 U.S. 740 (1984), the Court placed limits on what the police can do in routine DWI cases. The Court held that the Fourth Amendment prohibits the police from making a warrantless nighttime entry into a suspect's house to arrest him or her for drunk driving if the offense is a misdemeanor for which state law does not allow any jail sentence. The fact that the police had an interest in preserving the evidence (because the suspect's blood-alcohol level might diminish while the police procured a warrant) was ruled insufficient to create the required exigent circumstance.

In *Welch*, the defendant had run his car off the road and abandoned it. By the time police officers arrived at the scene and learned from a witness that the defendant was either inebriated or very ill, the defendant had gone home and fallen asleep. The officers checked the vehicle's registration and learned that the defendant lived close by. Without obtaining a warrant, they went to the suspect's home and arrested him. The Wisconsin Supreme Court held that the officers' actions were justified by exigent circumstances.

The U.S. Supreme Court reversed that decision, saying that "an important factor to be considered when determining whether any exigency exists is the gravity of the underlying offense for which the arrest is being made. . . . Application of the exigent circumstances exception in the context of a home entry should rarely be sanctioned when there is probable cause to believe that only a minor offense has been committed." Implicit in this is the assumption that, had the offense been serious (such as if the driver had seriously injured somebody before running off the road and abandoning his car), the warrantless search of his home would have been allowed. The Court concluded that in this case there was no immediate pursuit of the defendant from the scene, nor was there any need to protect either the public or the defendant, as he had abandoned the vehicle and was at home sleeping. Only the need to preserve the evidence remained, and that was not enough, given the type of offense involved and the state's treatment of it as a civil matter, to justify the warrantless intrusion.

In 2013, in *Missouri v. McNeely* the Court reaffirmed and clarified its decision in *Missouri v. McNeely* (2013) *Schmerber*, holding that the normal reduction over time of the level of alcohol in the bloodstream did not automatically create exigent circumstances justifying a warrant-less taking of a blood sample.

In this case Tyler McNeely was stopped by a Missouri state police officer, Matt Winder, after he observed McNeely speeding and crossing the centerline. Upon approaching McNeely, Officer Winder observed signs of intoxication, including blood-shot eyes and slurred speech. After McNeely failed a series of field-sobriety tests, Officer Winder arrested him and placed him in his cruiser to take him to the station for booking and the administration of a breath-test to measure his blood alcohol content. When McNeely stated he would not take a breath-test, Officer Winder drove McNeely to a local hospital for a blood test. Officer Winder instructed the nurse to take a blood sample, over McNeely's objections. Officer Winder never attempted to obtain a search warrant. After testing, McNeely's blood alcohol level was found to be above the legal limit and he was charged with driving while intoxicated. At trial, McNeely filed a motion to suppress his blood test, claiming it violated his Fourth Amendment rights to take the blood sample without first obtaining a search warrant. The trial court granted the motion. The Missouri Supreme Court affirmed the trial court, arguing that while the U.S. Supreme Court had ruled in *Schmerber v. California* (1966) that the drawing of a nonconsensual, warrantless blood sample was allowed due to exigent circumstances, the Court also indicated that this standard should be applied to the totality of the circumstances in each case. The Missouri Supreme Court concluded that the likeli-hood that blood alcohol levels will be reduced if a blood or breath sample is not taken quickly does not of itself create exigent circumstances. On examining the totality of the circumstances, the Missouri Supreme Court concluded that it was a routine DWI case, and that there were no exigent circumstances. The Court agreed, noting that the *Schmerber* ruling was issued after careful consideration of the specific circumstances of that case, and that future cases should be subject to the same case-by-case consid-eration when deciding whether there were exigent circumstances present to justify a warrantless blood sample to be taken in alcohol-related cases.

THE SPECIAL NEEDS BEYOND LAW ENFORCEMENT EXCEPTION

The Court has carved out a series of exceptions to the warrant requirement, collectively known as the special needs beyond law enforcement exception. What such **special needs exceptions** have in common is that they are not police searches (although some-times the police are asked to help) but instead involve searches conducted by other public agencies that perform tasks related to law enforcement. The Court has repeat-edly held that these types of searches may be made *without a warrant* and on *less than probable cause*. This section looks at each of these examples. The following situations illustrate the special needs exception to the warrant and probable cause requirements, as determined by the Court in decided cases:

◆ Public school searches
◆ Testing students for drugs
◆ Airport searches
◆ Searches of probationers and parolees

special needs exceptions
an exception to the requirements of a warrant and probable cause under the Fourth Amendment; it allows warrantless searches and searches on less-than-probable cause in cases where there are needs to be met other than those of law enforcement, such as the supervision of high school students, probationers, and parolees.

Public School Searches

In *New Jersey v. T.L.O.*, 469 U.S. 325 (1985), the Court resolved an issue that had long bothered public school students, teachers, and administrators. The Court said that public school teachers and administrators *do not need a warrant or probable cause* to search a student they believe is violating the law or school rules. What they do need are *reasonable grounds* (lower than probable cause) for suspecting that the search will turn up evidence that the student has violated or is violating either the law or the rules of the school.

In *T.L.O.*, a teacher at a New Jersey high school discovered a student and her companion smoking cigarettes in a school restroom in violation of school rules. She took them to the principal's office, where they met with the assistant vice principal. When the student denied that she had been smoking, the assistant vice principal demanded to see her purse. On opening the purse, he found a pack of cigarettes and also noticed a package of cigarette rolling papers, which are commonly associated with the use of marijuana. He then searched the purse thoroughly and found marijuana, a pipe, plastic bags, a fairly substantial amount of money, and other items that implicated her in marijuana dealing.

The student moved to suppress this evidence in juvenile court, alleging that the search was illegal for lack of probable cause and a warrant. The Supreme Court rejected her allegation, saying that the Fourth Amendment prohibition against unreasonable searches and seizures applies to searches conducted by public school officials, but the school's legitimate need to maintain a positive learning environment requires some easing of the Fourth Amendment restrictions. Therefore, public school officials do not need a warrant or probable cause to conduct a search. All they need are *reasonable grounds* to suspect that the search will turn up evidence that the student has violated or is violating either the law or the rules of the school.

The *T.L.O.* ruling applies only when the search and seizure are done by public school teachers and administrators. It does not apply to police officers, who are bound by the probable cause and warrant requirements even in school searches which they conduct on their own. The only possible exception is if the officers perform the search at the request of school authorities.

Safford Unified School District v. Redding (2009)

Twenty-four years later, the Court set a limit to school searches when it held that the search of a student's underwear without reasonable suspicion of a violation of school rules is unconstitutional (*Safford Unified School District v. Redding*, 557 U.S. 364 [2009]). In this case, a thirteen-year-old student, Savana Redding, was suspected by the assistant principal of the school of giving prohibited pills to other students. Redding denied all this and gave permission for the search of her belongings. The administrators

---

HIGHLIGHT ❯ **Searches of Students and the Fourth Amendment**

"[The accommodation of the privacy interests of schoolchildren with the substantial need of teachers and administrators for freedom to maintain order in the schools does not require strict adherence to the requirement that searches be based on probable cause to believe that the subject of the search has violated or is violating the law. Rather, the legality of a search of a student should depend simply on the reasonableness, under all the circumstances, of the search."

Source: *New Jersey v. T.L.O.*, 469 U.S. 325 (1985).

searched her backpack and found nothing. The assistant principal then took the student to the office of the school nurse so her clothing could be searched. There the student was made to remove her outer clothing, then they told her to "pull her bra out and shake it, and to "pull out the elastic on her underpants, thus exposing her breasts and pelvic area to some degree." No drugs or other contraband were found. The student's mother later sued the school authorities and school district, claiming that the strip search was unconstitutional and that those involved should be held civilly liable because they violated a clearly established constitutional right.

On appeal the Court agreed with the student and held that the search violated her constitutional rights. However, the administrators and school district were not held civilly liable because they did not violate a "clearly established constitutional right," which is required for civil liability. The majority opinion distinguished this case from *New Jersey v. T.L.O.*, saying that the school authorities in *Redding* went beyond what was allowed in the *T.L.O* case. Of importance to the Court was that there was no "reasonable suspicion" in *Redding* to justify the highly intrusive search.

Testing Non-College Students for Drugs

Can school administrators test non-college students for drugs? Any form of drug testing, whether it be of police officers or students, involves a potential violation of the Fourth Amendment because it is a form of search and seizure. The Court has held that drug testing high school student athletes does not require individualized suspicion and that random drug testing is constitutional (*Vernonia School District v. Acton* (515 U.S. 646 [1995]). In this case, the Vernonia School District discovered that some of their high school athletes had participated in illicit drug use. The school authorities then adopted a policy that authorized random urinalysis drug testing of its student-athletes. James Acton was denied participation in the football program when he and his parents refused to consent to drug testing. On appeal, the Court held that the drug-testing policy was valid, saying that the constitutionality of a search is determined by "balancing the intrusion on the individual's Fourth Amendment interests against the promotion of legitimate governmental interests." Finding that the privacy interests involved when collecting urine samples are "negligible," the Court concluded that high school athletes are under state supervision when they are in school and are subject to greater control than free adults.

Vernonia School District v. Acton (1995)

Seven years later, the Court extended this holding in *Board of Education of Independent School District No. 92 of Pottawatomie County et al. v. Earls*, 536 U.S. 822 (2002), another case involving middle and high school students. The Court held that the random urinalysis testing policy that applied to all middle and high school students participating in any extracurricular activity, not just athletics, was constitutional. The Court stressed that the random drug testing was "a reasonable means of furthering the School District's important interest in preventing and deterring drug use among its schoolchildren."

Do the *T.L.O.*, *Acton*, and *Earls* Decisions Apply to College Students? This was not addressed by the Court in any of the preceding cases, but the answer is no, because most college students are adults, so the in loco parentis justification (which is the basis for special needs searches in public elementary and high schools) does not apply. Lower courts have held that college students, regardless of age, are considered adults for the purpose of determining constitutional rights. Nonetheless, there are reasons to believe that drug testing college students will be deemed valid in cases where there is evidence of drug use by students involved in athletics or other college or university programs where sufficient justification, whatever that might be, for drug testing exists.

Airport Searches

Airport searches come under special needs and therefore do not need probable cause, reasonable suspicion, or even mere suspicion. They are a day-to-day reality of modern air travel and are done routinely. Airport searches are based on proven safety needs. Long before the tragic events of 9/11, airport searches had drawn approval from the courts. In *United States v. Davis*, 482 F.2d 893 (9th Cir. 1973), the Court said, "The need to prevent airline hijacking is unquestionably grave and urgent. . . . A pre-boarding screening of all passengers and carry-on articles sufficient in scope to detect the presence of weapons or explosives is reasonably necessary to meet the need."

United States v. Bell (1972)

The Fourth Amendment issues in searches and seizures at airports are many, among them: the preboarding request for identification, the search of a passenger's carry-on luggage, the search of a passenger's checked baggage, and the search of the person. Although Fourth Amendment issues have been an ongoing source of dispute, a great majority of search and seizure challenges filed by airplane passengers have been rejected by the courts. One court of appeals judge (*United States v. Bell*, 464 F.2d 667 [1972]) years ago justified airport searches in this way:

> When the risk is the jeopardy to hundreds of human lives and millions of dollars of property inherent in the pirating or blowing up of a large airplane, that danger alone meets the test of reasonableness, so long as the search is conducted in good faith for the purpose of preventing hijacking or like damage and with reasonable scope and the passenger has been given advance notice of his liability to such a search so that he can avoid it by choosing not to travel by air.

The use of police dogs to sniff containers and luggage to detect contraband at airports does not constitute a search. No warrant or probable cause is needed as long as the container or luggage is located in a public place. In *United States v. Sullivan*, 625 F.2d 9 (4th Cir. 1980), the court said, "It cannot be considered a search within the protection of the Fourth Amendment for a dog to sniff bags handled by an airline. There can be no reasonable expectation of privacy when any passenger's bags may be subjected to close scrutiny for the protection of public safety."

The invasiveness of some recent airport searches has raised concerns about constitutionality, particularly the federal Transportation Security Administration (TSA) authorization of the use of full-body scans in airports. It can be argued that the use of full-body scanners produce images of virtually naked bodies and grossly violate a passenger's right to privacy. The courts, however, have put a stop to a practice that a great majority of the public is willing to accept because it helps to ensure travel safety.

Searches of Probationers and Parolees

Griffin v. Wisconsin (1987)

In probation cases, the Court has held that a state law or agency rule permitting probation officers to search probationers' homes without a warrant and based on reasonable grounds (lower than probable cause) is a reasonable response to the special needs of the probation system and is therefore constitutional (*Griffin v. Wisconsin*, 483 U.S.

868 [1987]). The Court added that the supervision of probationers is a special need of the state that justifies a departure from the usual warrant and probable cause requirements.

In *United States v. Knights*, 534 U.S. 112 (2001), the Court held that a warrantless search by an officer of a probationer's apartment, supported by reasonable suspicion and authorized by the judge as a condition of probation, is valid under the Fourth Amendment under the special needs exception. The Court said that the totality of the circumstances is what determines whether a search is reasonable under the Fourth Amendment. Some states allow warrantless searches of probationers' homes by probation officers based on *mere suspicion*, an even lower degree of certainty than reasonable grounds. Although the Supreme Court has not ruled on this issue, lower courts have upheld the practice based on the twin concepts of probationers' *diminished constitutional rights* and *special needs*.

United States v. Knights (2001)

As for parolees (those released from prison after having served a part of their sentence), the Court has held that the suspicionless search of a parolee by a law enforcement officer is valid under the Fourth Amendment (*Samson v. California*, 547 U.S. 843 [2006]). In this case (also discussed in Chapter 4), the police officer, who knew Samson, stopped him and asked questions. Samson was searched, and the officer found methamphetamine in a cigarette box in Samson's shirt pocket. The officer later admitted that he stopped Samson solely because he knew he was on parole. Convicted of drug possession, Samson sought to exclude the evidence, saying it was the product of an unconstitutional search. The Court rejected his claim, ruling that the search was valid because convicted offenders have diminished constitutional rights and that, technically, parolees are under the custody of the Department of Corrections and are therefore still prisoners. The Court recognized the continuum of state-imposed punishments, saying that "on this continuum, parolees have fewer expectations of privacy than probationers, because parole is more akin to imprisonment than probation is to imprisonment." Although the Court did not address the issue directly, it noted that one of the conditions of Samson's parole (a common condition for release on parole) was that the parolee consent to being searched "with or without a warrant and with or without cause."

Samson v. California (2006)

In summary, probationers and parolees have minimal constitutional rights under the Fourth Amendment. The issue is important because probationers and parolees disproportionately commit more crimes than those who have had no prior convictions, and the number of people either on probation or parole continues to increase.

The Police and Special Needs

The special needs exception to the warrant and probable cause requirements is a fast-developing area of the law on searches and seizures. The Court will likely add other situations in the future similar to those discussed earlier that it considers as qualifying under the category of special needs. Like many other legal terms, *special needs* has no fixed meaning and therefore develops and evolves as the need arises.

The special needs exception, however, is of no day-to-day concern in policing because the searches are conducted by administrative officials, not by the police. There are instances, though, when the police are asked by administrative officials (as in school searches, searches in juvenile detention centers, and searches by probation officers) to help. In these cases, whether it is an administrative search (and therefore falls under special needs) or a police search (and therefore subject to the probable cause and warrant requirement) is determined by this test: Did administrative officials ask the police for help during the search, or are the administrative officials being used by the police as an excuse to search things and places they otherwise cannot search or seize because they lack probable cause? If administrators use the police for help, then it is a special needs search. Conversely, if the administrators are used by the police to do something they otherwise could not legally do, then it is a regular police search and needs a warrant and probable cause to be valid.

Police Searches and Special Needs Searches Compared

Police Searches	Special Needs Searches
Done by the police	Not done by the police but by other public officers such as school authorities, probation or parole officers, or work supervisors
Need for a warrant	No need for a warrant
Need for probable cause	No need for probable cause; reasonable suspicion is usually enough
Purpose is law enforcement	Purpose is not law enforcement but such other goals as to provide a better learning environment, rehabilitation, or supervision

ADMINISTRATIVE SEARCHES AND INSPECTIONS

administrative searches

searches conducted by government investigators to determine whether there are violations of government rules and regulations.

Michigan v. Clifford (1984)

Administrative searches are searches conducted by government investigators to determine whether there are violations of government rules and regulations. These searches are usually authorized by local ordinances or regulations of administrative agencies and are generally conducted by agents or investigators of these agencies rather than by the police. In some jurisdictions, the warrant issued is known as an *administrative* instead of a *judicial* warrant. In a case involving a prosecution for arson, the Court provided the following distinctions between the need for administrative warrants and a criminal search warrant and what these warrants require (*Michigan v. Clifford*, 464 U.S. 287 [1984]):

> If the primary object is to determine the cause and origin of a recent fire, an administrative warrant will suffice. To obtain such a warrant, fire officials need show only that a fire of undetermined origin has occurred on the premises, that the scope of the proposed search is reasonable and will not intrude unnecessarily on the fire victim's privacy, and that the search will be executed at a reasonable and convenient time.
>
> If the primary object of the search is to gather evidence of criminal activity, a criminal search warrant may be obtained only on a showing of probable cause to believe that relevant evidence will be found in the place to be searched. If evidence of criminal activity is discovered during the course of a valid administrative search, it may be seized under the "plain view" doctrine. This evidence may then be used to establish probable cause to obtain a criminal search warrant.

Administrative Searches and Law Enforcement Searches Compared

Administrative Searches	Law Enforcement Searches
Done by administrative agents or investigators, not by the police.	Done by law enforcement personnel.
Purpose is enforcement of administrative regulations.	Purpose is enforcement of criminal laws.
Consent or warrant is needed, except for highly regulated businesses.	Consent or warrant is always needed.
Probable cause is not needed, but agents must show that the place inspected is subject to administrative rules, ordinances, or regulations.	Probable cause is always needed unless consent is given.

WARRANTLESS SEARCHES MUST BE CONTEMPORANEOUS

Contemporaneous search is a search that must occur at the same time as, or very close in time and place to, the arrest. A contemporaneous search is illegal if conducted long after the arrest. In one case, the police arrested several smugglers and seized the foot-locker in which they believed marijuana was being transported. One hour after the arrest, after the suspects were in jail, the officers opened and searched the footlocker without a warrant. The Court invalidated the search, saying that it was "remote in time and place from the arrest" (*United States v. Chadwick*, 433 U.S. 1 [1977]).

However, the custodial search may be deemed "incident to arrest" even when carried out later than the time of arrest, if there was a valid reason for the delay. For example, in *United States v. Edwards*, 415 U.S. 800 (1974), a suspect was arrested and jailed late at night, but a search for evidence in his clothing was not conducted until the following morning. The Court said that the delayed search was justified because substitute clothing was not available for the suspect's use at the time of the booking.

contemporaneous search
the search must occur at the time as, or very close in time and place to, the arrest.

United States v. Chadwick (1977)

THE ANNOUNCEMENT REQUIREMENT

The rules for announcements in search and seizure cases are exactly the same as those for arrests. In brief, knock-and-announce is required by the Constitution. There are exceptions to this rule, however.

Constitutional law and many state statutes require that an officer making an arrest or executing a search warrant announce his or her purpose and authority before break-ing into a dwelling. The goal is to allow voluntary compliance and avoid violence. Breaking into the premises without first complying with the announcement require-ment may or may not invalidate the entry and any resulting search, depending on the law or court decisions in that state. The announcement requirement is discussed in detail in Chapter 6.

OTHER SEARCH AND SEIZURE ISSUES

This section examines ten specific search and seizure issues:

- ◆ Use of police dogs in searches
- ◆ Searches and seizures of computers
- ◆ Searches and seizures of text messages
- ◆ Searches and seizures of e-mails
- ◆ Drug testing public employees, including police officers
- ◆ Searches and seizures of public employees other than drug testing
- ◆ Squeezing luggage on a bus
- ◆ Searches and seizures by private persons
- ◆ Searches by off-duty officers
- ◆ Surgery to remove a bullet from a suspect

The Use of Police Dogs in Searches

United States v. Place (1983)

The Court has determined that dog sniffs are not searches and are therefore not protected by the Fourth Amendment (*United States v. Place*, 462 U.S. 696 [1983]). In this case, an airport traveler, who was suspected of carrying drugs, had his luggage subjected to dog sniffs. Based on the dog sniffs by a drug-detection dog, government agents obtained a warrant to search the luggage. The search found cocaine. The suspect was later charged with and convicted of a drug offense. He claimed that the sniff test by the police dog constituted an unconstitutional search under the Fourth Amendment. On appeal, the Court disagreed, saying that since the sniff did not require opening the luggage or exposing the luggage contents to public view, it constituted something less than a Fourth Amendment search. But the evidence obtained in this case was thrown out anyway based on some other grounds.

In a later case, *Illinois v. Caballes*, 543 U.S. 405 (2005), the Court held that "a dog sniff conducted during a concededly lawful traffic stop that reveals no information other than the location of a substance that no individual has any right to possess does not violate the Fourth Amendment." In this case, the driver was stopped for speeding. While one officer was issuing the warning ticket, another officer walked around the car with his drug-detection dog. The dog alerted the officers to the car's trunk. Searching the trunk, the officers found marijuana and arrested the driver. On appeal for drug possession, the driver alleged that the search was illegal because there was no probable cause to conduct the search. The Court rejected the claim and held that there was probable cause to search based on the dog's sniff. Because the sniff "revealed no information other than the location of a substance that no individual has any right to possess," the search was legal.

Florida v. Jardines (2013)

In *Florida v. Jardines* (569 U.S. --- [2013]) the Supreme Court clarified when police officers can use drug dogs to search private residences. In this case, based on an unverified tip that Jardines was growing marijuana plants in his home, the Miami-Dade Police Department arrived at Jardines's home with a surveillance team, which included a trained drug detection dog, Franky. Without a search warrant or consent from Jardines, a police officer led Franky from the police vehicle parked on the public street onto the property and up onto the front porch of the home. Once on the front porch, Franky alerted, indicating the presence of drugs inside the house. Based on the alert given by Franky, the police obtained a warrant and returned the next day to search Jardines's home; the search revealed multiple marijuana plants. Jardines was arrested and charged with drug trafficking. At trial, he filed a motion to suppress the evidence found during the search of his home, arguing that the sniff search conducted on his front porch violated the Fourth Amendment because it occurred on private property. The trial court granted the motion. The Florida Third District Court of Appeals

---

HIGHLIGHT > The Use of Drug Dogs and the Fourth Amendment

"[T]he use of a well-trained narcotics-detection dog—one that does not expose noncontraband items that otherwise would remain hidden from public view, during a lawful traffic stop, generally does not implicate legitimate privacy interests. In this case, the dog sniff was performed on the exterior of respondent's car while he was lawfully seized for a traffic violation. Any intrusion on respondent's privacy expectations does not rise to the level of a constitutionally cognizable infringement."

Source: *Illinois v. Caballes*, 543 U.S. 405 (2005).

reversed the trial court's decision and the Florida Supreme Court then reinstituted the trial court's decision to suppress the evidence. The Supreme Court affirmed the decision of the Florida Supreme Court. The Court held that when police bring a drug sniffing dog onto someone's front porch this action constitutes a search and a trespass. While the public is allowed to stand upon someone's front porch, this does not authorize the police to bring a drug dog onto the porch in order to "search" the house via the drug dog's sense of smell. Previous rulings by the Court have established the front porch of a home is part of the curtilage, and therefore enjoys the same protections from unreasonable searches as the home.

The difference between this case and the previous dog-sniffing cases decided by the Court is that *United States v. Place* (1980), involved dog-sniffing the luggage of a man who was detained in an airport, and *Illinois v. Caballes* (2005) involved a police dog sniffing a motor vehicle during a traffic stop—both cases involved dog sniffs in public places. In contrast, the *Jardines* case involves police dog sniffing the front door of a home, a private and highly protected property.

Searches and Seizures of Computers

Searches and seizures of computers and other electronic gadgets (such as laptops, personal digital assistants, and cell phones) have increasingly become problems in policing because these devices are being used by criminals more frequently. The good news is that the police now use computers to solve crimes; the bad news is that criminals also use computers to plan and commit crimes. Two issues arise in computer searches: (1) Are these searches constitutional or are they Fourth Amendment violations, and (2) what procedures must law enforcement use to preserve the evidence seized?

Legal Requirements In general, searches and seizures of computers have the same legal requirements as any other type of seizure, meaning there must be a warrant based on probable cause. A manual on computer searches, titled *Computer Searches* (issued by the District Attorney's Office of Alameda County, California), states that there are two requirements for the issuance of a warrant to search a computer: (1) "probable cause to believe the data to be seized exists, is evidence of a crime, and is presently located at the place to be searched," and (2) "a reasonably detailed description of the place to be searched and the data to be seized."[1] Both requirements are similar to those for non-computer searches.

Probable Cause in Computer Searches Probable cause is likely established if the suspect is in possession of incriminating data, if the data are stored on a computer, and if the computer is likely to be found in the place to be searched.[2] The requirement for a description of the place to be searched is similar to what is required for other types of warrants; the warrant must "contain a reasonably detailed description of the home or office that will be searched." Describing the hardware or software to be searched also needs particularity.

Computers and Reasonable Expectation of Privacy How is reasonable expectation of privacy determined for computers? A Justice Department publication says:

> To determine whether an individual has a reasonable expectation of privacy in information stored in a computer, it helps to treat the computer like a closed container such as a briefcase or file cabinet. The Fourth Amendment generally prohibits law

enforcement from accessing and viewing information stored in a computer without a warrant if it would be prohibited from opening a closed container and examining its contents in the same situation.[3]

There is no reasonable expectation of privacy, however, in the following cases: (1) when a person has made such information openly available, (2) when the contents of stolen computers are involved, (3) when the control of the computer has been given to a third party, and (4) when the owner loses control of the file.[4]

Searches and Seizures of Text Messages in a Cell Phone

United States v. Wurie (2013)

In two cases decided together in 2013, the Supreme Court for the first time dealt with the applicability of the Fourth Amendment to searches of cell phones. In *United States v. Wurie*, Boston police officers observed Brima Wurie conduct a drug sale from his vehicle. The officers then arrested Wurie, conducted a search of Wurie's person, and seized two cell phones. Later, while at the police station one of the cellphones, an old-fashioned "flip" phone, rang repeatedly. The officers inspected the phone and noticed that it was receiving a number of calls from a number identified as "my house." The officers opened the phone, obtained the phone number for "my house," and inspected the screen saver of the phone, which featured a young woman and a small child. The officers obtained an address for the number and went to the location. A young woman who matched the picture on the phone answered the door. The officers then obtained a search warrant and conducted a search of the premises, where they found a large amount of crack cocaine, drug paraphernalia, and firearms. The state then charged Wurie with multiple offenses. Wurie moved to suppress the evidence on the ground that the initial search of the flip phone violated his Fourth Amendment rights. The District Court denied his motion, and he was convicted and sentenced to 262 months in prison. The First Circuit Court of Appeals reversed, holding that the search incident exception to the Fourth Amendment did not allow police officers to search the digital contents of a cell phone. The Supreme Court granted certiorari, along with *California v. Riley*.

California v. Riley (2013)

In *California v. Riley*, police officers in San Diego arrested David Riley for driving with a suspended driver's license. They impounded and searched the vehicle; the search uncovered two handguns. The government then charged Riley with two felonies related to these firearms. The search also revealed several items that pointed to Riley being involved in the "Bloods" street gang. At the time of his arrest Riley was carrying a so-called "smart phone." The officers searched the contents of the phone at the scene of arrest and again at the station. The phone contained evidence of "Blood" activity, including a recent shooting. The state then charged Riley for his participation in this shooting. Riley moved to suppress the evidence from the search of his cell phone, contending that there were no exigent circumstances to justify the warrantless search. Riley was eventually convicted. The California Court of Appeals affirmed the conviction. The Supreme Court then granted certiorari, and combined the case with *Wurie* case.

The Supreme Court reversed both convictions. The Court noted that warrantless searches incident to arrest are justified to ensure the safety of the arresting officer and protect against the destruction of evidence, but that such warrantless searches do not extend to the contents of cell phones. Cell phones, by their nature, do not pose a danger to the arresting officer, and the act of confiscating the phone prevents the destruction of any evidence contained in the phone, and there is therefore no need to examine the contents of the phone. The Court acknowledged the wealth of personal information contained in a modern cell phone. The Court affirmed that the Fourth Amendment was constructed in order to prevent the government from arbitrarily intruding on this type of personal information.

Government Seizure of E-mails

No Court decision has thus far addressed the specific issue of government seizure of e-mails. A 2007 decision of the federal Court of Appeals for the Sixth Circuit, however, is informative on this issue. The court of appeals upheld, with modification, a district court order prohibiting the government from seizing e-mails from an Internet service provider (ISP) account of a resident of the Southern District of Ohio without notice to the account holder and an opportunity for a hearing (*Warshak v. United States* [6th Cir. 2007]).

Warshak v. United States (2007)

In *Warshak*, federal government agents investigated Steven Warshak and the company he owned for possible mail and wire fraud, money laundering, and other federal offenses. The government agents obtained an order from a U.S. magistrate judge directing the ISP to turn over to government agents information related to Warshak's e-mail account with the Internet service provider. This was done without any type of hearing or prior notification. The issuance of the order was based on the provisions of the Stored Communications Act (SCA), which was passed in 1986 and codified as a federal statute (18 U.S.C., § 2701). These provisions relate to the accessibility of "stored wire and electronic communications and transactional records." The government later appealed a district court's preliminary injunction limiting the government's access to the defendant's e-mail. Rejecting the government's claim to broad access, the court of appeals said:

> [W]e have little difficulty agreeing with the district court that individuals maintain a reasonable expectation of privacy in e-mails that are stored with, or sent or received through, a commercial ISP. The content of e-mail is something that the user "seeks to preserve as private," and therefore may be constitutionally protected.

In sum, the federal Court of Appeals for the Sixth Circuit held in *Warshak* that an e-mail holder or subscriber must be given prior notice and an opportunity to be heard before seizure, or the government must show that the account holder maintained no expectation of privacy and therefore enjoys no Fourth Amendment protection.

In an era of pervasive use of e-mails by the government and private sectors, the issue of law enforcement searches and seizures of e-mails for investigative purposes will ultimately have to be resolved by the Court.

Drug Testing Public Employees, Including Police Officers

Drug testing public employees, including police officers and other law enforcement personnel, is a common practice and needs to be addressed as an issue. Is it an allowable form of Fourth Amendment search and seizure? The Court has not directly addressed the constitutionality of drug testing police officers, but in 1989 it decided two cases on the issue of drug testing public employees. Neither decision, however, provides definite answers for police officers because they were based on the peculiar facts in those cases.

In the first case, the Court, in a 5-to-4 split, held that the U.S. Customs Service's drug-testing program for employees seeking promotion or transfer to positions involving interdiction of illegal drugs or requiring the carrying of firearms constitutes a search within the meaning of the Fourth Amendment. That search was deemed by the Court to be constitutional because of the government's compelling interest in public safety and in safeguarding borders, and because of the diminished privacy of employees who seek such positions (*National Treasury Employees Union v. Von Raab*, 489 U.S. 656 [1989]).

National Treasury Employees Union v. Von Raab (1989)

The second case involved drug testing private railroad employees in accordance with Federal Railroad Administration regulations. The regulations require private railroads (under government regulation) to administer blood and urine tests to railroad employees involved in train accidents and fatal accidents. Railroads are also authorized to administer breath and urine tests following certain other accidents. The Court held that this constituted a search under the Fourth Amendment (*Skinner v. Railway Labor Executives Association*, 489 U.S. 602 [1989]). Again, the Court considered the search to be constitutional, because there was a justification for it, namely, the safety-sensitive tasks of the employees. The nature of their task justified the departure from the usual search requirements of warrant and probable cause.

Skinner v. Railway Labor Executives Association (1989)

The *Von Raab* and *Skinner* cases hold that warrantless drug testing programs of public employees (or of private employees subject to government regulation) are reasonable and do not in themselves violate Fourth Amendment rights. There are strong grounds to believe that the same tests also apply to police officers, because they carry firearms and are responsible for enforcing the law and maintaining public order. It should be noted that both these cases involved mandatory testing, not testing at random. Whether or not completely random mandatory drug testing of police officers is constitutional has not been specifically resolved by the Court.

A purely random type of testing in which employees are required to give urine or other forms of sample at any time for drug tests has been declared by most lower courts to be unconstitutional because it can be arbitrary and subject to abuse. On the other hand, systematic testing has been held by courts to be constitutional. This form of testing provides that employees can be tested based on a systematic process of random selection, such as a lottery of names, numbers, or positions. Court decisions have also upheld drug testing of employees during annual physical examinations or when they seek promotion to higher or more sensitive positions.

Drug testing public employees based on reasonable suspicion that they are using drugs (as distinguished from purely arbitrary drug testing) has been upheld by most lower courts because it is justified by a degree of certainty. Unless the Court addresses the specific issue of police drug testing, the safer policy is to test based on reasonable suspicion.

Searches and Seizures of Public Employees Other Than Drug Testing

The leading case on government searches of government employees offices is *O'Connor v. Ortega* (480 U.S. 709 [1987]). In that case, the Court held that "the realities of the workplace" made certain types of privacy expectations among public employees unreasonable when the intrusion was by a supervisor rather than by law enforcement agents. The Court concluded that a warrant requirement would "seriously disrupt the routine conduct of business"; therefore, the standard of reasonableness, rather than probable cause or reasonable suspicion, was sufficient for work-related searches by public employers.

In this case, O'Connor was an administrator-psychiatrist in a state hospital. He was suspected of improprieties in administering the program. Suspicions consisted of improprieties in the acquisition of a computer, sexual harassment of a female hospital employee, and taking inappropriate disciplinary action against a resident physician who was under his supervision. While on administrative leave, and supposedly for inventory purposes, hospital officials searched his office and seized personal items from his desk and file cabinets. These were used in a subsequent administrative proceeding that resulted in his discharge. He then filed a civil liability lawsuit against the hospital officials, saying that he had a reasonable expectation of privacy in his office and that the search violated his Fourth Amendment right. On appeal, the Court held: (1) O'Connor, as an employee, had an expectation of privacy in his desk and file cabinets, but that (2) "requiring an employer to obtain a warrant whenever the employer wishes to enter an employee's office, desk, or file cabinet for a work-related purpose would seriously disrupt the routine conduct of business and would be unduly burdensome" and would come in the way of the government's need for "supervision, control, and the efficient operation of the workplace."

In a more recent case, the Court held that the warrantless search of a police officer's electronic message was not a violation of his constitutional rights. Citing *O'Connor v. Ortega*, the Court held that "a warrantless search to investigate work-related misconduct of a government employee is reasonable if it is justified at its inception and is reasonably work-related" (*City of Ontario v. Quon*, 560 U.S. --- [2010]). This case involved a member of the SWAT team of the Ontario, California Police Department. The department had a policy that employees did not have an expectation of privacy and could be subjected to monitoring without notice as to their computer, Internet, and e-mail use. There was no specific policy about text messages, but employees were told that the department would treat text messages like it would e-mails. Quon was investigated and later disciplined for improper use of the electronic equipment entrusted to him for use. He appealed, alleging a violation of his right against unreasonable searches and seizures. The Court held that the search was valid. The Court based its decision on the following assumptions: (1) employee Quon had a privacy right; (2) the review of his text messages constituted a search; and (3) intrusion into the electronic belongings of an employee is similar to a physical intrusion on an employee's office space. The Court concluded, however, that the search was valid because it was justified at its inception and reasonably work related in scope. In sum, work-related searches by the government of public employees, police officers included, do not need a warrant or probable cause. They do retain a reasonable expectation of privacy, but all that is needed for a valid search is a work-related justification.

City of Ontario v. Quon (2010)

Squeezing Luggage in a Bus

A traveler's luggage is an "effect" and is protected by the Fourth Amendment. Therefore, officers may not physically manipulate (such as squeeze) the luggage to inspect it without a warrant or probable cause. In *Bond v. United States*, 529 U.S. 334 (2000), Bond was riding on a Greyhound bus when a border patrol agent boarded the bus to check the immigration status of passengers. The agent went to the back of the bus. On the way back to the front, he squeezed a canvas bag above Bond's seat and felt that it contained a brick-like object. Bond admitted owning the bag and agreed to allow the agent to open it. The agent found methamphetamine. Bond later appealed his conviction, saying that the search by the officer violated his constitutional right.

The Court based its decision on the usual tests for searches and seizures: First, Bond had an expectation of privacy. He sought to preserve that privacy "by using an opaque bag and placing it directly above his seat." Second, that expectation of privacy is "one that society is prepared to recognize as reasonable." The Court concluded that "although there is expectation that the luggage will be handled by other passengers or bus employees, there is no expectation that the luggage will be physically manipulated in an exploratory manner," which was what the police did. The Court further said that "a physically invasive inspection is more intrusive than a visual inspection; therefore the law enforcement officer's physical manipulation of the luggage violated the Fourth Amendment."

Searches and Seizures by Private Persons

Searches and seizures by private persons do not come under Fourth Amendment protection, because the constitutional amendments apply only to acts of government agencies and officers. This is true even if the act by the private person is illegal.

Evidence obtained by private persons is admissible in court as long as they acted purely on their own and the police did not encourage or participate in the private search and seizure. For example, suppose Alex breaks into his neighbor's house because he suspects his neighbor of having stolen his TV. Alex recovers the set and now brings a case of robbery against his neighbor. The TV is admissible in evidence because the Fourth Amendment protection against unreasonable searches and seizures applies only to acts of government officers, not to private persons. However, Alex may be liable for breaking into and entering his neighbor's house in a separate criminal case.

Note also that the evidence is not admissible if a police officer participated in, ordered, or encouraged Alex to make the search. If a government official helps in a search or seizure by a private citizen, then the Fourth Amendment protections apply. It is immaterial whether the government officer proposed the idea or merely joined in while the search was in progress. If he or she was involved in any way before the object of the search was completely accomplished, the law says the officer participated in it; the evidence secured is therefore inadmissible.

Searches by Off-Duty Officers

A search by an off-duty officer is usually considered a government search. Many jurisdictions consider police officers to be law enforcement officers twenty-four hours a day. If this were not the rule, it would be convenient for police officers to conduct searches while off-duty and therefore subvert the Fourth Amendment. Although this issue has not been litigated in court, the rule probably will be the same even in jurisdictions where police officers are considered on duty at all times.

Surgery to Remove a Bullet from a Suspect

In *Winston v. Lee*, 470 U.S. 753 (1985), the Court held that a proposed surgery to remove a bullet from a suspect's chest for use as evidence would involve such severe intrusion on his interest in privacy and security that it would violate the Fourth Amendment and could not be allowed unless the government demonstrated a compelling need for it. The surgery could not be constitutionally undertaken, even though probable cause existed and the suspect was provided with all procedural safeguards, because the government failed to establish the compelling need for such surgery.

This decision is significant because in a previous case, *Schmerber v. California*, 384 U.S. 757 (1966), the Court held that a state may, over the suspect's objections, have a physician extract blood if he or she is suspected of drunken driving, without violating his or her Fourth Amendment right not to be subjected to unreasonable searches and seizures. However, according to the *Schmerber* decision, the holding that the Constitution does not forbid a state's minor intrusions into an individual's body under stringently limited conditions in no way indicates that it permits more substantial intrusions or intrusions under other conditions.

In the *Lee* case, the state of Virginia sought to compel Lee, a suspect in an attempted armed robbery who had allegedly been wounded by gunfire in that attempt, to undergo a surgical procedure under a general anesthetic for removal of the bullet lodged in his chest. Prosecutors alleged that the bullet would provide evidence of the suspect's guilt. Lee opposed the surgery. The Court concluded that the procedure was an example of the "more substantial intrusion" cautioned against in the *Schmerber* case and held that to permit the procedure to take place would violate the suspect's right to be secure in his person, as guaranteed by the Fourth Amendment.

The Court did not say that evidence retrievals of this nature could never be undertaken simply because they were per se intrusive. Instead, it used a balancing test, stating that "the medical risks of the operation, although apparently not extremely severe, are a subject of considerable dispute." But the Court also said that, "although the bullet may turn out to be useful . . . in prosecuting respondent, the Commonwealth [of Virginia] failed to demonstrate a compelling need for it."

This case appropriately ends this chapter because it reaffirms two important principles in search and seizure cases: (1) the more intrusive the search, the greater is the protection afforded by the Constitution, and (2) in highly intrusive searches, such as this one, the government must demonstrate a compelling need for the intrusion. Compelling need is a more difficult justification for the government to establish than just probable cause.

SUMMARY

- The Fourth Amendment and the right to privacy are the two constitutional rights limiting the powers of the police in search and seizure cases.
- A reasonable expectation of privacy exists when these two requirements are present: (1) the person must have exhibited an actual expectation of privacy, and (2) the expectation must be one that society is prepared to recognize as reasonable.
- There are two kinds of seizures: with a warrant (the rule) and without a warrant (the exception).

- Some types of searches do not need a warrant. These are searches incident to a lawful arrest, searches with consent, searches under exigent circumstances, and searches in hot pursuit of dangerous suspects.
- Two non-police searches do not need a warrant: special needs and administrative searches.
- Reasonableness governs the scope of a search. In search cases, it is useful for officers to remember this rule: Do not search for an elephant in a matchbox.

- When making an arrest, the police may search the area of immediate control.
- Drug testing elementary and high school students taking part in athletics and other school programs is valid.
- Searches and seizures of computers, e-mails, and related devices and data are governed by the Fourth Amendment, but case law and statutes are still evolving.

REVIEW QUESTIONS

1. Assume someone is talking on her cell phone with her parents while standing in the hallway of a university building between classes. She is telling them confidential things she does not want anybody else to hear. Does she have a reasonable expectation of privacy? Justify your answer.
2. What are the four requirements of a valid search warrant? Discuss each.
3. What categories of items are subject to search and seizure?
4. "Police officers executing a search warrant must always knock-and-announce before entry; otherwise the search is invalid." Is this statement true or false? Justify your answer.
5. Distinguish between administrative and law enforcement searches.
6. What does the phrase *area of immediate control* mean?
7. What are special needs searches? Give examples. How do they differ from police searches?
8. What is the exigent circumstances exception to the warrant requirement? Give examples.
9. What is the rule concerning searches of students by public school teachers and administrators? Does the same rule apply to school searches by police? Explain.
10. "The scope and manner of a search must be reasonable." Explain what this statement means.
11. Summarize the rules on computer searches. Are they similar to or different from other forms of searches?
12. "Searches of texts and e-mails are subject to the same rules as searches of things under the Fourth Amendment." Is this statement true or false? Justify your answer.

TEST YOUR UNDERSTANDING

1. Officers Joe and Bob were executing a search warrant for a shotgun allegedly used in a murder. They knocked at the house of the suspect and waited a full minute. When there was no response, they broke in and conducted a search but did not find the shotgun. They were later sued for unlawful entry. Was their entry unlawful? Justify your answer.
2. John, a student, had a bad fight with his girlfriend, Gail. They agreed to split up. Prior to that, Gail was living with John in his apartment and had her own key. When John left for class, Gail immediately went to the police and reported that John was selling drugs in his apartment. She said she was John's girlfriend and was living in the apartment with him. Without obtaining a warrant, the police went to the apartment and asked Gail to open the door and let them in. She did, and the police found heroin, which they seized. Was the seizure valid? State your reasons.
3. Mary and Sis were roommates in a dormitory but only for a few days because it was the start of the semester. On their third evening together, the campus police knocked on their door and asked if they could come in and "look around." When asked why, they told both occupants that they had reports from the other dormitory occupants that drugs were being sold from the room. Mary, a psychology major, readily gave consent, but Sis, a criminal justice student, refused to give consent, saying the police had to have a warrant based on probable cause to be able to come in. Based on Mary's consent, the police entered the room anyway and found drugs—ironically, on the desk owned by Mary. The police seized the drugs. Prosecuted for drug possession and sale, Mary sought exclusion of the evidence, saying his roommate had expressly objected to the police entry. You are the judge. Will you admit or exclude the evidence against Mary? Justify your answer based on cases decided by the Court.
4. Assume you are a police officer in the Boston Police Department. You are executing a search warrant issued by a judge. The warrant says you are to search the home of Jane, a high-profile

suspect in various drug deals. Discuss the extent and scope of what you can search. Will you search Jane's living room, kitchen, dining room, bedroom, and garage? Assume Jane has two vehicles parked in her covered garage. Can you also search those? Justify the scope of your search.

5. Chris, a crack dealer, was shot by the police during a police raid of a crack house. The bullet hit Chris in the leg and stayed there. Assume you are a judge. The officers come to you seeking a warrant for the removal by surgery in a hospital of the bullet lodged in Chris's leg. You are the judge. Will you issue the warrant? Justify your decision.

RECOMMENDED READINGS

Jennifer Cook. Note. *Discretionary warrantless searches and seizures and the Fourth Amendment: A need for clearer guidelines*. South Carolina Law Review, 410-440 (2001).

Orin S. Kerr. *An equilibrium-adjustment theory of the Fourth Amendment*. Harvard Law Review, vol. 125, p. 476 (2011).

Edward J. Imwinkelried. *The dangerous trend blurring the distinction between a reasonable expectation of confidentiality in privilege law and a reasonable expectation of privacy in fourth amendment jurisprudence*. Loyola Law Review, vol. 57, p. 1 (2011).

Tracey Maclin. *The good and bad news about consent searches in the supreme court*. McGeorge Law Review, 39, no. 27 (2008).

Aaron Stanley. *The continuing evolution of consent and authority in digital search and seizure*. Fordham Intellectual Property, Media & Entertainment Law Journal, 19 (2008): 179.

Seth W. Stoughton. *Modern police practices: Arizona v. Gant's illusory restriction of vehicle searches incident to arrest*. Virginia Law Review, vol. 97, p. 1727 (2011).

James Tomkovicz. *Divining and designing the future of the search incident to arrest doctrine: Avoiding instability, irrationality, and infidelity*. University of Illinois Law Review, 2007, 1417-76.

NOTES

1. *Computer Searches*, by the District Attorney's Office in Alameda County, California, *http://www.acgov.org/da/pov/documents/web.htm*.

2. Ibid.

3. *Searching and Seizing Computers and Obtaining Electronic Evidence in Criminal Investigations*. Computer Crime and Intellectual Property Section, Criminal Division, U.S. Department of Justice, July 2002.

4. Ibid.

CHAPTER 8

Motor Vehicle Stops, Searches, and Inventories

LEARNING OBJECTIVES

1. Differentiate how vehicle stops are separate from a vehicle search.
2. Differentiate when probable cause and reasonable suspicion are required for vehicle stops or a vehicle search.
3. Identify and explain the effect of the major court decisions in the development of the motor vehicle exception to the Fourth Amendment.
4. When given an example of a vehicle stop or a vehicle search, you will determine if the stop or search is lawful and why.
5. Describe what actions that a law enforcement officer may take after a lawful traffic stop.
6. Relate how *Arizona v. Gant* affected law enforcement in relation to past practices regarding search incidental to arrest and motor vehicle searches.
7. Identify and explain the effect of the major court decisions in the development of the motor vehicle exception to the Fourth Amendment.
8. Describe the circumstances in which an inventory search may be lawful.
9. When provided with examples, you will determine if the stop or search was lawful and why.

KEY TERMS

pretextual stops

sobriety checkpoint

vehicle impoundment

vehicle inventory

Larry St. Pierre/Shutterstock.com

THE TOP 5 IMPORTANT CASES

in Motor Vehicle Stops, Searches, and Inventories

◼ *CARROLL V. UNITED STATES* (1925) The search of an automobile does not require a warrant because the vehicle can be moved quickly out of the locality or jurisdiction in which the warrant must be sought.

◼ *NEW YORK V. BELTON* (1981) Once a driver has been arrested, the police may conduct a warrantless search of the passenger compartment of the automobile. The police may examine the contents of any container found within the passenger compartment as long as they may reasonably believe it might contain something that could pose a danger to the officer or hold evidence of the offense for which the suspect has been arrested.

◼ *UNITED STATES V. ROSS* (1982) If the police legitimately stop a car and have probable cause to believe that it contains contraband, they can conduct a warrantless search of the car. Every part of the vehicle in which the contraband might be stored may be inspected, including the trunk and all receptacles and packages that could possibly contain the object of the search.

◼ *ARIZONA V. GANT* (2009) Searches of motor vehicles incident to arrest when the arrestee is no longer in the vehicle is valid only if it is reasonable to believe that evidence of the reason for the arrest might be found in the vehicle.

◼ *UNITED STATES V. JONES* (2012) The warrantless use of a tracking device on a motor vehicle to monitor its movements is unconstitutional.

S TOPS AND SEARCHES of motor vehicles are an important and highly visible part of routine police patrol. They will continue to require the attention of the courts in the coming years as the number of motor vehicles on the road grows and vehicle technology become more sophisticated. Questions about what the police can and cannot do in motor vehicle cases are addressed by the Court each year. This trend will continue as the case law on motor vehicles becomes more extensive and refined. It is important that the police be familiar with the laws on motor vehicle stops and searches because a large percentage of arrests and searches are either made in or related to motor vehicles, and a lot of day-to-day police work involves motor vehicles.

The law on vehicle stops and searches is best understood if discussed under three general headings: vehicle stops, vehicle searches, and vehicle inventories. Each is governed by different Fourth Amendment and other legal rules, so we will

Table 8.1 Summary of the Rules for Vehicle Stops, Searches, and Inventories

	Need a Warrant?	Need Probable Cause?
To stop a vehicle	No	No, but need reasonable or articulable suspicion of suspect's involvement in criminal activity or a traffic violation
To search a vehicle	No	Yes
To inventory a vehicle	No	No, but must be guided by department policy

discuss them separately. States also have their own motor vehicle laws that are not discussed here.

Carroll v. United States (1925)

Carroll v. United States, 267 U.S. 132 (1925), decided in 1925, is arguably the most important case involving motor vehicles ever decided by the Court. It is, however, a *vehicle search* rather than a *vehicle stop* case and is therefore discussed in this chapter under vehicle searches. We begin with a discussion on vehicle stops, which often precede vehicle searches.

Table 8.1 summarizes the rules for vehicle stops, searches, and inventories—the three types of vehicle searches and seizures discussed in this chapter. The rest of the chapter expands on the table; understanding the chapter material will be easier if you learn this table first.

VEHICLE STOPS

Delaware v. Prouse (1979)

A form of seizure occurs every time a motor vehicle is stopped, so the Fourth Amendment prohibition against unreasonable searches and seizures applies. In *Delaware v. Prouse*, 440 U.S. 648 (1979), the Court said, "The Fourth and Fourteenth Amendments are implicated in this case because stopping an automobile and detaining its occupants constitute a 'seizure' within the meaning of those Amendments, even though the purpose of the stop is limited and the resulting detention quite brief." A *stop* is the brief detention of a person when the police officer has reasonable suspicion, in light of his or her experience, that criminal activity is about to take place. The courts have long held that motor vehicles, because of their mobility, should be governed by a

Illinois v. Lidster (2004)

different set of Fourth Amendment rules. This was emphasized by the Court in *Illinois v. Lidster*, 540 U.S. 419 (2004), when it stated that the "Fourth Amendment does not treat a motorist's car as his castle."

In this section, we examine the rules that govern vehicle stops. They are summarized as follows:

- The most important rule is that law enforcement officers must have reasonable suspicion that the occupants are involved in criminal activity before making a stop.
- Roadblocks are an exception to the reasonable suspicion rule.
- Officers are limited in what they can do after making a stop.
- Traffic stops that are only pretexts for vehicle searches are valid.
- Consent searches do not require that detainees be advised that they are free to leave.
- Arresting occupants for non-jailable offenses is valid.
- Passengers can be arrested during a stop.

We will look at each of these rules and the cases that established them.

The General Rule for Stops

Although a vehicle stop is a form of seizure, a motorist is not fully protected by the Fourth Amendment. Because the vehicle stop is less intrusive, neither a warrant nor probable cause is required. *Nonetheless, some type of justification is necessary for a valid stop; a stop by a police officer for no reason or without any justification is illegal.* In *United States v. Cortez*, 449 U.S. 411 (1981), the Court ruled that there must be at least a reasonable suspicion to justify an investigatory stop of a motor vehicle in connection with possible involvement in criminal activity. In *Cortez*, the Court stated:

United States v. Cortez (1981)

> Based upon that whole picture, the detaining officers must have a particularized and objective basis for suspecting the particular person stopped of criminal activity. . . . First, the assessment must be based upon all of the circumstances. The analysis proceeds with various objective observations, information from police reports, if such are available, and consideration of the modes or patterns of operation and certain kinds of lawbreakers. . . . The second element contained in the idea that an assessment of the whole picture must yield a particularized suspicion is the concept that the process just described must raise a suspicion that the particular individual being stopped is engaged in wrongdoing.

A lower court has also said, "The police do not have an unrestricted right to stop people, either pedestrians or drivers. The 'good faith' of the police is not enough, nor is an inarticulate hunch. They must have an articulable suspicion of wrongdoing, done or in prospect" (*United States v. Montgomery*, 561 F.2d 875 [1977]).

United States v. Montgomery (1977)

The warrantless exception in motor vehicle stop cases does not give the police unlimited authority to stop vehicles. Some justification is necessary, but it does not have to be probable cause. Some courts say *reasonable suspicion* is needed; other courts use the term *articulable suspicion*. Whatever term a jurisdiction uses, the level of certainty necessary for the police to be able to stop a vehicle is about the same—lower than probable cause but higher than mere suspicion. It is the same level of certainty that is needed in stop and frisk cases (discussed in Chapter 5).

In *United States v. Arvizu*, 534 U.S. 266 (2001), the Court held that a reasonable suspicion determination in automobile stop cases is based on the totality of the circumstances rather than each act viewed separately. In this case, the U.S. Border Patrol operated a checkpoint in an isolated area in Arizona. Some roads circumvented this checkpoint and were routinely used by smugglers to avoid detection. Because of this, sensors were placed along those roads to detect vehicular traffic.

United States v. Arvizu (2001)

An officer responded when a sensor was activated. He followed the suspect vehicle for several miles and observed several suspicious behaviors, including the following: the time the vehicle was on the road coincided with a shift change for roving patrols in the area; the roads the vehicle took were remote and not well-suited for the vehicle type; the vehicle slowed dramatically upon first observing the officer; the driver of the vehicle would not look at the officer when passing; the children in the vehicle seemed to have their feet propped up on some cargo; the children waved mechanically at the officers as if being instructed; and the vehicle made turns that would allow it to completely avoid the checkpoint. Based on these observations, the officer stopped the vehicle. After obtaining consent from the driver, Arvizu, the officer searched the vehicle and found drugs. Convicted of drug possession, Arvizu appealed, claiming that none of these factors, taken individually, constituted reasonable suspicion.

The Court disagreed, saying that "in making reasonable suspicion determinations, reviewing courts must look at the totality of the circumstances of each case to see whether the detaining officer has a particularized and objective basis for suspecting legal wrongdoing." This case is significant in vehicle stop cases for several reasons, including: (1) in determining reasonable suspicion, officers can rely on a number of factors that in isolation may not constitute reasonable suspicion, and (2) in determining reasonable suspicion, officers may "draw on their own experiences and specialized training to make inferences from and deductions about the cumulative information available." Both of these factors make it easier for officers to establish reasonable suspicion.

What the Police Can Do after a Vehicle Stop

Stopping the vehicle is not an end in itself; it is only a means to determine whether a criminal activity has occurred or is about to occur. What follows after a stop is important for both the officer's protection and the admissibility of any seized evidence. There are many things an officer may do after a valid stop, including the following actions.

Order the driver to get out of the vehicle. Once a vehicle is lawfully stopped for a traffic violation, the officer may order the driver to get out, even without suspecting criminal activity. If the officer then reasonably believes that the driver may be armed and dangerous, he or she may conduct a limited protective frisk for a weapon that might endanger his or her personal safety (*Pennsylvania v. Mimms*, 434 U.S. 106 [1977]).

Pennsylvania v. Mimms (1977)

For example, suppose Frank is stopped by the police for running a red light. Frank may be asked to get out of the car. If, after Frank complies, the officer reasonably believes that Frank may be armed and dangerous, then Frank may be frisked. If an illegal weapon is found during the frisk, then Frank may be arrested. Conversely, if the officer does not believe that the driver may be armed and dangerous, all the officer can do is ask the driver to get out of the car. If there is no belief that the driver is armed and dangerous, a subsequent frisk is illegal even if the initial traffic stop was legal.

MYTH vs. REALITY

MYTH A passenger in a vehicle may not be ordered out of the vehicle by a police officer during a traffic stop unless the officer has probable cause to believe the passenger has committed a crime.

FACT The Supreme Court has held that the police may order the driver and any passengers out of a vehicle during a routine traffic stop as a matter of course.

Order passengers to get out of the vehicle. The Court has long held that the driver of a car may be automatically required to get out of a car after a valid stop—whether or not the officer is concerned about personal safety. For a long time it was unclear whether that rule applied to vehicle passengers. But in *Maryland v. Wilson*, 519 U.S. 408 (1997), the Court ruled that police officers may also order passengers to get out of motor vehicles during traffic stops.

Maryland v. Wilson (1997)

In *Wilson*, a state trooper stopped a motor vehicle clocked at 65 miles per hour where the posted limit was 55 miles per hour. During the pursuit, the trooper noticed three occupants in the car. As the trooper approached what turned out to be a rented car, the driver got out and met him halfway. He produced a valid driver's license but was trembling and appeared extremely nervous. The trooper also noticed that one of the passengers, Wilson, was sweating and appeared extremely nervous. The trooper ordered Wilson out of the car. As Wilson got out, crack cocaine fell to the ground. Arrested and charged with possession of cocaine, Wilson argued during his trial that ordering him out of the car constituted an unreasonable seizure.

The trial court and the state court of appeals agreed, but the Supreme Court reversed the decision, noting that the "danger to an officer from a traffic stop is likely to be greater when there are passengers in addition to the driver in the stopped car." It added that the government's "legitimate and weighty interest in protecting officers prevails against the minimal infringement on the liberties of both the car driver and the passengers." This decision provides a bright-line rule saying that an officer making a traffic stop may also order passengers to get out of the car pending completion of the stop.

Ask the driver to produce required documents. An officer has the authority, after a valid stop, to ask the driver to show a driver's license and other documents that state laws require. A number of states require that the driver produce the vehicle registration and proof of insurance in addition to a driver's license. The justification for this authorization is that operating a motor vehicle on public highways is a privilege rather than a right. Virtually all states consider a refusal to produce the required documents a criminal offense, and the driver can be punished accordingly.

Question the driver and passengers. Once a valid stop has been made, the officer may question the driver and passengers without giving the *Miranda* warnings. The Court has said that the roadside questioning of a motorist pursuant to a routine traffic stop (provided it is not an arrest) does not constitute custodial interrogation and therefore does not require the *Miranda* warnings (*Berkemer v. McCarty*, 468 U.S. 420 [1984]). But, although the officer may ask questions, the driver and passengers have a constitutional right not to respond. Such a refusal to respond, however, may be taken into consideration by the officer in determining whether there is probable cause to arrest or search.

Berkemer v. McCarty (1984)

Locate and examine the VIN. Federal rules require that all vehicles sold in the United States have a vehicle identification number (VIN). The VIN must be displayed on the dashboard that it can be read from outside the car through the windshield. The Court has decided that motorists have no reasonable expectation of privacy with respect to the VIN located on the vehicle's dashboard, even if objects on the dashboard prevent

HIGHLIGHT › Asking the Passenger to Get Out of the Car

"We must therefore now decide whether the rule of *Mimms* applies to passengers as well as to drivers. On the public interest side of the balance, the same weighty interest in officer safety is present regardless of whether the occupant of the stopped car is a driver or passenger. Regrettably, traffic stops may be dangerous encounters. On the personal liberty side of the balance, the case for the passengers is in one sense stronger than that for the driver. There is probable cause to believe that the driver has committed a minor vehicular offense, but there is no such reason to stop or detain the passengers. But as a practical matter, the passengers are already stopped by virtue of the stop of the vehicle. The only change in their circumstances which will result from ordering them out of the car is that they will be outside of, rather than inside of, the stopped car. Outside the car, the passengers will be denied access to any possible weapon that might be concealed in the interior of the passenger compartment. It would seem that the possibility of a violent encounter stems not from the ordinary reaction of a motorist stopped for a speeding violation, but from the fact that evidence of a more serious crime might be uncovered during the stop. And the motivation of a passenger to employ violence to prevent apprehension of such a crime is every bit as great as that of the driver. . . . In summary, danger to an officer from a traffic stop is likely to be greater when there are passengers in addition to the driver in the stopped car. While there is not the same basis for ordering the passengers out of the car as there is for ordering the driver out, the additional intrusion on the passenger is minimal. We therefore hold that an officer making a traffic stop may order passengers to get out of the car pending completion of the stop".

Source: *Maryland v. Wilson*, 519 U.S. 408 (1997).

New York v. Class (1986)

the VIN from being observed from outside the car (*New York v. Class*, 475 U.S. 106 [1986]). In *New York v. Class* (1986), two New York City police officers stopped a motor vehicle for traffic violations. One of the officers looked for the VIN. He reached into the car's interior to move some papers that were obscuring the area of the dashboard where he believed the VIN was located. While doing that, the officer saw a gun protruding from underneath the driver's seat and seized it. The driver, Class, was arrested and later convicted of criminal possession of a weapon. On appeal, he sought exclusion of the gun, claiming the search was illegal. The Court disagreed, saying that since the VIN was in plain view on the dashboard, Class did not have a reasonable expectation of privacy.

Seize items in plain view. After a valid stop, the officer may seize illegal items in plain view. The seizure then establishes probable cause, which justifies an arrest. For example, suppose officers lawfully stop a car to issue the driver a citation for speeding. While writing out the citation, the officers see contraband in the passenger compartment. The officers may seize the contraband and place the driver under arrest. They may then search the driver and the vehicle.

Require a breathalyzer test. All fifty states require drivers suspected of drunk driving to take Breathalyzer tests. The limit in all fifty states is a blood alcohol level of 0.08 or higher. Refusal to take the test or test failure (because the alcohol level is beyond that allowed by law) may lead to suspension of the person's driver's license and, in some cases, jail time. Some states allow a civil case to be filed against those refusing to take the test in addition to DWI charges.

An interesting legal issue is whether a driver who fails a Breathalyzer test (and therefore may have his or her license revoked) may also be criminally charged with drunk driving. Some argue that this constitutes two prosecutions for the same offense; others maintain that there is no double jeopardy because license suspensions are administrative, not criminal, proceedings. Lower courts are divided. Courts in a number of states have ruled that these two proceedings arising from the same act constitute double jeopardy; the highest courts of several states have held otherwise. But the U.S. Supreme Court has not ruled on the issue, so uncertainty remains.

South Dakota v. Neville (1983)

In *South Dakota v. Neville* (459 U.S. 553 [1983]), the Court held that a South Dakota state law that permitted the prosecutor to comment on the refusal of a DWI defendant to take a blood alcohol level test did not violate defendant's right against self-incrimination, reasoning that the state had the right to force the defendant to take such a test anyway. Refusal to take the test could be brought by the prosecutor to the attention of the judge or jury during trial.

Search the passenger compartment for weapons. If an officer has reasonable suspicion that the motorist he or she has stopped is dangerous and may be able to gain control of a weapon in the car, the officer may conduct a search of the passenger compartment.

Michigan v. Long (1983)

This is the case even if the motorist is no longer inside the car (*Michigan v. Long*, 463 U.S. 1032 [1983]). This search should be limited to areas in the passenger compartment where a weapon might be found or hidden. The authorization for a brief search for a weapon is an extension of stop and frisk rather than an arrest. A routine stop to issue a traffic ticket, in which the officer does not have reason to fear for his or her safety, does not authorize the police to search the vehicle's passenger compartment.

May arrest if probable cause develops. A stop may immediately turn into an arrest *if probable cause develops.* For example, suppose an officer stops a vehicle for speeding and orders the driver to get out of the car. The officer senses danger to himself, frisks the driver, and finds an illegal weapon. The officer may then arrest the driver for the weapon possession and search the entire passenger compartment incident to the arrest. He or she may also conduct a full body search of the arrested driver.

Search the vehicle if probable cause is established. After a vehicle is stopped, what officers observe may evolve into probable cause to believe that the car contains the fruits and instrumentalities of crime or contraband, thus justifying a full warrantless search of the vehicle. For example, in *Colorado v. Bannister*, 449 U.S. 1 (1980), the police stopped Bannister's automobile to issue him a speeding ticket. While writing out the citation, the officer made two observations: (1) Bannister and his companion fit a broadcasted description of persons involved in the theft of auto parts and (2) there were wrenches and other materials in the back seat that could have been used for that crime. The Court held that what the officer observed established probable cause to justify a warrantless search because, had a magistrate been present while Bannister's car was stopped, the police could have obtained a warrant on the information the officer possessed. The warrantless search was therefore proper under the automobile exception.

Colorado v. Bannister (1980)

Probable cause to search must exist prior to the search of the car; otherwise, the search is illegal. For example, Officer Peters stops a car because it is weaving erratically on the road. Immediately after stopping the car, Officer Peters sees open liquor containers in the front and back seats, which are prohibited. There is now probable cause to search the car further for more evidence. If drugs are found in the course of the search, the evidence is admissible in court. By contrast, Officer Quinn stops a car because of an illegal right turn. Inside are five teenagers who say they are coming home from a basketball game at a local park. Assume that Officer Quinn has no probable cause, based on her observations, to believe an offense has been or is being committed. Nonetheless, Officer Quinn searches the car on the assumption that teenagers are more likely to drink and use drugs. If she finds drugs, the evidence will not be admissible in court, because Officer Quinn had no probable cause and was on a virtual fishing expedition when she searched the car. The officer may, however, look around the car (under the plain view rule) but cannot search it.

Search passengers' belongings. The Court's decision in *Wyoming v. Houghton*, 526 U.S. 295 (1999) settled another important issue concerning what officers can do after a vehicle stop. The Court has ruled that police officers who have probable cause to search a car may inspect passengers' belongings found in the car if they are capable of concealing the object of the search. In *Wyoming v. Houghton* (1999), a Wyoming Highway Patrol officer stopped a motor vehicle in which Houghton was riding. While questioning the (male) driver for a traffic violation, the officer noticed a hypodermic needle in the driver's shirt pocket. When the driver admitted using the needle to inject drugs, the passengers were ordered out of the car. The officer then searched the passenger compartment of the vehicle. On the back seat, he found a purse that Houghton claimed was hers. After finding methamphetamines and drug paraphernalia in the purse, he arrested Houghton. She appealed her felony conviction for possession of drugs, claiming that the search of a passenger's personal belongings inside an automobile is a violation of Fourth Amendment rights.

Wyoming v. Houghton (1999)

The Court disagreed, saying that police officers who have probable cause to search a car may also inspect passengers' belongings found in the car if they are capable of concealing the object of the search. The Court cited two justifications for the search: (1) the passenger's reduced expectation of privacy and (2) "the governmental interest in effective law enforcement [which] would be appreciably impaired without the ability to search the passenger's belongings, because an automobile's ready mobility creates the risk that evidence or contraband will be permanently lost while a warrant is obtained." But although they may search passengers' belongings, officers may not conduct body searches of passengers (*United States v. Di Re*, 332 U.S. 581 [1948]). The only time a body search is allowed is when the passenger has been arrested.

United States v. Di Re (1948)

May arrest for a non-jailable offense. The Court has held that the Fourth Amendment does not forbid a warrantless arrest for a minor criminal offense punishable only by a fine, such as a misdemeanor seat belt violation (*Atwater v. City of Lago Vista*, 532 U.S. 318 [2001]). This case, *Atwater v. City of Lago Vista* (2001), settles an issue to which previously there was no definitive answer: How can a suspect be arrested without a warrant for an offense whose maximum penalty does not include serving time in jail or prison?

Atwater v. City of Lago Vista (2001)

In *Atwater*, Texas law required all front seat passengers to wear a seat belt; failure to do so was a crime punishable by a fine of not more than $50. Texas law also expressly authorized the police officer to arrest without a warrant if a person was found in violation of the law, although the police could issue a citation instead of making an arrest. An officer observed Atwater driving a vehicle with her two young children in the front seat; no one was wearing a seat belt. Arrested and later fined $50, she appealed her conviction, saying it was unconstitutional because, under common law, violators of non-jailable minor offenses could not be arrested.

The Court disagreed, saying that such laws are now present in all fifty states and that "there is no historical evidence that the framers or proponents of the Fourth Amendment . . . were at all concerned about warrantless arrests by local constables and other peace officers." The Court concluded by saying: "We simply cannot conclude that the Fourth Amendment . . . forbade peace officers to arrest without warrant for misdemeanors not amounting to or involving breach of the peace"; hence, arrests for non-jailable offenses are constitutional.

May search based on consent. Even if there is no probable cause or reasonable suspicion, the officer may search the car if valid consent is given. The Court has said that an officer, after validly stopping a car, may ask the person in control of the vehicle for permission to search (*Schneckloth v. Bustamonte*, 412 U.S. 218 [1973]). Such consent must be intelligent and voluntary, although it does not have to be in knowing (meaning the police do not have to inform a driver that he or she has the right to refuse consent). Consent may be given verbally, or in writing. The burden is on the officer to prove, if challenged, that valid consent was obtained.

Schneckloth v. Bustamonte (1973)

Traffic Stops as Pretexts for Vehicle Searches

The temporary detention of a motorist based on probable cause to believe that he or she has violated a traffic law is valid, even if a reasonable officer would not have stopped the motorist in the absence of some other law enforcement objective (*Whren v. United States*, 517 U.S. 806 [1996]). In *Whren*, plainclothes vice officers were patrolling a

Whren v. United States (1996)

high-drug-crime area in an unmarked car when they saw a vehicle with youthful occupants waiting at an intersection. The vehicle remained at the intersection for an unusually long time. The officers made a U-turn and headed toward the vehicle, whereupon it suddenly made a right turn without signaling and took off at an unreasonable speed. The officers overtook the vehicle when it stopped at a red light. One of the officers approached the vehicle and observed two large plastic bags of what appeared to be crack cocaine in Whren's hands. At trial, the defendant sought to suppress the evidence, saying that, based on departmental policy, the plainclothes officers would not normally have dealt with this type of civil traffic violation; therefore, it was merely a **pretextual stop**—a stop used as a pretext to search the vehicle—in this case, to determine whether the occupants had drugs.

pretextual stop
a valid stop that is used as a pretext to search a vehicle.

The Court ruled that the temporary detention of the vehicle based on probable cause to believe that traffic laws had been broken did not violate the Fourth Amendment, even if the officers would not have stopped the vehicle without some additional law enforcement objective (in this case they suspected the vehicle might be involved in drug sales activity). The Court in effect ruled that whether ordinarily the police officers "would have" (subjective test) made the stop is not the test for validity; instead, the test is whether the officers "could have" made the stop. The fact that they "could have" made a valid stop because there was a traffic violation made the stop valid even though the actual purpose of the stop was to look for drugs.

An added factor made the traffic stop in *Whren* highly questionable. Police regulations in that jurisdiction permitted plainclothes officers (who made the arrest in this case) in unmarked cars to stop vehicles and enforce traffic laws "only in the case of a violation that is so grave as to pose an immediate threat to the safety of others." Such was not the case here, and so the plainclothes officers did not follow departmental policy. The Court concluded that the fact that local law enforcement practices did not allow such stops was irrelevant because, if Fourth Amendment issues were decided based on departmental policy, it would make the Fourth Amendment protections vary from place to place.

Exhibit 8.1 A Summary of What Officers May Do after a Valid Motor Vehicle Stop

- Order the driver to get out of the vehicle (*Pennsylvania v. Mimms* [1977]).
- Order passengers to get out of the vehicle (*Maryland v. Wilson* [1997]).
- Ask the driver to produce documents required by state law (state laws).
- Question the driver and passengers without *Miranda* warnings (*Berkemer v. McCarty* [1984]).
- Locate and examine the vehicle identification number (*New York v. Class* [1986]).
- Seize items in plain view (plain view doctrine).
- Require drunk-driving suspects to take a Breathalyzer test (state laws).

- Search the passenger compartment for weapons if there is reasonable suspicion of a threat to officer safety (*Michigan v. Long* [1983]).
- Search the vehicle (*Colorado v. Bannister* [1980]).
- Search passenger belongings (*Wyoming v. Houghton* [1999]).
- May arrest if probable cause is established (Fourth Amendment principle).
- May arrest for a non-jailable traffic offense (*Atwater v. City of Lago Vista* [2001]).
- May search based on a valid consent (general Fourth Amendment principle).

Note, however, that although pretextual stops are constitutional, they may be invalidated by state courts based on state law or the state constitution. For example, in *State v. Ladson*, 979 P.2d 833 (Wa., 1999), a case decided three years after *Whren*, the supreme court of the state of Washington held that there is no pretextual stop exception to the warrant requirement under the state's constitution. Therefore, pretextual stops in the state of Washington are not valid.

Washington v. Ladson (1999)

Searches with Consent and Freedom to Leave

The Court has held that a police officer does not need to inform the defendant that he or she is free to leave for a consent to search to be valid (*Ohio v. Robinette*, 519 U.S. 33 [1996]). In *Ohio v. Robinette* (1996), an Ohio deputy sheriff stopped the defendant for speeding, gave him a verbal warning, returned his driver's license, and then asked whether he was carrying contraband, drugs, or weapons in his car. The defendant replied "no" but then consented to a search of his car. The search revealed a small amount of marijuana and a controlled substance. At trial, Robinette argued that the consent given was invalid because, even in cases of lawful detention, the suspect must first be informed by the officer that he or she is "legally free to go" before consent to search can validly be given.

Ohio v. Robinette (1996)

The Court disagreed, saying that "the Fourth Amendment does not require that a lawfully seized defendant be advised that he is 'free to go' before his consent to search will be recognized as voluntary." Again, however, the evidence obtained may not be admissible if state law requires that such information be given before consent to search is sought.

Passengers Are Also "Seized" in Traffic Stops

The Court has determined that the passenger of a vehicle, like the driver, is also considered "seized" within the meaning of the Fourth Amendment during a traffic stop (*Brendlin v. California*, 551 U.S. 1 [2007]). In *Brendlin*, a police officer stopped a vehicle to verify a temporary license tag, even though the officer admitted there was nothing unusual about the permit. The officer recognized a passenger in the vehicle, Bruce Brendlin, as probably on parole and asked him to identify himself. After verifying that Brendlin was a parole violator and had a warrant for his arrest, the officer arrested him. A search incident to the arrest found a syringe cap. Brendlin moved to suppress the evidence as the fruit of a stop without probable cause. That motion was denied, and Brendlin pleaded guilty to drug charges. He later appealed, saying that even though he was merely a passenger, he was also seized within the meaning of the Fourth Amendment when the car was stopped and therefore could assert his Fourth Amendment rights. The Court agreed, saying that the test in these cases is whether a reasonable person in the position of the passenger would have "reasonably believed" himself or herself to be detained and subject to the authority of the police. The Court concluded that under the circumstances of this case, passenger Brendlin would have reasonably believed he was detained and subject to police authority.

Brendlin v. California (2007)

The Court stressed, however, that the ruling in *Brendlin* does not extend to instances of "incidental motor vehicle restrictions," such as when motorists are forced to slow down or stop because other vehicles are being detained. It must also be noted that the Court in this case resolved a narrow legal issue: whether a passenger in a vehicle is considered seized when a vehicle is stopped. It said yes, and therefore Brendlin had "standing" and could challenge the constitutionality of the seizure of the evidence used against him.

Arrests of Vehicle Passengers

May the police arrest the passengers of a car in addition to the driver? The Court says yes—if there is probable cause to believe that a crime has been committed in a motor vehicle and it is not clear who committed it, and as long as there is reasonable inference from the circumstances that the person arrested could have committed it (*Maryland v. Pringle*, 540 U.S. 366 [2003]).

Maryland v. Pringle (2003)

In *Pringle*, the police stopped a car for speeding. Pringle was a passenger. When the driver opened the glove compartment to get the car registration, the officer saw a large amount of rolled-up money. After issuing the driver a warning, the officer asked for and received permission to search the vehicle. The officer found $753 and five plastic bags of cocaine. None of the three people in the car admitted ownership of the drugs and money, so the officer arrested all of them.

Was the arrest of the passengers valid? The Court said yes because, based on the circumstances, the officer had probable cause to believe that the passengers could have committed the crime. The Court added this standard: "To determine whether an officer had probable cause to make an arrest, a court must examine the events leading up to the arrest" before making a decision. Given the circumstances of this case, the Court ruled, "it is an entirely reasonable inference from the facts here that any or all of the car occupants had knowledge of, and exercised dominion and control over, the cocaine . . . either solely or jointly." Note that *Pringle* does not automatically authorize officers to arrest passengers in the car. Instead, the arrest of passengers must be based on probable cause that they, not just the driver, are involved in the crime.

Roadblocks Do Not Need Reasonable Suspicion

Roadblocks are an exception to the rule that vehicle stops must be justified by suspicion of the occupant's involvement in criminal activity. Roadblocks are used by police for a variety of purposes. Five types of roadblocks are discussed here, four of which have been upheld as constitutional by the courts even without individualized suspicion of criminal activity. Not all roadblocks, however, are constitutional, as the cases discussed here show.

MYTH vs. REALITY

MYTH Police must have probable cause to believe a crime has occurred in order to put up a sobriety checkpoint or roadblock.

FACT The Supreme Court has held that police may put up a sobriety checkpoint or roadblock without probable cause, because the roadblock serves a compelling state interest and is a limited intrusion on privacy.

Roadblocks to control drunk driving are constitutional. In *Michigan Department of State Police v. Sitz*, 496 U.S. 444 (1990), the Court held that **sobriety checkpoints**, a form of roadblock in which the police stop every vehicle for the purpose of investigating and controlling drunk driving, do not violate the Fourth Amendment protection against unreasonable searches and seizures and are therefore constitutional.

Michigan Department of State Police v. Sitz (1990)

sobriety checkpoints
a form of roadblock in which the police stop every vehicle for the purpose of controlling drunk driving.

In the *Sitz* case, the Michigan State Police Department established a highway checkpoint program. Pursuant to established guidelines, checkpoints were to be set up at selected sites along state roads. All vehicles passing through the checkpoint were to be stopped and their drivers checked for signs of intoxication. If officers suspected the driver was intoxicated, they were to pull the vehicle to the side of the road and conduct further tests; all other drivers would be permitted to resume their journey. During the only operation of the checkpoint, which lasted about an hour and fifteen minutes, they checked 126 vehicles, with an average delay of twenty-five seconds. Officers arrested two individuals for DWI, including Sitz. He challenged these guidelines and the Michigan sobriety checkpoint practice in the courts as violating the Fourth Amendment.

The Supreme Court rejected the challenge, saying that sobriety checkpoints are a form of seizure, but one that is reasonable because the "measure of intrusion on motorists stopped briefly at sobriety checkpoints is slight." The *Sitz* case is significant, because for a long time lower courts had given conflicting decisions about the constitutionality of sobriety checkpoints. Courts in twenty-one states had upheld them, whereas courts in twelve states had declared them unconstitutional. However, the Supreme Court ruled that the police may establish highway checkpoints in an effort to catch drunk drivers.

It is important to note that the *Sitz* case does not allow the police to make random stops; it authorizes well-conceived and carefully structured sobriety checkpoints, such as Michigan's, that leave virtually no discretion to the officers operating the checkpoint. This eliminates the danger of police conducting arbitrary stops.

In *Sitz*, the Court adopted the balancing test applied in *Delaware v. Prouse*, 440 U.S. 647 (1979), which focused on three factors to determine the constitutionality of what the police do in these cases: (1) the gravity of the public concerns served by the seizure, (2) the degree to which the seizure advances the public interest, and (3) the severity of the interference with individual liberty. Although sobriety checkpoints are constitutional, they may be prohibited by departmental policy or state law.

Roadblocks to control the flow of illegal aliens are constitutional. Stops in the form of roadblocks for brief questioning, routinely conducted at permanent checkpoints, are consistent with the Fourth Amendment, so it is not necessary to obtain a warrant before setting up such a checkpoint (*United States v. Martinez-Fuerte*, 428 U.S. 543 [1976]).

United States v. Martinez-Fuerte (1976) involved a fixed checkpoint set up not at the border but in the interior, where all vehicles were stopped. After the stop, certain

United States v. Martinez-Fuerte (1976)

 **HIGHLIGHT** › **Vehicle Stops and Roadblocks Compared**

Similarities

- Police may ask questions.
- Police may "look around" the exterior of the vehicle and look in the windows of the vehicle.

- Police may use dogs to sniff the vehicle.
- Searches are not allowed unless there is probable cause.
- Police may arrest the occupants if there is probable cause.

Differences

Stop	Roadblock
Needs reasonable suspicion of involvement in criminal activity	No need for reasonable suspicion
Applies to specific vehicles	Applies to all vehicles or is based on random selection
Must be based on specific activity that amounts to reasonable suspicion	Cannot be used for unspecified law enforcement systematic functions, such as to obtain general information about criminal activity

motorists were referred to a secondary inspection area, where they could be questioned and their vehicles searched if it seemed justified. The Court permitted such "suspicion-less" stops in the interest of controlling the flow of illegal aliens.

Roadblocks to check for a driver's license and vehicle registration are constitutional. Establishing a roadblock to check driver's licenses and vehicle registrations is legitimate (*Town of Castle Rock v. Gonzales* [2005]). In the process, if the officers see evidence of other crimes, they are not required to close their eyes; they have the right to take reasonable investigative steps. However, police officers may not stop a single vehicle for the sole purpose of checking the driver's license and vehicle registration. To do that, the officers must reasonably believe that the motorist has violated a traffic law. Mere suspicion is not enough.

Town of Castle Rock v. Gonzales (2005)

Roadblocks because of a hit-and-run accident are constitutional. The Court held in *Illinois v. Lidster*, 540 U.S. 419 (2004), that police checkpoints set up to obtain information from motorists about a hit-and-run accident are valid under the Fourth Amendment. In *Lidster*, the police in Lombard, Illinois, set up a highway checkpoint to obtain information from motorists about a hit-and-run accident. The checkpoint was set up at about the same time of night and at the same location as the hit-and-run accident that had happened about one week earlier. Police officers stopped every vehicle for ten to fifteen seconds, asked the occupants if they had seen anything related to the accident, and handed them a flyer asking for their assistance. As Robert Lidster approached the checkpoint, his van swerved, almost hitting an officer. The officer smelled alcohol on Lidster's breath, so he directed him to a side street where another officer administered a sobriety test, which Lidster failed. They arrested him. Lidster was later convicted of driving under the influence of alcohol. He appealed, saying that the police checkpoint violated his Fourth Amendment rights.

The Court rejected his challenge, saying that the checkpoint stop was constitutional, citing three reasons: (1) "the relevant public concern was grave," (2) "the stop advanced this grave public concern to a significant degree," and (3) "more importantly, the stops interfered only minimally with liberty of the sort the Fourth Amendment seeks to protect."

Roadblocks to detect criminal wrongdoing are unconstitutional. Although vehicle road-blocks or checkpoints are constitutional for some purposes, they are unconstitutional if used to detect evidence of ordinary criminal wrongdoing (*Indianapolis v. Edmond*, 531 U.S. 32 [2000]).

Indianapolis v. Edmond (2000)

In *Indianapolis v. Edmond* (2000), Indianapolis, Indiana, police set up a program of vehicle checkpoints to detect illegal drugs. The roadblocks were operated during daylight hours and clearly marked by signs. The locations of the roadblocks were planned well in advance, and a predetermined number of vehicles were to be stopped. After the stop, an officer required the driver to produce a driver's license and registration. Only if the officer developed particularized suspicion of illegality was the driver detained. The total time of the stop averaged less than five minutes. Edmond and others were stopped at the checkpoints. They later brought suit, claiming the stops violated the Fourth Amendment because they lacked individualized reasonable suspicion.

On appeal, the Court agreed, saying that the roadblocks they had approved in prior cases were for purposes of controlling drunk driving, controlling the flow

HIGHLIGHT ❯ Summary of U.S. Supreme Court Cases on the Constitutionality of Roadblocks

Michigan Department of State Police v. Sitz (1990) Roadblocks to control drunk driving are constitutional.
United States v. Martinez-Fuerte (1976) Roadblocks to control the flow of illegal aliens are constitutional.
Delaware v. Prouse (1979) Roadblocks to check for a driver's license and vehicle registration are constitutional.

Illinois v. Lidster (2004) Roadblocks to obtain information from motorists about a hit-and-run accident are constitutional.
Indianapolis v. Edmond (2000) Roadblocks to detect evidence of ordinary criminal wrongdoing are unconstitutional.

---

of illegal aliens, and checking driver's licenses and vehicle registrations. The difference between those cases and *Edmond* was that in *Edmond* the purpose was to detect criminal wrongdoing, in particular the sale and possession of drugs. The Court acknowledged that the drug problem is severe, but it does not justify setting up roadblocks that have no clear relationship to the wrongdoing the police sought to reduce. The Court concluded by saying: "We have never approved a checkpoint program whose primary purpose was to detect evidence of ordinary criminal wrongdoing. Rather, our checkpoint cases have recognized only limited exceptions to the general rule that a seizure must be accompanied by some measure of individualized suspicion."

In summary, roadblocks are an exception to the need for reasonable suspicion in motor vehicle cases. Court decisions say this: Properly designed roadblocks for specific purposes are valid, but roadblocks for general crime control are unconstitutional. If the purpose is crime control (such as to detect drugs in a vehicle), there must be individualized suspicion before a police officer can stop motor vehicles.

VEHICLE SEARCHES

A valid stop does not automatically give police officers the authority to search a vehicle. A vehicle stop is *totally* different from a vehicle search, and each is governed by different rules. A stop does not need a warrant, but there must be reasonable suspicion that the vehicle is involved in some criminal activity for the stop to be valid. The rule for searches is different: In vehicle searches, probable cause must be present; reasonable suspicion is not sufficient.

The general rule is that *the search of an automobile does not require a warrant*. A vehicle search is therefore an exception to the warrant requirement of the Fourth Amendment. However, there are two requirements for warrantless vehicle searches: (1) probable cause and (2) the vehicle must be mobile, meaning capable of being driven away at any time. A vehicle that is up on blocks, missing an essential part, or being repaired and therefore cannot be driven away is not mobile. A warrant is needed to search immobilized vehicles even if there is probable cause. As in other types of searches, reasonableness governs the scope of the search; a fishing expedition for evidence is not allowed.

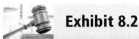

Exhibit 8.2   Portrait of a Texas Department of Public Safety Trooper

On the Road Again *by Kristin Edwards*

Department of Public Safety Trooper Jack Dean had a lot on his mind when he started his shift on April 30. The night before, a trooper had been killed in the line of duty, and updates were coming over the radio constantly about the incident.

"The guy that did this is hiding somewhere, and it's just a matter of time before we find him," he said evenly, not allowing his emotion get in the way of the facts. "He'll either get caught or he'll kill himself."

While his matter-of-fact treatment of the event made Dean seem somewhat cut off, his attitude proved to be much more focused on others than he initially let on.

"I think everybody in Huntsville knows what I do—I take people to jail," he said. "At the same time, there are a lot of things people don't realize about the job we do. If they did, they would look at us in a completely different way."

According to Dean, DPS troopers are allowed to work in any part of the state because they have jurisdiction everywhere.

"We can literally go wherever we want to work, because we're not required to stay in any specific areas or any particular county," he said. "I can go to Montgomery County or Trinity County if I want to, because we have jurisdiction throughout the state."

In addition to the traffic-related work Dean said troopers are known for, he and other troopers actually take on an extensive amount of other responsibilities.

"I don't mind taking calls for the county at all," he said. "In fact, we're trained in all aspects of the law, meaning everything from traffic to domestic issues. Basically, we can handle any kind of regular police work as well as what troopers are known for."

Because of the extra duties troopers can easily pick up, they have been given an opportunity to develop close working relationships with other local law enforcement agencies.

"We have an excellent working relationship with the Huntsville Police Department and the Walker County Sheriff's Department," he said. "There's no power struggle; they don't mind us working in the city,

and they can always call us if they need assistance just as we can always call them if we need assistance."

Of course, troopers have a multitude of technological advantages to their work. Just on the console of Dean's Dodge Charger, there are eight different light controls, siren controls, and a radio he uses to communicate back and forth with dispatch. The car also has a digital camera that can save everything outside and inside of the car onto a hard drive.

"Everything that happens once you pull someone over is recorded onto a DVD, which is saved to a hard drive," he said, replacing an old DVD with a new one and labeling the old one with appropriate dates. "People think you can go out and do racial profiling, but you just can't do it because everything is on this tape. You can't hide who you pull over, how you act, any of it."

As well, Dean's car has a dual system radar, which allows him to track the speeds of two vehicles at once and identify the faster one. Speeding has proven to be a somewhat subjective infraction in Dean's work, such as when he stops vehicles for traveling just over the speed limit.

"If I see them going even five over in a dangerous area, I stop them," he said.

Probable cause

During the course of his shift, Dean stopped vehicles for driving without a license plate light, for having tinted windows which may or may not have been darker than the legal allowed limit, and for swerving.

"I'm not going to write a ticket for not having a license plate or not having a light in your license plate, but those things are a great way to stop people to see what else is going on. The majority of my DWI's come out of license plate lights being out, or other minor infractions of the law. I've stopped people for things like that and found myself looking at people with warrants in the city."

Without fail, Dean followed standard procedure to the letter when pulling over a vehicle. After locating a safe spot to pull over, he checks for other vehicles and any other circumstances before usually bringing the driver to stand with him on the shoulder.

"We conduct most of our business outside of the car," he said. "If a car would come along, we have our tires turned so the car would go out in the road and hopefully miss us. The most important thing I try to do is relax because you have to talk to people like they're human beings. You speak nicely, look them in the eye and show respect, and nine times out of 10, they show you respect back."

At one point, Dean pulled a man over who spoke little to no English, and he asked him to step out of the car and removed the man's wallet from his back pocket. During the entire stop, both Dean and the man seemed relaxed and friendly.

"He spoke very little English, but they teach us enough Spanish to get by with what we need," Dean said. "I also speak a little bit of German, at least enough to hold a conversation."

Dean said he has actually had to use his German a few times.

"There have been situations where I've stopped people from Germany who are used to driving on the Autobahn," he said. "They'll be going over 100 on the Interstate, but then you get them stopped, and they're really nice."

DWI arrests

The week of the ride-along, Dean said he had arrested two college-aged students for DWIs, but he said that was rare.

"I probably don't arrest 10 college kids a year for DWIs," he said. "The majority of the arrests I make are among the older crowd, in that 30 to 60 age range. The oldest person I ever arrested for DWI was a 72-year-old man, and the youngest was actually 17."

Dean said the stigma of having a certain blood alcohol content equating to drunkenness is a complete lie.

"Being drunk is about the loss of your mental and physical capacities," he said. "I've pulled over a lot of people who were under the legal limit, and they were still intoxicated, no doubt."

The majority of DWI arrests Dean has made, however, have included several cases where the legal blood alcohol limit was far surpassed.

"The most drunk I have ever seen someone was this small female," he said. "She weighed about 105 pounds and had a blood alcohol content of about .35, which is nearly five times over the legal limit."

"She couldn't speak very well, and she had been driving all over the road."

Dean said he has also pulled impaired drivers over not for alcohol consumption, but because they were under the influence of prescription drugs.

"I'd say my DWIs are caused by 70 percent alcohol and 30 percent drugs—we're really starting to see a lot more use of prescription medications than just a few years ago," he said. "The three most common include Soma, Xanax and Hydrocodone."

"It's especially dangerous because drivers under the influence of these drugs display the same symptoms as someone who's been drinking."

Late in the evening, Dean pulled a truck over that was swerving between lanes, which could have indicated alcohol or drug use.

As it turned out, the woman driving the truck had been in an argument with her boyfriend, who was in the passenger seat.

"I hope you win," Dean said to the boyfriend, grinning to himself as he walked back to the car.

At one scene, a friend of Dean's named Shawn Nettles discussed the work he had seen him complete over the years.

In his experience, Nettles said he had seen more human compassion and fairness in Dean's work than he thought the public would imagine.

"People look at troopers like they're robots, like they're a different kind of person entirely," he said. "As for me, I look at him as a friend."

The Leading Case on Vehicle Searches

The leading (and also the earliest) Supreme Court case on automobile searches is *Carroll v. United States*, 267 U.S. 132 (1925). In this case, decided way back in 1925, Carroll was convicted for transporting "intoxicating spirituous liquor" (sixty-eight quarts of bonded whiskey and gin, in violation of the National Prohibition Act). He appealed his conviction, saying that it was wrong for the trial court to admit two of the sixty-eight bottles because they had been seized by law enforcement officers without a warrant. The officers countered that they had had probable cause to believe that the automobile contained bootleg liquor. They said that if they had taken the time to obtain a warrant, the car, which they had stopped on a highway, would have disappeared.

The Court agreed that the warrantless search of the automobile was reasonable, because it would have been gone if the officers had tried to obtain a warrant. After a discussion of various laws, the Court said:

> [T]he guaranty of freedom from unreasonable searches and seizures by the Fourth Amendment has been construed, practically since the beginning of the government, as recognizing a necessary difference between a search of a store, dwelling house, or other structure in respect of which a proper official warrant readily may be obtained and a search of a ship, motor boat, wagon, or automobile for contraband goods, *where it is not practicable to secure a warrant, because the vehicle can be quickly moved out of the locality or jurisdiction in which the warrant must be sought* (emphasis added).

Although in *Carroll* the Court ruled that there is no need for a warrant to search vehicles "where it is not practicable to secure a warrant," subsequent Court decisions have held that warrantless vehicle searches are constitutional even if there is time to obtain one.

The "automobile exception" to the warrant requirement is justified by five considerations (*Robbins v. California*, 453 U.S. 420 [1981]):

Robbins v. California (1981)

1. The mobility of motor vehicles often makes obtaining a judicial warrant impractical.
2. A diminished expectation of privacy surrounds the automobile.
3. A car is used for transportation, not as a residence or a repository of personal effects.
4. The car's occupants and contents travel in plain view.
5. Automobiles are necessarily highly regulated by the government.

IN ACTION   *THE LICENSE AND REGISTRATION CHECKPOINT*

Durham, North Carolina, police set up a roadblock on Elliot Road, a major road that runs through town and close by the Duke University campus. Their intention is to stop every vehicle that passes through this roadblock and ask the driver to produce his or her driver's license and vehicle registration. State law requires drivers to carry these documents with them any time they are operating a motor vehicle. The officers also hope to determine if any of the drivers may be transporting drugs, as there have been a number of arrests for drug use and sale in the area, particularly on the Duke University campus.

After stopping and verifying the driver's license and registration, the police ask the drivers if they can search their vehicles. Those drivers who give consent have their vehicles searched; those who do not give consent are detained roadside while a narcotics detection dog sniffs the detained vehicle; the sniff is usually done within five minutes.

1. Is the roadblock to check license and registration valid?
2. Is the search of a vehicle, with the driver's consent, valid?
3. Is the use of the dog to sniff the detained vehicle valid?

CASE BRIEF — *Carroll v. United States, 267 U.S. 132 (1925)*

The Leading Case on Vehicle Search

Facts: Officers observed the automobile of Carroll while on a regular patrol from Detroit to Grand Rapids. The same officers had been in contact with Carroll twice in the four months prior to this sighting. In September, the officers attempted to buy illegal liquor from Carroll, but he was alerted to their true identity and did not produce the contraband. In October, the officers recognized Carroll's automobile returning to Grand Rapids from Detroit (a city possessing an international boundary and that was known as a city from which illegal liquor was regularly imported). The officers gave chase and eventually apprehended Carroll and his passenger. He and his passenger were ordered out of the car. No liquor was visible in the front seat of the automobile. Officers then opened the rumble seat and looked under the cushions, again finding no liquor. One of the officers then tore open the seat cushion, and discovered 68 bottles of gin and whiskey. Carroll was arrested and convicted of transporting intoxicating liquor.

Issue: *May officers search an automobile without a search warrant but with probable cause that it contains illegal contraband?* Yes.

Decision: The Court affirmed the decision of the federal district court.

Holding: The risk of the vehicle being moved from the jurisdiction, or the evidence being destroyed or carried off, justifies a warrantless search as long as the search is conducted with probable cause that the vehicle contains contraband.

Case Significance: The general rule is that searches may be conducted only if a warrant has been issued. There are several exceptions to this rule, however, with searches of automobiles one of them. This case, decided in 1925, created the so-called automobile exception to the warrant requirement, which states that warrantless searches of motor vehicles are valid as long as there is probable cause to believe that there are seizable items in the vehicle. The justification for this exception is the mobile nature of the automobile.

Excerpts from the Opinion: [T]he guaranty of freedom from unreasonable searches and seizures by the Fourth Amendment has been construed, practically since the beginning of the government, as recognizing a necessary difference between a search of a store, dwelling house, or other structure in respect of which a proper official warrant readily may be obtained and a search of a ship, motor boat, wagon, or automobile for contraband goods, where it is not practicable to secure a warrant, because the vehicle can be quickly moved out of the locality or jurisdiction in which the warrant must be sought.

Having thus established that contraband goods concealed and illegally transported in an automobile or other vehicle may be searched for without a warrant, we come now to consider under what circumstances such search may be made. It would be intolerable and unreasonable if a prohibition agent were authorized to stop every automobile on the chance of finding liquor, and thus subject all persons lawfully using the highways to the inconvenience and indignity of such a search. Travelers may be so stopped in crossing an international boundary because of national self-protection reasonably requiring one entering the country to identify himself as entitled to come in, and his belongings as effects which may be lawfully brought in. But those lawfully within the country, entitled to use the public highways, have a right to free passage without interruption or search unless there is known to a competent official, authorized to search, probable cause for believing that their vehicles are carrying contraband or illegal merchandise.

Note that, although *Carroll* is acknowledged as the "mother" of all motor vehicle cases, it is primarily a vehicle *search* case, not a vehicle *stop* case. (Read the Case Brief to learn more about this case.)

The Objective Reasonableness Rule in Vehicle Searches

Florida v. Jimeno (1991)

The Court decided in *Florida v. Jimeno*, 500 U.S. 248 (1991), that valid consent justifies a warrantless search of a container in a car if it is objectively reasonable for the police to believe that the scope of the suspect's consent permitted them to open that container.

In *Florida v. Jimeno*, a Dade County police officer overheard Jimeno arranging what appeared to be a drug transaction over a public telephone. The officer followed Jimeno's car, observed him make an illegal right turn at a red light, and stopped him to issue a traffic citation. After informing Jimeno why he had been stopped, the officer told Jimeno he had reason to believe Jimeno was carrying narcotics in his car and asked permission to search. The officer explained that Jimeno did not have to grant permission, but Jimeno said he had nothing to hide and gave consent to the search, whereupon the officer found a kilogram of cocaine in a brown paper bag on the floor of the passenger compartment. Jimeno appealed his conviction, saying that his consent to search the vehicle did not extend to closed containers found inside the vehicle.

The Court disagreed, stating that a search is valid if it is objectively reasonable for the police to believe that the scope of the suspect's consent permits them to open a container. This case differs from *U.S. v. Ross* (discussed next), in which the police had probable cause to search the car. Here, there was no probable cause, but there was consent to search. This ruling defines what officers can do in car searches where there may not be probable cause but where consent to search is given.

Automatic Searches during Traffic Citations Are Unconstitutional

In *Knowles v. Iowa*, 525 U.S. 113 (1998), the Court held that a state law authorizing a vehicle search during the issuance of a traffic citation violates the Fourth Amendment unless there is consent (see Figure 8.1) or probable cause.

Knowles v. Iowa (1998)

In the *Knowles* case, Knowles was stopped for speeding and issued a citation, although he could have arrested the driver for speeding. The officer then conducted a full search of Knowles's car, where he found marijuana and drug paraphernalia. The state of Iowa had a law providing that the issuance of a citation instead of an arrest "does not affect the officer's authority to conduct an otherwise lawful search." This was interpreted by the Iowa Supreme Court to mean that officers could "conduct a full-blown search of an automobile and driver in those cases where police elect not to make a custodial arrest and instead issue a citation—that is, a search incident to citation." Convicted of possession of drug paraphernalia, Knowles appealed, claiming that the search was unconstitutional.

The Court agreed, saying that such searches, even if authorized by state law, violate the Fourth Amendment. They can be done only if there is valid consent or probable cause, neither of which was present in this case.

The mere issuance of a citation does not justify a full-blown search. However, this decision does not include items in plain view, because such items are not protected by the Fourth Amendment. For example, suppose Officer Roberts stops a pickup truck and issues a citation. Officer Roberts cannot automatically conduct a full-blown search of the car, as she could if there was probable cause to arrest the driver or search the car. But nothing prevents Officer Roberts from looking in the windows of the car to see if there are seizable items. If there are, these can validly be seized under the plain view doctrine (see Chapter 9).

WARRANTLESS VEHICLE SEARCHES

As noted previously in this chapter, warrantless searches of motor vehicles after a stop are constitutional as long as (1) the officer has probable cause for the search and (2) the

FIGURE 8.1 Voluntary Consent for Search and Seizure of Automobile

DATE: _____

I, _____ , having been informed of my constitutional right not to have a search made of the automobile hereinafter mentioned without a search warrant and of my right to refuse such a search, hereby authorize _____ _____ and _____ , police officers of the Houston Police Department, to conduct a complete search of my automobile, _____ which is a _____ located at _____ _____

These officers are authorized by me to take from my automobile any letters, papers, materials, or any other property which they may desire. This permission is being given by me to the above named officers voluntarily without threats or promises of any kind and is given with my full and free consent.

SIGNED: _____

WITNESSES:

_____

_____

Source: Official consent form of the Houston Police Department.

vehicle is mobile, meaning it can be driven away at any time. There are a number of things an officer can do after the vehicle is stopped. These are discussed in this section.

Police May Search Passenger Compartments

Once a driver has been arrested, the police may conduct a warrantless search of the passenger compartment of the car. This means they may examine the contents of any container found within the passenger compartment, as long as it may reasonably be thought to contain something that might pose a danger to officers or to hold evidence related to the offense for which the suspect has been arrested.

New York v. Belton (1981)

In *New York v. Belton*, 453 U.S. 454 (1981), a New York state officer noticed an automobile traveling at an excessive rate of speed. The officer gave chase and ordered the car to pull over to the side of the road. The officer asked to see the driver's license; in the process, he smelled burned marijuana and saw on the floor of the car an envelope marked "Supergold." He placed the four occupants under arrest, picked up the envelope, and found marijuana inside it. He then searched the passenger compartment and on the back seat found a black leather jacket belonging to Belton; in one of the pockets of the jacket he discovered cocaine. During the trial, Belton moved to suppress the cocaine, claiming it was not within the area of his immediate control, so its seizure was illegal. The Supreme Court rejected this contention, saying that the police may conduct a warrantless search of the passenger compartment of a car incident to a lawful arrest because that space is within the suspect's area of immediate control.

Belton is significant because it defines the extent of allowable search inside an automobile after a lawful arrest. Prior to *Belton*, there was confusion about whether the police could search parts of the automobile outside the driver's wingspan. The Court expanded the area of allowable search to the whole compartment, including the back seat; it also authorized the opening of containers found in the passenger compartment that might contain the object sought. However, *Belton* did not authorize the search of the trunk or under the hood of the car.

Lower courts interpreted the *Belton* decision as allowing the police to conduct a search incident to arrest of the passenger compartment of a vehicle even after the driver had been arrested and secured in a police vehicle. This became standard police practice. Then, in 2009, the Supreme Court called a halt to the practice. In *Arizona v. Gant*, 556 U.S. 332 (2009), the Court held that the police can search the passenger compartment of a motor vehicle after the driver has been arrested, but "only if the arrestee is within reaching distance of the passenger compartment at the time of the search or if it is reasonable to believe the vehicle contains evidence of the offense of arrest."

Arizona v. Gant (2009)

In this case, Gant was arrested for driving on a suspended license, handcuffed, and locked in a patrol car before officers searched his car, where they found cocaine in a jacket in the car. At trial, he moved to suppress the evidence, claiming that the search could not be justified as within the area of immediate control. The trial court denied the motion to suppress and Gant was convicted. On appeal, the Court held that police officers have the authority to search the passenger compartment of a vehicle immediately after an occupant's arrest but only if it is reasonable to believe that the arrestee might access the vehicle at the time of the search or that the vehicle contains evidence of the offense of arrest. The Court said:

> Police may search a vehicle incident to a recent occupant's arrest only if the arrestee is within reaching distance of the passenger compartment at the time of the search or it is reasonable to believe the vehicle contains evidence of the offense of arrest. When these justifications are absent, a search of an arrestee's vehicle will be unreasonable unless police obtain a warrant or show that another exception to the warrant requirement applies.

The Court claimed it was not overruling *Belton* but merely clarifying it, but the end result is the same—it put an end to the practice of conducting a search of the passenger compartment incident to arrest once the suspect is no longer in the immediate vicinity.

Police May Search Trunks and Closed Packages

If the police legitimately stop a car and have probable cause to believe that it contains contraband, they may conduct a warrantless search of the car. This search can be as thorough as a search authorized by a warrant issued by a magistrate. Therefore, every part of the vehicle in which the contraband might be stored may be inspected, including the trunk and all receptacles and packages (*United States v. Ross*, 456 U.S. 798 [1982]).

United States v. Ross (1982)

In *United States v. Ross*, after making a valid vehicle stop and arrest for a narcotics sale, one of the officers opened the car's trunk and found a closed brown paper bag. Inside the bag were glassine bags containing heroin. The officer then drove the car to police headquarters, where another warrantless search of the trunk revealed a zippered leather pouch containing cash. During the trial, the suspect argued that the police officers should not have opened either the paper bag or the leather pouch found in the trunk without first obtaining a warrant. The Supreme Court disagreed and allowed the evidence to be admitted.

The *Ross* case is important because it further defines the scope of police authority in searches of vehicles. In *Belton*, the Court specifically refused to address the issue of whether the police may open the trunk of a car in connection with a warrantless search incident to a valid arrest. Although based on slightly different facts, as it involved a warrantless search based on probable cause, *Ross* addressed that issue and authorized such action. But it went further, holding that any packages or luggage found in the trunk that could reasonably be thought to contain the items for which the officers have probable cause to search may also be opened without a warrant. Ross has therefore greatly expanded the scope of allowable warrantless car searches, focusing the search on the whole automobile as the possible source of evidence. Opening the brown paper bag and the pouch was legitimate by extension of police authority to conduct a warrantless search of the car. (Read the Case Brief to learn more about this case.)

Police May Search Containers in a Car

California v. Acevedo (1991)

The Court held in *California v. Acevedo*, 500 U.S. 565 (1991), that the police may search a *container* located in a car without a search warrant even though they lack probable cause to search the *car* as a whole and have probable cause to believe only that the container itself contains contraband or evidence. In *Acevedo*, the police in Santa Ana, California, observed Acevedo leaving an apartment known to contain marijuana carrying a brown paper bag the size of marijuana packages the police had seen earlier. The police had probable cause to search the brown paper bag because a federal drug agent in Hawaii had phoned earlier and said that the bag contained marijuana. Acevedo placed the bag in his car's trunk and then drove away. The police stopped the car, opened the trunk and the bag, and found marijuana.

Acevedo pleaded guilty to possession of marijuana for sale but later appealed his conviction, saying that the marijuana should have been suppressed as evidence. He claimed that, even if the police had probable cause to believe the container itself contained contraband, they did not have probable cause to search the car.

The Supreme Court ultimately disagreed with Acevedo, saying that probable cause to believe that a container in a car holds contraband or seizable evidence justifies a warrantless search of that container even in the absence of probable cause to search the car.

United States v. Chadwick (1977)

Acevedo is significant because it reverses two earlier Court rulings on essentially the same issue. In a 1977 case, *United States v. Chadwick*, 433 U.S. 1 (1977), the Court held that the police could seize movable luggage or other closed containers from a car but could not open them without a warrant, because a person has a heightened privacy expectation for such containers even if they are in a car. That case involved the seizure by government agents in Boston of a 200-pound padlocked footlocker that contained marijuana. Upon arrival by train from San Diego, the footlocker was placed in the trunk of Chadwick's car, whereupon it was seized by the agents and opened without a warrant. The Court declared the warrantless search of the footlocker unjustified.

Two years later, in *Arkansas v. Sanders*, 442 U.S. 753 (1979), the Court ruled unconstitutional the warrantless search of a suitcase located in a vehicle when there was probable cause to search only the suitcase but not the vehicle. In this case, the police had probable cause to believe that the suitcase contained marijuana. The police watched as the suspect placed the suitcase in the trunk of a taxi, which was then driven away. The police pursued the taxi for several blocks and then stopped it. They found the suitcase in the trunk, searched it, and found marijuana. Again, however, the Court refused to extend the warrantless search doctrine enunciated in *Carroll* to searches of personal luggage if the only justification for the search was that the luggage was located in an automobile that was lawfully stopped by the police.

Arkansas v. Sanders (1979)

The Court in *Acevedo* rejected *Chadwick* and *Sanders* and instead reiterated its ruling in the *Carroll* and *Ross* cases. In *Carroll*, the Court held that a warrantless search of an automobile was valid based on probable cause to believe that the vehicle contained evidence of a crime and in light of the vehicle's likely disappearance. In *Ross*, the Court allowed the warrantless search of a container found in a car where there was probable cause to search the car and as long as the opening of the container was reasonable—given the object of the search. *Acevedo* extended the *Carroll–Ross* line of cases in that it allows the warrantless search of a container as long as there is probable cause to believe that the container holds contraband, even if there is no probable cause to search the car itself. In essence, *Acevedo* (probable cause for the *container* but not for the car) is the opposite of *Ross* (probable cause for the *car* but not for the container), but the effect is the same—it expands the power of the police to conduct warrantless car searches.

Unresolved: Searches of Locked Trunks or Glove Compartments

Whether the police may open a *locked* (as opposed to a closed) glove compartment or trunk was not addressed by the Court in *New York v. Belton*, 453 U.S. 454 (1981) or in any other case involving a warrantless arrest situation. In a footnote to *Belton*, the Court stated:

> "Container" here denotes any object capable of holding another object. It thus includes closed or open glove compartments, consoles, or other receptacles located anywhere within the passenger compartment, as well as luggage, boxes, bags, clothing, and the like. Our holding encompasses only the interior of the passenger compartment of an automobile and does not encompass the trunk.

At least one state supreme court has held, however, that consent to search a car does not authorize police officers to pry open a locked briefcase found in the car's trunk (*State v. Wells*, 539 So.2d 464 [Sup. Ct. Fla. 1989]).

State v. Wells (1989)

In general, consent to search does not mean consent to open a locked container unless the key is given voluntarily to the police or the police lawfully obtain possession of the key. The search will most likely be valid, however, if the trunk is opened by pressing a release button inside the car. What is highly questionable is the forcible opening of locked glove compartments or car trunks. Such intrusions, if necessary, are best done with a warrant.

The Leading Case on the Search of Car Trunks and Closed Packages in Trunks

Facts: Police in Washington, D.C., received information from an informant that Ross was selling narcotics kept in the trunk of his car, which was parked at a specified location. The police drove to the location, spotted the person and car that matched the descriptions given by the informant, and made a warrantless arrest. The officers opened the car's trunk and found a closed brown paper bag containing heroin. The officers then drove the car to police headquarters, where another warrantless search of the trunk revealed a zippered leather pouch containing cash. Ross was charged with possession of heroin with intent to distribute. He sought to suppress the heroin and cash as evidence, alleging that both were obtained in violation of his constitutional rights because there were no exigent circumstances that would justify a warrantless search.

Issue: *After a valid arrest, may the police open the trunk of the car and containers found therein without a warrant and in the absence of exigent circumstances?* Yes.

Holding: When the police have probable cause to justify a warrantless search of a car, they may search the entire car and open the trunk and any packages or luggage found therein that could reasonably be thought to contain the items for which they have probable cause to search.

Case Significance: The *Ross* case is important in that it further defines the scope of police authority in vehicle searches. The Court's *Belton* decision had specifically refused to address the issue of whether the police could open the trunk of a car in connection with a search incident to a valid arrest. *Ross* addressed that issue and authorized such an action. But it went beyond that: Any packages or luggage found in the car that could reasonably be thought to contain the items for which there was probable cause to search could also be opened without a warrant. *Ross* has therefore greatly expanded the scope of allowable warrantless search, limited only by what is reasonable.

Excerpts from the Decision: As we have stated, the decision in *Carroll* was based on the Court's appraisal of practical considerations viewed in the perspective of history. It is therefore significant that the practical consequences of the *Carroll* decision would be largely nullified if the permissible scope of a warrantless search of an automobile did not include containers and packages found inside the vehicle. Contraband goods rarely are strewn across the trunk or floor of a car; because by their very nature such goods must be withheld from public view, they rarely can be placed in an automobile unless they are enclosed within some form of container. . . . The Court in *Carroll* held that "contraband goods concealed and illegally transported in an automobile or other vehicle may be searched for without a warrant." As we noted in *Henry v. United States*, the decision in *Carroll* "merely relaxed the requirements for a warrant on grounds of practicability." It neither broadened nor limited the scope of a lawful search based on probable cause.

A lawful search of fixed premises generally extends to the entire area in which the object of the search may be found and is not limited by the possibility that separate acts of entry or opening may be required to complete the search. Thus, a warrant that authorizes an officer to search a home for illegal weapons also provides authority to open closets, chests, drawers, and containers in which the weapon might be found. A warrant to open a footlocker to search for marijuana would also authorize the opening of packages found inside. A warrant to search a vehicle would support a search of every part of the vehicle that might contain the object of the search. When a legitimate search is under way, and when its purpose and its limits have been precisely defined, nice distinctions between closets, drawers, and containers, in the case of a home, or between glove compartments, upholstered seats, trunks, and wrapped packages, in the case of a vehicle, must give way to the interest in the prompt and efficient completion of the task at hand.

Searches When the Arrested Suspect Is Not in the Vehicle—Questions Remain

In *York v. Belton*, the driver was in the car when arrested, and the search took place after the occupants were placed under arrest. Would the *Belton* holding apply in cases where the initial contact with the police and the arrest took place outside the motor vehicle? In *Thornton v. United States*, 541 U.S. 615 (2004), the Court said yes; *Belton* would nonetheless apply, thus expanding further the concept of area of immediate control in motor vehicles.

Thornton v. United States (2004)

In *Thornton*, an officer became suspicious when Thornton slowed down to avoid driving next to the officer. The officer pulled over so that he could get behind Thornton and check his license plate. The check revealed the tags did not belong to the car Thornton was driving. Thornton pulled into a parking lot, parked, and got out of his vehicle. The officer stopped Thornton after he left the car and asked about the tags on the car. Thornton consented to a pat-down search. The officer felt a bulge in Thornton's pocket and asked him if he had illegal narcotics. Thornton then admitted he had drugs and retrieved two bags from his pocket, one containing marijuana and the other crack cocaine. The officer arrested Thornton, handcuffed him, and placed him in the back seat of the patrol car. The officer then searched Thornton's vehicle and found a handgun under the driver's seat.

After being convicted for possession of drugs and the firearm, Thornton sought exclusion of the handgun, saying it was illegally obtained because it was not in his area of immediate control since he was outside the vehicle when the arrest took place. The Court disagreed, saying that the *Belton* principle of allowable search of the passenger compartment applied even if the arrest took place outside the vehicle.

Five years after *Thornton*, however, the Court limited the scope of *Thornton* and held that the police can search the passenger compartment of a motor vehicle after arrest but "only if the arrestee is within reaching distance of the passenger compartment at the time of the search or if it is reasonable to believe the vehicle contains evidence of the offense of arrest" (*Arizona v. Gant*, 556 U.S. 332 [2009], discussed previously in this chapter). *Gant* is important because it limits the scope of *Thornton*, which allowed the search of the vehicle even if the arrest took place when the suspect was outside the car and no longer in a position to harm the officers or destroy evidence. *Gant* clarifies the issue of the reach of *Thornton*, saying that car searches after an arrest of the driver are still limited and that the area of immediate control in car searches applies only to areas where "it is reasonable to believe that the arrestee might access the vehicle at the time of the search or that the vehicle contains evidence of the offense of arrest." In sum, *Gant* limits *Thornton*, which some had interpreted as giving the police virtually unlimited authority to search motor vehicles after an arrest even if the driver was no longer in the vehicle. *Gant* imposes significant limits on the searches of the passenger compartment of a vehicle incident to the arrest of the driver.

OTHER MOTOR VEHICLE SEARCH AND SEIZURE ISSUES

Issues related to vehicle searches, including searches that are not contemporaneous, warrantless searches when there is time to obtain a warrant, warrantless seizures of vehicles found in public places, warrantless searches of motor homes, the use of electronic devices to detect cars, and immigration and border searches of vehicles, are discussed in this section.

Searches That Are Not Contemporaneous

The cases previously discussed involved car searches conducted *contemporaneously*, meaning at the time of or immediately after the arrest. Sometimes, however, the officer may not be able to conduct a search contemporaneously. In these cases, the rule is that, if the police have probable cause to stop and search an automobile on the highway, they may also take the automobile to the police station and search it there without a warrant. The ruling in *Ross* was later used to justify the warrantless search of a container even though there was a significant delay between the time the police stopped the vehicle and the time they performed the search of the container.

United States v. Johns (1985)

In *United States v. Johns*, 469 U.S. 478 (1985), customs officers stopped two trucks suspected of carrying marijuana. Officers removed several sealed packages believed to contain marijuana and placed them in a government warehouse. Three days later, officers opened them without a warrant and found marijuana. The Court said that neither *Ross* nor any other case establishes a requirement that a vehicle search occur immediately as part of the vehicle inspection or soon thereafter; a three-day delay before making the search is permissible. The search still must be done within a reasonable time, but the burden of proving unreasonableness is on the defendant.

Warrantless Searches When There Is Time to Obtain a Warrant

Closely related to the issue of contemporaneous searches is whether the police may conduct a warrantless search even if there is time to obtain a warrant. The answer is yes. This is different from a contemporaneous search (where a warrant could not have been obtained) in that this type of search assumes that the police could have obtained a warrant because they had time to do so but did not. For example, suppose the police, having probable cause, stopped Wilma's car on the highway and arrested her for robbery. There was probable cause to search the car, but the police instead towed the car to the police station and searched it there. This warrantless search is proper, because the police had probable cause to search when the vehicle was first stopped on the highway, and that probable cause justified a later search without a warrant.

Florida v. Meyers (1984)

Maryland v. Dyson (1999)

Florida v. Meyers, 466 U.S. 380 (1984), stands for the principle that a vehicle may be searched under the automobile exception to the Fourth Amendment even if it has been immobilized and released to the custody of the police. And in *Maryland v. Dyson*, 527 U.S. 465 (1999), the Court reiterated the rule that, if the police have probable cause to search a car, they do not need a warrant even if there was ample opportunity to obtain one.

Warrantless Seizures of Vehicles Found in Public Places

Florida v. White (1999)

In *Florida v. White*, 526 U.S. 23 (1999), the Court held that "the Fourth Amendment does not require the police to obtain a warrant before seizing an automobile from a public place if they have probable cause to believe it is forfeitable contraband."

In *White*, officers had previously observed White using his car to deliver cocaine but did not arrest him at that time. However, they did arrest him several months later at his workplace on unrelated charges. During the arrest, the officers seized White's car without a warrant, claiming they were authorized to do so because the car was subject to forfeiture under the Florida Contraband Forfeiture Act. They searched the car and found two pieces of crack cocaine in the ashtray. Convicted of a state drug violation, White moved to suppress the evidence seized during that search, saying his Fourth Amendment rights had been violated.

On appeal, the Court disagreed, holding that the search and seizure was valid because the car itself constituted forfeitable contraband under state law and probable cause was present. The Court added that, "because the police seized respondent's

vehicle from a public area—respondent's employer's parking lot—the warrantless seizure also did not involve any invasion of respondent's privacy."

Warrantless Searches of Motor Homes

The Court has held that motor homes are automobiles for purposes of the Fourth
Amendment and are therefore subject to the automobile exception: They can be
searched without a warrant. However, the application of this decision is limited to a
motor home capable of being driven on the road and located in a place not regularly
used for residential purposes. The Court decision in *California v. Carney*, 471 U.S. 386   *California v. Carney* (1985)
(1985), specifically stated that the case does not resolve whether the automobile excep-
tion applies to a motor home "situated in a way or place that objectively indicates that
it is being used as a residence."

In the *Carney* case, federal narcotics agents had reason to believe that Carney was
exchanging marijuana for sex with a boy in a motor home parked in a public parking
lot in downtown San Diego. The vehicle was outfitted to serve as a residence. The
agents waited until the youth emerged and convinced him to return and ask the defendant to come out. When the defendant came out, an agent entered the motor home
without a warrant and found marijuana lying on a table. During the trial, the defendant sought to suppress the evidence, saying that it was excludable because it was
obtained without a warrant.

The Court disagreed, saying that the evidence was admissible. The Court noted
that the vehicle in question was readily mobile, that there was a reduced expectation
of privacy stemming from its use as a licensed motor vehicle, and that it was situated
as to suggest that it was being used as a vehicle, not a residence. The Court refused to
distinguish motor homes from ordinary automobiles simply because motor homes are
capable of functioning as dwellings, saying that motor homes lend themselves easily
to use as instruments of illicit drug traffic and other illegal activity.

The Use of Electronic Devices to Monitor Vehicles

The constitutionality of the use of electronic devices to monitor vehicles has been
addressed by the Court over the years in a trilogy of cases. In the first case, the Court
held that a person traveling in a car on a public road has *no reasonable expectation of
privacy*, so visual surveillance by the police does not constitute a search. Moreover, the
Fourth Amendment does not prohibit the police from supplementing their sensory
faculties with technological aids to help the police identify the car's location (*United*   *United States v. Knotts*
States v. Knotts, 460 U.S. 276 [1983]). In *Knotts*, state narcotics agents, with the coopera-   (1983)
tion of a chemical supply company, installed an electronic tracking device, or beeper,
in a container of chloroform. When a man who the agents suspected of manufacturing
controlled substances turned up at the chemical company to purchase chloroform, the
bugged can was sold to him. The agents used both the beeper signal and visual surveillance to follow the suspect to a house, where the container was placed in another car.
The second car then proceeded into another state, where the agents lost both visual
and beeper contact. However, the beeper signal was picked up again by a monitoring
device aboard a helicopter. By this means, the agents learned that the container was
located in or near a secluded cabin owned by Knotts. Armed with this and other information, the agents obtained a search warrant and discovered a secret drug laboratory.

The Court held that the police actions in this case were valid and the evidence admissible, saying that by using the public roadways, the driver of the car voluntarily conveyed to anyone that he was traveling over particular roads and in a particular direction. Moreover, no expectation of privacy extended to the visual observation of the automobile arriving on private premises after leaving the public highway, nor to movements of objects such as the drum of chloroform outside the cabin in the "open fields." The *Knotts* case, however, did not address the issue of monitoring vehicles in private places.

United States v. Karo (1984)

That issue was addressed in *United States v. Karo*, 468 U.S. 705 (1984), decided a year later. In *Karo*, government agents, upon learning that Karo had ordered some cans of ether from a government informant (to use in extracting cocaine), obtained a court order authorizing the installation and monitoring of a beeper in one of the cans. The agents installed the beeper with the informant's consent, and the can was subsequently delivered to Karo. Over a period of months, the beeper enabled the agents to monitor the can's movements to a variety of locations, including several private residences and two commercial storage facilities. Based on the information gathered, the agents obtained a search warrant for one of the homes. When the evidence obtained from that warrant was introduced in court, Karo objected, but the evidence was admitted and he was convicted. He later appealed his conviction, claiming a violation of his Fourth Amendment rights because of the way the information used in obtaining the warrant was gathered. The Court agreed, saying that the monitoring of a beeper in a private dwelling, a location not open to visual surveillance, violated the rights of individuals to privacy in their own homes. Although the monitoring here was less intrusive than a full search, it revealed facts that the government was interested in knowing and that it could not otherwise have obtained legally without a warrant. Nevertheless, the evidence obtained was not suppressed because there was a lot of evidence other than that obtained through use of the beeper to establish probable cause for the issuance of the warrant. The crucial difference between *Knotts* and *Karo* is that the monitoring in *Knotts* was in a public place, whereas that in *Karo* involved the use of a beeper in a private dwelling.

United States v. Jones (2012)

The latest case in this trilogy of cases involving the monitoring of vehicles was decided by the Court in 2012. In *United States v. Jones* (565 U.S. [2012]), the Court held that the attachment of a GPS device to a vehicle, and the use of that device to monitor the vehicle's movements, constituted a search and violated Jones' constitutional rights. In *Jones*, government agents, without a warrant, attached a tracker to his jeep and used it to follow Jones for one month. The initial multiple charges of "conspiracy to distribute and possession with intent to distribute various drugs" were dismissed. But, miffed by the dismissal, prosecutors later filed a conspiracy charge against Jones and his business partner. They were convicted, but they appealed, claiming a violation of their Fourth Amendment rights because of the warrantless tracking. The Court held that the government agent violated Jones's constitutional right by placing the GPS unit on the vehicle. The Court said that "the Government's physical intrusion on an 'effect' ('persons, houses, papers, and effects') for the purpose of obtaining information constituted a 'search.'" The decision was based on a variety of grounds, including the historical property-based interpretation of the Fourth Amendment and the newer concept of the right to privacy.

Immigration and Border Searches of Vehicles

The Fourth Amendment protection against unreasonable searches and seizures does not apply in immigration and border searches, particularly of motor vehicles. There is

"The text of the Fourth Amendment reflects the close connection to property, since otherwise it would have referred simply to 'the right of the people to be secure against unreasonable searches and seizures'; the phrase 'in their persons, houses, papers, and effects' would have been superfluous. . . . Consistent with this understanding, our Fourth Amendment jurisprudence was tied to common-law trespass, at least until the later half of the 20th century. Thus, in *Olmstead v. United States* . . ., we held that wiretaps attached to telephone wires on the public streets did not constitute a Fourth Amendment search because 'there was no entry of the houses or offices of the defendants.'"

"Our later cases, of course, have deviated from that exclusively property-based approach. In *Katz v. United States*, we said that 'the Fourth Amendment protects people, not places,' and found a violation in attachment of an eavesdropping device to a public telephone booth. Our later cases have applied the analysis of Justice Harlan's concurrence in that case, which said that a violation occurs when government officers violate a person's 'reasonable expectation of privacy.'"

Source: *United States v. Jones* (2012), citations omitted.

no need for reasonable suspicion or probable cause for government agents to be able to stop, search, and seize. The scope of border searches is also much more extensive than in non border searches. In *United States v. Flores-Montano*, 541 U.S. 149 (2004), the Court held that the government's authority to conduct suspicionless inspections at the border includes the authority to remove, disassemble, and reassemble a vehicle's fuel tank.

United States v. Flores-Montano (2004)

In this case, Manuel Flores-Montano attempted to enter the United States at a point of entry in Southern California. Immigration officers asked Flores-Montano to leave his vehicle for secondary inspection. During the inspection, the officer noticed that the gas tank sounded solid, so he requested a mechanic's help in removing it. When the gas tank was removed, the inspector found thirty-seven kilograms of marijuana. Flores-Montano later sought suppression of the evidence, claiming the inspector did not have any reasonable suspicion he was engaged in criminal activity and that reasonable suspicion was required under the Fourth Amendment to remove the gas tank.

The Court ruled that "the government's authority to conduct suspicionless inspections at the border includes the authority to remove, disassemble, and reassemble a vehicle's fuel tank," adding that "on many occasions, we have noted that the expectation of privacy is less at the border than it is in the interior." It is clear from this case that (1) there is no need for suspicion, reasonable suspicion, or probable cause for border inspectors to conduct a vehicle search and (2) the extent of allowable search (removing the gas tank, disassembling, and then reassembling it) is much more extensive than in non border searches.

OTHER VALID CAR SEARCHES

Other circumstances that may justify warrantless car searches include the following:

◆ *Accident cases.* Sometimes, because of an accident or other circumstances, a car must remain in a location where it is vulnerable to theft or intrusion by vandals. If the police have probable cause to believe that the vehicle contains a weapon or a similar device that would constitute a danger if it fell into the wrong hands, they may make a warrantless search for the particular item (*Cady v. Dombrowski*, 413 U.S. 433 [1973]).

Cady v. Dombrowski (1973)

- *Cases in which the vehicle itself has been the subject of crime.* An officer who has probable cause to believe that a car has been the subject of burglary, tampering, or theft may make a limited warrantless entry and investigation of those areas that are reasonably believed to contain evidence of ownership.
- *Cases in which the vehicle is believed abandoned.* A limited search of an automobile in an effort to ascertain ownership is allowable when the car has apparently been abandoned or when the arrested driver is possibly not the owner and does not otherwise resolve the matter of ownership.

VEHICLE INVENTORY SEARCHES

In this section, we examine warrantless vehicle inventory searches that take place immediately after an arrest and those of vehicles impounded by the police.

Immediately after an Arrest

vehicle inventory
the police list the personal effects and properties they find in the vehicle.

The Court has decided two cases addressing the validity and scope of **vehicle inventory** searches, in which the police list the personal effects and properties they find in the vehicle, without a warrant immediately after an arrest.

In the first case, *Colorado v. Bertine*, 479 U.S. 367 (1987), the Court held that warrantless inventory searches of the person and possessions of arrested individuals are permissible under the Fourth Amendment. Bertine was arrested for driving under the influence of alcohol. After he was taken into custody and before the arrival of a tow truck to impound his van, an officer inventoried the van in accordance with departmental procedures. During the inventory search, the officer opened a backpack and found controlled substances, drug paraphernalia, and money. Bertine challenged the admissibility of the evidence, saying that a warrant was needed to open the closed backpack. The Court rejected his challenge, saying that the police must be allowed to conduct warrantless inventory searches to secure an arrestee's property from loss or damage and to protect the police from false claims. Because closed containers may hold items that need to be secured, the police must be allowed to open them without a warrant.

Colorado v. Bertine (1987)

The *Bertine* case specified two prerequisites for the valid inventory search of a motor vehicle: (1) the police must follow standardized procedures (to eliminate their uncontrolled discretion to determine the scope of the search) and (2) there must be no bad faith on the part of the police (in other words, the inventory search must not be used as an excuse for a warrantless search).

Florida v. Wells (1990)

In a subsequent case (*Florida v. Wells*, 495 U.S. 1 [1990]), the Court ruled that a police department's "utter lack of any standard policy regarding the opening of closed containers encountered during inventory searches requires the suppression of contraband found in a locked suitcase removed from the trunk of an impounded vehicle and pried open by police after the driver's arrest on drunken driving charges."

In the *Wells* case, Wells gave the Florida Highway Patrol permission to open the trunk of his car following his arrest for DWI. An inventory search turned up a locked suitcase in the trunk. The officers opened the suitcase and found marijuana. Wells sought to reverse his conviction for drug possession on appeal, saying that the marijuana found in his locked suitcase should not have been admitted as evidence. The Court agreed to suppress the evidence, saying that, "absent any Highway Patrol policy with the opening of closed containers . . . the instant search was insufficiently regulated to satisfy the Fourth Amendment."

The message for the police from the *Bertine* and *Wells* cases is clear: A standardized policy is a must in cases where the police list the personal effects and properties found in the vehicle after impoundment. Such a policy, said the Court, "prevents individual police officers from having so much latitude that inventory searches are turned into a ruse for a general rummaging in order to discover incriminating evidence." It is also clear from the preceding cases that opening a closed container or a locked suitcase is allowed in a vehicle inventory search but *only* if specifically authorized by departmental policy. The absence of a departmental policy authorizing the opening of closed or locked containers means that such opening is prohibited. But if such a departmental policy is in place, officers may inspect the outside and inside of a vehicle in the process of taking an inventory, including the passenger compartment, the trunk, and any containers found in the vehicle—as long as such a search is conducted for legitimate reasons, not as a fishing expedition.

Vehicles Impounded by Police

The police have authority for **vehicle impoundment** for various reasons, such as when the vehicle has been used for the commission of an offense or when it should be removed from the streets because it impedes traffic or threatens public safety. When the police lawfully impound a vehicle, they may conduct a routine inventory search without warrant or probable cause to believe that the car contains seizable evidence. This type of search is distinguished from searches immediately after an arrest, where the vehicle is not necessarily impounded. The leading case on impoundment searches is *South Dakota v. Opperman*, 428 U.S. 364 (1976).

In this case, Opperman's illegally parked car was taken to the city impound lot, where an officer, observing articles of personal property in the car, proceeded to inventory it. In the process, he found a bag of marijuana in the unlocked glove compartment. The Court concluded that, "in following standard police procedures, prevailing throughout the country and approved by the overwhelming majority of courts, the conduct of the police was not 'unreasonable' under the Fourth Amendment."

The ruling legitimizes car inventories, but the Court also made it clear in *Opperman* and other cases that inventory searches must be guided by departmental policy, so that the inventory becomes merely an administrative function by the police. Inventory

vehicle impoundment
takes place when the police take control of a vehicle for law enforcement reasons.

South Dakota v. Opperman (1976)

---

searches conducted solely for the purposes of discovering evidence are illegal regardless of what is discovered in the course of the inventory. In the words of the Court, "Our view that standardized criteria or established routine must regulate the opening of containers is based on the principle that an inventory search must not be a ruse for a general rummaging in order to discover incriminating evidence" (*Florida v. Wells*, 495 U.S. 1 [1990]).

It is true that when vehicles are abandoned or illegally parked or when the owner is arrested, the courts permit the vehicles to be impounded and inventoried. But that rule should not apply when the driver has been arrested for a minor traffic violation, primarily because the police are expected to give the suspect a reasonable opportunity to post bail and obtain his or her prompt release. In *Dyke v. Taylor Implement Manufacturing Company*, 391 U.S. 216 (1968), a driver who had been arrested for reckless driving was at the courthouse to make bail when his vehicle was searched. The Court concluded that the search of the vehicle could not be deemed incident to impoundment, because the police seemed to have parked the car near the courthouse merely as a convenience to the owner, who, if he were soon to be released from custody, could then have driven it away.

Another issue in car impoundment is whether other alternatives to impoundment should be explored before placing the vehicle under police control (at least in cases in which the vehicle itself has not been involved in the crime). A number of lower courts have held that when an arrestee requests that his or her car be either parked in the vicinity of the arrest or that it be turned over to a friend, the police must honor this request.

THE IMPORTANCE OF STATE LAWS AND DEPARTMENT POLICIES IN VEHICLE STOPS, SEARCHES, AND INVENTORIES

The rules discussed in this chapter on motor vehicle searches are based primarily on U.S. Supreme Court decisions. They do not reflect state law or law agency regulations in specific police departments, which may vary greatly. State law and departmental policies may limit what the police can do. Where state law or departmental policy is more limiting than Court decisions, an officer must follow state law and departmental policy. They are binding on the police officer, regardless of what the Court held in the cases discussed in this chapter.

◆ *Example 1*: The Court has decided that, if the police have probable cause to stop and search an automobile on the highway, they may take it to the police station and search it there without a warrant—thus doing away with the contemporaneousness requirement. Assume, however, that, according to state law and departmental policy, once the car is brought to the police station and the driver detained, the police must obtain a warrant before conducting a search of the car. In that case, a warrant must be obtained; otherwise, the search is illegal and the evidence obtained inadmissible.

◆ *Example 2*: Despite what the Court has said, assume that state law or departmental policy prohibits officers from automatically ordering drivers or passengers to get out of the car or from making pretextual traffic stops. Those limitations are binding on the police officer and must be followed despite what the Court said in the *Mimms* and *Whren* cases (which are discussed in this chapter) about what police officers can do constitutionally. The more limiting policy governs police conduct.

Regarding the law on vehicle stops, the following guidelines apply:

- There is no need for a warrant or probable cause to legally stop a motor vehicle, but there must be reasonable suspicion of involvement in criminal activity.
- Reasonable suspicion is determined by the totality of circumstances.

After a valid stop, an officer may legally do the following things:

- Order the driver and passengers to get out of the vehicle.
- Ask the driver to produce a driver's license and other documents required by state law.
- Ask questions to the driver and passengers.
- Locate and examine the vehicle identification number (VIN).
- Require drunk-driving suspects to take a Breathalyzer test, based on reasonable suspicion.
- Search the passenger compartment for weapons if there is reasonable suspicion.
- Search the vehicle if there is probable cause.
- Search passengers' belongings if there is probable cause.
- Make an arrest if there is probable cause.
- Search the car if there is consent, even without probable cause.

Roadblocks for specific purposes do not need reasonable suspicion, but roadblocks for general law enforcement purposes are unconstitutional.

For vehicle searches, the following guidelines apply:

- Warrantless vehicle searches are valid, but probable cause is required.
- Searches of passengers' belongings are valid.
- Searches of passenger compartments are valid.
- Searches of trunks and closed packages found in trunks are valid.
- There is no authoritative Court decision on whether searches of locked trunks or glove compartments are constitutional.

- Searches of vehicles do not need to be made immediately after an arrest.
- Warrantless vehicle searches are valid even if there was time to obtain a warrant.
- The extent of car searches is governed by the objective reasonableness rule.
- Searches of motor homes without a warrant are valid.
- A warrant is sometimes needed for the use of electronic tracking devices to locate cars.

REVIEW QUESTIONS

1. Compare and contrast the legal requirements for motor vehicle stops and searches. How are they similar? How are they different?
2. Why is a roadblock set up to catch drunk drivers constitutional while a roadblock to catch lawbreakers is not?
3. Give reasons why vehicle stops are based on reasonable suspicion instead of probable cause.
4. State four things an officer can do after a vehicle stop based on general law enforcement authority.
5. What are pretextual traffic stops? Are they valid or invalid? Why?
6. Assume a car is stopped by the police and the driver is arrested because the police found drugs in the trunk of the car. The police also arrest the passenger. The passenger claims her arrest is invalid. Is it? Justify your answer.
7. Assume a driver is stopped by the police for making an illegal turn. The penalty for that offense is a fine of $200 and no jail time. Discuss whether or not the driver can be arrested by the police for that offense. What are the legal issues involved if the driver is arrested?
8. After an arrest of a vehicle driver, can the police validly do the following:
   a. Search the car's glove compartment?
   b. Search the trunk of the car?

c. Search a briefcase in the trunk of the car?

d. Search the passenger compartment?

e. Search the car, which is now in the police station, one hour after the arrest?

9. Suppose evidence is obtained by the police while making an arrest that is not authorized by state law for a minor offense. Is the evidence obtained by the police admissible in court?

10. Assume that a police officer has made a valid arrest of a driver for possession of drugs. Discuss the extent of the officer's power to search as a result of that arrest.

11. "A police officer who makes a valid stop is authorized to ask the driver to get out of the car and then frisk the driver for officer protection." Is this statement true or false? Explain.

12. *Carroll v. United States* is arguably the most important case ever decided on vehicle searches. What did that case say, and why is it important?

TEST YOUR UNDERSTANDING

1. Steve was arrested in a rest stop by a police officer for speeding on the highway. He was arrested about ten yards from his car. The officer nonetheless searched the car and found illegal weapons. At trial, Steve sought to exclude the weapons, saying they were not in the area of immediate control when seized. You are the judge. Will you admit or exclude the evidence? Discuss the case history of this issue and then justify your ruling.

2. Officer Ann stops a motor vehicle that violated traffic rules and issues a citation. She then goes ahead and searches the car because state law authorizes her to do that if she has reasonable suspicion that a crime has been committed or is about to be committed. Is her search of the car, based on reasonable suspicion and as authorized by state law, valid? Explain your answer.

3. Highway patrol officer Tom stopped a vehicle on the freeway for speeding. Prior to issuing a ticket for speeding, Officer Tom looked around the car and asked the driver to open the glove compartment. The driver voluntarily complied. Drugs were found in the glove compartment. Officer Tom then arrested the driver and searched the whole car, including a briefcase marked "private" that was found in the trunk of the car. Was the search of the trunk valid? Was the search of the briefcase valid? Justify your answers.

4. Officer Albert was a Chicago detective who, after weeks of investigation, arrested a murder suspect in her home based on an arrest warrant. Immediately after the arrest, Officer Albert searched the suspect's car, found in her driveway, for possible incriminating evidence. The search yielded drugs, which Officer Albert confiscated. Was the warrantless search of the car in the suspect's driveway valid? Explain your answer.

5. Officer Frank arrested a suspect, observed driving on a city street, for robbery, based on a warrant. The driver and his car were brought to the police station, where the driver was booked and detained because he could not post bail. The day after the arrest, Officer Frank searched the vehicle without a warrant and found incriminating evidence that linked the suspect to the robbery. During trial, the suspect sought to exclude the evidence, saying it was obtained without a warrant and therefore the search was illegal. You are the judge. Will you admit or exclude the evidence? Justify your ruling.

RECOMMENDED READINGS

Wayne LaFave. *The "routine traffic stop" from start to finish: Too much "routine," not enough Fourth Amendment*. 102 Michigan Law Review, 1843–1905 (2004).

Kenneth Gavsie. *Making the best of Whren: The problems with pretextual traffic stops and the need for restraint*. 50 Florida Law Review, 385–403 (1998).

David Harris. *Driving while back and all other traffic offenses*. Journal of Criminal Law and Criminology, 544 (Winter 1997).

Martin O'Connor. *Vehicle searches—The automobile exception: The Constitution al ride from Carroll v. United States to Wyoming v. Houghton.* 16 Touro Law Review, 393 (Winter 2000).

Mark Richardson. *The vulnerable passenger: an analysis of the constitutionality of Terry frisking vehicle passengers not suspected of criminal activity in Arizona v. Johnson.* 89 Nebraska Law Review, 515 (2011).

Cynthia Lee. *Package bombs, footlockers, and laptops: What the disappearing container doctrine can tell us about the fourth amendment.* 100 Journal of Criminal Law & Criminology, 1403–1494 (Fall 2010), no. 4.

CHAPTER 9

Plain View, Open Fields, Abandonment, and Border Searches

LEARNING OBJECTIVES

1. Distinguish what searches or seizures are not protected under the Fourth Amendment.
2. Define the legal doctrine of plain view.
3. Define the legal doctrine of open fields.
4. Define the legal doctrine of abandonment.
5. Compare and contrast the following doctrines: plain view, plain view and touch, plain view and odor.
6. When given examples, you will determine if the property is curtilage or not and why.
7. When given examples, you will determine if the property is considered an exception under open fields or not and why.
8. When given examples, you will determine if the property is abandoned or not and why.
9. Explain the legal guidelines for border searches and checkpoints.
10. Compare and contrast the legal doctrines of plain view and abandonment.

KEY TERMS

abandonment

curtilage

extended border search

factory surveys

inadvertence

open fields doctrine

open view

plain odor doctrine

plain touch doctrine

plain view doctrine

Sinisa Drakulic/Shutterstock.com

in Searches and Seizures Not Fully Protected by the Fourth Amendment: Plain View, Open Fields, Abandonment, and Border Searches

■ *HESTER V. UNITED STATES* (1924) "The special protection accorded by the Fourth Amendment to the people in their persons, houses, papers, and effects is not extended to the open fields."

■ *UNITED STATES V. RAMSEY* (1977) "Searches made at the border pursuant to the long-standing right of the sovereign to protect itself by stopping and examining persons and property crossing into this country, are reasonable simply by virtue of the fact that they occur at the border."

■ *OLIVER V. UNITED STATES* (1984) A place that has a posted "No Trespassing" sign, has a locked gate (with a footpath around it), and is located more than a mile from the owner's house has no reasonable expectation of privacy and is considered an open field, unprotected by the Fourth Amendment.

■ *UNITED STATES V. DUNN* (1987) Whether an area is considered a part of the curtilage and therefore covered by the Fourth Amendment rests on four factors: (1) the proximity of the area to the home, (2) whether the area is in an enclosure surrounding the home, (3) the nature and uses of the area, and (4) the steps taken to conceal the area from public view.

■ *HORTON V. CALIFORNIA* (1990) The Fourth Amendment does not prohibit the warrantless seizure of evidence in plain view, even though the discovery of the evidence was not inadvert.

THIS CHAPTER DISCUSSES four situations related to searches and seizures that have one important element in common: they do not enjoy full Fourth Amendment protection. They do not need a warrant or probable cause. These situations are plain view, open fields, abandonment, and border searches. These four situations constitute some form of "looking" and "taking" by the government. The legal rules and requirements in these four instances differ and thus they are discussed separately. All four situations involve contact with or action by the police, but they constitute seizure of items or things, not of people. In these cases, ownership of the item seized cannot be established (in the case of plain view, open fields, or abandonment) or the property interest is subordinate to a higher need for security (as in border searches).

The contacts discussed in this chapter differ from the contacts discussed in Chapter 6 that are also unprotected by the Fourth Amendment. Those discussed in Chapter 6 are such contacts with the police as:

◆ Asking questions of people they meet
◆ Asking a vehicle driver to get out of a car after stopping her
◆ Boarding a bus and asking questions that a person is free to refuse to answer
◆ Driving alongside a person "to see where he was going"

These contacts with the police involve people, not items, but are also unprotected by the Fourth Amendment because they are only minimally intrusive.

THE PLAIN VIEW DOCTRINE

The plain view doctrine holds that police officers have the right to seize items that are plainly within their view as long as they have the legal right to be in the position to see the items. This section discusses the application of this doctrine. We begin with the case that defined the plain view doctrine and then examine: (1) the requirements of the doctrine; (2) situations in which it applies; (3) how it is used as a justification for admitting evidence into court; (4) the change in the Court's ruling on inadvertent viewing; (5) the application of plain view to open spaces, motor vehicles, and the use of mechanical devices; and (6) a comparison of plain view with open view, plain touch, and plain odor.

Plain View Defined

plain view doctrine
items that are within the sight of an officer who is legally in the place from which the view is made may properly be seized without a warrant as long as such items are immediately recognizable as subject to seizure.

The **plain view doctrine** states that items that are within the sight of an officer who is legally in the place from which the view is made may properly be seized without a warrant—so long as such items are immediately recognizable as subject to seizure. What the officer sees in plain view can be seized without having to worry about the Fourth Amendment. In the words of the Court, "It has long been settled that objects falling in the plain view of an officer who has a right to be in a position to have that view are subject to seizure and may be introduced in evidence" (*Harris v. United States*, 390 U.S. 234 [1968]).

Harris v. United States (1968)

In *Harris v. United States*, a police officer searched an impounded automobile in connection with a robbery. While opening the door, the officer saw, in plain view, the automobile registration card belonging to the victim of the robbery. Harris was charged with robbery. At trial, he moved to suppress the automobile registration card, claiming it was obtained illegally because the officer had no search warrant, although he had time to obtain one. On appeal, the Court admitted the evidence, saying that the automobile registration card was in plain view and therefore did not need a warrant to be seized.

Although generally considered an exception to the search warrant requirement, that is not correct. Plain view is really not a search at all, so the Fourth Amendment does not apply, because there is no search by the police for that specific item. No warrant or probable cause is necessary; the officer simply seizes what is seen, not something that has been searched for. Seeing the item is usually accidental and unexpected, although it does not have to be.

Requirements of the Doctrine

Three basic requirements of the plain view doctrine must be met for the evidence to be seized legally by the police:

◆ The officer must have gained awareness of the item solely by seeing it.
◆ The officer must be in that physical position legally.
◆ It must be immediately apparent that it is a seizable item.

Awareness of the Item through Sight Awareness of the seizable item must be gained solely through the officer's sight, not through the other senses—hearing, smelling, tasting, or touching. This means that the item must be *plainly visible* to the officer. For example, suppose that while executing a search warrant for a stolen computer, an officer sees marijuana on the suspect's nightstand. The marijuana may be seized because the officer knows through the sense of sight that the item is illegal and therefore seizable. But if the officer merely suspects that there is marijuana in the apartment because of the smell, as might occur if it were hidden in a drawer, its seizure in the course of a search cannot be justified under the plain view doctrine. Of course, it may be seized validly without a warrant if the officer can establish probable cause and the presence of exigent circumstances.

The Location of the Officer The officer must not have done anything illegal to get to the spot from which he or she sees the items in question. An officer comes to be in a place properly in a number of ways: (1) when serving a search warrant, (2) while in "hot pursuit" of a suspect, (3) having made entry after obtaining valid consent, and (4) when making a valid arrest with or without a warrant. For example, suppose that while executing a search warrant for a stolen television, an officer sees gambling slips on a table. She may properly seize them, even though they were not included in the warrant, as long as her presence on the premises is legal. By contrast, a police officer who forces his way into a house and then sees drugs on the table cannot validly seize the drugs, because he entered the house illegally. What the officer sees subsequent to an illegal entry can never cure the initial illegality.

Recognition of the Item Recognition of the items in plain view must be immediate and not the result of further prying or examination. In other words, the items must be out in the open, and it must be "immediately apparent" that they are seizable. For example, suppose an officer sees something that she immediately recognizes as drug paraphernalia. She may seize it under plain view. By contrast, suppose that after a valid entry, the officer sees a laptop computer she suspects is stolen. She calls the police station to ask for the serial number of the laptop reported stolen earlier and, after verification of the number, seizes the laptop. This seizure cannot be justified under the plain view doctrine, because the item was not immediately recognizable as subject to seizure. The officer had to do some investigating before it became apparent the laptop computer was in fact stolen. The evidence may be seized, however, if the seizure will can be justified based on other legal grounds, such as exigent circumstances.

The "immediately apparent" requirement must be based on *probable cause*, not on any lesser degree of certainty, such as reasonable suspicion (*Arizona v. Hicks*, 480 U.S. 321 [1987]). In *Arizona v. Hicks*, a bullet fired through the floor of Hicks's apartment injured a man below, prompting the police to enter Hicks's apartment to search for the

Arizona v. Hicks (1987)

suspect, weapons, and other potential victims. An officer discovered three weapons and a mask. He also noticed several pieces of stereo equipment, which seemed out of place in the ill-appointed apartment. The officer therefore read and recorded the serial numbers of the equipment, moving some of the pieces in the process. A call to police headquarters confirmed that one of the pieces of equipment was stolen; a later check revealed that the other pieces were also stolen. Hicks was convicted of robbery.

On appeal, Hicks sought suppression of the evidence, saying that the search was illegal. The Court agreed, noting that with plain view there must be probable cause to believe that the items being searched are, in fact, contraband or evidence of criminal activity. A lesser degree of certainty—such as reasonable suspicion, as in this case—would not suffice.

Texas v. Brown (1983)

On the other hand, "certain knowledge"—a higher degree of certainty than probable cause—is not necessary. For example, in *Texas v. Brown*, 460 U.S. 730 (1983), an officer stopped a car at night to check the driver's license. He shone his flashlight into the car's interior and saw the driver holding an opaque green balloon knotted about a half-inch from the tip. The officer also saw white powder in the open glove compartment. In court, the officer testified that he had learned from experience that inflated, tied-off balloons were often used to transport narcotics. The Court concluded that the officer had probable cause to believe that the balloon contained narcotics, so the warrantless seizure was justified under plain view (*Texas v. Brown*, 460 U.S. 730 [1983]).

Situations in Which the Doctrine Applies

In police work, there are many situations in which the plain view doctrine applies and thus the items seen may be seized without a warrant. Among these are the following:

◆ Making an arrest with or without a warrant
◆ In hot pursuit of a fleeing suspect
◆ During a search incident to a valid arrest
◆ While on patrol
◆ Making a car inventory search
◆ Conducting an investigation in a residence
◆ Making an entry into a home after obtaining valid consent

This list is illustrative, not comprehensive. In sum, the plain view doctrine applies to every aspect of police work so long as all three of the requirements of plain view are met.

One of Many Justifications for Admission of Evidence

The plain view doctrine is only one of many possible legal justifications for admitting in court evidence obtained by the police. It is used as a legal justification for seizure only if all three requirements are met. The absence of one of these elements means that the evidence is not admissible under plain view, but it may still be admissible under another legal doctrine. For example, suppose an officer arrests a suspect at home by authority of an arrest warrant. While there, the officer sees in the living room several computers that he suspects may be stolen. He telephones the police department to give the serial numbers and is informed that those computers have been reported stolen. At this stage, the officer has probable cause to seize the items.

The officer cannot seize them under plain view, because the items were not immediately recognizable as subject to seizure. Ordinarily, the officer would need a warrant to seize the computer, but warrantless seizures may be justified if the officer can establish exigent circumstances (such as that the computers would most likely be hauled away by the other occupants if the officer left the house). The computers are then admissible in court under the probable cause and exigent circumstances exception, but not under plain view.

Inadvertence Is No Longer Required

For a long time, inadvertence was one of the plain view requirements. **Inadvertence** means that the officer must have no prior knowledge that the evidence was present in the place; the discovery must be purely accidental. In the words of one court, "The plain view doctrine is properly applied to situations in which a police officer is not searching for evidence against the accused but nevertheless inadvertently comes across an incriminating object" (*United States v. Sedillo*, 496 F.2d 151 [9th Cir. 1974]).

In *Coolidge v. New Hampshire*, 403 U.S. 443 (1971), the Supreme Court said, "The . . . discovery of evidence in plain view must be inadvertent. . . . But where the discovery is anticipated, where the police know in advance the location of the evidence and intend to seize it, the situation is altogether different." However, the Court has expressly abandoned the inadvertence requirement. In *Horton v. California*, 496 U.S. 128 (1990), the Court stated, "The Fourth Amendment does not prohibit the warrantless seizure of evidence in plain view even though the discovery of the evidence was not inadvertent. Although inadvertence is a characteristic of most legitimate plain view seizures, it is not a necessary condition."

In *Horton*, a police officer determined that there was probable cause to search Horton's home for the proceeds from a robbery and for weapons used in the robbery. The affidavit filed by the officer referred to police reports that described both the weapons and the proceeds, but for some reason the warrant issued by the magistrate only authorized a search for the proceeds. When the officer went to Horton's home to execute the warrant, he did not find the stolen property (proceeds), but he did see the weapons in plain view and seized them. At trial, the officer testified that, while he was searching Horton's home for the proceeds, he was also interested in finding "other evidence" related to the robbery. Tried and convicted, Horton argued on appeal that the weapons should have been suppressed because their discovery was not inadvertent.

inadvertence
the officer must have no prior knowledge that the evidence was present in the place; the discovery must be purely accidental.

United States v. Sedillo (1974)

Coolidge v. New Hampshire (1971)

Horton v. California (1990)

HIGHLIGHT ⟩ Requirements of the Plain View Doctrine

All three of the following requirements must be met for the item to be seized legally; the absence of one means the plain view doctrine does not apply:

1. The awareness of the item must be through use of the sense of sight.

2. The officer must be legally in the place from which the item is seen.

3. It must be immediately apparent that the item is subject to seizure.

Inadvertence is no longer a requirement for plain view.

The Court disagreed, saying that, "although inadvertence is a characteristic of most legitimate plain view seizures, it is not a necessary condition." The Court expressly rejected the inadvertence requirement, noting that: (1) evenhanded law enforcement is best achieved by the application of objective standards of conduct rather than by standards that depend on the officer's subjective state of mind and (2) the suggestion that the inadvertence requirement is necessary to prevent the police from conducting a general search is not persuasive. In this case, "the scope of the search was not enlarged in the slightest by the omission of any reference to the weapons in the warrant." The Court held that the evidence was admissible.

The *Horton* decision means that most plain view cases will still be the result of inadvertence (meaning that the officer sees a seizable item that he or she did not expect to see), but in the process of serving a warrant, an officer may also seize an item he or she knew beforehand would be there even if the item is not listed in the warrant as one of those to be seized.

Read the Case Brief to learn more about the *Horton* case.

CASE BRIEF

Horton v. California, 496 U.S. 128 (1990)

The Leading Case on "Plain View" and Inadvertence

Facts: A police officer determined that there was probable cause to search the suspect Horton's home for the proceeds of a robbery and weapons used in the robbery. The affidavit filed by the officer referred to police reports that described both the weapons and the proceeds, but the warrant that was issued only authorized a search for the proceeds. When the officer went to Horton's home to execute the warrant, he did not find the stolen property (proceeds) but did find the weapons in plain view and seized them. At the trial, the officer testified that while he was searching Horton's home for the proceeds, he was also interested in finding other evidence related to the robbery. Tried and convicted, Horton argued on appeal that the weapons should have been suppressed during the trial because their discovery was not "inadvertent."

Issue or Issues: *Is inadvertence a necessary element of the plain view doctrine?* No.

Decision: The judgment of the California Supreme Court was affirmed.

Holding: "The Fourth Amendment does not prohibit the warrantless seizure of evidence in plain view even though the discovery of the evidence was not inadvertent. Although inadvertence is a characteristic of most legitimate plain view seizures, it is not a necessary condition."

Case Significance: This case does away with the requirement that for plain view to apply, the discovery of the evidence must be inadvertent, or accidental. The police officer in this case knew that the evidence was there. It was, in fact, described in the officer's affidavit, but for some reason the warrant issued by the magistrate only authorized a search for the proceeds. The Court said that the seizure was valid, nonetheless, for the following reasons:

1. "The items seized from petitioner's home were discovered during a lawful search authorized by a valid warrant."
2. "When they were discovered, it was immediately apparent to the officer that they constituted incriminating evidence."
3. "The officer had probable cause, not only to obtain a warrant to search for the stolen property, but also to believe that the weapons and handguns had been used in the crime he was investigating."
4. "The search was authorized by the warrant."

Excerpts from the Opinion: Justice Stewart [in *Coolidge v. New Hampshire*, 403 U.S. 443 (1971)] concluded that the inadvertence requirement was necessary to avoid a violation of the express constitutional requirement that a valid warrant must particularly describe the things to be seized. He explained: "The rationale of the exception to the warrant requirement, as just stated, is that a plain view seizure will not turn an initially valid (and therefore limited) search into a 'general' one, while the inconvenience of procuring a warrant to cover an inadvertent discovery is great. But where the discovery is anticipated, where the police know in advance the location of the evidence and intend to seize it, the situation is altogether different. The requirement of a warrant to seize imposes no inconvenience whatever, or at least none which is constitutionally cognizable in a legal system that regards warrantless searches as 'per se unreasonable' in the absence of 'exigent circumstances.'"

We find two flaws in this reasoning. First, evenhanded law enforcement is best achieved by the application of objective standards of conduct, rather than standards that depend upon the subjective state of mind of the officer. The fact that an officer is interested in an item of evidence and fully expects to find it in the course of a search should not invalidate its seizure if the search is confined in area

and duration by the terms of a warrant or a valid exception to the warrant requirement. If the officer has knowledge approaching certainty that the item will be found, we see no reason why he or she would deliberately omit a particular description of the items to be seized from the application of a search warrant. Specification of the additional item could only permit the officer to expand the scope of the search. On the other hand, if he or she has a valid warrant to search for one item and merely a suspicion concerning the second, whether or not it amounts to probable cause, we fail to see why that suspicion should immunize the second item from seizure if it is found during a lawful search for the first.

Second, the suggestion that the inadvertence requirement is necessary to prevent the police from conducting general searches, or from converting specific warrants into general warrants, is not persuasive because that interest is already served by the requirements that no warrant be issued unless it "particularly describes the place to be searched and the persons or things to be seized," and that a warrantless search be circumscribed by the exigencies which justify its initiation.

Plain View and Open Spaces

Plain view usually applies when the officer is within an enclosed space (such as a house, an apartment, or an office)—hence, the term used by some courts of a "prior valid intrusion into a constitutionally protected area." It also applies when the officer is out in the open, such as out on the street on patrol. In open spaces, however, a distinction must be made between *seeing* and *seizing*. For example, suppose that, while walking around an apartment complex, an officer sees illegal weapons through a window. This is also plain view. The difference between this scenario and one in which the officer is in the apartment itself is that here the officer cannot make an entry into the apartment to seize the items without a warrant unless he or she obtains consent or establishes exigent circumstances.

When the officer is in an enclosed space (such as a house or apartment), *seizing automatically follows seeing* as a matter of natural sequence. By contrast, when an entry is needed, seeing and seizing become two separate acts because of the need for a legal entry. In the absence of consent or exigent circumstances, the officer needs a warrant if he or she must make some form of entry before seizing the item. An exigent circumstance would exist, for example, if the officer could establish that the evidence would most likely no longer be available unless immediate action were taken. Without an exigent circumstance, the officer must obtain a warrant.

Plain view also applies to items seen from outside fences or enclosures. For example, suppose an officer on patrol sees marijuana plants inside a fenced yard. This falls under plain view, but the officer needs a warrant to enter the fenced yard to seize the marijuana.

Plain View and Motor Vehicles

Plain view also applies to motor vehicles. For example, suppose that, while out on patrol, Officer Roberts observes a car parked on the street, looks at the front seat, and sees drugs and drug paraphernalia. This scenario falls under plain view. Whether Officer Roberts can seize these items without a warrant, however, is not clear, particularly if the vehicle is closed and locked. This is different from the usual plain view situation, in which seeing immediately leads to seizing because no further entry is necessary. The Supreme Court has not addressed this issue. In view of this uncertainty, the better practice is for Officer Roberts to obtain a warrant to gain entry to the vehicle, unless entry could be made without using force (as when Officer Roberts obtains possession of the key), consent were given, or exigent circumstances were present that would justify immediate entry.

Plain View and Mechanical Devices

The use of mechanical devices by the police does not affect the applicability of the plain view doctrine. For example, the use of a flashlight by an officer to look into the inside of a car at night does not constitute a search under the Fourth Amendment. Evidence that would not have been discovered and seized without the use of a flashlight is nonetheless admissible in court (*Texas v. Brown*, 460 U.S. 730 [1983]). The same is true for the use of binoculars. In *United States v. Knotts*, 460 U.S. 276 (1983), the police use of a beeper (electronic tracking device) to monitor the whereabouts of a person traveling in a car on public highways did not turn the surveillance into a search. Such monitoring on a public highway was considered by the Court to fall under the plain view doctrine.

United States v. Knotts (1983)

The officer does not need to be standing upright for plain view to apply. For example, in the *Brown* case, the police officer who legally stopped the automobile bent down so that he could see what was inside the car. The Court said that the fact that the officer got into an unusual position to see the contents of the vehicle did not prevent the plain view doctrine from applying.

Plain View and Open View Compared

Some lower courts distinguish between plain view and open view. They apply plain view to cases in which the officer has made a "prior valid intrusion into a constitutionally protected area" (meaning when the officer is inside an enclosed space, such as a house or an apartment) and apply the term **open view** to instances when the officer is out in open space (such as the sidewalk) but sees an item within an enclosed area. The Supreme Court, however, has not made this distinction, so the discussion of plain view in this text includes the concept of open view.

open view
applies to instances when the officer is out in open space but sees an item within an enclosed area.

Plain View and Plain Touch Compared

As discussed in Chapter 3, probable cause is usually established through the use of the officer's five senses—sight, touch, smell, hearing, and taste. Plain view refers to the sense of sight, which is the most common way probable cause is established.

Does a similar doctrine apply to the sense of touch? Although not as well known or as extensively developed in case law as plain view, recent Court decisions have reaffirmed the existence of the **plain touch** (some call it "plain feel") **doctrine.** This doctrine holds that if an officer touches or feels something that is immediately identifiable as seizable, the object can be seized as long as such knowledge amounts to probable cause. The most recent Court case on plain touch is *Minnesota v. Dickerson*, 508 U.S. 366 (1993), discussed in Chapter 5 in the context of stop and frisk. The Court in *Dickerson* excluded the evidence obtained, because the officer went beyond what is allowable in a pat-down frisk when he proceeded to "squeeze, slide, and manipulate" the item he felt in the suspect's jacket and which he admitted was not a dangerous weapon.

The Court, however, refused to go along with the Minnesota Supreme Court's rejection of the doctrine of plain touch, saying that "the very premise of *Terry* [*Terry v. Ohio*, 392 U.S. 1 (1968)], after all, is that officers will be able to detect the presence of weapons through the sense of touch," and further added: "We think this doctrine [referring to plain view] has an obvious application by analogy to cases in which an officer discovers contraband through the sense of touch during an otherwise lawful search." The Court then concluded, "If a police officer lawfully pats down a suspect's outer clothing and feels an object whose contour or mass makes its identity immediately apparent, there has been no invasion of the suspect's privacy beyond that already authorized by the officer's search for weapons; if the object is contraband, its warrantless seizure would be justified by the same practical considerations that inhere in the plain-view context."

The Court in *Dickerson* would probably have held the evidence admissible if the officer had testified that during the pat-down he touched something that, although not a weapon, he immediately knew from his background and experience and the totality

plain touch doctrine
if an officer touches or feels something that is immediately identifiable as seizable, the object can be seized as long as such knowledge amounts to probable cause.

Minnesota v. Dickerson (1993)

Terry v. Ohio (1968)

IN ACTION   *A PRIVATE POKER GAME OVERHEARD*

Officer Roberts is assigned to foot patrol in the neighborhood adjacent to Washington State University, in the small college town of Pullman, Washington. This neighborhood is comprised primarily of fraternity and sorority houses and rental apartments. This beat has a transient population of students and an unusually high incidence of break-ins.

Officer Roberts regularly patrols this beat. He often walks through the parking lots of the buildings and the alleyways behind them, checking to make sure doors are locked and looking for signs of a possible break-in, such as a broken window. One afternoon, as he is walking in the alley behind a twelve-unit apartment building, he overhears voices coming from an open window. He pauses and listens, and he hears several people discussing how to sort out and bag up cocaine. He peers through a partially open window, and sees what he believes is a large quantity of cocaine on the living room table.

Convinced that the occupants of this apartment are engaged in drug possession and distribution, Officer Roberts walks up to the apartment's door and knocks on it. The door is opened by an occupant, and Officer Roberts asks if he can come in. The occupant says "No," but while this exchange takes place, Officer Roberts is able to see into the living room, and he again observes a large quantity of cocaine on a table in the living room. He steps past the person at the door and seizes the cocaine. He then arrests all of the occupants.

1. *Was Officer Roberts's looking through the window valid under the plain view doctrine? Explain.*
2. *Was Officer Roberts's observation of the cocaine while standing at the open door valid under the plain view doctrine? Explain.*
3. *Was Officer Roberts's seizure of the cocaine in the living room valid under the plain view doctrine? Explain.*

of circumstances was contraband. That would have been a clear case of plain feel leading to probable cause.

Plain View and Plain Odor Compared

plain odor doctrine
if an officer smells something that is immediately recognizable as seizable, that object can be seized as long as that knowledge amounts to probable cause.

United States v. Johns (1985)

According some courts, there exists a **plain odor doctrine**, wherein if an officer smells something that is immediately recognizable as seizable, that object can be seized as long as that knowledge amounts to probable cause. Courts usually cite the case of *United States v. Johns*, 469 U.S. 478 (1985), in which the Court said that "whether [the] defendant ever had a privacy interest in the packages reeking of marijuana is debatable." This language suggests there is no reasonable expectation of privacy in something which is immediately recognizable (by its odor) as contraband.

This issue has not been directly addressed by the Court; most plain view cases involve the sense of sight and, more recently, the sense of touch. In the absence of any definitive pronouncement from the Court, it is better to limit the "plain" doctrine, for now, to the twin senses of sight and touch. Note, however, that the sense of smell is one of the senses that can establish probable cause. Plain odor, however, has not been clearly established thus far as a legal doctrine by the Court.

THE OPEN FIELDS DOCTRINE

In this section, we define the open fields doctrine, identify areas not included in this doctrine, define and discuss curtilage, examine the significance of *Oliver v. United States* (1984) in expanding the open fields doctrine, look at the impact of sense-enhancement technology and beepers (electronic tracking devices) on this doctrine, and then compare the open fields and plain view doctrines.

The Open Fields Doctrine Defined

open fields doctrine
items in open fields are not protected by the Fourth Amendment and can be taken by an officer without a warrant or probable cause.

Hester v. United States (1924)

The **open fields doctrine** states that items in open fields are not protected by the Fourth Amendment's guarantee against unreasonable searches and seizures, so they can properly be taken by an officer without a warrant or probable cause. The Fourth Amendment protects only "houses, papers, and effects" against unreasonable searches and seizures. Open fields do not come under "houses, papers, and effects," so the constitutional protection does not apply. In the words of Justice Oliver Wendell Holmes, "The special protection accorded by the Fourth Amendment to the people in their persons, houses, papers, and effects is not extended to the open fields" (*Hester v. United States*, 265 U.S. 57 [1924]). In that case, the Court added that the distinction between open fields and houses "is as old as the common law."

Areas Not Included in Open Fields

Certain areas come under the protection of the Fourth Amendment and therefore cannot be classified as open fields. These areas include houses. Courts have interpreted the term *houses* under the Fourth Amendment broadly, applying it to homes (owned, rented, or leased), apartments, hotel or motel rooms, hospital rooms, and even sections not generally open to the public in places of business. *Black's Law Dictionary* defines a *house* as a "structure that serves as living quarters for one or more persons or families."[1] Under this definition, a homeless person can have a "house" that is protected against unreasonable searches and seizures as long as whatever shelter there is has a reasonable expectation of privacy.

Curtilage

Curtilage is "the area to which extends the intimate activity associated with the 'sanctity of a man's home, and the privacies of life'" (*Boyd v. United States*, 116 U.S. 616 [1886]). In general, "curtilage has been held to include all buildings in close proximity to a dwelling, which are continually used for carrying on domestic employment; or such place as is necessary and convenient to a dwelling and is habitually used for family purposes" (*United States v. Potts*, 297 F.2d 68 [6th Cir. 1961]). Curtilage is considered a part of the house and is therefore protected against unreasonable searches and seizures. Officers need a warrant and probable cause to seize items in the curtilage.

Curtilage may encompass a variety of places, including the following:

◆ *Residential yards.* Courts disagree on whether yards are part of the curtilage. If members of the public have access to the yard at any time, it is probably not curtilage. But if only members of the family have access to it, it may be part of the curtilage.
◆ *Fenced areas.* A fence around a house makes the immediate environs within that fence a part of the curtilage, because the owner clearly intended that area to be private and not open to the general public.
◆ *Apartment houses.* Areas of an apartment building that are used in common by all tenants (such as a laundry room, pool, or yard) are not considered part of any tenant's curtilage.
◆ *Barns and other outbuildings.* Outbuildings are usually considered part of the curtilage if they are used extensively by the family, are enclosed by a fence, or are close to the house. The farther such buildings are from the house, the less likely it is that they will be considered part of the curtilage.
◆ *Garages.* Garages are usually considered part of the curtilage unless they are far from the house and seldom used.

Open fields begin where curtilage ends. Fourth Amendment protection applies only to the home and the curtilage, not to open fields (see Figure 9.1). It is important to note that open fields include areas that are neither open nor fields—the key here is that open fields are all areas that are not part of the curtilage.

curtilage
"the area to which extends the intimate activity associated with the 'sanctity of a man's home, and the privacies of life.'"

Boyd v. United States (1886)
United States v. Potts (1961)

HIGHLIGHT ⟩ A Comprehensive Definition of Curtilage

"A piece of ground commonly used with the dwelling house. A small piece of land, not necessarily enclosed, around the dwelling house, and generally includes the buildings used for domestic purposes in the conduct of family affairs. A courtyard or the space of ground adjoining the dwelling house necessary and convenient and habitually used for family purposes and the carrying on of domestic employments. A piece of ground within the common enclosure belonging to a dwelling house, and enjoyed with it, for its more convenient occupation."

Source: *Black's Law Dictionary*, 7th ed. (St. Paul, MN: West, 1999).

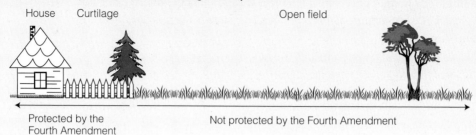

FIGURE 9.1 The Relationship between Houses, Curtilage, and Open Fields

Next, we will look at the case that defined how curtilage is determined, and the case that determined whether evidence gathered from aerial surveillance of curtilage was admissible.

The Test to Determine Curtilage *United States v. Dunn* How is curtilage determined? The Court ruled in *United States v. Dunn*, 480 U.S. 294 (1987), that determining whether an area is considered a part of the curtilage and therefore covered by Fourth Amendment protections rests on four factors:

United States v. Dunn (1987)

1. The proximity of the area to the home
2. Whether the area is in an enclosure surrounding the home
3. The nature and uses of the area
4. The steps taken to conceal the area from public view

The Court added this caution, however:

> We do not suggest that combining these factors produces a finely tuned formula that, when mechanically applied, yields a "correct" answer to all extent-of-curtilage questions. Rather, these factors are useful analytical tools only to the degree that, in any given case, they bear upon the centrally relevant consideration—whether the area in question is so intimately tied to the home itself that it should be placed under the "umbrella" of Fourth Amendment protection.

Applying these factors in *Dunn*, the Court concluded that the barn in this case could not be considered part of the curtilage. In *Dunn*, after learning that a codefendant had purchased large quantities of chemicals and equipment used in the manufacture of controlled substances, drug agents obtained a warrant to place an electronic tracking device, or beeper, in some of the equipment. The beeper ultimately led agents to Dunn's farm. The farm was encircled by a perimeter fence, with several interior fences of the type used to hold livestock. Without a warrant, officers entered the premises, climbing over the perimeter fence, interior fences, and a wooden fence that encircled a barn, approximately 50 yards from the respondent's home. En route to the barn, the officers crossed two barbwire fences and one wooden fence. Without entering the barn, the officers stood at a locked gate and shone a flashlight into the barn, where they observed what appeared to be a drug laboratory. Officers returned twice the following day to confirm the presence of the laboratory, each time without entering the barn. Based on information gained from these observations, officers obtained a search warrant and seized incriminating evidence from the barn.

Dunn was convicted of conspiracy to manufacture controlled substances. On appeal, he sought exclusion of the evidence, saying that: (1) a barn located 60 yards from a house and 50 yards from a second fence surrounding the house is part of the curtilage and therefore could not be searched without a warrant, and (2) the officers committed trespass en route to the barn. The Court disagreed, saying that, judged in terms of the four tests (enumerated previously), this particular barn could not be considered a part of the curtilage, despite the presence of three fences.

The Court added that the concept of *physical trespass is no longer the test* that determines whether the Fourth Amendment applies. Instead, the test is *whether there exists a reasonable expectation of privacy* that deserves protection. In this case, despite the presence of fences, there was none. But the Court added that, although the barn itself was part of the open field, the inside of the barn was protected by the Fourth Amendment, and so a warrant was needed for a lawful entry.

The good news about *Dunn* is that in it the Court laid out the test lower courts should use to determine whether a barn, building, garage, or the like is part of the curtilage. The bad news is that these factors are difficult for trial courts to apply with precision. Given the existing tests, what is curtilage to one court may not be curtilage to another.

Aerial Surveillance of Curtilage The fact that a space is part of a home's curtilage does not mean it is automatically entitled to constitutional protection against any and all intrusions. In *California v. Ciraolo*, 476 U.S. 207 (1986), the Court decided that the constitutional protection against unreasonable search and seizure is not violated by the naked-eye aerial observation by the police of a suspect's fenced backyard, which admittedly is a part of the curtilage.

In this case, police in Santa Clara, California, received an anonymous phone tip that marijuana was being grown in Ciraolo's backyard. The backyard was shielded from public view by a 6-foot-high outer fence and a 10-foot-high inner fence completely enclosing the yard. On the basis of the tip, officers trained in marijuana identification obtained an airplane and flew over the suspect's house at an altitude of 1,000 feet. They readily identified the plants growing in the yard as marijuana. A search warrant was obtained on the basis of the naked-eye observation by one of the officers, supported by a photograph of the surrounding area taken from the airplane. Officers executed the warrant and seized the marijuana plants. In a motion to suppress the evidence, Ciraolo alleged that the warrantless aerial observation of the yard violated the Fourth Amendment.

The Court rejected Ciraolo's contention, saying that no Fourth Amendment right was violated. The Court admitted that Ciraolo "took normal precautions to maintain his privacy" by erecting the fence, but added:

> The area is within the curtilage and does not itself bar all police observation. The Fourth Amendment protection of the home has never been extended to require law enforcement officers to shield their eyes when passing by a home on public thoroughfares. Nor does the mere fact that an individual has taken measures to restrict some views of his activities preclude an officer's observations from a public vantage point where he has a right to be and which renders the activities clearly visible. . . . The observations by Officers Shutz and Rodriguez in this case took place within public navigable airspace, in a physically nonintrusive manner; from this point they were able to observe plants readily discernible to the naked eye as marijuana. . . . On this record, we readily conclude that respondent's expectation that his garden was protected from such observation is unreasonable and is not an expectation that society is prepared to honor.

California v. Ciraolo (1986)

MYTH vs. REALITY

MYTH Police cannot lawfully seize contraband in the open field if they are trespassing on private property when they discover the contraband.

FACT Police may seize contraband in the open field even if they are trespassing when they discover it, as the Fourth Amendment does not apply to open fields.

In the *Ciraolo* case, the airplane flew over the suspect's house at an altitude of 1,000 feet to make the observations. Suppose the flight had been made by the police in a helicopter at a height of only 400 feet. Would the evidence still have been admissible? In *Florida v. Riley*, 488 U.S. 445 (1989), the Court answered yes, saying that, as long as the police are flying at an altitude at which Federal Aviation Administration (FAA) regulations allow members of the public to fly (the FAA sets no minimum flying altitude for helicopters), such aerial observation is valid because, in the absence of FAA prohibitions, the homeowner would have no reasonable expectation of privacy from such flights. Note, however, that these cases involved mere "looking" or "peering," but not entering, so the degree of intrusion was minimal.

A Broader Meaning of Open Fields

In a 1984 decision, *Oliver v. United States*, 466 U.S. 170 (1984), the Supreme Court gave the open fields doctrine a broader meaning. In this case, the Court said that it is legal for the police to enter and search unoccupied or underdeveloped areas outside the curtilage without either a warrant or probable cause, as long as the place comes under the category of "fields," even if the police had to pass a locked gate and a "No Trespassing" sign. The field in this case was secluded and not visible from any point of public access. The Court defined the term *open fields* to include "any unoccupied or underdeveloped area outside the curtilage"—a definition sufficiently broad to include the heavily wooded area where the defendant's marijuana crop was discovered by the police.

The significance of *Oliver* is that it reaffirms the doctrine that the "reasonable expectation of privacy" standard in Fourth Amendment cases does not apply when the property involved is classified as an open field. The Court stressed that steps taken to protect privacy—such as planting the marijuana on secluded land, erecting a locked gate (but with a footpath along one side), and posting "No Trespassing" signs around the property—do not necessarily establish a reasonable expectation of privacy. The test, according to the Court, is not whether the individual chooses to conceal assertedly private activity, but instead whether the government's intrusion infringes upon personal and societal values protected by the Fourth Amendment. The fact that the government's intrusion upon an open field (as in this case) is a trespass according to common law does not make it a "search" in the constitutional sense, so the Fourth Amendment does not apply.

The *Oliver* case involved a warrantless observation of a marijuana patch located more than a mile from Oliver's house. The *Dunn* case involved the warrantless observation of a barn located just 60 yards from a house and 50 yards from a wooden fence that, in turn, was within a bigger perimeter fence. In both cases, the Court concluded that neither property could be considered a part of the curtilage and therefore was treated as open field.

The *Dunn*, *Ciraolo*, and *Oliver* cases all tell us that the concept of curtilage has become restricted and that of open field has been significantly expanded by the Court, thus giving law enforcement officials greater leeway in search and seizure cases. The relationship among houses and buildings, curtilage, and open fields may generally be stated as follows: Houses and buildings are the most protected, then comes curtilage, and then come open fields. Houses, buildings, and curtilage are protected by the Fourth Amendment; open fields are not. (Read the Case Brief to learn more about the *Oliver* case.)

Definition: Items in open fields are not protected by the Fourth Amendment guarantee against unreasonable searches and seizures, so they can be seized by an officer without a warrant or probable cause.

Key Court decision: "[O]pen fields do not provide the setting for those intimate activities that the Amendment is intended to shelter from government interference or surveillance. There is no societal interest in protecting the privacy of those activities, such as the cultivation of crops, that occur in open fields" (*Oliver v. United States*, 466 U.S. 170 [1967]).

Curtilage: "The area to which extends the intimate activity associated with the 'sanctity of a man's home, and the privacies of life'" (*Boyd v. United States*, 116 U.S. 616 [1886]).

Test to determine curtilage: If a person has a reasonable expectation of privacy in a place, it is part of the curtilage and is protected by the Fourth Amendment.

Applications: Aerial surveillance of curtilage is valid. Also, an area may be an open field despite the presence of a locked gate and a "No Trespassing" sign.

CASE BRIEF   *Oliver v. United States, 466 U.S. 170* (1984)

The Leading Case on "Open Fields"

Facts: Acting on reports that marijuana was grown on the Oliver's farm, but without a search warrant, probable cause, or exigent circumstances, police officers went to the farm to investigate. They drove past Oliver's house to a locked gate with a "No Trespassing" sign but with a footpath around one side. Officers followed the footpath around the gate and found a field of marijuana more than a mile from Oliver's house. He was charged with and convicted of manufacturing a controlled substance.

Issue or Issues: *Is a place that is posted with a "No Trespassing sign," has a locked gate (with a footpath around it), and is located more than a mile from the owner's house considered an open field?* Yes.

Decision: The decision of the Court of Appeals for the Sixth Circuit was affirmed.

Holding: A place where the property owner posts a "No Trespassing" sign that has a locked gate but with a footpath around it, located more than a mile from the house, has no reasonable expectation of privacy and is considered an open field. Therefore, it is legal for the police to enter that area without a warrant or probable cause, because it is unprotected by the Fourth Amendment.

Case Significance: This case makes clear that the reasonable expectation of privacy doctrine does not apply when the property involved is an open field. The Court

defines what areas enjoy the protection extended by the reasonable expectation of privacy doctrine. The Court stressed that steps taken to protect privacy—such as planting marijuana on secluded land, erecting a locked gate (but with a footpath along one side), and posting "No Trespassing" signs around the property—do not in and of themselves establish a reasonable expectation of privacy, so the property comes under open fields. Therefore, the police could enter the property without a warrant or probable cause. The test to determine whether the property comes under a reasonable expectation of privacy or is considered an open field is not whether the individual chooses to conceal assertedly private activity, but whether the government's intrusion infringes upon the personal and societal values protected by the Fourth Amendment."

Excerpts from the Opinion: No single factor determines whether an individual legitimately may claim under the Fourth Amendment that a place should be free of government intrusion not authorized by warrant. . . . In assessing the degree to which a search infringes upon individual privacy, the Court has given weight to such factors as the intention of the Framers of the Fourth Amendment . . . the uses to which the individual has put a location . . . and our societal understanding that certain areas deserve the most scrupulous protection from government invasion.

In this light, the rule of *Hester v. United States* [265 U.S. 57 (1924)] that we reaffirm today, may be understood as providing that an individual may not legitimately demand privacy for activities conducted out of doors in fields, except in the area immediately surrounding the home. . . . This rule is true to the conception of the right to privacy embodied in the Fourth Amendment. The Amendment reflects the recognition of the Founders that certain enclaves should be free from arbitrary government interference. For example, the Court since the enactment of the Fourth Amendment has stressed "the overriding respect for the sanctity of the home that has been embedded in our traditions since the origins of the republic."

We concluded, from the text of the Fourth Amendment and from the historical and contemporary understanding of its purposes, that an individual has no legitimate expectation that open fields will remain free from warrantless intrusion by government officers.

Open Fields and Sense-Enhancement Technology

Kyllo v. United States
(2001)

In *Kyllo v. United States*, 533 U.S. 27 (2001), the Court held that using a technological device to explore the details of a home that would previously have been unknowable without physical intrusion is a search and is presumptively unreasonable without a warrant.

In *Kyllo*, officers suspected Kyllo of growing marijuana in his home. They used a thermal imaging device from across the street (therefore an open field) to examine the heat radiating from his house. The scan showed that the roof over the garage and a side wall of the house were relatively hot compared to the rest of his house and substantially hotter than neighboring homes. Based on this information, on utility bills, and on tips from informants, the officers obtained a search warrant for Kyllo's home. The search revealed more than 100 marijuana plants. Appealing his conviction, Kyllo argued that the use of the thermal imaging device without a warrant constituted an illegal search of his home. The federal prosecutor argued that thermal imaging does not constitute a search because: (1) it detects "only heat radiating from the external surface of the house" and therefore there was no entry and (2) it did not detect private activities occurring in private areas because "everything that was detected was on the outside."

The Court disagreed, saying that the Fourth Amendment draws "a firm line at the entrance of the house." The Court said further:

> The very core of the Fourth Amendment stands the right of a man to retreat into his own home and there be free from unreasonable governmental intrusions. With few exceptions, the question whether a warrantless search of a home is reasonable and hence constitutional must be answered no. . . . We think that obtaining by sense-enhancement technology any information regarding the interior of the home that could not otherwise have been obtained without physical intrusion into a constitutionally protected area constitutes a search, at least where (as here) the technology in question is not in general public use. . . . On the basis of this criterion, the information obtained by the thermal images in this case was the product of a search.

The significance of *Kyllo* for the open fields doctrine is that the use of electronic devices from an open field may constitute a violation of the Fourth Amendment if such use obtains information that would not otherwise be obtainable from the open field alone. The use of thermal imaging in *Kyllo* was deemed by the Court as equivalent to physical intrusion into a home, although through the use of sense-enhancing technology rather than actual entry by a law enforcement officer.

Open Fields and Plain View Compared

Open fields and items in plain view are similar in that neither is protected by the Fourth Amendment; there is no need for a search warrant or probable cause to obtain the item. The differences between open fields and items in plain view before the law are summarized in the following list:

Open Fields	Plain View
Seizable item is not in a house, dwelling, or curtilage.	Seizable item usually is in a house, dwelling, or curtilage.
Items hidden from view may be seized.	Only items not hidden from view may be seized.
Awareness of the item may be through the sense of sight, hearing, smell, touch, or taste.	Awareness of the item must be through the sense of sight.
The item must be in an open space.	The item may be in an enclosed or open space.

ABANDONMENT

Items that are abandoned are not protected by the Fourth Amendment. This section defines abandonment and then looks at the factors that determine whether an item has been abandoned, when motor vehicles may be declared abandoned, and how police actions affect abandonment issues; it concludes with a comparison between abandonment and the plain view doctrine.

Abandonment Defined

Abandonment is defined as the giving up of a thing or item absolutely, without limitation as to any particular person or purpose. Abandonment implies giving up possession, ownership, or any reasonable expectation of privacy. Abandoned property is not protected by the Fourth Amendment guarantee against unreasonable searches and seizures, so it may be seized without a warrant or probable cause. For example, if a car is left in a public parking lot for so long that it is reasonable to assume that the car has been abandoned, the police may seize the car without a warrant.

> **abandonment**
> the giving up of a thing or item without limitation as to any particular person or purpose.

Abandoned property does not belong to anyone, because the owner has given it up. This is the case even if the item was given up involuntarily, such as when items are thrown out of a house or car for fear of discovery by the police. If the police find such property, they may therefore seize it and introduce it as evidence in a criminal proceeding. For example, suppose the police approach a group of juveniles in an apartment complex parking lot to quiet them down because of complaints from nearby residents. One of the juveniles throws away an envelope, which is retrieved by the police and later ascertained to contain drugs. The recovery is legal, and the evidence is usable in court.

Guidelines for When Items Are Considered Abandoned

Abandonment is frequently difficult to determine, but the two basic guidelines are: (1) where the property is left and (2) the intent to abandon the property.

Where the Property Is Left This section looks at whether property left in an open field, public place, or private premises is abandoned. It also considers the issue of whether trash should be considered abandoned.

Property Left in an Open Field or Public Place Property discarded or thrown away in an open field or public place is considered abandoned. For example, drugs discarded by a suspect in an airport restroom when she realizes she is under surveillance, or drugs thrown by the suspect from a speeding car when he realizes that the police are closing in, would be considered abandoned.

Property Left on Private Premises Property may sometimes be considered abandoned on private premises if circumstances indicate that the occupant has left the premises. For example, if a suspect pays his bill and checks out of a hotel room, items left behind that are of no apparent value but that the police can use as evidence—such as photographs or newspaper clippings—are considered abandoned property and may be seized by the police.

If the occupant has not left the premises, there is no abandonment. For example, suppose that, while "looking around" the house after receiving valid consent, the police see the occupant grab a package containing marijuana from the kitchen table and throw it into the bedroom. That package might be seized by the police, but not under the abandonment doctrine, because the property is still in the house. However, the seizure might still be justified under plain view or probable cause and exigent circumstance.

California v. Greenwood (1988)

Is Trash or Garbage Abandoned? The Court decided in *California v. Greenwood*, 486 U.S. 35 (1988), that garbage left outside the curtilage of a home for regular collection is considered abandoned and therefore may be seized by the police without a warrant. In this case, the Court said that "having deposited their garbage in an area particularly suited for public inspection . . . [the owners] could have no reasonable expectation of privacy in the inculpatory items that they discarded" (here, items indicating narcotics use). There is no Fourth Amendment protection if trash is left in an area accessible to the public, so no warrant or probable cause is needed. By contrast, leaving trash in the curtilage of a home (not accessible to the public but where trash collectors are allowed to enter) would not be considered abandonment, so Fourth Amendment protections would apply.

This means that the police would need a warrant to enter the premises and retrieve that trash. May trash obtained by trash collectors be legally turned over to the police? Once trash is gathered by trash collectors, it loses its reasonable expectation of privacy even if obtained inside a curtilage. It may therefore be voluntarily turned over to the police by trash collectors. Problems may arise, however, if this is done at the request of the police. In these cases, trash collectors may be seen as acting as agents of the police and doing something the police cannot legally do. Court decisions have not addressed this issue authoritatively.

The Intent to Abandon the Property The intent to abandon is generally determined objectively—by what a person does. Throwing items away in a public place shows an intent to abandon; denial of ownership when questioned about an item also constitutes abandonment. For example, suppose that, when questioned by the police, a suspect denies that a confiscated wallet belongs to him. If, in fact, the suspect owns that wallet, it may now be considered abandoned. Failure to claim something over a long period of time also indicates abandonment; the longer the period, the clearer the intent. But the prosecution must prove that there was, in fact, an intent to abandon the item.

"[A] person does not retain a reasonable expectation of privacy in trash once it leaves the curtilage. A trash collector who enters the curtilage to collect trash subsequently turned over to police is considered a private actor for Fourth Amendment purposes when acting in the scope of a routine trash collection.

"Law enforcement officers who request assistance from trash collectors should ensure that they do nothing that exceeds the routine performance of their duties."

Source: Thomas V. Kukura, "Trash, Inspections, and the Fourth Amendment," *FBI Law Enforcement Bulletin*, February 1991, p. 32.

Abandonment of Motor Vehicles

An article in the *FBI Law Enforcement Bulletin* sheds light on the issue of motor vehicle abandonment. The author states that courts consider four key factors in determining whether a vehicle has been abandoned.[2]

1. Flight from the vehicle by the person in an apparent effort to avoid apprehension by law enforcement.
2. Where, and for how long, a vehicle is left unattended. The author notes that "a person who leaves a car in a traveled lane of a busy highway should expect the police to remove the car with some promptness; the more difficult abandonment question is presented when a person parks a vehicle lawfully. Unless other factors are present, such as flight, abandonment is only found in such cases where the vehicle is parked on someone else's property either without authorization or for a period of time that exceeds the permission granted."
3. The condition in which the vehicle is left unattended. Quoting a lower court decision, the author writes, "One who chooses to leave luggage in an unlocked, burned-out automobile at the side of a highway in the country can fairly be thought to have a much lower expectation of privacy."
4. Denial, by a person who is present, of possession or ownership of the vehicle. The author gives the example of the case of three men who, when approached by customs agents after the three had loaded the contents of two boxes into the rear of a car, denied any knowledge of the car or its cargo (understandably, because the agents discovered 30 milligrams of cocaine in the car).

Police Actions and Abandonment

The police activities that led to the abandonment must be legal, or else the evidence obtained is not admissible in court. For example, suppose the police, for no justifiable reason, decide to search a pedestrian one evening. Terrified, the pedestrian throws away what turns out to be a bag of cocaine. The cocaine cannot be used in evidence, because the abandonment was caused by illegal police conduct. Or suppose police officers stop a motor vehicle on the highway for no justifiable reason. Just before the vehicle stops, the driver throws away a pistol that is later ascertained to have been a weapon used in a robbery. The pistol is not admissible in evidence, because the abandonment was caused by illegal police conduct.

Definition: The giving up of a thing or item absolutely, without limitation as to any particular person or purpose.

Factors determining when items are considered abandoned: (1) Property left in an open field or public place is abandoned; (2) for property left on private premises, it depends on whether the occupant has left the premises; (3) for trash or garbage, it depends on where it

is left; and (4) intent to abandon is determined by what a person does.

Motor vehicles: Abandonment of motor vehicles is determined by four key factors: (1) flight from the vehicle, (2) where and for how long a vehicle is left unattended, (3) the condition in which the vehicle is left unattended, and (4) denial of possession or ownership of the vehicle.

Abandonment and Plain View Compared

An abandoned item and an item in plain view are similar in that neither is protected by the Fourth Amendment; there is no need for a search warrant or probable cause to obtain the items. Differences between the two are summarized in the following list:

Abandonment	Plain View
Owner or possessor has given up possession of item.	Owner or possessor has not given up possession of item.
Seized item may be legal or illegal.	Seized item must be illegal.
Discovery of item may be through the sense of sight, touch, hearing, smell, or taste.	Discovery of item must be through the sense of sight.

BORDER SEARCHES

A "border" does not just mean a territorial border, areas where one country is adjacent to the other, as is the case with the United States and Mexico or Canada. It also means places where first entry is made into a country, such as the international airports in Chicago, or New York. Full Fourth Amendment protections do not apply at immigration borders, particularly at the point of entry, be it by land or air. The general rule is that searches may be conducted by immigration, border, and customs agents in the absence of probable cause, reasonable suspicion, or suspicion. This is justified by the compelling state interest in stopping illegal immigration and the flow of prohibited goods into the country.

United States v. Ramsey (1977)

In *United States v. Ramsey*, 431 U.S. 606 (1977), the Court held that "searches made at the border, pursuant to the long-standing right of the sovereign to protect itself by stopping and examining persons and property crossing into this country, are reasonable simply by virtue of the fact that they occur at the border."

The rules for border stops and searches are governed by immigration laws, case law, and agency policies. This section examines the following issues:

◆ Temporary detention of persons believed to be illegal
◆ The use of strip, body cavity, and X-ray searches
◆ Detention of alimentary canal smugglers
◆ Disassembling the gas tank of a motor vehicle
◆ Searching vehicles away from the border

- ◆ Stopping vehicles at checkpoints
- ◆ Factory survey of aliens

Temporary Detention of Aliens Believed to Be Illegal

For the purpose of questioning, an immigration officer may detain against his or her will an individual reasonably believed to be an alien. In *Au Yi Lau v. United States Immigration and Naturalization Service*, 445 F.2d 217, 223 (9th Cir.) (1971), the Ninth Circuit Court of Appeals stated:

> Immigration officers, in accordance with the Congressional grant of authority found in Section 287(a)(1) of the Immigration and Naturalization Act, may make forcible detentions of a temporary nature for the purposes of interrogation under circumstances created by reasonable suspicion, not arising to the level of probable cause to arrest, that the individual so detained is illegally in this country.

The person searched does not need to be entering the country. Anyone found in a border area is subject to search on the basis of reasonable suspicion, including visitors, employees, and transportation workers.

Au Yi Lau v. United States Immigration and Naturalization Service (1971)

Detention of Persons for Questioning in a Border Area

The Court has held that a roving patrol cannot detain persons for questioning in an area near the border solely because the occupants of the vehicle "looked Mexican" (*United States v. Brignoni-Ponce*, 422 U.S. 873 [1975]).

In this case, a roving border patrol stopped a vehicle south of San Clemente, California, and questioned the driver and his two passengers about their citizenship. The officers later admitted that the only reason they stopped the vehicle was that its three occupants appeared to be of Mexican descent. As a result of the questioning, the officers learned that the passengers were illegal aliens. All three were arrested and the driver was charged with knowingly transporting illegal immigrants. The driver later claimed that the testimonies of the two passengers against him were the fruit of an illegal seizure. The Court agreed, saying that stopping a motor vehicle inside the United States solely because the occupants "looked Mexican" was unconstitutional. Said the Court: "Even if they saw enough to think that the occupants were of Mexican descent, this factor alone would justify neither a reasonable belief that they were aliens. . . . The likelihood that any given person of Mexican ancestry is an alien is high enough to make Mexican appearance a relevant factor, but standing alone it does not justify stopping all Mexican-Americans to ask if they are aliens."

United States v. Brignoni-Ponce (1795)

Strip, Body Cavity, and X-ray Searches

A strip search (removing a person's clothing) is allowed in border searches but only if there is reasonable suspicion for it. The same rule applies to body cavity searches, and X-ray searches. The Supreme Court has not addressed these types of searches, but lower courts that have done so have consistently upheld them. These types of searches have one element in common: they are more intrusive and therefore need reasonable suspicion as a justification. A border search may be conducted even without suspicion, but these more intrusive searches need some justification to be valid. Thus, the Fourth Amendment does not apply in full in border search, but it does apply minimally.

Detention of Alimentary Canal Smugglers

United States v. Montoya de Hernandez (1985)

In a case involving the alimentary canal smuggling of narcotics across the nation's borders, *United States v. Montoya de Hernandez*, 473 U.S. 531 (1985), the Court held that reasonable suspicion (instead of probable cause) is sufficient to permit customs agents at the border to detain a traveler suspected of engaging in this offense. The Court also concluded that agents were justified in detaining a traveler (who was suspected of having swallowed balloons containing drugs) for 27 hours before they found drugs in her rectum and arrested her. The Court emphasized that such detention was necessary because of "the hard-to-detect nature of alimentary canal smuggling and the fact that the detention occurred at the international border." The Court took into account the needs of law enforcement under those circumstances and concluded that what the customs agents did was reasonable. Had this not been an immigration and border seizure case, the Court would not have considered the length of time involved to be reasonable.

Disassembling the Gas Tank

United States v. Flores-Montano (2004)

In a 2004 border case, *United States v. Flores-Montano*, 541 U.S. 149 (2004), the Court held that "the government authority to conduct suspicionless inspections at the border includes the authority to remove, disassemble, and reassemble a vehicle's fuel tank." In this case, Flores-Montano attempted to enter the United States at a border crossing. A customs inspector examined the vehicle and asked him to leave it for secondary inspection. At the secondary station, another customs inspector tapped on the gas tank and noted it sounded solid. The inspector then asked a mechanic to help remove the gas tank. When the inspector opened an access plate, he found 37 kilograms of marijuana. Flores-Montano sought suppression of the evidence, claiming that the inspectors did not have reasonable suspicion he was engaged in criminal activity and that reasonable suspicion was required to remove a gas tank. The Court disagreed and held the disassembly valid. It reasoned that "[t]he Government's interest in preventing the entry of unwanted persons and effects is at its zenith at the international border. Time and again, we have stated that searches made at the border, pursuant to the long-standing right of the sovereign to protect itself by stopping and examining persons and property crossing into this country, are reasonable simply by virtue of the fact that they occur at the border," adding that "we have long recognized that automobiles seeking entry into this country may be searched." This case illustrates the extensive power of the government in border searches.

Searching Vehicles Away from the Border

extended border searches
searches made inside the U.S. border.

While searches at border crossings are not subject to Fourth Amendment protection, searches made once the person is inside the U.S. border (called **extended border searches**) are subject to different rules. For example, in *Almeida-Sanchez v. United States*, 413 U.S. 266 (1973), the Court held that the warrantless search of a Mexican citizen's car 25 air miles north of the Mexican border was unconstitutional. In that case, the border patrol conducted a warrantless search of the car of a Mexican citizen who was a holder of a valid work permit. The search yielded marijuana, which was used to convict the petitioner. He appealed, alleging that his constitutional rights were violated.

Almeida-Sanchez v. United States (1973)

The Court agreed, saying that the search was not a border search or the functional equivalent thereof and therefore needed probable cause or a warrant. Distance from the border makes a difference in the Fourth Amendment protection given. Border patrol agents can detain and question the occupants of a car so long as they have reasonable suspicion.

Stopping Vehicles at Fixed Checkpoints

It is permissible for border officials to stop vehicles at reasonably located, fixed checkpoints (such as those set up in the interior of the country) to question occupants of vehicles even without reasonable suspicion that the vehicles contain illegal aliens. Moreover, no warrant is needed before setting up a checkpoint for immigration purposes (*United States v. Martinez-Fuerte*, 428 U.S. 543 [1976]). Note, however, that stopping vehicles at fixed checkpoints and questioning occupants after the stop (which is constitutional) is different from roving border patrols stopping vehicles away from the border and questioning occupants without reasonable suspicion (which is unconstitutional). This is because the stopping and questioning at fixed checkpoints are not arbitrary, whereas stopping and questioning away from the border without reasonable suspicion can be arbitrary and open to abuse.

United States v. Martinez-Fuerte (1976)

Factory Survey of Aliens

Immigration officials sometimes conduct **factory surveys**, in which officials pay surprise visits to factories and ask employees questions to determine if they are illegal aliens: "What is your nationality?" "Where were you born?" and so on. The Court has declared that this type of brief questioning does not constitute a Fourth Amendment "seizure," so no probable cause or reasonable suspicion for suspecting a particular worker of being an illegal alien needs be shown before conducting the survey (*Immigration and Naturalization Service v. Delgado*, 466 U.S. 210 [1984]).

factory surveys
surprise visits to factories by officials to determine if employees are illegal aliens.

Immigration and Naturalization Service v. Delgado (1984)

Summary of Case Law on Border Stops and Searches

Court decisions indicate that the Fourth Amendment does not fully apply at immigration borders or their equivalent, such as international airports, seaports, or other places of entry. Those seeking entry into the United States, whether they are citizens or noncitizens, have minimal Fourth Amendment rights at the border. They can be stopped and asked questions without reasonable suspicion; their vehicles and belongings can be searched extensively without probable cause; and they can be strip-searched, although only based on reasonable suspicion.

Once noncitizens are legally inside the United States, however, they are entitled to constitutional protection. The tragic events of 9/11 have intensified litigation aimed at defining the basic rights of foreigners and citizens at the border, particularly those suspected of involvement in terrorist activities. Advanced technology and more detailed procedures are being used in border searches to detect illegal entries and the inflow of prohibited items. This area of law is fast-changing through national legislation, court decisions, and administrative regulations. It will continue to change as long as the threat to national security is present.

- Plain view is defined as follows: Items that are within the sight of an officer who is legally in a place from which the view is made, and who had no prior knowledge that the items were present, may properly be seized without a warrant—as long as the items are immediately recognizable as subject to seizure.

- Plain view has three requirements: (1) awareness of the item must be through use of the sense of sight; (2) the officer must be legally in the place from which the item is seen; and (3) it must be immediately apparent that the item is subject to seizure.

- Inadvertence is no longer a plain view requirement.

- Plain view applies to open spaces and to motor vehicles.

- Plain view applies even if mechanical devices are used.

- The rule on open fields is: Items in open fields are not protected by the Fourth Amendment guarantee against unreasonable searches and seizures, so they can be seized by an officer without a warrant or probable cause.

- Curtilage is defined as: "the area to which extends the intimate activity associated with the sanctity of a man's home, and the privacies of life."

- The test to determine curtilage is: If a person has a reasonable expectation of privacy in a place, it is part of the curtilage and is protected by the Fourth Amendment.

- Aerial surveillance of curtilage is valid. An area may be an open field despite a locked gate and a "No Trespassing" sign.

- Abandonment is defined as: the giving up of a thing or item absolutely, without limitation as to any particular person or purpose.

- Four factors determine when items are considered abandoned: (1) Property left in an open field or public place is abandoned; (2) for property left on private premises, it depends on whether the occupant has left the premises; (3) for trash or garbage, it depends on where it is left; and (4) intent to abandon is determined by what a person does.

- Abandonment of motor vehicles is determined by four factors: (1) flight from the vehicle, (2) where and for how long a vehicle is left unattended, (3) the condition in which the vehicle is left unattended, and (4) denial of possession or ownership of the vehicle.

- Fourth Amendment protections do not fully apply at immigration borders, but once inside the border some protections are afforded.

- The suspicionless disassembling of a tank of a motor vehicle at the border is valid.

- Vehicles may be stopped at fixed checkpoints and occupants questioned.

- A warrant or probable cause is required for vehicle searches that take place away from the border.

REVIEW QUESTIONS

1. What is the plain view doctrine? Discuss its three requirements.
2. "If the three requirements for the plain view doctrine are not met, any evidence seized is not admissible in court." Is this statement true or false? Explain your answer.
3. What is inadvertence? Is it a plain view requirement? Give an example of inadvertence.
4. What is curtilage? How is curtilage determined?
5. What are open fields? Are they protected or unprotected by the Fourth Amendment? Explain.
6. In what ways are plain view and open fields similar? In what ways are they different?
7. "A homeless person who sleeps underneath a bridge that is part of a state highway has no Fourth Amendment protection because that person is in an open field." Is this statement true or false? Justify your answer.

8. Explain how *Oliver v. United States* has changed the concept of open fields. How does the new concept differ from the old one?

9. "The use of sense-enhancing technology to explore the inside details of a home is constitutional as long as it is done from a public place." Is this statement true or false? Justify your answer.

10. State the differences between abandonment and plain view. As a police officer, which would you prefer—finding evidence in plain view or finding evidence that is abandoned? Why?

11. "The Fourth amendment does not apply at all in border searches." Is this statement true or false? Explain your answer.

12. "Immigration officials may check vehicles at border checkpoints as well as locations inside the border as long as they have suspicion that illegal immigrants are in the vehicle." Is this statement true or false? Explain your answer.

TEST YOUR UNDERSTANDING

1. Assume you are a police officer who sees a car in a parking lot that has obviously not been moved or driven in months. Is that car abandoned? Justify your answer based on the three factors that determine abandonment.

2. Assume you are a police officer serving a search warrant for drugs. While inside the suspect's house, you see a flat-screen television in the living room that you think is stolen. After checking the television's serial number, you call the police station and determine that the television is in fact stolen. You seize the flat-screen television. Is that television admissible in court under plain view? Is it admissible at all as evidence? Explain.

3. While on patrol, Wilma, a police officer, sees what she is certain are marijuana plants inside the fence of a local residence. She goes inside the fence and seizes the plants. Are the seized plants admissible in evidence during a criminal trial? Justify your answer.

4. While on patrol in a neighborhood of student apartment complexes, Fred, a sheriff's deputy, sees illegal drugs through the window of an apartment building. He sees people inside the apartment, and they also see him. He knocks at the door, but the occupants refuse him entry. He forces entry anyway and seizes the drugs. Is the seizure valid? Why or why not?

5. Assume you are a border patrol agent assigned to a city located near the Arizona-Mexico border. One day, you see a truck loaded with people who, from your experience, look like they just arrived after crossing the Mexican border, which is located only 20 miles away. (In other words, based on their clothing, hairstyles, and mannerisms, they do not look like U.S. residents.) You stop the vehicle and begin asking questions. However, you cannot get a coherent answer because none of the vehicle's occupants speak English (and you do not speak Spanish). You take the occupants of the vehicle into custody because you suspect, based on the totality of circumstances, that they are illegal immigrants who just crossed the border. Was the arrest valid? Explain.

6. Officer Jones of the Police Department of Brazos State University was informed by one of the dormitory resident assistants that student Tim had drugs in his room in a campus fraternity house. Acting on this information, Officer Jones knocked at Tim's door and asked if he could look around. Officer Jones was admitted by Tim. He immediately saw a suspicious bag on Tim's desk. But before Officer Jones could seize it, Tim ran to the table, grabbed the pound of marijuana, and threw it out the window and onto the campus street below. Officer Jones hurriedly went down and recovered the contraband. Assume you are the prosecuting attorney in the case against Tim. What is your best ground for admissibility of this evidence in a criminal prosecution—plain view, abandonment, open fields, or none of the above? Select one, give reasons for your choice, and state why you would not choose the others.

RECOMMENDED READINGS

Valerie Bell, Craig Hemmens, Nichole Gerhard. "Getting touchy-feely: Application of the plain view doctrine to plain touch, plain smell, and plain hearing situations by the United States courts of appeal and district courts." *Criminal Justice Studies* 23(1): 3–20 (2010).

Evan B. Citron. "Say hello and wave goodbye: The legitimacy of plain view seizures at the threshold of the home." 74 *Fordham Law Review* 2761 (2005).

Catherine Hancock. "Justice Powell's garden: The Ciraolo dissent and Fourth Amendment protection for curtilage-home privacy." 44 *San Diego Law Review*: 551 (2007).

Carrie Leonetti. "Open fields in the inner city: Application of the curtilage doctrine to urban and suburban areas." 15 *George Mason University Civil Rights Law Journal* 297 (2005).

Brendan Peters. "Fourth Amendment yard work: Curtilage's mow-line rule. *Stanford Law Review* 56: 943–80 (2004).

Rowan Themer. "A man's barn is not his castle: Warrantless searches of structures under the 'open fields doctrine.'" *Southern Illinois University Law Journal*, 33: 139–55 (2008).

Victoria Wilson. Laptops and the border search exception to the Fourth Amendment: Protecting the United States borders from bombs, drugs, and the pictures from your vacation. *Miami Law Review* 65: 999 (2011).

NOTES

1. *Black's Law Dictionary*, 5th ed. (St. Paul, MN: West, 1979), p. 665.
2. John Gales Sauls, "Search of abandoned property: Fourth Amendment considerations," *FBI Law Enforcement Bulletin*, May 1994, pp. 29–31.

CHAPTER 10

Lineups and Other Means of Pretrial Identification

LEARNING OBJECTIVES

1. Compare and contrast the three procedures used in pretrial identification: lineups, showups, and photographic identifications.
2. Discuss the four constitutional rights that may be invoked during a lineup or showup.
3. Explain what rights from the Fourth and Fifth Amendments do not apply to pretrial identification.
4. List what factors render eyewitness testimony and identification unreliable.
5. Describe the legal guidelines for a lawful pretrial identification.
6. Compare and contrast the effect of the filing of charges on the legal guidelines for pretrial identification as compared to charges not being formally filed.
7. Compare and contrast other forms of pretrial identification.
8. Explain the standard for admissibility of scientific or technical testimony under *Daubert v. Merrell Dow Pharmaceuticals*.

KEY TERMS

brain fingerprinting
Daubert doctrine
DNA testing
facial recognition technology
Frye doctrine
Kirby rule
lineup
photographic identification
showup
Wade–Gilbert rule

Skocko/Shutterstock.com

THE TOP 5 IMPORTANT CASES

in Lineups and Other Means of Pretrial Identification

UNITED STATES V. WADE (1967) A police lineup or other face-to-face confrontation after the accused has been formally charged with a crime is considered a "critical stage of the proceedings," so the accused has a right to have counsel present.

GILBERT V. CALIFORNIA (1967) Police identification procedures that are "fraught with dangers of suggestion" are invalid because they violate the accused's right to due process.

KIRBY V. ILLINOIS (1972) There is no right to counsel at police lineups or identification procedures prior to the time the suspect is formally charged with a crime.

NEIL V. BIGGERS (1972) Identification procedures must be fair. To determine whether the procedures were fair, courts must consider all the circumstances leading to the identification. Courts will find the procedure was unfair only when, in light of all such circumstances, it was so suggestive as to give rise to a real and substantial likelihood of irreparable misidentification.

DAUBERT V. MERRELL DOW PHARMACEUTICALS, INC. (1993) Federal courts now allow the admission of expert testimony pertaining to scientific, technical, or other specialized knowledge that will assist the judge or jury in understanding the evidence or in determining the fact in issue. The *Daubert* doctrine replaces the *Frye* doctrine (still used in most state courts) as the standard for admissibility of scientific evidence in federal courts.

THE POLICE USE a variety of procedures to verify that a suspect who has been taken into custody is, in fact, the person who committed the crime being investigated. The identification procedures serve the dual functions of identifying suspects and providing evidence at trial. The police generally use three procedures for the immediate identification of suspects:

◆ A lineup, at which a victim of or witness to a crime is shown several possible suspects at the police station for identification

◆ A showup, at which only one suspect is shown to the witness or victim, usually at the scene of the crime and immediately following a quick arrest of the suspect

◆ Photographic identification, at which photographs of possible suspects are shown to the victim or witness

Four constitutional rights are often invoked by suspects during each of these pretrial identification stages:

◆ The right to counsel
◆ The right to due process
◆ The right against unreasonable searches and seizures
◆ The right against self-incrimination

The three identification procedures and the four constitutional rights of suspects during these proceedings are the main topics of discussion in this chapter. Their relationship and interaction are summarized in the following chart.

In addition to eyewitness identifications, the police have other available tools for identifying suspects, most of which are more scientific and reliable. This chapter discusses some of them and some of the legal issues involved in their use. These are DNA testing, polygraph examination, Breathalyzer tests, handwriting and hair sample analyses, fingernail scrapings, and brain fingerprinting.

Here is a summary of eyewitness identification and suspects' constitutional rights. It is important that this chart be learned well so the discussion that follows on eyewitness identifications and rights of the accused does not become confusing.

Summary of Eyewitness Identification and Suspects' Constitutional Rights

	Right to Counsel?	Right to Due Process?	Right against Unreasonable Search and Seizure?	Right against Self-Incrimination?
Lineups	Yes, if after a formal charge; no, if before a formal charge	Yes	No	No
Showups	Yes, if after a formal charge; no, if before a formal charge	Yes	No	No
Photographic Identification	No	Yes	No	No

LINEUPS

Black's Law Dictionary defines a **lineup** as "a police identification procedure by which the suspect in a crime is exhibited, along with others with similar physical characteristics, before the victim or witness to determine if he can be identified as having committed the offense."[1] The same source says, "Lineup involves and requires lining up of a number of individuals from which one of those lined up may or may not be identified as committer of a crime, and there cannot be a one-man lineup."

lineup
a police identification procedure where the suspect is shown to a victim or witness for purposes of identification.

Lineup procedures vary from one department to another, but a lineup always involves a victim or a witness at the police station trying to identify a suspect from a group of usually five or more individuals. Lineups are often conducted with one-way mirrors so that those in the lineup cannot see the person making the identification. Some departments photograph the lineup as a possible defense if its fairness is challenged later.

Right to Counsel during Lineups—It Depends

The right to counsel during lineups must be considered in terms of two stages: prior to the filing of a formal charge and after the filing of a formal charge.

FIGURE 10.1 Lineup Form

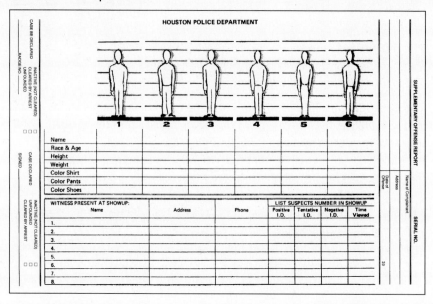

Source: Official lineup form of the Houston Police Department.

No Right to Counsel Prior to a Formal Charge: *Kirby v. Illinois* A suspect in a lineup has no right to a lawyer if he or she has not been *formally charged with an offense*, meaning before an indictment, information, preliminary hearing, or arraignment (*Kirby v. Illinois*, 406 U.S. 682 [1972]).

Kirby v. Illinois (1972)

In *Kirby v. Illinois*, a robbery suspect was identified by the victim in an identification procedure at the police station. No lawyer was present in the room during the identification, nor was Kirby advised by the police of any right to the presence of counsel. Kirby later was convicted of robbery and appealed his conviction. The Court held that Kirby was not entitled to the presence and advice of a lawyer during a lineup or other face-to-face confrontation, *because he had not been formally charged with an offense*. This is known as the **Kirby rule**. (See the Case Brief to learn more about the *Kirby* case.) The identification process in which he participated was a matter of routine police investigation and thus was not considered a "critical stage of the prosecution." Only when the proceeding is considered a "critical stage of the prosecution" is a suspect entitled to the presence and advice of counsel.

Kirby rule
a person who has not been formally charged with an offense is not entitled to a lawyer during a lineup.

The Court has not defined what "critical stage" means, except to say that counsel is needed in such other proceedings as custodial interrogations before or after charges have been filed (*Miranda v. Arizona*, 384 U.S. 436 [1966]) and in preliminary hearings to determine whether there is sufficient evidence to bring the case to a grand jury (*Coleman v. Alabama*, 399 U.S. 1 [1970]).

Miranda v. Arizona (1966)

Coleman v. Alabama (1970)

Most lower courts have held that taking the accused into custody under an arrest warrant is equivalent to filing a formal charge. But if the lineup is conducted after a warrantless arrest, formal charges have not yet been filed; the suspect therefore has no right to the presence of counsel. In these cases, though, officers must be careful not to violate the suspect's right to due process (discussed shortly). Some states require the presence of counsel for the suspect at all lineups whether before or after formal charges are filed. The stage at which formal charges are considered to have been filed varies from state to state and even from one court to another, so it is best to know the law in a particular jurisdiction.

Right to Counsel after Formal Charge In contrast, a lineup or other face-to-face confrontation after the accused has been formally charged with an offense is considered a critical stage of the proceedings; therefore, the accused has a right to have counsel present (*United States v. Wade*, 388 U.S. 218 [1967]). As with other rights, however, the right to counsel at this stage may be waived by the suspect.

United States v. Wade (1967)

In the *Wade* case, the suspect was arrested for bank robbery and later indicted. He was subsequently assigned a lawyer to represent him. Fifteen days after the lawyer was assigned, an FBI agent, without notice to Wade's lawyer, arranged to have two bank employees observe a lineup of Wade and five or six other prisoners in a courtroom of the local county courthouse. Each person in the lineup wore strips of tape like those allegedly worn by the robber during the bank robbery. On request, each said something like "Put the money in the bag," the words allegedly uttered by the robber. Wade was tried for the offense and convicted. He appealed, claiming that the bank employees' courtroom identifications were unconstitutional because the lineup violated his rights to protection against self-incrimination and to the assistance of counsel.

The Court rejected the first claim but upheld the second. The Court noted that there is a grave potential for prejudice, intentional or not, in the pretrial lineup, which might do damage at trial. Because the presence of counsel can often avert prejudice and ensure a meaningful confrontation at trial, the lineup is a "critical stage of the prosecution" at which the accused is as much entitled to the aid of counsel as at the trial itself.

Is the filing of a formal charge a logical dividing line by which to determine whether an accused should have a right to counsel in cases involving pretrial identification? The Supreme Court says yes. In the *Kirby* case, the Court said that "the initiation of judicial criminal proceedings is far from a mere formalism," adding that "it is . . . only then that the adverse positions of government and defendant have solidified . . . [A] defendant finds himself faced with the prosecutorial forces of organized society and immersed in the intricacies of substantive and procedural criminal law."

CASE BRIEF

Kirby v. Illinois, 406 U.S. 682 (1972)

The Leading Case on the Right to Counsel during a Lineup before Formal Charges Are Filed

Facts: A man named Willie Shard reported to the Chicago police that the previous day, on a Chicago street, two men had robbed him of a wallet containing traveler's checks and a Social Security card. The following day, two police officers stopped Kirby and a companion named Bean. When asked for identification, Kirby produced a wallet that contained three traveler's checks and a Social Security card, all bearing the name of Willie Shard. Papers with Shard's name on them were also found in Bean's possession. The officers took Kirby and his companion to a police station. Only after arriving at the police station and checking the records there did the arresting officers learn of the Shard robbery. A patrol car was dispatched to Shard's place of employment, and it brought him to the police station. Immediately upon entering the room in the police station where Kirby and his companion were seated at a table, Shard identified them as the men who had robbed him two days earlier. No lawyer was present in the room, and neither Kirby nor his companion had asked for legal assistance or been advised by the police of any right to the presence of counsel. Kirby was convicted of robbery and appealed his conviction, alleging that his identification should have been excluded because it was extracted unconstitutionally.

Issue or Issues: *Was Kirby entitled to the presence and advice of a lawyer during this pretrial identification stage?* No.

Decision: The decision of the Appellate Court of Illinois was affirmed.

Holding: There is no right to counsel at police lineups or identification procedures prior to the time the suspect is formally charged with the crime.

Case Significance: *Kirby* was decided five years after *United States v. Wade*. It clarified an issue that was not directly resolved in *Wade:* whether the

ruling in *Wade* applies to cases in which the lineup or pretrial identification takes place prior to the filing of a formal charge. The Court answered this question in the negative, saying that what happened in *Kirby* was a matter of routine police investigation; hence, it was not considered a "critical stage of the prosecution." The Court reasoned that a post-indictment lineup is a critical stage, whereas a pre-indictment lineup is not.

Excerpts from the Opinion: The initiation of judicial criminal proceedings is far from a mere formalism. It is the starting point of our whole system of adversary criminal justice. For it is only then that the government has committed itself to prosecute, and only then that the adverse positions of government and defendant have solidified. It is then that a defendant finds himself faced with the prosecutorial forces of organized society, and immersed in the intricacies of substantive and procedural criminal law. It is this point, therefore, that marks the commencement of the "criminal prosecutions" to which alone the explicit guarantees of the Sixth Amendment are applicable.

In this case, we are asked to import into a routine police investigation an absolute constitutional guarantee historically and rationally applicable only after the onset of formal prosecutorial proceedings. We decline to do so. Less than a year after *Wade* and *Gilbert* were decided, the Court explained the rule of those decisions as follows: "The rationale of those cases was that an accused is entitled to counsel at any 'critical stage of the prosecution,' and that a post-indictment lineup is such a 'critical stage.'" We decline to depart from that rationale today by imposing a per se exclusionary rule upon testimony concerning an identification that took place long before the commencement of any prosecution whatever.

Critics of the Court maintain that the boundary between "prior to" and "after" filing is artificial and that any identification of the suspect at any stage is important in establishing guilt or innocence. The Court rejects this, saying the difference is significant enough to require the presence of counsel in one and not in the other. (See the Case Brief to learn more about the *Wade* case.)

In a companion case to *Wade, Gilbert v. California*, 388 U.S. 263 (1967), the Court held that requiring a suspect to give a handwriting sample without a lawyer present does not violate the suspect's right to avoid compulsory self-incrimination or the right to counsel. The lineup procedure, however, was invalid. In the *Gilbert* case, the lineup was conducted in an auditorium in which about a hundred witnesses to alleged offenses by the suspect were gathered. They made wholesale identification of the suspect in one another's presence. Aside from being legally deficient because of the absence of counsel, this procedure, the Court said, was "fraught with dangers of suggestion."

The two cases led to the rule defining at what point counsel must be allowed at lineups. We will look at this rule and examine the relationship between the right to counsel and the *Miranda* warnings, the role of the lawyer during lineups, and what happens when the counsel for the suspect fails to appear.

The Wade–Gilbert Rule Together, the decisions in *United States v. Wade* and *Gilbert v. California* are known in legal circles as the **Wade–Gilbert rule**, as distinguished from the *Kirby* rule (taken from *Kirby v. Illinois*) discussed earlier. According to *Wade–Gilbert*, after being formally charged with a crime, a suspect in a lineup or other confrontation is entitled to have a lawyer present. Failure to provide a lawyer at a lineup after a formal charge has been filed against the suspect makes the evidence inadmissible. However, it does not automatically exclude the testimony of the witness if he or she can identify the accused in court without having to rely on the earlier lineup identification (*Gilbert v. California*, 388 U.S. 263 [1967]).

Wade–Gilbert rule
after being formally charged with a crime, a suspect in a lineup or other confrontation is entitled to have a lawyer present.

To determine that this in-court testimony is admissible, the judge must conclude that the testimony is "purged of the primary taint" caused at the lineup. For example, suppose the police require Bob, a suspect, to appear in a lineup without a lawyer after he has been indicted by a grand jury. The victim identifies Bob as the person who assaulted her. This identification is invalid because Bob was not assigned a lawyer. However, if it can be established in court that the victim would have identified Bob in court anyway without the lineup (if, for instance, it is established that she, in fact, saw Bob a couple of times before the lineup or had a good view of him at the time of the crime), then the identification may be admissible because the judge may determine that it has been purged of the illegality associated with the lineup.

A suspect cannot refuse to appear in the lineup even if their lawyer advises against appearing. The lawyer is present primarily to observe the proceedings. If the suspect cannot afford a lawyer, the state must appoint one. A lawyer may be appointed temporarily just for the lineup to protect a suspect from possible prejudicial actions by the police. The assumption is that even a temporary counsel can adequately protect a suspect's right to due process.

In summary, the answer to the question of whether a suspect has a right to a lawyer during lineups is as follows:

◆ Before a formal charge is filed: No (*Kirby v. Illinois* [1967]).
◆ After a formal charge is filed: Yes (*Wade v. Gilbert* [1967] *and Gilbert v. California* [1967]).

The Right to Counsel and the *Miranda* Warnings Why is a suspect not entitled to a lawyer during a police lineup prior to the filing of formal charges and yet is entitled to the *Miranda* warnings (which state that the suspect has a right to a lawyer and that, if the suspect cannot afford a lawyer, the state will provide one) immediately upon arrest even if he or she is still out in the streets? The answer is that the *Miranda* warnings must be given any time a police officer interrogates a suspect who is in custody. This rule protects the suspect's right against self-incrimination. By contrast, lineups do not involve any form of interrogation, and therefore the danger of self-incrimination is merely physical, not testimonial or communicative, to which the Fifth Amendment right applies.

The Lawyer during the Lineup   The main role of a lawyer is to make sure the procedure is fair. The lawyer's function is that of an "interested observer" who makes sure that things are done right and that the suspect's due process rights are not violated. The Supreme Court, however, has not provided any authoritative guidelines on the role of a lawyer during lineups. Most commentators believe the lawyer should, at the very least, observe the proceedings—including taking notes or making a recording—and be able to state any objection to the proceedings. Others have suggested that the lineup procedure should be treated as an adversarial proceeding in which the lawyer may question the witnesses, make objections, and have any reasonable recommendations respected by the police. No guidelines have been set by the Supreme Court. Most jurisdictions follow the "observe the proceeding" rule for the lawyer and allow nothing beyond that.

CASE BRIEF

United States v. Wade,
388 U.S. 218 (1967)

The Leading Case on the Right to Counsel after Formal Charges Are Filed

Facts: A man with a small piece of tape on each side of his face entered a bank, pointed a pistol at a cashier and the vice president of the bank, and forced them to fill a pillowcase with the bank's money. The man then drove away with an accomplice. An indictment was returned against Wade. Wade was arrested and counsel was appointed. Fifteen days later, without notice to his counsel, Wade was placed in a lineup to be viewed by the bank personnel. Both employees identified Wade as the robber, but in court they admitted seeing Wade in the custody of officials prior to the lineup. At trial, the bank personnel re-identified Wade as the robber and the prior lineup identifications were admitted as evidence. Wade was convicted of bank robbery.

Issue or Issues: *Should the courtroom identification of an accused be excluded as evidence because the accused was exhibited to the witness before trial at a post-indictment lineup conducted for identification purposes and without notice to and in the absence of the accused's appointed lawyer? Yes.*

Decision: The Court vacated and remanded the decision of the District Court for the Eastern District of Texas.

Holding: A police lineup or other face-to-face confrontation after the accused has been formally charged with a crime is considered a "critical stage of the proceedings"; therefore, the accused has the right to have counsel present. The absence of counsel during such proceedings renders the evidence obtained inadmissible.

Case Significance: The *Wade* case settled the issue of whether an accused has a right to counsel after the filing of a formal charge. The standard used by the Court was whether identification was a "critical stage of the proceedings." The Court, however, did not say exactly what this phrase meant; hence, lower courts did not know where to draw the line. In a subsequent case, *Kirby v. Illinois* (see the Case Brief), the Court said that any pretrial identification prior to the filing of a formal charge was not part of a "critical stage of the proceedings," and therefore no counsel was required. The *Wade* case did not authoritatively state what is meant by "formal charge" either, so that phrase has also been subject to varying interpretations, depending on state law or practice.

Excerpts from the Decision: Since it appears that there is grave potential for prejudice, intentional or not, in the pretrial lineup, which may not be capable of reconstruction at trial, and since presence of counsel itself can often avert prejudice and assure a meaningful confrontation at trial, there can be little doubt that for Wade the post-indictment lineup was a critical stage of the prosecution at which he was as much entitled to such aid [of counsel] . . . as at the trial itself. Thus both Wade and his counsel should have been notified of the impending lineup, and counsel's presence should have been a requisite to conduct of the lineup, absent an "intelligent waiver." Concern is expressed that the requirement will forestall prompt identifications and result in obstruction of the confrontations. As for the first,

we note that in the two cases in which the right to counsel is today held to apply, counsel had already been appointed and no argument is made in either case that notice to counsel would have prejudicially delayed the confrontations.

Moreover, we leave open the question whether the presence of substitute counsel might not suffice where notification and presence of the suspect's own counsel would result in prejudicial delay. And to refuse to recognize the right to counsel for fear that counsel will obstruct the course of justice is contrary to the basic assumptions upon which this Court has operated in Sixth Amendment cases. We rejected similar logic in *Miranda v. Arizona* concerning presence of counsel during custodial interrogation. In our view, counsel can hardly impede legitimate law enforcement; on the contrary, for the reasons expressed, law enforcement may be assisted by preventing the infiltration of taint in the prosecution's identification evidence. That result cannot help the guilty avoid conviction but can only help assure that the right man has been brought to justice.

During a pretrial lineup, lawyers should be accorded all professional courtesies but need not be allowed to control the proceedings; nor should an attorney's disruptive presence be tolerated. If the lawyer acts improperly, it is best to invite the judge or the district attorney to witness the proceedings. Counsel should not be allowed to question the witness before, during, or after the lineup; however, if an attorney asks to speak to his or her client prior to or after the lineup, he or she should be allowed to do so. If the suspect has an attorney (that is, after the suspect has been formally charged with the offense), the attorney must be notified of the lineup in advance.

If the main role of a lawyer during the lineup is as an observer (unless local practice provides otherwise), how does the suspect benefit from the lawyer's presence? One justice of the Court has answered thus: "Attuned to the possibilities of suggestive influences, a lawyer could see any unfairness at a lineup, question the witnesses about it at trial, and effectively reconstruct what had gone on for the benefit of the jury or trial judge" (*United States v. Ash*, 413 U.S. 300 [1973]).

United States v. Ash (1973)

What If the Lawyer Fails to Appear? A police officer has a number of options if the lawyer, after having been duly informed of the lineup, fails to show up:

◆ Ask the suspect if he or she is willing to waive the right to counsel; such a waiver is valid as long as it is voluntary and intelligent.
◆ Postpone the lineup to another time when counsel can be present.
◆ Get a substitute counsel for the lineup.
◆ If the preceding options are not feasible, conduct a photo lineup: Those appearing are photographed or videotaped in one room, and the witness is kept isolated in a different room. The photograph or tape is then shown to the witness. The theory is that "because there is no constitutional right to have counsel present when a suspect's photograph is shown to witnesses for identification, the Sixth Amendment is not implicated."[2]

Right to Due Process Applies in Lineups

A suspect has a right to *due process* in a lineup. Due process means "fundamental fairness." This means that the lineup must not be unfair; that is, it must not be impermissibly suggestive. In the words of the Court: "The influence of improper suggestion upon identifying witnesses probably accounts for more miscarriages of justice than any other single factor—perhaps it is responsible for more such errors than all other factors combined" (*United States v. Wade*, 388 U.S. 218 [1967]).

Neil v. Biggers (1972)

In determining what is fair or unfair in identification procedures, courts generally consider all the circumstances leading up to the identification. Courts will find the procedure was unfair only when, in light of the totality of the circumstances, the identification procedure is so *impermissibly suggestive* as to give rise to a real and substantial likelihood of irreparable misidentification (*Neil v. Biggers*, 409 U.S. 188 [1972]). When that point is reached is determined by the trial court, with some guidelines provided by the Supreme Court, as the cases discussed in this chapter show. Recall that, in *Gilbert v. California*, 388 U.S. 263 (1967), the Court held that a lineup conducted in an auditorium where the defendant was identified by about a hundred witnesses violated the suspect's due process rights, because the procedure was "fraught with dangers of suggestion." Similarly, the use of force to compel the suspect to appear in a lineup may also make the proceeding so suggestive as to violate the suspect's due process rights.

Foster v. California (1969)

In *Foster v. California*, 394 U.S. 440 (1969), the Court found that a pretrial identification by the sole witness to the crime violated due process. In the Foster case, the suspect was lined up with two other men several inches shorter. The suspect was close to six feet tall, whereas the two other men were short—"five feet five or six." Only the suspect wore a jacket similar to the one worn by the robber. When the lineup produced no positive identification, the police used a one-man showup of the suspect. Because even the showup was inconclusive, the police later used a second lineup in which only the suspect was a repeater from the earlier lineup.

The Court said that the suspect's due process rights were violated, because under those conditions the identification of the suspect was inevitable. The Court said: "The suggestive elements in this identification procedure made it all but inevitable that [the witness] would identify petitioner whether or not he was in fact 'the man.' In effect, the police repeatedly said to the witness, 'This is the man.'"

Examples of impermissibly suggestive identification procedures are: (1) the suspect is African-American, and there is only one person of that race in the lineup; (2) before the lineup, the police give hints to the witness about the physical characteristics of the suspect; (3) the suspect in the lineup is in jail clothes or wearing handcuffs; and (4) the police allow witnesses to talk to each other and share observations before the lineup takes place.

No Unreasonable Search and Seizure Is Involved in Lineups

Schmerber v. California (1966)

In *Schmerber v. California*, 384 U.S. 757 (1966), the defendant claimed a violation of the guarantee against unreasonable search and seizure during pretrial identification. At the request of a police officer, a sample of Schmerber's blood was taken by a doctor in a hospital for use as evidence in a drunk-driving case. The defendant raised the issue on appeal, claiming that the police should have obtained a warrant before extracting blood from him.

The Court rejected this claim, saying that the officer might reasonably have believed that he was confronted with an emergency in which the delay necessary to obtain a warrant, under the circumstances, would have led to the destruction of the evidence. The Court added, "Particularly in a case such as this, where time had to be taken to bring the accused to a hospital and to investigate the scene of the accident, there was no time to seek out a magistrate and secure a warrant. Given these special facts, we conclude that the attempt to secure evidence of blood-alcohol content in this case was an appropriate incident to petitioner's arrest."

Claims of unreasonable search and seizure in pretrial identification procedures are few and, when raised, do not succeed. They fail because they basically allege, as in *Schmerber*, that the police should have obtained a warrant before conducting the identification procedure.

Compelling a suspect to appear in a lineup or showup is a form of seizure, but it is usually easily justified under the numerous exceptions to the warrant rule, such as the exigent circumstances justification invoked by the police in *Schmerber*. Moreover, many lineups occur after a warrant has been issued or the suspect has been brought before a magistrate. In these cases, the search and seizure challenge becomes moot because of the issuance of a warrant.

No Right against Self-Incrimination Is Involved in Lineups

MYTH vs. REALITY

MYTH A suspect in a lineup cannot be required to speak, because of the privilege against self-incrimination.

FACT The privilege against self-incrimination does not apply to lineups when a suspect is not required to "speak his guilt" by providing testimonial evidence.

Suspects may think they cannot be required to appear in a lineup or showup because it forces them to incriminate themselves. That claim appears logical—indeed, it is incriminating to be pointed out as the culprit in a lineup or to be identified in a showup. However, the Supreme Court has repeatedly rejected this claim. The rule is that a suspect may be required to appear in a police lineup before or after being charged with an offense. The reason is that the right against compulsory self-incrimination applies only to evidence that is testimonial or communicative, which occurs when a suspect is required to "speak his guilt"—or communicate orally. It does not extend to *physical self-incrimination*, which involves the physical body or objects.

Courts have decided that the government can force a suspect to do the following because they involve only the giving of physical, not testimonial, evidence:

◆ Appear in a police lineup before or after formal charge.
◆ Give a blood sample, even unwillingly, as long as proper conditions are present; even if state law allows a suspect to refuse to take a blood-alcohol test, a refusal may be constitutionally introduced as evidence of guilt in court.
◆ Submit to a photograph.
◆ Give handwriting samples.
◆ Submit to fingerprinting.
◆ Repeat certain words or gestures or give voice exemplars (the voice here is used as an identifying physical characteristic, not as oral testimony).

The rule that the Fifth Amendment right not to incriminate oneself protects only against self-incrimination that is testimonial or communicative rather than physical was reiterated in *Schmerber v. California*, 384 U.S. 757 (1966). Following the *Schmerber* decision, the Court ruled in *United States v. Wade*, 388 U.S. 218 (1967) that appearance in a police lineup is a form of physical, not testimonial, self-incrimination and therefore is not protected by the Fifth Amendment. There is no self-incrimination even if the suspect is required to "speak up" for identification by repeating phrases such as "Put the money in the bag." This is because the purpose of having the suspect speak up is not to evaluate what is said, which would be testimonial, but to determine the level, tone, and quality of voice, which are physical properties.

It follows from the *Schmerber* ruling that a suspect does not have a constitutional right to refuse to appear or participate in a lineup. A suspect who is in the custody of the police may be required to appear in a lineup. However, the use of force to compel a suspect's appearance is inadvisable because it might constitute a violation of the suspect's right to due process. If the suspect is not in custody, appearance in a lineup may be compelled only by court order. If a suspect refuses to appear despite a court order, he or she may be held in contempt of court and kept in jail. A suspect's refusal to cooperate in the identification procedure may also be commented on by the prosecution during the trial. Alternatively, if a suspect refuses to participate in a lineup, the police might be justified in arranging a showup, in which only the suspect is viewed by the witness.

SHOWUPS

showup
one-on-one confrontation between a suspect and a witness to crime.

A **showup** is defined as a "one-on-one confrontation between a suspect and a witness to crime." It usually takes place either: (1) shortly after the crime has occurred or (2) in circumstances where a lineup is not feasible. As in the case of lineups, the rights to counsel and due process apply; the rights to protection against unreasonable searches and seizures and against self-incrimination do not.

Right to Counsel during Showups—It Depends

As in the case of lineups, the right to counsel during showups must be considered in terms of two stages: prior to the filing of a formal charge and after the filing of a formal charge.

Prior to a Formal Charge In most cases, the police bring a suspect to the scene immediately after the commission of a crime, to be identified by the victim or other eyewitnesses. Because the suspect has not been charged with a crime, there is no right to counsel (*Kirby v. Illinois*, 406 U.S. 682 [1972]). For example, suppose that, minutes after a purse is snatched, a suspect fitting the description given by the victim is apprehended several blocks away and is brought back to the scene of the crime for identification by the victim. The suspect has no right to counsel even if he or she requests it. If the police question the suspect, however, they must give the *Miranda* warnings, because the situation has escalated beyond a police lineup, where no questions are asked, to a custodial interrogation, which then triggers *Miranda*.

Moore v. Illinois (1977)

After a Formal Charge The rule is different once the adversarial judicial criminal proceedings are initiated. In *Moore v. Illinois*, 434 U.S. 220 (1977), a rape suspect appeared in court, without counsel, for a preliminary hearing to determine whether his case should be sent to the grand jury and to set bail. After the suspect's appearance before the judge, the rape victim was asked by the prosecutor if she saw the perpetrator in the courtroom. She then pointed to the suspect. During the trial, this identification was admitted in court over the defendant's objections. But on appeal, the Supreme Court held that this violated the defendant's right to counsel; because the adversarial criminal proceedings had been initiated at that time, the defendant was entitled to a lawyer at that form of showup.

Right to Due Process Applies in Showups

The leading case on the right to due process in showups is *Neil v. Biggers*, 409 U.S. 188 (1972). In this case, a rape victim could give no description of her attacker other than that he was a black man wearing an orange-colored shirt and that he had a high-pitched voice. The victim was assaulted in her dimly lighted kitchen and then forcibly taken out of the house and raped under a bright, full moon. The victim went through a number of photographs and was shown several lineups but could not make a positive identification. The police arrested the defendant seven months later on information supplied by an informant. The defendant was brought before the victim alone. The police showed the victim the defendant's orange-colored shirt and asked her if she could identify the defendant's voice (from an adjoining room). No other voices were provided for comparison.

The Court held that, although the confrontation procedure itself was suggestive, the totality of circumstances made the identification reliable. Among the factors considered by the Court were "the opportunity of the witness to view the criminal at the time of the crime, the witness's degree of attention, the accuracy of the witness's prior description of the criminal, the level of certainty demonstrated by the witness at the confrontation, and the length of time between the crime and the confrontation." Considering all these factors, the Court concluded that the totality of circumstances showed that the identification was reliable, saying:

> The victim spent a considerable period of time with her assailant, up to half an hour. She was with him under adequate artificial light in her house and under a full moon outdoors, and at least twice, once in the house and later in the woods, faced him directly and intimately. She was no casual observer, but rather the victim of one of the most personally humiliating of all crimes. Her description to the police, which included the assailant's approximate age, height, weight, complexion, skin texture, build, and voice, might not have satisfied Proust, but was more than ordinarily thorough. She had "no doubt" that respondent was the person who raped her.

The courts take five factors into account when determining whether, in the totality of circumstances, the suspect's due process rights have been violated during a showup (*Neil v. Biggers*, 409 U.S. 188 [1972]):

- The witness's opportunity to view the criminal at the time of the crime
- The witness's degree of attention at that time
- The accuracy of any prior description given by the witness
- The level of certainty demonstrated by the witness at the identification
- The length of time between the crime and the identification

Although *Neil v. Biggers* is a photographic showup case, the test to determine the violation of a suspect's due process rights should be the same in lineups and photographic identifications because they are all forms of eyewitness identification. In sum, *Neil v. Biggers* is the leading case on eyewitness identification procedures and the right to due process. In every case, the question courts ask is: Was the procedure fair or was it unduly suggestive?

Stovall v. Denno (1967)

In *Stovall v. Denno*, 388 U.S. 293 (1967), the Court ruled a showup in a hospital valid because the possible unfairness of the showup was justified by the urgent need to confront the suspect because the only living eyewitness, who was hospitalized, was in danger of dying. In this case, the defendant, Stovall, was convicted and sentenced to die for murdering a certain Dr. Behrendt. Stovall was arrested the day after the murder and, without having been given time to obtain a lawyer, was taken by police officers to the hospital to be viewed by Mrs. Behrendt, who had been seriously wounded by her husband's assailant. After observing Stovall and hearing him speak, when she was told to do so by an officer, Mrs. Behrendt identified him as the murderer of her husband. On appeal, Stovall claimed a violation of his right to due process.

The Court rejected his claim, quoting with approval the findings of the state court of appeals, which said:

> Here was the only person in the world who could possibly exonerate Stovall. Her words, and only her words, "He is not the man," could have resulted in freedom for Stovall. The hospital was not far distant from the courthouse and jail. No one knew how long Mrs. Behrendt might live. Faced with the responsibility of identifying the attacker, with the need for immediate action and with the knowledge that Mrs. Behrendt could not visit the jail, the police followed the only feasible procedure and took Stovall to the hospital room. Under these circumstances, the usual police station lineup, which Stovall now argues he should have had, was out of the question.

Showups, however, have been criticized because of their unreliability. In a 2005 decision, the Wisconsin State Supreme Court had these strong words about showups:

> We conclude that evidence obtained from an out-of-court showup is inherently suggestive and will not be admissible unless, based on the totality of circumstances, the procedure was necessary. . . . A lineup or photo array is generally fairer than a showup, because it distributes the probability of identification among the number of persons arrayed, thus reducing the risk of a misidentification. In a showup, however, the only option for the witness is to decide whether to identify the suspect.[3]

No Unreasonable Search and Seizure Is Involved in Showups

As in the case of lineups, showups are not considered unreasonable searches and seizures, because the circumstances usually warrant them. They are usually conducted at the scene of the crime (as when the victim is taken to the scene to identify an alleged purse snatcher) and immediately following the quick arrest of the suspect. Showups are a form of intrusion, but they are usually justified under the exigent circumstances exception because of the absence of an opportunity to obtain a warrant. Moreover, the degree of intrusion is usually minimal and necessary under the circumstances.

No Right against Self-Incrimination Is Involved in Showups

As in the case of lineups, showups do not violate the prohibition against self-incrimination because, although self-incriminatory, the self-incrimination involved is real or physical, not testimonial or communicative.

PHOTOGRAPHIC IDENTIFICATIONS

Photographic identification (also known as a photo array or mug-shot identification) is a process in which a victim or witness is shown photographs of possible suspects. Only the right to due process applies in this form of pretrial identification.

No Right to Counsel in Photographic Identification

There is no right to counsel when the prosecution seeks to identify the accused by displaying photographs to witnesses prior to trial (*United States v. Ash*, 413 U.S. 300 [1973]). This is true even if the suspect has already been formally charged with the crime. In this case, the defendant was charged with five counts of bank robbery. In preparing for trial, the prosecutor decided to use a photographic display to determine whether the witnesses he planned to call would be able to make in-court identifications of the accused. Shortly before the trial, an FBI agent and the prosecutor showed five color photographs to the four witnesses who had tentatively identified the black-and-white photograph of Ash. Three of the witnesses selected the picture of Ash, but one was unable to make any selection.

This post-indictment identification provided the basis for Ash's claim on appeal that he was denied the right to counsel at a "critical stage" of the prosecution. The Court disagreed, holding that photographic identification is not like a lineup, because the suspect is not present when the witnesses view the photographs. Because the main reason for lawyers' presence at lineups is to prevent suspects from being disadvantaged by their ignorance and failure to ascertain and object to biased conditions, there is no need for lawyers when the suspects are absent.

Right to Due Process Applies in Photographic Identification

As in the case of lineups and showups, the right to due process applies, meaning that the photographic identification must not be unduly suggestive. In photographic identifications, a number of photographs must be shown to avoid charges of impermissible suggestion. In addition, there should be nothing in the photographs that focuses attention on a single person. For example, if the suspect is Hispanic, the photographs should feature several Hispanic individuals. To do otherwise would be fundamentally unfair to the suspect and would violate due process.

In *Simmons v. United States*, 390 U.S. 377 (1968), witnesses identified a bank robbery suspect from six photos obtained from a relative a day after the crime. This was followed by an in-court identification of the suspect by the same five witnesses. The Court held that the photographic identification was not unnecessarily suggestive so as to create a "very substantial likelihood of irreparable misidentification." Among the factors the Court took into account were the seriousness of the crime, the need for immediate apprehension, and the fact that the risk of misidentification was small.

Simmons v. United States (1968)

In another case, *Manson v. Brathwaite*, 432 U.S. 98 (1977), the Court held that the showing of a single photograph to a witness was unnecessarily suggestive, but the Court nonetheless admitted the identification based on the totality of circumstances.

Manson v. Brathwaite (1977)

In this case, Glover, an undercover state police officer, purchased heroin from a seller through the open doorway of an apartment while standing for two or three minutes within two feet of the seller in the hallway, which was illuminated by natural light. A few minutes later, Glover described the seller to another police officer as "a colored man, approximately five feet eleven inches tall, dark complexioned, black hair, short Afro style, and having high cheekbones, and of heavy build." The other officer, suspecting that the defendant was the seller, left a police photograph of the suspect in Glover's office, who viewed it two days later and identified the individual in the photograph as the seller. The photograph was introduced during the trial as the picture of the suspect, and an in-court identification was made.

On appeal, the Court agreed with the trial court that the examination of the single photograph was unnecessarily suggestive but ruled that the identification in court did not have to be excluded. The Court noted that "Glover, no casual observer but a trained police officer, had a sufficient opportunity to view the suspect, accurately described him, positively identified respondent's photograph as that of the suspect, and made the photograph identification only two days after the crime." The photograph identification alone would have violated the defendant's due process right, but the totality of circumstances justified admission of the court identification.

This case reiterates previous Court decisions holding that the suggestiveness of the identification procedure is but one of the factors courts should take into account in determining whether a suspect's due process rights were violated. Much more important than a single factor is the totality of the circumstances. The Court in *Brathwaite* also restated the main concern of the Court in identification cases, saying, "Reliability is the linchpin in determining the admissibility of identification testimony for confrontations."

No Unreasonable Search and Seizure Is Involved in Photographic Identification

Photographic identification does not involve any unreasonable search and seizure because no search or seizure takes place, as long as the photographs are obtained legally. Showing photographs does not come under the Fourth Amendment, nor is it unduly intrusive.

No Right against Self-Incrimination Is Involved in Photographic Identification

There is no self-incrimination when photographs are shown because, as in the case of lineups and showups, the self-incrimination involved is real or physical, not testimonial or communicative.

HIGHLIGHT > **Due Process and Photographic Identification**

"We hold that each case must be considered on its own facts, and that convictions based on eye-witness identification at trial following a pretrial identification by photograph will be set aside on that ground only if the photographic identification procedure was so impermissibly suggestive as to give rise to a very substantial likelihood of irreparable misidentification. This standard accords with our resolution of a similar issue in *Stovall v. Denno* (388 U.S. 293 [1967]), and with decisions of other courts on the question of identification by photograph."

Source: *Simmons v. United States*, 390 U.S. 377 (1968).

Alice Smith is walking home from work when a man comes up from behind her, pushes her into an alleyway, and demands she give him her purse. Witness Jim Franklin sees the crime and runs to the aid of Ms. Smith; the robber runs away. The police are called. Officer Roberts responds and gets the robbery suspect's description from both Smith and Franklin. Officer Roberts is acquainted with a possible suspect (Bob) who lives in the area and has committed similar offenses in the past (that is, using the same modus operandi, or M.O.). Officer Roberts goes to the police station and obtains a mug shot of suspect Bob. Officer Roberts returns to the scene of the crime and shows the mug shot to Ms. Smith and Witness Franklin. Officer Roberts asks, "Is this him?" Ms. Smith and Jim Franklin both say yes. Based on this evidence, Officer Roberts arrests suspect Bob. During the trial, both Ms. Smith and Jim Franklin identify the suspect in the courtroom as the offender.

1. *Were Officer Roberts' actions at the scene appropriate? If not, what should Officer Roberts have done differently?*
2. *Are Ms. Smith's and Jim Franklin's identifications at trial valid? Why or why not?*

PROBLEMS WITH EYEWITNESS IDENTIFICATION

Eyewitness identification has been the focus of intense attention and investigation in the last few years because it has been associated with numerous cases of false convictions. Once considered highly reliable evidence, eyewitness identification has declined in reliability and become the subject of changes in legislation and court decisions.

There are many problems associated with eyewitness identification. The most common ones are that it is "hopelessly unreliable" and lacks prescribed guidelines. These two issues are discussed here as are some of the efforts are reform.

"Hopelessly Unreliable"

All three forms of eyewitness identification—lineups, showups, and photographic identification—have raised serious concerns among lawyers and criminal justice professionals because of their proven unreliability in many cases. Eyewitness identification used to be considered the most damning piece of evidence against a suspect. Numerous studies show, however, that eyewitness identification is not always reliable and that other forms of circumstantial evidence (DNA or fingerprints, for example) are far more accurate in identifying suspects or proving guilt.

A U.S. Department of Justice report notes that eyewitness testimony is far from infallible and that "even honest and well-meaning witnesses can make errors, such as identifying the wrong person or failing to identify the perpetrator of a crime."[4] A journal article written by noted authorities John Turtle, R. C. L. Lindsay, and Gary Wells says that "there are approximately 100 documented cases in the U.S. in which a convicted person who has served time in prison has been exonerated by DNA evidence indicating that someone else committed the crime. It has been estimated that of those 100 cases, over 75% were primarily the result of mistaken eyewitness identification of the convicted suspect."[5]

MYTH vs. REALITY

MYTH An eyewitness identification by a witness is more reliable than other methods of identifying a suspect.

FACT Scientific studies have demonstrated that eyewitness identifications are often incorrect.

In *Wisconsin v. Dubose*, 205 WI 126 (2005), the Wisconsin Supreme Court summarized the state of research on eyewitness testimony as follows:

> Over the last decade, there have been extensive studies on the issue of identification evidence, research that is now impossible for us to ignore. . . . These studies confirm that eyewitness testimony is often "hopelessly unreliable." The research strongly supports the conclusion that eyewitness misidentification is now the single greatest source of wrongful convictions in the United States, and responsible for more wrongful convictions than all other causes combined.

No Prescribed Guidelines

Given the pervasive skepticism about the reliability of eyewitness evidence, the pressure is on for police departments and prosecutors to ensure that identification procedures are fair and reliable. Despite the frequent use of lineups for suspect identification, standards and guidelines vary from state to state and even within a state. A state of Virginia crime commission found that many law enforcement agencies within that state "have no written policies on lineup procedures, and . . . smaller departments often lack the resources needed to produce reliable lineups."[6] That study also says that "currently there is no law requiring Virginia police and sheriff's departments to have a written policy on conducting lineups."

In cases of photographic identification, studies show that "when witnesses are shown all six photos at once—rather than one at a time—a natural tendency kicks in to compare faces and judge which looks most like the one they remember. They make a relative judgment as opposed to a true recognition," according to experts.[7] Many states do not have prescribed legislative or administrative guidelines for police departments to follow, and so practices vary from one department to another.

In sum, studies on eyewitness testimony show low reliability and flawed procedures. The evidence is strong that eyewitness testimony has led to numerous wrongful convictions, even in death penalty cases. Courts and legal scholars have expressed skepticism over its credibility; thus, law enforcement agencies across the nation are revising their procedures to ensure that procedures are fair and highly reliable based on the totality of circumstances and not simply on mere eyewitness identification.

Legislative and Judicial Responses

Some states have enacted legislation to make their lineup and eyewitness identification procedures more reliable. Illinois, Maryland, West Virginia, Wisconsin, Ohio, and North Carolina have passed laws that seek to minimize misidentifications. The states of Georgia, Vermont, and Virginia are studying the problem further, while other jurisdictions have adopted voluntary guidelines.[8] In 2011, the state of Texas passed a law requiring that all law enforcement agencies of the state "adopt, implement, and as necessary amend a detailed written policy regarding the administration of photography and live lineup identification procedures" (Article 38.10 of the Texas Code of Criminal Procedure). Each law enforcement agency is expected to come up with its own guidelines, which took effect in June 2012. To help enforce the mandate and to facilitate work among the local agencies, the Bill Blackwood Law Enforcement Management Institute of Texas (LEMIT) was commissioned to write a model procedure for voluntary adoption by state law enforcement agencies. Among its recommendations is the concept of a *blinded lineup*, referring to a procedure whereby the suspect is not known to the person who conducts the lineup. Other states have passed reform legislation, but with differing provisions about how to make the process more reliable.

The biggest response, however, and which will likely have a more immediate impact on the pervasive problem of misidentification, is a decision from the New Jersey Supreme Court, *State v. Henderson* (27 A.3d 872 [N. J. 2011]). See the Highlight Box on *State v. Henderson* for details.

State v. Henderson (2011)

A study by a special master in the New Jersey case estimated that more than 2,000 studies related to the subject had been published since the Supreme Court's original 1977 decision. The court added: "From social science research to the review of actual police lineups, from laboratory experiments to DNA exonerations, the record proves that the possibility of mistaken identification is real." More than a dozen factors were listed that should be considered when judges during trial assess the reliability of a witness's identification. Among these are "the amount of time the witness had to observe the event, how close the witness was to the suspect, whether the witness was under the influence

HIGHLIGHT › *State v. Henderson*—New Jersey Supreme Court Ruling on Eyewitness Identification

State v. Henderson (**A-8-08**) (**062218**), **Supreme Court of New Jersey (2011)** is a significant decision because for the first time a state supreme court closely examined the controversial issue of eyewitness identification and then mandated that massive changes be made to a state's eyewitness identification procedures. In this case, defendant Henderson alleged that an eyewitness mistakenly identified him as an accomplice to a murder. He argued that the identification was unreliable because the officers investigating the case intervened during the identification process and thus unduly influenced the eyewitness. The trial court refused to exclude the evidence, saying the behavior of the police officers was not impermissively suggestive. Henderson was convicted and appealed to the New Jersey Supreme Court. That court agreed to hear the case and, fully aware of the controversy surrounding eyewitness testimony, appointed a special master (a person appointed to help the judge on certain judicial matters) to "evaluate scientific and other evidence about eyewitness identification." After hearing seven experts and producing more than 2,000 pages of transcripts—along with hundreds of scientific studies—the special master issued a report saying that:

> Study after study revealed a troubling lack of reliability in eyewitness identifications. From social science research to the review of actual police lineups, from laboratory experiments to DNA exonerations, the record proves that the possibility of mistaken identification is real. Indeed, it is now widely known

that eyewitness misidentification is the leading cause of wrongful convictions across the country.

The court adopted the report and then ordered changes in the state's eyewitness identification procedures. It concluded that:

> The current legal standards for assessing eyewitness identification evidence must be revised because it does not offer an adequate measure for reliability; does not sufficiently deter inappropriate police conduct; and overstates the jury's ability to evaluate identification evidence. Two modifications to the standard are required. First, when defendants can show some evidence of suggestiveness, all relevant systems and estimator variables should be explored at pretrial hearings. Second, the court system must develop enhanced jury charges on eyewitness identification for trial judges to use. Defendant is entitled to a new pretrial hearing consistent with this opinion to determine the admissibility of the eyewitness evidence introduced at his trial.

Question: How do you think the U.S. Supreme Court would decide this case if brought to it and accepted on appeal? Either way the Court might rule, it would be a Court decision of immense significance to police departments. Meantime, recent laws in some states are taking the lead in forcing changes to how police departments conduct police lineups and secure eyewitness testimony.

of alcohol or drugs, whether the witness was identifying someone of a different race and the length of time that had elapsed between the crime and the identification."[9]

Perry v. New Hampshire (2012)

Despite the focus and attention on eyewitness testimony, it must be noted that the U.S. Supreme Court in 2012 upheld its original decision on the standard for excludible eyewitness identification promulgated in *Manson v. Brathwaite*, 432 U.S. 98 (1977). The Court held in *Perry v. New Hampshire*, 565 U.S. --- (2012), that the issue whether the police used an "unnecessarily suggestive identification procedure" is to be judged based on a two-pronged test: (1) whether the police in fact used an unnecessarily suggestive procedure, and, if they did (2) whether that procedure "so tainted the resulting identification as to render it unreliable and thus inadmissible." The Court held that "the Due Process Clause does not require a preliminary judicial inquiry into the reliability of an eyewitness identification when the identification was not procured under unnecessarily suggestive circumstances arranged by law enforcement." The Court concluded that the due process clause only prohibits the "introduction of evidence when inclusion of the evidence is so extremely unfair that its inclusion would violate fundamental concepts of justice."

EYEWITNESS IDENTIFICATION GUIDELINES

The National Institute of Justice of the U.S. Department of Justice (DOJ) released a research report in 2001 titled "Eyewitness Evidence: A Guide for Law Enforcement."[10] The major study involved a thirty-four-member working group of top criminal justice professionals in law enforcement, law, psychology, and other fields. Their recommendations are supported by social science research of the past twenty years, which "combines research and practical perspectives." The group's task was to identify the best practices in the field of eyewitness evidence and "relay this information to criminal justice professionals who can practically apply this knowledge."

The guidelines have not been enacted into law, and therefore their adoption by law enforcement agencies is optional. Nonetheless, this work constitutes the most comprehensive and authoritative effort by the DOJ, or any other law enforcement agency, to produce guidelines that ensure fair and legally defensible identification procedures. These guidelines are reproduced here because they are currently the most frequently used models in numerous jurisdictions that are establishing or revising pretrial identification guidelines. The guidelines are for lineups, showups, and photographic identifications.

HIGHLIGHT ❯ What Is a "Double-Blind" Lineup Procedure?

In a recent and influential book, *Convicting the Innocent*—cited by the New Jersey Supreme Court in *State v. Henderson*—University of Virginia law professor Brandon L. Garrett says this about the double-blind lineup procedure that is now being used by the police in a number of jurisdictions: "There is one straightforward way to ensure that police do not engage in suggestive conduct during lineup procedure. That's to use a double-blind procedure, in which the administering officer does not know which person in the lineup or array is the suspect, so he cannot influence the witness, intentionally or not."

Other recommendations include warning the witness that the suspect may not be in the lineup. This helps ensure that the witness is not be under pressure to identify anybody in that lineup as a suspect.

Source: Brandon L. Garrett, *Convicting the Innocent* (Harvard University Press, 2011).

For Lineups

The report offers guidelines for composing and presenting lineups.

Composing In composing a live lineup, the investigator should:

◆ Include only one suspect in each identification procedure.

◆ Select fillers (non-suspects) who generally fit the witness's description of the perpetrator. When the description of the perpetrator provided by the witness is limited or inadequate, or when the description of the perpetrator differs significantly from the appearance of the suspect, fillers should resemble the suspect in significant features.

◆ Consider placing suspects in different positions in each lineup, both across cases and with multiple witnesses in the same case. Position the suspect randomly unless, where local practice allows, the suspect or the suspect's attorney requests a particular position.

◆ Include a minimum of four fillers per identification procedure.

◆ When showing a new suspect, avoid reusing fillers in lineups shown to the same witness.

◆ Complete uniformity of features is not required. Avoid using fillers who so closely resemble the suspect that a person familiar with the suspect might find it difficult to distinguish the suspect from the fillers.

◆ Create a consistent appearance between the suspect and fillers with respect to any unique or unusual feature (for example, scars, tattoos) used to describe the perpetrator by artificially adding or concealing that feature.

Summary: The foregoing procedures will result in a photo or live lineup in which the suspect does not unduly stand out. An identification obtained through a lineup composed in this manner may have stronger evidentiary value than one obtained without these procedures.

Presenting In presenting a live lineup, the investigator should:

◆ Instruct the witness that he or she will be asked to view a group of individuals.

◆ Instruct the witness that it is just as important to clear innocent persons of suspicion as to identify guilty parties.

◆ Instruct the witness that individuals present in the lineup may not appear exactly as they did on the date of the incident, because features such as head and facial hair are subject to change.

◆ Instruct the witness that the person who committed the crime may or may not be present in the group of individuals.

◆ Assure the witness that, regardless of whether or not an identification is made, the police will continue to investigate the incident.

◆ Instruct the witness that procedure requires the investigator to ask the witness to state in his or her own words how certain he or she is of any identification.

Summary: Instructions provided to the witness prior to presentation of a lineup will likely improve the accuracy and reliability of any identification obtained from the witness and can facilitate the elimination of innocent parties from the investigation.

FIGURE 10.2 Sample Witness Certification Form for Lineups

Reference No.:   Offense: Date of Offense:

Witness:

Time, Date, and Place of Live Lineup:

Persons present:

Instructions:

In a moment, I am going to show you a series of individuals. The person who committed the crime may or may not be included. I do not know whether the person being investigated is included.

The investigation will continue whether or not you make an identification. Even if you identify someone during this procedure, I will continue to show you all individuals in the series. Keep in mind that things like hair styles, beards, and mustaches can be easily changed.

You should not feel you have to make an identification. It is as important to exclude innocent persons as it is to identify the perpetrator. The individuals will be shown to you one at a time. Take as much time as you need to look at each one. After each individual, I will ask you "Is this the person you saw [Insert description of act]?" Take your time answering the question. If you answer "Yes," I will then ask you, "In your own words, can you describe how certain you are?"

Because you are involved in an ongoing investigation, in order to prevent compromising the investigation, you should avoid discussing this identification procedure or its results.

Do you understand the way the lineup procedure will be conducted and the other instructions I have given you?

Consent to Participate:

I have read these instructions, or they have been read to me, and I understand the instructions. I am prepared to view the individuals, and I will follow the instructions provided on this form.

Signed: _____

     (Witness)

I certify that I have translated and read the instructions to the witness.

Signed: _____

     (Translator, if applicable)

Signed: _____

     (Lineup Administrator)

Identification Result:

I have picked number _____   Signed: _____

                                     (Witness)

I did not pick anyone _____   Signed: _____

                                     (Witness)

Source: College of Criminal Justice, Sam Houston State University, *Model Policy on Eyewitness Identification, State of Texas*, drafted and designed by the Law Enforcement Management Institute of Texas (LEMIT), 2012, for recommended but optional use in law enforcement agencies.

For Showups

When conducting a showup, the investigator should:

◆ Determine and document, prior to the showup, a description of the perpetrator.
◆ Consider transporting the witness to the location of the detained suspect to limit the legal impact of the suspect's detention.

When multiple witnesses are involved, the investigator should:

◆ Separate witnesses and instruct them to avoid discussing details of the incident with other witnesses.
◆ If a positive identification is obtained from one witness, consider using other identification procedures (for example, a lineup or photo array) for the remaining witnesses.
◆ Caution the witness that the person he or she is looking at may or may not be the perpetrator.
◆ Obtain and document a statement of certainty for both identifications and non-identifications.

Summary: The use of a showup can provide investigative information at an early stage, but the inherent suggestiveness of a showup requires careful use of procedural safeguards.

For Photographic Identifications

In completing a photo lineup, the investigator should:

◆ Include only one suspect in each identification procedure.
◆ Select fillers (non-suspects) who generally fit the witness's description of the perpetrator. When the description of the perpetrator provided by the witness is limited or inadequate, or when the description of the perpetrator differs significantly from the appearance of the suspect, fillers should resemble the suspect in significant features.
◆ If multiple photos of the suspect are reasonably available to the investigator, select a photo that resembles the suspect's description or appearance at the time of the incident.
◆ Include a minimum of five fillers per identification procedure.
◆ Complete uniformity of features is not required. Avoid using fillers who so closely resemble the suspect that a person familiar with the suspect might find it difficult to distinguish the suspect from the fillers.
◆ Create a consistent appearance between the suspect and fillers with respect to any unique or unusual feature (for example, scars, tattoos) used to describe the perpetrator by artificially adding or concealing that feature.
◆ Consider placing suspects in different positions in each lineup both across cases and with multiple witnesses in the same case. Position the suspect randomly in the lineup.
◆ When showing a new suspect, avoid reusing fillers in lineups shown to the same witness.
◆ Ensure that no writings or information concerning previous arrest(s) will be visible to the witness.

- View the spread, once completed, to ensure that the suspect does not unduly stand out.
- Preserve the presentation order of the photo lineup. In addition, preserve the photos themselves in their original condition.

Many law enforcement agencies have shifted from the old method to the new method of conducting a lineup. Under the old method, the investigating officer was allowed to administer the lineup, photographic identification, or showup. This officer knew the identity of the suspect. In the new method, fillers must resemble the suspect or person of interest, and an impartial administrator in the department (someone who does not know the identity of the suspect) presents the lineup. The new method minimizes the possibility of bias and unfairness.

OTHER MEANS OF IDENTIFYING SUSPECTS

In addition to lineups, showups, and photographic arrays, the police often use other identification procedures, such as DNA testing, polygraph examinations, Breathalyzer tests, handwriting and hair sample analyses, and brain fingerprinting. The admissibility of these forms of scientific evidence in court varies. Constitutional rights may also be involved in each procedure.

DNA Testing

DNA testing results are admissible as evidence. In this section, we look at the background of DNA testing, some of the legal issues testing has created, the reliability of testing, the need for a national database, and the future of DNA testing.

DNA testing
compares a suspect's DNA with DNA recovered during the investigation.

Background A relatively new but powerful tool in suspect identification and crime solving is **DNA testing**, which matches the suspect's DNA with DNA recovered from the scene of the crime (such as that found in semen or blood). DNA stands for deoxyribonucleic acid, which is the chemical that carries a person's genetic information. Known in some circles as genetic fingerprinting, DNA may be recovered from a variety of sources, including semen, blood, hair, skin, sweat, and saliva.

A publication of the National Institute of Justice, "What Every Law Enforcement Office Should Know about DNA Evidence," offers this simplified account of how DNA evidence works:

> DNA is similar to fingerprint analysis in how matches are determined. When using either DNA or a fingerprint to identify a suspect, the evidence collected from the crime scene is compared with the "known" print. If enough of the identifying features are the same, the DNA or fingerprint is determined to be a match. If, however, even one feature of the DNA or fingerprint is different, it is determined not to have come from that suspect.[11]

If DNA testing is performed properly, the chances of the method producing a false match are several hundred thousand to one and sometimes several million to one.[12] DNA evidence, because it is so accurate, makes it much easier for police to locate suspects and prosecutors to obtain convictions.

Although DNA research goes back to the nineteenth century, DNA testing first gained prominence in England in the mid-1980s. It quickly caught the fancy of the law enforcement community and prosecutors in the United States as a fool-proof means of suspect identification. Since then it has been used as a crime-detecting tool in many countries. When first introduced in a U.S. court in 1987, DNA typing was billed as the "greatest advance in forensics since the discovery of fingerprints."[13] In *United States v. Jakobetz*, 955 F.2d 786 (1992), a federal court of appeals ruled that "the district court properly exercised its discretion in admitting the DNA profiling evidence proffered by the government in this case; we also conclude that courts facing a similar issue in the future can take judicial notice of the general theories and specific techniques involved in DNA profiling." In addition to affirming the trial court's admission of the evidence, *Jakobetz* featured a lengthy discussion of the science and technology of DNA testing and the reasons it is reliable. (See Exhibit 10.1.)

United States v. Jakobetz (1992)

DNA Exonerations and Some Legal Issues DNA testing has been useful for the police in identifying suspects, and it has also led to the exoneration of some defendants. The latest figures from the Innocence Project, an organization active in the work of freeing innocent defendants, show that there have been 329 post-conviction DNA exonerations in thirty-seven different states since the first such exoneration in 1989. Of these exonerations, seventeen involved death row inmates. The average length of time served by those exonerated is thirteen and a half years, and the total number of years spent beyond bars for wrongful conviction was approximately 3,800 years. Only about half of those exonerated through DNA testing have been financially compensated for their wrongful conviction. The federal government, twenty-seven states, and the District of Columbia have passed laws that compensate individuals who were wrongfully incarcerated. Other states deal with wrongful convictions on a case-by-case basis.

Although the admissibility of DNA testing results as evidence is settled, other legal questions have arisen. In 2009, the U.S. Supreme Court held that prisoners have no constitutional right to after-conviction DNA testing that might prove their innocence (*District Attorney's Office of the Third Judicial District v. Osborne*, 557 U.S.--- [2009]). In this case, Osborne was convicted of kidnapping and sexual assault in Alaska, based on the testimony of his codefendant and the victim. Part of the evidence against him was the result of a DNA test that indicated that Osborne could not be excluded as the possible perpetrator. On appeal, he sought access to the DNA evidence so he could, at his own expense, conduct more precise DNA testing that he hoped would establish his innocence. The state of Alaska refused, saying that other evidence established his guilt anyway. Moreover, there is no Alaska law that gives convicted defendants the right of access to post-conviction DNA testing. Osborne filed a civil liability lawsuit in federal court, claiming that his right to due process was violated. The Court disagreed, holding that a defendant has no constitutional right to access evidence for DNA testing after the defendant has received a fair trial and is seeking such evidence to reverse a conviction. The defendant is entitled to access to DNA evidence prior to and during trial, under the provisions of the Constitution. But once convicted, such right no longer exists. Under the facts of his case, Osborne was not entitled to such access.

Problems concerning the admissibility of DNA evidence continue to bother some courts. DNA evidence and its admissibility came under heavy scrutiny and challenge during the celebrated O. J. Simpson criminal trial, a trial that did little to increase public confidence in the reliability of DNA testing and the way it is administered in some government laboratories. Despite these problems, DNA testing methods over the past decade have improved tremendously, to the point where courts routinely accept DNA evidence and juries have come to expect it in many cases.

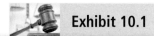

Exhibit 10.1 ● **What Every Law Enforcement Officer Should Know about DNA Evidence**

Identifying DNA Evidence

Since only a few cells can be sufficient to obtain useful DNA information to help your case, the following list identifies some common items of evidence that police may need to collect, the possible location of the DNA on the evidence, and the biological source containing the cells. Just because an officer cannot see a stain does not mean there are not enough cells for DNA typing. Further, DNA does more than just identify the source of the sample; it can place a known individual at a crime scene, in a home, or in a room where the suspect claimed not to have been. It can refute a claim of self-defense and put a weapon in the suspect's hand. It can change a story from an alibi to one of consent. The more officers know how to use DNA, the more powerful a tool it becomes.

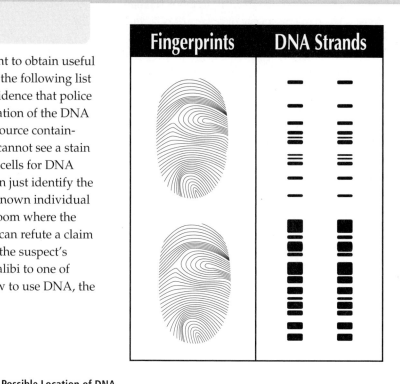

Evidence	Possible Location of DNA on the Evidence	Source of DNA
baseball bat or similar weapon	handle, end	sweat, skin, blood, tissue
hat, bandanna, or mask	inside	sweat, hair, dandruff
eyeglasses	nose or ear pieces, lens	sweat, skin
facial tissue, cotton swab	surface area	mucus, blood, sweat, semen, earwax
dirty laundry	surface area	blood, sweat, semen
toothpick	tips	saliva
used cigarette	cigarette butt	saliva
stamp or envelope	licked area	saliva
tape or ligature	inside/outside surface	skin, sweat
bottle, can, or glass	sides, mouthpiece	saliva, sweat
used condom	inside/outside surface	semen, vaginal or rectal cells
blanket, pillow, sheet	surface area	sweat, hair, semen, urine, saliva
"through and through" bullet	outside surface	blood, tissue
bite mark	person's skin or clothing	saliva
fingernail, partial fingernail	scrapings	blood, sweat, tissue

Source: National Institute of Justice, "What Every Law Enforcement Officer Should Know about DNA Evidence," *http://www.ncjrs.gov/nij/DNAbro/id.html.*

Unassailable Scientific Reliability Considered by some to be the gold standard of criminal evidence, the consensus is that the scientific foundation of DNA testing is solid and unassailable. If competently interpreted, the test is reliable and the results are admissible in court. It is generally accepted that each person's DNA is unique except for the DNA of identical twins, and that the chances of similarity in DNA are infinitesimally small. There is no question that DNA technology is scientifically reliable. Under existing evidence rules on admissibility (the *Frye* doctrine or the *Daubert* doctrine, both discussed later in this chapter), DNA testing easily satisfies both standards.

The legal controversy, however, centers around the skill of technicians who conduct the tests and the validity of their interpretations. The chair of a National Academy of Sciences panel looking into DNA testing has recommended that laboratories analyzing DNA should be held to higher standards in the way the tests are performed and interpreted. Admitting that, when performed properly, DNA testing can be invaluable in solving crimes, the panel also called for adherence to very strict standards to ensure that the "technique is performed properly in crime laboratories and that its results are accurate." It further urged that scientists set the standards for admissibility. Judges and jurors should not be put in a position where, based on complex data, they have to decide whether a laboratory test result is reliable.[14]

DNA technology has made giant strides over the years. Years ago, a DNA test required a sizable sample (such as a blood or semen stain) with high-quality DNA, and the test took several weeks. Today, DNA can be obtained from a single shaft of hair, and DNA tests can be conducted in a matter of days. DNA testing results constitute convincing evidence, but jurors are nonetheless free to disregard it, as they are any type of evidence.

A National DNA Database The federal government has opened a national DNA database aimed at significantly reducing the number of rapes and other crimes by identifying and catching repeat offenders earlier. As one source describes it, the "FBI's Combined DNA Index System (CODIS) is a national database into which law-enforcement officials around the country can upload DNA information about criminals." It adds that "states participating in the program (almost all have joined) can draw from the common DNA basket when investigating unsolved crimes. So far, more than 1.2 million profiles have been registered."[15] Although CODIS has critics worried about possible violations of civil liberties, one big plus going for it is that it has already cleared numerous innocent, wrongfully convicted people in the United States through DNA testing.

All fifty states and the FBI now have laws or other forms of authorization allowing the collection of DNA samples from convicted offenders. These samples form profiles that are compared against available DNA profiles of biological evidence. The DNA databases include information on the range of included offenses and on some characteristics of offenders, such as whether they are adults or juveniles. The data collected are extensive and a major help in solving crimes, but their use is controlled and limited. For example, criminal penalties are imposed for such acts as tampering with the samples or records, the improper entry of DNA samples into the database, improper access and use, and improper disclosure of DNA information.[16]

In *Maryland v. King*, --- U.S. --- 2013, the Supreme Court held that it is constitutional to take DNA samples from felony arrestees who are booked on serious charges because the collection and analysis of DNA serves a legitimate government interest, that of accurately identifying arrestees.

Maryland v. King (2013)

In this case, King was arrested for first- and second-degree assault for menacing a group of people with a shotgun in Wicomico County, Maryland. During his booking, a buccal swab was taken from the inside of King's cheek to gather a DNA sample. Maryland law allowed police to collect a DNA sample from anyone arrested for a "violent" felony, including burglary. Under this procedure the defendant was arraigned and the DNA was processed and entered into a database. Upon analyzing the DNA taken from King, it was discovered that it matched the DNA collected from the victim of a rape in 2003. King was subsequently charged with that rape. At the rape trial King filed a motion to suppress the DNA evidence taken at his booking, claiming that the Maryland DNA Collection Act violated the Fourth Amendment. King was convicted of rape and sentenced to life in prison without the possibility of parole. On appeal, the Court of Appeals of Maryland held that the collection of DNA samples from felony arrestees was an unlawful seizure, as King had an expectation of privacy in his DNA.

The Supreme Court reversed the decision of the Court of Appeals of Maryland and held that it is constitutional to take DNA samples from felony arrestees who are booked on serious charges because the collection and analysis of DNA serves a legitimate government interest, that of accurately identifying arrestees. The Court asserted that the accurate identification of arrestees ensures that the correct person has been arrested and can provide information on their criminal history to inform bail decisions. The buccal swab of the inside of an arrestee's cheek did not, according to the Court, intrude upon their reasonable expectation of privacy of a suspect who has been arrested. Furthermore, the buccal swab is minimally invasive and unlikely to threaten the health or safety of the arrestee.

The Future of DNA Testing DNA testing has proved to be an effective tool in suspect identification. It has come a long way since the mid-1980s, when it first came to the attention of the police. The federal government, the states, and local agencies are all spending a great deal of money to improve their DNA-testing capability. Those expenditures will continue to grow as both prosecution and defense become more aware of how DNA is a potent tool for establishing guilt or innocence. It is a win-win situation in the search for justice. A publication by the National Institute of Justice, "Eyewitness Evidence: A Guide for Law Enforcement," summarizes efforts to improve DNA technology in the fight against crime:

◆ "The development of 'DNA chip technology' that uses nanotechnology to improve both speed and resolution of DNA evidence analysis. This technology will reduce analysis time from several hours to several minutes and provide cost-effective miniaturized components.

HIGHLIGHT What Is CODIS?

"CODIS (Combined DNA Index System), is an electronic database of DNA profiles that can identify suspects, similar to the AFIS (Automated Fingerprint Identification System) database. Every State in the Nation is in the process of implementing a DNA index of individuals convicted of certain crimes, such as rape, murder, and child abuse. Upon conviction and sample analysis, perpetrators' DNA profiles are entered into the DNA database. Just as fingerprints found at a crime scene can be run through AFIS in search of a suspect or link to another crime scene, DNA profiles from a crime scene can be entered into CODIS. Therefore, law enforcement officers have the ability to identify possible suspects when no prior suspect existed."

Source: National Institute of Justice, "What Every Law Enforcement Officer Should Know about DNA Evidence," *http://www.ncjrs.gov/nij/DNAbro/ id.html.*

- "The development of more robust methods to enable more crime labs to have greater success in the analysis of degraded, old, or compromised items of biological evidence.
- "Advanced applications of various DNA analysis methods, such as Short Tandem Repeats (STRs), Single Nucleotide Polymorphisms (SNPs), mitochondrial DNA analysis (mtDNA), and Y-chromosome DNA analysis.
- "The use of animal, plant, and microbial DNA to provide leads that may link DNA found on or near human perpetrators or victims to the actual perpetrator of the crime.
- "Technologies that will enable DNA identification of vast numbers of samples occasioned by a mass disaster or mass fatality incident.
- "Technologies that permit better separation of minute traces of male sexual assailant DNA from female victims."[17]

DNA testing is doubtless an effective instrument in the search for justice, both for the state and for the wrongfully accused or convicted. Its potential for crime solving is still unfolding, but its effects are already dramatic. Future years will see the effectiveness of DNA testing enhanced and its use become more common. Those changes bode well for the police and defendants in their common quest for evidence that truly serves the ends of justice.

Polygraph Examinations

In contrast to the universal admissibility of DNA evidence, most courts refuse to admit the results of polygraph (more popularly known as "lie detector") tests in either civil or criminal proceedings. The only exception is if admissibility is agreed to by both parties. The reliability of polygraphs is questionable, particularly when the test is administered by an unqualified operator. In the words of one observer, "Polygraphy is very

---

HIGHLIGHT   **New DNA Uses for the Fight against Crime**

A 2011 *Time* article, "Are Familial DNA Searches a Brilliant Tool for Solving Crimes or a Dangerous Abuse of Privacy?" tells of a murder, twenty-three years earlier, where detectives identified a suspect using familial DNA searching. The article says that this type of search "enables cops, under certain circumstances, to track down a suspect by cross-referencing a DNA sample from a parent, sibling or child, often without the relative's knowledge." The test has been used in the United Kingdom for nearly a decade and holds great potential for solving crimes in the United States. The article adds, however, that it also raises important individual privacy issues.*

DNA testing has also found a niche as a crime-solving tool in crimes other than rape or murder. An article in the *Houston Chronicle*, titled "DNA: It's Not Just for Homicides Anymore," tells how DNA tests are also now being used by many police departments to solve property crimes through

"touch DNA." The article describes a burglary where all it took to solve was a cigarette butt found in the burglarized home of a nonsmoker. The evidence was sent to the crime lab and it found a DNA match to a husband-and-wife team. DNA tests can also be performed on "evidence containing either skin cells or bodily fluids, like blood and saliva—from property crime cases such as car break-ins and home invasions." The downside, states the article, is that such DNA use for property crimes would require an upgrade of the city's DNA testing facility, which would cost millions of dollars. On the positive side, the article states that after a "match" is found, the likelihood that the accused would plead guilty goes way up, thus saving the county a lot of money.†

Time, December 5, 2011, pp. 41–45.
†*Houston Chronicle*, December 7, 2009, p. B1.

different from other scientific evidence. It is in essence the opinion of the polygrapher. The underlying scientific basis for polygraphy has always been the subject of heated controversy."[18] Despite progress in technology, most courts still consider it "junk science" because of its lack of reliability.

Aside from the problem of unqualified operators, many scholars believe that people who are adept at deception or who have convinced themselves that they are telling the truth can "beat" the polygraph. After interviewing polygraph experts from the CIA, FBI, and other agencies, a committee of the National Academy of Sciences has concluded that "it is possible to fool a lie detector, especially if the subject is being screened for general criminal or spy activity and not for some specific act."[19]

Frye v. United States (1923)

Frye doctrine
for scientific evidence to be admissible at trial, the procedures used must be sufficiently established to have gained general acceptance in the particular field to which they belong.

Polygraph results fail to conform to the **Frye doctrine** and are therefore inadmissible as evidence in court. This doctrine, enunciated in *Frye v. United States*, 293 F. 1013 (D.C. Cir. 1923), states that, before the results of scientific tests will be admissible as evidence in a trial, the procedures used must be sufficiently established to have gained general acceptance in the particular field to which they belong. Although some states, by case law or statute, have abandoned the *Frye* doctrine in favor of more liberal rules, it is still the test used in most states.

By contrast, the Court has held that in federal cases, the *Frye* doctrine has been replaced by the adoption of the Federal Rules of Evidence, Rule 702, which provides, in part:

> **A.** Witness qualified as an expert by knowledge, skill, experience, training, or education, may testify thereto in the form of an opinion or otherwise, if:
> 1. the testimony is based upon sufficient facts or data,
> 2. the testimony is the product of reliable principles and methods, and
> 3. the witness has applied the principles and methods reliably to the facts of the case.

Daubert doctrine
allows the admission in court of expert testimony pertaining to scientific, technical, or other specialized knowledge that will assist the trier of fact to understand the evidence or to determine a fact in issue.

These rules embody the **Daubert doctrine**, which allows the admission in court of expert testimony pertaining to "scientific, technical, or other specialized knowledge" that will "assist the trier of fact to understand the evidence or to determine a fact in issue" (*Daubert v. Merrell Dow Pharmaceuticals, Inc.*, 509 U.S. 579 [1993]). It is clearly an easier test to meet than the *Frye* test. In federal courts, the admissibility of polygraph results is now left to the discretion of the trial court judge. This is not true in most state courts, where strict rules prohibit the admission into evidence of polygraph results. Moreover, some states by law prohibit the polygraph examination of a complainant by the police for any complaint.

Daubert v. Merrell Dow Pharmaceuticals, Inc. (1993)

United States v. Scheffer (1998)

In *United States v. Scheffer*, 523 U.S. 303 (1998), the Court held that a prohibition against the admissibility in court of polygraph evidence in favor of a defendant does not violate his or her constitutional right to present a defense. In that case, the results of a polygraph examination of an airman indicated that there was no deception in his denial that he used drugs. He sought to introduce that evidence to help exonerate himself, but military rules of evidence prohibited the admission of polygraph evidence in court-martial proceedings. Convicted of using drugs, the airman appealed, claiming that excluding the exonerating polygraph evidence violated his constitutional right to present a defense.

The Court disagreed, holding that there was no violation of Scheffer's constitutional right. Significantly, the Court assessed the state of polygraph evidence reliability as follows:

To this day, the scientific community remains extremely polarized about the reliability of polygraph techniques. Some studies have concluded that polygraph tests overall are accurate and reliable. Others have found that polygraph tests assess truthfulness significantly less accurately—that scientific field studies suggest the accuracy rate of the "control question technique" polygraph is "little better than could be obtained by the toss of a coin," that is, 50 percent. This lack of scientific consensus is reflected in the disagreement among state and federal courts concerning both the admissibility and reliability of polygraph evidence.

The Office of Technology Assessment has stated that "there is at present only limited scientific evidence for establishing the validity of polygraph testing." It also stated that its review of twenty-four relevant studies meeting minimal acceptable scientific criteria found that correct detections ranged from about 35 to 100 percent.[20] The mathematical chance of misidentification is highest when the polygraph is used for screening purposes. In the words of one writer:

> Departmental policy should recognize that [the] polygraph is not a perfect investigative process and that polygraph results, both examiner opinions following chart evaluation and [even] confessions and admissions obtained from examinees, are subject to error. Therefore, results should be considered in the context of a complete investigation. They should not be relied upon to the exclusion of other evidence or used as the sole means of resolving questions of verity.[21]

Even if reliability were to increase in the near future, polygraph tests might still find limited use in criminal proceedings because of objections based on self-incrimination. It can be argued, with some justification, that forcing a person to take a polygraph examination and using the results against the person would violate the right to protection against compulsory self-incrimination because the nature of the examination is testimonial or communicative instead of real or physical. Issues pertaining to the right to counsel and due process might also arise, but chances of their being upheld in court probably would be minimal.

Breathalyzer Tests

All states and the District of Columbia have laws against drunk driving that make it a crime to drive with a blood alcohol concentration (BAC) at a prohibited level of 0.08 percent or above. One publication describes how Breathalyzer test results are used in criminal prosecutions:

> The breath alcohol reading is used in criminal prosecutions in two ways. Unless the suspect refuses to submit to chemical testing, he will be charged with a violation of the illegal *per se* law: that is, it is a misdemeanor throughout the United States to drive a vehicle with a BAC of .08% or higher. . . . While BAC tests are not necessary to prove a defendant was under the influence, laws in most states require the jury to presume that he was under the influence if his BAC was over .08% when driving. This is a rebuttable presumption, however [meaning it can be overcome by evidence to the contrary]: the jury can disregard the test if they find it unreliable or if other evidence establishes a reasonable doubt.[22]

There are various consequences for drunk-driving violations, including incarceration, forfeiture of vehicles that are driven while the driver is impaired by alcohol use, and license suspension. Forty-three states and Washington, D.C., also have laws prohibiting the possession by drivers or passengers of open containers of alcohol in the

HIGHLIGHT ▷ A Comparison of the *Frye* and the *Daubert* Doctrines for Admissibility in Court of Scientific Testimony

Similarities

Both doctrines are based on court rulings. The *Frye* doctrine was laid out by a federal court of appeals in 1923; the *Daubert* doctrine was enunciated by the U.S. Supreme Court in a federal case in 1993. Both have since been enacted into law for use in state *(Frye)* or federal *(Daubert)* courts.

Differences

Frye Doctrine	*Daubert* Doctrine
◆ Allows the admission in court of expert scientific testimony if the procedures used are sufficiently established to have gained acceptance in the particular field to which they belong	◆ Allows the admission in court of expert scientific testimony if it will assist the trier of fact to understand the evidence or to determine a fact in issue
◆ Focus of the standard is acceptance by peers in that field	◆ Focus of the standard is whether it will help the judge or jury determine and understand the facts in the case
◆ A strict standard for admission of scientific evidence in court	◆ A liberal standard for admission of scientific evidence in court
◆ Used in most state courts	◆ Used in federal courts and some state courts

passenger compartment of a motor vehicle.[23] Most jurisdictions suspend the driver's license if the suspect refuses to submit to a Breathalyzer test.

The results of Breathalyzer tests have been challenged based on scientific inaccuracy caused by improperly calibrated equipment or poorly trained officers. Some states have strict rules and procedures governing the use and administration of Breathalyzer tests, and adherence to these prescribed rules and procedures is mandatory. In one case, the Supreme Court of Ohio ruled that "tests of breath, blood or urine for alcohol content must closely comply with state regulations designed to minimize errors."[24]

In sum, the reliability of Breathalyzer tests has long been recognized in courts, but legal issues persist about the fairness of their administration and adherence to procedures prescribed by state law.

Handwriting Samples

Courts have consistently ruled that obtaining handwriting samples for use in criminal prosecutions does not violate a suspect's right against self-incrimination under the Fifth Amendment. In *Gilbert v. California*, 388 U.S. 263 (1967) (discussed earlier in this chapter), the Court held that the admission of a handwriting sample did not violate the Fifth Amendment. In that case, the Court cited a previous ruling in *Schmerber v. California*, 384 U.S. 757 (1966), which held that "the Fifth Amendment offers no protection against compulsion to submit to fingerprinting, photographing, or measurements, to write or to speak for identification, to appear in court, to stand, to assume a stance, or to make a particular gesture." This is because the right against self-incrimination prohibits the admission of testimonial evidence but does not prohibit the incriminatory use of physical evidence. In a later case, *United States v. Mara*, 410 U.S. 19 (1973), the Court declared: "Handwriting, like speech, is repeatedly shown to the public and there is no more expectation of privacy in the physical characteristics of a person's script than there is in the tone of his voice."

United States v. Mara (1973)

In sum, obtaining a handwriting sample from a suspect is constitutional because handwriting is considered public. Consent for obtaining it is advisable but is not a requirement for its admissibility as evidence in court.

Hair Samples

Hair samples are used with more frequency in criminal prosecutions to prove guilt. One advantage of using hair samples is that it keeps information (such as drug use) for a long period of time. Court cases have arisen questioning the constitutionality of this use. In *Coddington v. Evanko* (2005), the U.S. Court of Appeals for the Third Circuit held that law enforcement officers may shave large amounts of hair from a suspect's head, neck, and shoulders, without a warrant, probable cause, or any basis for suspecting that the hair would provide evidence of crime."[25]

Coddington v. Evanko (2005)

In *Coddington*, the Pennsylvania state trooper's hair was cut by his superiors because they had received confidential information of Coddington's cocaine use. They cut the hair from Coddington's "head, neck, and a small section in the area of his left shoulder blade." Additional hair was taken from Coddington while he was in the home of a retired state police trooper by the retired trooper's wife, a retired beautician. Test results from the hair samples did not show any evidence of cocaine use or use of any other illegal drugs. Coddington sued his superiors, claiming a violation of his constitutional rights against unreasonable searches and seizures and his right to privacy. His lawsuit was dismissed.

He appealed to the federal Third Circuit Court of Appeals, which upheld the dismissal, saying that "the only hair that was taken was above the body surface and on public display, and that hair was taken in [a] proper manner." This ruling followed a 1982 decision from the same court that held that "taking hair samples from visible parts of a suspect's body does not invade any reasonable expectation of privacy," and therefore does not amount to a Fourth Amendment search.[26]

Although held by courts as valid, one source recommends that "sample collection should be performed by a responsible authority respecting the legal, ethical and human rights of the person to be tested for drugs of abuse. Hair samples should be obtained in a non–drug-contaminated environment by an appropriately trained individual, not necessarily a physician. A sufficient amount of sample should be collected so that a repeat analysis or a confirmation analysis by another laboratory can be performed should it be needed."[27]

Brain Fingerprinting

Brain fingerprinting is a new and controversial tool in solving crimes. The technique was invented by Lawrence Farwell, a neuroscientist trained at the University of Illinois. It is characterized as "a real-time psycho-physiological assessment of a subject's response to stimuli in the form of words or pictures presented on a computer monitor. As a forensic method, the test assesses the subject's knowledge of a crime scene or of the instrumentalities or fruits of a crime, and it can also be used to assess knowledge of the particulars of an alibi scene or sequence of events."[28]

brain fingerprinting assesses a suspect's response to stimuli in the form of words or pictures presented on a computer monitor.

Although it does not claim to prove the suspect's guilt or innocence, brain fingerprinting supposedly provides "extremely strong scientific evidence that the record of the time of the crime stored in the suspect's brain does or does not contain the salient facts about the crime, and does or does not contain the salient facts about the alibi."[29] It has generated national attention for possible use in crime detection, such as whether a person has been trained as a terrorist and other events that have effects on a person's memory. At least one state court has ruled that brain fingerprinting results are admissible in court. But a recent study by J. Rosenfeld of Northwestern University suggests that "in the presence of learned countermeasures, the wider class of P300-based tests, which includes the brain fingerprinting technique, may give results close to those obtained by chance."[30] This form of evidence is still new, and its admissibility will continue to be tested in court based on the *Frye* or the *Daubert* standard.

Facial Recognition Technology

facial recognition technology
a way of identifying suspects by comparing drivers license photos with pictures of convicts in a high-tech analysis of chin widths and nose sizes.

Facial recognition technology is a way of identifying suspects by "comparing driver's license photos with pictures of convicts in a high-tech analysis of chin widths and nose sizes." Still in its early stages, it is now used by the FBI to search for and identify fugitives. This approach relies on biometric information that is unique to each person. Such biometrics include fingerprints and DNA. Other possible sources are iris patterns in the eye, voices, scent, and the way a person walks.

One publication describes the complex technology this way:

> Some facial recognition algorithms identify faces by extracting landmarks, or features, from an image of the subject's face. For example, an algorithm may analyze the relative position, size, and/or shape of the eyes, nose, cheekbones, and jaw. These features are then used to search for other images with matching features. Other algorithms normalize a gallery of face images and then compress the face data, only saving the data in the image that is useful for face detection. A probe image is then compared with the face data.[31]

Although the technology is still new, it has found limited use in other countries and in some agencies in the United States, particularly the U.S. Department of State. Whether the evidence obtained can be used by the police in court is an issue that is yet to be addressed by the courts. As in all cases of scientific means of identification, admissibility will be determined based on the *Frye* or *Daubert* legal tests.

SUMMARY

Lineups

- A lineup is a police identification procedure in which the suspect in a crime is exhibited, along with others with similar physical characteristics, before the victim or witness to determine if the suspect committed the offense.
- The right to counsel applies after a formal charge has been filed but not before.

- The role of a lawyer during a lineup is to make sure the procedure is fair, but the lawyer must not be allowed to control the proceedings.
- The right to due process applies and is violated if the identification procedure is impermissibly suggestive.

- The right to protection against unreasonable searches and seizures does not apply.
- The right to protection against self-incrimination does not apply, because the self-incrimination involved is physical, not testimonial.

Showups

- A showup is one-to-one confrontation between a suspect and a witness to a crime.
- The right to counsel applies after a formal charge has been filed but not before.
- The right to due process applies and is violated if the identification procedure is impermissibly suggestive.
- The right to protection against unreasonable searches and seizures does not apply.
- The right to protection against self-incrimination does not apply, because the self-incrimination involved is physical, not testimonial.

Photographic Identifications

- A photographic identification is a process in which a victim or witness is shown photographs of possible suspects in a one-on-one situation.
- The right to counsel does not apply.
- The right to due process applies and is violated if the identification procedure is impermissibly suggestive.
- The right to protection against unreasonable searches and seizures does not apply.
- The right to protection against self-incrimination does not apply, because the self-incrimination involved is physical, not testimonial.
- Lineups and eyewitness identifications are controversial because they are "hopelessly unreliable."
- A lot of changes are being made to lineups and eyewitness identification procedures.
- Other means of pretrial identification and their admissibility in court include the following:
  - DNA testing—results admissible
  - Polygraph examination—results not admissible
  - Breathalyzer tests—results admissible
  - Handwriting samples—results admissible
  - Hair samples—results admissible
  - Brain fingerprinting—too early to tell
  - Facial recognition technology—too early to tell

REVIEW QUESTIONS

1. What four constitutional rights are likely to be invoked by suspects during the pretrial identification stage? Briefly discuss how each applies to lineups, showups, and photographic displays.
2. "A suspect is entitled to a lawyer during a police lineup." Is this statement true or false? Explain your answer.
3. "A suspect's right to protection against self-incrimination is violated in a police lineup." Is this statement true or false? Justify your answer.
4. What can the police do if a suspect refuses to appear in a lineup?
5. "A suspect is entitled to counsel during a lineup." Is this statement true or false? Discuss your answer.
6. Discuss what is wrong with eyewitness identification.
7. Discuss current efforts to change the way the police conduct lineups.
8. What is DNA testing? Why are DNA test results admissible as evidence in court?
9. Discuss the impact of DNA testing on prosecutions and defendants. Which side has benefited more from DNA technology?
10. Distinguish between the *Frye* and the *Daubert* doctrines as tests of the admissibility in court of scientific evidence. Which test would a defense lawyer want the trial court to use, and why? Would the answer be the same for the prosecutor? Explain.
11. Discuss why the results of polygraph examinations are not admissible in most courts.
12. Are the results of Breathalyzer tests admissible in court? Briefly summarize the rules in various states on drunk driving.
13. What is brain fingerprinting? Are brain fingerprinting results admissible in court? Why or why not?

TEST YOUR UNDERSTANDING

1. Suspect Joe was arrested by the police in downtown San Francisco. He was charged with robbery. He asked for a lawyer and was given a

public defender. A week later, Joe was made to appear in a police lineup. He refused, saying that he would do so only if his lawyer was present during the lineup. He further objected to the lineup on the grounds that it would violate his constitutional right to due process and protection against self-incrimination and that it was also a violation of his Fourth Amendment right against unreasonable searches and seizures. You are the judge in the case. Will you uphold or reject Joe's allegations? Analyze each allegation and give reasons for your decision.

2. Assume you are a suspect and are made to appear in a police lineup. You are suspected of a sexual assault allegedly committed by "a Hispanic who was about 5 feet 8, wore jeans, and spoke with an accent." You are Hispanic, about 5 feet 10, and one of three Hispanics of similar height in the lineup. All three of you speak with an accent; all three of you are wearing jeans. You are identified by the victim after you are made to repeat the statement "I will kill you if you shout." Were your constitutional rights violated, and if so, what specific right(s)? Support your answer.

3. Assume you are a lawyer who has a client against whom a charge for rape has been filed. You are later informed that the police have the DNA results of some epithelial (skin) cells found on the victim's clothes, and this evidence matches your client's DNA, which was obtained—against his strenuous objections—while he was arrested and held in detention for a few hours in the local jail. The police obtained your client's DNA pursuant to state law, which provides that "all persons arrested for any offense must be subjected to DNA testing." State all possible arguments you can use in court to challenge the case against your client. Given these facts, would you advise your client to plead guilty? Justify your response.

4. A defendant in a rape case (six feet tall, Asian, 170 pounds in weight, and 18 years old) is placed by the police in a traditional police lineup, meaning a simultaneous instead of a sequential lineup. Five other people are in the lineup, all male: a Hispanic who is 40 years old and 5 feet 5 inches in height, another Asian who is 17 years old and 150 pounds in weight, a black male who is 20 years

old and 6 feet 2 inches tall, a white person who is 30 years old and 5 feet 7 inches tall, and another white person who is 35 years old, and weighs around 120 pounds. The defendant was identified by the victim in this lineup. Assume you are a lawyer for the defendant. You challenge the lineup composition on appeal, saying it is unfair to your client. Do you think your challenge will succeed? Justify your response.

5. Assume you are defending a murder suspect whose DNA was found, along with those of other suspects, in a crime scene. The primary evidence against your client is the DNA recovered from the crime scene, along with that of others. The others were acquitted during trial because one witness testified to not seeing them at the crime scene and the evidence at trial was inconclusive as to them. In your client's case, however, a former girlfriend testified that she was in the same house when the crime took place and that your client did it. Your client is convicted. Assume you are convinced that a new DNA test will show that your client could not have committed the murder and that somebody else did it. On appeal, you ask for a retest of the DNA, but the appellate court turns you down. Will you have a strong case if you appeal to the U.S. Supreme Court? State your reasons.

RECOMMENDED READINGS

James M. Doyle. *True Witness: Cops, Courts, Science, and the Battle against Misidentification*. New York: Palgrave Macmillan (2005).

Christopher Domin. Mitigating evidence? The admissibility of polygraph results in the penalty phase of a capital trial. *UC Davis Law Review* 2010/04/01, vol. 43, p. 1461.

Brandon L. Garrett, *Convicting the Innocent: Where Criminal Prosecutions Go Wrong*. Harvard University Press, Cambridge, MA. (2011).

Technical Working Group for Eyewitness Evidence. *Eyewitness Evidence: A Guide for Law Enforcement*. National Institute of Justice, U.S. Department of Justice, NCJ 178240.

Sandra Guerra Thompson. Eyewitness identifications and state courts as guardians against wrongful conviction. *The Ohio State Journal of Criminal Law*, vol. 7, p. 603 (2010).

What Every Law Enforcement Officer Should Know about DNA Evidence. National Institute of Justice, U.S. Department of Justice, *http://www.ncjrs.gov/pdffiles1/nij/bc000614.pdf.*

NOTES

1. Henry C. Black, *Black's Law Dictionary*, 6th ed., abridged (St. Paul, MN: West, 1991), p. 641.
2. Larry Rissler, "The Role of Defense Counsel at Lineups," *FBI Law Enforcement Bulletin*, February 1980, p. 24.
3. *Wisconsin v. Dubose*, 205 WI 126 (No. 2003AP1690-CR [2005]).
4. Technical Working Group for Eyewitness Evidence, "Eyewitness Evidence: A Guide for Law Enforcement," National Institute of Justice, U.S. Department of Justice, October 1999, *http://www.ncjrs.gov/txtfiles1/nij/178240.txt.*
5. John Turtle, R. C. L. Lindsay, and Gary L. Wells, "Best Practice Recommendations for Eyewitness Evidence Procedures: New Ideas for the Oldest Way to Solve a Case," *Canadian Journal of Police & Security Services* 1(1): March 2003, p. 3.
6. Dara McLeod, "Problems with Police Lineups," *Virginia Lawyers' Weekly*, *http://www.vachiefs.org/vacp/news/2005-02-8.html.*
7. "Police Lineup Methods Often Flawed, Experts Say," *Miami Herald*, August 4, 2005.
8. Brandon L. Garrett, *Convicting the Innocent* (Harvard University Press, 2011), p. 252.
9. Benjamin Weiser, "In New Jersey, Rules Are Changed on Witness IDs," *The New York Times*, August 24, 2011, p. 11.
10. Available electronically at *http://www.ncjrs.gov/txtfiles1/nij/178240.txt.*
11. National Institute of Justice, U.S. Department of Justice, "What Every Law Enforcement Officer Should Know about DNA Evidence," *http://www.ncjrs.gov/pdffiles1/nij/bc000614.pdf.*
12. *Houston Chronicle*, August 8, 1992, p. A3.
13. "Courtroom Genetics," *U.S. News & World Report*, January 27, 1992, pp. 60–61.
14. *New York Times*, April 15, 1992, p. 1.
15. "Privacy v. Security, Special Edition: Criminal Justice," *Time Magazine* (1), p. 4.
16. Seth Axelrad, "Survey of State DNA Database Statutes," ASLME (American Society of Law, Medicine and Ethics), *www.aslme.org/dna_04/grid/guide.pdf.*
17. Supra note 16.
18. U.S. Deputy Solicitor General Michael Dreeben, as quoted in the *Houston Chronicle*, November 4, 1997, p. A9.
19. *Houston Chronicle*, October 9, 2002, p. 15A.
20. *Houston Chronicle*, November 23, 1985, sec. 3, p. 1.
21. R. Ferguson, "Polygraph Policy for Model Law Enforcement." *FBI Law Enforcement Bulletin*, July 1987, p. 7.
22. "Breathalyzer," Wikipedia entry, *http://en.wikipedia.org/wiki/Breathalyzer.*
23. "DWI/DUI Laws of U.S. States," Alcohol: Problems and Solutions, *http://www2.potsdam.edu/hansondj/DrivingIssues/1104284869.html.*
24. "DUI Tests Must Now Be Accurate," Alcohol: Problems and Solutions, *http://www2.potsdam.edu/hansondj/InTheNews/DrinkingAndDriving/1070544548.html.*
25. *Coddington v. Evanko*, 112 Fed. App. 835 (C.A. 3rd, 2004).
26. Ibid.
27. "Statement of the Society of Hair Testing Concerning the Examination of Drugs in Human Hair," *http://www.soht.org/html/Statements.html.*
28. "Brain Fingerprinting Testing in the Case of *Harrington v. State*," *http://www.brainwavescience.com/LegalIssuesin-Admissibility.php.*
29. "Brain Fingerprinting Testing Ruled Admissible in Court," *http://www.brainwavescience.com/Ruled%20Admissable.php.*
30. "Brain Fingerprinting," Wikipedia entry, *http://en.wikipedia.org/wiki/Brain_fingerprinting.*
31. "Facial Recognition System," Wikipedia, http://en.wikipedia.org/wiki/Facial_recognition_system

CHAPTER 11

Confessions and Admissions:
Miranda v. Arizona

LEARNING OBJECTIVES

1. Differentiate between admission and confession.
2. Explain how *Miranda v. Arizona* changed the rules of admissibility to the "three question test."
3. Determine, when given a scenario, whether the *Miranda* warning should be advised and why.
4. Discuss the elements of the *Miranda* warning.
5. Analyze the *Miranda* warning and determine the constitutional origin for the rights within the warning.
6. Define the legal concept of custodial interrogation and determine what constitutes custody and interrogation.
7. Explain the "three question test" of *Miranda*.
8. Understand that the Supreme Court requires waivers to the *Miranda* warning must be intelligent and voluntary; the student will define those terms.
9. Explain the effect of *Edwards v. Arizona* upon questioning by law enforcement.
10. Describe the legal development of the *Miranda* warning from original decision to present-day application.

KEY TERMS

admission

collateral derivative evidence

confession

custodial interrogation

custody

deprived of freedom in a significant way

Edwards rule

functional equivalent of an interrogation

general on-the-scene questioning

harmless error rule

intelligent waiver

interrogation

Miranda rule

Mirandized

public safety exception

voluntary statement

voluntary waiver

volunteered statement

waiver

THE TOP 5 IMPORTANT CASES

in Confessions and Admissions: *Miranda v. Arizona*

■ *MIRANDA V. ARIZONA* (1966) Law enforcement officers must give suspects the following warnings whenever there is a custodial interrogation: (1) You have a right to remain silent. (2) Anything you say can be used against you in a court of law. (3) You have a right to the presence of an attorney. (4) If you cannot afford an attorney, one will be appointed for you prior to questioning. (5) You may terminate this interview at any time.

■ *EDWARDS V. ARIZONA* (1981) Once the suspect has invoked the right to remain silent, the suspect cannot be questioned again about the same offense unless he or she initiates further communication, exchanges, or conversations with the police.

■ *BERKEMER V. MCCARTY* (1984) A person subjected to custodial interrogation must be given the *Miranda* warnings regardless of the nature or severity of the offense. Exception: The roadside questioning of a motorist detained pursuant to a routine traffic stop does not constitute a custodial interrogation, so there is no need to give the *Miranda* warnings.

■ *ARIZONA V. FULMINANTE* (1991) The harmless error rule is applicable to cases on appeal involving confessions.

■ *DICKERSON V. UNITED STATES* (2000) *Miranda v. Arizona* governs the admissibility in federal and state courts of confessions and admissions given during a custodial interrogation by the police. The *Miranda* warnings are a constitutional rule; therefore, any law passed by Congress that overturns *Miranda* is unconstitutional.

THE FIFTH AMENDMENT to the U.S. Constitution provides that "no person shall . . . Be compelled in any criminal case to be a witness against himself, nor be deprived of life, liberty, or property, without due process of law." This right has been a source of controversy and has generated a host of issues, some of which are still unresolved. The main question is this: When are confessions and admissions admissible as evidence in a criminal trial, and when are they excludable? The answers are not simple, but this chapter's discussion should provide some insights.

One case stands out far above all other cases on the admissibility of confessions and admissions. That case is *Miranda v. Arizona*, 384 U.S. 436 (1966). *Miranda* is perhaps the best known criminal procedure decision ever issued by the Supreme Court, and it was and remains controversial. It is perhaps the only U.S. Supreme Court decision that has led to the creation of a new word, one that is widely used by police, prosecutors, defense lawyers, and judges: **Mirandized**, meaning that the suspect has

Miranda v. Arizona (1966)

Mirandized
a term used by law enforcement officers to indicate that the suspect has been given the *Miranda* warnings.

Miranda rule

evidence obtained by the police during custodial interrogations cannot be used in court during trial unless the defendant was first informed of the right not to incriminate himself or herself and the right to a lawyer.

been given the *Miranda* warnings. By the **Miranda rule** evidence obtained by the police during custodial interrogations cannot be used in court during trial unless the defendant was first informed of the right not to incriminate himself or herself and the right to a lawyer. (Mirandized), and unless that right was waived intelligently and voluntarily.

BEFORE *MIRANDA*

Before the *Miranda* decision, the only test for whether a confession was admissible into court was whether it was voluntary, based on a totality of the circumstances test. The problem was determining what constituted a *voluntary* confession?

Voluntary Confessions

Before the *Miranda* decision, the Supreme Court decided the admissibility of confessions and admissions on a case-by-case basis. The sole test was whether the confession was voluntary or involuntary, based on a totality of the circumstances. Voluntariness was determined by the courts based on whether the suspect's will was "broken" or "overborne" by the police during interrogation and taking into account all of the facts and circumstances in the case. This approach did not provide much guidance to the lower courts because the Supreme Court had failed to set any definitive guidelines by which the admissibility of confessions could be determined. In general, the Court held that confessions obtained by force or coercion could not be used in court; conversely, confessions were admissible if they were voluntary. *Voluntariness* was the standard used, but the meaning of that word was difficult to determine and changed over the years.

In criminal justice, a **confession** means that a person says he or she committed the act; an **admission** means that the person owns up to something related to the act but may not have committed it.

Originally, only confessions or statements obtained by physical force (such as beating, whipping, or maiming) were considered inadmissible. Later, courts recognized that coercion could be mental as well as physical. Even then, the hard question remained: At what point did physical or mental (psychological) coercion become so excessive as to render the confession involuntary? Clearly, physical torture was prohibited, but what about a push, a shove, a slap, or a mere threat? As for mental coercion, suppose the police did not physically abuse the suspect but simply detained him "until he talked"—was that coercion? If so, how long must the detention last before the confession could be considered coerced? A few hours? A day? A week?

confession

a person says he or she committed the act.

admission

a person admits to something related to the act but may not have committed it.

Four Cases Illustrating the Pre-*Miranda* Voluntariness Test

The following four cases, all decided prior to *Miranda*, give a glimpse into the evolution of the Court's rulings and illustrate the difficulty the Court faced in prescribing a clear criterion for the admissibility of confessions or statements before the *Miranda* decision. Each case was decided on the old voluntariness standard and under circumstances that could hardly be replicated in other cases. This led to confusing and conflicting

The terms *confession* and *admission* are often used as though they are interchangeable; they are not. A confession is more incriminating than an admission. Here are examples:

Confession: "Yes, I shot him."

Admission: "Yes, I was there, but I did not shoot him. I do not know who did."

If you are a prosecutor, you would prefer a confession. It makes your job easier.

If you are a defense lawyer, you would prefer that your client had made an admission, not a confession. That makes your job easier.

If you are the defendant, you would wish you did not give the police either a confession or an admission. Either way, you may be in trouble!

---

decisions in the lower courts, a confusion that was largely eliminated by the *Miranda* decision.

Coercion and Brutality—Confession Not Valid A deputy sheriff, accompanied by other persons, took a suspect (Brown) to a murder scene where he was questioned about the crime. Brown denied his guilt and was hanged by a rope from the limb of a tree for a period of time. He was then let down, after which he again denied his guilt. He was next tied to the tree and whipped, but he still refused to confess and was allowed to go home. Later Brown was seized again and whipped until he confessed.

The Court reversed the conviction and held that the confession was a product of utter coercion and brutality and thus violated the Fourteenth Amendment right to due process.

Deception—Confession Not Valid The defendant was suspected of murder in New York. About ten days after the murder, Spano telephoned a close friend who was a rookie police officer in the New York Police Department. Spano told his friend that he (Spano) had taken a terrific beating from the murder victim, and, because he was dazed, did not know what he was doing when he shot the victim. The officer relayed this information to his superiors. Spano was brought in for questioning, but his attorney advised him not to answer any questions. The department called in the rookie friend and told him to inform Spano that his telephone call had caused the officer a lot of trouble. The officer was instructed to win sympathy from Spano for the sake of the officer's wife and children. Spano initially refused to cooperate, but after his friend's fourth try, he finally agreed to tell the police about the shooting. Spano was convicted and appealed.

The Court said that the use of deception as a means of psychological pressure to induce a confession was a violation of the defendant's constitutional rights, and therefore the Court excluded the evidence.

Confession Not Voluntary—Confession Not Valid The defendant was charged with murder and found guilty by a jury. While in jail pending trial, Rogers was questioned about the killing. The interrogation started during the afternoon of the day of his arrest and continued through the evening. During the interrogation, Rogers was allowed to smoke and was given a sandwich and some coffee. At no time was he ever subjected to violence or threat of violence by the police. Six hours after the start of the interview,

Rogers still refused to give any information. The police then indicated that they were about to have Rogers's wife taken into custody, whereupon Rogers indicated his willingness to confess. The confession was introduced as evidence during the trial, and Rogers was convicted.

The Court held that the confession by Rogers was involuntary, and therefore not admissible, on the grounds that the accused did not have complete freedom of mind when making his confession.

Suspect Denied Counsel at the Police Station—Confession Not Valid Escobedo was arrested for murder and interrogated for several hours at the police station, during which time he was persuaded to confess. During the interrogation, Escobedo repeatedly asked to see his lawyer, who was also at the police station at that time and who demanded to see him. The police refused both requests and proceeded to interrogate Escobedo. He eventually confessed, was tried, and was convicted.

On appeal, the Court held that Escobedo was denied his right to counsel, so no statement taken during the interrogation could be admitted against him at the trial. The Court said that "where, as here, the investigation is no longer a general inquiry into the unsolved crime but has begun to focus on a particular suspect . . . no statement elicited by the police during the investigation may be used against him at a criminal trial."

Escobedo v. Illinois was an easy case for the Court to decide because the police had indeed grossly violated Escobedo's right to counsel. However, the *Escobedo* case left two issues unsettled: (1) Did the right to counsel apply only when the facts were similar to those in *Escobedo* (the suspect was accused of a serious offense, was being questioned at the police station, and had asked to see his lawyer, and the lawyer was present and demanded to confer with his client)? and (2) What did the Court mean when it said that the right to counsel could be invoked when the investigation had begun to "focus on a particular suspect"? Did this phrase refer to when a suspect was under investigation, had been arrested, had been charged with an offense, or had been arraigned? Because of its unique facts, the *Escobedo* case raised more questions than it answered. Trial courts disagreed on the meaning of *Escobedo*, particularly the interpretation of the term *focus*, leading to conflicting decisions. Further guidance from the Court became necessary. *Escobedo* therefore set the stage for *Miranda* and, in fact, made *Miranda* necessary because the confusion created in the lower courts by *Escobedo* had to be cleared up.

MIRANDA REJECTS VOLUNTARINESS AS THE SOLE TEST

In *Miranda*, the Court rejected voluntariness as the sole test to determine whether statements from suspects are admissible in court. Voluntariness is still required under *Miranda*, but it is assumed from a "yes" answer to all three questions the trial court must ask:

1. Were the *Miranda* warnings given?
2. If they were given, was there a waiver?
3. If there was a waiver, was it intelligent and voluntary?

Miranda, in effect, established a three-question test for admissibility.

1. If the statement was voluntary but the *Miranda* warnings were not given when they should have been (because there was a custodial interrogation), the evidence cannot be admitted in court.
2. Even if the statement was voluntary and the *Miranda* warnings were given, the statement is not admissible if the government cannot establish that there was a waiver.
3. If the statement was voluntary, the *Miranda* warnings were given, and there was a waiver, but the waiver was not intelligent and voluntary, the evidence obtained is not admissible in court.

The three tests can be illustrated as follows:

◆ *Question 1: Were the* Miranda *warnings given?* Example: Assume that after her arrest and in response to questions asked without the *Miranda* warnings, Suspect Alice gives the police a confession that is 100 percent voluntary. The evidence cannot be used in court because Alice was not given her *Miranda* warnings.
◆ *Question 2: If they were given, was there a waiver?* Example: Assume that Suspect Bob was given the *Miranda* warnings. However, the prosecutor could not prove in court that Bob in fact waived his rights prior to giving a confession. The evidence is not admissible.
◆ *Question 3: If there was a waiver, was it intelligent and voluntary?* Example: Assume that Suspect Jane gave a voluntary statement to the police after being given the *Miranda* warnings. During the trial, however, the prosecutor could not prove that Jane's waiver was intelligent and voluntary. The evidence is not admissible.

For judges, the importance of *Miranda* lies in the shift from the old voluntariness test to a new and clear standard that is easier to apply. Instead of determining voluntariness on a case-by-case basis, which took a lot of time, after *Miranda*, judges only need to ascertain the answers to the three questions. If the answers are yes to all three questions, then the evidence is admissible; conversely, if at least one of the answers is a no, the evidence is not admissible. Determining the admissibility of confessions or admissions based on *Miranda* is therefore easier and less time-consuming.

It must be emphasized that voluntariness is still a requirement for admissibility, but it is no longer the sole focus of the trial court's initial inquiry. Involuntary confessions are not admissible under *Miranda*, but voluntariness is assumed if the answers to the three questions are all yes. Trial courts no longer need to investigate specific facts in each case to determine if the statement was in fact voluntary.

The Court summarized these rules in *Missouri v. Seibert*, 542 U.S. 600 (2004), when it said:

Missouri v. Seibert (2004)

> *Miranda* conditioned the admissibility at trial of any custodial confession on warning a suspect of his rights; failure to give the prescribed warnings and obtain a waiver of rights before custodial questioning generally requires exclusion of any statements obtained. Conversely, giving the warnings and getting a waiver has generally produced a virtual ticket of admissibility.

THE BASICS OF *MIRANDA V. ARIZONA*

Although people are familiar with the words in the *Miranda* warnings, few know the details of the case that brought them into everyday law enforcement language. In this section, we look at the *Miranda* case, the warnings, the constitutional requirements, when *Miranda* warnings must be given, a comparison with the right to counsel, when the *Miranda* rights may be waived, and what is required to make a waiver stand up in court.

The Case

Miranda v. Arizona, 384 U.S. 436 (1966), decided by a narrow 5-to-4 vote, is undoubtedly the best-known and arguably the most significant law enforcement case ever decided by the U.S. Supreme Court. Because of its importance, the case deserves detailed discussion. We will look at the facts of the case, the legal issues, the Court's decision, and its significance.

The Facts Ernesto Miranda was arrested at his home in Phoenix, Arizona, and taken to a police station for questioning in connection with a rape and kidnapping. Miranda was then twenty-three years old, poor, and a ninth-grade dropout. The officers interrogated him for two hours, after which they emerged from the interrogation room with a written confession signed by Miranda. The confession was admitted as evidence during the trial. Miranda was convicted of rape and kidnapping and sentenced to twenty to thirty years imprisonment on each count. The Arizona Supreme Court affirmed the conviction; Miranda appealed to the U.S. Supreme Court.

The Legal Issues Must the police inform a suspect who is subject to a custodial interrogation of his or her constitutional rights involving self-incrimination and counsel prior to questioning for the evidence obtained to be admissible in court during the trial?

The Court's Decision Evidence obtained by the police during custodial interrogation of a suspect cannot be used in court during the trial unless the suspect was first informed of the right not to incriminate himself or herself and of the right to counsel. The Court said:

> We hold that when an individual is taken into custody or otherwise deprived of his freedom by the authorities and is subject to questioning, the privilege against self-incrimination is jeopardized. Procedural safeguards must be employed. . . . He must be warned prior to any questioning that he has a right to remain silent, that anything he says can be used against him in a court of law, that he has a right to the presence of an attorney, and that if he cannot afford an attorney one will be appointed for him prior to any questioning if he so desires. Opportunity to exercise these rights must be afforded to him throughout the interrogation.

***Miranda's* Significance** *Miranda v. Arizona* had a huge impact on day-to-day crime investigation. It drew a bright-line rule for admissibility of confessions and admissions and led to changes that have since become an accepted part of routine police work. No other law enforcement case initially generated more controversy within and outside police circles. Supporters of the *Miranda* decision hailed it as properly protective of individual rights, whereas critics accused the Court of being soft on crime and of coddling criminals.

The 5-to-4 split among the justices served to fan the flames of the controversy in its early stages, with opponents of the ruling hoping that a change in Court composition would hasten its demise. But that has not happened, nor is it likely to happen. The *Miranda* warnings, with variations, have been adopted in other countries and have in fact become a popular export of the U.S. criminal justice system.

Miranda is unusual because a Court decision seldom tells the police exactly what they should do. In *Miranda*, the Court did not simply say that a constitutional right was violated; it went further and prescribed in no uncertain terms what the police should do. In clear language, the Court mandated that a suspect "must be warned prior to any questioning that he has a right to remain silent, that anything he says can be used against him in a court of law, that he has a right to the presence of an attorney, and that if he cannot afford an attorney one will be appointed for him prior to any questioning if he so desires." Seldom has the Court been as specific in its instructions about what the police should do.

Miranda also clarified some of the ambiguous terms used in *Escobedo*. "By custodial interrogation," said the Court, "we mean questioning initiated by law enforcement officers after a person has been taken into custody or otherwise deprived of his freedom of action in any significant way." It then added this footnote: "This is what we meant in *Escobedo* when we spoke of an investigation which had focused on an accused." Yet the focus test used in *Escobedo* was abandoned by the Court in later cases; in its place, the custodial interrogation test was used to determine whether the *Miranda* warnings needed to be given. The *Escobedo* case *brought the right to counsel to the police station prior to trial*; the *Miranda* case went beyond the police station and *brought the right to counsel out into the streets* if custodial interrogation was to take place.

The *Miranda* Warnings

Miranda mandates that the following four warnings must be given to a suspect or accused prior to custodial interrogation:

- You have a right to remain silent.
- Anything you say can be used against you in a court of law.
- You have a right to the presence of an attorney.
- If you cannot afford an attorney, one will be appointed for you prior to questioning.

Almost all law enforcement departments in the United States add a fifth warning: "You have the right to terminate this interview at any time." This additional statement, however, is not constitutionally required under the *Miranda* decision.

Most police departments direct officers to issue the warnings as given here (taken directly from the *Miranda* decision). However, in some cases, warnings that are not worded exactly as given here may still comply with *Miranda*, provided the defendant is given adequate information concerning the right to remain silent and to have an attorney present. For example, in *Duckworth v. Eagan*, 492 U.S. 195 (1989), the police gave the following warnings: "You have a right to talk to a lawyer for advice before we ask you any questions, and to have him with you during questioning. You have the right to the advice and presence of a lawyer even if you cannot afford to hire one. We have no way of giving you a lawyer, but one will be appointed for you, if you wish, if and when you go to court." The last part of that warning—"if you wish, if and when you go to court"—was challenged as ambiguous and therefore inadequate.

Duckworth v. Eagan (1989)

The Court disagreed, saying that the warning, although ambiguous, was sufficient to inform the suspect of his rights. The Court added that this does not require that lawyers always be available. It is enough that the suspect is informed of his or her right to an attorney and to appointed counsel, and that, if the police cannot provide appointed counsel, they will not question the suspect until and unless there is a valid waiver. The Court also stated, "If the individual indicates in any manner any time prior to or during questioning that he wishes to remain silent, the interrogation must cease." If it does not cease, any information obtained by the police is not admissible as evidence in court unless the government can prove that the defendant knowingly and intelligently waived that right.

The ruling in *Duckworth* was reaffirmed by the Court twenty-one years later. In *Florida v. Powell* (559 U.S. — [2010]), the Court held that informing a suspect that he has a right to an attorney prior to questioning complies with the *Miranda* requirements. In that case, Powell was charged and convicted in Florida of being a felon in possession of a firearm. He was sentenced by a Florida state court to ten years in prison. On appeal, he argued that his *Miranda* warnings were invalid because the form used by the Tampa Police Department did not explicitly state that he had a right to an attorney during questioning. The Court disagreed, saying that *Miranda* "does not dictate the words in which the essential information must be conveyed. Rather, to determine whether police warnings are satisfactory, the inquiry is simply whether the warnings reasonably conveyed to a suspect his rights as required by *Miranda*." In sum, substantial conveyance rather than a word-by-word repetition of what the Court originally said in *Miranda* is all that is required.

Florida v. Powell (2010)

MYTH vs. REALITY

MYTH Police must give the *Miranda* warnings exactly as the Supreme Court specified.

FACT Police do not have to give the *Miranda* warnings verbatim but must provide warnings which adequately convey the four components of the *Miranda* warnings.

Miranda Required by the Constitution, Not Just by Judges

In what was described as the most serious challenge to the *Miranda* rule since the decision came out in 1966, a three-judge panel in the federal Court of Appeals for the Fourth Circuit held, in 1999, that voluntary confessions given without the *Miranda* warnings do not have to be excluded in federal court prosecutions and that congressional law overrules *Miranda* in federal courts. That ruling generated extensive publicity and was promptly appealed to the U.S. Supreme Court. The Court resolved the issue, holding that *Miranda v. Arizona* governs the admissibility in federal and state courts of confessions and admissions given during custodial interrogation by the police. Giving the *Miranda* warnings is required by the Constitution, and therefore any law passed by Congress that seeks to overturn the *Miranda* decision is unconstitutional (*Dickerson v. United States*, 530 U.S. 428 [2000]).

Dickerson v. United States (2000)

The facts in *Dickerson v. United States* (2000) are that Dickerson was arrested and made incriminating statements to police. Before his trial, he moved that the statements be suppressed because he had not received his *Miranda* warnings prior to being interrogated. His statements were voluntary, but they were made without having been given the *Miranda* warnings. The federal district court granted the motion to suppress, but the court of appeals overturned it, stating that 18 U.S.C. § 3501, passed by Congress in response to the *Miranda* decision, prevailed and only required a finding by a court that the confession was given voluntarily.

Note that 18 U.S.C. § 3501 was part of a law passed by Congress in 1966 right after the *Miranda* decision came out, but a ruling on the constitutionality of that law was never made by the U.S. Supreme Court because the law was not enforced by the federal government—until *Dickerson*. That law sought to overturn the Court decision in *Miranda* by providing that the admissibility of confessions and admissions in federal court is determined by whether or not they were made voluntarily, not by whether or not they complied with the *Miranda* warnings. Rejecting the constitutionality of

18 U.S.C. § 3501, the Court said: "In sum, we conclude that *Miranda* announced a constitutional rule that Congress may not supersede legislatively."

Dickerson is significant because it settled an important issue: Can the *Miranda* decision be overruled by laws passed by Congress or state legislatures? The Court answered that *Miranda* is not just a rule of evidence; therefore, it cannot be undone by legislation, as Congress had tried to do. Rather, it is a constitutional requirement and therefore only a constitutional amendment can do away with the *Miranda* warnings. Because of this decision, the *Miranda* warnings are here to stay unless the Court, in future years, changes its mind about their being required by the Constitution, or if there is a constitutional amendment. Had the decision been different, federal cases immediately would have been governed by the provisions of the federal law. Some state legislatures probably would have passed similar legislation, leading to the admissibility of confessions and admissions being governed by different rules. That would have signaled the end of *Miranda* as a rule for all police departments to follow.

Miranda Must Be Given for All Offenses Except Routine Traffic Stops

Should the *Miranda* warnings be given for all offenses or only for some? The Court answered this important question in *Berkemer v. McCarty*, 468 U.S. 420 (1984). The Court's answer can be summarized as follows:

Berkemer v. McCarty (1984)

- ◆ *The rule.* A person subjected to custodial interrogation must be given the *Miranda* warnings regardless of the nature or severity of the offense and whether the person goes to jail or not. This includes felonies, misdemeanors, and petty and traffic offenses.
- ◆ *The only exception.* The roadside questioning of a motorist detained pursuant to a routine traffic stop does not require the *Miranda* warnings.

Read the Case Brief to learn more about *Berkemer v. McCarty*.

Four years later, the Court reiterated the principle that the stop of a motorist for a traffic violation, although representing a Fourth Amendment seizure of the person, is not sufficiently custodial to require the *Miranda* warnings (*Pennsylvania v. Bruder*, 488 U.S. 9 [1988]). However, traffic offenses that involve more than roadside questioning pursuant to a routine traffic stop need the *Miranda* warnings. In general, the arrest of a driver in connection with a traffic offense triggers the *Miranda* warnings, because that no longer is a case of roadside questioning pursuant to a routine traffic stop.

Pennsylvania v. Bruder (1988)

These rules can be illustrated as follows:

- ◆ *Example 1.* Fred is stopped by an officer for driving while intoxicated. State law allows the officer to arrest the driver for this traffic offense, so he arrests Fred and takes him to the police station for booking. If the officer asks anything other than preliminary questions (such as name and address), Fred must be given the *Miranda* warnings. Otherwise, statements Fred makes will not be admissible in court.
- ◆ *Example 2.* Matt is stopped by an officer for failure to stop at a stop sign. The officer asks Matt questions and then issues a citation or releases Matt. The officer does not have to give Matt the *Miranda* warnings even if she asks Matt questions.

In sum, the *Miranda* warnings must be given when the suspect is interrogated for any type of offense—whether it is a felony, misdemeanor, or petty traffic offense. The only exception is roadside questioning of a motorist detained pursuant to a routine traffic stop.

CASE BRIEF

Berkemer v. McCarty,
468 U.S. 420 (1984)

The Leading Case on Types of Offenses That Require *Miranda* Warnings

Facts: After observing McCarty's car weaving in and out of a highway lane, Officer Williams of the Ohio State Highway Patrol forced McCarty to stop and get out of the car. Noticing that McCarty was having difficulty standing, the officer concluded that he would be charged with a traffic offense and would not be allowed to leave the scene, but McCarty was not told that he would be taken into custody. When McCarty could not perform a field sobriety test without falling, Officer Williams asked if he had been using intoxicants, whereupon McCarty replied that he had consumed two beers and had smoked marijuana a short time before. The officer then formally arrested McCarty and drove him to a county jail, where a blood test failed to detect any alcohol in his blood. Questioning was resumed, and McCarty again made incriminating statements, including an admission that he was "barely" under the influence of alcohol. At no point during this sequence was McCarty given the *Miranda* warnings. He was subsequently charged with operating a motor vehicle under the influence of alcohol and/or drugs, a misdemeanor under Ohio law. He pleaded "no contest" but later filed a writ of habeas corpus, alleging that the evidence obtained should not have been admitted in court.

Issue or Issues: *Was evidence obtained by the police without giving the suspect the Miranda warnings admissible in a prosecution for a misdemeanor offense?* No.

Holding: The Court decided that: (1) a person subjected to custodial interrogation must be given the *Miranda* warnings regardless of the nature or severity of the offense of which the person is suspected or for which he or she was arrested, but that (2) the roadside questioning of a motorist detained pursuant to a routine traffic stop does not constitute custodial interrogation, so there is no need to give the *Miranda* warnings.

Case Significance: This case settled two legal issues that had long divided lower courts. It is clear now that once a suspect has been placed under arrest for any offense, whether it is a felony or a misdemeanor, the *Miranda* warnings must be given before interrogation. This rule is easier for the police to follow than the requirement of determining if the arrest was for a felony or a misdemeanor before giving the warning. The Court

said that the purpose of the *Miranda* warnings, which is to ensure that the police do not coerce or trick captive suspects into confessing, is applicable equally to misdemeanor and felony cases.

The second part of the decision is equally important; it identifies a particular instance when the warnings do not need to be given. There is no custodial interrogation in a traffic stop because it is usually brief and the motorist expects that, although a citation may be forthcoming, in the end he or she will likely be allowed to continue on his or her way. However, if a motorist who has been detained is thereafter subjected to treatment that renders him or her "in custody" for practical purposes, then he or she is entitled to be given the *Miranda* warnings.

Excerpts from the Opinion: Two features of an ordinary traffic stop mitigate the danger that a person questioned will be induced "to speak where he would not otherwise do so freely." First, detention of a motorist pursuant to a traffic stop is presumptively temporary and brief. The vast majority of roadside detentions last only a few minutes. A motorist's expectations, when he sees a policeman's light flashing behind him, are that he will be obliged to spend a short period of time answering questions and waiting while the officer checks his license and registration, that he may then be given a citation, but that in the end he most likely will be allowed to continue on his way. In this respect, questioning incident to an ordinary traffic stop is quite different from stationhouse interrogation, which frequently is prolonged, and in which the detainee often is aware that questioning will continue until he provides his interrogators the answers they seek.

Second, circumstances associated with the typical traffic stop are not such that the motorist feels completely at the mercy of the police. To be sure, the aura of authority surrounding an armed, uniformed officer and the knowledge that the officer has some discretion in deciding whether to issue a citation, in combination, exert some pressure on the detainee to respond to questions. But other aspects of the situation substantially offset these forces. Perhaps most importantly, the typical traffic stop is public, at least to some degree. Passersby, on foot or in other cars, witness the interaction of officer and motorist. This exposure to public view both reduces the ability of an unscrupulous policeman to use illegitimate means to elicit self-incriminating statements and diminishes the motorist's fear that, if he does not cooperate, he will be subjected to abuse. In short, the atmosphere surrounding an ordinary traffic stop is substantially less "police dominated" than that surrounding the kinds of interrogation at issue in *Miranda* itself, and in the subsequent cases in which we have applied *Miranda*.

Distinguishing *Miranda* from the Right to Counsel

Although often associated with a suspect's right to counsel, *Miranda v. Arizona* is in fact based on the Fifth Amendment right to protection against self-incrimination, not on the Sixth Amendment right to counsel. *Miranda* warnings 1 and 2, as noted previously, protect the right not to incriminate oneself. Warnings 3 and 4 are right-to-counsel warnings, but they are there primarily to protect suspects against compulsory self-incrimination. In other words, a suspect is entitled to a lawyer during interrogation so that the right against self-incrimination may be protected. *Miranda* is but a small slice of the big right-to-counsel pie, although it is more often used in police work. Even if the proper *Miranda* warnings are given, the evidence is not admissible if the right to counsel under the Sixth Amendment is violated.

In *Massiah v. United States*, 377 U.S. 201 (1964), the Court held that incriminating statements are not admissible in court if the defendant was questioned without an attorney present after the defendant was charged with a crime and had obtained an attorney. This case was decided two years before *Miranda* (1966) but has since been reiterated by courts in subsequent cases involving the right to counsel.

Massiah v. United States (1964)

In a subsequent case, *United States v. Henry*, 447 U.S. 264 (1980), the Court held that the government violates a defendant's Sixth Amendment right to counsel by intentionally creating a situation likely to induce the accused to make incriminating statements without the presence of a lawyer. In *this* case, Henry was indicted for armed robbery. While he was in jail, government agents contacted one of his cell mates, who was an informant, and instructed him to be alert to any statements Henry made but not to initiate any conversations regarding the robbery. After the informant was released, he was contacted by the agents and paid for the information he provided concerning Henry's incriminating statements about the robbery. Convicted, Henry appealed, saying that the testimony of the informant should have been excluded. The Court agreed, holding the informant's testimony inadmissible. The Court believed it probable that the informant used his position to secure incriminating information and therefore probably acted beyond "mere listening" for information. The Court added that, although the government agent told the informant not to initiate any questioning of Henry, the agent must have known that the informant was likely to do so anyway. More important, in *Henry*, the basis for the appeal was a violation of the right to counsel, not the right to protection against self-incrimination—as was the case in *Miranda*.

United States v. Henry (1980)

In *Fellers v. United States*, 540 U.S. 519 (2004), the Court held that the proper standard to use when determining whether statements made by a defendant after an indictment are admissible in court is the Sixth Amendment right to counsel, not the Fifth Amendment right against self-incrimination. In this case, Fellers claimed that both his Sixth Amendment right to counsel and his Fifth Amendment *Miranda* rights were violated when the statements he made at his home and then later at the jail were used against him during the trial. Fellers was under indictment when both questionings took place. If his Fifth Amendment right against self-incrimination had been used as the

Fellers v. United States (2004)

standard for admissibility, then his statements while in jail would have been admissible because he was given the *Miranda* warnings and had waived his Fifth Amendment right before giving the confession. However, he claimed that the jail statement was inadmissible because it violated his Sixth Amendment right to counsel in that it was the fruit of an unlawful interrogation at his home (after indictment and when he had a lawyer) and therefore should have been excluded even if he was given the *Miranda* warnings.

The Court agreed, saying that in previous cases "this Court has consistently applied the deliberate-elicitation standard in subsequent Sixth Amendment cases . . . and has expressly distinguished it from the Fifth Amendment custodial-interrogation standard." Because the officers interrogated the defendant at his home without counsel after he had been indicted, the absence of his lawyer made his statement in his home inadmissible. His subsequent statement in jail was also inadmissible because it was fruit of the poisonous tree.

In cases involving confessions and admissions, the Fifth Amendment protection against compulsory self-incrimination and the Sixth Amendment right to counsel, although different, are closely intertwined. Giving the *Miranda* warnings may make the statement admissible under the Fifth Amendment right against self-incrimination, but that same statement may still be excluded under the Sixth Amendment right to counsel if the defendant, at the time of questioning, has been assigned or obtained a lawyer for his or her defense. Thus, in some cases, in addition to giving the *Miranda* warnings, the police must ascertain whether or not the suspect already has or has been assigned a lawyer for that case.

In sum, the *Miranda* warnings and the right to counsel are not one and the same right. Some cases primarily involve the *Miranda* warnings and are self-incrimination cases; others, like *Henry*, involve the right to counsel before or after indictment. The rule is that, after a suspect has obtained counsel and is in custody, interrogation about any offense that is likely to elicit incriminating answers—in the absence of a lawyer—violates the suspect's right to counsel.

Miranda May Be Waived Knowingly and Intelligently

In *Miranda*, the Court said, "After . . . warnings have been given, and such opportunity [to exercise these rights] afforded him, the individual may knowingly and intelligently

---

 **HIGHLIGHT** ❯ *Miranda* **Warnings and the Right to Counsel Compared**

Miranda Warnings	Right to Counsel
Come under the Fifth Amendment right against self-incrimination	Comes under the Sixth Amendment
Apply only during custodial interrogation	Applies in many proceedings—before trial, during trial, and during an appeal of a conviction
Given by the police	Lawyer is either retained by the suspect or assigned by a judge
Given in the absence of a lawyer	Once defendant has a lawyer, defendant cannot be questioned in the absence of a lawyer unless the right is waived
Must be given every time there is a custodial interrogation about any offense except routine traffic stops	Once given, is violated only if the interrogation deals with the same offense but not if it is about other offenses, even if closely related

waive these rights and agree to answer questions or make a statement." A **waiver** is an intentional giving up of a known right or remedy. The rights under *Miranda* may be waived expressly or implicitly, but the Court said that "a heavy burden rests on the government to demonstrate that the defendant knowingly and intelligently waived his privilege against self-incrimination and his right to retained or appointed counsel."

The following aspects of a valid waiver need further discussion:

◆ What is meant by an intelligent and voluntary waiver?
◆ Can a valid waiver be presumed from a suspect's silence after the warnings?
◆ Is a waiver "following the advice of God" valid?
◆ Is a waiver after a prolonged interruption valid?
◆ Is a waiver that a suspect has withdrawn valid?

What Is Meant by an Intelligent and Voluntary Waiver? The *Miranda* decision specifically states that the prosecution must prove that the defendant intelligently and voluntarily waived his or her right to silence and to counsel. An **intelligent waiver** means one given by a suspect who knows what he or she is doing and who is sufficiently competent to waive his or her rights. Intelligent waiver is difficult for the prosecution to prove in cases involving a suspect who is drunk, under the influence of drugs, is in a state of trauma or shock, is seriously injured, is senile, or is very young. There is no definite guidance from the courts in these cases; the best policy is for the police either to wait until the suspect's competency is restored (even if temporarily) or to be certain that the suspect understands the warnings.

A **voluntary waiver** is one that is not the result of any threat, force, or coercion and is made of the suspect's own free will. It is determined based on a totality of circumstances. In one case, a suspect in the killing of an undercover officer, who was in the intensive care unit of the hospital and under heavy sedation, was asked by the police if he had shot anyone. The suspect replied, "I can't say; I have to see a lawyer." The Court said that the statements obtained by the police were not "the product of his free and rational choice" and could not be used even for impeachment purposes (*Mincey v. Arizona*, 437 U.S. 385 [1978]). The Court added:

> It is hard to imagine a situation less conducive to the exercise of a "rational intellect and a free will" than Mincey's. He had been seriously wounded just a few hours earlier, and had arrived at the hospital "depressed almost to the point of coma," according to his attending physician. Although he had received some treatment, his condition at the time of . . . interrogation was still sufficiently serious that he was in the intensive care unit. He complained to [the detective] that the pain in his leg was "unbearable." He was evidently confused and unable to think clearly about the events of that afternoon or the circumstances of his interrogation, since some of his written answers were on their face not entirely coherent.

Moreover, the waiver must be shown on the record. Quoting from an earlier case, the Court in *Miranda* said, "Presuming waiver from a silent record is impermissible. The record must show, or there must be evidence which shows, that an accused was offered counsel but intelligently and understandingly rejected the offer. Anything less is not a waiver." The waiver does not have to be written or expressed, but it must be proved by the prosecution.

"Intelligent and Voluntary" Must Be Proved by Prosecution The Court in *Miranda* held that the prosecution has a "heavy burden . . . to demonstrate that the defendant knowingly

waiver
an intentional giving up of a known right or remedy.

intelligent waiver
one given by a suspect who knows what he or she is doing.

voluntary waiver
a waiver that is not the result of any threat, force, or coercion.

Mincey v. Arizona (1978)

and intelligently waived his privilege against self-incrimination and his right to a retained or appointed counsel." If that burden is not met, the evidence obtained is inadmissible even if it is voluntary. Although a written waiver is not constitutionally required, most police departments have a written waiver form that suspects are asked to sign. The written waiver may be a part of the written confession, either before or after the statement by the accused, or be attached to it. If witnesses to the waiver are available (such as police officers, other police personnel, or private persons), they may be asked to sign the waiver to strengthen the showing of voluntariness (see Figure 11.1). If the confession is typewritten, it is a good practice to have the defendant read it and, in his or her own handwriting, correct any errors. This procedure reinforces the claim of a valid waiver. In the absence of a written waiver, the issue boils down to the testimony of the suspect against the testimony of the police officer that the waiver was in fact voluntary. A written waiver makes the claim of voluntariness by the police more credible.

In juvenile cases, the waiver of rights is usually governed by state law. In many states, there is a minimum age below which a juvenile cannot waive his or her rights. In other states, the waiver is valid only if signed by a parent or guardian and/or signed in the presence of a lawyer.

Signed Waiver Not Required A signed waiver is not required. Refusal by the suspect to sign a waiver form does not necessarily mean that there is no valid waiver. The Court has said that "the question is not one of form but rather whether the defendant in fact knowingly and voluntarily waived the rights delineated in *Miranda*" (*North Carolina v. Butler*, 441 U.S. 369 [1979]). A written waiver, however, makes it easier to prove a valid waiver in court.

Express Waiver Not Required The failure to make an explicit statement regarding the waiver does not determine whether the evidence is admissible. Instead, the trial court must look at all the circumstances to determine whether a valid waiver in fact has been made. An express waiver, although easier to establish in court, is not required (*North Carolina v. Butler*, 441 U.S. 369 [1979]). The court will most likely take into account a variety of considerations, such as the age of the suspect, whether the suspect was alone with the officers at the time of interrogation or was in the presence of other people, the time of day, and the suspect's mental condition at the time of questioning.

Can a Valid Waiver Be Presumed from Suspect's Silence after the Warnings? No. The Court in *Miranda* said that a waiver cannot be presumed from silence after the defendant has been warned of his or her rights. The trial court cannot presume a waiver from the failure of the accused to complain after being given the warning or from the fact that the accused spoke with the police after the warnings were given (*Teague v. Louisiana*, 444 U.S. 469 [1980]). The Court has not decided authoritatively whether a nod or a shrug constitutes a valid waiver.

Is a Waiver "Following the Advice of God" Valid? Yes. The admissibility of statements made when the mental state of the suspect interferes with his or her "rational intellect" and "free will" is governed by state rules of evidence rather than by Supreme Court decisions on coerced confessions. Such statements are therefore not automatically excluded; admissibility instead depends on state rules (*Colorado v. Connelly*, 479 U.S. 157 [1986]).

MYTH vs. REALITY

MYTH Police must obtain a signed waiver for a confession to be admissible after they give the *Miranda* warnings.

FACT Police do not have to obtain a signed waiver; the waiver may be verbal. The better practice, however, is to obtain a signed waiver.

North Carolina v. Butler (1979)

Teague v. Louisiana (1980)

Colorado v. Connelly (1986)

FIGURE 11.1 The Miranda Warnings in English and Spanish

Date _____ Time _____

Location _____

Name _____ DOB _____

Signature _____

WARNING TO BE GIVEN BEFORE TAKING
ANY ORAL OR WRITTEN CONFESSION

1. You have the right to remain silent and not make any statement at all and that any statement you make may be used against you and probably will be used against you at your trial;
2. Any statement you make may be used as evidence against you in court;
3. You have the right to have a lawyer present to advise you prior to and during any questioning;
4. If you are unable to employ a lawyer, you have the right to have a lawyer appointed to advise you prior to and during any questioning;
5. You have the right to terminate this interview at any time.

SPANISH VERSION

1. Tiene usted el derecho de mantener su silencio y decir absolutamente nada. Cualquier declaración que usted haga se podrá usar en su contra en la causa en que se le acusa.
2. Cualquier declaración que usted haga se podrá usar como evidencia en su contra en corte.
3. Tiene usted el derecho de tener un abogado presente para que él le aconseje antes de que se le hagan preguntas y durante el tiempo que se le esté haciendo preguntas.
4. Si no puede emplear un abogado, tiene usted el derecho a que se le asigne un abogado para que él le aconseje antes de o durante el tiempo que se le hagan preguntas.
5. Tiene usted el derecho de terminar esta entrevisa en cualquier momento que usted desee.

Source: Official form of the Houston Police Department, Houston, Texas, 2008.

In *Colorado v. Connelly*, Connelly approached a uniformed Denver police officer and confessed that he had murdered someone and wanted to talk to the officer about it. The officer advised Connelly of his *Miranda* rights. Connelly indicated that he understood his rights and wanted to talk about the murder. After a homicide detective arrived, Connelly was again advised of his *Miranda* rights and again indicated that he wanted to speak with the police. Connelly was then taken to the police station, where he told officers that he had come from Boston to confess to the murder. When he became visibly disoriented, he was sent to a state hospital. In an interview with a psychiatrist, Connelly revealed that he was "following the advice of God" in confessing to the murder. He sought exclusion of the evidence during trial, saying that the confession was, in effect, coerced.

The Court rejected the challenge, saying that confessions and admissions are involuntary and invalid under the Constitution *only if the coercion is exerted by the police*, not if exerted by somebody else—in this case, allegedly, by God. The police did not act improperly or illegally, so the confession was constitutionally admissible.

Is a Waiver after a Prolonged Interruption Valid? In *Miranda*, the Court hinted that, even if there is a waiver, if there is a prolonged interruption before an interrogation is resumed, it is best to give the *Miranda* warnings again. Although no time has been specified, "prolonged interruption" should be taken to mean an interruption of several hours. The longer the time lapse, the greater is the need to give the warnings again. For example, suppose a suspect is give the *Miranda* warnings and waives his rights. The police interrogate him for a while, but then take a break for several hours. When the officers resume their interrogation, the suspect should be given the *Miranda* warnings again. There is no clear answer regarding the length of a time lapse before the warnings must be given again. The better practice is to give the warnings whenever there is a significant lapse of time and when in doubt.

Is a Waiver That Suspect Has Withdrawn Valid? A suspect may withdraw a waiver once given. If the waiver is withdrawn, the interrogation must stop immediately. However, evidence obtained before the waiver is withdrawn is admissible in court. For example, suppose a suspect waives her rights and agrees to talk to the police. She gives incriminating information but changes her mind after fifteen minutes of questioning. The interrogation must cease immediately, but any statements she made prior to changing her mind are admissible.

Is a Defendant's Understanding of the *Miranda* Rights and Not Invoking Those Rights Equivalent to a Waiver? Yes. In *Berghuis v. Thompkins*, 560 U.S. — (2010), Thompkins, a murder suspect, was interrogated by two Michigan police officers for almost three hours. He was given his *Miranda* warnings but remained silent throughout the interrogation. At the end of the interrogation, however, he was asked if he prayed to God to forgive him for what he had done. He answered, "Yes." He was convicted, but later appealed his conviction saying that his right against self-incrimination was violated when the officers continued to ask him questions even when he wished to remain silent. The Court disagreed, saying that Thompkins did not invoke his right to remain silent through his actions and, therefore, the police validly continued to interrogate him. The Court added that a waiver cannot be implied based on a suspect's understanding of the right and then failing to invoke that right. What is needed is an "unambiguous" waiver of the right. Moreover, Thompkins waived that right when he "knowingly and voluntarily" made a statement to the police.

custodial interrogation
an interrogation that takes place while a suspect is in custody.

WHEN MUST THE *MIRANDA* WARNINGS BE GIVEN?

When must the *Miranda* warnings be given? This question is crucial in policing. Answer: Whenever there is "**custodial interrogation**." Knowing this phrase avoids a lot

HIGHLIGHT ❭ What Happened to Ernesto Miranda?

Ernesto Miranda was later retried (under an assumed name to avoid publicity) for the same offenses of rape and kidnapping. There is no double jeopardy when a defendant is retried after a successful appeal; the appeal is considered a waiver of the right against double jeopardy. His original confession was not used in the second trial, but he was reconvicted on the basis of other evidence. After serving time in prison, Miranda was released on parole. He was killed in 1972 in a skid-row card game in Phoenix, Arizona. The police gave his alleged assailant the *Miranda* warnings.

of misunderstanding. The key words that need to be understood well and separately are "custodial" and "interrogation."

Courts assume that custodial interrogations are inherently coercive; therefore, the *Miranda* warnings are needed to ensure that suspects' statements are voluntary. In *Escobedo v. Illinois* (discussed previously), the Court stated that the warnings must be given as soon as the investigation has "focused" on the individual as a suspect. In *Miranda*, the Court abandoned the focus of the investigation test and replaced it with the custodial interrogation standard. In other words, a person who is the focus of an investigation is entitled to the *Miranda* warnings if that person is under custodial interrogation. That phrase, in turn, means that the suspect is: (1) in custody *and* (2) under interrogation. Both factors must be present; otherwise, there is no custodial interrogation. Here are examples:

◆ *Example 1.* Suspect Sam is in custody but is not being questioned—there is no need for the *Miranda* warnings.
◆ *Example 2.* Suspect Martha is being interrogated but is not in custody—there is no need for the *Miranda* warnings.

Next, we will discuss each component of this term, *custodial interrogation*, separately.

When Is the Suspect in Custody?

A suspect is in **custody** in two situations:

1. When the suspect is *under arrest* **or**
2. When the suspect is not under arrest but is *"deprived of freedom in a significant way."*

custody
when the suspect is under arrest or deprived of freedom in a significant way.

In the words of the Court, the test that determines whether a person is in custody for *Miranda* purposes is "whether the suspect has been subjected to a formal arrest or to equivalent restraints on his freedom of movement" (*California v. Beheler*, 463 U.S. 1121 [1983]). Moreover, whether a person is in custody is determined not by just one fact but by the totality of the circumstances. Each of these situations deserves an extended discussion.

California v. Beheler (1983)

Custody Situation 1: When the Suspect Is under Arrest The rule is clear that, when a person is under arrest, the *Miranda* warnings must be given prior to an interrogation. It makes no difference whether the arrest is for a felony or a misdemeanor. When, then, is a suspect under arrest? The answer is whenever the four elements of arrest are present: intent, authority, custody, and understanding (as discussed in Chapter 6).

◆ *Example 1.* A suspect is arrested by virtue of a warrant. En route to the police station, the officer questions the suspect about the crime. The suspect must first be given the *Miranda* warnings.
◆ *Example 2.* A suspect is arrested without a warrant because the police have probable cause to make a warrantless arrest (as when a crime is committed in the presence of the police). If the suspect is questioned by the police at any time after the arrest, the suspect must first be given the *Miranda* warnings.

The brief questioning of a person by the police is not an arrest if the police officer intends to let the person go after the brief detention. Also, stopping a motor vehicle for the purpose of issuing the driver a ticket or citation is not an arrest, so the *Miranda* warnings are not needed even if the police ask questions.

deprived of freedom in a significant way

when a person's freedom of movement is limited by the police and a reasonable person in the same circumstances would feel he or she was in custody.

Escobedo v. Illinois (1964)

Thompson v. Keohane (1995)

Stansbury v. California (1994)

Yarborough v. Alvarado (2004)

Custody Situation 2: When the Suspect Is Not under Arrest But Is Deprived of Freedom in a Significant Way This is the more difficult situation. When is a person **deprived of freedom in a significant way** so as to be considered in custody for purposes of *Miranda*? The answer is when the person's freedom of movement is limited by the police and a reasonable person in the same circumstances would feel he or she was in custody. Therefore, even if the investigation has focused on a person, the *Miranda* warnings need not be given unless the defendant will not be allowed to leave after the questioning. Focus of the investigation is no longer the test (as it was under *Escobedo v. Illinois* in 1964) to determine if the *Miranda* warnings must be given; custodial interrogation is now the test.

Whose Perception Determines Whether a Suspect Has Been Deprived of Freedom? Whose perception determines whether a suspect has been deprived of freedom in a significant way—that of the police or that of the suspect? In *Berkemer v. McCarty*, 468 U.S. 420 (1984), the Court said that a "policeman's unarticulated plan has no bearing on the question whether a suspect was 'in custody' at a particular time; the only relevant inquiry is how a reasonable man in the suspect's position would have understood his position." In a subsequent case, *Thompson v. Keohane*, 516 U.S. 99 (1995), the Court was more specific when it said: "Two discrete inquiries are essential to the determination (whether a person is under custody): first, what were the circumstances surrounding the interrogation; and second, given those circumstances, would a reasonable person have felt he or she was not at liberty to terminate the interrogation and leave?" It is not sufficient that a suspect thinks that he is not free to go. The test is whether a reasonable person in the suspect's position would conclude that he is not free to go. This test is based on the totality of the circumstances and is therefore determined on a case-by-case basis.

A 1994 case clarifies what the Court means by "in custody." In *Stansbury v. California*, 511 U.S. 318 (1994), the Court rejected the "subjective test" by the officer and adopted instead the "objective test" in determining whether a person is in custody. The Court said that "an officer's subjective and undisclosed view concerning whether the person being interrogated is a suspect is irrelevant to the assessment of whether the person is in custody," adding that "in determining whether an individual was in custody, a court must examine all of the circumstances surrounding the interrogation, but the ultimate inquiry is simply whether there [was] a 'formal arrest or restraint on the freedom of movement' of the degree associated with a formal arrest."

In sum, police intent is less important than the circumstances surrounding the interrogation when determining whether a person is in custody. A person may be in custody even if he or she is at home, in the office, or on the street. The objective test (meaning whether a reasonable person under the same circumstances would conclude that he or she was not free to go) determines whether a person actually is in custody.

In *Yarborough v. Alvarado*, 541 U.S. 652 (2004), the Court held that a police officer did not need to consider a suspect's age or previous history with law enforcement to determine whether the suspect was in custody for purposes of the *Miranda* warnings. In that case, the police interviewed 17-year-old Michael Alvarado at the police station as a suspect in a crime. He was not under arrest, and he was not given the *Miranda* warnings. He confessed to the crime, was prosecuted, and was convicted of second-degree murder and attempted robbery. In a habeas corpus petition, he sought exclusion of his confession, saying that although he was "in custody" he was not given the *Miranda* warnings.

The Court held that "determining whether a suspect is actually in custody has always been based on objective criteria like whether he had been brought to the police station by police or had come of his own accord." The Court then added that "requiring officers to consider individual characteristics of a suspect when determining whether he is in custody, such as the suspect's age or previous history with law enforcement, would make the test a subjective one that would be more difficult for officers to understand and abide by."

Here are some specific issues related to custodial situation 2 (where the suspect is not under arrest but is deprived of freedom in a significant way):

◆ *Questioning at the police station.* For example, suppose the police invite a suspect to come to the police station "to answer a few questions." This type of interrogation requires the *Miranda* warnings because a police station lends a "coercive atmosphere" to the interrogation. The exceptions to this general rule are: (1) if the suspect goes to the police station on his or her own and knows that he or she is free to leave at any time, and (2) if the suspect goes to the police station upon invitation of the police but is told that he or she is not under arrest and is free to leave at any time.

◆ In *Oregon v. Mathiason*, 429 U.S. 492 (1977), the police suspected a parolee of involvement in a burglary. The suspect came to the police station in response to an officer's message that the officer would "like to discuss something with you." It was made clear to the suspect that he was not under arrest but that the police believed he was involved in the burglary. The suspect confessed, but he later sought to exclude the evidence. The Court said that the *Miranda* warnings are necessary only if the suspect is in custody "or otherwise deprived of freedom in a significant way." Since those things had not occurred, the confession was admissible.

Oregon v. Mathiason (1977)

◆ *Questioning in a police car.* Questioning in police cars generally requires the *Miranda* warnings because of its custodial nature. The warnings must be given even if the suspect has not been placed under arrest. The reason is that questioning in police cars tends to be inherently coercive—the suspect is being deprived of freedom in a significant way.

◆ *Questioning when the suspect is not free to leave.* When the police will not allow the suspect to leave their presence, will not leave the suspect alone, or will not leave if asked to do so by the suspect, then the *Miranda* warnings must be given. If the police consider the suspect's attempt to leave or his or her refusal to answer questions as reason enough to stop the suspect from leaving or to arrest him or her formally, then the *Miranda* warnings must be given. Clearly, under these conditions, the suspect is being deprived of freedom in a significant way.

◆ *Questioning in the home.* Whether the *Miranda* warnings must precede questioning in a suspect's home depends on the circumstances of the case. The Court has held that the questioning of a suspect in his bedroom by four police officers at 4 A.M. required the *Miranda* warnings (*Orozco v. Texas*, 394 U.S. 324 [1969]). In a later case, however, the Court held that statements obtained by Internal Revenue Service agents during a noncustodial, noncoercive interview with a taxpayer under criminal tax investigation, conducted in a private home where the taxpayer occasionally stayed, did not require the *Miranda* warnings as long as the taxpayer had been told that he was free to leave (*Beckwith v. United States*, 425 U.S. 341 [1976]).

Orozco v. Texas (1969)

Beckwith v. United States (1976)

Note that, in both the *Orozco* and *Beckwith* cases, the investigation had already focused on the suspect. Under the old *Escobedo* standard, therefore, the warnings ought to have been given in both cases. The key consideration under *Miranda*, however, is whether the suspect's freedom of movement has been limited in a significant way—whether the suspect is truly free to leave after the questioning. In *Orozco*, aside from the coercive nature of the questioning, the suspect was not free to leave after the questioning, whereas in *Beckwith*, the suspect was free to go.

◆ *Questioning a person who is in custody for another offense.* Any time the suspect being questioned for another offense is in jail or prison, the *Miranda* warnings must be given because the suspect is in custody. For example, suppose a prison inmate serving a state sentence is questioned by federal agents regarding a completely separate offense. The suspect is entitled to the *Miranda* warnings even though no federal criminal charges are contemplated at the time of questioning. Failure to give the *Miranda* warnings when the suspect is in jail or prison means that the evidence obtained cannot be used in a criminal trial. However, there is no need for jail or prison officials to give the *Miranda* warnings in prison disciplinary cases, as these are administrative proceedings. A defendant who is in custody for another offense is not under arrest, at least for this second offense, but is certainly being deprived of freedom in a significant way. A safe policy in situations where the suspect is "deprived of freedom in a significant way" is this: When in doubt, give the *Miranda* warnings so as not to jeopardize the admissibility of any evidence obtained.

◆ *Questioning juveniles.* The Court has held that age must be considered when questioning a juvenile to determine if in that juvenile's mind he or she was in custody at the time of the interrogation (*J.D.B. v. North Carolina*, 564 U.S. — [2011]). In this case, J.D.B., a 13-year-old juvenile who was a special education student, was questioned by the police about a burglary. He was released, but was interrogated a second time after one of the stolen items, a digital camera, was suspected to be in his possession. He was removed from class and interrogated in a school conference room for nearly an hour. He was not initially informed of his *Miranda* rights, nor did the police notify his grandmother, his legal guardian, about the questioning. The police did not tell J.D.B. that he could contact his grandmother, nor did they inform him he could leave at any time. However, they did this after the investigator threatened J.D.B. he could be sent to a detention facility and after which J.D.B. had confessed to the offense.

J.D.B. v. North Carolina (2011)

An adjudication hearing (a hearing to determine if the juvenile is delinquent or not) was later held in which J.D.B. was declared a delinquent. The public defender representing J.D.B. filed a motion to suppress the confession, saying that no *Miranda* warnings were given before the confession. On appeal, the Court decided to send the case back to the state court to determine whether J.D.B. was in custody when he was interrogated. Said the Court: "It is beyond dispute that children will often feel bound to submit to police questioning when an adult in the same circumstances would feel free to leave." The Court added that youths are not adults and that the "reasonable person" standard must be applied when the police try to determine the issue of custody. In sum, the Court held that the age of a juvenile suspect must be taken into consideration in determining whether a suspect felt he or she was under custody or not. This case is significant because in determining whether an adult is in custody, the usual objective test is applied. This is a clear rule that can be easily applied in most cases. In cases involving juveniles, however, the objective test is modified in that the age of the juvenile must be taken into account to determine if, given the circumstances, that the juvenile (using the standard of reasonableness) felt he or she was in custody.

◆ *Prison inmates*. The Court has held, in *Howes v. Fields* (2012), that the questioning of an inmate is not custodial because the inmate if the inmate is told he could leave the interview at any time. Imprisonment alone does not mean a suspect is in "custody" for *Miranda* purposes.

Howes v. Fields (2012)

In this case, while in prison on an unrelated charge, inmate Randall Fields was removed from the general population and taken to a conference room where he was questioned regarding the sexual abuse of a 13-year-old boy by armed police officers unassociated with the prison. Fields was not informed of his *Miranda* rights; however, he also remained unrestrained during the interrogation and was told he could leave the room at any time. During the seven-hour questioning, Fields made statements to the officers that later proved significant in his conviction for criminal sexual conduct. After his conviction, Fields sought habeas corpus relief, stating that his right to due process had been violated when statements made during the questioning were used as evidence against him even though he had not been Mirandized prior to the interrogation. The Court disagreed, upholding the conviction on the ground that Fields was not in custody for purposes of the *Miranda* warnings.

When Is the Suspect under Interrogation?

This is the second half of the phrase "custodial interrogation" that answers the question, When must the *Miranda* warnings be given? There are two situations in which a suspect is under **interrogation**:

◆ When the police ask questions that tend to incriminate
◆ When the police ask no questions but, through their actions, create the functional equivalent of an interrogation

interrogation
when the police ask questions that tend to incriminate or create the functional equivalent of an interrogation.

When the Police Ask Incriminating Questions Most interrogations fall into this category, with questions aimed at obtaining what may be an admission or confession from the suspect: "Did you kill her?" "Where is the gun?" "Why did you do it?" Note, however, that police do not have to give the *Miranda* warnings when asking identification or routine booking questions: "What is your name?" "Where do you live?" "Do you have a driver's license?" Such questions are not self-incriminatory, so no warning is necessary.

Rhode Island v. Innis (1980)

When the Police Create the Functional Equivalent of an Interrogation There are instances when no questions are being asked by the police, but the circumstances are so conducive to making a statement or giving a confession that the courts consider them to be the **functional equivalent of an interrogation.** In *Rhode Island v. Innis*, 446 U.S. 291 (1980), the Court said:

functional equivalent of an interrogation
instances in which no questions are actually asked by the police but in which the circumstances are so conducive to making a statement or confession that the courts consider them to be the equivalent of interrogation.

> A practice that the police should know is reasonably likely to evoke an incriminating response from a suspect thus amounts to interrogation. But since the police surely cannot be held accountable for the unforeseeable results of their words or actions, the definition of interrogation can extend only to words or actions on the part of the police officers that they would have known were reasonably likely to elicit an incriminating response.

In specific cases, the Court has clarified the issue further in the following scenarios.

When Police Appeal to the Defendant's Religious Interests In one case, *Brewer v. Williams*, 430 U.S. 387 (1977), the suspect in a murder case turned himself into the police. His lawyer told him he would not be interrogated or mistreated. On the drive from Davenport, Iowa (where he had turned himself in), to Des Moines, Iowa (where he was facing the charge), the officer gave the suspect the now-famous "Christian burial" speech. The officer called the suspect "Reverend" and indicated that the parents of the missing girl should be entitled to give a Christian burial to the poor child who had been snatched away from them on Christmas Eve. The defendant then showed the officers where the body could be found.

The Court said that the evidence obtained was not admissible because of a violation of the suspect's right to counsel. The defendant had clearly asserted this right, and there was no evidence of knowing and voluntary waiver. Moreover, although there was no actual interrogation, the Court held that an interrogation nonetheless occurred when the police, knowing the defendant's religious interests, made remarks designed to appeal to those interests and thus induce the defendant to confess. Although *Brewer* is a right-to-counsel case, it illustrates the type of police behavior that is considered the functional equivalent of an interrogation.

When Two Officers Converse between Themselves Compare the *Brewer* case to *Rhode Island v. Innis*. In *Innis*, the officers were conversing between themselves while they had the suspect in the back of the car. The suspect had been arrested in connection with the shotgun robbery of a taxicab driver. The officers talked about the fact that it would be a terrible thing if one of the handicapped students from the school near the crime scene were to find a loaded shotgun and get hurt. The conversation between the two officers was within the hearing of the suspect. The suspect then interrupted the police and told them the location of the shotgun. The Court held that this did not constitute interrogation, so the volunteered evidence was admissible (*Rhode Island v. Innis*, 446 U.S. 291 [1980]). What the police did in this case was not the functional equivalent of an interrogation.

Arizona v. Mauro (1987)

When a Conversation between a Suspect and His Wife Is Recorded by an Officer In *Arizona v. Mauro*, 481 U.S. 520 (1987), the police received a call that a man had just entered a store claiming that he had killed his son. When officers reached the store, the man admitted to committing the act and directed officers to the body. He was then arrested and advised of his *Miranda* rights. He was taken to the police station, where he was again given the *Miranda* warnings. The suspect then told the officers that he did not want to make any more statements until a lawyer was present. At that time, the police stopped questioning him. The suspect's wife was in another room, and when the police questioned her, she insisted on speaking with the suspect. The police allowed the meeting on the condition that an officer be present to tape the conversation. The tape was later used to impeach the suspect's contention that he was insane at the time of the murder. During the trial, the suspect sought the exclusion of the taped conversation, saying that he should have been given the *Miranda* warnings prior to the recording.

The Court disagreed, saying that a conversation between a suspect and their spouse that is recorded by and in the presence of an officer does not constitute the functional equivalent of an interrogation under *Miranda*, so the evidence was admissible. The Court added that what the police did was merely "arrange a situation" in which there was a likelihood that the suspect would say something incriminating.

The practice in some jurisdictions of recording police custodial interrogations is controversial and fueled by the issue of innocent convictions about which much has been reported in the mass media. The main goal of advocates is to minimize false confessions, particularly in felonies and death penalty cases. One source says that, "One reform that will prevent convictions based on false confessions is the electronic recording of stationhouse interrogations of felony suspects."* The same source lists the advantages of recording custodial interviews. These include protection "against baseless charges of improper police conduct," making it "easier for some suspects to confess, because many of them find it easier to admit verbally to committing a crime, rather than writing out or signing a written confession," and deterring "improper police conduct during custodial interviews." It then says that, "recordings increase public trust in police conduct because they show that the police have nothing to hide."

Despite what proponents perceive as a win-win situation in that it supposedly benefits the police, suspects, and the public, the move toward recording police interrogations has not been received with much enthusiasm by the police. Thus, its adoption has been stymied. A few states, by law, have mandated the recording of police interrogations, but most states have not. Studies are underway in a number of states. Various issues have come up, such as whether the recording should apply to all custodial interrogations or only to those considered serious, the legal consequences for failure to record, and whether the evidence should be admissible in court if it is not recorded. Some judges have excluded unrecorded confessions for some offenses if there is no state law mandating their admissibility. The state courts of Alaska and Minnesota have ruled that interrogations must be recorded if they are to be admissible in some serious offenses. A few police departments have adopted

electronic recording of interrogations on their own; others are mandated by law. The same article, noted previously, ends with the observation that, "This is a growing trend among state legislatures and courts to require electronic recording of custodial interrogations in police facilities, and among law enforcement agencies to do so voluntarily even though it is not required."

Despite continuing efforts from advocacy groups, notably the Innocence Project, resistance to custodial interrogations has been persistent, caused by fear in law enforcement agencies (led by the FBI, which has not adopted it) about the implications of mandatory recording for police agencies. Those fears have yet to be publicly and clearly articulated, but they are there. One policy review states that the "greatest beneficiaries of a mandatory video recording rule are not criminal suspects and defense attorneys, but police and prosecutors." The article further states that a National Institute of Justice survey found that "nearly every police department that had videotaped interrogations found the policy useful." The source enumerates the benefits of custodial interrogation for innocent suspects, the criminal justice system, and public safety. Addressing the issue of recording costs, the policy review says that "in surveys of more than 450 police and sheriff's departments that record, no officers have reported that the costs were prohibitive enough to warrant abandoning the practice." Moreover, funding may not be the main issue because funding sources are available both from public and private sources.

Should police departments be required, by law or administrative policy, to record police custodial interrogations? What do you think are its benefits and disadvantages?

*Source: Thomas P. Sullivan, Andrew W. Vail, and Howard W. Anderson III, "The Case for Recording Police Interrogations," *Litigation*, vol. 34, no. 3, Spring 2008.

LEADING DECISIONS ON THE *MIRANDA* WARNINGS

Over the decades since *Miranda* was decided in 1966, the Court has resolved numerous issues about its meaning and application. Leading decisions after *Miranda* may be divided into three categories:

◆ Situations that require the *Miranda* warnings
◆ Situations not requiring or not fully applying the *Miranda* warnings
◆ Situations where the *Miranda* warnings are not needed

Situations That Require the *Miranda* Warnings

The cases discussed first are those holding that the evidence obtained was not admissible, thus requiring that the *Miranda* warnings should have been given.

Further Questioning about the Same Offense after a Suspect Asks for a Lawyer In *Edwards v. Arizona*, 451 U.S. 477 (1981), a suspect was charged with robbery, burglary, and murder. At his first interrogation, he asked for a lawyer. The interrogation was stopped. The next day, the suspect still had not seen a lawyer, but he talked to two detectives and implicated himself in the crimes. The confession, admittedly voluntary, was ruled inadmissible in court because it had not been established that the suspect had waived his right to counsel "intelligently and knowingly." The Court said that, once a suspect invokes the right to remain silent, the suspect cannot be questioned again for the same offense unless he or she initiates further communication, exchanges, or conversation with the police. This is known as the **Edwards rule**.

In *Edwards*, the suspect did not initiate further communication. Instead, the police came back the next morning and gave the suspect his *Miranda* warnings a second time. Because Edwards had learned by that time that another suspect had already implicated him in the crime, he gave an incriminating statement. The Court held that the evidence obtained was inadmissible.

In a subsequent case, *Minnick v. Mississippi*, 498 U.S. 146 (1991), the Court held that, once the suspect requests a lawyer, the interrogation must stop—whether the defendant confers with the lawyer or not. The Fifth Amendment is violated when the suspect requests a lawyer, is given an opportunity to confer with the lawyer, and then is forced to talk to the police without the lawyer being present. Prior consultation with the lawyer is not enough. The lawyer must be present at all subsequent questionings; otherwise, the evidence obtained is not admissible.

Further Questioning about an Unrelated Offense after a Suspect Asks for a Lawyer Following the *Edwards* rule, the Court said in *Arizona v. Roberson*, 486 U.S. 675 (1988), that invoking the *Miranda* rights in one offense also invokes the *Miranda* rights for an unrelated offense. In that case, Roberson, after having been given his *Miranda* warnings, advised the police that he wanted an attorney. The police stopped questioning him. Three days later, however, while Roberson was still in custody, another police officer, who did not know that Roberson had previously invoked his right to an attorney, again advised him of his *Miranda* rights and then interrogated him about an unrelated burglary. Roberson incriminated himself. During the trial, he sought exclusion of the evidence, relying on the *Edwards* rule.

The Court agreed, saying that this case came under the bright-line rule enunciated in *Edwards*, so the evidence could not be admitted. The rule is now clear: Once the *Miranda* rights are invoked by a suspect in one offense, that suspect cannot be interrogated further for that or an unrelated offense.

Questioning about a Second Offense When the Suspect Has a Lawyer for a Different but Related Offense In *Texas v. Cobb*, 532 U.S. 162 (2001), the Court held that the police may question a suspect about a second offense while the suspect has a lawyer for a

---

Edwards v. Arizona (1981)

Edwards rule

once a suspect invokes the right to remain silent, he or she cannot be questioned again for the same offense unless he or she initiates further communication, exchanges, or conversation with the police.

Minnick v. Mississippi (1991)

Arizona v. Roberson (1988)

Texas v. Cobb (2001)

different, although factually related, offense. Although *Cobb* is a right-to-counsel case, it has significance for police questioning of suspects and deserves discussion in this chapter and section.

Cobb was indicted for burglary in Huntsville, Texas, and was assigned a lawyer to represent him. He confessed to the burglary but denied involvement in the brutal killing of a woman and a child during that burglary. While free on bond in the burglary case and having moved to Odessa, Texas, Cobb had a conversation there with his father in which he confessed to the killings. On his own, the father told the Huntsville police by telephone about his son's confession. The Huntsville police told the father to go to the Odessa police station. He did and gave a statement. A warrant was issued; the Odessa police arrested Cobb and gave him the *Miranda* warnings before interrogating him. Cobb confessed to the murders, saying he committed them in the course of the burglary.

Charged with and convicted of capital murder, Cobb appealed, saying his right to counsel was violated when he was interrogated by the Odessa police for the murders without securing the permission of his lawyer for the burglary case. The Court rejected his appeal, saying that the Sixth Amendment right to counsel is "offense specific," meaning it applies only to that particular offense for which a lawyer has been assigned and not to other offenses even if they are closely "factually related." Because the offenses of burglary and murder are different offenses in Texas, as elsewhere, the assignment of a lawyer for the burglary did not mean that the lawyer's permission had to be sought by the police before asking the suspect about the murders, which were committed during the burglary.

To avoid possible confusion, the *Roberson* and *Cobb* cases must be clearly distinguished. First, in the *Roberson* case, the suspect, after having been given the *Miranda* warnings, asked for an attorney. In the *Cobb* case, the suspect did not ask for an attorney even after receiving the *Miranda* warnings. Second, in the *Roberson* case, the

---

IN ACTION   A CONFESSION AFTER A REQUEST FOR A LAWYER

Suspect Dawn is detained by store security detectives at a large retail chain for shoplifting. Store detectives place handcuffs on Dawn, place her in a locked security office, and contact the police.

Officer Smith is dispatched to the store. In her investigation, Officer Smith reads the store detective's report and establishes probable cause to arrest Suspect Dawn. Officer Smith removes the store detective's handcuffs from D's wrists, places her own handcuffs on Dawn, and advises Dawn that she is under arrest. Officer Smith then reads Dawn the *Miranda* warnings and asks Dawn, "Would you like to make a statement?" Dawn responds, "No, I want a lawyer." Officer Smith then transports Dawn to the police station. Officer Smith submits her police report detailing the arrest.

Several hours later, Detective Jones is assigned to the case. Detective Jones places Dawn in the interview room, reads Dawn the *Miranda* warnings, and asks her if she would "like to talk." Dawn says yes and subsequently confesses to the shoplifting.

1. *Is Dawn's confession to Detective Jones admissible? Why or why not?*
2. *What if Detective Jones did not know that Dawn had previously been Mirandized by Officer Smith—would D's statement then be admissible?*

questioning was for an unrelated offense, whereas in the *Cobb* case, the questioning was for a factually related, although different, offense.

Questioning a Defendant without a Lawyer after an Indictment When a defendant is questioned by police agents without a lawyer present after an adversarial judicial proceeding (such as an indictment) has been started, the evidence is not admissible. The Court ruled in *United States v. Henry*, 447 U.S. 264 (1980), that incriminating statements made to a government informant sharing a suspect's jail cell were not admissible in evidence, because they violated the suspect's right to a lawyer.

In *Henry*, the defendant was indicted for armed robbery of a bank. While the defendant was in jail awaiting trial, government agents contacted an informant who was confined in the same cell block as Henry. An FBI agent instructed the informant to be alert to any statements Henry made but not to initiate conversations with or question him regarding the charges against him. After the informant was released from jail, he reported to the FBI agent that he and Henry had engaged in conversation and that Henry had made incriminating statements about the robbery. The informant was paid for giving the information. The Court excluded the evidence, saying that the government had violated Henry's Sixth Amendment right to a lawyer by intentionally creating a situation likely to induce the accused to make incriminating statements in the absence of a lawyer. The right was violated even if the defendant was not explicitly questioned, because the incriminating information was secured in the absence of a lawyer and after the defendant had been indicted.

Suspect Asking for a Lawyer during the Reading of *Miranda* Warnings Once a suspect has clearly invoked his or her right to counsel, nothing the suspect says in response to further interrogation may be used to cast doubt on that invocation. An invocation of rights may be made very early in the process, such as during the interrogator's reading of the suspect's *Miranda* rights. Therefore, the questioning of an in-custody suspect may have to end even before it starts (*Smith v. Illinois*, 469 U.S. 91 [1984]).

Smith v. Illinois (1984)

In *Smith v. Illinois*, the defendant was interrogated by the police. They informed him that they wanted to talk about a particular robbery and then began to advise him of his rights. As they read the suspect each right, they asked if he understood. They gave him warnings on the right to silence and on the state's right to use what he might say. Then they gave him the right-to-counsel warning as follows: "You have a right to consult a lawyer and to have a lawyer present with you when you're being questioned. Do you understand that?"

The suspect responded, saying, "Uh, yeah. I'd like to do that."

The officer continued with the rest of the *Miranda* warnings. When the suspect was asked whether he wanted to talk without a lawyer, he replied, "Yeah and no, uh. I don't know what's that, really."

The officer replied, "Well, you either have to talk to me at this time without a lawyer being present, and if you do agree to talk with me without a lawyer being present you can stop at any time you want to."

The suspect agreed to talk and made some incriminating statements before cutting off the questioning with a request for counsel. The Court held that the evidence obtained could not be admitted in court because the suspect had invoked the right to counsel even before the giving of the *Miranda* warnings was completed.

Interrogation during Detention When Detention Is the Functional Equivalent of an Arrest There are situations where a suspect has not been arrested but the circumstances are such that the person is, in fact, considered arrested by the Court. In *Kaupp v. Texas*, 538 U.S. 626 (2003), the Court held that a confession must be suppressed if it was obtained during a detention when officers did not have probable cause for an arrest and where the detention amounted to the functional equivalent of an arrest.

Kaupp v. Texas (2003)

In *Kaupp*, officers investigating the disappearance of a girl had Kaupp and the girl's half-brother as the main suspects. The half-brother confessed to the killing and implicated Kaupp. The half-brother had failed a polygraph test three times, but Kaupp had passed his polygraph. Given the results, the officers did not believe they had probable cause to obtain an arrest warrant for Kaupp based solely on the half-brother's confession. Subsequently, officers went to Kaupp's home at 3 A.M. and, after his father let them in, went to his bedroom, awakened him with a flashlight, and told him, "We need to go and talk." Kaupp said, "Okay." He was then handcuffed and taken to a patrol car. After going to the scene where the body had been recovered, officers took Kaupp to the sheriff's office. Kaupp was taken to an interview room; the handcuffs were removed, and he was read his *Miranda* warnings. After initially denying any involvement in the crime, Kaupp admitted to having some part but did not confess to the murder for which he was later tried.

During the trial, he sought exclusion of his confession, but the trial court rejected his motion, saying that Kaupp had consented to go with the officers when he answered "Okay" when the officer told him, "We need to go and talk." The trial court also said that the handcuffs were placed on Kaupp not because he was under arrest but for officer safety.

On appeal, the Court upheld Kaupp's contention, saying that the officers had created a situation where a reasonable person would not have felt free to leave, and that Kaupp's detention, although not declared by the officers as such, in fact amounted to the functional equivalent of an arrest for which there was no probable cause. His arrest was invalid, and the confession obtained by the police was therefore ruled inadmissible.

Giving the *Miranda* Warnings Only after the Police Obtain an Unwarned Confession

In *Missouri v. Seibert*, 542 U.S. 600 (2004), the Court held that giving the *Miranda* warnings only after the police obtained an unwarned confession violates the

A Summary of Cases after *Miranda v. Arizona* Where the Evidence Obtained Was Not Admissible in Court

Case	How Was Evidence Obtained?	Evidence Admissible?
United States v. Henry (1980)	Questioning after indictment	No
Edwards v. Arizona (1981)	No valid waiver of right to counsel	No
Smith v. Illinois (1984)	Interrogation after invocation of right to counsel during questioning	No
Arizona v. Roberson (1988)	Interrogation about second offense after invoking *Miranda* for first offense	No
Minnick v. Mississippi (1991)	Questioning after request for lawyer	No
Kaupp v. Texas (2003)	Detention without probable cause that amounted to the functional equivalent of an arrest	No
Missouri v. Seibert (2004)	Giving *Miranda* warnings but only after the police obtain an unwarned admission	No

Miranda rule; therefore, statements made after the *Miranda* warnings are given are not admissible even if these statements repeat those given before the *Miranda* warnings were read to the suspect. *Seibert* is important because it declares invalid a questionable practice in some law enforcement departments (see the Case Brief for more on *Missouri v. Seibert*).

CASE BRIEF

Missouri v. Seibert, 542 U.S. 600 (2004)

The Leading Case on Admissibility of Physical Evidence from an Unwarned Confession

Facts: Seibert's son had cerebral palsy. When he died in his sleep, Seibert feared charges of neglect because of bedsores on his body. In her presence, two of her teenaged sons and two of their friends planned to burn the family's mobile home to conceal the death of the son. They also planned to leave a mentally ill teenager who was living with the family in the mobile home to avoid giving the appearance that the son had been left alone. In the fire, the mentally ill teenager died. Five days later, the police awoke Seibert at 3 A.M. in the hospital where one of her sons was being treated for burns. She was arrested and taken to the police station.

The officer making the arrest was told not to read her the *Miranda* warnings. At the station, Seibert was left in an interrogation room for about twenty minutes, then she was interrogated for about forty minutes without being read her *Miranda* warnings. After she admitted she knew the teenager was meant to die in the fire, she was given a twenty-minute break. The officer then turned on a tape recorder, gave Seibert the *Miranda* warnings, obtained a signed waiver of rights, and then resumed the interrogation. At the beginning of the interrogation, the officer confronted Seibert with her unwarned statements and essentially reacquainted her with the statements she had made prior to her *Miranda* warnings.

At a suppression hearing to exclude the statements, the officer admitted he had made a conscious decision to withhold the *Miranda* warnings based on an interrogation technique he had been taught by the police department— which was to question first, give the warnings, then repeat the questioning "until I get the answer she's already provided once."

Issue or Issues: *Are statements made after a suspect is given the* Miranda *warnings that repeat unwarned statements he or she made admissible in court?* No.

Decision: The decision of the Supreme Court of Missouri was affirmed.

Holding: Giving the *Miranda* warnings after an interrogation has already occurred and an unwarned confession has been obtained by the police does not effectively comply with *Miranda*'s constitutional requirement even if the subsequent confession repeats the statements made before the warnings were given; therefore, statements obtained in this manner are not admissible in court.

Case Significance: The Court in this case struck down an established practice in some police departments. In an earlier case, *Oregon v. Elstad*, the Court admitted a confession obtained after the police gave the *Miranda* warnings—even though the suspect had previously made statements before the warnings were given. This practice was subsequently used by police training organizations, in what became known as a "question-first" two-step interrogation technique. Following this procedure, a police officer first interrogates a person without the *Miranda* warnings. Once a confession is obtained, the *Miranda* warnings are then given. The officer resumes the interrogation and obtains a warned confession similar to the unwarned confession that has been given. In *Seibert*, however, the Court held this practice violative of *Miranda* and therefore held the evidence inadmissible.

The Court said that there are several distinctions between this case and *Elstad* (where the evidence obtained was admissible despite a prior unwarned statement). These include "the completeness and detail of the questions and answers in the first round of interrogation, the overlapping content of the two statements, the timing and setting of the first and the second statements, the continuity of police personnel, and the degree to which the interrogator's questions treated the second round as continuous with the first." The overriding consideration in these types of two-interrogation cases is whether the two interrogations (the unwarned and the warned) can be seen as separate and distinct interrogations, where a reasonable person would believe he or she is free to disregard the first and assert his or her rights in the second. In the *Seibert* case, the Court stated, "At the opposite extreme are the facts here [as opposed to the facts in the *Elstad* case], which by any objective measure reveal a police strategy adapted to undermine the *Miranda* warnings. The unwarned interrogation was conducted in the station house, and the questioning was systematic, exhaustive, and managed with psychological skill. When the police were finished there was little, if anything, of incriminating potential left unsaid. The warned phase of questioning proceeded after a pause of only fifteen to twenty minutes, in the same place as the unwarned segment. When the same officer who had conducted the first phase recited the *Miranda* warnings, he said nothing to counter the probable misimpression that the advice that anything Seibert said could be used against her also applied to the details of the inculpatory statement previously elicited. In particular, the police did not advise that her prior statement could not be used."

Therefore, the issue whether or not a subsequent warned admission or confession is admissible after the suspect has given an unwarned admission or confession depends on the facts and circumstances of the case. If the facts and circumstances are closer to *Elstad*, the statement is admissible, but if they are closer to *Seibert*, then the statement is not admissible.

Excerpts from the Opinion: The object of question-first is to render *Miranda* warnings ineffective by waiting for a particularly opportune time to give them, after the suspect has already confessed. . . . The threshold issue when interrogators question first and warn later is thus whether it would be reasonable to find that in these circumstances the warnings could function effectively as *Miranda* requires. Could the warnings effectively advise the suspect that he had a real choice about giving an admissible statement at that juncture? Could they reasonably convey that he could

choose to stop talking even if he had talked earlier? For unless the warnings could place a suspect who has just been interrogated in a position to make such an informed choice, there is no practical justification for accepting the formal warnings as compliance with *Miranda*, or for treating the second state of interrogation as distinct from the first, unwarned and inadmissible segment. . . .

There is no doubt about the answer that proponents of question-first give to this question about the effectiveness of warnings given only after successful interrogation, and we think their answer is correct. By any objective measure, applied to circumstances exemplified here, it is likely that if the interrogators employ the technique of withholding warnings until after interrogation succeeds in eliciting a confession, the warnings will be ineffective in preparing the suspect for successive interrogation, close in time and similar in content. After all, the reason that question-first is catching on is as obvious as its manifest purpose, which is to get a confession the suspect would not make if he understood his rights at the outset; the sensible underlying assumption is that with one confession in hand before the warnings, the interrogator can count on getting its duplicate with trifling additional trouble. Upon hearing warnings only in the aftermath of interrogation and just after making a confession, a suspect would hardly think he had a genuine right to remain silent, let alone persist in so believing once the police began to lead him over the same ground again. A more likely reaction on a suspect's part would be perplexity about the reason for discussing rights at that point, bewilderment being an unpromising frame of mind for knowledgeable decision. What is worse, telling a suspect that "anything you say can and will be used against you," without expressly excepting the statement just given, could lead to an entirely reasonable inference that what he has just said will be used, with subsequent silence being of no avail.

Situations Not Requiring or Not Fully Applying the *Miranda* Warnings

In the next set of cases, the Court held that the evidence obtained was admissible despite the absence of the *Miranda* warnings, thus rejecting *Miranda* or not applying it in full.

Questioning on an Unrelated Offense after the Suspect Indicates Desire to Remain Silent Suppose a suspect indicates a desire to remain silent (as opposed to asking for a lawyer) after being given the *Miranda* warnings. May that suspect be interrogated again? The answer is yes as long as five conditions are met: (1) The suspect is given the *Miranda* warnings prior to the first interrogation; (2) the first interrogation stops as soon as the defendant indicates a desire to remain silent; (3) the questioning is resumed only after a significant period of time has lapsed (although the Court has not specified how long is long enough); (4) the suspect is again given the *Miranda* warnings; and (5) the second questioning is about crimes not covered in the first interrogation (*Michigan v. Mosley*, 423 U.S. 96 [1975]).

Michigan v. Mosley (1975)

In *Michigan v. Mosley*, Mosley was arrested in connection with a series of robberies and was given the *Miranda* warnings. He declined to discuss the robberies but did not indicate any desire to consult with a lawyer. More than two hours later, another detective, after again giving the *Miranda* warnings, questioned Mosley about an unrelated offense—a murder. Mosley gave an incriminating statement, which was used in his murder trial. Convicted, he appealed, saying that he should not have been asked any questions after he exercised his right to remain silent. The Court disagreed, admitting the evidence and saying that Mosley's second interrogation about another offense took place only after a significant time lapse and after a fresh set of warnings was given.

This scenario, in which a suspect indicates a *desire to remain silent*, should be distinguished from one in which the suspect indicates a *desire to see a lawyer*—as was the case in *Edwards v. Arizona*. In *Edwards*, decided six years after *Mosley*, the Court held that, once a suspect indicates a desire for a lawyer, police officers must not question the suspect again—unless the suspect initiates the conversation. The Court apparently does not consider the desire to remain silent as highly protected as the desire to see a lawyer, and therefore the evidence is admissible as long as the five conditions listed are present. *Mosley* is a *Miranda* warning case, whereas *Edwards* is considered by the Court to be a right-to-counsel case; hence, the rules are different.

After a Knowing and Voluntary Waiver, Questioning until the Suspect Clearly Requests a Lawyer The Court held in *Davis v. United States*, 512 U.S. 452 (1994), that the statement "I think I want a lawyer before I say anything else" by a suspect, after a knowing and voluntary waiver of his or her *Miranda* rights, does not constitute an invocation of the right to counsel because it is merely an ambiguous request for a lawyer.

Davis v. United States (1994)

In *Davis*, a navy sailor who was charged with the murder of another sailor had earlier waived his rights to remain silent and to counsel, both orally and in writing. Ninety minutes into the interrogation, however, Davis said, "Maybe I should talk to a lawyer." When agents inquired if he was asking for an attorney, Davis replied that he was not. The interrogation continued, and Davis's statements were used to convict him of murder. At his court-martial hearing, Davis moved to suppress the statements obtained after he suggested that he might need a lawyer. The Court admitted the evidence, saying that, unless a suspect makes a statement that a reasonable interrogator under the circumstances would interpret as an unambiguous request for counsel, the right to counsel under *Miranda* is not considered invoked. The Court added that in cases in which the suspect's statement is unclear, it is entirely proper for law enforcement officers to clarify whether the suspect, in fact, wants to see a lawyer. Seeking clarification from the suspect does not violate *Miranda*.

Using a Voluntary but Inadmissible Statement to Impeach a Defendant's Credibility Trustworthy statements taken in violation of *Miranda* may be used to impeach the credibility of a defendant who takes the witness stand. The jury must be instructed that the confession may not be considered as evidence of guilt but only as a factor in determining whether the defendant is telling the truth (*Harris v. New York*, 401 U.S. 222 [1971]).

Harris v. New York (1971)

Note, however, that the admission or confession cannot be used in court for any purpose whatsoever if it was obtained involuntarily.

For example, suppose a suspect confesses to the police even though she was not given the full *Miranda* warnings (she may have been warned that she has a right to remain silent but not of her right to a lawyer). The evidence is not admissible in court to prove her guilt. But suppose further that she takes the witness stand during the trial and testifies that she knew nothing at all about the crime. The confession may be used by the prosecutor to challenge her credibility as a witness. In this case, the confession is voluntary. But if the confession is involuntarily obtained (for example, through threats by the police), it cannot be used for any purpose, not even for impeachment.

Using an Inadmissible Statement to Obtain Collateral Derivative Evidence Trustworthy statements obtained in violation of *Miranda* may be used to obtain **collateral derivative evidence** (meaning evidence of a secondary nature that is related to the case but not directly a part of it). For example, in *Michigan v. Tucker*, 417 U.S. 433 (1974), the police interrogated a suspect without giving the *Miranda* warnings. In the process, they obtained from the suspect the name of a person (the collateral derivative evidence) who eventually became a prosecution witness. The Court held that, although the defendant's own statements could not be used against him because they were obtained in violation of *Miranda*, the prosecution witness's testimony had been purged of its original taint and was therefore admissible.

collateral derivative evidence
evidence of a secondary nature that is related to the case but not directly a part of it.

Michigan v. Tucker (1974)

Interrogating without Informing the Suspect of All Crimes A suspect's waiver of *Miranda* rights is valid even if he or she believes the interrogation will focus merely on minor crimes, but the police bring up a different and more serious crime (*Colorado v. Spring*, 479 U.S. 564 [1987]).

Colorado v. Spring (1987)

In *Colorado v. Spring*, Spring and a companion shot a man during a hunting trip in Colorado. An informant told federal agents that Spring was engaged in interstate trafficking in stolen firearms and that he had participated in the murder. Spring was arrested in Kansas City and advised of his *Miranda* rights. He signed a statement indicating that he understood and waived his rights. He was asked about the firearms transaction (which had led to his arrest) and also whether he had ever shot a man. Spring answered yes but denied the shooting in question. He confessed to the murder later, however, after having been given the *Miranda* warnings again. Tried and convicted, he appealed, saying that he should have been informed of all crimes about which he was to be questioned before there could be a valid waiver of his *Miranda* rights.

The Court rejected his challenge, saying that the Constitution does not require that a suspect know and understand every possible consequence of a waiver of a Fifth Amendment privilege. There was no allegation here that Spring failed to understand that privilege or that he did not understand the consequences of speaking freely.

Oral Confessions Are Admissible An oral confession is admissible even if the suspect tells the police he will talk with them but will not make a written statement without a lawyer present (*Connecticut v. Barrett*, 479 U.S. 523 [1987]).

Connecticut v. Barrett (1987)

In *Connecticut v. Barrett*, Barrett was arrested in connection with a sexual assault. Upon his arrival at the police station, he was advised of his *Miranda* rights and signed a statement saying he understood his rights. Barrett then said that he would not give a written statement in the absence of counsel but would talk to the police about the incident. In two subsequent interrogations, Barrett was again advised of his rights and signed a statement of understanding. On both occasions, he gave an oral statement admitting his involvement in the sexual assault but refused to make or sign a written statement. After being convicted of sexual assault, he appealed, alleging that his oral statements should not be admissible in court.

The Court rejected his challenge, saying that refusal by a suspect to put his or her statement in writing does not make an admission or confession inadmissible, as long as the police can establish that the *Miranda* warnings were given and the waiver was intelligent and voluntary. Note, however, that the admissibility of oral statements may be the subject of limiting rules in some states. For example, state law might provide that oral confessions are admissible only if corroborated by other evidence indicating guilt, such as a weapon or eyewitnesses.

Confession Admissible Despite Failure to Inform the Suspect of a Retained Attorney In *Moran v. Burbine*, 475 U.S. 412 (1986), the Court held that a suspect's waiver of the Fifth Amendment right to remain silent and to have counsel present during custodial interrogation is not nullified either by the failure of police officers to inform the suspect that the attorney retained on his or her behalf by a third party is attempting to reach the suspect or by misleading information given to the attorney by the police regarding their intention to interrogate the suspect at that time.

In this case, the failure of police officers to inform a suspect that the attorney retained for him by his sister was attempting to reach him did not make the evidence obtained inadmissible. If the officer knows, however, that the defendant has retained a lawyer, and the lawyer wants to be present during interrogation, that must be respected.

United States v. Patane (2004)

The Physical Fruits of an Unwarned but Voluntary Statement In an important case, *United States v. Patane*, 543 U.S. 630 (2004), the Court held that failure to give the *Miranda* warnings to a suspect does not require the suppression of the physical fruits of a suspect's unwarned but voluntary statements.

Patane was arrested for harassing his ex-girlfriend. He was released on bond, subject to a restraining order that prohibited him from contacting her. Patane violated the restraining order by telephoning her. An investigating police officer was given information by a probation officer that Patane had an illegal handgun. The officer went to Patane's home, inquired about his attempts to contact his ex-girlfriend, and then arrested Patane for violating the restraining order. When another officer tried to read Patane his *Miranda* warnings, Patane interrupted and said he knew his rights. After that, the officers made no further attempts to read Patane his *Miranda* rights. They then asked him about the handgun, and Patane told them where it was located. Patane was arrested for being a felon in possession of a firearm. Tried and convicted, he appealed, saying that the failure of the officers to give him the *Miranda* warnings required suppression of the handgun, which was the physical fruit of his unwarned but voluntary statements. The Court disagreed, saying that Patane's constitutional right against self-incrimination was not violated because the evidence involved (the handgun) was physical, not testimonial (spoken).

Note that in this case, the focus was on the admissibility of the handgun that was obtained without the suspect being given the *Miranda* warnings and after he had asserted that he knew his rights. The statement itself was deemed voluntary. Given the suspect's statement that he knew his rights and the fact that what was recovered was a pistol, the Court concluded that the suspect's right against self-incrimination was not violated. The Court refused to apply the fruit of the poisonous tree doctrine (which holds that evidence obtained resulting from other evidence that is illegally obtained is not admissible in court) in this case, because that doctrine applies only to violations of the Fourth Amendment guarantee against unreasonable searches and seizures and is unrelated to the *Miranda* rule, which is based on the Fifth Amendment.

In a case decided in 2010, the Court held that the *Edwards* rule did not require the suppression of a suspect's statements that were obtained two weeks after the initial interrogation at which the suspect claimed his right to remain silent (*Maryland v. Shatzer*, 559 U.S. — [2010]). In this case, Shatzer was interrogated in 2003, while he was in a Maryland prison, by the Hagerstown Police Department. The interrogation was in connection with allegations that he sexually abused his child. That investigation was subsequently dropped, but was reopened in 2006 upon the urging of Shatzer's wife, who said her child could now make more specific allegations about the sexual abuse. Two months later, Shatzer, while still in prison, was interrogated for the same 2003 offense by another detective from the same police department. The detective knew that Shatzer had previously been investigated for the same offense, but was not aware that he had, at that time, invoked his *Miranda* right to remain silent. At the 2006 interview, Shatzer was advised of his *Miranda* rights. He waived them and then confessed to sexually abusing his child.

Maryland v. Shatzer (2010)

Shatzer was charged with that offense and convicted. On appeal, he claimed that his 2006 confession was invalid because his invocation of his *Miranda* rights in 2003 was still applicable in 2006. The Court disagreed, saying that "when a suspect has been released from custody and returned to normal life before the police later attempt interrogation, there is little reason to believe that the confession was coerced." Thus, the confession was admissible.

Situations in Which the *Miranda* Warnings Are Not Needed

When are the *Miranda* warnings not needed? The easy and quick answer is *whenever there is no custodial interrogation.* The *Miranda* case itself and subsequent Court decisions have identified a number of situations in which there is no need to give the *Miranda* warnings. These are:

◆ When the officer does not ask any questions
◆ During general on-the-scene questioning
◆ When the statement is volunteered
◆ When asking a suspect routine identification questions
◆ When questioning witnesses who are not suspects
◆ In stop-and-frisk cases
◆ During lineups, showups, or photographic identifications
◆ When the statement is made to a private person
◆ When a suspect testifies before a grand jury
◆ When there is a threat to public safety
◆ When an undercover officer poses as an inmate and asks questions

A Summary of Cases Rejecting *Miranda* or Not Applying *Miranda* in Full: Statements in These Cases Are Admissible

Case	How Was Evidence Obtained?	Evidence Admissible?
Harris v. New York (1971)	Impeachment of credibility	Yes
Michigan v. Tucker (1974)	Collateral derivative evidence	Yes
Michigan v. Mosley (1975)	Questioning on an unrelated offense	Yes
New York v. Quarles (1984)	Threat to public safety	Yes
Berkemer v. McCarty (1984)	Roadside questioning of motorist pursuant to routine traffic stop	Yes
Oregon v. Elstad (1985)	Confession obtained after warnings given following earlier voluntary but unwarned admission	Yes
Moran v. Burbine (1986)	Failure of police to inform suspect of attorney retained for him	Yes
Kuhlmann v. Wilson (1986)	Informant in same cell	Yes
Colorado v. Connelly (1986)	Confession following advice of God	Yes
Connecticut v. Barnett (1987)	Oral confession	Yes
Colorado v. Spring (1987)	Shift to another crime	Yes
Arizona v. Mauro (1987)	Conversation with defendant's wife recorded	Yes
Pennsylvania v. Bruder (1988)	Curbside stop for traffic violation	Yes
Duckworth v. Eagan (1989)	Variation in warning	Yes
Michigan v. Harvey (1990)	Impeachment of testimony	Yes
Illinois v. Perkins (1990)	Officer posing as inmate	Yes
Pennsylvania v. Muniz (1990)	Routine questions and videotaping for DWI	Yes
Arizona v. Fulminante (1991)	Harmless involuntary confessions	Yes
Davis v. United States (1994)	No clear request to see attorney	Yes
Texas v. Cobb (2001)	Interrogation for closely related offense while having lawyer for first offense	Yes
United States v. Patane (2004)	Obtained physical evidence after failure to give the *Miranda* warnings	Yes
Maryland v. Shatzer (2010)	Interrogation for same offense two years later after original invocation of *Miranda* rights.	Yes

When the Officer Does Not Ask Any Questions The *Miranda* warnings are unnecessary when the police do not ask questions of the suspect. *Miranda* applies only if the police interrogate the suspect; if they do not ask questions, no warnings need to be given. For example, suppose Andy is arrested by the police because of an arrest warrant. If the police do not question Andy during the time he is in police custody, the *Miranda* warnings do not need to be given. In many states, the magistrate gives the *Miranda* warnings when the arrested person is brought before him or her for initial appearance or presentment.

During General on-the-Scene Questioning *Miranda* warnings do not have to be given prior to **general on-the-scene questioning**, meaning questioning at the scene of the crime for the purpose of gathering information about the people involved. This is because the Court, in *Miranda*, noted: "In such situations the compelling atmosphere inherent in the process of in-custody interrogation is not necessarily present."

general on-the-scene questioning
questioning at the scene of the crime.

A distinction must be made, however, between general on-the-scene questioning and questioning at the scene of the crime after the police have focused on an individual, which requires the *Miranda* warnings. Consider these two examples:

◆ *Example 1.* Bob has been stabbed fatally in a crowded bar. A police officer arrives and questions people at the scene of the crime to determine whether anyone saw the actual stabbing. This is considered general on-the-scene questioning, for which there is no need to give the *Miranda* warnings.

◆ *Example 2.* Assume instead that upon arrival at the bar, the officer sees Frank with a bloody knife in his hands. The officer's suspicion will doubtless be focused on Frank. Therefore, any questioning of Frank requires the *Miranda* warnings even though such questioning is at the scene of the crime.

When the Statement Is Volunteered A person who volunteers a statement does not have to receive *Miranda* warnings before speaking. A **volunteered statement** is one given by a suspect without interrogation. For example, suppose Mike enters the police station and announces, "I just killed my wife." The statement is admissible in court because it was volunteered. A volunteered statement is different from a **voluntary statement**, which is a statement given without coercion and of the suspect's own free will. For example, Suspect John confesses to a burglary after being given the *Miranda* warnings and consenting to a valid waiver. A volunteered statement is always voluntary, but a voluntary statement is not often volunteered.

volunteered statement
one given by the suspect without interrogation.

voluntary statement
a statement given without coercion and of the suspect's own free will.

When Asking a Suspect Routine Identification Questions When asking questions about a suspect's identification, such as "What is your name?" "Where do you live?" "How long have you lived here?" the *Miranda* warnings are not required (*Pennsylvania v. Muniz*, 496 U.S. 582 [1990]).

Pennsylvania v. Muniz (1990)

In *Pennsylvania v. Muniz*, Muniz was arrested for driving while under the influence of alcohol. He was taken to a booking center and was told that his actions and voice would be videotaped. He was asked seven questions regarding his name, address, height, weight, eye color, date of birth, and current age, which he answered. He later sought exclusion of his answers, saying he was not given the *Miranda* warnings before those questions were asked.

The Court disagreed, saying that Muniz's answers were admissible because these questions fall within a "routine booking question" exception to the *Miranda* rule. The Court felt that these questions were requested for record-keeping, not for the purpose of criminal investigation. No possible self-incrimination was involved; hence, the *Miranda* warnings were not needed.

When Questioning Witnesses Who Are Not Suspects When the person being interrogated is merely a witness to a crime, not a suspect, the *Miranda* warnings are not needed. However, if the officer suspects during the questioning that the witness might be involved in the offense, then the warnings must be given. For example, assume that Officer Roberts interviews Fred about the rape of a neighbor committed the previous night. In the course of the interrogation, Officer Roberts decides that Fred is a suspect because of his inconsistent answers, nervous behavior, and a record of sexual offenses. At that stage, Fred must be given his *Miranda* warnings because the situation has shifted from Fred being a witness to Fred being a suspect in the crime.

In Stop-and-Frisk Cases There is no need to give the *Miranda* warnings if a person is stopped by the police and asked questions to determine if criminal activity is about to take place or has taken place. In this brief encounter the suspect is not deprived of freedom in a significant way. The purpose of the stop is to determine whether criminal activity is about to take place, and the purpose of a frisk is to protect the officer. In neither case is custodial interrogation involved. Note, however, that once a stop-and-frisk situation turns into an arrest, the *Miranda* warnings must be given if the suspect is interrogated.

During Lineups, Showups, or Photographic Identifications No *Miranda* warnings need to be given during lineups, showups, or photographic pretrial identifications. The reason is that these pretrial identification procedures are not protected by the Fifth Amendment guarantee against self-incrimination because the evidence obtained is physical in nature and does not constitute testimonial self-incrimination.

When the Statement Is Made to a Private Person *Miranda* does not apply to statements or confessions made to private persons. Protection against compulsory self-incrimination applies only to interrogations initiated by law enforcement officers. Incriminating statements made by the accused to friends or cellmates while in custody are admissible even if made without the *Miranda* warnings. This is because the Bill of Rights does not apply to the actions of private persons as long as they are purely private.

When a Suspect Testifies before a Grand Jury In an interrogation of a potential criminal defendant before a grand jury, the *Miranda* warnings are not required, even if the prosecutor intends to charge the witness with an offense. This is because grand jury questioning does not constitute custodial interrogation. The theory is that such interrogation does not present the same opportunities for abuse as custodial interrogation by the police. Questioning in a grand jury room is different from custodial police interrogation (*United States v. Mandujano*, 425 U.S. 564 [1976]). The evidence obtained may be held inadmissible, however, if state law requires the giving of the *Miranda* warnings even in grand jury proceedings. State laws that give more rights to suspects than the Constitution does are binding on government agencies in that state.

When There Is a Threat to Public Safety In *New York v. Quarles*, 467 U.S. 649 (1984), the Court carved out a **public safety exception** to the *Miranda* rule, saying that, when questions asked by police officers are reasonably prompted by concern for public safety, the responses are admissible in court even though the suspect was in police custody and not given the *Miranda* warnings.

In the *Quarles* case, a woman approached two police officers who were on patrol, told them that she had just been raped, described her assailant, and said that the man had just entered a nearby supermarket and was carrying a gun. One officer entered the store and spotted Quarles, who matched the description given by the woman. Quarles ran toward the rear of the store but was eventually apprehended. The officer noticed that Quarles was wearing an empty shoulder holster. After handcuffing the suspect, the police asked where the gun was; Quarles nodded toward some empty cartons, where the gun was found. The suspect was given the *Miranda* warnings only after the gun was recovered. The Court said that the gun was admissible as evidence under the public safety exception.

public safety exception
responses to questions by the police without the *Miranda* warnings are admissible if the questions are reasonably prompted by concerns for public safety.

New York v. Quarles (1984)

The public safety exception is best limited to cases in which a criminal act has just been committed and there is immediate danger to the public; otherwise, it might be abused. It should not apply to cases in which the danger to public safety is not immediate or serious.

When an Undercover Officer Poses as an Inmate and Asks Questions In *Illinois v. Perkins*, 496 U.S. 292 (1990), the Court decided that an undercover law enforcement officer posing as a fellow inmate did not need to give the *Miranda* warnings to a suspect in jail before asking questions that might produce an incriminating response.

Illinois v. Perkins (1990)

In this case, the police placed undercover agent Parisi in a jail cell block with the suspect Perkins, who had been detained on charges unrelated to the murder that Parisi was investigating. When Parisi asked Perkins if he had ever killed anybody, Perkins made statements incriminating himself in the murder. He was subsequently charged, tried, and convicted. On appeal, he sought to exclude the evidence, claiming that he should have been given the *Miranda* warnings before being asked the incriminating question by Parisi.

The Court disagreed, saying that the doctrine must be enforced strictly but only in situations in which the concerns underlying that decision are present. These concerns were not present there, because the essential ingredients of a police-dominated atmosphere and compulsion were absent. The Court said that a coercive atmosphere is "not present when an incarcerated person speaks freely to someone whom he believes to be a fellow inmate and whom he assumes is not an officer having official power over him." The Court then added that in such circumstances *Miranda* does not forbid mere strategic deception by taking advantage of a suspect's misplaced trust.

MIRANDA CASES ON APPEAL: THE HARMLESS ERROR RULE

harmless error rule
a rule stating that an error made by the trial court in admitting illegally obtained evidence does not lead to a reversal of the conviction if the error is determined to be harmless. The prosecution has the burden of proving that the error is in fact harmless.

The **harmless error rule** provides that harmless errors during trial in civil or criminal cases do not require a reversal of the judgment by an appellate court. Conversely, if the error is *harmful*, the judgment must be reversed. In *Arizona v. Fulminante*, 499 U.S. 279 (1991), the Court ruled that the harmless error rule is applicable to cases involving involuntary confessions. But the burden of proving harmless error rests with the prosecution and must be established "beyond a reasonable doubt." This is significant because prior to *Fulminante* the rule was that the erroneous admission into evidence by the trial court

Arizona v. Fulminante (1991)

HIGHLIGHT ▸ **Police Acceptance of *Miranda***

Despite their initial reaction of dismay, the police seem to have adjusted to *Miranda* fairly well. Under the circumstances, the Court is probably willing to "live with" a case that has become part of American culture, especially if it continues to view the case as a serious effort to strike a proper balance between the need

for police questioning and the need to protect a suspect against impermissible police pressure.

Source: Yale Kamisar, in *The Oxford Companion to the Supreme Court of the United States*, ed. Kermit L. Hall (New York: Oxford University Press, 1992), p. 555.

of an involuntary confession led to an automatic reversal of the conviction on appeal regardless of whether the admission was harmless or harmful. That has now changed.

The facts of the case are sad, and the Court decision was complex, with three issues decided by the Court on close votes. Fulminante was suspected by police of having murdered his stepdaughter, but no charges were filed against him. He left Arizona for New Jersey, where he was later convicted on an unrelated charge of firearms possession. While incarcerated in a federal prison in New York on that charge, Fulminante was befriended by a fellow inmate, Sarivola, who was serving a sixty-day sentence for extortion. Sarivola later became an informant for the FBI. Sarivola offered Fulminante protection from the other inmates (which Fulminante needed because of the rumor that he was a child murderer) in exchange for the truth. Fulminante admitted to Sarivola that he had driven his stepdaughter to the desert on his motorcycle, choked and sexually assaulted her, and made her beg for her life before shooting her twice in the head. After his release from prison, Fulminante also confessed to Sarivola's wife about the same crime. Indicted for first-degree murder, Fulminante sought exclusion of his confessions to Sarivola and Sarivola's wife. The trial court admitted the confession; Fulminante was convicted and sentenced to death.

On appeal, the Court addressed three issues raised by Fulminante:

◆ Should the harmless error rule apply to *Miranda* confessions on appeal? Yes.
◆ Was Fulminante's confession voluntary? No, it was coerced.
◆ Was the admission of Fulminante's confession by the trial court a harmless error in his conviction? No, because the government failed to establish beyond a reasonable doubt that the admission was a harmless error.

The Court decision meant that Fulminante was to be given a new trial, but the involuntary confession could not be admitted.

Under the *Fulminante* rule, the reversal of a conviction on appeal in *Miranda*-type cases involves two steps. The first step is determining whether the confession is voluntary or involuntary. If the confession is voluntary, then the admission by the trial court of the evidence is proper. If it is involuntary, the second step becomes necessary—determining whether the admission of such evidence by the trial court was a harmless error. The burden of proof rests with the prosecution. If the admission constitutes a harmless error (as determined by the appellate court), the conviction is affirmed. Conversely, the conviction is reversed: (1) if the error is deemed harmful by the appellate court, or (2) if the prosecution fails to establish beyond a reasonable doubt that the error was harmless (as was the situation in *Fulminante*).

SUMMARY

The *Miranda* warnings consist of these statements:

◆ You have a right to remain silent.
◆ Anything you say can be used against you in a court of law.

◆ You have a right to the presence of an attorney.
◆ If you cannot afford an attorney, one will be appointed for you prior to questioning.
◆ You have the right to terminate this interview at any time.

Certain issues have surrounded the *Miranda* case:

◆ *Importance: Miranda* sets the standard for admissibility of admissions or confessions.
◆ *Standard for admissibility before* Miranda: Voluntariness.
◆ *Standard for admissibility after* Miranda: Three questions: (1) Were the *Miranda* warnings given? (2) Was there a waiver? (3) If so, was the waiver intelligent and voluntary? The answer to all three questions must be yes.
◆ *When must the* Miranda *warnings be given?* Whenever there is a custodial interrogation.
◆ *When is a person in custody?* When under arrest or deprived of freedom in a significant way.
◆ *When is a person under interrogation?* When being asked questions or when the police create a situation that is likely to elicit a confession or admission.
◆ *For what offenses must the* Miranda *warnings be given?* All offenses—felonies and misdemeanors—except routine traffic stops.
◆ *Can the* Miranda *rights be waived?* Yes, but the government must prove that the waiver was intelligent and voluntary.
◆ *What is the rule for* Miranda *cases on appeal?* Conviction is reversed if the admission of excludable evidence by the trial court is harmful; conviction is not reversed if the admission of excludable evidence is harmless.

In some instances, the *Miranda* warnings are not needed:

◆ When no questions are asked by the officer
◆ During general on-the-scene questioning
◆ When the statement is volunteered
◆ When questioning a suspect about their identification
◆ When questioning witnesses
◆ In stop-and-frisk cases
◆ During lineups, showups, or photographic identifications
◆ When the statement is made to a private person
◆ When the suspect appears before a grand jury
◆ When there is a threat to public safety

REVIEW QUESTIONS

1. What was the old standard for the admissibility of confessions and admissions? Explain why that standard was difficult to apply.
2. How did *Miranda v. Arizona* change the standard for admissibility of confessions and admissions? In your opinion, is it a change for the better? Explain your answer.
3. Assume that the state legislature of Washington passes a law providing that confessions are admissible in state court criminal cases as long as they are voluntary, even without the *Miranda* warnings. Is that law constitutional? Cite a case precedent and reasons for your answer.
4. Distinguish between the *Miranda* warnings and the right to counsel. In what ways are they similar? In what ways are they different?
5. Explain what custodial interrogation means.
6. Assume a college student is a suspect in a campus burglary case. He is being asked questions by the campus police in his dormitory room with his roommate present. Must the police give him the *Miranda* warnings? Explain your answer.
7. "The *Miranda* warnings must be given every time the police interrogate a suspect in connection with an offense." Is that statement true or false? Discuss your answer.
8. What is meant by the functional equivalent of an interrogation? Give an example.
9. Distinguish between the subjective test and the objective test used in determining whether a person is in custody for purposes of the *Miranda* warnings. Which test would a police officer prefer the courts use and why?
10. A police officer has obtained an oral confession from a suspect even though she failed to give the suspect the *Miranda* warnings because before she could do that, the suspect admitted to having committed the crime under investigation. Is that confession of any use to police in court during trial? Justify your answer.
11. Based on Court decisions, give four situations when the *Miranda* warnings are not needed and explain why.
12. What is the harmless error rule on appeal? Give an example of its application in *Miranda* cases.

1. Ed robbed an apartment and kidnapped its sole occupant. Charged with both offenses, Ed was assigned a lawyer for the robbery but not for the kidnapping. Discuss whether Ed may be questioned by the police for the kidnapping in the absence of his lawyer.

2. Sam, a university student, ran a red light and was stopped by the police. He was asked to get out of his car and was questioned about why he ran a red light and was speeding. Sam gave unsatisfactory answers. The police looked around the car and saw a suspicious package. They asked if they could open it; Sam said yes. The package turned out to contain drugs. The police asked Sam for the source of the drugs. Sam said he got it from his dormitory roommate. The police then went to Sam's room and found more drugs. During the trial, Sam claimed he should have been given the *Miranda* warnings by the police. Based on the officer's failure to give the *Miranda* warnings, are any of the drugs confiscated admissible in evidence? Justify your answer.

3. Officer Peters went to Greg's house, a 19-year-old gang member. Greg's family knew Officer Peters because he lived in the same neighborhood and was a family friend. Officer Peters talked to Greg's parents and told them he had information about Greg's involvement in a murder. The officer asked the parents to appeal to their son to cooperate with the police. The parents called Greg into the room and asked him to "tell Officer Peters the truth." At first Greg denied involvement, but after repeated questioning by his parents, Greg admitted his part in the murder, which he committed with two other gang members. During the trial, Greg sought exclusion of his statement, saying he should have been given the *Miranda* warnings by Officer Peters. You are the judge. Will you exclude or admit the statement? Justify your answer.

4. Defendant Jones claims he was in custody when interrogated by the police about a murder. Officer Smith denies that claim and says that custody and arrest were farthest from his mind when he and Jones (they knew each other because they lived in the same neighborhood) chatted on the street one day about the murder of a neighbor whom they both knew. You are the judge who is presiding in Jones's murder trial. Whose claim prevails—that of Jones or Officer Smith? What standard will you use to justify your ruling?

5. The police are transporting a suspect in a police car for interrogation in the police station. During the long drive, the officers asked the suspect to which church he belongs. He said he worshipped every Sunday in a local church that adhered to strict rules about the Bible and belief in God. The police then say that their own church also had the same strict rules about living the righteous life. There was no further conversation other than that. A few minutes later, however, the suspect started to sob and then confessed that he did kill his wife in a fit of jealousy. He later signed a statement confession to the crime. Is that confession admissible during trial? State why or why not.

6. A 17-year-old juvenile, who is the best student in his high school class, is being asked questions by a police officer in the school principal's office about an alleged rape that took place in school grounds. You are that officer. Should you give that juvenile the *Miranda* warnings? Justify you're answer.

RECOMMENDED READINGS

Fred E. Inbau. *Law and police practice: Restrictions on the law of interrogation and confessions.* 89 Journal of Criminal Law and Criminology 1393, 1403 (1999).

Yale Kamisar. *On the fortieth anniversary of the* Miranda *case: Why we needed it, how we got it— and what happened to it.* 5 Ohio State Journal of Criminal Law 163 (2007).

Charles D. Weisselberg. *Saving Miranda (Miranda v. Arizona, 86 S.Ct. 1602 [1966],* Cornell Law Review, 109–192 (1998).

Kit Kinports. *The Supreme Court's love-hate relationship with* Miranda. Journal of Criminal Law & Criminology, Spring 2011, vol. 101, issue 2, pp. 375–440.

Baker, Liva. *Miranda: Crime Law and Politics*. New York: Atheneum, 1985.

Smith, and Albert W. Alschuler. *The Privilege against Self-Incrimination: Its Origins and Development*. Chicago: University of Chicago Press, 1997.

Leo, Richard A. *Police Interrogation and American Justice*. Cambridge, Mass.: Harvard University Press, 2008.

Levy, Leonard. *The Origins of the Fifth Amendment: The Right against Self-Incrimination*. London: Oxford University Press, 1968.

CHAPTER 12

Basic Constitutional Rights of the Accused during Trial

LEARNING OBJECTIVES

1. Identify five of the basic rights given to the accused during trial.
2. Diagram the level development of the right to counsel during trial.
3. Describe the process for selecting a jury for trial.
4. Compare and contrast the different meanings of due process.
5. Differentiate between the two challenges use to disqualify prospective jurors.
6. Determine, when provided different situations, whether the defendant or the accused is entitled to right to counsel at that point.
7. Explain the different methods of obtaining counsel.
8. Describe when counsel is determined to be ineffective.
9. Compare and contrast the privilege of self-incrimination between the accused and a witness.
10. List methods to ensure a fair and impartial trial for the accused.

KEY TERMS

Brady rule

challenge for cause

court-appointed counsel

hung jury

immunity

indigent defendant

jury of peers

nonunanimous verdict

peremptory challenge

petty offense

physical self-incrimination

privilege of a witness

privilege of the accused

procedural due process

retained counsel

sequestration

serious offense

substantive due process

testimonial or communicative self-incrimination

transactional immunity

use and derivative use immunity

voir dire

Junial Enterprises/Shutterstock.com

THE TOP 5 IMPORTANT CASES

in Basic Constitutional Rights of the Accused During the Trial

■ *GIDEON V. WAINWRIGHT* (1963) The Sixth Amendment right to counsel is applicable to state proceedings through the due process clause of the Fourteenth Amendment. The right to counsel applies every time an accused is charged with a felony offense.

■ *BRADY V. MARYLAND* (1963) Due process is violated when the prosecution suppresses evidence favorable to an accused upon request where the evidence is material either to guilt or to punishment.

■ *BATSON V. KENTUCKY* (1986) A prosecutor's use of peremptory challenges to exclude members of the defendant's race from the jury solely on racial grounds violates the equal protection rights of both the defendant and the excluded jurors.

■ *LOCKHART V. MCCREE* (1986) Persons who are unwilling to vote for the death penalty under any circumstances may be disqualified from a capital offense jury.

■ *J. E. B. V. ALABAMA* (1994) The equal protection clause prohibits discrimination based on gender in the selection of jurors.

It is better that ten guilty persons escape than that one innocent suffer.
—Sir William Blackstone (1723–1780)

THE CONSTITUTIONAL rights guaranteed in the Bill of Rights are most highly protected during the trial stage of a criminal proceeding. This is when the adversarial process, which characterizes the U.S. criminal justice process, is at its peak. The government is represented by the prosecutor, and the accused is championed by the defense lawyer, who has been either retained by the accused or appointed by the state. The judge, a neutral party, presides over the trial, setting the rules for the lawyers to follow. In bench trials, the judge also determines the facts; in jury trials, that function is performed by the jury. This adversarial process supposedly ensures that truth will emerge and justice is fairly administered. This does not always turn out to be the case, but the expectation and the ideal are always there.

The Constitution guarantees the accused fundamental rights during trial, the most important of which are discussed in this chapter. The constitutional rights discussed in this chapter cannot be reduced or taken away by federal or state laws, but federal and state governments can add additional rights. Three examples illustrate this.

◆ *Example 1.* There is no constitutional right to a twelve-member jury trial, but the federal government and most states provide for twelve-member juries by statute or by provision in the state constitution.
◆ *Example 2.* The Constitution does not guarantee a defendant the right to appeal a criminal conviction, but the federal government and all states provide for the right to appeal, by either state law or a provision of the state constitution.
◆ *Example 3.* There is no constitutional right to a jury trial in juvenile proceedings, but a jury hearing may be given by state law.

This chapter discusses five basic rights of the accused, which are:

◆ The right to a trial by jury
◆ The right to counsel
◆ The right to due process
◆ The right against self-incrimination
◆ The right to a fair and impartial trial

There are other constitutional rights that are not discussed in this chapter because, although they are important, these rights are of immediate concern not to the police but to the courts. These other constitutional rights, which are summarized briefly at the end of this chapter, are:

◆ The right to protection against double jeopardy
◆ The right to confront witnesses
◆ The right to compulsory process to obtain witnesses
◆ The right to a speedy and public trial
◆ The right to proof of guilt beyond a reasonable doubt

THE RIGHT TO TRIAL BY JURY

Article III, Section 2, Clause 3 of the Constitution provides that "[t]he Trial of all Crimes, except in cases of Impeachment, shall be by Jury." The Sixth Amendment also provides that "In all criminal prosecutions, the accused shall enjoy the right to a speedy and public trial, by an impartial jury of the State and district wherein the crime shall have been committed." We will now look at issues surrounding trial by jury, including the following:

◆ Voir dire
◆ Jury size
◆ Unanimous versus nonunanimous verdicts
◆ Serious versus petty offenses
◆ The selection of the jury
◆ Disqualification based on race or gender

Voir Dire

Voir dire is a process whereby potential jurors are assembled in court and questioned by the judge or attorneys so either side can determine if they should be chosen for or disqualified from membership in a trial jury. It is a French term literally meaning "to speak the truth"; its avowed purpose is the identification of individuals who are qualified to serve on a jury. Noted writers Wayne LaFave, Jerold Israel, and Nancy King maintain that the voir dire serves three legitimate functions. The first is "to elicit information which would establish a basis for challenges for cause." The second is "to facilitate the intelligent use of peremptory challenges," and the third is "that of indoctrinating the potential jurors on the merits of the case and developing rapport."[1] The questions to be asked by lawyers during the voir dire process are determined by the judge, who exercises a great deal of discretion when setting limits. Decisions by the trial judge about which questions can or cannot be asked are almost always upheld by an appellate court, if challenged. Typically, potential jurors are asked to complete a questionnaire from which the judge or lawyers get a written glimpse at the backgrounds of the jury pool. This saves time during the question and answer period. In highly publicized cases, the voir dire may take days or weeks and can be a contentious process. It has been said, with a grain of truth, that despite public avowals, neither side in a case is really interested in a neutral jury. Instead, both sides want jurors who will likely be sympathetic to their cause.

> **voir dire**
> a process whereby potential jurors are assembled in court and questioned by the judge or attorneys so either side can determine if they should be chosen for or disqualified from membership in a trial jury.

Jury Size

A jury of twelve is not required by the Sixth Amendment in criminal or civil trials; that number, however, is often required by state or federal law. In *Williams v. Florida*, 399 U.S. 78 (1970), the Supreme Court upheld a Florida law providing for a six-member jury in all state criminal cases except those involving the death penalty. The minimum number of jurors is six. Juries of fewer than six members are unconstitutional, because there would be too few jurors to provide for effective group discussion and it would diminish the chances of drawing from a fair, representative cross section of the community—thus impairing the accuracy of fact-finding (*Ballew v. Georgia*, 435 U.S. 223 [1978]). Although most juries are composed of either twelve or six members, any number between six and twelve is constitutional. Whether death penalty cases can be decided by juries of fewer than twelve is an issue the Court has not addressed. Given the severity of the punishment involved, the Court probably would not approve a jury of fewer than twelve people in death penalty cases.

> *Williams v. Florida* (1970)

> *Ballew v. Georgia* (1978)

Unanimous versus Nonunanimous Verdicts

The Constitution does not require that guilty verdicts in criminal cases be unanimous. In federal criminal cases, a unanimous jury verdict is required, but a **nonunanimous verdict** suffices in some state trials. For example, in *Apodaca v. Oregon*, 406 U.S. 404 (1972), the Court held that a 10-to-2 vote for conviction is constitutional. And in *Johnson v. Louisiana*, 406 U.S. 356 (1972), the Court upheld the constitutionality of a 9-to-3 vote for conviction. The Court has not decided whether an 8-to-4 or a 7-to-5 vote for conviction would also be constitutional; no states presently allow such verdicts.

> **nonunanimous verdict**
> a verdict by a jury that is not the result of a unanimous vote.

> *Apodaca v. Oregon* (1972)
> *Johnson v. Louisiana* (1972)

What this means is that a state can provide for a less-than-unanimous verdict for conviction and that such a procedure is constitutional. Currently, forty-five states require unanimity in criminal cases, but twenty-nine states do not require unanimity in civil trials. The vote needed to convict varies among jurisdictions that do not require unanimity, ranging from two-thirds in Montana to five-sixths in Oregon. All states require a unanimous verdict in capital cases. The Court prohibits a finding of guilty by less than a six-person majority; therefore, in a six-person criminal trial, the jury must always be unanimous in finding guilt.

The Court has rejected the argument that permitting a nonunanimous verdict violates the reasonable doubt standard for conviction in criminal cases, saying that disagreement among jurors would not in itself establish that there was a reasonable doubt as to the defendant's guilt. Reasonable doubt refers to the thinking of an individual juror, not to a split vote among the jurors, even though that vote be narrow. A **hung jury** is a jury that cannot come to a unanimous agreement (in jurisdictions where unanimity is required) to convict or to acquit. When this happens, the defendant can be tried again at the discretion of the prosecutor. There is no constitutional limit to the number of times an accused can be tried again after a hung jury. This decision is left to the discretion of the prosecutor.

hung jury
a jury that cannot come to a unanimous agreement to convict or to acquit.

Serious versus Petty Offenses

Despite the wording of Article III, Section 2, Clause 3 of the Constitution, which states that "[t]he Trial of all Crimes . . . shall be by Jury," the Court has ruled that the Constitution guarantees a jury trial only when a *serious offense* is charged. Such offenses must be distinguished from mere "petty" offenses. For purposes of the constitutional right to a trial by jury, a **serious offense** is one for which more than six months' imprisonment is authorized (*Baldwin v. New York*, 399 U.S. 66 [1970]). In making this determination, courts look at the maximum possible sentence that may be imposed. An offense is considered serious if the maximum punishment *authorized* by statute is imprisonment for more than six months, regardless of the penalty *actually* imposed; therefore, the accused is entitled to a jury trial. For example, suppose Jane is tried

serious offense
for purposes of a jury trial, one for which more than six months imprisonment is authorized.

for theft, the maximum penalty for which is one year in jail. If Jane is denied a jury trial, convicted, and sentenced to five months in jail, the conviction must be reversed because the proceedings violated Jane's right to a trial by jury even though the actual penalty imposed was less than six months.

By contrast, an offense whose maximum penalty is six months or less is considered a **petty offense** for purposes of the right to a trial by jury (regardless of how that offense is classified by state law); therefore, the defendant has no constitutional right to a jury trial. The Court has ruled that when a state treats drunk driving as a petty offense, no jury trial is needed even if other peripheral sanctions (such as a fine and automatic loss of one's driver's license) may also be imposed (*Blanton v. North Las Vegas*, 489 U.S. 538 [1989]). However, some states classify drunk driving as a serious offense for which the maximum penalty is more than six months of confinement. In those states, a jury trial is constitutionally required.

Significantly, the Court has held that a defendant who is prosecuted in a single case for more than one petty offense does not have a constitutional right to a trial by jury even if the total potential penalty exceeds six months (*Lewis v. United States*, 518 U.S. 322 [1996]). In *Lewis*, the defendant was charged in a single proceeding with two counts of mail obstruction. Each charge carried a penalty of six months' imprisonment. The defendant argued that he was entitled to a jury trial because he faced a total imprisonment of up to one year for the two petty offenses. On appeal, the Court disagreed, saying that the "scope of the Sixth Amendment does not change just because a defendant faces multiple charges" and that "where we have a judgment by the legislature that an offense is petty, we do not look to the potential prison term faced by a particular defendant who is charged with more than one such petty offense."

In sum, the maximum authorized penalty for one offense determines whether a defendant is entitled to a jury trial, not the total penalty the defendant faces in cases of multiple charges. If no punishment is prescribed by statute, the offense is considered petty when the actual sentence imposed is six months or less.

Selecting a Jury of Peers

The Supreme Court's interpretation of the Sixth Amendment requires that trial juries in both federal and state criminal trials be selected from "a representative cross-section of the community." It also guarantees trial by a **jury of peers**. This phrase does not mean that, say, a student facing criminal charges must have a jury of students or that female defendants must have an all-female jury. What it does mean is that jury service cannot be consciously restricted to a particular group. For example, excluding women from juries or giving them automatic exemptions, with the result that jury panels are almost totally male, is invalid (*Taylor v. Louisiana*, 419 U.S. 522 [1975]). Likewise, the exclusion of persons because of race, creed, color, or national origin is unconstitutional.

Disqualification of Jurors Based on Race

A prosecutor's use of **peremptory challenges**—challenges for which no reason is stated, as opposed to **challenges for cause**, for which legal reasons for the challenge must be stated—to exclude members of the defendant's race from a jury solely on racial grounds violates the equal protection rights of both the defendant and the excluded jurors (*Batson v. Kentucky*, 476 U.S. 79 [1986]). In *Batson v. Kentucky*, a trial judge in Kentucky

petty offense
for purposes of a jury trial, it is an offense whose maximum penalty is six months or less.

Blanton v. North Las Vegas (1989)

Lewis v. United States (1996)

MYTH vs. REALITY

MYTH A defendant has the right to a jury of peers, and that means the jury must include people similar in age or race or gender to the defendant.

FACT A defendant's right to a jury of peers means only that the jury must come from the same community as where the crime occurred and be representative of the community generally, not the defendant specifically.

jury of peers
a jury that is not consciously restricted to a particular group.

Taylor v. Louisiana (1975)

peremptory challenges
a challenge to exclude a potential juror for which no reason is stated.

challenges for cause
a challenge to exclude a potential juror based on legal reasons.

conducted the examination of the jury and excused certain jurors for cause. After that, the prosecutor used his peremptory challenges to strike all four black persons from the jury pool, resulting in an all-white jury. On appeal, the Court reaffirmed the principle announced in an 1880 case (*Strauder v. West Virginia*, 100 U.S. 303 [1880]), saying that "the State denies a black defendant equal protection of the laws when it puts him on trial before a jury from which members of his race have been purposefully excluded." Interestingly, however, the prosecution's racially motivated use of peremptory challenges to exclude people from the trial jury does not violate the defendant's Sixth Amendment right to a trial by an impartial jury (*Holland v. Illinois*, 493 U.S. 474 [1990]). But the Court did hint that such a challenge could have been raised as a violation of the constitutional right to equal protection under the Fourteenth Amendment. Because that challenge was not raised in this case, the result was different from that of *Batson*.

Strauder v. West Virginia (1880)

Holland v. Illinois (1990)

In *Batson*, the Court outlined the three steps courts must follow in resolving cases of peremptory jury disqualification based on race:

◆ *Step 1.* The side making the allegation (usually the defense) must establish a *prima facie* (meaning at first sight) case of discrimination based on race or other forbidden grounds.
◆ *Step 2.* The burden then shifts to the side that made the peremptory strike to come up with a race-neutral explanation for the strike.
◆ *Step 3.* The trial court is then required to decide whether the side opposing the peremptory challenges has proved purposeful discrimination.

To illustrate the three-step process, suppose Defendant Alex is tried and convicted by an all-white jury. Alex alleges that potential African American jurors were scratched from the jury pool by the prosecutor because of race. If Alex establishes a prima facie case that race was, in fact, the reason for their disqualifications (admittedly difficult to do in peremptory challenges because no reason is given), then the burden shifts to the prosecutor to establish that race was not the basis for removing them from the jury pool. The trial court must then decide whether Alex has, in fact, proved discrimination based on race.

Johnson v. California (2005)

In *Johnson v. California*, 543 U.S. 499 (2005), the Court held that "permissible inferences of discrimination were sufficient to establish a prima facie case of discrimination under *Batson*, shifting the burden to the prosecution to explain adequately the racial exclusion by offering permissible race-neutral justifications for the strikes." These "permissible inferences of discrimination" make it easier for defendants to challenge racial discrimination during peremptory challenges (where no reason needs to be given by either side when striking a juror from the list, which often results in disqualification of racial minorities).

Snyder v. Louisiana (2008)

In *Snyder v. Louisiana*, 552 U.S. 472 (2008), the Court concluded that the trial judge acted improperly in upholding the peremptory strikes of the black jurors, saying that the reasons given by the prosecution for striking the jurors applied equally well to the white jurors that the prosecutor did not strike. Allen Snyder, an African American, was charged with and tried for murder in Louisiana. The prosecutor used peremptory challenges to strike all five African Americans in the jury pool. Snyder, tried by an all-white jury, was found guilty and given the death penalty. On appeal, his lawyers argued that the striking of all the black jurors constituted discrimination in violation of the equal protection clause. The Court reversed the trial judge's ruling, which upheld the prosecutor's strikes, saying that the judge committed clear error in holding that the strikes were not based on race considerations and therefore violated *Batson*. The fact that the white jurors, to whom the reasons for striking the black jurors applied equally, were left on the jury clearly indicated that striking the African American jurors was based on race.

The Court has also held that the Constitution prohibits a criminal defendant, as well as the prosecution, from engaging in purposeful discrimination on the grounds of race in the exercise of peremptory challenges (*Georgia v. McCullum*, 505 U.S. 42 [1992]). In this case, several white defendants were charged with assaulting two African Americans. Before the jury selection process began, the trial judge denied the prosecution's motion to prohibit defendants from exercising their peremptory challenges in a racially discriminatory manner, as the prosecution expected the defendants would do. On appeal, the Court said that in previous cases it had held that the exercise of racially discriminatory peremptory challenges violates the equal protection clause of the Fourteenth Amendment when the offending challenges are made by the state and, in civil cases, when they are made by private litigants. The Court held that the prohibition should also be extended to discriminatory challenges made by criminal defendants.

Georgia v. McCullum (1992)

Is racial underrepresentation in the venire panel sufficient in itself to establish racial discrimination in jury selection? The Court said no, holding that "underrepresentation of African Americans in a jury pool does not, of itself, establish a constitutional violation (*Berghuis. v. Smith* (559 U.S. — [2010]). In this case Smith, an African American, was arrested and charged with murder. The jury panel included approximately 100 people, but only three were African American. Smith was convicted of second-degree murder and possession of a firearm; he was sentenced to life in prison without possibility of parole. On appeal, Smith claimed that his right to a jury trial was violated because his jury was not drawn from a "cross section" of the community. The Court disagreed, saying that underrepresentation of a racial group in and of itself in a jury pool does not establish a constitutional violation. What is needed, instead, is for the defendant to establish three facts: "(1) the excluded group is a distinct group; (2) there is an unfair and unreasonable disproportion in the venires from which juries are selected; and (3) the underrepresentation is due to a systematic exclusion of the group in the jury selection process." The defendant in this case failed to establish these. The Court added that it is not enough that defendant simply identifies a number of factors or practices that, theoretically, could cause racial underrepresentation. In sum, the burden of proof falls heavily on the person making allegations of racial underrepresentation.

Berghuis. v. Smith (2010)

May a white defendant object to the exclusion of black jurors from the jury through the use of a peremptory challenge, and vice versa? The answer is yes. The defendant does not need to be a member of the group excluded to invoke successfully the equal protection clause (*Powers v. Ohio*, 499 U.S. 400 [1991]). In *Powers v. Ohio*, Powers, a white man, objected to the prosecution's use of peremptory challenges to remove seven African Americans from the jury. The Court upheld his challenge on appeal, saying that under the equal protection clause a defendant may object to the race-based exclusion of jurors through peremptory challenges even though the defendant and the excluded jurors are not of the same race. And, in a 1998 case, the Court extended that decision, ruling that a white defendant had reason to complain of discrimination against blacks in the selection of the grand jury (*Campbell v. Louisiana*, 523 U.S. 392 [1998]).

Powers v. Ohio (1991)

Campbell v. Louisiana (1998)

Disqualification of Jurors Based on Gender

J.E.B. v. Alabama (1994)

The Court has held that the Constitution forbids discrimination in the selection of jurors based on "gender" or "on the assumption that an individual will be biased in a particular case solely because the person happens to be a woman or a man" (*J.E.B. v. Alabama*, 511 U.S. 127 [1994]). This case involved a paternity and child support trial in which the state used nine of its ten peremptory challenges to remove male jurors, resulting in an all-female civil jury. The state assumed that male jurors would be biased in favor of a man in a child support–paternity lawsuit. In holding that the disqualifications violated the equal protection clause, the Court said that "the conclusion that litigants may not strike potential jurors solely on the basis of gender does not imply the elimination of all peremptory challenges," as some had feared, adding that "so long as gender does not serve as a proxy for bias, unacceptable jurors may still be removed." Although this case involved peremptory challenges in a civil case, there is every reason to believe that it also applies to criminal cases in terms of both peremptory challenges and challenges for cause. (To learn more about this case, read the Case Brief.)

The principles and cases involving challenges based on race and gender represent an attempt by the Court to ensure that all juries are selected in a nondiscriminatory manner and that race and gender are not factors, whether in challenges for cause or in peremptory challenges. However, because peremptory challenges are made without giving reasons, it is difficult to determine whether a peremptory challenge is based on race—unless the results are clear, obvious, and provable, or one party admits to such bias.

The controversy over peremptory challenges silently based on race and gender may extend to similar challenges based on other grounds. Although discrimination based on race and gender has generated the most attention in recent years, factors such as lifestyle, mental disability, religion, class, ethnicity, national origin, occupation, economic status, and physical status may gain prominence in an era of inclusion and increasing diversity. Although some of these issues have been raised in lower courts, the U.S. Supreme Court has thus far not addressed them.

CASE BRIEF

J.E.B. v. Alabama, 511 U.S. 127 (1994)

The Leading Case on Gender Discrimination in Jury Trials

Facts: The state of Alabama filed a complaint for paternity and child support against J.E.B. on behalf of the mother of a minor child. The trial court assembled a panel of thirty-six potential jurors: twelve males and twenty-four females. Three jurors were excused for cause, leaving ten males and twenty-three females in the jury pool. The state of Alabama used nine of its ten peremptory challenges to remove male jurors; the male defendant used nine strikes to remove female jurors. The result was an all-female jury. Even before the jury was impaneled, the petitioner objected to the peremptory challenges by the state, saying that they were exercised against male jurors solely on the basis of gender. Trial was held, and the jury found the petitioner to be the father of the child; he was ordered to pay child support. He appealed.

Issue or Issues: *Does the Constitution prohibit discrimination in jury selection based on gender?* Yes.

Decision: The decision of the Court of Civil Appeals of Alabama was reversed and remanded.

Holding: "The Equal Protection Clause of the Constitution prohibits discrimination in jury selection on the basis of gender, or on the assumption that an individual will be biased in a particular case solely because that person happens to be a woman or a man."

Case Significance: This case extends the *Batson* ruling, which prohibits discrimination based on race in jury peremptory challenges, to discrimination based on gender, hence proscribing both types of discrimination. The petitioner in this case was a man who alleged that his equal protection rights were violated because the state of Alabama used its peremptory challenges to strike males from the jury, the result being an all-female jury that found him to be the father of the child and required him to pay child support. The Court upheld the challenge, saying that gender discrimination in jury selection is unconstitutional. The Court added, however, that "[t]he conclusion that litigants may not strike potential jurors solely on the basis of gender does not imply the elimination of all peremptory challenges. So long as gender does not serve as a proxy for bias, unacceptable jurors may still be removed, including those who are members of a group or class that is normally subject to 'rational basis' review and those who exhibit characteristics that are disproportionately associated with one gender." What is prohibited are challenges based on bias simply because a potential juror is a male or a female and is therefore expected to vote in a certain way. Peremptory challenges based on gender bias are usually difficult to prove because they are made without any reasons given. There are cases such as this one, however, in which the obvious reason for the strikes was gender bias. In these types of cases, the constitutional prohibition applies.

Excerpts from the Opinion: Discrimination in jury selection, whether based on race or on gender, causes harm to the litigants, the community, and the individual jurors who are wrongfully excluded from participation in the judicial process. The litigants are harmed by the risk that the prejudice which motivated the discriminatory selection of the jury will infect the entire proceedings. The community is harmed by the State's participation in the perpetuation of invidious group stereotypes and the inevitable loss of confidence in our judicial system that state sanctioned discrimination in the courtroom engenders. When state actors exercise peremptory challenges in reliance on gender stereotypes, they ratify and reinforce prejudicial views of the relative abilities of men and women. Because these stereotypes have wreaked injustice in so many other spheres of our country's public life, active discrimination by litigants on the basis of gender during jury selection "invites cynicism respecting the jury's neutrality and its obligation to adhere to the law." The potential for cynicism is particularly acute in cases where gender related issues are prominent, such as cases involving rape, sexual harassment, or paternity. Discriminatory use of peremptory challenges may create the impression that the judicial system has acquiesced in suppressing full participation by one gender or that the "deck has been stacked" in favor of one side.

 HIGHLIGHT ⟩ **Quick Summary of the Right to Trial by Jury**

- ◆ Voir dire is the process whereby potential jurors are assembled in court and questioned by the judge or attorneys for purposes of jury selection.
- ◆ A jury of twelve is not required by the Constitution, but that number is often required by state or federal law.
- ◆ Unanimous verdicts are not required by the Constitution.
- ◆ A jury trial is constitutionally required in serious offenses, meaning offenses for which more than six months imprisonment is authorized.

- ◆ A jury of peers is one which is not consciously restricted to a particular group; instead, it should represent a cross-section of the community.
- ◆ There are two kinds of jury challenges: peremptory challenge and challenge for cause.
- ◆ It is unconstitutional to disqualify jurors based on race or gender.

THE RIGHT TO COUNSEL

A second basic right discussed in this chapter is the right to counsel. The Sixth Amendment to the Constitution provides that "in all criminal prosecutions, the accused shall enjoy the right . . . to have the Assistance of Counsel for his defense."

This right has been held applicable to the states since the 1963 decision in *Gideon v. Wainwright*, 372 U.S. 335 (1963). A defendant has the right to be represented by counsel at "every critical stage" of the criminal proceeding. The meaning of the term *critical stage* has been determined by the Court on a case-by-case basis. (Read the Case Brief to learn more about this case.)

The right to counsel is available throughout the criminal justice process but is constitutionally required in the following proceedings which the Court considers a "critical stage" (the standard the Court has consistently used to determine if counsel is constitutionally required) in the criminal justice process:

- Custodial interrogations (the police must give the *Miranda* warnings)
- Lineups (if formal charges have been filed)
- Initial appearance
- Preliminary examination
- Arraignment
- Trial (discussed in this chapter)
- Sentencing
- Appeal from a conviction (if available to others)

A lawyer is *not* required by the Constitution in the following proceedings but may be required by state or federal law:

- Criminal investigation
- Arrest (unless the suspect is interrogated)
- Grand jury proceedings
- Habeas corpus proceedings
- Probation or parole revocation

This chapter discusses only a small, albeit the most important, slice of the right-to-counsel pie—the right to counsel during trial. We will examine the following topics:

- Why counsel is needed during trial
- How counsel is obtained
- The responsibility of the defense lawyer
- The right to court-appointed counsel during the trial
- The difficulty of proving ineffective assistance of counsel
- Claims of ineffective counsel in death penalty cases
- The right to act as one's own counsel
- Automatic reversal of a conviction for denying defendant a paid lawyer

Why Counsel Is Needed

In *Powell v. Alabama*, 287 U.S. 45 (1932), the Court stated the justification for the right to counsel in criminal proceeding. The Powell case was one of the two famous "Scottsboro cases" (the other was *Norris v. Alabama*, 294 U.S. 587 [1935]), in which nine black youths were charged with the rape of two white girls. Justice Sutherland wrote this often quoted statement on why an accused needs counsel during the trial:

> Even the intelligent and educated layman has small and sometimes no skill in the science of the law. Left without aid of counsel, he may be put on trial without a proper

charge, and convicted upon incompetent evidence irrelevant to the issue or otherwise inadmissible against him. Without counsel, though he may not be guilty, he faces the danger of conviction because he does not know how to establish his innocence.

Despite the importance of the assistance of a lawyer during trial, as this quotation indicates, the Court in 2004 held that if a defendant says that he or she wishes to plead guilty without the assistance of counsel, the trial judge need not spell out all the possible consequences before accepting the plea (*Iowa v. Tovar*, 541 U.S. 77 [2004]). For the waiver of the right to counsel during the plea stage to be "full knowing, intelligent, and voluntary," it is enough that the trial court inform the accused of the nature of the charges filed, the right to have counsel, and the possible range of penalties the court can impose. There is no need for the accused to be informed that his defense will be jeopardized or that he or she will lose the opportunity to get an independent opinion of whether it is prudent to plead guilty.

Iowa v. Tovar (2004)

How Counsel Is Obtained

The term *right to counsel* refers to either *retained counsel* or *court-appointed counsel*. Most of the discussion here is limited to the right to court-appointed counsel, because most criminal cases deal only with that issue. However, we begin with a discussion of retained counsel.

Retained counsel is an attorney chosen and paid by the accused. While states are not required by the Sixth Amendment to allow representation by retained counsel in any proceedings in which it has no Sixth Amendment obligation to appoint

Retained counsel
an attorney chosen and paid by the accused.

 HIGHLIGHT 〉 **The Extent of the Constitutional Right to a Lawyer in Criminal Proceedings**

Type and Sequence of Proceedings	Right to a Lawyer?
1. Criminal investigation	No
2. Arrest	No, unless interrogated
3. Custodial interrogation	Yes (*Miranda* warnings required)
4. Lineups	Yes, if formal charges have been filed; no, if formal charges have not been filed
5. Initial appearance	Yes
6. Preliminary examination	Yes
7. Grand jury (in states where required)	No
8. Arraignment	Yes
9. Trial	Yes, except for offenses that do not involve jail or prison time
10. Sentencing	Yes, except for offenses that do not involve jail or prison time
11. Appeal from a denial to withdraw a guilty plea	Yes
12. Appeal from conviction	Yes, if available to others
13. Habeas corpus (after appeal is exhausted)	No, but may be given by state or federal law
14. Probation revocation	No, but may be given by state law
15. Parole revocation	No, but may be given by state law

NOTE: The standard the U.S. Supreme Court uses to determine whether the right to a lawyer is given by the Constitution is this: Is the proceeding a "critical stage"? That is, is the defendant "compelled to make a decision which may later be formally used against him or her"?

counsel for the indigent, most jurisdictions allow retained counsel to be present even in proceedings involving misdemeanors punishable only by a fine—offenses for which the Constitution does not require states to provide counsel to indigents.

A defendant's right to hire an attorney of his or her own choosing (as opposed to an attorney provided by the state for an indigent) may be limited by the trial court to avoid a possible conflict of interest (*Wheat v. United States*, 486 U.S. 153 [1988]). In *Wheat v. United States*, the defendant and others were charged with conspiracy to distribute drugs. Two days before trial, one of the defendants asked to replace his counsel with another attorney who represented two of the other alleged co-conspirators. These two co-conspirators had either already pleaded guilty to the charges or were getting ready to do so. The prosecution objected to the change of counsel, alleging a conflict of interest if the same lawyer represented all three defendants because, for some reason, that would have limited cross-examination by the prosecutor.

The trial court refused to allow the change of counsel by the defendant, saying that it would indeed create a conflict of interest, a decision upheld by the Court on appeal. In sum, a defendant's right to hire his or her own lawyer may be limited by the trial court if there is a compelling justification for it, such as a conflict of interest.

Wheat v. United States (1988)

Automatic Reversal of a Conviction for Denying Defendant a Paid Lawyer

In a case decided in 2006, the Court held that denying a criminal defendant paid counsel of his own choosing is a "structural error" that automatically violates the Sixth Amendment right to counsel (*United States v. Gonzalez-Lopez*, 548 U.S. 140 [2006]). In this case, the defendant hired an attorney, Joseph Low, as his lawyer in a federal criminal trial. The judge refused to allow Low to represent the defendant because the judge said Low had violated a court rule in a previous case, a finding by the judge that turned out on appeal to be a mistake. Tried and convicted, the defendant appealed his conviction, claiming that the Sixth Amendment guarantees him the right to have his own paid lawyer. This right, he said, was violated because the denial by the judge was based on the judge's wrong interpretation of the court rule. The Court upheld his claim and overturned his conviction, saying that although the usual hurdle in effective counsel cases is that "defendant must prove that the result would likely have been different had his right not been violated," structural errors involving the right to counsel did not use this strict test. Said the Court: "It is impossible to know what different choices the rejected counsel would have made, and then to quantify the impact of those different choices on the outcome of the proceeding." Such an exercise would constitute speculation, where any type of test would be difficult to apply.

United States v. Gonzalez-Lopez (2006)

court-appointed counsel
a defense lawyer appointed by the court for a defendant who is too poor to pay.

Court-Appointed Counsel for Indigent Defendants **Court-appointed counsel** is an attorney appointed by the judge and paid by the county or state to represent an "indigent" accused at a "critical stage" in the criminal proceedings. More than half of felony defendants are classified as **indigent defendants**, yet the Court has not set a uniform rule to determine indigency. In general, a defendant is indigent if he or she is too poor to hire a lawyer. Standards used by judges include being unemployed, not having a car, not having posted bail, and not owning a house. The judge enjoys wide discretion in determining indigency, and that determination is rarely reversed on appeal. A number of jurisdictions provide some guidance for judges to consider in determining indigency. Indigency therefore varies from one jurisdiction or judge to another. The American Bar Association (ABA)

indigent defendants
a defendant who is too poor to hire a lawyer.

recommends the following standard: "Counsel should be provided to any person who is financially unable to obtain adequate representation without substantial hardship to himself or his family." It adds that a lawyer should not be denied "to any person merely because his friends or relatives have resources adequate to retain counsel or because he has posted or is capable of posting bond."[2]

The method of appointing counsel for an indigent defendant also varies. In some jurisdictions, judges use a list containing the names of available and willing attorneys, who are then assigned to cases on a rotating basis. In others, judges make assignments at random, assigning any lawyer who may be available in the courtroom at the time of the appointment. Still other jurisdictions employ full-time public defenders to handle indigent cases. The decision to create a public defender's office is usually driven by considerations of cost-effectiveness. From an economic perspective, the bigger the city or county, the more attractive the public defender model becomes.

Much has been written about the lack of quality of legal representation provided by court-appointed counsel. Problems abound, including the lack of financial support, lack of training, insufficient support systems for investigation, and heavy case loads. In an issue brief for the American Constitution Society for Law and Policy, titled "Assessing the Indigent Defense System," Professor Erica J. Hashimoto states that "At this point . . . we certainly have sufficient data to establish that defenders in some jurisdictions have unmanageable caseloads, and there appears to be no dispute that lawyers with those types of caseloads cannot provide effective assistance." Reviewing data from the Bureau of Justice Statistics (BJS), she says that in 1999, from the 100 largest counties, "those offices received 719,660 non-capital cases; 1,612,046 misdemeanors; 13,053 appeals; and 277,000 juvenile cases. This means that each attorney received (in addition to any cases they had on their caseload at the beginning of the year) an average of 100 felonies, 225 misdemeanors, 2 appeals, and 39 juvenile cases, in addition to a slew of probation revocations and other types of cases."[3] Primarily due to lack of funding and sufficient political attention, legal representation for indigent defendants in the United States continues to suffer as it has in the past.

HIGHLIGHT › How Indigent Defendants Get Legal Representation

The National Legal Aid & Defender Association says that there are three basic models for the delivery of defense services to "low income people" facing criminal charges:

1. *The staffed public defender model*, with employees on salary.
2. *The assigned counsel model*, where individual private attorneys are appointed to provide defense services, either from an ad hoc list maintained by the courts or through some more systematic organization of services.
3. *The contract model*, where individual attorneys or firms contact to provide some or all of a jurisdiction's indigent defense services.

The same source adds the following information:

Today, the majority of indigent defense in the United States is provided through a public defender model, particularly in larger urban jurisdictions.

More than half of the nation's counties still use the assigned counsel model.

Most states have organized some form of statewide defender services, whether in oversight, funding or both. Some states provide statewide services for a particular kind of representation, such as appeals or capital representation.

Source: National Legal Aid & Defender Association, "Frequently Asked Questions," http://www.nlada.org/Defender/Defender_Public/Defender_Public_Home.

Fuller v. Oregon (1974)

An indigent defendant has no right to designate an attorney of his or her choice. The selection of a defense lawyer is made purely at the discretion of the court, although the judge may allow the accused some input in the process. Some states provide counsel to defendants but specify as a condition of probation or parole that the defendant reimburse the state or county for the fees of the appointed lawyer. Such laws are valid as long as they exempt indigents who cannot afford to pay (*Fuller v. Oregon*, 417 U.S. 40 [1974]).

The Responsibility of the Defense Lawyer Is to the Client

It may surprise and disappoint many victims of crime to learn that, in the U.S. system of justice, the loyalty of a defense lawyer is not to the public but solely to the client. This means that a defense lawyer is not an agent of the state but instead is obligated to give the client the best possible defense, whether the client is innocent or guilty. In the U.S. system of justice, lawyers have an obligation to defend the guilty. Some lawyers do not even want to know whether their client is innocent or guilty, believing that guilt or innocence should not affect the way they do their job. This loyalty to the client comes from the adversarial model of criminal justice, in which both sides in a criminal case (the prosecution and the defense) are adversaries expected to fight fairly before a neutral judge or jury. Out of this fight, the truth is supposed to emerge. That does not always happen, but the system is supposed to work that way.

The limits on the conduct of lawyers when defending a client come from two sources: a professional code of ethics and the penal code. A defense lawyer cannot do anything which is *unethical* or *illegal*. Should they do that, a defense lawyer may be disciplined by the judge or professional organization, including disbarment. Prosecution might follow if the lawyer commits a criminal act. Working for the good of the community, however, is not among the responsibilities expected of a lawyer when defending an accused. To put it crudely, the welfare of the client is paramount; other considerations are unimportant. The conduct of lawyers is monitored by state bar associations and by the judiciary. The ABA has developed Model Rules of Professional Conduct. States' codes of professional responsibility vary, although most codes or rules are based on the model rules of the ABA. The interpretation and enforcement of these rules may not conform to what the public expects, adding to the poor public perception of the legal profession.

The Right to Court-Appointed Counsel during the Trial Has Exceptions

Although the Sixth Amendment extends to "all criminal prosecutions," the Court has held that the right to court-appointed counsel applies only in the following types of criminal cases:

Argersinger v. Hamlin (1972)

◆ When the crime charged is a serious offense (*Gideon v. Wainwright*, 372 U.S. 335 [1963])
◆ When the crime charged is a misdemeanor for which the defendant faces a possible jail sentence (*Argersinger v. Hamlin*, 407 U.S. 25 [1972])

To illustrate these two decisions, suppose John is charged with robbery, a serious offense in that jurisdiction. John, if indigent, is entitled to court-appointed counsel during the trial. John would also be entitled to a lawyer if indigent and charged with a misdemeanor for which he faced a possible jail sentence. However, if John is charged with a traffic violation for which no jail sentence is attached, John is not entitled to a lawyer.

Despite *Gideon* and *Argersinger*, the Court later held that the state is not required to appoint counsel for an indigent defendant charged with a serious offense that is punishable by imprisonment if the defendant is not, in fact, sentenced to prison (*Scott v. Illinois*, 440 U.S. 367 [1979]).

Scott v. Illinois (1979)

In *Scott*, the defendant was tried without a lawyer for the crime of shoplifting. The maximum penalty prescribed by state law for the offense was a fine of $500, or a year in prison, or both. Scott was convicted and sentenced to pay a fine of $50. On appeal, the Court affirmed the conviction, saying that the "federal Constitution does not require a state trial court to appoint counsel for a criminal defendant such as petitioner." Under *Scott*, the state is arguably not required to provide counsel, whether an indigent defendant is charged with a serious offense or a misdemeanor, if the defendant is not sentenced to prison (for example, when the judge assigns the defendant to community service or imposes a fine). States do have the option of providing appointed counsel for all misdemeanor defendants, and many states follow that policy.

Although juvenile proceedings are not criminal in nature, a juvenile is nonetheless entitled to court-appointed counsel if the proceeding can lead to commitment in an institution in which the juvenile's freedom is restricted (*In re Gault*, 387 U.S. 1 [1967]).

In re Gault (1967)

CASE BRIEF

Gideon v. Wainwright, 372 U.S. 335 (1963)

The Leading Case on the Right to Court-Appointed Counsel

Facts: Gideon was charged in a Florida state court with breaking and entering a pool room with intent to commit a misdemeanor, an act classified as a felony under Florida law. Appearing in court without funds and without a lawyer, Gideon asked the court to appoint a lawyer for him. The court refused, saying that under Florida law the only time the court could appoint a lawyer to represent an accused was when the crime charged was a capital offense. Gideon conducted his own defense and was convicted.

Issue or Issues: *Does the Constitution require appointment of counsel for an indigent person who is charged in a state court with a felony offense?* Yes.

Decision: The decision of the Supreme Court of Florida was reversed and remanded.

Holding: The Sixth Amendment requires that a person charged with a felony offense in a state court be appointed counsel if he or she cannot afford it.

Case Significance: This case mandates that when an indigent person is charged with a felony in a state court,

counsel must be provided. This settled a controversy among lower courts, which had inconsistent rulings on the type of offense an indigent had to be charged with in order to be entitled to a lawyer. An earlier decision (*Betts v. Brady*, 316 U.S. 455 [1942]), which held that the requirement that counsel be provided to all indigent defendants in federal felony trials, did not extend to the states. This was overruled in the *Gideon* case when the Supreme Court held that the rule applied to criminal proceedings in state courts as well. Since 1963, both federal and state felony defendants must be given court-appointed counsel if indigent. Note that the *Gideon* case required the appointment of counsel for indigents only in felony cases. This was later extended to misdemeanor cases in *Argersinger v. Hamlin*, 407 U.S. 25 (1972). Although not a case directly involving the police, the *Gideon* case is included here because it is helpful for the police to know what types of indigent offenders are entitled to a court-appointed lawyer during trial.

Excerpts from the Opinion: In our adversary system of criminal justice, any person haled into court, who is too poor to hire a lawyer, cannot be assured a fair trial unless counsel is provided for him. This seems to us to be an obvious truth. Governments, both state and federal, quite properly spend vast sums of money to establish machinery to try defendants accused of crime. Lawyers to prosecute are everywhere deemed essential to protect the public's interest in an orderly society. Similarly, there are few defendants charged with crime, few indeed, who fail to hire the best lawyers they can get to prepare and present their defenses. That government hires lawyers to prosecute and defendants who have the money hire lawyers to defend are the strongest indications of the widespread belief that lawyers in criminal courts are necessities, not luxuries. The right of one charged with crime to counsel may not be deemed fundamental and essential to fair trials in some countries, but it is in ours. From the very beginning, our state and national constitutions and laws have laid great emphasis on procedural and substantive safeguards designed to assure fair trials before impartial tribunals in which every defendant stands equal before the law. This noble ideal cannot be realized if the poor man charged with a crime has to face his accusers without a lawyer to assist him.

Proving Ineffective Assistance of Counsel Is Difficult

A defendant may challenge his or her conviction on the grounds that the lawyer at trial was so incompetent as to deprive the defendant of effective assistance of counsel. Although this claim is frequently raised, it is difficult to prove and therefore seldom succeeds. The meaning of "effective assistance of counsel" bothered lower courts for years because of the absence of a clear standard. However, in two 1984 cases, the Court clarified the issue by specifying the following criteria:

United States v. Cronic (1984)

◆ A claim of ineffective assistance of counsel can be made only by pointing out specific errors made by the trial counsel. It cannot be based on an inference drawn from the defense counsel's inexperience or lack of time to prepare, the gravity of the charges, the complexity of the defense, or the accessibility of witnesses to counsel (*United States v. Cronic*, 466 U.S. 648 [1984]).

Strickland v. Washington (1984)
Lockhart v. Fretwell (1993)

◆ The Court assumes that effective assistance of counsel is present unless the adversarial process is so undermined by counsel's conduct that the trial cannot be relied upon to have produced a just result. An accused who claims ineffective counsel must show the following: (1) deficient performance by counsel and (2) a reasonable probability that but for such deficiency the result of the proceeding would have been different (*Strickland v. Washington*, 466 U.S. 668 [1984]). In a 1993 case (*Lockhart v. Fretwell*, 506 U.S. 364 [1993]), however, the Court made the standard for reversal of conviction even more difficult: "To show prejudice under *Strickland*, a defendant must demonstrate that *counsel's errors are so serious as to deprive him of a trial whose result is fair or reliable, not merely that the outcome would have been different*."

Under these standards, mere generalizations about the quality of the lawyer or the inadequacy of his or her efforts will not suffice. Specificity is required, and the burden is on the defendant to show a reasonable probability that if the lawyer's performance had not been deficient, the results would have been different. This is difficult to establish, and, in most cases, the accused needs another lawyer who knows enough law to be able to prove this. For example, suppose that, after conviction, defendant Gary alleges that he had ineffective counsel because the lawyer assigned by the court to defend him (as an indigent) had limited experience handling criminal cases and finished last in his law school class. This will not suffice to establish ineffective counsel.

Instead, Gary must specify the errors the defense lawyer committed that contributed to his conviction. Likewise, a mere error of law in advising a defendant to enter a guilty plea does not in itself constitute the denial of effective counsel. The test is whether the mistake was "within the range of competency" of most criminal defense lawyers. However, if the lawyer fails to follow state procedural rules, resulting in the dismissal of the appeal, this represents ineffective assistance of counsel.

Claims of Ineffective Counsel in Death Penalty Cases

In recent years, the Court has had to decide a number of cases involving claims of ineffective counsel, particularly in death penalty cases. Some of these claims have succeeded, others have failed. It is difficult to identify a common standard whereby the Court decides these challenges. The bottom line is that the Court examines the facts and decides whether counsel was effective or ineffective on a case-by-case basis.

Claims of Ineffective Counsel Succeeded in These Cases:

1. *Failure to Conduct Reasonable Investigation.* In a case involving the death penalty, the Court held that the defendant's Sixth Amendment right to effective counsel was violated by his lawyer's failure to conduct a reasonable investigation into his social history and mitigating factors (*Wiggins v. Smith*, 539 U.S. 510 [2003]). The Court said that the evidence that the lawyer failed to discover and present was "powerful" and could have made a difference in the sentence that was imposed (death); therefore, the defendant was prejudiced by the lawyer's poor performance.

2. *A Negligent Lawyer.* In another case, the Court held that the Sixth Amendment right to effective counsel requires the lawyer to obtain materials that the lawyer knew the prosecution would likely use at the sentencing stage of a criminal trial for murder (*Rompilla v. Beard*, 545 U.S. 374 [2005]). In this case, Rompilla was charged with and convicted of murder in Pennsylvania. During the sentencing stage, and in an effort to have the death penalty imposed, the prosecution presented to the jury Rompilla's prior rape and assault conviction, both aggravating circumstances. The jury sentenced him to death. On appeal, Rompilla's new lawyers claimed ineffective counsel during trial because the defense lawyer did not present mitigating evidence about Rompilla's troubled childhood and mental problems. The Court upheld Rompilla's claim of ineffective counsel, saying that counsel's failure to examine the file on his prior conviction for rape and assault, despite counsel's knowledge that the evidence would likely be presented at the sentencing stage, justified a finding of ineffective counsel. The Court said that had the defense lawyer examined those records, he would have found mitigating evidence about the defendant's troubled childhood and mental problems that could have saved him from the death penalty.

3. *A Sleeping Lawyer.* In *Burdine v. Johnson* (5th Cir. 2001), which generated extensive national publicity, a defense lawyer for a capital offense defendant in Texas kept falling asleep during the trial. Convicted and sentenced to death, the defendant appealed, claiming he was denied constitutional right to effective counsel. A panel for the Fifth Circuit Court of Appeals first rejected the defendant's claim, but the full appeals court agreed to hear the case, concluded that Burdine did not have the benefit of effective counsel and therefore ordered a new trial. The U.S.

Wiggins v. Smith (2003)

Rompilla v. Beard (2005)

Supreme Court refused to hear the case on appeal; thus the decision to give Burdine a new trial was upheld.

Maples v. Thomas (2010)

4. *An Abandoned Defendant.* In a recent case, the Court held that an Alabama death row inmate "should not be prevented from appealing because he missed a deadline after his lawyers dropped his case and failed to tell him" (*Maples v. Thomas*, No. 10-63 [2010]). The majority held that the "two lawyers did not alert Alabama court authorities that they were withdrawing, so that when a court clerk sent papers to the lawyers, the firm's mailroom sent them back unopened and marked, "Return to Sender Left Firm" and "Returned to Sender Attempted Unknown."" The Court concluded that defendant was virtually abandoned by the lawyers and was "left unrepresented at a critical time . . . and he lacked any clue of any need to protect himself." The Court then reversed a decision by the U.S. Court of Appeals for the eleventh circuit against Maples who had been convicted and sentenced to death for two murders.

Claims of Ineffective Counsel Failed in These Cases:

Yarborough v. Gentry (2003)

Bell v. Cone (2002)

1. *Lawyer Cites Defendant's Shortcomings.* The Court held that the lawyer's closing argument in a case, in which he admitted some of the defendant's shortcomings, did not deprive the defendant of effective assistance of counsel, because the summation brought out several key points (*Yarborough v. Gentry*, 540 U.S. 1 [2003]).

2. *A Silent Lawyer.* In *Bell v. Cone*, 505 U.S. 685 (2002), the Court allowed a death sentence to stand even though the defendant's lawyer failed to make an argument to the jury to save his life. In this case, Cone was tried and found guilty of capital murder. During the sentencing stage, the sequence was for the prosecution to argue first, then the defense lawyer, and then the prosecutor again. A junior prosecutor argued first for the prosecution. The defense lawyer then decided to waive his argument because under court rules the prosecutor could not argue a second time if the defense lawyer waived the argument. This was done by the defense lawyer as a strategy so that the senior prosecutor, who was a highly effective lawyer and who was going to give the second prosecution argument, could not speak. The jury gave the defendant the death penalty anyway, even without the second argument by the prosecution. Cone appealed, claiming ineffective counsel. In this case, the Court upheld the sentence, saying that Cone's constitutional right was not violated because what the defense lawyer did as a strategy was reasonable.

3. *A Lawyer Who Had the Victim as a Client.* In this case, Mickens was convicted of murder and sentenced to death. He claimed ineffective assistance of counsel because he discovered, after trial, that his attorney had previously represented the victim on unrelated charges, which were pending at the time of the murder. This was never revealed to Mickens by the lawyer or by the court, although the court had knowledge of the representation. This, Mickens argued, created a conflict of interest that resulted in ineffective representation. The Court rejected his claim, saying that a defendant who claims that the right to counsel was violated because of a conflict of interest must show that the conflict had a negative effect on the attorney's representation and that there was a reasonable probability that the result would have been different. The Court concluded that

"dual representation" in and of itself merely represents a "theoretical division of loyalties" and did not require a reversal of the results (*Mickens v. Taylor*, 535 U.S. 162 [2002]).

Claim of Ineffective Counsel during Plea Bargaining

As noted in this chapter, the right to counsel is pervasive and starts with the initial encounter with the police if the suspect is in custody and is interrogated by the police. Until recently, however, the Court had not decided a case involving the right to counsel during plea bargaining. In 2012, the Court held that "the Sixth Amendment right to effective assistance of counsel extends to the consideration of plea offers that lapse or are rejected (*Missouri v. Frye*, — U.S. — [2012]). In *Frye*, the defendant was charged with driving with a revoked license. Having been convicted of the offense three times before, he was charged with an offense that under Missouri law carried a maximum of a four-year prison term. Before trial, the prosecutor sent Frye's lawyer a letter offering two plea bargains, one of which included an offer to change the charge to a misdemeanor, which would have carried a ninety-day sentence. The lawyer did not tell Frye about these offers and they expired. Frye later pleaded guilty to the offense without a plea bargain and was given a three-year sentence. While in prison he sought post-conviction relief, saying that his counsel's failure to inform him of the earlier plea offers constituted ineffective assistance of counsel. He testified that he would have pleaded guilty to the misdemeanor had he been informed by his lawyer about it. On appeal, the Court agreed, saying: "Plea bargains have become so central to today's criminal justice system that defense counsel must meet responsibilities in the plea bargain process to render the adequate assistance of counsel that the Sixth Amendment requires at critical stages of the criminal process."

Missouri v. Frye (2012)

The Right to Act as One's Own Counsel

Under certain conditions, an accused has a constitutional right to waive counsel and represent himself or herself in a criminal proceeding (*Faretta v. California*, 422 U.S. 806 [1975]). In *Faretta*, the defendant had a high school education, had represented himself before, and did not want a public defender to represent him, because of the public

Faretta v. California (1975)

 HIGHLIGHT > **A Quick Summary of the Right to Counsel**

- ◆ The right to counsel in criminal proceedings is extensive—from the time of custodial interrogations up to trial.
- ◆ There are two types of counsel: retained and court-appointed.
- ◆ Indigent defendants must be provided counsel at government expense.
- ◆ Indigent defendants are usually assigned counsel based on three models: the staffed public defender model, the assigned counsel model, and the contract model.

- ◆ The responsibility of a defense lawyer is to the client, not to society or the state.
- ◆ The right to court-appointed counsel during the trial has exceptions.
- ◆ Claim of ineffective assistance of counsel is difficult for a convicted person to establish.
- ◆ Defendants have a constitutional right to act as one's own counsel provided the following are met: awareness of the right to counsel, express waiver, and competence of the accused.

defender's heavy caseload. The right to self-representation does not require legal skills, but in cases in which the defendant is ignorant or too inexperienced, the request to act as his or her own counsel will probably be denied by the court.

Before an accused can be permitted to waive counsel and represent himself or herself, the following constitutional requirements must be met:

- *Awareness of the right to counsel.* The court must fully advise the accused of his or her right to be represented by counsel.
- *Express waiver.* The accused's waiver of counsel cannot be inferred from his or her silence or from his or her failure to request the appointment of counsel.
- *Competency of the accused.* The trial judge must determine whether the accused is: (1) competent to waive the right to counsel and (2) competent to make an intelligent choice in the case. In determining the defendant's competency to make an intelligent choice, the court must make the defendant aware of the dangers and disadvantages of self-representation. An accused who elects to represent himself or herself cannot later claim ineffective counsel.

THE RIGHT TO DUE PROCESS

A third basic right of the accused discussed in this chapter is the right to due process. There are two due process clauses in the U.S. Constitution. The Fifth Amendment (applicable to federal prosecutions) provides that "No person shall be held to answer for a capital, or otherwise infamous crime, . . . nor be deprived of life, liberty, or property, without due process of law; nor shall private property be taken for public use, without just compensation." A second due process clause is found in Section 1 of the Fourteenth Amendment (applicable to state prosecutions), which provides that "No state shall make or enforce any law which shall abridge the privileges or immunities of citizens of the United States; nor shall any state deprive any person of life, liberty, or property, without due process of law; nor deny to any person within its jurisdiction the equal protection of the laws."

procedural due process
the legal process that is to be followed, depending upon the type of proceeding involved.

The Many Meanings of Due Process

Due process essentially means "fundamental fairness," but it has no fixed meaning that applies to all situations. Due process has two aspects: **procedural due process** and **substantive due process**. Procedural due process is what is involved in criminal procedure. What process is due varies from one case to another, depending on the type of proceeding and what is at stake for the individual. For example, due process during a criminal trial is different from due process in probation or parole revocation proceedings or in prison disciplinary proceedings. What rights are due in a particular proceeding is ultimately decided by the courts.

substantive due process
there are aspects of a person's life that cannot be regulated by the government because they are so basic and private to the individual.

In contrast, substantive due process means that there are aspects of a person's life that cannot be regulated by the government because they are so basic and private to the individual. An example is the Court decision in *Roe v. Wade* (410 U.S. 113 [1973]), which holds that abortion cannot be totally regulated by the government because to do that is to intrude into one of the most basic and private rights of a woman, which should be beyond total government control.

Roe v. Wade (1973)

Any time fundamental fairness is an issue, due process can likely be raised. Because of its elastic nature, the right to due process is manifested in many forms in criminal proceedings. Its broadest application is in the incorporation controversy (the issue whether the rights in the Bill of Rights should be applicable to the States, discussed in Chapter 1). Another application is in the right to a fair and impartial trial in its many forms (discussed in this chapter). In sum, the right to due process is a convenient source of many rights for the accused in a criminal proceeding. An example is the *Brady* rule, which has been repeatedly invoked by convicted defendants in criminal proceedings. The *Brady* rule is based on due process. We will look at what the rule says and how it affected cases that came after the ruling.

The *Brady* Rule on Disclosure of Evidence to the Accused

Due process is protected to the utmost during criminal trials. In a criminal proceeding, the prosecutor has a duty to disclose evidence favorable to a defendant; failure to disclose violates a defendant's constitutional right to due process. This obligation was first declared in *Mooney v. Holohan*, 294 U.S. 103 (1935), when the Court said that the "due process requirement is not satisfied by mere notice and hearing if the state, through prosecuting officers acting on state's behalf, has contrived conviction through pretense of trial which in truth is used as a means of depriving defendant of liberty through deliberate deception of court and jury by presentation of testimony known to be perjured."

Mooney v. Holohan (1935)

The *Holohan* principle was reiterated almost three decades later in *Brady v. Maryland*, 373 U.S. 83 (1963). *Brady* involved a case in which the defendant admitted participating in the crime but claimed that his companion did the actual killing. Prior to the trial, Brady's lawyer requested that the prosecutor allow him to examine the companion's statements made outside of court. The prosecutor showed some of these to Brady's lawyer but withheld the statement in which the companion admitted doing the actual killing. The defense did not know about that statement until after Brady had been tried, convicted, and sentenced.

Brady v. Maryland (1963)

On appeal, the Supreme Court reversed Brady's conviction, saying that "the suppression by the prosecution of evidence favorable to an accused upon request violates due process where the evidence is material either to guilt or to punishment, irrespective of the good faith or bad faith of the prosecution." This holding, better known as the **Brady rule**, has been interpreted and refined by the Court in subsequent cases.

Brady rule
the prosecutor has a duty to disclose evidence favorable to a defendant.

Cases after *Brady*

One of the cases that interpreted *Brady* was *United States v. Agurs*, 427 U.S. 97 (1976). In *Agurs*, the Court said that the defendant's failure to request that favorable evidence be shown to the defense did not free the government of all obligation, but that the prosecutor's failure in this particular case did not violate the defendant's right to due process.

United States v. Agurs (1976)

In *Agurs*, the Court distinguished three situations that can give rise to a *Brady* claim:

1. Where previously undisclosed evidence revealed that the prosecution introduced trial testimony that it knew or should have known was perjured

2. Where the Government failed to comply with a defense request for disclosure of some specific kind of exculpatory evidence

3. Where the Government failed to volunteer exculpatory evidence never requested, or requested only in a general way

In this case, however, the Court stated:

> [The] prosecutor's failure to tender [defendant's] criminal record to the defense did not deprive respondent of a fair trial . . . where it appears that the record was not requested by defense counsel and gave rise to no inference of perjury, that the trial judge remained convinced of respondent's guilt beyond a reasonable doubt after considering the criminal record in the context of the entire record, and that the judge's firsthand appraisal of the entire record was thorough and entirely reasonable.

In essence, the Court in *Agurs* limited the defendant's right to discovery procedure under the circumstances described in that case.

United States v. Bagley (1985)

In *United States v. Bagley*, 473 U.S. 667 (1985), the Court held that, "regardless of request, favorable evidence is material, and constitutional error results from its suppression by the government, if there is a reasonable probability that, had the evidence been disclosed to the defense, the result of the proceeding would have been different."

Kyles v. Whitley (1995)

Another case on disclosure of evidence and the right of an accused to due process is *Kyles v. Whitley*, 514 U.S. 419 (1995). In *Kyles*, the Court held that, because the effect of the state-suppressed evidence favorable to the defendant raised a reasonable probability that its disclosure would have produced a different result at trial, the conviction had to be reversed.

In this case, Kyles was convicted of first-degree murder in Louisiana and sentenced to death. Later, it was revealed that the state had failed to disclose certain evidence favorable to the accused, including the following: (1) contemporaneous eyewitness statements taken by the police following the murder, (2) various statements made to the police by an informant who was never called to testify, and (3) a computer printout of license plate numbers of cars parked at the crime scene on the night of the murder, which did not contain the number of Kyles's car. The Court held that this evidence, taken together, raised a reasonable probability that its disclosure would have produced a different result at trial; hence, the conviction was reversed.

Strickler v. Greene (1999)

In a 1999 case, *Strickler v. Greene*, 527 U.S. 263 (1999), the Court held that the prosecution's failure to disclose evidence, in the form of interview notes from a detective that seriously undermined the truthfulness of the only eyewitness's testimony in a murder case, did not violate the *Brady* rule because the evidence was not material to the issue of guilt or innocence. In this case, the only eyewitness to the crime testified at trial that she had an exceptionally good memory and that she had absolutely no doubt that she had identified the defendant correctly. But it was later learned that the notes of her interview with a detective showed that she could not identify the defendant during that first interview. On appeal, the Court held that the failure by the prosecution to disclose the detective's notes did not require a reversal of the conviction because the defendant had not shown by reasonable probability that disclosure of the notes would have changed the results of the trial.

The latest rule states that if the circumstances surrounding the nondisclosure raise a "reasonable probability" that the disclosure would have made a difference in the trial's result, the defendant's due process right has been violated and the conviction must be reversed. But undisclosed favorable evidence that is not material to the issue

HIGHLIGHT ❯ A Quick Summary of the Right to Due Process

- ◆ Due process essentially means fundamental fairness.
- ◆ It has two aspects: procedural due process and substantive due process.
- ◆ In criminal proceedings, procedural due process is the aspect of the right that is often invoked.
- ◆ The *Brady* rule is based on due process; it states that the prosecutor has a duty to disclose evidence favorable to a defendant and that failure to disclose violates a defendant's constitutional right.

- ◆ Based on several rulings after *Brady*, the current rule on disclosure of evidence by the prosecution is: If the circumstances surrounding the nondisclosure raise a "reasonable probability" that the disclosure would have made a difference in the trial's result, the defendant's due process right has been violated and the conviction must be reversed. But undisclosed favorable evidence that is not material to the issue of guilt or innocence does not lead to a reversal of the conviction.

of guilt or innocence does not lead to a reversal of the conviction. The constitution does not require a perfectly fair trial for the accused to be convicted. In the words of Justice Byron White, "Due process does not require that every conceivable step be taken, at whatever cost, to eliminate the possibility of convicting an innocent person" (*Patterson v. New York*, 432 U.S.197 [1977]). The trial must be fair, but not necessarily faultless.

Patterson v. New York (1977)

THE RIGHT AGAINST SELF-INCRIMINATION

A fourth basic right of the accused is the right against self-incrimination. The prohibition against compulsory self-incrimination springs from the Fifth Amendment provision that "no person . . . shall be compelled in any criminal case to be a witness against himself." This guarantee is designed to restrain the government from using force, coercion, or other such methods to obtain any statement, admission, or confession that might be used by the police to take the place of other evidence. The right applies to criminal, civil, or administrative proceedings if the answer sought tends to incriminate the witness in a subsequent criminal case.

This section focuses on the scope of the provision, the privileges of both the accused and witnesses during a trial, immunity, and how the right against self-incrimination is waived.

The Prohibition Applies Only to Testimonial Self-Incrimination, Not to Physical Self-Incrimination

The prohibition against self-incrimination extends only to testimonial or communicative self-incrimination; it does not prohibit **physical self-incrimination**, which involves real or physical evidence. For example, the accused can be forced to submit to reasonable physical or psychiatric examinations, and the prosecution may introduce the evidence obtained—such as fingerprints, footprints, blood or urine samples, or voice identifications. Also, a defendant can be forced to stand up for identification in the courtroom, to put on certain items of clothing, or to give a handwriting sample (*Gilbert v. California*, 388 U.S. 263 [1967]).

physical self-incrimination
involves real or physical evidence.

Gilbert v. California (1967)

In contrast, **testimonial** or **communicative self-incrimination** is that which in itself explicitly or implicitly relates a factual assertion or discloses information. It is in the form of verbal or oral communication. For example, a question that asks whether the defendant killed the deceased is testimonially self-incriminating because it asks for a factual assertion or disclosure of information of a nonphysical nature.

The Fifth Amendment's protection extends only to natural persons, meaning human beings. Corporations or partnerships (which are considered persons by law) cannot claim the privilege, so the records of such entities cannot be withheld on these grounds. For example, suppose a corporation faces charges of violating labor laws. The corporation may be required to produce its official books and records even if they contain incriminating evidence. The search and seizure of a person's private papers in accordance with a legal process, with or without a warrant, does not violate the right to protection against self-incrimination—at least if the information on the papers was written voluntarily, not obtained by testimonial compulsion. This is because the protection given to books and papers under the Fifth Amendment is very limited. Although they are perhaps the products of a mental process (such as a diary), the books or documents themselves constitute physical evidence.

South Dakota v. Neville
(1983)

Another aspect of the right to protection against self-incrimination is discussed in *South Dakota v . Neville*, 459 U.S. 553 (1983). That case involved a South Dakota law that permitted a person suspected of driving while intoxicated to refuse to submit to a blood alcohol test but also authorized revocation of the driver's license of anyone who refused to take the test. The statute permitted such a refusal to be used against the driver as evidence of guilt during the trial. The Supreme Court held that the admission into evidence of a defendant's refusal to submit to a blood alcohol test does not violate the defendant's Fifth Amendment right to protection against compulsory self-incrimination. A refusal to take the test, after a police officer has lawfully requested it, is not an act coerced by the officer and therefore is not protected by the Fifth Amendment. The Court said that any self-incrimination resulting from a blood alcohol test is physical in nature, not testimonial or communicative, so it is not protected by the Fifth Amendment. This case legalized the practice used in some states of giving DWI suspects a choice to take or refuse a blood alcohol test and then using a refusal as evidence of guilt later in court.

Testimonial and Nontestimonial Self-Incrimination Compared

In a case of importance to the police, the Court held that "statements are nontestimonial (and therefore admissible in court) when made in the course of police interrogation under circumstances objectively indicating that the primary purpose of interrogation is to enable police assistance to meet an ongoing emergency" (*Davis v. Washington*, 547 U.S. 813 [2006]). Defendant Davis was arrested by the police after Michelle McCottry called 911 and told the operator that Davis had beaten her. Davis was later charged with violating a domestic no-contact order. The 911 tape was admitted into evidence and Davis was convicted. He appealed his conviction, saying that his constitutional right to cross-examination was violated by the admission of the tape recording into evidence since there was no opportunity to cross-examine.

Davis v. Washington (2006)

The Court disagreed and upheld his conviction, saying that the issue was whether the statements were testimonial (protected by the Fifth Amendment) or nontestimonial (not protected). The facts of this case show that the statement was nontestimonial and therefore could be admitted at trial. The Court made this distinction: "Statements are non-testimonial when made in the course of police interrogation under circumstances objectively indicating that the primary purpose of the interrogation is to enable police assistance to meet an ongoing emergency." In contrast, statements "are testimonial when the circumstances objectively indicate that there is no such ongoing emergency, and that the primary purpose of the interrogation is to establish or prove past events relevant to later criminal prosecution."

This decision is significant because police departments receive all kinds of 911 calls every day that they routinely record, including those that may be highly incriminating to the accused. This case considers such evidence admissible in court because it is nontestimonial and therefore is not protected by the Fifth Amendment.

Two Separate Privileges during Trial

The privilege against compulsory self-incrimination during trials guarantees two separate privileges: the *privilege of the accused* and the *privilege of a witness*.

IN ACTION   *SELF-INCRIMINATING WRITING ON THE WALL*

Pleasantville police officers Fred and Barney were dispatched to investigate a robbery alarm call at the Hop-In liquor store. Central dispatch advised the responding units that they had attempted to call the store by phone, but there had been no answer. Upon arrival at the Hop-In, responding officers found the front door standing wide open and a male store clerk lying on the floor inside, deceased from an apparent gunshot wound to the chest. The cash register was empty and the store had been ransacked.

Officers quickly reviewed the store's security videotape for evidence. The video depicted two male suspects, one wearing a red hooded sweatshirt and the other wearing a green T-shirt and blue baseball cap. Officers broadcast the suspects' descriptions to other Pleasantville officers, and within an hour, two suspects were under arrest for the robbery and murder of the store clerk. The suspects were identified as Larry and Moe. Larry and Moe were booked into the Pleasantville jail and placed in separate cells pending follow-up by Pleasantville detectives.

The following morning Detective Smith interviewed the suspects separately about the robbery and murder. Detective Smith advised each of the suspects of his rights under *Miranda*. Both Larry and Moe refused to make any statement (invoking their Fifth Amendment protections) and demanded that they be placed back in their respective cells. Detective Smith called for jail guards to take the suspects back to their cells. As the guards were doing so,

they noticed graffiti on the jail cell walls. In Moe's cell, the wall read, "Sorry God for what I have done, no one was meant to die." In Larry's cell, the wall read, "I am innocent of murder, I may be guilty of robbery, but I didn't kill anyone, it was Moe!"

Larry and Moe are charged criminally for the robbery and murder of the store clerk. During the trial the prosecutor attempts to enter the writings on the jail cell walls as evidence against both defendants. The prosecutor calls the jail guards as witnesses to testify that the graffiti writings were not on the wall prior to Larry and Moe being placed in their individual cells. The attorneys for Larry and Moe object to the writings being admitted as evidence. They base their objection on the fact that each defendant had clearly invoked his Fifth Amendment rights.

The judge advises the courtroom that she will need a few minutes to review the defendants' objection and orders the court into a thirty-minute recess. Now it is your turn to be the judge. While reviewing defense counsels' objection, you must decide the following:

1. Should the writings be allowed into the trial as evidence?
2. Can Moe's writings be used against him? Why or why not?
3. Can Larry's writings be used against him? Why or why not?
4. Can Larry's writings be used against Moe? Why or why not?

privilege of the accused
the privilege not to testify during trial.

Griffin v. California (1965)

United States v. Robinson (1988)

The Privilege of the Accused The defendant in a criminal case has the **privilege of the accused** not to take the stand and not to testify. The Court has ruled that the accused "may stand mute, clothed in the presumption of innocence." Moreover, prosecutors cannot comment on a defendant's assertion of the right not to testify. No conclusion of guilt may be drawn from the failure of the accused to testify during the trial. Therefore, the prosecutor is not permitted to make any comment or argument to the jury suggesting that the defendant is guilty because he or she refused to testify (*Griffin v. California*, 380 U.S. 609 [1965]).

However, this rule has been modified by the concept of *fair response*, which provides that a prosecutor's statement to the jury, during closing arguments, that the defendant could have taken the witness stand but refused to do so is proper as long as it is in response to defense counsel's argument that the government did not allow the defendant to explain his or her side of the story (*United States v. Robinson*, 485 U.S. 25 [1988]). Unless it is in the context of a fair response, the comments of a prosecutor suggesting that the defendant must be guilty because he or she refused to take the stand will lead to a reversal of the conviction.

The privilege to remain silent and not to take the stand applies in all stages of a criminal proceeding, starting when the suspect is first taken into custody. It applies in criminal prosecutions or contempt proceedings but not in situations in which there is no prosecution and no accused, such as grand jury investigations or legislative or administrative hearings. Once an accused takes the witness stand in his or her own defense, he or she waives the privilege not to testify. Therefore, the accused must answer all relevant inquiries about the crime for which he or she is on trial. This is one reason defense lawyers may not want the accused to take the witness stand, particularly if the accused has a bad record or a background that is better kept undisclosed.

privilege of a witness
any witness, other than an accused on the witness stand, has the privilege to refuse to disclose any information that may tend to incriminate him or her.

United States v. Balsys (1998)

The Privilege of a Witness Any witness, other than an accused on the witness stand, has the **privilege of a witness** to refuse to disclose any information that may "tend to incriminate" him or her. The reason for this is that the witness is not on trial; he or she is in court merely to provide information about what happened. A question tends to incriminate a witness if the answer would directly or indirectly implicate that witness in the commission of a crime. The privilege does not apply if the answer might expose the witness to civil liability; but if the facts involved would make the witness subject to both civil and criminal liability, the privilege may be claimed. However, the privilege cannot be claimed merely because the answer would hold the witness up to shame, disgrace, or embarrassment.

The answer to the question does not need to prove guilt to give rise to the privilege. All that is needed is a reasonable possibility that the answer would "furnish a link in the chain of evidence needed to prosecute." In one case, the Court held that a witness, an immigrant from Lithuania, could be forced to testify in a case in the United States even if the testimony given might subject that witness to prosecution (for Nazi war crimes) in another country—Lithuania (*United States v. Balsys*, 524 U.S. 666 [1998]).

The witness's privilege protects only against the possibility of prosecution, so if a witness could not be or can no longer be prosecuted, he or she can be compelled to testify. Several examples will help illuminate this provision.

- *Example 1.* If the *statute of limitations*—a law providing that a crime must be prosecuted within a certain period of time—has run out on the crime, the witness can be forced to answer the question.
- *Example 2.* If the witness has been acquitted and therefore cannot be prosecuted again, he or she can be forced to answer the question.
- *Example 3.* If the witness is assured of immunity, he or she can be forced to answer an incriminating question.

The decision whether a witness's answer tends to incriminate him or her is made by the hearing officer or judge immediately after the question is asked and the opposing lawyer objects on the grounds that the question is self-incriminatory. The decision is appealable only after the trial, so the witness must testify if so ordered or face contempt proceedings.

The following list summarizes the distinctions between these two privileges:

Privilege of the Accused	Privilege of a Witness
An accused cannot be forced to testify.	A witness can be forced to testify if ordered by the court.
A refusal cannot be commented on by the prosecution.	A refusal can result in a contempt citation.
An accused who testifies cannot refuse to answer incriminating questions because the privilege at that stage is considered waived.	A witness who testifies can refuse to answer questions that might result in criminal prosecution.

The Grant of Immunity

There are many situations in which the government grants immunity to a witness or a codefendant in return for his or her testimony. **Immunity** in criminal cases means that the person granted immunity will not be prosecuted in a criminal case, either fully or partially—depending on the type of immunity granted—for testimony given before a grand jury, in court, or in some other proceeding from which prosecution could otherwise have resulted. Immunity is usually given when the testimony of the witness is crucial to proving the government's case or when the government needs further information for investigative purposes.

immunity
the person granted immunity will not be prosecuted in a criminal case.

A witness who is granted immunity from prosecution may be forced to testify because the reason for the privilege (protection from self-incrimination) no longer exists. Once immunity is granted, a witness who still refuses to testify can be held in contempt of court.

The authority to grant immunity varies from one jurisdiction to another, but it is generally granted by law (which usually lists a category of witnesses who may be granted immunity), a grand jury, judges, or prosecutors. In a growing number of cases, such as drug possession, the same act may constitute a crime under both federal and state laws. The question then arises whether a grant of immunity from prosecution in one jurisdiction, state or federal, disqualifies the witness from claiming the privilege in another jurisdiction. The rules governing the grant of immunity are as follows:

- If a state has granted the witness valid immunity, the federal government is not permitted to make use of the testimony (or any of its fruits) in a federal prosecution against the witness (*Murphy v. Waterfront Commission*, 378 U.S. 52 [1964]). Therefore, the witness may be forced to testify in the state proceedings.

Murphy v. Waterfront Commission (1964)

- The Supreme Court has not decided whether a state should be allowed to use compelled testimony given in federal court under a grant of federal immunity. However, its use would probably be prohibited under the reasoning of the *Murphy* case.
- Testimony given under a grant of immunity in a state court cannot be used as evidence against the witness in the court of another state.

Transactional and Use and Derivative Use Immunity Compared

Does the grant of immunity to a witness exempt the witness in full from further criminal prosecution? Not necessarily; instead, it depends on the type of immunity that is given. There are two types of immunity: transactional and use and derivative use. With **transactional immunity**, the witness can no longer be prosecuted for any offense whatsoever arising out of that act or transaction. In contrast, **use and derivative use immunity** means that the witness is assured only that *his or her testimony and evidence derived from it* will not be used against him or her in a subsequent prosecution. But the witness can be prosecuted on the basis of evidence other than his or her testimony, if the prosecutor has such independent evidence. Transactional immunity is full immunity, whereas use and derivative use immunity is partial immunity.

In *Kastigar v. United States*, 406 U.S. 441 (1972), the Court decided that prosecutors only have to grant use and derivative use immunity to compel an unwilling witness to testify. The witness is not constitutionally entitled to transactional immunity before he or she can be compelled to testify. In the *Kastigar* case, the witness refused to testify under a grant of use and derivative use immunity, claiming that the Fifth Amendment guarantee against compulsory self-incrimination requires that transactional immunity be given before a witness can be forced to testify. The Court disagreed, saying that use and derivative use immunity is sufficient for purposes of Fifth Amendment protection; the granting of transactional immunity is not required.

The similarities and differences of transactional immunity and use and derivative use immunity are summarized as follows:

Similarities

If given, the witness can be forced to testify because self-incrimination no longer exists. Refusal to testify can result in contempt of court.

The witness has no constitutional right to either type of immunity.

Giving it is purely discretionary with whomever is authorized by law or policy to give it.

Differences

Transactional immunity is full immunity; if given, the witness can no longer be prosecuted.

Use and derivative use immunity is partial immunity; if given, the witness can still be prosecuted based on evidence other than his or her testimony.

How the Right Is Waived

A witness's right to protection against self-incrimination may be waived through the following actions:

- *Failure to assert.* The witness is the holder of the privilege, and only the witness (or his or her lawyer) can assert it. If the witness fails to assert the privilege at the time an incriminating question is asked, the privilege is waived.

---

transactional immunity
full immunity, meaning the witness can no longer be prosecuted for any offense arising out of that act or transaction.

use and derivative use immunity
partial immunity, meaning the witness can still be prosecuted on the basis of evidence other than his or her testimony, if the prosecutor has such independent evidence.

Kastigar v. United States (1972)

- *Partial disclosure.* When the witness discloses a fact that he or she knows to be self-incriminating, the witness also waives his or her privilege with respect to all further facts related to the same transaction.
- *Taking the witness stand.* When the witness is also the accused and voluntarily takes the stand, he or she must answer all relevant inquiries about the charge for which he or she is on trial. The accused is therefore "fair game" on all such matters during the cross-examination.

THE RIGHT TO A FAIR AND IMPARTIAL TRIAL

The last basic right of the accused discussed in this chapter is the right to a fair and impartial trial. The Sixth and Fourteenth Amendments guarantee the accused a fair trial by an impartial jury. What this guarantee basically means is that the circumstances surrounding the trial must not be such that they unduly influence the jury. Undue influence usually takes the form of publicity so massive that it becomes prejudicial to the accused.

The Prohibition against Prejudicial Publicity

Two basic principles of the U.S. system of criminal justice are that: (1) a person must be convicted by an impartial tribunal, and (2) a person must be convicted solely on the basis of evidence admitted at the trial. The publicity given to a notorious case before

 HIGHLIGHT **A Quick Summary of the Right against Self-Incrimination**

- The Fifth Amendment right against self-incrimination applies only to testimonial self-incrimination; it does not apply to physical self-incrimination.
- A law that allows the refusal of a suspect to submit to a blood alcohol test to be used as evidence in court and also authorizes revocation of the driver's license for such refusal does not violate the Fifth Amendment right against self-incrimination.
- There are two separate privileges against self-incrimination during trial: the privilege of the accused and the privilege of a witness. The privilege of the accused holds that the accused does not have to testify during his or her trial. Once the accused takes the witness stand, he or she must answer all questions asked, whether they be self-incriminatory or not. The privilege of a witness, other than an accused on the witness stand, states that the witness

may refuse any information that may "tend to incriminate" him or her.
- Immunity from prosecution may be given to a witness. Once given, the witness must testify even if the testimony is self-incriminatory. Testimony given under a grant of immunity in a state court cannot be used as evidence against the witness in the court of another state.
- Immunity is of two kinds: transactional (full) and use and derivative use (partial) immunity. In transactional immunity, the witness can no longer be prosecuted for any offense arising out of that act of transaction. Use and derivative use immunity means that the witness is assured only that his or her testimony and evidence derived from it will not be used against that witness in a subsequent prosecution.

or during a trial may bias a jury or create a significant risk that the jury will consider information other than the evidence produced in court. Here are two examples:

Irvin v. Dowd (1961)

- ◆ *Example 1.* Headlines announced that Dowd had confessed to six murders and twenty-four burglaries, and reports were widely circulated that Dowd had offered to plead guilty. Ninety percent of the prospective jurors interviewed expressed an opinion that Dowd was guilty, and eight out of twelve jurors finally seated, familiar with the material facts, held such a belief. The Court held that Dowd had been denied due process, stressing that this was a capital case (*Irvin v. Dowd*, 366 U.S. 717 [1961]).

Rideau v. Louisiana (1963)

- ◆ *Example 2.* Police arranged to have Bob's prior confession shown several times on local television. The Court held that Bob had, in effect, been "tried" thereby—and that no actual prejudice needed to be shown to establish a denial of due process under such circumstances (*Rideau v. Louisiana*, 373 U.S. 723 [1963]).

Controlling Prejudicial Publicity

In an effort to control prejudicial publicity, the judge has the power to take several steps: change the venue, sequester the jury, grant a continuance, issue a gag order, or control the press.

Change of Venue A defendant claiming undue pretrial publicity or other circumstances that would endanger his or her right to a fair and impartial trial locally can move to have the venue (place) of the trial changed to another county, from which more impartial jurors can be drawn. This is allowable in both felony and misdemeanor cases.

sequestration
keeping jurors together during the trial and strictly controlling contact with the outside world.

Sequestration If there is a danger that jurors will be exposed to prejudicial publicity during the trial, some states permit **sequestration**—keeping jurors together during the trial and strictly controlling contact with the outside world—at the judge's discretion immediately following jury selection and continuing for the duration of the trial. A few states automatically sequester the jury throughout the trial, but most states sequester jurors only for serious cases and then only after the case is given to the jury for deliberation.

Continuance If the prejudice is severe, a *continuance* (postponement) may be granted to allow the threat to an impartial trial to subside.

Imposing a Gag Rule The judge may impose a gag rule prohibiting the various parties in the trial from releasing information to the press or saying anything in public about the trial. Gag orders usually include the participating attorneys, witnesses, the police, and members of the jury. These orders are valid for the duration of the trial. However, the validity of a gag order beyond the duration of the trial is suspect because it may run afoul of constitutional rights.

Controlling the Press This is a very difficult problem for the judge because of the First Amendment guarantee of freedom of the press. The press has the right to attend a criminal trial, but the media may be excluded if specific findings indicate that closure is necessary for a fair trial. The media do not have a Sixth Amendment right to attend a pretrial hearing in a criminal case. Generally, it is difficult to justify attempts to control the kinds of news items the news media can report in connection with a criminal case—even where such items may create a "clear and present danger" of an unfair trial for the accused. Courts usually prohibit the taking of photographs or the televising of courtroom proceedings. In a number of states, however, the televising of courtroom proceedings is left to the discretion of the trial judge.

If the judge allows the televising of court proceedings, care must be taken not to create a "carnival atmosphere" inside the courtroom. The Supreme Court reversed the conviction in *Sheppard v. Maxwell*, 384 U.S. 333 (1966), because press coverage was too intrusive. The Court found the coverage so distracting to the judge, jurors, witnesses, and counsel that it created a "carnival atmosphere" and denied the defendant a fair trial.

Sheppard v. Maxwell (1966)

HIGHLIGHT › A Quick Summary of the Right to a Fair and Impartial Trial

The Sixth Amendment to the Constitution guarantees the accused a fair trial by an impartial jury. This means that the circumstances surrounding the trial must not be such that they unduly influence the jury. To ensure this, courts are given the authority to control prejudicial publicity. Among these are:

- ◆ changing the venue
- ◆ sequestration
- ◆ continuance
- ◆ imposing a gage rule and
- ◆ controlling the press.

Exhibit 12.1 Other Constitutional Rights of the Accused during Trial That Are Not Discussed in This Chapter

The Right to Protection against Double Jeopardy

- ◆ *Source of the right.* Sixth Amendment.
- ◆ *Definition.* Successive prosecution of a defendant for the same offense by the same jurisdiction.
- ◆ *When does it attach?* In a jury trial, when a competent jury has been sworn; in a trial before a judge, when the first witness has been called and sworn.

The Right to Confront Witnesses

- ◆ *Source of the right.* Sixth Amendment.
- ◆ *What it includes.* The right to cross-examine witnesses, to be physically present during trial, to physically face witnesses at trial, and to know the identity of prosecution witnesses.

The Right to Compulsory Process to Obtain Witnesses

- ◆ *Source of the right.* Sixth Amendment.
- ◆ *What it includes.* The power to require the appearance of witnesses and the right to present a defense which, in turn, includes defendant's right to present witnesses and his or her own version of the facts.

The Right to a Speedy and Public Trial

- ◆ *Source of the right.* Sixth Amendment.
- ◆ *Definition of a speedy trial.* A trial free from unnecessary and unwanted delay. If the delay is due to willful delay tactics by the accused, the accused will be deemed to have waived the right.
- ◆ *Definition of a public trial.* A trial that can be seen and heard by persons interested in ensuring that the proceedings are fair and just.

The Right to Proof of Guilt Beyond a Reasonable Doubt

- ◆ *Source of the right.* No specific constitutional provision but inferred from the due process clauses of the Fifth and Fourteenth Amendments.
- ◆ *Definition.* Difficult to define with precision. The definition varies from one state to another and even from court to court within a state. No specific definition is constitutionally required as long as "taken as a whole, the instructions correctly convey the concept of reasonable doubt" (whatever that means).

The right to trial by jury is guaranteed in the Bill of Rights.

- *Source of the right.* Sixth Amendment.
- *Size* of the jury. The jury may number from six to twelve.
- *Unanimous verdict.* Not required by the Constitution.
- *When is a jury trial required?* When more than six months' imprisonment is authorized for the offense, even if the accused gets a lower sentence.
- *What is a jury of peers?* A jury whose membership is not consciously restricted to a particular group.
- *What is unconstitutional in jury selection?* Disqualification of jurors based on race, gender, creed, color, national origin, and other prohibited categories.

The right to counsel is guaranteed in the Bill of Rights.

- *Source of the right.* Sixth Amendment.
- *Why counsel is needed.* The defendant's lack of skill in the law might result in a wrongful conviction.
- *Two types of counsel.* Retained by defendant and court-appointed (if indigent).
- *Proceedings at which the right to counsel applies.* All serious offenses, as well as misdemeanors for which the defendant faces a possible jail sentence.
- *Right to effective assistance of counsel.* Guaranteed, but it is difficult to establish ineffective counsel on appeal.
- *Right to act as one's own counsel.* Allowed, but only if the accused is aware of his or her right to counsel, if there is an express waiver, and if the accused is competent.

The right to protection against self-incrimination is guaranteed in the Bill of Rights.

- *Source of the right.* Fifth Amendment.
- *Scope of the right.* Applies only to testimonial, not physical, self-incrimination.

- *Two separate privileges during trial.* The privilege of the accused and the privilege of a witness.
- *Effect of a grant of immunity.* The person can be forced to testify.
- *Types of immunity.* Transactional and use and derivative use.

The right to due process is guaranteed in the Bill of Rights.

- *Source of the right.* Fifth and Fourteenth Amendments.
- *Basic meaning.* Fundamental fairness for the accused.
- *Latest rule.* If the circumstances surrounding the nondisclosure raise a "reasonable probability" that the disclosure would have made a difference in the trial's result, the defendant's due process right has been violated and the conviction must be reversed.

The right to a fair and impartial trial is guaranteed in the Bill of Rights.

- *Source of the right.* The Sixth and Fourteenth Amendments.
- *What it means.* The circumstances surrounding the trial must not be such that they unduly influence the judge or jury.
- *Ways a judge may control prejudicial publicity.* Change of venue, sequestration, continuance, issuance of a gag rule, and control of the press.

REVIEW QUESTIONS

1. Assume that the Nebraska legislature passes a law providing that all crimes in Nebraska are to be tried by a six-member jury. Assume further that the same law also provides that a 5-to-1 vote for conviction results in conviction. Is that law constitutional? Explain your answer.
2. There are two kinds of challenges the prosecutor and the defense lawyer can use when selecting

a jury. How do these challenges differ? Which challenge is bad for the defendant, and why?

3. Sam, a man accused of rape, was tried and convicted by a jury made up of all women. Was his constitutional right to trial by a jury of peers violated? Justify your answer.

4. A college criminal justice student is charged with selling drugs in a dormitory. Such a crime is a felony in the state. She has taken a few college courses in law and has some knowledge of criminal procedure and constitutional rights. Can she waive her right to a lawyer and insist on defending herself?

5. Discuss the extent of the right to counsel in criminal proceedings—from the initial encounter with the police (for allegedly beating up a boyfriend) all the way up to conviction and appeal to a higher court.

6. Discuss the responsibility of a defense lawyer in the U.S. system of justice.

7. What is the meaning of the phrase "effective assistance of counsel"? Discuss why it is hard for a prisoner to prove that his or her lawyer during trial was ineffective.

8. What does the *Brady* rule say? How has the *Brady* rule been broadened or narrowed by subsequent Court decisions? State the current rule.

9. "The Fifth Amendment prohibits all types of self-incrimination and applies to all types of court cases." Is this statement true or false? Explain your answer.

10. Compare and contrast the protection against compulsory self-incrimination of an accused and of a witness.

11. Are recorded 911 calls to police departments admissible as evidence against an accused in court? Give reasons for your answer.

12. What is the effect of a grant of immunity on a witness? What happens if a witness refuses to testify even after a grant of immunity?

TEST YOUR UNDERSTANDING

1. Assume you are a lawyer for Defendant Will in a prosecution for bribery against a high government official. Your client, a codefendant, is given a choice by the prosecutor between transactional immunity and use and derivative use immunity. Which immunity would you advise your client to take and why?

2. Assume that Henry, an indigent Hispanic male, was charged in Colorado with a misdemeanor. The offense carries a maximum ten-month jail sentence, if convicted. He was tried without a lawyer before a jury of six white women. He was convicted on a 5-to-1 vote; the jury gave him a two-month sentence in the local jail. Explore all possible constitutional issues in the case, and state how the Court will likely decide each issue if brought to it on appeal.

3. Jim, a prison inmate in Illinois, is serving the first six months of a five-year sentence for robbery. He seeks release, claiming that he had ineffective counsel because the lawyer assigned to him during the trial graduated from an unaccredited law school (although he passed the bar examination), was last in his class of 75 students, never had a defendant acquitted in five years of law practice, and was sometimes under the influence of drugs during the trial. Assume all these statements are true. You are a federal judge hearing the case. Is Jim's claim of ineffective counsel valid or not? Support your decision.

4. Assume you are a judge in state court presiding over a high-profile criminal case in which the governor, who is married and has five children, allegedly killed his campaign manager (who was also his mistress) because she wanted to break off their relationship. The case has generated tremendous publicity in the local and national media. Discuss the following: (a) what constitutional issues might arise during the trial, given the nature of the case; and (b) what you, as the trial judge, can do to avoid the conviction being reversed by the U.S. Supreme Court on those issues if raised on appeal.

RECOMMENDED READINGS

William V. Dorseano III. *Reexamining the right to trial by jury.* SMU Law Review 1695 (2001).

Anthony Lewis. *Keynote address (Symposium on indigent criminal defense in Texas).* South Texas Law Review 1050–1057 (2001).

James S. Montana, Jr. *Right to counsel: Courts adhere to bright-line limits.* 16 Criminal Justice 4 (2001).

Stephen Gillers. *Guns, fruits, drugs, and documents: A criminal defense lawyer's responsibility for real evidence.* Stanford Law Review 2011, vol: 63, p. 813.

Justin Goetz. *Hold fast the keys to the kingdom: Federal administrative agencies and the need for Brady disclosure.* Minnesota Law Review 2011, vol: 95, p. 1424.

NOTES

1. Wayne R. LaFave, Jerold H. Israel, & Nancy J. King, *Criminal Procedure*, 3rd. ed. (St. Paul, MN, West Group Publishing, 2000), p. 1037.

2. ABA Standards, Providing Defense Services, Sec. 6.1.

3. Erica J. Hashimoto, "Assessing the Indigent Defense System," issue brief, American Constitution Society for Law and Public Policy (Washington, DC, 2005), September 2010, at 10–11.

CHAPTER 13

Sentencing, the Death Penalty, and Other Forms of Punishment

LEARNING OBJECTIVES

1. Explain the four goals and objectives of punishment.
2. Compare and contrast the types of sentencing.
3. Describe the five types of criminal punishments.
4. Compare and contrast sentencing disparity and disproportionate sentencing.
5. Describe the legal development regarding the use of the death penalty.
6. Compare and contrast prisoner rights from the old approach to the new approach.
7. Differentiate between the types of probation.
8. Define the types and uses of intermediate sanctions.
9. Explain the use of sentencing guidelines in reducing sentencing disparity.

KEY TERMS

bifurcated trial
blended sentencing
community service
concurrent sentence
consecutive sentence
determinate sentence
due process
electronic monitoring
fine
forfeiture
indeterminate sentence
intensive probation
intermediate sanction
mandatory sentence
monetary penalty
new approach to prisoners' rights
old approach to prisoners' rights
parole
positive school of criminology
presumptive sentences
probation
restitution
sentencing
sentencing disparity
sentencing guidelines
shock probation
special conditions

WilleeCole/Shutterstock.com

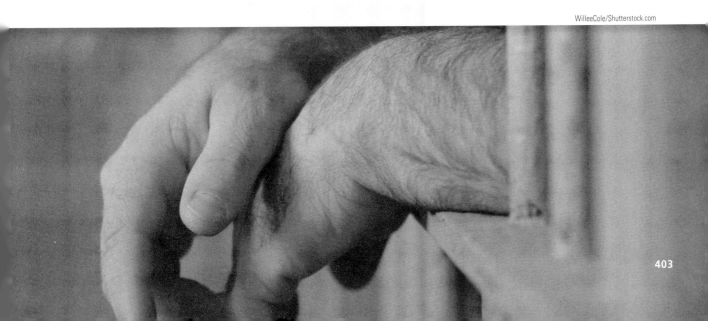

THE TOP 5 IMPORTANT CASES

in Sentencing, the Death Penalty, and Other Forms of Punishment

▶ *WEEMS V. UNITED STATES* (1910) A sentence that is disproportionate to the offense is unconstitutional because it constitutes cruel and unusual punishment.

▶ *GREGG V. GEORGIA* (1976) Death penalty laws that have sufficient safeguards against arbitrary and capricious imposition are constitutional.

▶ *ROPER V. SIMMONS* (2005) The death penalty for juveniles is unconstitutional.

▶ *WOLFF V. MCDONNELL* (1974) Prisoners are entitled to due process in prison disciplinary proceedings that can result in loss of good-time credit or punitive segregation.

▶ *BAZE V. REESE* (2008) The use of a three-drug combination to execute offenders does not constitute cruel and unusual punishment and is constitutional.

THIS CHAPTER discusses topics that are not a part of day-to-day policing but are closely associated with police work. They deserve discussion because the daily work of the police often leads to court trial, conviction, and punishment of the defendant. In policing, success is sometimes measured by whether conviction results and, if it does, the sentence imposed on the criminal. What eventually happens to the defendant can give satisfaction, but it can also result in frustration if the officer believes justice has not been served by the verdict or the sentence imposed.

In the U.S. system of justice, punishment is the domain of corrections officials. Nonetheless, the punishment meted out to offenders is important if police work is to have meaning for both the offender and the public. This chapter deals with issues that are not the main concerns of police officers but are the result of police work. We start with sentencing, followed by a discussion of the death penalty and other types of punishment courts impose. We end with a discussion of the rights of victims.

SENTENCING

sentencing
the formal pronouncement of punishment following conviction in a criminal prosecution.

Sentencing is defined as the formal pronouncement of punishment following conviction in a criminal prosecution. Sentences are imposed by a judge, but some jurisdictions allow jury sentencing. Sentencing authorities usually enjoy discretion in deciding on the sentence to be imposed. This discretion is found in state penal codes, which can provide for a wide range between the minimum and maximum penalties for an offense. No punishment is imposed without authorization by state law.

In most state and federal penal codes, a fixed or specified range of punishment is prescribed. An example is this provision in the Texas Penal Code, which states:

Texas Penal Code, Section 21.07. Public Lewdness

(a) A person engages in any of the following acts in a public place or, if not in a public place, he is reckless about whether another is present who will be offended or alarmed by his:

   (1) act of sexual intercourse;

   (2) act of deviate sexual intercourse;

   (3) act involving contact between the person's mouth or genitals and the anus or genitals of an animal or fowl.

(b) An offense under this section is a Class A misdemeanor. Class A misdemeanors in Texas are punished by a fine not to exceed $4,000, confinement in jail for a term not to exceed one year, or both such fine and confinement.

Aside from stating the penalty to be imposed for a criminal act, the preceding law illustrates another characteristic of criminal laws: they are specific about what conduct is prohibited. Specificity is required because vague criminal laws are unconstitutional because they fail to properly inform a potential offender of the prohibited conduct and are therefore unfair. Laws that are unfair violate the constitutional right to **due process**, which means fundamental fairness.

due process
fundamental fairness.

The Goals and Objectives of Sentencing

Sentencing goals and objectives generally fall into four categories:

◆ Rehabilitation—removing or remediating presumed causes of crime by providing economic, psychological, or socialization assistance to offenders to reduce the likelihood of continuing crime.

◆ Deterrence—sanctioning convicted offenders to reduce crime by making the public and the offender aware of the certainty and severity of punishment for criminal behavior.

◆ Incapacitation—separating offenders from the community to reduce the opportunity for further commission of crime.

◆ Retribution—punishing offenders to express societal disapproval of criminal behavior without specific regard to prevention of crime by the offender or among the general public.

The preceding sentencing goals are not mutually exclusive and often overlap. For example, imprisonment can be a deterrent, retributive, and incapacitative; community service can achieve the goals of rehabilitation and deterrence; the death penalty is retributive but also accomplishes *specific* deterrence and incapacitation; probation can be rehabilitative and retributive, but it does not incapacitate because the offender is still in the community.

In some cases, these goals are irreconcilable. For example, the death penalty is the ultimate form of retribution but is never rehabilitative; imprisonment seldom leads to rehabilitation, but it is retributive and incapacitative; and community service is likely to rehabilitate but does not incapacitate. Each state determines the goals and objectives of its sentencing laws.

Sentencing Disparity

positive school of criminology
advocates that the penalty should "fit the offender" instead of the offense.

Giving sentencing authorities discretion reflects the philosophy of the **positive school of criminology**, which advocates that the penalty should fit the offender instead of the offense. Wide discretion in sentencing results in **sentencing disparity**, meaning different sentences are given for similar crimes committed under similar circumstances. For example, the Texas Penal Code provides for imprisonment of five to ninety-nine years for first-degree felonies. Therefore, defendant Joe can get five years and defendant Bob can get ninety-nine years for the same type of crime committed under similar circumstances. Sentencing disparity is hard to remedy because appellate courts seldom reverse or modify a sentence imposed by the trial court if it is within the statutory limit, as in the preceding examples.

sentencing disparity
different sentences given for similar crimes committed under similar circumstances.

To avoid huge sentencing disparity, some states dictate **mandatory sentences**, which allow no room for discretion. This means the judge or jury must impose the sentence specified by law and cannot deviate from it. Critics consider mandatory sentences inflexible and contrary to the needs of individualized justice. To remedy this, other states provide for **presumptive sentences**, under which a specified sentence is set by law for an offense, but the sentencing authority is given limited discretion based on the presence of mitigating or aggravating circumstances. Sentencing disparity exists, not only among judges in a state, but also from one state to another. An offense may be punished severely in Texas and lightly in Washington. This type of variation persists because punishment of offenders in the United States is a state concern, where justice is determined by state legislatures and reflects consensus among political constituents.

mandatory sentences
sentences that must be imposed by the judge or jury; no deviation is allowed.

presumptive sentences
a specified sentence is set by law, but may be increased or decreased depending on the presence of aggravating or mitigating circumstances.

When Is a Sentence Considered Cruel and Unusual Punishment?

The Eighth Amendment to the Constitution, which prohibits cruel and unusual punishment, does not generally apply to sentences. It applies instead to the treatment of prisoners or detainees. For example, conditions in prisons can be so bad as to constitute cruel and unusual punishment. The Eighth Amendment has also been invoked in death penalty cases, where the death penalty itself and its procedures have been challenged as cruel and unusual. These challenges have not succeeded.

There are instance, however, when the sentence imposed violates the prohibition against cruel and unusual punishment. This happens if the punishment meted out is grossly disproportionate to the offense committed. To use an extreme example, a law imposing life imprisonment on first-time shoplifters would be unconstitutional because the punishment is grossly disproportionate to the offense. The earliest case on this issue was decided more than 100 years ago, in *Weems v. United States*, 217 U.S. 349 (1910). In that case, Weems, a U.S. government official stationed in the Philippines (then a territory of the United States), was charged with falsifying an official document. The monetary amounts of the false entries involved were small, but Weems was convicted and sentenced to fifteen years of hard labor, the wearing of chains, the lifelong loss of certain rights, and the payment of a huge fine and court costs. On appeal, the Court pronounced the punishment disproportionate to the offense and said it constituted cruel and unusual punishment. (Read the Case Brief to learn more about this case.)

Weems v. United States (1910)

Eighty-one years later, the Court modified the *Weems* decision and said that mandatory and disproportionate sentences are not unconstitutional as long as they are not

Harmelin v. Michigan (1991)

"grossly disproportionate" to the offense committed (*Harmelin v. Michigan*, 501 U.S. 957 [1991]). What is "grossly disproportionate," however, is hard to determine with certainty. It varies from one judge or jury to another. Disproportionate sentencing has reemerged as an issue in the "three strikes and you're out" sentencing guidelines that have been passed in some states. These guidelines impose heavy penalties on repeat offenders. The sentences resulting from such guidelines are deemed constitutional unless they are grossly disproportionate to the offense committed and there is no hope for release.

Sentencing Guidelines

To reduce sentencing disparity, **sentencing guidelines** have been adopted by the federal government and some states. The Federal Sentencing Guidelines, adopted in 1987, prescribe a uniform sentencing policy for convicted defendants in federal courts. Nearly half of the states also have sentencing guidelines, although the provisions and format vary from one state to another. Sentencing guidelines are either mandatory or discretionary, but legislative intent on guidelines is sometimes disregarded by the courts because some judges consider guidelines unwarranted intrusions into the purely judicial function of sentencing.

sentencing guidelines
guidelines that provide structure for judges by specifying the sentencing range that should be imposed for offenses.

Federal Sentencing Guidelines Sentencing disparity has long been a concern in criminal justice. Historically, sentences were set in the penal code of various states and without accompanying recommended guidelines. That changed when Congress passed the Comprehensive Crime Control Act of 1984. Embedded in that legislation was the Sentencing Reform Act, which created the U.S. Sentencing Commission. The Commission established federal sentencing guidelines which are designed with the following goals:

◆ incorporate the purposes of sentencing (i.e., just punishment, deterrence, incapacitation, and rehabilitation);

◆ provide certainty and fairness in meeting the purposes of sentencing by avoiding unwarranted disparity among offenders with similar characteristics convicted of similar criminal conduct, while permitting sufficient judicial flexibility to take into account relevant aggravating and mitigating factors;

◆ reflect, to the extent practicable, advancement in the knowledge of human behavior as it relates to the criminal justice process.[1]

The Sentencing Reform Act introduced several innovations to existing sentencing practices. Among those innovations were the limiting of judicial discretion; providing

HIGHLIGHT ❯ What Are Sentencing Guidelines?

"Sentencing guidelines provide structure at the criminal sentencing stage by specifically defining offense and offender elements that should be considered in each case. After considering these elements using a grid or worksheet scoring system, the guidelines recommend a sentence or sentence range. Options usually include some period of incarceration (prison or jail), probation, or an alternative sanction. Goals of guidelines vary, but an underlying theme is that offenders with similar offenses and criminal histories be treated alike. Guidelines vary considerably in terms of whether they are promulgated by the legislature or judiciary, when judges must follow the recommendations; and what rights are afforded to those who disagree with imposed guidelines sentences."

Source: Neal B. Kauder & Brian J. Ostrom, *State Sentencing Guidelines: Profiles and Continuum*, National Center for State Courts, p. 3.

for appellate review of sentences, requiring reasons for sentences stated on the record, and the abolition of parole.

The guidelines give federal judges "fair and consistent sentencing ranges" to consult at sentencing. Judges are to consider both the "seriousness of the criminal conduct" and the "defendant's criminal record." Using the severity of the offense, federal crimes are assigned in the guidelines to one of forty-three "offense levels." Then each offender is assigned to one of six "criminal history categories" depending upon the extent and recency of that past misconduct. (See Table 13.1.)

The guidelines were initially considered mandatory. But they were immediately challenged in court as violative of a defendant's Sixth Amendment right to trial by jury. In *United States v. Booker* (543 U.S. 220 [2005]) the Court held that "the imposition of an enhanced sentence under the federal sentencing guidelines based on the sentencing judge's determination of a fact . . . that was not found by the jury or admitted by the defendant violated the Sixth Amendment." In the same case, however, the Court instructed judges to take the guidelines into consideration when sentencing, but to "tailor the sentences in light of other statutory concerns." As a result, the guidelines were subsequently amended and made advisory instead of mandatory. Thus, federal guidelines help federal judges determine the sentence to be imposed, but judges need not issue sentences within the guidelines. The sentence imposed, however, must be justified and is subject to appellate review. Departures from the guidelines are also authorized under certain conditions.

United States v. Booker (2005)

State Sentencing Guidelines Following the lead of the federal government, thirty-two states now have sentencing guidelines but they vary in goal and purpose. They also vary in such details as grid or worksheet structure; commission membership; whether there are enforceable rules for guideline use; whether reasons are required for the sentence imposed; and whether there is an appellate review of defendant-based challenges to the sentences. Each state uses guidelines to serve its own purpose, criminal law and sentencing being mainly the concern of the states. Each state determines how those who violate its laws are to be punished.

Sentencing Juvenile Offenders

The juvenile justice system is based on the concept of *parens patriae* ("the state is parent") and uses different terminology than the adult criminal justice system. For example, juveniles are not "arrested" by the police; they are instead "taken into custody." They are not "tried" by the courts; they are "adjudicated." They are not "sentenced," but are instead "dispositioned." Despite differences in terminology, the adult and juvenile justice systems are basically similar, but the roles of judges differ in each. In adult justice, the judge is a neutral person who presides over a legal fight between the prosecutor and the defense attorney. Sentences are imposed by the judge or jury within limits specified by law or sentencing guidelines. In juvenile cases, the judge acts as a "wise parent" whose primary concerns are the welfare and future of the juvenile. Adjudication proceedings are not as formal as criminal trials for adults. The judge plays a more active role, and the rules of evidence sometimes do not apply.

Judges and juries enjoy wide latitude in juvenile dispositions. Depending on the seriousness of the offense, this ranges from the juvenile being sent back to his

Table 13.1 Guidelines: Federal Sentencing Tables

SENTENCING TABLE
(in months of imprisonment)

	Offense level	Criminal History Category (Criminal History Points)					
		I (0 or 1)	II (2 or 3)	III (4, 5, 6)	IV (7, 8, 9)	V (10, 11, 12)	VI (13 or more)
	1	0–6	0–6	0–6	0–6	0–6	0–6
	2	0–6	0–6	0–6	0–6	0–6	1–7
	3	0–6	0–6	0–6	0–6	2–8	3–9
	4	0–6	0–6	0–6	2–8	4–10	6–12
Zone A	5	0–6	0–6	1–7	4–10	6–12	9–15
	6	0–6	1–7	2–8	6–12	9–15	12–18
	7	0–6	2–8	4–10	8–14	12–18	15–21
	8	0–6	4–10	6–12	10–16	15–21	18–24
	9	4–10	6–12	8–14	12–18	18–24	21–27
Zone B	10	6–12	8–14	10–16	15–21	21–27	24–30
	11	8–14	10–16	12–18	18–24	24–30	27–33
Zone C	12	10–16	12–18	15–21	21–27	27–33	30–37
	13	12–18	15–21	18–24	24–30	30–37	33–41
	14	15–21	18–24	21–27	27–33	33–41	37–46
	15	18–24	21–27	24–30	30–37	37–46	41–51
	16	21–27	24–30	27–33	33–41	41–51	46–57
	17	24–30	27–33	30–37	37–46	46–57	51–63
	18	27–33	30–37	33–41	41–51	51–63	57–71
	19	30–37	33–41	37–46	46–57	57–71	63–78
	20	33–41	37–46	41–51	51–63	63–78	70–87
	21	37–46	41–51	46–57	57–71	70–87	77–96
	22	41–51	46–57	51–63	63–78	77–96	84–105
	23	46–57	51–63	57–71	70–87	84–105	92–115
	24	51–63	57–71	63–78	77–96	92–115	100–125
	25	57–71	63–78	70–87	84–105	100–125	110–137
	26	63–78	70–87	78–97	92–115	110–137	120–150
Zone D	27	70–87	78–97	87–108	100–125	120–150	130–162
	28	78–97	87–108	97–121	110–137	130–162	140–175
	29	87–108	97–121	108–135	121–151	140–175	151–188
	30	97–121	108–135	121–151	135–168	151–188	168–210
	31	108–135	121–151	135–168	151–188	168–210	188–235
	32	121–151	135–168	151–188	168–210	188–235	210–262
	33	135–168	151–188	168–210	188–235	210–262	235–293
	34	151–188	168–210	188–235	210–262	235–293	262–327
	35	168–210	188–235	210–262	235–293	262–327	292–365
	36	188–235	210–262	235–293	262–327	292–365	324–405
	37	210–262	235–293	262–327	292–365	324–405	360–life
	38	235–293	262–327	292–365	324–405	360–life	360–life
	39	262–327	292–365	324–405	360–life	360–life	360–life
	40	292–365	324–405	360–life	360–life	360–life	360–life
	41	324–405	360–life	360–life	360–life	360–life	360–life
	42	360–life	360–life	360–life	360–life	360–life	360–life
	43	life	life	life	life	life	life

Source: *Federal Sentencing Guidelines Manual*, 2011, p. 407.

CASE BRIEF

Weems v. United States, 217 U.S. 349 (1910)

The Leading Case on Disproportionate Sentences

Facts: Weems, a U.S. government officer stationed in the Philippines (the Philippines was at that time a U.S. territory, and the U.S. Supreme Court had jurisdiction over it), was charged with falsifying an official document. The complaint charged that while Weems was acting as the disbursing officer of the Bureau of Coast Guard and Transportation of the U.S. government of the Philippines, he sought to deceive and defraud the U.S. government, the Philippine Islands, and its officials. The falsification was committed by entering into the cash book, as paid out, wages to lighthouse employees in the amounts of 204 pesos and 408 pesos, both small amounts. Weems was convicted and sentenced to fifteen years of hard labor, the wearing of chains, the lifelong loss of certain rights, and the payment of a fine of 4,000 pesos and court costs.

Issue or Issues: *Does a sentence that is disproportionate to the offense committed violate the Eighth Amendment prohibition against cruel and unusual punishment?* Yes.

Decision: The decision of the Supreme Court of the Philippines was reversed.

Holding: A sentence that is disproportionate to the offense committed violates the Eighth Amendment ban on cruel and unusual punishment.

Case Significance: This is the earliest case on disproportionate sentencing decided by the Court. The Court held that the punishment was more severe than the crime warranted. The Court noted that there were only two degrees of punishment for this particular crime in the Philippine Islands, neither of which fit the plaintiff's case. The trial court simply chose something in between. More important to the Court, however, was the arbitrary manner in which the punishment was chosen and the wording of the law. The punishments for fraud of any degree were extreme. Even after an offender had served sentence at

"hard and painful labor," the punishment continued. The offender faced losing rights of family and property for life. The Court reiterated that the Constitution prohibits cruel and unusual punishment and Weems's sentence was both.

Decided in 1910, this case was later modified by *Harmelin v. Michigan*, 501 U.S. 957 (1991). In *Harmelin*, the Court held that mandatory and disproportionate sentences are not necessarily unconstitutional as long as they are not "grossly disproportionate" to the offense committed. This is the current standard for cruel and unusual punishment in sentences.

Excerpts from the Opinion: These parts of his penalty endure for the term of imprisonment. From other parts there is no intermission. His prison bars and chains are removed, it is true, after twelve years, but he goes from them to a perpetual limitation of his liberty. He is forever kept under the shadow of his crime, forever kept within voice and view of the criminal magistrate, not being able to change his domicile without notice to the "authority in charge of his surveillance," and without permission in writing. He may not seek, even in other scenes, and among other people, to retrieve his fall from rectitude. Even that hope is taken from him and he is subject to tormenting regulations that, if not so tangible as iron bars and stone walls, oppress as much by their continuity, and deprive of essential liberty. No circumstance of degradation is omitted. It may be even the cruelty of pain is not omitted. He must bear a chain night and day. He is condemned to painful as well as hard labor. . . . Such penalties for such offenses amaze those who have formed their conception of the relation of a state to even its offending citizens from the practice of American commonwealth, and believe that it is a precept of justice that punishment for crime should be graduated and proportioned to offense.

or her parents to, in some cases, the juvenile being sent to an adult prison. Juveniles are "dispositioned" according to provisions of a state juvenile code or family law. Juvenile proceedings are technically civil proceedings, although most constitutional rights adults enjoy are now also available to juveniles. As a result of the increase in juvenile crime in the 1990s, legislatures got tough on juveniles and enacted laws that tend to blur the distinctions between adult and juvenile justice. This is particularly true in the sentencing process, where many states have expanded the sentencing options of judges or juries that handle criminal cases. This approach is called **blended sentencing** and is characterized as a middle ground between juvenile and adult punishments.

blended sentencing sentences given to juveniles that combine juvenile and adult sentences.

In most states, the release of a juvenile from state institutions is not set during the disposition proceeding by the juvenile court judge. Instead, it is determined by two factors: (1) when the juvenile reaches the age of adulthood (in many states this is at age 18), and (2) if the juvenile is deemed by juvenile authorities to be fit for release even

FIGURE 13.1 Blended Sentencing Options Create a Middle Ground between Juvenile Sanctions and Adult Sanctions

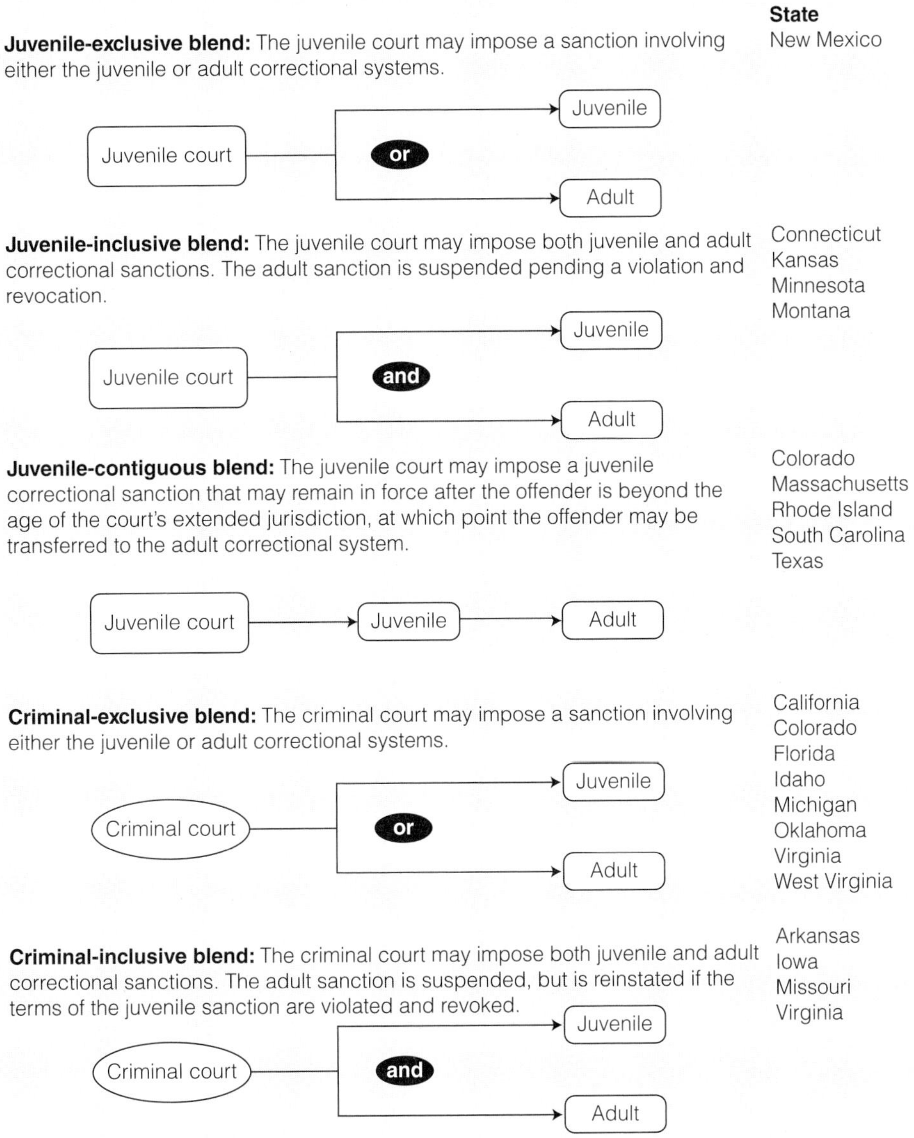
State
Juvenile-exclusive blend: The juvenile court may impose a sanction involving either the juvenile or adult correctional systems.
New Mexico
Juvenile court
or
Juvenile
Adult
Juvenile-inclusive blend: The juvenile court may impose both juvenile and adult correctional sanctions. The adult sanction is suspended pending a violation and revocation.
Connecticut
Kansas
Minnesota
Montana
Juvenile court
and
Juvenile
Adult
Juvenile-contiguous blend: The juvenile court may impose a juvenile correctional sanction that may remain in force after the offender is beyond the age of the court's extended jurisdiction, at which point the offender may be transferred to the adult correctional system.
Colorado
Massachusetts
Rhode Island
South Carolina
Texas
Juvenile court
Juvenile
Adult
Criminal-exclusive blend: The criminal court may impose a sanction involving either the juvenile or adult correctional systems.
California
Colorado
Florida
Idaho
Michigan
Oklahoma
Virginia
West Virginia
Criminal court
or
Juvenile
Adult
Criminal-inclusive blend: The criminal court may impose both juvenile and adult correctional sanctions. The adult sanction is suspended, but is reinstated if the terms of the juvenile sanction are violated and revoked.
Arkansas
Iowa
Missouri
Virginia
Criminal court
and
Juvenile
Adult

Source: Adapted from Howard N. Snyder and Melissa Sickmund, *Juvenile Offenders and Victims: 1999 National Report* (Washington, D.C.: Office of Juvenile Justice and Delinquency Prevention, 1999), p. 108.

before reaching the age of adulthood. A realistic scenario in juvenile court sentencing might go like this:

> Juvenile Court Judge: "I am sending you to a youth institution as part of your rehabilitation."
> Juvenile Offender: "For how long, Judge? When can I go home?"
> Juvenile Court Judge: "I don't know. That is up to the authorities there."

TYPES OF SENTENCES

Criminal sentences may be classified into five categories:

- ◆ Death penalty
- ◆ Imprisonment
- ◆ Probation
- ◆ Intermediate sanctions
- ◆ Fines, forfeiture, and restitution

More than one type of punishment may be imposed for a crime. For example, the death penalty may carry with it the payment of restitution; imprisonment may include property forfeiture; and probation may include having to perform community service. The various types of sentences are discussed in this section of the chapter, beginning with the most controversial punishment—the death penalty.

The Death Penalty

The most severe penalty for crime is death. As of 2015, thirty-two states and the federal government had death penalty laws, although many states have not executed an offender in years (see Exhibit 13.1). This ultimate form of punishment has been used in the United States from the earliest years of its history without much legal controversy. It was not until the early 1970s that the constitutionality of the death penalty drew greater Court attention. Prior to that, the death penalty cases that reached the Court dealt with the procedure used for execution rather than the constitutionality of the penalty itself. For example, in 1878, the Court found that execution by firing squad was not cruel and unusual (*Wilkerson v. Utah*, 99 U.S. 130 [1878]). And in 1890, electrocution as a form of execution was found to be constitutional (*In re Kemmler*, 136 U.S. 436 [1890]).

Wilkerson v. Utah (1878)
In re Kemmler (1890)

The Death Penalty Is Declared Unconstitutional (1972) In the 1970s, the Court decided two death penalty cases, four years apart, each resulting in a different conclusion. *Furman v. Georgia* and *Gregg v. Georgia* constitute the foundation cases and are, arguably, the most widely known cases on the death penalty.

Furman v. Georgia (1972)

In *Furman v. Georgia*, 408 U.S. 238 (1972), three defendants were convicted by a jury in state court and sentenced to death. Two of the defendants were convicted of rape and the other of murder. On appeal, the Court held that the imposition and carrying out of the death penalty in that case was unconstitutional. But of the five justices who voted against constitutionality, three based their vote on the equal protection clause of the Fourteenth Amendment, while the other two justices based their vote on the prohibition against cruel and unusual punishment. The justices who based their opposition on

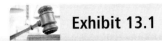

Exhibit 13.1 · **Facts about the Death Penalty**

1015 18th St. NW, Suite 704
Washington, DC 20036
Phone: 202-289-2275
Fax: 202-289-7336
dpic@deathpenaltyinfo.org
www.deathpenaltyinfo.org

DEATH PENALTY INFORMATION CENTER
Facts about the Death Penalty
Updated: July 19, 2012

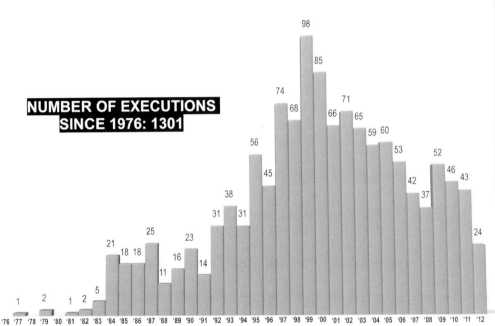

NUMBER OF EXECUTIONS SINCE 1976: 1301

DEATH PENALTY STATES (33)
Alabama
Arizona
Arkansas
California
Colorado
Delaware
Florida
Georgia
Idaho
Indiana
Kansas
Kentucky
Louisiana
Maryland
Mississippi
Missouri
Montana
Nebraska
Nevada
New Hampshire
North Carolina
Ohio
Oklahoma
Oregon
Pennsylvania
South Carolina
South Dakota
Tennessee
Texas
Utah
Virginia
Washington
Wyoming
U.S. Gov't
U.S. Military

NON-DEATH PENALTY STATES (17)
Alaska
Connecticut*
Hawaii
Illinois
Iowa
Maine
Massachusetts
Michigan
Minnesota
New Jersey
New Mexico*
New York
North Dakota
Rhode Island
Vermont
West Virginia
Wisconsin
District of Columbia
Inmates remain on death row.

Race of Defendants Executed

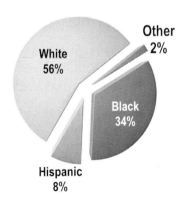

- White: 731
- Black: 446
- Hispanic: 100
- Other: 24

Race of Victims in Death Penalty Cases

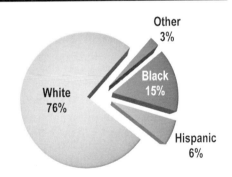

Over 75% of the murder victims in cases resulting in an execution were white, even though nationally only 50% of murder victims generally are white.

Source: Facts about the Death Penalty, Death Penalty Information Center, www.deathpenaltyinfo.org/documents/FactSheet, p. 1.

the equal protection clause said that the penalty was applied in a "freakish and wanton" manner. Too much discretion was vested in the sentencing authority; thus the penalty could be applied selectively and capriciously. Unless those infirmities were removed from the statute, the penalty could not be imposed because it violated the equal protection clause. After the *Furman* decision, thirty-five states and the federal government revised their capital punishment statutes so as to eliminate equal protection problems, thus setting the stage for another major death penalty case four years later.

Gregg v. Georgia (1976)

The Death Penalty Is Declared Constitutional (1976) Four years after *Furman*, the Court decided *Gregg v. Georgia*, 428 U.S. 153 (1976). In *Gregg*, the Court held that the death penalty is not per se (in itself) cruel and unusual punishment and may be imposed if the sentencing authority is given guidance by law so as to remove arbitrariness and capriciousness from the sentencing process. Defendant Gregg was charged with two counts of first-degree murder and two counts of robbery. Gregg and a traveling companion were picked up by two motorists while hitchhiking in Florida. The next morning the bodies of the two motorists were discovered in a ditch near Atlanta. Gregg was tried, convicted, and sentenced to death. In accordance with Georgia law in capital cases, it was a **bifurcated trial**, meaning that the trial had two stages: one for determining guilt, and the other for determining the punishment. In addition to a bifurcated trial, Georgia law also required that the jury consider aggravating and mitigating circumstances, and provided for automatic appeal to the Georgia Supreme Court, thereby ensuring that the death penalty would be imposed only in a limited number of cases. In a 7-to-2 vote, the Court held that the death penalty is not per se cruel and unusual punishment. It can be imposed if arbitrariness and capriciousness in its imposition are removed. The Georgia law was found to be constitutional because it had sufficient provisions to ensure that the imposition of the death penalty would not be capricious or arbitrary.

bifurcated trial
the trial has two stages: the guilt or innocence stage and the punishment stage.

See Exhibit 13.2 for details about state-by-state executions since the *Gregg* decision in 1976.

Important Death Penalty Decisions after *Gregg v. Georgia* The 1976 *Gregg* decision settled the issue of constitutionality of the death penalty, but the Court continues to decide death penalty cases every year. The following are some of the more important cases decided by the Court on death penalty issues.

Woodson v. North Carolina (1976)

- *Are mandatory death penalty laws constitutional?* No, mandatory death *penalty* laws are not constitutional. They violate the prohibition against cruel and unusual punishment because they fail to take into consideration the individual characteristics of the criminal and the circumstances of the case (*Woodson v. North Carolina*, 428 U.S. 280 [1976]).

Lockhart v. McCree (1986)

- *Can prospective jurors who oppose the death penalty be disqualified?* Yes, prospective jurors whose opposition to the death penalty is so strong as to prevent or impair their performance as jurors in the sentencing phase of a trial may be removed for cause from jury membership (*Lockhart v. McCree*, 476 U.S. 162 [1986]).

Ford v. Wainwright (1986)

- *Can an inmate who was sane during the commission of the crime but has since become insane be executed?* No, a person who is insane cannot be executed, because they lack the capacity to understand what is happening (*Ford v. Wainwright*, 477 U.S. 399 [1986]).

Exhibit 13.2 • State-by-State Executions Since 1976

NUMBER OF EXECUTIONS BY STATE SINCE 1976

	Total	2011	2012		Total	2011	2012
Texas	483	13	6	Nevada	12	0	0
Virginia	109	1	0	Utah	7	0	0
Oklahoma	99	2	3	Tennessee	6	0	0
Florida	73	2	2	Maryland	5	0	0
Missouri	68	1	0	Washington	5	0	0
Alabama	55	6	0	Nebraska	3	0	0
Georgia	52	4	0	Pennsylvania	3	0	0
Ohio	47	5	1	Kentucky	3	0	0
North Carolina	43	0	0	Montana	3	0	0
South Carolina	43	1	0	U.S. Gov't	3	0	0
Arizona	32	4	4	Idaho	3	1	1
Louisiana	28	0	0	Oregon	2	0	0
Arkansas	27	0	0	Connecticut	1	0	0
Mississippi	21	2	6	New Mexico	1	0	0
Indiana	20	0	0	Colorado	1	0	0
Delaware	16	1	1	Wyoming	1	0	0
California	13	0	0	South Dakota	1	0	0
Illinois	12	0	0				

EXECUTIONS BY REGION*

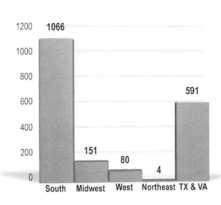

*Federal executions are listed in the region in which the crime was committed.

DEATH SENTENCING

The number of death sentences per year has dropped dramatically since 1999.

Year	1995	1996	1997	1998	1999	2000	2001	2002	2003	2004	2005	2006	2007	2008	2009	2010	2011
Sentence	312	315	266	294	277	224	158	165	151	139	139	125	120	121	118	104	78*

Source: Bureau of Justice Statistics: "Capital Punishment, 2010." *Projected, based on DPIC's research.

MENTAL DISABILITIES

- *Intellectual Disabilities:* In 2002, the Supreme Court held in *Atkins v. Virginia* that it is unconstitutional to execute defendants with 'mental retardation.'
- *Mental Illness:* The American Psychiatric Association, the American Psychological Association, the National Alliance for the Mentally Ill, and the American Bar Association have endorsed resolutions calling for an exemption of the severely mentally ill.

JUVENILES

- In 2005, the Supreme Court in *Roper v. Simmons* struck down the death penalty for juveniles. 22 defendants had been executed for crimes committed as juveniles since 1976.

WOMEN

- There were 62 women on death row as of January 1, 2012. This constitutes less than 2% of the total death row population. 12 women have been executed since 1976. (NAACP Legal Defense Fund, January 1, 2012).

DETERRENCE

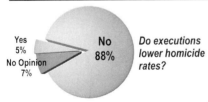

Do executions lower homicide rates?

- According to a survey of the former and present presidents of the country's top academic criminological societies, 88% of these experts rejected the notion that the death penalty acts as a deterrent to murder. (Radelet & Lacock, 2009)

- A report by the National Research Council, titled Deterrence and the Death Penalty, stated that studies claiming that the death penalty has a deterrent effect on murder rates are "fundamentally flawed" and should not be used when making policy decisions (2012).

- Consistent with previous years, the 2010 FBI Uniform Crime Report showed that **the South had the highest murder rate. The South accounts for over 80% of executions.** The Northeast, which has less than 1% of all executions, tied with the West for the lowest murder rate.

Murder Rates per 100,000 (2010)

Source: Facts about the Death Penalty, Death Penalty Information Center, www.deathpenaltyinfo.org/documents/FactSheet.pdf, p. 3.

McCleskey v. Kemp (1987)

♦ *Based on studies of statistical discrimination, is the execution of racial minorities unconstitutional?* No, a statistical study suggesting racial discrimination in the imposition of death sentences does not make the death penalty unconstitutional. What is needed is that the "petitioner must prove that decision-makers in his case acted with discriminatory purpose." Proof of discrimination by statistical studies does not suffice (*McCleskey v. Kemp*, 481 U.S. 279 [1987]).

Penry v. Lynaugh (2002)

♦ *Can a mentally retarded defendant be given the death penalty?* No. The execution of mentally retarded defendants (the term used by the Court) violates the Eighth Amendment prohibition against cruel and unusual punishment (*Atkins v. Virginia*, 536 U.S. 304 [2002]). This case overrules a previous case, *Penry v. Lynaugh*, decided thirteen years previously.

♦ *Can a third party challenge the constitutionality of a death sentence?* No, only the person on whom the death penalty is imposed can challenge its constitutionality (*Whitmore v. Arkansas*, 495 U.S. 149 [1990]).

Whitmore v. Arkansas (1990)

Roper v. Simmons (2005)

♦ *Can juveniles who commit crimes at age 16 or 17 be given the death penalty?* No, imposing the death penalty on juveniles who commit crimes at age 16 or 17 constitutes cruel and unusual punishment (*Roper v. Simmons*, 543 U.S. 551 [2005]). This decision overrules a previous case, *Stanford v. Kentucky*, decided sixteen years previously.

♦ *Can families of victims in death penalty cases present victim impact statements?* Yes, victim impact statements concerning the characteristics of the victim and the emotional impact of the crime on the victim's family do not violate the prohibition against cruel and unusual punishment (*Payne v. Tennessee*, 495 U.S. 149 [1990]).

Payne v. Tennessee (1990)

♦ *Can a judge, on his or her own, determine the presence of aggravating circumstances and then increase the punishment imposed to death?* No, a judge alone cannot do that. The determination of aggravating circumstances that elevates the penalty to death must be made by a jury, serving as the fact-finder (*Ring v. Arizona*, 536 U.S. 584 [2002]).

Ring v. Arizona (2002)

♦ *Is the lethal injection procedure for execution (using three drugs) currently followed in the state of Kentucky constitutional?* Yes, the lethal injection procedure for execution followed in Kentucky (and other states) is constitutional and does not violate the constitutional prohibition against cruel and unusual punishment (*Baze v. Rees*, 553 U.S. 35 [2008]). (Read the Case Brief to learn more about this issue.)

Baze v. Rees (2008)

Kennedy v. Louisiana (2008)

♦ *Is it constitutional to impose the death penalty for a crime where the victim's life was not taken?* No, it is cruel and unusual punishment to impose the death penalty for the rape of a child because the crime did not result in the child's death (*Kennedy v. Louisiana*, 554 U.S. 407 [2008]).

MYTH vs. REALITY

MYTH The death penalty may be imposed for crimes other than first-degree murder.

FACT The death penalty may only be imposed in cases where the defendant has been convicted of first-degree murder and the jury has found the existence of aggravating circumstances.

Imprisonment

The second type of sentence is imprisonment, which can be in a jail or prison. Jails are confinement places usually reserved for detainees and minor offenders. They are operated by cities or counties and are usually under the supervision and control of a sheriff. In contrast, prisons are funded, and controlled by either the state or the federal government. Most prisons do not hold detainees, although many include persons whose cases are on appeal. Jails and prisons may be distinguished as follows:

Baze v. Rees, 553 U.S. 35 (2008)

The Leading Case on the Constitutionality of Lethal Injection

Facts: Ralph Baze and Thomas Bowling were both convicted of two counts of capital murder and sentenced to death in Kentucky. Kentucky's form of execution is the lethal injection of three drugs: sodium thiopental, to render unconsciousness; pancuronium bromide, to paralyze the lungs; and potassium chloride, which induces cardiac arrest. As part of Kentucky's lethal injection protocol, those persons responsible for inserting the intravenous (IV) catheters into the prisoner must be qualified personnel with at least one year's professional experience. Kentucky uses a certified phlebotomist and an emergency medical technician (EMT) to perform these functions. The warden and deputy warden stay in the execution chamber with the prisoner, and if the prisoner is not unconscious within sixty seconds of administering the first drug, sodium thiopental, a second dose of the drug is administered before injecting the other two drugs. Between injections, members of the execution team flush the IV lines with saline to prevent clogging of the lines.

Issue or Issues: *Does Kentucky's lethal injection procedure violate the Eighth Amendment prohibition against cruel and unusual punishment?* No.

Decision: The decision of the Kentucky State Supreme Court was affirmed.

Holding: Kentucky's lethal injection procedure does not violate the Eighth Amendment because it does not present a substantial or objectively intolerable risk of serious harm. "A State's refusal to adopt proffered alternative procedures may violate the Eighth Amendment only where the alternative procedure is feasible, readily implemented, and . . . significantly reduces a substantial risk of severe pain."

Case Significance: This case, decided in 2008, was considered one of the most serious challenges to the death penalty since the 1976 decision in *Gregg v. Georgia*. It came during a time of strong doubts about the wisdom and constitutionality of the death penalty, primarily because of the risk of executing innocent defendants. Massive publicity about defendants, including those on death row, who were freed because DNA evidence proved they were innocent, caused the public to pause and ask if the country had executed an innocent person in the past or if it will do so in the future.

Prior to the decision in this case, there was massive media publicity and predictions that it would put the issue of the death penalty to its final and deserved rest. To the disappointment of death penalty opponents, the case did not turn out to be that significant. Instead, it focused on a narrow issue: whether Kentucky's method of execution constituted cruel and unusual punishment. The federal government and at least thirty states use the same combination of drugs as used by Kentucky. Were Kentucky's procedure declared unconstitutional, it would have forced the other states and the federal government to find new ways to execute defendants by lethal injection.

Excerpts from the Opinion: Petitioners do not claim that lethal injection or the proper administration of the particular protocol adopted by Kentucky by themselves constitute the cruel or wanton infliction of pain. Quite the contrary, they concede that "if performed properly," an execution carried out under Kentucky's procedures would be "humane and constitutional." That is because, as counsel for petitioners admitted at oral argument, proper administration of the first drug, sodium thiopental, eliminates any meaningful risk that a prisoner would experience pain from the subsequent injections of pancuronium and potassium chloride.

Instead, petitioners claim that there is a significant risk that procedures will not be properly followed—in particular, that the sodium thiopental will not be properly administered to achieve its intended effect—resulting in severe pain when the other chemicals are administered. Our cases recognize that subjecting individuals to a risk of future harm—not simply actually inflicting pain—can qualify as cruel and unusual punishment. To establish that such exposure violates the Eighth Amendment, however, the conditions presenting the risk must be "sure or very likely to cause serious illness and needless suffering," and give rise to "sufficiently imminent dangers." *Helling v. McKinney*, 509 U.S. 25, 33, 34–35 (1993). We have explained that to prevail on such a claim there must be a "substantial risk of serious harm," an "objectively intolerable risk of harm" that prevents prison officials from pleading that they were "subjectively blameless for purposes of the Eighth Amendment." *Farmer v. Brennan*, 511 U.S. 825 (1994).

(continued)

Much of petitioner's case rests on the contention that they have identified a significant risk of harm that can be eliminated by adopting alternative procedures. Given what our cases have said about the nature of the risk of harm that is actionable under the Eighth Amendment, a condemned prisoner cannot successfully challenge a State's method of execution merely by showing a slightly or marginally safer alternative. Instead, the proffered alternatives must effectively address a "substantial risk of serious harm." To qualify, the alternative procedure must be feasible, readily implemented, and in fact significantly reduce a substantial risk of severe pain. If a State refuses to adopt such an alternative in the face of these documented advantages, without a legitimate penological justification for adhering to its current method of execution, then a State's refusal to change its method can be viewed as "cruel and unusual" under the Eighth Amendment.

Jails	Prisons
Usually for minor offenders (misdemeanants)	Usually for serious offenders (felons)
Hold detainees and convicts	Hold only those who have been convicted or whose cases are pending appeal
Established and funded by local governments	Established and funded by state or federal governments
Administered by the sheriff or chief of police	Administered by a state or federal correctional officer

Types of Prison Sentences Several terms are used for the various types of sentences, but these terms are used differently in different states and jurisdictions. For example, *determinate sentences* may be called *fixed sentences* or *mandatory sentences* in some places. However, the definitions used here provide general guidelines.

Determinate versus Indeterminate Sentences Sentences involving imprisonment may be classified as either determinate or indeterminate. **Determinate sentences** specify the period of incarceration based on guidelines. A sentence of five years in the penitentiary for robbery is a determinate sentence (some jurisdictions call it a fixed sentence). Other determinate sentences provide limited discretion, such as a sentence for burglary at a minimum of one year and a maximum of two years. By contrast, an **indeterminate sentence** gives wide discretion to the sentencing authority. An example is a sentence that provides for a minimum of five years and a maximum of life imprisonment.

Concurrent versus Consecutive Sentences If the defendant is convicted of two or more crimes, or is already serving a sentence on some other offense, the sentence can be a **concurrent sentence** (served at the same time) or a **consecutive sentence** (served one after the other, or "stacked"). This decision is usually discretionary with the judge. In the absence of specific indication, sentences are to be served concurrently. For example, Fred is tried and convicted of two robberies. He is sentenced to five years in prison for each conviction. If the sentences are imposed concurrently, Fred will serve a total of five years. If the sentences are imposed consecutively, Fred will stay in prison for ten years. If nothing is noted in the sentence, the penalties are to be served concurrently, meaning that Fred will serve five years.

Old versus New Approach to Prisoners' Rights Prisoners in the United States used to be viewed as "slaves of the state." This meant they had no rights whatsoever other than the basic rights to life and food. Prison authorities wielded a lot of power and could do just about anything they wanted with prisoners. The courts followed a hands-off policy and refused to accept cases filed by prisoners. The policy of nonintervention was

determinate sentence
a sentence that specifies the period of incarceration based on guidelines.

indeterminate sentence
a sentence that gives wide discretion to the sentencing authority.

concurrent sentence
sentences served at the same time.

consecutive sentence
sentences served one after the other.

justified by the following: (1) the prisoners were being punished and thus deserved the treatment they received; (2) prison administrators were deemed the experts on how prisons ought to be administered and therefore received significant deference from the courts; and (3) the public did not know what was going on in prisons and did not care.

The hands-off days are gone; we now live in the hands-on era, in which the philosophy of the courts toward prisoners' rights has changed dramatically. The clearest indication of this change is that courts now hear prison cases regularly. The **old approach to prisoners' rights** held that "lawful incarceration brings about the necessary withdrawal of many privileges and rights, a restriction justified by considerations underlying our prison system." This has given way to the new philosophy, which states that "prisoners retain all the rights of free citizens except those on which restriction is necessary to assure their orderly confinement or to provide reasonable protection for the rights and physical safety of all members of the prison community."

Under the **new approach to prisoners' rights**, only three government interests justify a different treatment of prisoners: (1) maintaining internal order and discipline, (2) securing the institution against unauthorized access or escape, and (3) rehabilitating prisoners. In this new approach, prisoners have the same rights as people in the free world, except those rights that can be denied them based on the three justifications. The burden of justifying these regulations, if challenged by prisoners in court, rests with prison authorities. Prison administrators obviously prefer the good old days because governing prisons was easier then. For example, under the old philosophy, it was easy for a prison warden to prohibit inmates from membership in outside organizations. Under the new philosophy, however, the warden must prove that the prohibition is related to one of the three justifications noted previously.

Rights of Prisoners Since adopting the hands-on policy in prison cases, the Court has decided many cases involving claims by inmates that their constitutional rights were violated by prison authorities. Some of the most significant prison law cases are described here.

- ◆ *When are prison regulations valid?* The standard is this: "A prison regulation that impinges on inmates' constitutional rights is valid only if it is reasonably related to a legitimate penological interest" (*Turner v. Safley*, 482 U.S. 78 [1987]).
- ◆ *Can prison wardens be held liable for bad prison conditions?* Yes, but prisoners must establish that prison conditions are the result of "deliberate indifference," meaning that the warden had a "culpable state of mind" (*Wilson v. Seiter*, 501 U.S. 294 [1991]). This is not an easy standard for prisoners to establish.
- ◆ *Do prisoners have a right to go to court?* Yes, but that right is violated only if a prisoner's attempt to pursue a legal claim is hindered by prison officials. Inadequacies in a state's delivery of legal services to inmates is insufficient as a basis for a lawsuit based on denial of access to court. What is needed is a showing of widespread actual injury to prisoners (*Lewis v. Casey*, 518 U.S. 343 [1996]).
- ◆ *Do prisoners have constitutional rights when being disciplined by prison authorities?* Yes, but only if the prison disciplinary proceedings can result in loss of good-time credit or punitive segregation (*Wolff v. McDonnell*, 418 U.S. 539 [1974]).
- ◆ *Is racial segregation in prison constitutional?* No, except when a compelling state interest (such as a racially motivated prison riot) justifies it (*Lee v. Washington*, 390 U.S. 333 [1968]).

old approach to prisoners' rights
prisoners had only a few rights because they are incarcerated.

new approach to prisoners' rights
prisoners have the same rights as people in the free world, except those rights that can be denied them for justified reasons.

Turner v. Safley (1987)

Wilson v. Seiter (1991)

Lewis v. Casey (1996)

Wolff v. McDonnell (1974)

Lee v. Washington (1968)

Hudson v. McMillian (1992)

♦ *Are prison authorities liable for use of nondeadly force?* Yes, but only if such force was used "maliciously and sadistically" to cause harm (*Hudson v. McMillian*, 503 U.S. 1 [1992]). What those terms mean is determined by courts on a case-by-case basis.

Estelle v. Gamble (1976)

♦ *Are prison authorities liable for lack of medical care?* The Court said yes, but only if there is "deliberate indifference" to inmates' medical needs. Deliberate indifference in medical needs cases means "unnecessary and wanton infliction of pain" by prison medical personnel or prison authorities (*Estelle v. Gamble*, 429 U.S. 97 [1976]).

Farmer v. Brennan (1994)

♦ *Are prison authorities liable for inmate-on-inmate violence?* The Court said yes, but the prisoner must prove that the prison authorities "know of and disregard an excessive risk of harm to the inmate." It is not enough for liability that "the risk was so obvious that a reasonable person should have noticed it" (*Farmer v. Brennan*, 511 U.S. 825 [1994]).

The guiding theme in these cases can be expressed as follows: Yes, inmates have constitutional rights, but they are *diminished*, meaning they are not as extensive as those enjoyed by people outside prison walls. What rights prisoners have are determined by the courts on a case-by-case basis.

parole
the prisoner is released before the end of his or her prison term, but subject to supervision by a parole officer.

Release on Parole Most states provide for the release of a prisoner on **parole**. In parole, the prisoner is released before the end of his or her prison term, but subject to supervision by a parole officer. The Court has held that prisoners released on parole are technically under the supervision of the jurisdiction's department of corrections and therefore can be treated as though they are still in prison. For example, a parolee can be stopped or searched by the police without suspicion or probable cause. Parole release is usually based on good prison behavior and is often used as an incentive for inmates to behave and work well while in prison. Parole is a relief to inmates because they are released early, but it also benefits the state because the cost of keeping an offender on community supervision is much less than that of keeping an offender in prison.

MYTH vs. REALITY

MYTH Inmates enjoy a wide variety of constitutional rights, similar to those enjoyed by people outside of prison.

FACT Inmates enjoy only limited constitutional rights; their conviction and incarceration limit most of their rights to a significant degree.

In states that have parole, a hearing is held before a parole board to determine a prisoner's fitness for release. Early release is discretionary with the board because, like probation, parole is an act of grace by the state rather than a right given to prisoners. Parole release is subject to conditions similar to those for probation (see the next section in this chapter) except that they can be more strict. Violation of the terms of parole leads to revocation of parole. The parolee is given a hearing and, if found to have violated the terms of parole, is sent back to prison to serve the remainder of their term.

Life Without Parole (LWOP) Most states have laws that provide for life without parole (LWOP). As the term implies, some prisoners cannot be paroled even if parole is allowed in that state. This form of imprisonment is imposed on particularly dangerous offenders who otherwise would have merited the death penalty. Life without parole often draws support from both liberals and conservatives, but for different reasons. Liberals like it because it spares the inmate from the death penalty; conservatives approve of it because it permanently removes a threat to society.

The Court recently held, however, that life sentences without parole on juveniles constitutes cruel and unusual punishment and are therefore unconstitutional

(*Miller v. Alabama*, 567 U.S. — [2012]). In a previous ruling, the Court had held that it is unconstitutional to impose a life sentence on a juvenile involved in a crime that did not include a killing. Miller extends that ruling to crimes involving murder.

Miller v. Alabama (2012)

Probation

The third type of sentence is **probation**. This is where a convicted offender is allowed to remain in the community, subject to court-imposed conditions and under the supervision of a probation officer. If the imposed conditions are violated, the probation may be revoked and the probationer imprisoned. Probation is the most widely used form of punishment for two reasons: it is less expensive, and it keeps the offender in the community. It is usually given to first-time or nonviolent offenders. Exhibit 13.3 provides statistical information about probation and also parole.

probation
a convicted offender is allowed to remain free in the community, subject to court-imposed conditions and under the supervision of a probation officer.

Probation Is a Privilege, Not a Right In most states, probation is given at the discretion of the judge or jury. A defendant cannot demand that the judge or jury grant probation. It is granted for a specified number of years, usually to coincide with the prison term that would have been served if the defendant were sent to prison. For example, Alice is sentenced to five years, but instead is placed on probation. Alice will be on probation for five years. Some states, however, provide that the probationer be discharged after having been on probation for a minimum number of years. For example, Jane is sentenced to seven years' probation. The law may provide that Jane may be discharged from probation and the court record dismissed after two years if during that time Jane does not violate any condition of probation. This type of probation is most often used in juvenile cases or for first-time adult offenders.

Kinds of Probation Probation variations include shock probation and intensive probation.

- **Shock probation** (also called shock incarceration, shock parole, or a split sentence) is a variation of probation used in some states. In shock probation an offender serves time in prison, after which he or she is discharged and placed on probation. The idea is to expose the offender to the harsh realities of prison life so as to deter him or her from further criminality.

- **Intensive probation** is a second variation. As the term implies, the probationer is supervised more closely than those on regular probation. For example, drug testing may be required once a week instead of once a month; home visits may take place once a week instead of once a month; and an evening curfew may be imposed. The probationer may also be subject to electronic monitoring. This condition requires the offender to wear an electronic monitor that tracks his or her whereabouts. Violations of any restrictions imposed (for example, the probationer may not be allowed to leave the state without permission) are electronically recorded and immediately known by the probation officer. Intensive probation is usually imposed on serious offenders or those who have had a history of violations. It is a last chance for the offender to stay in the community; a violation sends the offender to prison.

shock probation
an offender serves time in prison, after which he or she is discharged and placed on probation.

intensive probation
the probationer is supervised more closely than in regular probation.

Exhibit 13.3 • **Probation and Parole Statistics**

U.S. Department of Justice
Office of Justice Programs
Bureau of Justice Statistics

November 2011, NCJ 236019

Probation and Parole in the United States, 2010

Lauren E. Glaze and Thomas P. Bonczar, *BJS Statisticians*

During 2010, the number of adults under community supervision declined by 1.3% from 4,954,600 at the beginning of the year to 4,887,900 at yearend (figure 1). The community supervision population includes adults on probation and adults on parole or any other post-prison supervision. (See text box on page 2.) This represented the second consecutive decline in the number of adults under community supervision.

The probation population decreased by 1.7%, which was also the second consecutive year of decline. The parole population increased by 0.3%. At yearend 2010, about 1 in 48 adults in the U.S. were under community supervision.

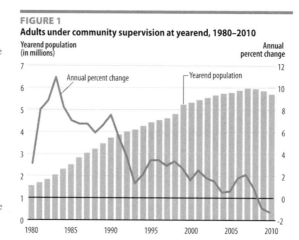

FIGURE 1

Adults under community supervision at yearend, 1980–2010

Note: Annual percent change was calculated as the difference between the January 1 and December 31 populations within the reporting year. See *Methodology* for more details.

HIGHLIGHTS

- The number of adult offenders under community supervision declined by 66,700 during 2010 to reach 4,887,900 offenders at yearend 2010.

- The overall decline in the community supervision population was due to a 1.7% decline in the probation population along with a 0.3% increase in the parole population.

- At yearend 2010, about 4,055,500 adults were on probation, and during 2010 more than 4.4 million adults moved onto or off probation.

- Probation entries (2,190,200) declined for the third consecutive year and probation exits (2,261,300) declined for the first time since 2006.

- Almost two-thirds (65%) of probationers completed their terms of supervision or were discharged early during 2010, the same percentage as in 2009.

- The rate of incarceration among probationers at risk of violating their conditions in 2010 (5.7%) remained at about the same level observed in 2000 (5.5%).

- At yearend 2010, an estimated 840,700 adults were on parole, and about 1.1 million offenders moved onto or off parole during the year. Both parole entries (down 0.5%) and exits (down 1.8%) declined during 2010.

- The state parole population declined by 0.3% during 2010. The number of adults on supervised release in the federal system increased by 4.9%, which contributed to the increase in the U.S. parole population.

- The percentage of parolees who completed their terms or were discharged early during 2010 (52%) was slightly higher than the level observed for 2009 (51%).

- Among parolees at risk of violating the conditions of their supervision, about 13% were reincarcerated during 2010, down from about 16% reincarcerated during 2000.

BJS

For a list of all publications in this series, go to http://bjs.gov/index.cfm?ty=pbse&sid=32.

Source: Bureau of Justice Statistics, http://bjs.ojp.usdoj.gov/index.cfm?ty=pbse&sid=42.

Conditions of Probation The judge has broad discretion in setting conditions of probation, following general conditions similar to those shown in Exhibit 13.4. The most common conditions of probation are that the probationer must:

◆ Not violate any state law or the laws of other states
◆ Report to the probation officer regularly
◆ Refrain from using drugs or alcohol and submit to drug testing
◆ Get a job and support his or her family
◆ Obtain permission from the probation officer or court before traveling

In addition, the judge may impose **special conditions**, meaning conditions tailored to meet the special needs of an offender. For example, a probationer might be forbidden from working in a place where children are found, or a drifter might be required to obtain a permanent job. Special conditions may include conditions not imposed on regular probationers. For example, a shoplifter may be required to stand near a particular store carrying a sign that reads, "I stole from this store." Or a sex offender may be required to have a sign posted in front of his or her residence that reads, "I am a sex offender." These conditions are valid as long as they are reasonable and related to the offense committed.

special conditions
conditions to meet the special needs of an offender.

The conditions attached to the probation must be accepted by the probationer; otherwise, probation may be withheld. Probation conditions are often listed in state statutes, but the conditions specified by law are usually merely suggestive—meaning that the judge may choose to impose some, all, or none of the conditions suggested by law.

Probation and Parole Compared

Similarities between Probation and Parole

Both are community-based corrections programs.
Both are less expensive than imprisonment.
Both are a privilege, not a right.
Both are subject to imposed conditions.
Both are usually supervised by probation or parole officers.
Time served on probation or parole counts for nothing if the offender is sent to prison.
Both are subject to revocation if conditions are violated.

Differences between Probation and Parole

Probation	Parole
Is given before the offender serves time in prison.	Is given after the offender has served time in jail or prison.
Means the offender is "halfway in."	Means the offender is "halfway out."
Probation agencies are usually under the supervision of the judiciary.	Parole agencies are usually under the supervision of the governor's office.
Probation agencies are usually local funded by county or city funds.	Parole agencies are usually state agencies, agencies, funded by state funds.
Probation revocation hearings are held by a judge.	Parole revocation hearings are conducted by a parole board or its representatives.

Probation Revocation If probation conditions are violated, the probationer may be sent to prison. This takes place only after a hearing and is usually initiated by the probation officer or agency. Probationers have constitutional rights during probation revocation proceedings. In addition to a hearing, probationers are given such basic

Exhibit 13.4 • Conditions of Probation in Clackamas County, Oregon

The Court may place the defendant on probation, which shall be subject to the following GENERAL CONDITIONS unless specifically deleted by the Court (ORS 137.540).

1. Pay supervision fees, fines, restitution or other fees ordered by the Court.
2. Not use or possess controlled substances except pursuant to a medical prescription.
3. Submit to testing of breath or urine for controlled substance or alcohol use if the probationer has a history of substance abuse or if there is a reasonable suspicion that the probationer has illegally used controlled substances.
4. Participate in a substance abuse evaluation as directed by the supervising officer and follow the recommendations of the evaluator if there are reasonable grounds to believe there is a history of substance abuse.
5. Remain in the state of Oregon until written permission to leave is granted by the supervising officer.
6. If physically able, find and maintain gainful full-time employment, approved schooling, or a full-time combination of both. Any waiver of this requirement must be based on a finding by the Court stating the reasons for the waiver.
7. Change neither employment nor residence without prior permission from the Department of Corrections or a county community corrections agency.
8. Permit the supervising officer to visit the probationer or the probationer's work site or residence and to conduct a walk-through of the common areas and of the rooms in the residence occupied by or under the control of the probationer.

9. Consent to the search of person, vehicle, or premises upon the request of a representative of the supervising officer if the supervising officer has reasonable grounds to believe that evidence of a violation will be found, and submit to fingerprinting or photographing, or both, when requested by the Department of Corrections or a county community corrections agency for supervision purposes.
10. Obey all laws, municipal, county, state, and federal.
11. Promptly and truthfully answer all reasonable inquiries by the Department of Corrections or a county community corrections agency.
12. Not possess weapons, firearms, or dangerous animals.
13. Report as required and abide by the direction of the supervising officer.
14. If under supervision for, or previously convicted of, a sex offense under ORS 163.305 to 163.465, and if recommended by the supervising officer, successfully complete a sex offender treatment program approved by the supervising officer and submit to polygraph examinations at the direction of the supervising officer.
15. Participate in a mental health evaluation as directed by the supervising officer and follow the recommendation of the evaluator.
16. If required to report as a sex offender under ORS 181.596, report with the Department of State Police, a chief of police, a county sheriff, or the supervisory agency: (a) when supervision begins; (b) within 10 days of a change of residence; and (c) once each year within 10 days of the probationer's date of birth.

Source: Clackamas County, "Conditions of Probation," http://www.co.clackamas.or.us/corrections/info.htm.

rights as: (1) a written notice of the alleged probation violation, (2) disclosure to the probationer of the evidence of violation, (3) the opportunity to be heard in person and to present evidence as well as witnesses, (4) the right to judgment by a detached and neutral hearing body, (5) the right to confront and cross-examine witnesses, and (6) the right to a written statement of the reasons for revoking the probation (*Gagnon v. Scarpelli*, 411 778 [1973]). The right to a lawyer during revocation proceedings is decided

Gagnon v. Scarpelli (1973)

on a case-by-basis basis. For example, a lawyer should be provided if the probationer has difficulty presenting his or her version of disputed facts or conducting the examination or cross-examination of witnesses. In some states, lawyers are provided to an indigent probationer during probation revocation.

Probation revocation is discretionary with the judge. In many cases, the judge gives heavy weight to the recommendation of the probation officer who supervised the offender. If probation is revoked, the judge may reduce the original prison sentence. However, the judge cannot increase the prison sentence originally imposed because doing so would constitute double jeopardy.

The same rights described earlier are also given to parolees in parole revocation proceedings.

Intermediate Sanctions

The fourth type of sentence are **intermediate sanctions**. These are a type of punishment that is less severe and costly than prison, but more restrictive than traditional probation. They reflect a type of punishment that takes into account the severity of the offense, the characteristics of the offender, and the needs of the community. These forms of punishment are midway between prison and probation. They have a common theme: to provide punishment that best fits the crime and are more rehabilitative. The programs range from community service to substance abuse treatment, day reporting, house arrest, electronic monitoring, halfway house placement, and boot camps. Intermediate sanctions are usually imposed on nonviolent or first-time offenders.

Community service places a convicted offender in an unpaid position with a nonprofit or tax-supported agency to perform a specified number of hours of work or service within a given time limit as a sentencing option or condition. Community service comes under a variety of official labels, among them court referral, volunteer work, service restitution, and symbolic restitution programs. There are as many types of programs as there are opportunities for service in the community. Among them are hospital work, helping the elderly, counseling drug offenders, and providing manual labor in public service jobs.

House arrest means the offender is confined to his or her own home, except when at work, in school, or undergoing treatment. This limits the offender's freedom of movement and ensures that he or she does not go to places that are conducive to a recurrence of the offense. House arrest punishes the offender, but it also ensures that there is some type of continuity in the offender's life.

Electronic monitoring involves an offender having an electronic monitor placed on their person (usually around the ankle) that constantly tracks the offender's location. It is imposed on offenders who are under curfew or prohibited from being in certain areas because of the nature of their offense. These are such places as liquor stores, gambling establishments, or elementary schools. Violations are monitored and immediately reported to designated officers.

Boot camps provide a military-style regimen for younger offenders and are designed to instill discipline, punish, and educate. Their premise is that some crimes are committed due to lack of discipline, and therefore boot camps can be rehabilitative and preventative.

Intermediate sanctions, although punishments in themselves, are also used extensively as conditions of probation and parole. For example, community service,

intermediate sanctions sanctions that less severe and less costly than prisons, but more restrictive than traditional probation.

community service places an offender in unpaid position with nonprofit or tax-supported agencies to perform a specified service.

electronic monitoring an offender is placed on an electronic monitor that constantly tracks his or her location.

boot camp a military-style institution intended to provide discipline and education as well as punishment, usually for younger and first-time offenders.

Eric is a Missouri resident and a sentenced offender. He was sentenced to three years of probation with the following conditions:

1. He must not violate any law of any state or any local ordinance.
2. He must report to Probation Officer Greg James monthly at a predetermined time.
3. He must not use any illegal substance or alcohol and must also submit to random testing.
4. He must obtain permission from Probation Officer James before traveling out of Missouri.

In his second year of probation, Eric was captured by store detectives stealing a satellite radio system from an electronics store in Orlando, Florida. The Orlando Police Department responded to the scene and investigated. After interviewing the store detectives, they issued Eric a misdemeanor appearance citation for shoplifting. The appearance citation contained a mandatory court date for the following month.

Approximately three months later, Probation Officer James received a letter from the local district court in Orlando, Florida. The letter informed James that probationer Eric was in Orlando in January, received a misdemeanor violation for shoplifting, and has since failed to report for the scheduled court date; a warrant has now been issued by the Orlando District Court. James reviewed probationer Eric's file and found no record of any request to leave the state for any type of travel. Eric's home address is listed as Springfield, Missouri.

Probation Officer James prepared all of the paperwork required to initiate probation revocation proceedings against Eric. James also sent Eric written notice that the terms of his probation had been breached and that his probation had been placed in jeopardy. The notice informed Eric that a hearing had been set for the probation revocation. During the hearing, Eric will have an opportunity to present evidence on his own behalf.

On the date of the hearing, Eric and James arrived at the courthouse to present their arguments before the presiding judge. During the hearing, Probation Officer James presented evidence supporting the alleged breach of the conditions of probation. He presented sworn statements from Orlando store detectives regarding the shoplifting incident and sworn statements from the Orlando police officer who issued Eric the misdemeanor appearance citation. Eric responded to the allegations by testifying that the Orlando misdemeanor case was a case of mistaken identity and that he was at home in Missouri during that time. James rebutted Eric's testimony by restating that his witnesses (through their sworn statements) could attest to the fact that Eric was in fact arrested in Orlando for shoplifting the satellite radio system on the date in question. At the close of all testimony, the judge sent the courtroom into a fifteen-minute recess so that he could review all of the testimony and reread the sworn statements from the absent witnesses.

Approximately fifteen minutes later, the judge returned to the bench and announced his decision that Eric had violated the conditions of his probation agreement and should now be sent back to prison to serve out the remainder of the original sentence. The judge added that Eric will face the shoplifting charges upon release from prison. The court then served Eric with a written order stating all of the reasons for the probation revocation.

1. *What conditions of probation did Eric violate, if any?*
2. *Was Probation Officer James justified in recommending that Eric's probation be revoked?*
3. *Was the judge justified in revoking Eric's probation?*
4. *Can Probationer Eric be prosecuted for shoplifting after release from prison, or would that constitute double jeopardy?*

---

substance abuse treatment, electronic monitoring, and boot camps are standard conditions for probationers and parolees in many states.

Fines, Forfeiture, and Restitution

The fourth type of sentence are fines, forfeiture, and restitution. These are considered intermediate sanctions in some states, but should be placed in a different category because they have one element in common: they involve the payment or loss of money or property, something that community sanctions may not have.

A **fine** is a monetary punishment imposed by the court upon a person convicted of a crime. The amount imposed may be set by the state or left to the discretion of the judge. A fine should be distinguished from a **monetary penalty**, which is a sum of money exacted by an administrative agency for the doing of or failure to do some act. A monetary penalty is imposed by an administrative agency, whereas a fine is imposed by the court. Payment of a penalty of $500 by a liquor store owner for failure to obtain a liquor license (a penalty) is different from paying a fine of $100 for driving while intoxicated. Fines are usually levied in petty offenses or misdemeanor cases, such as traffic violations.

Forfeiture is the taking by the state of a person's specific property without compensation. It can be imposed in civil or criminal cases. It seeks to ensure that the offender does not benefit from the fruits or fortune obtained through crime. For example, illegal drugs from drug dealers are seized and forfeited to the government. The same is true with homes or property obtained as a result of organized crime. It is a way whereby offenders are punished without the full benefit of all the constitutional rights afforded defendants in criminal cases. Through forfeiture, government agents can deprive criminals of ill-gotten wealth in situations where a criminal case may be weak. The property forfeited goes to the government and can be designated for specific purposes. For example, money obtained through forfeiture from drug dealers can be allocated to help finance the war on drugs.

Restitution means a victim is restored to his or her original position prior to loss or injury, or placed in the position he or she could have been in, had the offense not occurred. The main difference between a fine and restitution is that the money paid for a fine goes to the state, whereas the money paid for restitution is given to the victim. Restitution and forfeiture differ in that restitution benefits the injured or deprived party, whereas forfeiture benefits the government. Restitution money is collected by the government and given to the injured party; in forfeiture, the money is seized by the government and becomes its property.

Fines, forfeiture, and restitution may be imposed along with other forms of punishment. For example, a fine can be levied and the defendant sent to jail. Or a defendant can be sent to prison for years and his or her property forfeited to the government. Or an offender can be sent to prison and made to pay restitution.

fine
monetary punishment.

monetary penalty
a sum of money exacted by an administrative agency for the doing of or failure to perform some act.

forfeiture
taking away the property of an offender without compensation.

restitution
a victim is restored to his or her original situation prior to the loss or injury.

CRIME VICTIMS' RIGHTS

Until a few decades ago, victims could not participate in the criminal justice process. They had no rights whatsoever and participated only as witnesses or spectators during trial. This was because the U.S. adversary system of justice assumes that the state is the offended party in a criminal case and therefore prosecutes the offender in the name of the state (thus criminal charges are usually designated as *People v. X*). Victims had no rights, nor did they have a say in the punishment to be imposed. This was true even in plea-bargained cases, which are usually informal proceedings and do not go to trial.

That situation has changed. The change started in 1982, when then-president Ronald Reagan appointed a task force which subsequently recommended that the Sixth Amendment of the U.S. Constitution be amended to include the rights of crime victims, but this did not happen. In 2004, Congress passed the Crime Victims' Rights Act (CVRA), which gives victims rights in federal criminal proceedings.

Victims' Rights in State Courts

All states now give victims rights by law or provisions in the state constitution. These rights are usually contained in a victims' bill of rights. Currently, thirty-one states have state victims' rights as constitutional amendments, meaning they cannot be taken away by mere legislation. These rights vary from state to state and usually apply only to victims of serious offenses, including those committed by juveniles. They do not usually apply to victims of misdemeanors.

In contrast to the federally guaranteed victims' rights, the following basic rights are usually given by state law:

◆ The right to be treated with dignity and compassion.
◆ The right to protection from intimidation and further harm.
◆ The right to receive compensation for damages.
◆ The right to equal treatment in court.
◆ The right to have their property returned promptly, if found by the police.[2]

As with sentencing guidelines, rights of victims, federal and state, are a comparatively recent development. But they are now well established and understandably popular with the public. They are here to stay.

Article 9, Section 2.1. Victims' Bill of Rights

Section 2.1.

(A) To preserve and protect victims' rights to justice and due process, a victim of crime has a right:

1. To be treated with fairness, respect, and dignity, and to be free from intimidation, harassment, or abuse, throughout the criminal justice process.
2. To be informed, upon request, when the accused or convicted person is released from custody or has escaped.
3. To be present at and, upon request, to be informed of all criminal proceedings where the defendant has the right to be present.
4. To be heard at any proceeding involving a post-arrest release decision, a negotiated plea, and sentencing.
5. To refuse an interview, deposition, or other discovery request by the defendant, the defendant's attorney, or other person acting on behalf of the defendant.
6. To confer with the prosecution, after the crime against the victim has been charged, before trial or before any disposition of the case and to be informed of the disposition.
7. To read presentence reports relating to the crime against the victim when they are available to the defendant.
8. To receive prompt restitution from the person or persons convicted of the criminal conduct that caused the victim's loss or injury.

9. To be heard at any proceeding when any post-conviction release from confinement is being considered.
10. To a speedy trial or disposition and prompt and final conclusion of the case after the conviction and sentence.
11. To have all rules governing criminal procedure and the admissibility of evidence in all criminal proceedings protect victims' rights and to have these rules be subject to amendment or repeal by the legislature to ensure the protection of these rights.
12. To be informed of victims' constitutional rights.

(B) A victim's exercise of any right granted by this section shall not be grounds for dismissing any criminal proceeding or setting aside any conviction or sentence.

(C) "Victim" means a person against whom the criminal offense has been committed or, if the person is killed or incapacitated, the person's spouse, parent, child or other lawful representative, except if the person is in custody for an offense or is the accused.

(D) The legislature, or the people by initiative or referendum, have the authority to enact substantive and procedural laws to define, implement, preserve and protect the rights guaranteed to victims by this section, including the authority to extend any of these rights to juvenile proceedings.

(E) The enumeration in the constitution of certain rights for victims shall not be construed to deny or disparage others granted by the legislature or retained by victims.

Source: Arizona Constitution, Article 9, Section 2.1.

SUMMARY

The four goals and objectives of sentencing are rehabilitation, deterrence, incapacitation, and retribution.

Sentencing disparity results from discretion given to sentencing authorities.

"Grossly disproportionate" sentences constitute cruel and unusual punishment.

The federal government and all states now have sentencing guidelines.

The five types of sentences are: the death penalty; imprisonment; probation; intermediate sanctions; and fines, forfeiture, and restitution.

The death penalty was declared unconstitutional by the Court in 1972, but declared constitutional in 1976.

Prisoners have diminished constitutional rights, but they do retain some rights.

Prisoners may be released on parole.

Most states now have life in prison without parole for vicious and violent offenders.

Probation is a privilege, not a right, meaning it can be given or withheld by the judge.

Judges have broad discretion in setting conditions of probation.

Probation means halfway in; parole means halfway out.

Intermediate sanctions are a type of punishment that is less severe and costly than prisons, but more restrictive than traditional probation.

Fines, forfeiture, and restitution have one common element: payment or loss of money or property.

Fines, forfeiture, and restitution differ based on who is benefited by the punishment and collection procedure.

Federal and state crime victims now have rights given by law or by constitutional amendment in some States.

REVIEW QUESTIONS

1. What are the goals and objectives of sentencing? Discuss each. Are these goals consistent or inconsistent with each other?

2. What is sentencing disparity and why does it exist? What can be done to reduce sentencing disparity?

3. What are sentencing guidelines? Discuss some of its features.

4. What is blended sentencing? Give its variations. Are you in favor of or against it?

5. Within a span of just four years during the 1970s, the Court, in the *Furman* and *Gregg* decisions, changed its mind on the constitutionality of the death penalty. What explains these decisions on such an important national issue within so short a time?

6. The Court has held that there are crimes where it is unconstitutional to impose the death penalty. What are those types of crimes?

7. Distinguish between the old approach and the new approach to prisoners' rights. Which approach would a sheriff who is in charge of a county jail that has 200 prisoners and detainees prefer for a court to use in a case filed by an inmate against him? Why?

8. "Prisoners have diminished constitutional rights." Explain what this statement means and then give examples *based on decided prison cases*.

9. In what ways are probation and parole similar? In what ways are they different?

10. What are intermediate sanctions? Give examples and a sentence definition of each.

11. How does restitution differ from a fine? Which would a crime victim prefer for the judge to impose? Why?

12. What are some rights that are now given to victims? Are those rights the same in federal and state courts?

13. Do you think it is a good idea to allow victims to address the defendant in court before sentencing? Why or why not?

TEST YOUR UNDERSTANDING

1. Assume you are a state legislator in North Carolina chairing a legislative committee that has been organized by the governor to revise North Carolina's sentencing laws. Seeking your guidance and leadership, your colleagues on the committee ask you to draft a statement identifying what the main purpose of North Carolina's sentencing laws should be. Which of the four main goals and objectives would you recommend? Justify your recommendation based on your personal beliefs about what sentencing ought to accomplish.

2. Assume you are a college student in Arizona who goes to a football game one weekend and later attends a raucous fraternity party. After midnight, and while you and four of your friends are slightly drunk, you drive back to your dormitory. En route, the five of you decide to "have more fun" and burglarize McDonald's, Burger King, and Taco Bell, three fast-food places in town that are near each other. You and your friends are caught by the police and later charged with three counts each of burglary. You are tried and found guilty. Assume that the laws in Arizona provide for a maximum of five years for burglary.

(a) How much time will you serve in prison?

(b) Will you and your four friends serve the same amount of time?

(c) Assume, further, that you are given maximum time for each of the three burglaries by the judge, but one of your friends, who in fact was the mastermind, was given the minimum penalty. You appeal your sentence, saying it is totally unfair. Will your appeal succeed? Why or why not?

3. You are the warden of a maximum-security prison in Florida, which has a population of 1,000 inmates. You issue a prison regulation prohibiting inmates from congregating in groups of more than three. You also prohibit inmates from having long hair and facial hair. An inmate takes you to court challenging the constitutionality of your regulations.

(a) What type of case will the inmate likely file in court?

(b) Who will win—you or the inmate? Justify your answer based on the new approach used by the courts in cases involving prisoners.

4. Assume that the legislature in your state passes a law (in response to a recent highly publicized case) that parents who brutalize their own children automatically get the death penalty when convicted, if the act results in severe permanent and serious injury to the child. Based on Court decisions, is that law constitutional?

RECOMMENDED READINGS

Nicholas N. Kittrie, Elyce H. Zenoff, and Vincent A. Eng. *Sentencing, Sanctions, and Corrections: Federal and State Law, Policy, and Practice*, 2nd ed. (New York: Foundation Press, 2002).

Norval Morris and Michael Tonry. *Between Prison and Probation: Intermediate Punishments in a Rational Sentencing System* (New York: Oxford University Press, 1991).

Michael Tonry. *Sentencing Matters* (New York: Oxford University Press, 1996).

NOTES

1. An Overview of the United States Sentencing Commission, published by the Office of Legislative and Public Affairs, United States Sentencing Commission, p. 1.

2. Charles Montaldo, "The Rights of Crime Victims: Every State Guarantees Victim Rights," http://crime.about.com/od/victims/a/rights.htm.

CHAPTER 14

Legal Liabilities of Law Enforcement Officers

LEARNING OBJECTIVES

1. Differentiate between the three categories of legal liability for a law enforcement officer.
2. Describe the elements of Section 1983 of Title 42 of the United States Code.
3. Compare and contrast the two types of state tort law: intentional and negligent.
4. Illustrate with examples of an intentional tort under state law.
5. Provide examples of a negligent tort under state law.
6. Describe possible defenses to legal liability under both federal and state tort law.
7. Compare a Section 1983 action under federal law with action taken under state tort law.
8. Compare and contrast vicarious liability with direct liability.
9. Describe actions that may be taken against an officer for misconduct in addition to legal liability.
10. Describe and provide examples of the legal concept of "color of law."

KEY TERMS

acting under color of law

acting within the scope of authority

assault

battery

clearly established constitutional right

deadly force

deep pockets theory

deliberate indifference

discretionary act

false arrest

false imprisonment

good faith

indemnification

intentional tort

municipal policy

municipal custom

negligence tort

official immunity

probable cause defense

public duty doctrine

punitive force

qualified immunity defense

reasonable force

Section 1983 case

special relationship

tort

under color of law

wrongful death

Ralf Kleemann/Shutterstock.com

THE **TOP 5** IMPORTANT CASES

in Legal Liabilities of Public Officers

■ *HARLOW V. FITZGERALD* (1982) Government officials performing discretionary functions are shielded from liability for civil damages as long as their conduct does not violate clearly established statutory or constitutional rights of which a reasonable person would have known.

■ *GROH V. RAMIREZ* (2004) An officer is not entitled to qualified immunity if "it would be clear to a reasonable officer that his conduct was unlawful in the situation he confronted."

■ *BROSSEAU V. HAUGEN* (2004) "Because the focus is on whether the officer had fair notice that her conduct was unlawful, reasonableness is judged against the backdrop of the law at the time of the conduct. If the law at that time did not clearly establish that the officer's conduct would violate the Constitution, the officer should not be subject to liability, or indeed, even the burdens of litigation."

■ *TOWN OF CASTLE ROCK V. GONZALES* (2005) The wrongful failure by the police to arrest a husband who violated a domestic relations court restraining order did not amount to a violation of a constitutional right under the Fourteenth Amendment due process clause and therefore does not result in liability under Section 1983.

■ *SCOTT V. HARRIS* (2007) "A police officer's attempt to terminate a dangerous high-speed car chase that threatens the lives of innocent bystanders does not violate the Fourth Amendment even when it places the fleeing motorist at risk of serious injury or death."

O NE OF THE UNFORTUNATE REALITIES of modern-day policing is a civil lawsuit filed by members of the public. U.S. society is litigation prone, and the police are a popular target because they exercise authority and are involved in highly charged and often emotional confrontations with the public. The police are generally appreciated and respected because they provide a needed service to the community and help others. But they are also sometimes disliked, if not despised, because some officers behave badly. Lawsuits have become so pervasive that there is probably no major police or law enforcement department in the country whose officers and supervisors have not been sued in state or federal court. Liability lawsuits are here to stay; hence, this chapter's material must be learned well.

This chapter focuses on lawsuits the public usually files against police officers. First, we look at the wider liability picture. Lawsuits are but a part of the broader liability picture that consists of the following actions: ethical violations, administrative

Table 14.1 Types of Conduct in Policing

Conduct in Question	Ethical Violation	Administrative Liability	Civil Liability	Criminal Liability
Being negative about policing in general	No	No	No	No
Not giving 100% effort to the job	Probably	Generally no	No	No
Accepting a free meal while on the job	Probably	Probably	No	No
Being rude or discourteous to a crime victim	Probably	No, unless specifically prohibited	No	No
Stopping drivers for minor traffic violations despite prohibition by agency policy	No	Yes	No	No
Making stops, seizures, or arrests based on a racial profile	Yes	Yes	Yes	No, unless specifically prohibited by law
Using excessive force on a suspect	Yes	Yes	Yes	Yes
Accepting bribes	Yes	Yes	Yes	Yes
Fatally shooting a suspect without justification	Yes	Yes	Yes	Yes

violations (meaning violations of agency rules), violations that lead to civil liabilities, and violations that lead to criminal liabilities. Ethical and criminal violations can lead to reprimands or dismissal from the job; civil liabilities lead to monetary payments for damages and attorney's fees; criminal liabilities result in criminal sanctions such as fines, probation, or incarceration in a prison or jail. The wider liability picture is illustrated in Table 14.1. In general, the more serious the conduct, the greater is the likelihood that all of the liabilities will be imposed if what happened violates ethics, agency rules, civil statutes, and criminal laws.

LAWSUITS AGAINST POLICE: AN OCCUPATIONAL HAZARD

Newspapers and sources that track liability lawsuits against law enforcement officers have featured the following headlines:

"U.S. to Pay $2 Million in Wrongful Terror Arrest"[1]
"66 Bullets Costs County $13 Million"[2]
"New York Will Pay $50 Million in 50,000 Illegal Strip-Searches"[3]
"The City of Los Angeles Agreed to Pay $15 Million to a Man Who Said Police Officers Shot Him in the Head and Chest and then Framed Him in the Attack"[4]
"Jury Assesses Damages of $256 Million for Motorist's Collision with Off-Duty Police Officer Which Left One Child Dead, One Quadriplegic, and One Paralyzed on One Side with a Damaged Brain"[5]
"Chicago Reaches $18 Million Settlement with Family of Unarmed Woman Shot and Killed by Officer at the Conclusion of a 31-Block Pursuit of the Vehicle in Which She Was Riding"[6]

Most officers will not be sued in the course of their careers. But although the fear of a lawsuit is often exaggerated, the effect on police officers can be constant and real. One study of police trainees at a regional law enforcement academy concludes that law enforcement candidates have real concerns about work-related lawsuits, fostering an "us-versus-them" attitude among officers.[7] Others believe that the courts have handcuffed law enforcement officers and made police work unattractive and dangerous.

Whatever the reaction, liability lawsuits are a presence in police work that is difficult to ignore.

Plaintiffs' lawyers maintain that lawsuits can result in long-term benefits to the department and the community, in that they focus on police misconduct and thus minimize its recurrence and protect the public from police abuses. Lawsuits also increase police consciousness of the rights of the public they serve and thus improve policing. Many departments train their police better because they fear litigation, and department policies have been changed in response to court orders. Financial appropriations for law enforcement have increased in many places because of fear by local or state politicians of a possible lawsuit that could cost the city or county a lot of money. The result of all these changes is a more professionalized police department. Indeed, plaintiffs' lawyers say, "Spend money now to improve your department, or pay big bucks later in a lawsuit."

AN OVERVIEW OF POLICE LEGAL LIABILITIES

Police legal liabilities (as opposed to non-legal liabilities, such as ethical violations) come from a variety of sources, but the whole arena of legal liabilities can be classified as in Table 14.2. As the table shows, police legal liability cases can be divided into liabilities under federal law and liabilities under state law. Each of these two categories can be further sub-classified into civil liability, criminal liability, or administrative liability.

Can an officer be liable under all of the above? The answer is yes, if all the elements for liability are present. For example, an act of an officer that leads to the wrongful death of a suspect may subject the officer to liability under state and federal laws. Under each, the officer may be held liable civilly, criminally, and administratively. The double jeopardy defense does not work in these cases because it applies only if there are successive prosecutions for the same offense by the same jurisdiction. Civil and criminal penalties may result from a single act, because "successive prosecution" requires that both cases be criminal; hence, double jeopardy does not apply if one case is criminal and the other civil. Criminal prosecutions may also take place in state court

Table 14.2 Overview of Police Liabilities

	Under Federal Law	Under State Law
Civil Liabilities	1. Title 42 of U.S. Code, Section 1983—Civil Action for Deprivation of Civil Rights 2. Title 42 of U.S. Code, Section 1985—Conspiracy to Interfere with Civil Rights 3. Title 42 of U.S. Code, Section 1981—Equal Rights under the Law	State tort law (for such acts as false arrest and false imprisonment, assault and battery, excessive use of force, wrongful death, or negligence)

Criminal Liabilities	1. Title 18 of U.S. Code, Section 242—Criminal Liability for Deprivation of Civil Rights
	2. Title 18 of U.S. Code, Section 241—Criminal Liability for Conspiracy to Deprive a Person of Rights
	3. Title 18 of U.S. Code, Section 245—Violations of Federally Protected Activities
		1. State penal code provisions specifically aimed at public officers for crimes such as:
		  a. Official oppression
		  b. Official misconduct
		  c. Violation of the civil rights of prisoners
		2. Regular penal code provisions punishing such criminal acts as assault, battery, false arrest, serious bodily injury, and homicide

Administrative Liabilities	1. Federal agency rules or guidelines vary from one agency to another	1. Agency rules or guidelines on the state or local level vary from one agency to another

and federal court for the same act. Separate federal and state prosecutions take place in different jurisdictions; because they do not meet the "same jurisdiction" requirement, there is no double jeopardy. There is also no double jeopardy if an officer is dismissed from employment and then prosecuted later or held civilly liable for the same act. This is because dismissal by the agency is administrative in nature and is neither a civil nor a criminal proceeding.

Although various legal remedies are available, plaintiffs usually sue for civil liabilities under federal or state tort law. The discussion in this chapter therefore focuses on these two types of liability:

◆ Civil liability under federal law (Section 1983 cases)
◆ Civil liability under state tort law

CIVIL LIABILITY UNDER FEDERAL LAW

Section 1983 case
a lawsuit filed under federal law that seeks damages from a police officer, supervisor, and/or department.

For purposes of police liability, a **Section 1983 case** (also referred to as a *civil rights case*) is defined as a lawsuit filed under federal law that seeks damages from a police officer, supervisor, and/or department on the ground that these defendants, acting under color of law, violated the plaintiff's constitutional rights or rights given by federal law. Section 1983 and state tort cases (discussed later in this chapter) are not mutually exclusive; in fact, plaintiffs are likely to sue under both laws and in the same lawsuit. For example, suppose Officer Jones tries to arrest a suspect, but the suspect flees. Officer Jones shoots the suspect, killing him instantly. In addition to a criminal case, Officer Jones will also

---

IN ACTION   *IGNORING THE MEDICAL COMPLAINTS OF A SUSPECT IN CUSTODY*

Pullman police officers were dispatched to the Wheatland apartment complex to investigate a loud noise complaint reported by a neighbor. The dispatcher advised the responding officers that the complaining witness reported hearing a very loud and volatile argument coming from apartment C2. During the investigation, Officer Hall learns that one of the suspects (Sam) has an outstanding warrant for his arrest. Officer Hall attempts to place Sam under arrest, but Sam resists and a struggle ensues. Officer Hall finally subdues Sam, places him under arrest, handcuffs him, and transports him to the Pullman jail facility.

Officer Hall completes the standard booking process for Sam. As Officer Hall is placing Sam inside his assigned cell, Sam states that his "heart hurts" and that he does not feel well—which he blames on the struggle that occurred during his arrest. Officer Hall does not see any visible injuries and orders Sam into his cell. Sam is placed in cell 4. Officer Hall tells Sam he has a case of "jail-itis." Officer Hall clears the incident and returns to his patrol duties.

About an hour later, Officer Hall is summoned to the police station by his supervisor, Sergeant Roberts. Sergeant Roberts informs Hall that prisoner Sam collapsed in his cell from a possible heart attack and was subsequently transported by ambulance to Pullman Hospital for emergency medical treatment. Sergeant Roberts advises Hall that Sam made allegations that he had requested medical treatment but had been ignored.

1. *Could Officer Hall's inaction translate into officer personal liability?*
2. *Could Officer Hall's inaction translate into liability for the Pullman Police Department?*
3. *Could Officer Hall's inaction translate into vicarious liability for Sergeant Roberts?*
4. *Could Officer Hall's inaction translate into administrative liability for Hall?*
5. *What should Officer Hall have done when Sam reported not feeling well?*

likely be charged civilly: (1) under Section 1983 for violating the suspect's constitutional right to due process, and (2) under state tort law for wrongful death.

What Section 1983 Provides

Liability under federal law is based on the provisions of Title 42 of the U.S. Code, Section 1983, Civil Action for Deprivation of Rights. That law provides:

> Every person who, under color of any statute, ordinance, regulation, custom, or usage, of any State or Territory, subjects, or causes to be subjected, any citizen of the United States or other persons within the jurisdiction thereof to the deprivation of any rights, privileges, or immunities secured by the Constitution and laws, shall be liable to the party injured in an action at law, suit in equity, or other proper proceeding for redress.

This law, commonly referred to as the civil rights law or Section 1983, is the most frequently used provision among the legal liability statutes available to plaintiffs. The law, originally passed by Congress in 1871, was then known as the Ku Klux Klan Law because it sought to control the activities of state officials who were also members of that organization. For a long time, the courts interpreted the law narrowly and seldom applied it. In 1961, however, the Court adopted a much broader interpretation, thus opening wide the door for liability lawsuits in federal courts.

Note that the provisions of the law says that "every person who, under color of any statute, ordinance, regulation, custom, or usage of any State or Territory...." Thus, the law, when passed by Congress in 1871, was not meant to apply to officials of the federal government. However, the Court in 1971 held that federal officers can also be held liable for constitutional violations in what is known as a *Bivens* action. In *Bivens*, the Court ruled that federal narcotics agents could be held liable under Section 1983 for violating a suspect's Fourth Amendment right (*Bivens v. Six Unknown Named Agents of the Federal Bureau of Narcotics*, 403 U.S. 288 (1971)). In sum, both state and federal law enforcement officers can be held civilly liable for violations of constitutional rights.

Bivens v. Six Unknown Named Agents of the Federal Bureau of Narcotics (1971)

Among the reasons for the popularity of Section 1983 cases among plaintiffs is that they are usually filed in federal court, where discovery procedures are more liberal. Moreover, the plaintiff, if successful, may recover attorney's fees in accordance with the Attorney's Fees Act of 1976. A police officer or agency can be held liable for damages as well as for plaintiff's attorney's fees. As noted previously, the same act by the police may be the basis of both a Section 1983 lawsuit and an action under state tort law. For example, arrest without probable cause may constitute false arrest under state tort law and a violation of the arrestee's Fourth Amendment right to protection against unreasonable search and seizure, compensable under Section 1983. In such cases, a plaintiff may combine his or her claims and sue under multiple legal theories in federal court.

Two Requirements for a Section 1983 Lawsuit to Succeed

For a Section 1983 lawsuit to succeed, plaintiff must prove both of the following elements:

1. The defendant was acting under color of law.
2. There was a violation of a right given by the Constitution or by federal law.

Unless both of these elements are proved by the plaintiff, the liability lawsuit fails.

acting under color of law
officer using power possessed by virtue of law.

Under Color of Law The phrase **acting under color of law** refers to the use of power possessed by virtue of law and made possible only because the officer is clothed with the authority of the state. The problem is that, although it is usually easy to identify acts that are wholly within the color of law (as when an officer conducts a search or makes an arrest while on duty), some acts are not as easy to categorize.

◆ *Example 1.* Suppose a police officer working during off-hours as a private security guard in a shopping center shoots and kills a fleeing shoplifter. Is he acting under color of law?

◆ *Example 2.* Suppose an officer arrests a felon during off-hours when she is not in uniform. Is she acting under color of law?

The answer usually depends on job expectations. Many police departments (by state law, judicial decision, or agency regulation) require police officers to act in their official police capacity twenty-four hours a day. In these jurisdictions, any arrest made, whether on or off duty, is made **under color of law**. In the case of police officers who "moonlight," courts have held that wearing a police uniform while acting as a private security agent, carrying a gun issued by the department, and informing department authorities of the second job combine to indicate that the officer is acting under color of law.

under color of law
when the officer uses power possessed by virtue of law and made possible only because the officer is clothed with the authority of the state.

Courts have interpreted color of law broadly to include state laws, local ordinances, and agency regulations. It does not simply refer to laws passed by legislative bodies. Moreover, it is not required that the act be authorized by law or agency policy. It suffices that the act is committed under the cloth of police authority even if it was not in fact authorized. An *officer acts under color of law even if he or she acts against lawful authority.* Thus, the concept includes clearly illegal acts committed by the officer by reason of position or opportunity. For example, suppose an officer arrests a suspect without probable cause or brutalizes a suspect in the course of an arrest. These acts are clearly illegal, but they come under color of law and may be the subject of a Section 1983 lawsuit.

MYTH vs. REALITY

MYTH Police officers are never liable for acts they engage in while off-duty.

FACT Police officers may be liable anytime they are "acting under color of law," and this may include times when the officer is off duty, if the officer used his or her position to advantage.

Violation of a Right The second element a plaintiff must prove in a Section 1983 case is that the right violated is a constitutional right or a right given by federal law. Violations of rights given by state law only cannot lead to liability under Section 1983. For example, neither the Constitution nor federal law gives the right to have a lawyer during a police lineup prior to being charged with an offense. Therefore, if an officer forces a suspect to appear in a lineup without a lawyer (assuming that right is given by state law), the officer is not liable under Section 1983. If the right is given by state law only, its violation may be actionable under state law or administrative regulation, but not under Section 1983.

The constitutional rights usually invoked by plaintiffs in Section 1983 lawsuits against police officers are:

◆ The Fourth Amendment right to protection against unreasonable searches and seizures. Example: Officer Thomas is sued because she allegedly arrested a suspect without probable cause.

◆ The Fifth Amendment right to protection against self-incrimination and the right to due process. Example: A defendant sues Officer White because she allegedly interrogated a suspect and threatened to "blow your head off" if he did not "tell the truth."

- ◆ The Sixth Amendment right to assistance of counsel. Example: Officer Smith is sued because she allegedly continued to interrogate a suspect even after the suspect informed her that he had a lawyer and had been instructed by his lawyer not to answer any questions asked by the police.
- ◆ The Fourteenth Amendment rights to due process and to equal protection of the laws. Example: Officer Yates issued by a suspect because he allegedly used unreasonable force when arresting the suspect and engaged in racial profiling.

It is not difficult for a plaintiff to sue under Section 1983 based on an alleged violation of a constitutional right by the police. This is because the rights given in the Bill of Rights and the other constitutional amendments are elastic and may accommodate many alleged violations. For example, a violation of the Fourth Amendment protection against unreasonable searches and seizures can be alleged just about any time an arrest or a search or seizure of things takes place. Violation of due process can be charged any time a person feels that he or she has suffered unfairness at the hands of the police. The constitutional right to equal protection has traditionally been applied to discrimination based on race, but some courts have applied it to gender, religion, and other types of discriminatory treatment. The right to privacy may include a host of violations that can form the basis of a Section 1983 lawsuit, ranging from searches and seizures to interception of electronic communications. The scope of these constitutional rights makes it quite easy to file a Section 1983 lawsuit against police officers. Proving these allegations, however, is an entirely different matter.

In *Chavez v. Martinez*, 538 U.S. 760 (2004), the Court reemphasized that a Section 1983 case succeeds only if there is a proven violation of a constitutional right or of a right guaranteed by federal law. In this case, the suspect filed a Section 1983 lawsuit alleging that his constitutional right against self-incrimination was violated when he was not given the *Miranda* warnings and the interrogation continued despite his telling the police: "I am not telling you anything until they treat me." The Court held that the failure to read *Miranda* warnings to Martinez did not violate his constitutional rights (because his statements were not used at his trial) and thus could not be grounds for a Section 1983 action.

Chavez v. Martinez (2004)

In *Town of Castle Rock v. Gonzales*, 545 U.S. 748 (2005), the Court held that the wrongful failure by the police to arrest a husband who violated a domestic relations court restraining order does not amount to a violation of a constitutional right under the Fourteenth Amendment due process clause and therefore does not result in civil liability under federal law (Section 1983).

Town of Castle Rock v. Gonzales (2005)

Although most lawsuits against the police under Section 1983 are based on alleged violations of constitutional rights, the police can also be held liable under this law for violations of federal laws. For example, the police may be held liable if they violate the provisions of the Federal Civil Rights Act of 1964 (which prohibits discrimination based on race, color, gender, or national origin) or the Americans With Disability Act of 1990, or myriad other federal laws.

Defenses in Section 1983 Cases

Several defenses are available in Section 1983 cases. The two defenses discussed here are the ones most often used by defendants in police civil liability cases:

1. The qualified immunity defense
2. The probable cause defense

Brosseau v. Haugen (2004)

The Qualified Immunity Defense The **qualified immunity defense** (also known as the *good faith defense*) in Section 1983 cases holds that an officer is not civilly liable unless he or she violated a clearly established statutory or constitutional right of which a reasonable person would have known (*Harlow v. Fitzgerald*, 457 U.S. 800 [1982]). There are two parts to this defense. In order for a plaintiff to show that an officer is not entitled to qualified immunity, the plaintiff must prove both of the following elements:

1. The officer has violated a clearly established statutory or constitutional right.
2. The violated right is one of which a reasonable person would have known.

If the plaintiff cannot prove one or both of these elements, then the qualified immunity defense succeed and no liability ensues.

When is a statutory or constitutional right considered "clearly established"? This legal issue has been the subject of several Court decisions. The Court has said that "reasonableness is judged against the backdrop of the law at the time of the conduct. If the law at that time did not clearly establish that the officer's conduct would violate the Constitution, the officer should not be subject to liability, or indeed, even the burden of litigation" (*Brosseau v. Haugen*, 125 S.Ct. 596 [2004]). In *Brosseau*, a police officer shot a suspect in the back while the suspect was trying to drive away from the officer. The suspect later sued, saying that his being shot by the officer constituted excessive force and violated his constitutional rights. The Court ruled that Officer Brosseau was entitled to qualified immunity because previous court cases did not clearly establish that shooting a fleeing suspect violated his constitutional right.

CASE BRIEF — *Scott v. Harris*, 550 U.S. 372 (2007)

The Leading Case on Police Liability in High-Speed Motor Vehicle Chases

Facts: A Georgia county deputy clocked Harris's vehicle traveling at 73 miles per hour on a road with a 55-miles-per-hour speed limit. When the deputy attempted to pull Harris over, he sped away, initiating a high-speed chase down a two-lane road at speeds exceeding 85 miles per hour. Officer Scott heard the radio communication and joined the pursuit along with other officers. After turning into a parking lot of a shopping center, Harris evaded officers by making a sharp turn, colliding with Scott's police car. Six minutes and nearly ten miles after the chase had begun, Scott attempted to terminate the pursuit. Prior to this, Scott received permission for the maneuver from his supervisor. Scott used his push bumper to ram the rear of Harris's vehicle, causing Harris to lose control of the vehicle. It left the roadway, ran down an embankment, overturned, and crashed. Harris was badly injured and rendered a quadriplegic.

Harris sued in federal court under Section 1983, alleging that the use of excessive force constituted an unreasonable seizure under the Fourth Amendment. Officer Scott claimed qualified immunity and wanted the case dismissed. The district court denied Scott's request. The Eleventh Circuit affirmed the denial, saying that Scott's actions constituted "deadly force" for which he could be held liable.

Issue or Issues: *(1) Can police officers constitutionally stop a motorist from fleeing by taking actions that place the motorist or bystanders at risk of serious injury or death? Yes. (2) Do police officers violate "clearly established" federal law by using what amounts to deadly force during a high-speed chase? No.*

Decision: The decision of the Court of Appeals for the Eleventh Circuit was reversed.

Holding: (1) "A police officer's attempt to terminate a dangerous high-speed car chase that threatens the lives of innocent bystanders does not violate the Fourth Amendment, even when it places the fleeing motorist at risk of serious injury or death." (2) Police officers do not violate "clearly established" federal law when they use what amounts to deadly force during a high-speed chase under circumstances similar to this case; therefore they are not civilly liable under federal law.

Case Significance: This case is a highly significant case for police officers because it gives them protection from civil liability under federal law (42 U.S.C. Section 1983) if they use deadly force (in this case the chase of suspect's motor vehicle and the maneuvers used by the police to stop suspect's vehicle) in connection with a vehicle chase as long as suspect's behavior constitutes a danger to the public. The Court held that the officer's actions were reasonable under the Fourth Amendment because the videotape of the car chase showed that, contrary to suspect's claim, his driving posed "an imminent threat to the lives of any pedestrians who might have been present, to other civilian motorists, and to the officers involved in the chase." The Court said it is reasonable for police officers to use deadly force to prevent harm to innocent bystanders, even if such use of deadly force puts the fleeing motorist at serious risk of injury or death. Although this was a motor vehicle case, it is reasonable to assume that the same standard of "an imminent threat to the lives of others" will likely be applied by the Court in police work even in non-motor vehicle cases.

In this case, the Court took the rather unusual step of actually viewing the video of the motor vehicle chase to make a finding of fact (usually a function of the trial court): The behavior of the suspect constituted a danger to the safety of others. The Court then weighed the need to prevent the harm suspect could have inflicted on others as opposed to the harm the officer could have inflicted, and did inflict, on the suspect. It concluded that the use of deadly force was reasonable. It also concluded that there was no violation of a "clearly established" constitutional right because lower court decisions on this issue varied, and therefore the right was not clearly established. This is a case of balancing public safety against the constitutional right of the accused. Under the circumstances of this case, public safety prevailed.

Excerpts from the Opinion: In determining the reasonableness of the manner in which a seizure is effected, "[w]e must balance the nature and quality of the intrusion on the individual's Fourth Amendment interests against the importance of the governmental interests alleged to justify the intrusion." *United States v. Place*, 462 U.S. 696, 703 (1983). Scott defends his actions by pointing to the paramount governmental interest in ensuring public safety, and [Harris] nowhere suggests this was not the purpose motivating Scott's behavior. Thus, in judging whether Scott's actions were reasonable, we must consider the risk of bodily harm that Scott's actions posed to respondent in light of the threat to the public that Scott was trying to eliminate. Although there is no obvious way to quantify the risks on either side, it is clear from the videotape that respondent posed an actual and imminent threat to the lives of any pedestrians who might have been present, to other civilian motorists, and to the officers involved in the chase.... It was respondent, after all, who intentionally placed himself and the public in danger by unlawfully engaging in the reckless, high-speed flight that ultimately produced the choice between two evils that Scott confronted. Multiple police cars, with blue lights flashing and sirens blaring, had been chasing respondent for nearly 10 miles, but he ignored their warning to stop. By contrast, those who might have been harmed had Scott not taken the action he did were entirely innocent. We have little difficulty in concluding it was reasonable for Scott to take the action that he did.

In *Scott v. Harris*, a case involving a high-speed vehicle chase that resulted in the suspect being badly injured, the Court held that the pursuing officer was not liable under Section 1983 despite serious injury to the suspect. The Court said there was no violation of a "clearly established" constitutional right because at the time the vehicle chase and injury took place, lower court decisions on cases involving similar facts varied on the issue of officer liability (*Scott v. Harris*, 550 U.S. 372 [2007]). Read the Case Brief to learn more about this case.

Scott v. Harris (2007)

Two years later, the Court held that school officials could not be held liable under Section 1983 because although a strip search violated an eighth-grader's Fourth Amendment rights, lower court decisions differed on whether highly intrusive strip searches (in this case the search of a student's undergarments for evidence of a possible violation of school regulations) in schools was constitutional or not (*Safford Unified School District #1 v. Redding*, 557 U.S. — [2009]). Although this case involved school officials, the interpretation of the term "clearly established constitutional right" should apply to law enforcement officers as well.

In sum, for a right to be "clearly established," it must be proved by the plaintiff that a reasonable police officer "would have understood that his or her acts were unlawful." Since case facts vary, determining whether the officer violated a **clearly established constitutional right** must be done on a case-by-case basis.

clearly established constitutional right
a right so established that a reasonable police officer would have known his or her act was unlawful.

Groh v. Ramirez (2004)

When is a right considered one "of which a reasonable person would have known"? In *Groh v. Ramirez*, 540 U.S. 551 (2004), the Court held that an officer was not entitled to qualified immunity because "it would be clear to a reasonable officer that his conduct was unlawful in the situation he confronted." Read the Case Brief to learn more about this case.

CASE BRIEF
Groh v. Ramirez, 540 U.S. 551 (2004)

The Leading Case on Police Liability for an Unconstitutional Search Warrant

Facts: Groh, an agent of the ATF, prepared an application for a search warrant based on information that weapons and explosives were located on Ramirez's farm. The application was supported by a detailed affidavit listing the items to be seized and describing the basis for his belief that the items were concealed on the property. Groh presented these documents, along with a warrant form he also completed, to a magistrate. The magistrate signed the warrant form. Although the application and affidavit described the contraband expected to be discovered, the warrant form only indicated that the place to be searched was Ramirez's home. The warrant did not incorporate any reference to the itemized list contained in the application or affidavit. The day after the magistrate signed the warrant, officers searched Ramirez's home but found no illegal weapons or explosives. Groh left a copy of the warrant at the home but did not leave a copy of the application. The following day, in response to a request from Ramirez's attorney, Groh faxed a copy of the application. No charges were filed against Ramirez, but he later filed suit, claiming his Fourth Amendment rights were violated by the nonspecific warrant. The district court granted Groh's motion for dismissal, saying that there had been no violation of Ramirez's rights, and that even if there had been such a violation, Groh would not be liable because of qualified immunity. The Ninth Circuit Court of Appeals reversed the district court's decision, holding that

the warrant was not valid because it failed to describe with particularity the place to be searched and the items to be seized. The case was then appealed to the U.S. Supreme Court.

Issue or Issues: *(1) Does a search warrant that does not particularly describe the persons or things to be seized, but does particularly describe them in the application that was filed with the judge, violate the Fourth Amendment? Yes. (2) Was the officer entitled to qualified immunity? No.*

Decision: The decision of the Court of Appeals for the Ninth Circuit was affirmed.

Holding: A search and seizure warrant that does not contain a particular description of the things to be seized is unconstitutional even if the application for the warrant contains such descriptions. An officer is not entitled to qualified immunity (meaning the good faith defense) if "it would be clear to a reasonable officer that his conduct was unlawful."

Case Significance: The application for a warrant submitted by the officer to the judge in this case clearly specified the items to be seized. However, the warrant itself did not specify those items, nor did the warrant incorporate by reference the application's itemized list. The Court concluded that the warrant was "plainly invalid." The purpose for the specificity requirement is to have "written assurance" that the judge "actually found probable cause for a search as broad as the affiant requested." The Court also said that "the particularity requirement's purpose is not limited to preventing general searches; it also assures the individual whose property is searched and seized of the executing officer's legal authority, his need to search, and the limits of his power to do so."

For purposes of civil liability, the Court held that the officer was "not entitled to qualified immunity despite the constitutional violation because it would be clear to a reasonable officer that his conduct was unlawful in the situation he confronted." It added, "Given that the particularity requirement is stated in the Constitution's text, no reasonable officer could believe that a warrant that did not comply with that requirement was valid." This case illustrates the meaning of the phrase "a clearly established constitutional right of which a reasonable person would have known." This phrase is the core of the qualified immunity defense in Section 1983 cases. Qualified immunity holds that an officer is not liable under Section 1983 unless there is "a violation of a clearly established constitutional right of which a reasonable person would have known." The implication of this decision for any law enforcement officer is that he or she must be fully aware of the basic constitutional rights of the public and make sure they are carefully observed. This applies to violations of any constitutional right and not just those under the Fourth Amendment.

Excerpts from the Opinion: The warrant was plainly invalid. The Fourth Amendment states unambiguously that "no Warrants shall issue, but upon probable cause, supported by Oath or affirmation, and *particularly describing* the place to be searched, and *the persons or things to be seized*" [emphasis added]. The warrant in this case complied with the first three of these requirements: It was based on probable cause and supported by a sworn affidavit, and it described particularly the place of the search. On the fourth requirement, however, the warrant failed altogether. Indeed, petitioner concedes that "the warrant ... was deficient in particularity because it provided no description of the type of evidence sought." ...

The fact that the application adequately described the "things to be seized" does not save the warrant from its facial invalidity. The Fourth Amendment by its terms requires particularity in the warrant, not in the supporting documents. And for good reason: "The presence of a search warrant serves a high function," and that high function is not necessarily vindicated when some other document, somewhere, says something about the objects of the search, but the contents of that document are neither known to the person whose home is being searched nor available for her inspection. We do not say that the Fourth Amendment forbids a warrant from cross-referencing other documents. But in this case the warrant did not incorporate other documents by reference, nor did either the affidavit or the application (which had been placed under seal) accompany the warrant.

In February of 2012, the Court decided another case on qualified immunity of police officers, but with results different from that of *Groh*. In *Messerschmidt v. Millender* (No. 10-704 [2012]), the Court held that the officers in that case enjoyed qualified immunity and therefore could not be held liable under Section 1983 for what their search based on a warrant. The facts in *Millender* are that Detective Curt Messerschmidt received a complaint from Shelly Kelly saying that she was afraid of being attacked by her boyfriend, Jerry Ray Bowen, while she moved out of her apartment. She sought police protection. Two police officers arrived, but they had to leave because they were called to an emergency. Kelly was then attacked by the boyfriend, who fired five shots at her vehicle while she was speeding away. She later met with Detective Messerschmidt and gave him the details of the attack. She further mentioned that the same boyfriend had attacked her previously and that he was a member of a gang. After a detailed investigation, Detective Messerschmidt verified that the boyfriend was in fact a member of two gangs and that he also had a record of previous convictions for firearms and ammunition offenses. Based on this, Detective Messerschmidt applied for a search warrant based on two affidavits he executed. In the first affidavit, Messerschmidt said that he had "extensive law

Messerschmidt v. Millender (2012)

enforcement experience and his specialized training in gang-related crimes." In the second affidavit, Messerschmidt stated why he believed there was probable cause for the search. The warrant application was approved by the supervisor as well as by a police lieutenant and a deputy district attorney. The warrant was subsequently issued and a search was conducted. During the search, the police recovered the boyfriend's shotgun and a box of .45-caliber ammunition.

The boyfriend later filed a Section 1983 action against the officers, saying that they had subjected him to an unreasonable search in violation of the Fourth Amendment. The Federal District Court decided in favor of the boyfriend, saying that "the firearm and gang-related aspects of the search warrant were overbroad and that the officers and gang-material aspects of the search warrant were overbroad." It held that the officers were not entitled to qualified immunity. The Court of Appeals for the Ninth Circuit agreed with the district court. On appeal, the Court held that, under the circumstances and facts of the case, the officers were entitled to qualified immunity and therefore could not be held liable. A number of factors tilted the Court's decision in favor of the officers. First was "the fact that a neutral magistrate has issued a warrant that, therefore, the officers acted in an objectively reasonable manner...." The Court conceded that, indeed, there are instances of possible liability and these are in cases where "it is obvious that no reasonably competent officer would have concluded that a warrant should issue." The Court did not consider this case as falling under that narrow exception, however, adding that "it would not be entirely unreasonable for an officer to believe that there was probable cause to search for all firearms and firearms-related materials," and that "it would not be unreasonable for an officer to conclude that Bowen (the boyfriend) owned other illegal guns."

What distinguishes *Millender* (where the officers were given qualified immunity) from *Groh* (where the officer was denied qualified immunity and therefore held liable) were the Court's conclusions that in *Millender*, it could not have been clear to the officers that they acted unconstitutionally, whereas in *Groh* it was "clear to the officer that his conduct was unlawful." In sum, if it would be clear to a reasonable police officer that his or her conduct was unlawful, then the officer cannot claim qualified immunity. Reasonableness, however, is ultimately a finding of fact to be decided by a jury or judge if the case goes to trial. What may be reasonable to one judge or jury may be unreasonable to another.

The good faith defense has three important implications for police officers and agencies:

1. Officers must know the basic constitutional and federal rights of the public they serve. Although officers should be familiar with these rights from college courses and police academy training, their knowledge needs constant updating in light of new court decisions in criminal procedure and constitutional law.
2. Police agencies have an obligation to inform their officers constantly of new cases that establish constitutional rights.
3. Agencies must update their manuals or guidelines regularly to reflect cases decided not only by the U.S. Supreme Court but also by federal courts in their jurisdiction.

Can the Use of Tasers Result in Legal Liability under Federal Law?

Many police departments in the United States use Tasers instead of guns to arrest suspects or subdue detainees. Tasers and stun guns have been described as "pistol-like devices that shoot electrical volts instead of bullets."* They are used by approximately 14,000 police and law enforcement agencies in the world. Tasers are generally considered an effective means of control that is not excessively violent and therefore spares the police from being sued for excessive use of force.

The issue whether the use of Tasers violates constitutional rights has not been addressed by the United States Supreme Court. A 2010 decision by the United States Court of Appeals for the Ninth Circuit, however, has held that the use of Tasers and stun guns can result in unreasonable searches and seizures in violation of the Fourth Amendment (*Bryan v. MacPherson*, 630 F.3d 805 [2010]) and consequently expose the officer and department to civil liability under federal law (42 USC Section 1983).

In this case, Officer MacPherson used his X26 Taser to arrest suspect Carl Bryan for a seatbelt infraction. Because of Bryan's odd and abusive behavior, the officer asked him to "stay in the car," but Bryan opened the door to get out. Bryan did not get back in the car when ordered to do so. Officer MacPherson then used his Taser and hit Bryan with a single dart in his left arm. The suspect fell to the ground, cut and bruised his face, and broke four teeth. Despite the suspect's odd behavior, the Court found that the officer use of the Taser constituted excessive force because the suspect "was obviously and noticeably unarmed, made no threatening statements or gestures, did not resist arrest or attempt to flee, but was standing inert twenty to twenty-five feet away from the officer."

Addressing the issue of whether Officer MacPherson used excessive force, the Court said that such allegations under the Fourth Amendment are examined using a general standard about whether the officer's action is objectively reasonable in light of the facts and circumstances confronting the officer. Reviewing previous cases, the Court then identified three criteria for balancing individual rights against the forceful act of the government under the Fourth Amendment. These are: (1) the nature and quality of the intrusion; (2) the governmental interest in the use of force; and (3) the balancing of competing interests. Analyzing the circumstances in this case, the Court concluded that the use by Officer MacPherson of the Taser was excessive. Having said that, the Court, however, did not hold the officer civilly liable because the officer "did not violate a clearly established constitutional right of which a reasonable person would have known."

The Court concluded by saying: "Based on these recent statements regarding the use of tasers, and the death of prior authority, we must conclude that a reasonable officer in Officer MacPherson's position could have made a reasonable mistake of law regarding the constitutionality of the taser use in the circumstances." In sum, *Bryan* holds that an officer can be held liable when using Tasers or stun guns, but only if such use was excessive as determined by surrounding circumstances. The determination is made by a jury or judge on a case-by-case basis.

* Taser is the brand name of the electronic control devices manufactured and marketed by the Arizona company Taser International.

The Probable Cause Defense in Search and Seizure Cases The second defense in Section 1983 cases discussed in this chapter is the **probable cause defense**. This means the officer is not liable in cases in which probable cause is present. It is a limited type of defense in that it applies only in Fourth Amendment cases where probable cause is required for the police to be able to act legally, such as in arrests and search and seizure cases. It cannot be used in cases alleging violations of other constitutional rights, such as the First, Fifth, Sixth, or Fourteenth Amendments.

probable cause defense
a reasonable good faith belief in the legality of the action taken.

One court has said that, for purposes of a legal defense in Section 1983 cases, probable cause simply means "a reasonable good faith belief in the legality of the action taken" (*Rodriguez v. Jones*, 473 F.2d 599 [5th Cir. 1973]). That ruling puts the probable cause expectation for Section 1983 cases lower than the concept of probable cause in search and seizure cases under the Fourth Amendment, where it is defined as "more

Rodriguez v. Jones (1973)

than bare suspicion; it exists when the facts and circumstances within the officers' knowledge and of which they had reasonably trustworthy information are sufficient in themselves to warrant a man of reasonable caution in the belief that an offense has been or is being committed" (*Brinegar v. United States*, 338 U.S. 160 [1949]). Thus, the probable cause requirement for a defense in Section 1983 cases is lower in certainty than that for an arrest or search. For example, suppose Officer Hill makes an arrest that is later determined to be without probable cause. According to *Rodriguez*, Officer Hill may be exempt from liability if he reasonably and in good faith believed at the time of the arrest that it was legal. The arrest itself, however, will not be valid.

Brinegar v. United States (1949)

CIVIL LIABILITY UNDER STATE TORT LAW

tort
a civil wrong in which the action of one person causes injury to the person or property of another, in violation of a legal duty imposed by law.

A second type of civil liability is liability under state tort law. **Tort** is defined as a civil wrong in which the action of one person causes injury to the person or property of another, in violation of a legal duty imposed by law. Tort law is oftentimes a product of judicial decisions over the years. It is not as precise or clear as criminal law, which is neatly laid out in a state's penal code and usually leaves no room for vagueness. State tort actions are the second most common form of lawsuit against police (Section 1983 cases are the most common). But more plaintiffs may be using the "state tort route" in the future if the Court continues to limit the use of Section 1983 cases as a remedy for violations of rights.

Types of State Tort Cases

There are two types of state tort cases:

1. Intentional tort
2. Negligence tort

intentional tort
occurs when there is an intention on the part of the officer to bring some physical harm or mental coercion upon another person.

Intentional Tort An **intentional tort** occurs when there is an intention on the part of the officer to bring some physical harm to or mental coercion upon another person. Intent is mental and thus difficult to establish. However, courts and juries generally are allowed to infer the existence of intent from the facts of the case. For example, suppose an officer takes a person to the police station in handcuffs for questioning. When charged with false arrest, the officer denies that he intended to place the person under arrest. The judge or jury probably will decide that intent to arrest was, in fact, present because the person was handcuffed and obviously not free to leave.

Intentional tort in itself comes in different forms, but there are five types that are commonly brought against police officers:

1. False arrest and false imprisonment
2. Assault and battery
3. Excessive use of nondeadly force
4. Excessive use of deadly force
5. Wrongful death

false arrest
when the officer makes an illegal arrest.

False Arrest and False Imprisonment In a tort case for **false arrest**, the plaintiff alleges that the officer has made an illegal arrest. A claim of false arrest also arises if the officer arrests the wrong person named in the warrant. An officer who makes a warrantless arrest bears the burden of proving that the arrest was, in fact, based on probable cause and that an arrest warrant was not necessary because the arrest came under one of the exceptions to the warrant rule. If the arrest is made with a warrant, the presumption is that probable cause exists, unless the officer obtained the warrant with malice, knowing that there was no probable cause (*Malley v. Briggs*, 475 U.S. 335 [1986]). An arrest with a warrant is therefore unlikely to result in civil liability for false arrest unless the officer serves a warrant that he or she knows to be illegal or unconstitutional. For example, if Officer Miller serves an unsigned warrant or one that is issued for the wrong person, Miller will be liable for false arrest despite the issuance of a warrant.

Malley v. Briggs (1986)

False arrest is a different tort from **false imprisonment**, but in police tort cases the two are virtually identical. This is because arrest necessarily means confinement, which is in itself an element of imprisonment. In both cases, the individual is restrained or deprived of freedom without legal justification. The cases do differ, however, in that a false arrest leads to false imprisonment, but false imprisonment is not necessarily the result of a false arrest. For example, a suspect may be arrested with probable cause (a valid arrest) but may be illegally detained in jail for several days without the filing of charges (false imprisonment). If an officer makes an arrest based on probable cause but later finds out that the person is innocent, continuing to hold the person constitutes false imprisonment even though the arrest was valid.

false imprisonment
when a person is placed in confinement without any valid reason.

Assault and Battery Although sometimes used as one term, assault and battery represent two separate acts. **Assault** is the intentional causing of an apprehension of harmful or offensive conduct; it is the attempt or threat (accompanied by the ability) to inflict bodily harm on another person. An assault is committed if the officer causes another person to think that he or she will be subjected to harmful or offensive contact. **Battery** is the intentional infliction of harmful or offensive bodily contact. Given this broad definition, the potential for battery exists every time an officer uses force on a suspect or arrestee. The main difference between assault and battery is that assault is generally menacing conduct that results in a person's fear of imminently receiving a battery, whereas battery involves unlawful, unwarranted, or hostile touching—however slight. In some jurisdictions, assault is attempted battery.

assault
the attempt or threat to inflict bodily harm on another person.

battery
the intentional infliction of harmful or offensive bodily contact.

Excessive Use of Nondeadly Force Any discussion of the use of force by police must be separated into use of *nondeadly force* and use of *deadly force*. Lumping the two together confuses the issue because different rules govern them. Excessive use of force, nondeadly or deadly, leads to liability under state tort law and also under Section 1983. The police are often charged with brutality or use of excessive force. The general rule is that nondeadly force may be used by police in various situations as long as such force is reasonable.

Reasonable force is force that a prudent and cautious person would use if exposed to similar circumstances; it is limited to the amount of force necessary to achieve legitimate results.

reasonable force
the force that a prudent and cautious person would use if exposed to similar circumstances.

For the purpose of day-to-day policing, it is best to think of nondeadly force as either reasonable or punitive, rather than as reasonable or unreasonable. This is because it is often hard for an officer to distinguish between what is reasonable force and what is unreasonable force, particularly when making split-second decisions when

punitive force
force that is meant to punish rather than control.

emotions are running high and personal safety (the officer's and other people's) is at risk. In contrast, an officer is more likely to know when he or she is using **punitive force**, which is force that is meant to punish rather than merely bring the situation under control. In police work, the use of reasonable force is always legal, whereas the use of punitive force is always illegal and exposes the officer, his or her supervisors, and the city to lawsuits.

deadly force
force that, when used, would lead a reasonable officer objectively to conclude that it poses a high risk of death or serious injury.

Excessive Use of Deadly Force **Deadly force** is defined as force that, when used, would lead a reasonable officer objectively to conclude that it poses a high risk of death or serious injury to its target. The general rules for the use of deadly force may be summarized as follows: In misdemeanor cases, the safest practice is for officers to refrain from using deadly force except for self-defense or the defense of the life of a third person. The use of deadly force in misdemeanor cases to prevent an escape raises questions of disproportionality; the designation of the offense as a misdemeanor denotes that the state does not consider such offenses as serious. Therefore, using deadly force to prevent the escape of a misdemeanant may constitute a disproportionate punishment.

In felony cases, the safest rule is to use deadly force only when the life of the officer or another person is in danger and the use of such force is immediately necessary to preserve that life. The use of deadly force is usually governed by specific departmental rules that must be followed strictly. If there are no departmental rules, state law must be followed.

wrongful death
when death occurs as a result of an officer's unlawful action or inaction.

Wrongful Death The question of **wrongful death** arises whenever death occurs as a result of an officer's action or inaction. An officer has a duty to use not merely ordinary care but a high degree of care in handling a weapon, or else he or she can become liable for wrongful death. Sometimes an officer is held liable because of failure to follow good police procedure. In one case, a police officer was held liable for $202,295.80 in a wrongful death action for shooting and killing a man suspected of buying marijuana, even though the officer thought he was shooting in self-defense. The judge concluded that the officer's fault in not following sound police procedure not only placed the officer in a position of greater danger but also imperiled the deceased suspect by creating a situation in which a fatal error was more likely (*Young v. City of Killeen*, 775 F.2d 1349 [5th Cir. 1985]).

Young v. City of Killeen (1985)

In summary, the types of intentional tort occur when the officer intends to inflict some physical harm or mental coercion on another person.

negligence tort
a tort that occurs when there is a breach of a common law or statutory duty to act reasonably toward those who may foreseeably be harmed by one's conduct.

Negligence Tort The second category of state tort is **negligence tort**. Unlike intentional tort, negligence tort does not involve any intent on the part of the officer. Instead, it is defined as the breach of a common law or statutory duty to act reasonably toward those who may foreseeably be harmed by one's conduct. This definition may be modified or superseded by specific state law providing for a different type of conduct, usually making it more restrictive than this definition. Negligence tort applies in many aspects of police work, five of which we will briefly discuss here:

1. Liability for failing to protect a member of the public
2. Liability for negligent use by police of motor vehicles
3. Liability for injury caused by a fleeing motorist-suspect
4. Liability for failure to respond to a call
5. Liability for failure to arrest drunk drivers

Liability for Failing to Protect a Member of the Public The task of a police officer may be simply stated as: the protection of life and property. Does this mean that the police are liable every time an injury to life or loss or destruction of property occurs? The answer is generally no, but there are exceptions.

The general rule is that there is no police liability for failing to protect a member of the public. This is because of the **public duty doctrine**, which holds that government functions are owed to the general public but not to specific individuals. Therefore, police officers who fail to prevent crime while acting within the scope of their official capacity are not liable to specific individuals for injury or harm that may have been caused by a third party. For example, the police would not be liable if Sue was assaulted, Tom was murdered, or McDonald's was burglarized. Without the protection of the public duty doctrine, nobody would ever want to be a police officer because of possible civil liability every time a crime is committed under the claim of failure to protect.

An exception to the public duty doctrine is when a **special relationship** exists. This is the one major and important exception to the public duty doctrine. Special relationship means that if a duty is owed to a particular person rather than to the general public, then a police officer or agency that breaches that duty can be held liable for damages. Special relationship has many meanings, depending on state law, court decisions, and agency regulations. What these situations have in common is that the duty of the police has shifted from protecting the public in general to protecting a particular person, so a special relationship has been established. Liability might be imposed in the instances noted next based on the special relationship exception to the public duty doctrine.

1. *When the police deprive an individual of liberty by taking him or her into custody.* In a Florida case, a person was arrested for possession of a lottery ticket. He was handcuffed by the police but then was stabbed by another person. The court ruled that once the suspect was handcuffed and taken into custody, a special relationship was created in which the city was responsible for his safety, just as though he had been incarcerated in the city jail. In this case, however, the court did not find the officers liable, because there was no negligence in their handling of the suspect. They were just as surprised as the arrestee when a woman ran up and stabbed him (*Sanders v. City of Belle Glade*, 510 So.2d 962 [Fla. App. 1987]).

2. *When the police assume an obligation that goes beyond the police duty to protect the general public.* For example, a man named Schuster provided New York City police officers with information that led to the arrest of a fugitive. The incident received considerable media attention, exposing Schuster as the individual who had assisted in the fugitive's capture. When Schuster received life-threatening phone calls, he notified the police. Several weeks later, Schuster was shot and killed. Schuster's family brought suit, alleging that the city police had failed to provide him with adequate protection and that New York City thereby had breached a special duty owed to individuals who provide the police with information about a crime. A New York court agreed, saying that "in our view the public (acting in this instance through the City of New York) owes a special duty to use reasonable care for the protection of persons who have collaborated with them in the arrest or prosecution of criminals" (*Schuster v. City of New York*, 154 N.E. 2d 534 [N.Y. 1958]).

public duty doctrine
government functions are owed to the general public but not to specific individuals, thus there is generally no liability for failing to protect a member of the public.

special relationship
if a duty is owed to a particular person rather than to the general public, then a police officer or agency that breaches that duty can be held liable.

Sanders v. City of Belle Glade (1987)

Schuster v. City of New York (1958)

Irwin v. Town of Ware
(1984)

Sorichetti v. City of
New York (1985)

3. *When protection is required by law.* Some states enact laws expressly protecting special groups or individuals. In other states, judicial decisions regard certain laws as protecting special groups or individuals even though they are not specifically protected by law. For example, in a case in Massachusetts, the police were found liable for failing to arrest a drunk driver who subsequently caused injury to the plaintiff. A special relationship was considered to have been created by the legislature in a state statute that prohibited drunk driving (*Irwin v. Town of Ware*, 467 N.E. 2d 1292 [Mass. 1984]).

4. *When protection is ordered by the court.* This situation is illustrated in *Sorichetti v. City of New York*, 482 N.E. 2d 70 (1985). The New York Court of Appeals upheld a judgment for $2 million against the New York City police for failure to protect a child who was under an order of protection issued by the court. The mother had obtained the order curtailing her husband's access to their child because of his violent tendencies. One weekend, the mother agreed to permit the husband to keep the child if he met her at the police station. At the station, the husband yelled to the wife that he was going to kill her and then pointed to the daughter and said, "You better do the sign of the cross before this weekend is up." The wife immediately asked the police to arrest her husband; the police replied that there was nothing they could do. The wife went to the police the next day and again demanded that they return her daughter and arrest her husband, but the police denied her request. That same weekend, the child was attacked by the father and suffered severe wounds. The appellate court upheld the huge damages award, saying that the court-issued protective order created a special relationship that required the police to take extra steps to protect the daughter from harm from a known source.

HIGHLIGHT ▶ Civil Lawsuits against the Police Can Be Expensive: An Illustrative Case

An issue of the *Houston Chronicle* had this headline: "Lawyer seeks $4.4 million for legal work." The article went on to say that a Houston lawyer "who won a $1.7 million civil rights settlement for two brothers who took photos of a 2002 drug raid, has asked a federal judge for $4.4 million in attorney's fees." Harris County commissioners (in Houston, Texas) had earlier agreed unanimously in an emergency meeting to pay $1.7 million to settle the case. In their lawsuit, the brothers had asked for $5 million in damages.

The settlement came "after nine days of testimony that focused on the Ibarras' arrests at their mother's Houston home." In their lawsuit, the Ibarra brothers maintained that "sheriff's deputies stormed their home without probable cause, destroyed film in their camera and arrested them after one of the brothers took pictures of a drug raid in progress at a neighbor's home." Lawyers for the officers said, "[T]he officers did not want their faces exposed because some of them worked in an undercover capacity and feared the pictures might threaten their safety." Interviewed later, two jurors suggested that they would have awarded the Ibarra brothers more than the amount for which the case was settled.

In addition to the $1.7 million payment to the plaintiffs, the county must pay "all attorney's fees, court costs and expenses incurred by both sides in the case." The lawyer for the plaintiffs asked the court to "double the $2.2 million in standard fees under a multiplier that accounts for a case's complexity and riskiness," saying that he "personally invested $130,000 because his clients were poor." He claimed that Harris County agreed to the award "to avoid the possibility of a historic multimillion-dollar verdict," adding that the $4.4 million in attorney's fees "would deter the county from fighting other legitimate civil rights claims."

Sources: *Houston Chronicle*, March 4, 2008, p. 1; *Houston Chronicle*, March 19, 2008, p. B4.

It is important to note, however, that *Sorichetti* was a state tort case filed in New York state court. If the same case were filed today under Section 1983 (in federal court and under federal law), the results would likely be different. This is because in 2005, the U.S. Supreme Court held that the wrongful failure by the police to arrest a husband who violated a domestic relations court restraining order does not amount to a violation of a constitutional due process right under the Fourteenth Amendment and therefore does not result in civil liability under Section 1983, which is a federal law (*Town of Castle Rock v. Gonzales*, 545 U.S. 748 [2005], discussed earlier in this chapter under Section 1983). The special relationship doctrine does not apply in Section 1983 cases, meaning that it applies only if the civil liability case is brought under state tort law and if state law provides for such type of liability.

5. *In some domestic abuse cases.* The rule is that the police do not have any liability in domestic abuse situations, because the duty to protect an abused spouse comes under the public duty doctrine. In some instances, however, a special relationship has been established, so failure to protect would lead to liability. In a 2003 case, a woman in Tennessee claimed that the county and sheriff's deputies failed to adequately protect her against her estranged husband, who allegedly set fire to her home while divorce proceedings were pending. The claim was based on the allegation that the deputies failed to arrest the husband for violating a protection order and therefore left him free to commit the arson. She was awarded $30,000 in damages against the county and $130,000 in damages against the two deputy sheriffs. Violation of the protection order created the special relationship that led to liability.

Other Sources of Police Civil Liability under State Tort Law

The situations described previously are examples of possible police liability based on the special relationship doctrine. In addition to special relationship, there are other sources of civil liability based on state tort laws, but not under Section 1983. Some of these include:

Negligent use of police vehicles
Injury caused by a fleeing motorist-suspect
Failure to respond to calls
Failure to arrest a drunk driver

Negligent Use of Police Vehicles As in other state tort negligence cases, the general rule is that there is no liability for police use of motor vehicles. If liability is imposed at all, it is usually based on police conduct that "shocks the conscience of the court" rather than on a lower standard. Liability under state law may also arise if there are violations of state law or departmental policy. Police departments have rules that officers must follow during vehicular chases. Failure to abide by departmental policy might establish a level of negligence that can lead to liability in a state tort action for the officer.

Injury Caused by a Fleeing Motorist-Suspect Some cases have been filed by third parties against police officers and departments, seeking damages for injuries caused by a fleeing motorist-suspect who, in the course of the pursuit, hits and injures a pedestrian. Most states hold that the police are not liable for injuries or harm caused by a fleeing violator, because the proximate cause of the injury was not the conduct of the police in making the chase but the negligent behavior of the fleeing violator.

Failure to Respond to Calls Numerous cases have been filed against the police based on alleged negligent failure to respond to calls for police help, including 911 calls. Most police departments encourage the public to call 911 in cases of emergency, and some have assured the public that such calls will be given priority and responded to promptly—even stating the number of minutes it will take the police to respond. The general rule, based on court decisions, is that the police cannot be held liable for either slow or improper response to calls for police help, including 911 calls, except when a special relationship exists between the police and the caller. It is not a good policy for police departments to ensure the public that they will respond within, say, five, ten, or fifteen minutes after receiving a 911 call. Such a policy may expose the department to liability in the event that the police are unable to live up to that promise.

Ashburn v. Anne Arundel County (1986)

Failure to Arrest a Drunk Driver Most states hold that police officers are not liable for injuries inflicted on the public by drunk drivers whom the police fail to arrest. Illustrative of this rule is a Maryland Court of Appeals decision (*Ashburn v. Anne Arundel County*, 510 A.2d 1078 [Md. 1986]). In this case, a police officer found Millham, intoxicated, sitting behind the wheel of a pickup truck in the parking lot of a 7-Eleven store. The officer told Millham to pull his truck to the side of the lot and to refrain from driving that evening, but he did not make an arrest. As soon as the officer left, Millham drove off and soon collided with the plaintiff, a pedestrian. After losing his left leg and suffering other injuries, the plaintiff brought suit.

On appeal, the Maryland Court of Appeals held that:

◆ The officer was not in a special relationship with pedestrians and therefore did not have a duty to prevent a driver from injuring pedestrians.
◆ The law that requires officers to detain and investigate a driver does not impose any duty on the police to prevent drivers from injuring pedestrians.

Special relationship may be created, however, after which liability ensues, if an arrest is mandated by law and the officer fails to arrest the drunk driver.

Official Immunity Is a Defense in State Tort Cases

official immunity
a defense in state tort cases if an act is discretionary, done in good faith, and the officer was acting within the scope of authority.

City of Lancaster v. Chambers (1994)

Various defenses are available in state tort cases, but the one most often used in state tort litigation is **official immunity** (some states call it *qualified immunity* or *partial immunity*). Its meaning varies slightly from state to state. Despite variations, common elements of the official immunity defense can be identified. One state court says that government employees are entitled to official immunity from lawsuits if the act involves the performance of their "discretionary duties, in good faith, as long as they are acting within the scope of their authority" (*City of Lancaster v. Chambers*, 883 S.W. 2d 650 [Tex. 1994]). This definition requires that, for the official immunity defense to succeed, three elements must be proved by the officer in court:

1. The act performed was a discretionary act.
2. The officer acted in good faith.
3. The officer acted within the scope of authority.

Discretionary Act A **discretionary act** is one that involves personal deliberation, decision, and judgment. The opposite of a discretionary act is a mandatory act. For example, the decision to arrest a suspect for a minor offense usually is left to the discretion of the officer; hence, it is discretionary. But using only lawful force when making an arrest is mandatory in that the police are required by the Constitution to respect the rights of arrested suspects. Also mandatory is obeying the law or following departmental policy.

discretionary act
an act that involves personal deliberation, decision, and judgment.

The Officer Acted in Good Faith In state tort cases, **good faith** means that the officer "acted in the honest belief that the action taken or the decision was appropriate under the circumstances." For example, making an arrest without a warrant on the reasonable belief that the suspect would otherwise flee would be acting in good faith. On the other hand, making a warrantless arrest without probable cause is not acting in good faith, because every officer knows that a valid warrantless arrest can be made only if there is probable cause.

good faith
when an officer "acts in the honest belief that the action taken or the decision was appropriate under the circumstances."

The Officer Acted within the Scope of Authority Acting within the scope of authority means that the officer is discharging the duties generally assigned. For example, an officer executing a search warrant or making an arrest by virtue of a warrant is acting within the scope of authority. The same is true of an officer who makes an arrest based on probable cause or who uses reasonable force in making an arrest. In contrast, an officer who beats up a suspect or who makes a vehicle stop without any justification is clearly acting outside the scope of authority.

acting within the scope of authority
when an officer is discharging the duties generally assigned.

Federal (Section 1983) and State Tort Cases Compared

The preceding discussion on federal (Section 1983) and state tort cases can be confusing, particularly because the same act by a police officer can lead to liability under both laws. It is important to remember that a single act by the police can violate both laws, and therefore cases may be filed under both laws. There is no double jeopardy because both are civil cases where double jeopardy does not apply. Even if both cases were criminal, double jeopardy would not apply anyway because the cases would come under different criminal jurisdictions, federal and state. The chart should help dispel the confusion. It summarizes the differences between federal and state civil liability laws:

Differences between Federal Section 1983 and State Tort Cases

Federal (Section 1983) Cases	State Tort Cases
Based on federal law.	Based on state law.
Law passed in 1871.	Tort law developed in court cases.
Usually filed in federal court.	Usually filed in state court.
Only public officials can be sued.	Public officials and private persons can be sued.
Basis for liability is violation of a constitutional right or a right given by federal law.	Basis for liability is injury to a person or the property of another in violation of a duty imposed by state law.
Good faith defense means the officer did not violate a clearly established constitutional or federal right which a reasonable person should have known.	Good faith defense usually means the officer acted in the honest belief that the action taken was appropriate under the circumstances.
Liability for negligence is based on deliberate indifference or conduct that shocks the conscience.	Liability for negligence is based on state law or court definition of negligence.

IF THE POLICE ARE SUED

What happens if police officers and the city are sued? Should they lose, who pays? This section examines these questions as we study what happens when the police officer, supervisor, and city or county are defendants.

The Police Officer as Defendant

The officer is an obvious liability target because he or she allegedly committed the violation. The rule is that if what happened can be blamed on the officer alone and on nobody else, the officer alone is liable. For example, suppose an officer, despite excellent training, brutalizes a suspect. If what happened is solely the fault of the officer, then the officer alone is liable. If sued, an officer has two immediate concerns: (1) Who will be his or her lawyer? and (2) If the jury finds liability, who will pay the damages?

MYTH vs. REALITY

MYTH If a police officer is sued, the police department will cover all of the costs of his or her defense.

FACT Police departments do not always cover the costs of defending a police officer who is sued. It depends on agency policy and whether the officer's conduct was egregious.

Who Will Be the Officer's Lawyer? Most state agencies, by law or official policy, provide representation to state law enforcement officers in civil actions. Such representation is usually undertaken by the state attorney general. The situation is different in local law enforcement agencies, where representation usually is decided on a case-by-case basis. This means that the local agency is under no obligation to provide a lawyer if an officer is sued, although most agencies will provide some form of representation unless what the officer did constitutes gross abuse of authority. If the agency provides a lawyer, it will probably be the district attorney, the county attorney, or another lawyer who works with the government in some capacity. In some cases, the officer is allowed to choose a lawyer, whose fees are then paid by the agency. This is ideal for the officer but unpopular with agencies because of the high cost. It is cheaper to use somebody already employed by the municipality (such as a county attorney or a district attorney) to represent an officer than to hire an outside lawyer.

indemnification
compensation for incurred hurt, loss, or damage.

Who Will Pay If the Officer Is Held Liable? A majority of states provide direct payment or reimbursement of any damages paid by its state employees. The amount states will pay for state employee liability varies considerably; some states set no limit, but most states do. If the court awards the plaintiff an amount larger than the maximum allowed by the agency, the state employee pays the difference. Although most state agencies provide some form of **indemnification**, meaning compensation for incurred hurt, loss, or damage, it does not follow that the agency will automatically indemnify every time liability is imposed. Most state agencies will pay if the employee acted within the scope of employment, but the agency will not indemnify if the employee's act was grossly, blatantly, or outrageously violative of individual rights or agency regulations, as determined by the court.

However, police officers are not state employees, and so these rules do not apply. Police officers are employees of the local government, be that a city, county, or municipality. The practices among local agencies vary from full payment or reimbursement for civil liability to no payment or reimbursement whatsoever. In some cases, legal representation and indemnification are provided for by policy; in other cases, there is no official policy at all, and so decisions are made by local policy makers on a case-by-case basis, depending on the merit of the case. Whatever may be the policy or practice on indemnification, many state and local agencies will not pay for punitive damages (as opposed to token or actual damages) imposed on a public employee, because the imposition of punitive (punishment-related) damages usually indicates that the employee acted outside the scope and course of employment and that the employee, not the agency, is being punished by the imposition of civil damages.

The Police Supervisor as Defendant

The term *police supervisors* includes anybody who supervises somebody in the hierarchy of that organization. It therefore includes police sergeants, lieutenants, captains, majors, sheriffs, and police chiefs. Supervisors can be held liable in three ways:

1. *Personal involvement.* If the supervisor personally participated in the act.
2. *Vicarious liability.* If the supervisor was not personally involved, but what happened can be linked to his or her negligence.
3. *Direct liability.* If the supervisor violated the rights of the officers given by the constitution, laws, agency policy, or contract.

Personal Involvement A police supervisor may be held liable if he or she participated in the act, ratified the act, directed the act, or was present at the time the act was committed and could have stopped it but did not. In these cases, the supervisor was personally involved in the act. Examples include the following:

◆ *Participated in the act.* A police chief takes part in the beating of a suspect.
◆ *Ratified the act.* A sheriff learns about the beating of a detainee after the fact but approves of the beating.
◆ *Directed the act.* A captain tells a subordinate to arrest a suspect even without probable cause.
◆ *Was present when the act was committed.* A sergeant is in the interrogation room when a suspect is beaten by other officers but does nothing to stop the beating.

In all of these situations, the supervisor had personal involvement in what happened and therefore can be held liable.

Vicarious Liability *Vicarious* means experienced through another; *vicarious liability* is indirect liability. In these cases, the supervisor did not have a direct hand in or intent to violate the right of the plaintiff, but through the negligence of the supervisor, the violation took place. A supervisor is liable if the illegal act by a subordinate comes under any of the following seven categories of a supervisor's negligence:

1. Negligent failure to train
2. Negligent failure to direct
3. Negligent failure to supervise
4. Negligent hiring
5. Negligent failure to discipline
6. Negligent assignment
7. Negligent entrustment

The level of negligence needed for supervisory liability in state tort cases varies from state to state. Most states, however, use deliberate indifference as the standard for negligence by supervisors. The U.S. Supreme Court has also ruled that in cases based on federal law (Section 1983), supervisory liability based on failure to train is based on "deliberate indifference" (*City of Canton v. Harris*, 489 U.S. 378 [1989]). There is no generally accepted definition of what **deliberate indifference** means. It is, however, a higher form of negligence than "mere indifference," but it is lower than "conduct that shocks the conscience." On a scale of 1 to 10 (1 being the slightest form of negligence), deliberate indifference is likely equivalent to a 7 or 8. Conduct that shocks the conscience is a 10.

The old defense by supervisors that "I did not know what my subordinate did, and therefore I should not be held liable" no longer works. Courts no longer use the standard of actual knowledge for supervisor liability; instead, they use the standard of "the supervisor should have known." This requires supervisors to know what goes on in their departments and not simply tell subordinates: "Go ahead, do what you want to do, but don't tell me about it."

Direct Liability Police officers have rights supervisors must respect. These rights come from various sources: the Constitution, federal law, state law, court decisions, agency policies, and collective bargaining agreements. Liability arises if the supervisor violates any of these rights. For example, a police chief is liable if he or she violates a police officer's freedom of religion or fails to provide due process in dismissals. Similarly, a sheriff is liable if he or she discriminates against women in the agency or sexually harasses a subordinate—both of which are violations of the Civil Rights Act of 1964. This area of law is complex and far beyond the scope of this chapter. It is mentioned here only to present the total supervisory liability picture. Violating the rights of subordinates is a frequent source of lawsuits in law enforcement and has resulted in an increasing number of civil liability awards against supervisors. It is a topic with which supervisors must be thoroughly familiar.

The City or County as Defendant

The inclusion of the city or county as defendant is rooted in the **deep pockets theory**, which means that, whereas officers and supervisors may have limited financial resources to pay the plaintiff, police agencies have a broader and deeper financial base.

States and state agencies generally cannot be sued and held liable under Section 1983, because they enjoy sovereign immunity ("the State can do no wrong") under the Eleventh Amendment to the Constitution. This does not mean, however, that state officials are

deliberate indifference
no fixed definition; generally a higher form of negligence than "mere indifference," but lower than "conduct that shocks the conscience."

City of Canton v. Harris
(1989)

deep pockets theory
officers generally have limited financial resources, but the city, county, or municipality has deeper pockets of funds.

HIGHLIGHT › **Responsibility to Stop Other Officers Who Inflict Punishment**

We believe it is clear that one who is given the badge of authority of a police officer may not ignore the duty imposed by his office and fail to stop other officers who summarily punish a third person in his presence or otherwise within his knowledge. That responsibility obviously obtains when the nonfeasor is a supervisory officer to whose direction misfeasor officers are committed. So, too, the same responsibility must exist as to nonsupervisory officers who are present at the scene of such summary punishments, for to hold otherwise would be to insulate nonsupervisory officers from liability for reasonably foreseeable consequences of the neglect of their duty to enforce the law and preserve the peace.
Source: *Byrd v. Brishke*, 466 F.2d 6 (7th Cir. 1972).

immune from liability. Sovereign immunity extends only to the state itself and its agencies; state officials may be sued and held liable just like local officials. Although states are generally immune from liability in Section 1983 cases, the same is not true in state courts. Many states have waived their sovereign immunity by law or court decisions. In these states, a liability lawsuit may be brought against the state itself.

The rule is different in cases involving cities and counties or municipalities because these are local governments. The Court has held that a municipality can be held liable if an unconstitutional action taken by an employee is caused by a **municipal policy** or **municipal custom** (*Monell v. Department of Social Services*, 436 U.S. 658 [1978]).

In *Webster v. City of Houston*, 735 F.2d 838 (5th Cir. 1984), the U.S. Court of Appeals for the Fifth Circuit defined "policy or custom" as follows:

1. *Policy.* A policy statement, ordinance, regulation, or decision that is adopted officially and promulgated by the municipality's lawmaking officers or by an official to whom the lawmakers have delegated policy-making authority. For example, liability arises if a police department has a policy that discriminates against women when hiring.
2. *Custom.* This is a persistent widespread practice of city officials or employees that, although not authorized by officially adopted and promulgated policy, is so common and well settled as to constitute a custom that fairly represents municipal policy. For example, liability ensues if the department does not have an official policy allowing racial profiling, but nonetheless knows it is persistent and does nothing to stop it.

The distinction is that a policy is usually written, whereas a custom is unwritten.

In a case decided in 2010, the Court held that the District Attorney's Office in New Orleans, Louisiana, could not be held liable under Section 1983 for inadequate training (*Connick v. Thompson*, 563 U.S. __ [2010]). In this case, Thompson brought a Section 1983 lawsuit against the Orleans Parish District Attorney's Office and various prosecuting attorneys in that office, claiming that they violated his constitutional right to due process by withholding evidence favorable to him that could have established his innocence. Thompson was previously convicted of murder and sentenced to death. On retrial, after a number of years on death row, he was found not guilty and released. He sued, claiming that the prosecutorial error in his case was caused by inadequate training. He was awarded $14 million in damages by the trial court. On appeal, however, the Court reversed, saying that the district attorney's office could not be held liable under Section 1983, because a single violation of a constitutional right (as was claimed by Thompson) did not suffice for liability. Instead, there must be "a pattern of abuse and a subsequent failure to establish a training program" for agency liability to ensue.

municipal policy
a statement, ordinance, regulation or decision that is officially adopted and promulgated by governmental authorities.

municipal custom
a persistent widespread practice that is so common or well settled as to constitute municipal policy.

Monell v. Department of Social Services (1978)

Webster v. City of Houston (1984)

Connick v. Thompson (2010)

OTHER CONSEQUENCES OF POLICE MISCONDUCT

The discussion in this chapter focuses primarily on the civil liabilities of the police. There are other sanctions, however, for improper police conduct. Four sanctions are discussed briefly in this section include:

◆ Criminal prosecution of police officers
◆ Administrative punishment for violations of department rules

◆ Exclusion of evidence illegally obtained (the exclusionary rule)
◆ Loss of law enforcement license

Prosecution under Federal and State Laws

Police officers are subject to criminal liabilities, which may be classified as follows:

Under Federal Law	Under State Law
1. Title 18 of U.S. Code, Section 242—Criminal Liability for Deprivation of Civil Rights	1. State penal code provisions specifically aimed at public officers for crimes such as: a. Official oppression b. Official misconduct c. Violation of the civil rights of prisoners
2. Title 18 of U.S. Code, Section 241—Criminal Liability for Conspiracy to Deprive a Person of Rights	2. Regular penal code provisions punishing such criminal acts as assault, battery, false arrest, serious bodily injury, and homicide
3. Title 18 of U.S. Code, Section 245—Violations of Federally Protected Activities	

For serious violations, criminal prosecution of police officers is always an option. As discussed previously, officers can be prosecuted in both federal and state courts for the same act. Because they are not the same jurisdiction, the prohibition against double jeopardy does not apply. Why do plaintiffs prefer to file civil cases instead of filing criminal cases so the officer can be prosecuted in criminal court? The answer probably lies in three realities: money, easier access to court, and higher chances of winning or getting a conviction.

Administrative Liability: Agency Investigation and Punishment

Internal police investigations result from a variety of officer misbehavior, ranging from charges of unethical conduct to allegations of criminal wrongdoing. Among the

HIGHLIGHT › Can the Police Sue Back?

Can the police retaliate by suing those who sue them? The answer is yes, and some departments have, in fact, struck back. The Fifth Circuit Court of Appeals has held that a city can criminally prosecute individuals for knowingly filing false complaints against the police (*Gates v. City of Dallas*, 729 F.2d 343 [5th Cir. 1984]). New York City has adopted a policy of countersuing individuals who have brought civil suits accusing police officers of brutality, asserting that it was the complainant who attacked the police. Nonetheless, the number of civil cases actually brought by the police against members of the public remains comparatively small.

The reality is that, although police officers may file tort lawsuits against arrestees or suspects, there are disincentives to doing so. For example, the officer will have to hire his or her own lawyer, a financial expense

that the officer is unlikely to recover from the defendant. Even if the officer wins the case, most of those who have encounters with the police are too poor to pay damages anyway. Thus, officers may prefer to get back at the suspect in a criminal case. States have criminal laws penalizing such offenses as assaulting a peace officer, resisting arrest or a search, hindering apprehension or prosecution, refusing to obey a police order, and committing aggravated assault. These offenses can be added to the original criminal charges filed against the person, thereby increasing the total penalty that may be imposed. Some officers also feel that the antagonistic treatment they sometimes receive from the public is simply part of police work, to be accepted without retaliation. In sum, there are alternatives to suing plaintiffs civilly that police might find more effective and convenient.

categories of sanctions discussed previously—civil, criminal, and administrative—the sanction that is imposed first and fastest is administrative. A major police act of misconduct results in immediate suspension, with or without pay, while the department investigates. Smaller departments leave the issue of discipline to supervisors, whereas large departments have internal affairs divisions that conduct investigations and recommend sanctions. Conduct that does not result in civil liability may nonetheless lead to an administrative sanction, particularly if it violates departmental policy.

The use of civilian review boards has long been advocated as a way to discipline officers. This approach, however, has been tried without much success. Although the use of civilian review boards is viewed by the public as an impartial way to investigate misconduct, police officers consider them selective and discriminatory. Their reaction is: "Why us and not other public officials as well?" Conversely, the public is wary of police departments investigating their own. Investigation by peers is suspect in any professional organization; it is worse when it involves the police, who have long had the reputation of drawing a "blue curtain" and a wall of secrecy between themselves and the public.

Exclusion of Illegally Obtained Evidence (The Exclusionary Rule)

The exclusionary rule, discussed extensively in Chapter 4, provides that any evidence obtained by the police in violation of the Fourth Amendment guarantee against unreasonable searches and seizures is not admissible in a criminal prosecution to prove guilt. The main purpose of the exclusionary rule is to deter police misconduct, the assumption being that there will be a strong disincentive for the police to misbehave if the evidence obtained thereby is not admitted. The underlying philosophy of the exclusionary rule is that, in a democratic society, it is better for nine guilty persons to go free than for one innocent person to be convicted. Whether or not the exclusionary rule is an effective deterrent to police misconduct is debatable; there are studies to support both sides. The controversy, however, is no longer significant because the exclusionary rule is here to stay. What the courts have done over the years is to refine it to determine when it does or does not apply.

The consequences of obtaining excludible evidence through improper conduct are not well defined. Although the evidence itself is excluded, the officer is usually left unpunished except in cases involving gross civil rights violations or in high-profile cases, where civil liabilities or criminal prosecutions might follow. The benefit of the doubt is usually resolved in favor of the police, perhaps with good reason. In some cases, the police do not know that what they are doing is wrong unless it is later declared illegal by a trial court. This may sometimes be a product of poor officer training, and therefore the fault is systemic rather than personal. There are proposals to admit the evidence during trial but criminally punish the officer who obtained the evidence illegally. This, however, is unrealistic. For example, what jury would convict an officer in a subsequent criminal case for improper seizure of evidence in a major drug trial that resulted in the conviction of the accused?

Loss of Law Enforcement License

Law enforcement officers are professionals licensed by the state. Improper police conduct may result in loss of license, which disqualifies an officer from law enforcement work. Like other forms of sanction, loss of license may be imposed with other punishments, particularly after a criminal conviction. It is an administrative sanction, but its effects can be permanent and far-reaching.

Loss of license can result from a violation of professional ethics as well as from other serious forms of misconduct. Ethical behavior is a generic term that covers a wide range of police conduct, from not accepting free coffee to not committing a criminal act. Most police departments and organizations subscribe to a code of ethics that prescribes professional expectations. Such codes resemble a code of ideal behavior rather than a criminal code. Sanctions for violations vary—from simple censure to firing from the department. In some cases, however, a serious violation of professional ethics results in criminal prosecution. Examples are accepting bribes or lying during police investigations. The code of ethics for law enforcement officers constitutes a broad umbrella that covers a host of misconduct. It differs from other means of police control in that it expects the officer to behave properly and professionally and is more prescriptive than punitive.

A frequent complaint from some segments of society is that some police officers lie. Although no reliable data or studies are available, most officers will likely concede that lies are sometimes told by officers in the course of police work. The results can be devastating for a suspect or defendant. The police usually win so-called swearing contests between a defendant and a police officer. Whatever the justification or excuse, lying by the police is not only unethical, it is also criminal (perjury, if under oath) and should never happen in law enforcement.

SUMMARY

Civil liability may occur under federal (Section 1983) cases.

◆ *Definition.* A Section 1983 case is a case usually filed in federal court in which the plaintiff seeks monetary damages and/or an injunction from a government official who, while acting within the scope of authority, violated the plaintiff's constitutional rights or a right given by federal law.

◆ *Two requirements for a Section 1983 lawsuit to succeed.* (1) The defendant must have been acting under color of law, and (2) there must have been a violation of a constitutional right or a right given by federal law.

◆ *Qualified immunity defense.* An officer is not civilly liable unless he or she violated a clearly established statutory or constitutional right of which a reasonable person would have known.

◆ *When it does not apply.* Section 1983 does not apply if the right violated was given by state law or agency policy, not by federal law.

Civil liability may occur under state tort law.

◆ *Definition.* Tort is a civil wrong in which the action of one person causes injury to the person or property of another in violation of a legal duty imposed by law.

◆ *Types of state tort cases.* (1) *Intentional tort* occurs when there is an intention on the part of the officer to bring some physical harm to or mental coercion upon another person. (2) *Negligence tort* occurs when there is a breach of a common law or statutory duty to act reasonably toward those who may foreseeably be harmed by one's conduct.

◆ *When negligence tort does not apply.* There is no liability under negligence tort for failing to protect a member of the public, because the officer is protected by the public duty doctrine. The public duty doctrine means that government functions are owed to the general public but not to specific individuals. Special relationship is an important exception to the public duty doctrine. It means that there may be liability in negligence cases if a duty is owed to a particular person rather than to the general public.

◆ *Defense often used in state tort cases.* Official immunity, which means that the officer is not liable if performing a discretionary duty in good faith and is acting within the scope of authority, is the most common defense in state tort cases.

◆ *When defendants are liable.* (1) A police officer is liable when what happened can be blamed solely on the officer and on nobody else. (2) A supervisor is liable when the supervisor is involved in the act or when what happened can be linked to one or all of the seven areas of supervisor negligence. (3) A city or county is liable when what happened was the result of policy or custom.

There are other possible consequences of police misconduct, including the following:

◆ Prosecution under federal and state laws
◆ Administrative investigations and punishment
◆ Exclusion of evidence illegally seized (the exclusionary rule)
◆ Loss of law enforcement license

REVIEW QUESTIONS

1. Give an overview of the types of legal liabilities to which police officers may be exposed in connection with their work.
2. What two elements are needed for civil cases under Section 1983 to succeed? Explain what each means.
3. What is the public duty doctrine? Explain its main exception.
4. What is the good faith defense in Section 1983 cases? How does it differ from the good faith defense in state tort cases?
5. Police officers are not liable in Section 1983 cases "unless they violate a clearly established constitutional or federally given right of which

a reasonable person would have known." Using decided cases, explain what is meant by a "clearly established constitutional right."

6. Give instances when an officer may be liable under state tort law.
7. What is the difference between reasonable force and unreasonable force in policing? Give an example of police use of reasonable force and then an example of police use of unreasonable force.
8. What is the public duty doctrine? What is its main exception, and what does that exception mean?
9. What does official immunity mean? Give an example of a situation in which a police officer has official immunity.
10. State the differences between federal Section 1983 and state tort cases.
11. When are police chiefs liable for the acts of their subordinates? Give examples.
12. When will the following be held liable if sued: the officer, the supervisor, and the police department?

TEST YOUR UNDERSTANDING

1. Assume a police officer brutally beats up a high school student who was suspected of dealing dope. Lawsuits are filed against the officer. Could the officer be liable under state tort law? On what basis? Could the officer also be liable under Section 1983? On what basis? Could the officer be prosecuted successively in criminal cases in state court and then in federal court? Would the constitutional protection against double jeopardy apply to the officer? Explain your answers.
2. Officer Harris, a police officer in Kansas, violated a court order by refusing to arrest Frank, a husband against whom a restraining order had been issued by the court. Officer Harris's refusal resulted in serious injury to Frank's wife and daughter. A case is brought against Officer Harris alleging a violation of Section 1983 (federal law) and a violation of Kansas state tort law. Will Officer Harris be liable under one or both of these laws? Justify your answer.
3. Jane, a university student, was arrested by the campus police because they had information

from her roommate that she was selling drugs in the dormitory and had drugs in her car. Based on this information and without obtaining a warrant, university police officers arrested Jane, bodily searched her, and also searched her car. The searches yielded no drugs. The police later learned that the information from the roommate was completely false and that the roommate intensely disliked Jane. Answer the following questions, justifying your answers: (a) Who will Jane's lawyer likely include in a lawsuit and why? (b) What defenses, if any, are available to the officers? (c) Will these defenses succeed?

RECOMMENDED READINGS

Stacey A. Blankenship, "How to Avoid Police Liability," *http://www.dklaw.com/Articles/PDF /SAB_Police.pdf.*

John J. Davis, "Police Misconduct and Civil Rights Law," *http://library.findlaw.com/1999 /Nov/1/126320.html.*

Jack Ryan, "Overview of Police Liability," Public Agency Training Council, *http://patc.com /weeklyarticles/liabilityoverview.shtml.*

Richard G. Schott. *Double exposure: Civil liability and criminal prosecution in federal court for police misconduct.* FBI Law Enforcement Bulletin, May 2008, vol. 77 issue 5, pp. 23–32.

Joanna C. Schwartz. *What police learn from lawsuits.* Cardozo Law Review 2012/02/01, vol. 33, p. 841.

NOTES

1. *Houston Chronicle*, November 30, 2006, p. A3.
2. *Houston Chronicle*, March 9, 2008, p. A16.
3. *New York Times*, March 21, 2001, p. 1.
4. *New York Times*, November 22, 2000, final edition, sec. A.
5. *Liability Reporter*, November 2001, p. 168.
6. *Liability Reporter*, July 2001, p. 102.
7. F. Scogins and S. Brodsky, "Fear of Litigation among Law Enforcement Officers," 10 *American Journal of Police* 45 (1991).

CHAPTER 15

Electronic Surveillance and the War on Terror

LEARNING OBJECTIVES

1. Compare and contrast the old approach versus the new approach to the constitutionality of electronic surveillance.
2. Discuss the expectation of privacy as it relates to *Katz v. United States*.
3. Compare the four laws that govern electronic surveillance: Title III of the Omnibus Crime Control and Safe Streets Act of 1968, the Electronic Communications and Privacy Act of 1986, the Communication Assistance for Law Enforcement Act of 1994, and the Foreign Intelligence Surveillance Act of 1979.
4. Identify arguments for and against electronic surveillance based upon legal decisions and legislation governing electronic surveillance.
5. Describe the responsibilities of the United States Department of Homeland Security.
6. Propose legal issues that have or may occur in regards to the "War on Terror."
7. Describe how the USA PATRIOT Act has increased the surveillance authority of law enforcement.
8. Identify examples of electronic surveillance that do not intercept communication.
9. When provided with scenarios will state what legal decision or legislation would be utilized for lawful surveillance.
10. Discuss the legality of law enforcement using GPS tracking devices on vehicles.

KEY TERMS

Communications Assistance for Law Enforcement Act (CALEA) of 1994

Community Oriented Policing Services (COPS)

Department of Homeland Security

Electronic Communications and Privacy Act (ECPA) of 1986

electronic surveillance

Foreign Intelligence Surveillance Act (FISA) of 1978

new concept of electronic surveillance

old concept of electronic surveillance

pen registers

Title III of the Omnibus Crime Control and Safe Streets Act of 1968

USA PATRIOT Act

Arina P Habich/Shutterstock.com

463

THE TOP 5 IMPORTANT CASES

in Terrorism and Electronic Surveillance

■ *KATZ V. UNITED STATES* (1967) Any form of electronic surveillance, including wiretapping, that violates a reasonable expectation of privacy constitutes a search under the Fourth Amendment. No physical trespass is required.

■ *KYLLO V. UNITED STATES* (2001) Using a technological device to explore details of a home that would have been unknowable without physical intrusion is a search and as such requires a warrant.

■ *HAMDI V. RUMSFELD* (2004) Due process requires that if a U.S. citizen is detained for charges of fighting against the United States as an enemy combatant, that person should be given a meaningful opportunity to contest the factual basis for his detention before a neutral decision maker.

■ *RASUL V. BUSH* (2004) Courts in the United States have the power to hear cases challenging the legality of the detention of foreign nationals captured abroad in connection with the fighting in Afghanistan and their detention in the Guantanamo Bay Detention Center in Cuba.

■ *UNITED STATES V. JONES* (2012) "The attachment of a global positioning system (GPS) tracking device to an individual's vehicle, and subsequent use of that device to monitor the vehicle's movements on public streets, constitutes a search or seizure within the meaning of the Fourth Amendment."

THIS CHAPTER discusses two important concepts in modern-day policing. The first is electronic surveillance; the second is the war on terror. Though seemingly not directly related, the relationship between these two topics is quite close in that the war on terror cannot be successfully waged without the use of modern electronic surveillance. Electronic surveillance has been a part of policing since society's use of technology started. Some law enforcement personnel maintain that a key function of law enforcement is understanding the recent technology and using it more efficiently to apprehend criminals than criminals can use technology to commit crime. In contrast to electronic surveillance, the war on terror is recent and not the main task of policing. Nonetheless, it is a part of modern-day policing, particularly in border areas and large cities that are likely terrorist attack sites.

ELECTRONIC SURVEILLANCE

We first discuss current laws on electronic surveillance because this is the area of more immediate concern to the police. The first major law on electronic surveillance was passed by Congress in 1968, but that law has since been modified by other federal laws that apply to every state and U.S. borders. In addition, states have enacted laws that may further limit what border agents and the police can do by way of electronic surveillance. It is an area of law that is constantly changing due to security needs and technological progress.

Electronic surveillance is defined as the use of electronic devices to monitor a person's activities or location. This type of search and seizure comes in many forms, such as eavesdropping, telephone tapping, "bugging," closed-circuit television, night vision, GPS tracking, electronic tagging, and Internet and computer surveillance. It differs from searches and seizures of things (discussed in Chapter 6) in that it uses modern technology and therefore changes the traditional concept of searches (looking) and seizures (taking). While searches and seizures of things usually require using the five senses, electronic surveillance uses technology to detect or gather information. It is generally nonintrusive and therefore creates different legal perspectives and problems under the Fourth Amendment.

electronic surveillance
the use of electronic devices to monitor a person's activities or location.

The use of electronic surveillance is regulated by the U.S. Constitution, federal law, and state statutes. The Fourth Amendment prohibition against unreasonable searches and seizures applies to electronic surveillance; so does the constitutional right to privacy. In addition, several federal and state laws further limit what the police can do. The rules on electronic surveillance are much more complex than the rules on searches and seizures of things, which are basically governed by U.S. Supreme Court decisions. In contrast, several long and complex federal and state laws govern what law enforcement agents can and cannot do in electronic surveillance. The complexities of electronic surveillance can be a source of concern for the police because some of these laws impose criminal penalties for violations. Constantly changing technology creates new issues that are a challenge for legislatures and courts to address.

This section looks at evolving concepts in electronic surveillance and the federal laws that govern electronic searches. It starts by examining the old and the new concepts of the constitutional use of electronic surveillance.

The Old Concept

The **old concept of electronic surveillance** held that electronic surveillance was unconstitutional only if there was a trespass. The first major case in electronic surveillance was *Olmstead v. United States*, 277 U.S. 438 (1928). *Olmstead* involved a bootlegging operation against which evidence was gathered through the use of wiretaps on telephone conversations. The Court held that wiretapping did not violate the Fourth Amendment unless there was "some trespass into a constitutionally protected area." Under this concept, evidence obtained through a bugging device placed against a wall to overhear a conversation in an adjoining office was admissible because there was no actual trespass. The Court said, "The Amendment does not forbid what was done here. There was no searching. There was no seizure. The evidence was secured by the use of the sense of hearing and that only. There was no entry of the houses or offices of the defendants."

old concept of electronic surveillance
electronic surveillance was unconstitutional only if there was a trespass.

Olmstead v. United States (1928)

This old concept prevailed from 1928 to 1967. In 1934, Congress passed the Federal Communications Act, which provided that "no person not being authorized by the sender shall intercept any communication and divulge or publish the existence, contents, substance, purport, effect or meaning of such intercepted communication to any person." In 1937, in *Nardone v. United States*, 302 U.S. 379 (1937), the Court interpreted this provision as forbidding federal agents, as well as other persons, from intercepting and disclosing telephone messages by the use of wiretaps. However, in 1942, in *Goldstein v. United States*, 316 U.S. 114 (1942), the Court held that wiretap evidence could be used against persons other than those whose conversations had been overheard and whose Fourth Amendment rights were therefore violated. That same year, the Court also held that the use of a "bug" (an electronic listening device that is not a wiretap on telephone lines) was not in violation of the Federal Communications Act, because the act applied only to actual interference with communication wires and telephone lines.

In 1961, the Court took a tougher view on electronic surveillance in the case of *Silverman v. United States*, 365 U.S. 505 (1961). In *Silverman*, the Court held that placing a "spike mike" in a building wall to allow police to overhear conversations within the building without a warrant violated the Fourth Amendment. The fact that the device, although tiny, actually penetrated the building wall was sufficient to constitute a physical intrusion in violation of the Fourth Amendment. In 1964, in *Clinton v. Virginia*, 377 U.S. 158 (1964), the Court further determined that evidence the police obtained by attaching an electronic device to the exterior wall of a building was illegally obtained. These decisions eroded the impact of the *Olmstead* decision.

The New Concept

The **new concept of electronic surveillance** holds that electronic surveillance is unconstitutional if it violates a reasonable expectation of privacy. The old concept of "some trespass into a constitutionally protected area" was not used by the Court in *Katz v. United States*, 389 U.S. 347 (1967). Under the new concept enunciated in *Katz*, a search occurs whenever there is police activity that violates a "reasonable expectation of privacy." Under this new concept, search activity includes any form of electronic surveillance, with or without actual physical trespass or wiretap.

In *Katz*, the police attached an electronic listening device to the outside of a public telephone booth that the defendant was using. Although there was no tapping of the line, the Court held that the listening device violated the defendant's reasonable expectation that his conversations, held in a public telephone booth, were private. The Court said that what Katz "sought to exclude when he entered the booth was not the intruding eye—it was the uninvited ear." He did not shed his right to do so simply because he made his calls from a place where he might be seen. The key phrase in determining intrusion is "reasonable expectation of privacy."

Aside from focusing on and popularizing the phrase *reasonable expectation of privacy* (the current standard used in Fourth Amendment cases), the *Katz* case is also significant because it makes the Fourth Amendment protection "portable," meaning its protections against unreasonable searches and seizures accompany people wherever they go and not just in the privacy of their homes or residences. In the words of the Court, the Fourth Amendment "protects people, not places." This concept is key to understanding the full extent of the protection afforded by the Fourth Amendment against any and all unreasonable searches and seizures, not just in electronic

---

Nardone v. United States (1937)

Goldstein v. United States (1942)

Silverman v. United States (1961)

Clinton v. Virginia (1964)

new concept of electronic surveillance electronic surveillance is unconstitutional if it violates a reasonable expectation of privacy.

Katz v. United States (1967)

MYTH vs. REALITY

MYTH The Fourth Amendment only applies to situations where police trespass or interfere with a person's house, papers, or effects.

FACT The Fourth Amendment applies whenever and wherever a person has a "reasonable expectation of privacy."

HIGHLIGHT › U.S. Supreme Court Cases on Electronic Surveillance: The Transition from the Old to the New Concept

Olmstead v. United States (1928) Wiretapping does not violate the Fourth Amendment unless there is "some trespass into a constitutionally protected area."

Nardone v. United States (1937) The Federal Communications Act forbids federal agents, as well as other persons, from interpreting and disclosing telephone messages through wiretaps.

Goldstein v. United States (1942) Wiretap evidence can be used against persons other than those whose conversations were overheard and whose Fourth Amendment rights were therefore violated.

Silverman v. United States (1961) Placing a spike mike in a building wall to allow police to overhear conversations

within the building without a warrant violates the Fourth Amendment.

Clinton v. Virginia (1964) Evidence the police obtained by attaching an electronic device to the exterior wall of a building was illegally obtained.

Katz v. United States (1967) The prohibition against unreasonable search and seizure is not limited to homes, office buildings, or other enclosed spaces. It applies even in public places where a person has a "reasonable expectation of privacy." The Court expressly overruled *Olmstead v. United States* (1928).

---

surveillance cases. A person enjoys the protection of the Fourth Amendment not only at home but also in a public place as long as these two elements are present: (1) there is a reasonable expectation of privacy, and (2) the expectation is acceptable to the public.

CASE BRIEF — Katz v. United States, 389 U.S. 347 (1967)

The Leading Case on the Right to Privacy

Facts: Katz was convicted in federal court of transmitting wagering information by telephone across state lines. Evidence of Katz's end of the conversation, overheard by FBI agents who had attached an electronic listening and recording device to the outside of the telephone booth from which the calls were made, was introduced at the trial. Katz sought to suppress the evidence, but the trial court admitted it. The court of appeals affirmed the conviction, finding that there was no Fourth Amendment violation, because there was "no physical entrance into the area occupied" by Katz. He appealed to the U.S. Supreme Court.

Issue or Issues: *Is a public telephone booth a constitutionally protected area such that obtaining evidence by attaching an electronic listening/recording device to the top of it violates the user's right to privacy?* Yes.

Decision: The decision of the Federal Court of Appeals for the Ninth Circuit was reversed.

Holding: Any form of electronic surveillance, including wiretapping, that violates a reasonable expectation of privacy constitutes a search. No actual physical trespass is required.

Case Significance: The *Katz* decision expressly overruled the decision in *Olmstead v. United States*, 277 U.S. 438 (1928), which found that wiretapping did not violate the Fourth Amendment unless there was some trespass into a "constitutionally protected area." In *Katz*, the Court said that the Fourth Amendment's coverage does not depend on the presence or absence of a physical intrusion into a given enclosure. The current test is that a search exists and therefore comes under the Fourth Amendment protection whenever there is a reasonable expectation of privacy. The concept that the Constitution "protects people rather than places" is significant, because it makes the protection of the Fourth Amendment "portable"—meaning it is carried by persons wherever they go, as long as their behavior and circumstances are such that they are entitled to a reasonable expectation of privacy.

Excerpts from the Opinion: The petitioner has phrased those questions as follows: (A) Whether a public telephone booth is a constitutionally protected area so that evidence obtained by attaching an electronic listening recording device to the top of such a booth is obtained in violation of the right to privacy of the user of the booth and (B) Whether physical penetration of a constitutionally protected area is necessary before a search and seizure can be said to be violative of the Fourth Amendment to the United States Constitution.

We decline to adopt this formulation of the issues. In the first place, the correct solution of Fourth Amendment problems is not necessarily promoted by incantation of the phrase "constitutionally protected area." Secondly, the Fourth Amendment cannot be translated into a general constitutional "right to privacy." That Amendment protects individual privacy against certain kinds of governmental intrusion, but its protections go further, and often have nothing to do with privacy at all. . . . Other provisions of the Constitution protect personal privacy from other forms of governmental invasion. . . . But the protection of a person's general right to privacy—his right to be let alone by other people . . . is, like the protection of his property and of his very life, left largely to the law of the individual States.

FOUR FEDERAL LAWS THAT GOVERN ELECTRONIC SURVEILLANCE

Electronic surveillance is governed by federal laws, which are often supplemented by state laws. In case of a conflict, however, federal laws prevail. The U.S. Congress has passed several laws on electronic surveillance and amends them to fit changing circumstances. Four laws deserve mention because they are the core pieces of legislation on electronic surveillance:

- ◆ Title III of the Omnibus Crime Control and Safe Streets Act of 1968
- ◆ The Electronic Communications and Privacy Act (ECPA) of 1986
- ◆ The Communications Assistance for Law Enforcement Act (CALEA) of 1994
- ◆ The Foreign Intelligence Surveillance Act (IFISA) of 1978

Following is a discussion of each.

Title III of the Omnibus Crime Control and Safe Streets Act of 1968

Title III of the Omnibus Crime Control and Safe Streets Act of 1968
government agents cannot tap or intercept wire communications except if a court order has authorized the wiretap, or if consent is given by one of the parties.

The use of wiretaps, electronic surveillance, and bugging devices is largely governed by the provisions of **Title III of the Omnibus Crime Control and Safe Streets Act of 1968** (better known as the *wiretap law*) and subsequent federal laws amending or supplementing it. This law is long and complex. Its main provision may, however, be summarized as follows: Law enforcement officers nationwide, federal and state, *cannot* tap or intercept wire communications or use electronic devices to intercept private conversations, except in two situations:

- ◆ If a court order has authorized the wiretap.
- ◆ If consent is given by one of the parties.

This section looks at these two exceptions and how state laws are affected by Title III.

Exception 1: If a Court Order Has Authorized the Wiretap For judges to be able to do this, the state must have passed a law authorizing the issuance of a court order. Without such a law, courts are not authorized to issue a judicial order. If the legislature has passed a law authorizing the issuance of a court order, then a judge may issue such an order as long as the following four requisites are present:

- There is probable cause to believe that a specific individual has committed one of the crimes listed in the act.
- There is probable cause to believe that the interception will furnish evidence of the crime.
- Normal investigative procedures have been tried and have failed or reasonably appear likely to fail or to be dangerous.
- There is probable cause to believe that the facilities or the place from which or where the interception is to be made are used in connection with the offense or are linked to the individual under suspicion.

Once law enforcement officials have obtained judicial authorization to intercept wire or oral communications, they do not have to obtain another judicial authorization to enable them to enter the premises to install the listening device. Such authorization to enter comes with the court order.

Exception 2: If Consent Is Given by One of the Parties Consent is one of the most often used exceptions to the court order requirements under Title III and has also been exempted from the warrant requirement by several court decisions. However, some states expressly prohibit by law, on pain of civil consequences or criminal prosecution, electronic eavesdropping or wiretapping even if consent is given by one of the parties. Such statutes take precedence over any consent given by one of the parties and must therefore be followed.

In *United States v. White*, 401 U.S. 745 (1971), the Court held that the Constitution does not prohibit a government agent from using an electronic device to record a telephone conversation between two parties if one party to the conversation consents. The Court has also ruled that the Fourth Amendment does not protect persons from supposed friends who turn out to be police informants. Thus, a person assumes the risk that whatever he or she says to others may be reported by them to the police; there is no police "search" in such cases. It follows that, if the supposed friend allows the police to listen in on a telephone conversation with the suspect, there is no violation of the suspect's Fourth Amendment rights. The evidence obtained is admissible because of the consent given by one party to the conversation (*On Lee v. United States*, 343 U.S. 747 [1952]).

United States v. White (1971)

On Lee v. United States (1952)

The Electronic Communications and Privacy Act (ECPA) of 1968

Title III of the Omnibus Crime Control and Safe Streets Act of 1968 continues to be the main federal law on electronic surveillance. In 1986, however, the U.S. Congress passed the **Electronic Communications and Privacy Act (ECPA)**, which amends and supplements the provisions of Title III. It is the second law that governs electronic surveillance. A series of law-oriented articles in the *FBI Law Enforcement Bulletin* discusses the main provisions of that law.[1]

According to the author, Robert Fiatal, the ECPA contains three provisions that relate to federal, state, and local law enforcement work[2]:

Electronic Communications and Privacy Act (ECPA) of 1986
amends and supplements the provisions of Title III.

1. It amends the law of nonconsensual interception of wire communications [wiretaps] and oral communications by a concealed microphone or electronic device [bugs].

2. It sets forth specific procedures for obtaining authorization to use pen registers [telephone decoders], which record the numbers dialed from a telephone, and trap-and-trace devices, which ascertain the origin of a telephone call.
3. It prescribes the procedure law enforcement officers must follow to obtain stored communications and records relating to communications services, such as telephone toll records and unlisted telephone subscriber information.

The ECPA has two aims: (1) to safeguard private electronic communications—such as in-transit and stored electronic mail (e-mail), computing services, and voice mail—from unauthorized government access and (2) to ban Internet and other electronic communication service providers from divulging the contents of those communications without the consent of the customer who originated the communication.[3]

The ECPA sets forth some rules to protect privacy relative to the use of cellular telephones, radio paging, customer records, and satellite communication. It also includes rules on workplace privacy in public or private employment. Under this law, "an employer cannot monitor employee telephone calls or electronic mail when employees have a reasonable expectation of privacy." It adds, however, that an employer is allowed to eavesdrop "if employees are notified in advance or if the employer has reason to believe the company's interests are in jeopardy."[4]

The ECPA provisions, particularly those enhancing the power of government to wiretap under various conditions, have become a focus of debate about individual privacy issues and the right of the government to uphold national security. Overall, the ECPA gives the government more power than it had in the past to conduct electronic surveillance in various law enforcement and security situations. Since its enactment in 1986, the ECPA has been amended by various laws, among them the USA PATRIOT Act of 2001 and its reauthorization acts in 2006, and the Foreign Intelligence Surveillance Act of 1978 (FISA) amendments of 2008, which also are discussed in this chapter.

The Communications Assistance for Law Enforcement Act (CALEA) of 1994

The third federal law governing electronic surveillance is the **Communications Assistance for Law Enforcement Act (CALEA) of 1994.** Recognizing the growing importance of cell phones, the U.S. Congress enacted **CALEA** to keep up with further advances in telecommunications technology. It has provisions relating to three primary techniques of lawfully authorized electronic surveillance devices: pen registers, trap-and-trace devices, and content interceptions. CALEA supplements and amends provisions of Title III of the Omnibus Crime Control and Safe Streets Act of 1968 and the ECPA.

CALEA's purpose is "to make clear a telecommunications carrier's duty to cooperate in the interception of communications for law enforcement purposes, and for other purposes."[5] Significantly, its provisions require the cell phone industry to design its systems to comply with new standards that would make it easier for the FBI to monitor calls. The act also left it to the Federal Communications Commission (FCC) to determine specific standards related to the FBI's authority to monitor more than just cell phone conversations.

After years of negotiations, in August 1999, the FCC announced rules that expanded the power of law enforcement agents to keep track of conversations and locate suspects. Among other things, the 1999 regulations authorize government agents: (1) to determine the general location of a cell phone user by identifying which cellular antenna the phone company used to transmit the beginning and end of any call under surveillance, (2) to identify all callers on a conference call and monitor such conversations even after the target of the inquiry is no longer part of the conversation, and (3) to determine whether suspects are making use of such cell phone features as call forwarding and call waiting.[6]

Do users of cellular telephones have a reasonable expectation of privacy? Although the Supreme Court has not resolved this issue, lower courts have said no. The reason is that cell phones transmit radio signals between a handset and a base unit that occasionally can be intercepted by other cordless telephones. In the words of one observer, "Those who seek privacy protection for their conversations on cordless telephones should remember that the airwaves are public." Despite the public nature of cell phone conversations, federal and local agents at present can monitor these calls only with a warrant.[7]

The Foreign Intelligence Surveillance Act (FISA) of 1978

As the name itself suggests, the **Foreign Intelligence Surveillance Act (FISA) of 1978** surveillance sets the procedure for foreign intelligence surveillance. Its purpose is the enhancement of the country's counterintelligence capacity. Over the years and after several amendments, the federal law now covers electronic eavesdropping, wiretapping, pen/trap orders, and obtaining business records. FISA permits electronic surveillance without or with a court order. Without a court order, the president, through the attorney general, may authorize electronic surveillance for a period of one year, but only if the purpose is gathering foreign intelligence information. If this is done, the attorney general is required to certify to the House Permanent Select Committee on Intelligence and the Senate Select Committee on Intelligence the conditions under which the surveillance was made.

The federal government may also conduct electronic surveillance with a court order. FISA itself provides for the creation of a Foreign Intelligence Surveillance Court (FISC) that is empowered to oversee requests for surveillance warrants by the FBI or other police agencies against suspected foreign agents inside the United States. FISC is located in the U.S. Department of Justice Building in Washington, DC, and has eleven judges who are all appointed by the chief justice of the Supreme Court. Before submitting the warrant application to FISC, the Justice Department reviews the application. Among other requirements, the application must contain the reasons for believing that the target person is a foreign agent and a "detailed description of the nature of the information sought and the type of communication or activities to be subject to surveillance."[8]

In summary, Title III of the Omnibus Crime Control and Safe Streets Act of 1968, the ECPA of 1986, CALEA of 1994, and FISA of 1978 are currently the four main laws governing electronic surveillance by law enforcement officials. However, each year Congress introduces laws seeking to meet the challenges of technological advances. Some state legislatures have also passed laws that supplement (but do not limit) federal laws. Electronic surveillance laws, however, are difficult to keep up with because they are detailed and complex because of the many facets they cover and the rapidly changing nature of the technologies they regulate. The discussion here merely touches the surface, the proverbial tip of the iceberg. The good news is that we now

Foreign Intelligence Surveillance Act (FISA) of 1978
sets the procedure for foreign intelligence.

have laws to guide law enforcement as it battles crimes involving the use of electronic technology; the bad news is that these laws are complex and always lag behind technological changes.

IN ACTION — A WARRANT FOR A WIRETAP BASED ON AN OVERHEARD CELL PHONE CONVERSATION

Jennifer Sandell has been a police officer for fourteen years. She has spent her entire career working for the Crawford Police Department. Two years ago, Sandell was promoted to the rank of sergeant and was transferred into Crawford's elite narcotics unit. Sergeant Sandell has had much success pursuing complex, well-organized drug rings. When not in pursuit of drug criminals, she enjoys shopping for the latest fashions at the Crawford Fashion Mall.

Yesterday Sandell descended on the shoe department at Larson's Department Store on a mission to find a pair of shoes to wear to her brother's upcoming wedding. Her shopping excursion took a strange twist when she overheard a cell phone conversation between the woman seated across from her and an unknown male party named "Reynolds" (Sandell heard the woman address her listener by this name no less than six times). Sandell overheard the woman make arrangements to buy a large amount of "happy juice" (a common slang term used to refer to LSD). Sandell was left with the impression that the deal was going to take place on Crawford's north border (an area known for drug activity) in the next week.

Based on what she had overheard, Sandell contacted Larson's store security and gave them a description and the location of the woman in the store. Identifying herself as an off-duty Crawford police sergeant, Sandell requested that they monitor the woman on their closed-circuit television system. Store security obliged and monitored the woman as she shopped in their store. They watched her make a credit card purchase at register 2 and proceed to an unoccupied vehicle in the parking lot, where they captured a digital "snapshot" of the vehicle's license plate along with a good description of the vehicle. Security officers provided Sandell with this information, which allowed Sandell to locate the woman at the vehicle. Sandell obtained the vehicle identification number and watched the woman drive out of the parking lot.

Today, Sergeant Sandell is back on duty and eager to follow up on her latest criminal lead. She briefs her unit at roll call and provides the following information gleaned from her preliminary investigation:

- The female suspect and "Reynolds" have been identified through Department of Motor Vehicle (DMV) records including photos. They are former high school classmates.
- The female suspect has an out-of-state criminal record that includes multiple arrests for narcotics trafficking over the past ten years. Her most recent arrest for a drug-related crime was within the past two years.
- The female suspect's residence has been identified, and the phone company has confirmed that there is a landline phone at that address. Sergeant Sandell possesses the female suspect's cell phone number and her landline phone number.
- Sergeant Sandell has developed probable cause to believe the suspect is a high-level dealer expecting a large shipment of narcotics (possibly hallucinogens), but the deal specifics remain a mystery—in other words, the where, when, and how of the planned transaction remain unknown.
- Sergeant Sandell has decided to establish a wiretap on the suspect's cell phone and home landline phone. She has limited the request to reveal only information related to the suspected criminal sale and shipment of drugs.
- Sergeant Sandell believes "Reynolds" is the wholesale dealer who will supply the now identified female suspect.

You are the judge from whom Sergeant Sandell seeks approval for the wiretaps. You have just concluded reading her warrant request for the wiretaps. The warrant's affidavit contains the information described.

1. *Do you approve the wiretaps?*
2. *If not, what reason(s) do you give Sergeant Sandell for denying the wiretap request?*

A Summary of the Four Major Federal Laws on Electronic Surveillance

Title III of the Omnibus Crime Control and Safe Streets Act of 1968 (the main law) forbids law enforcement officers from tapping or intercepting wire communications or using electronic devices to intercept private conversations, except if (1) there is a court order authorizing the wiretap, or (2) consent is given by one of the parties.

The Electronic Communications and Privacy Act (ECPA) of 1986 (1) amends the law of nonconsensual interception of wire communications and oral communications by a concealed microphone or electronic device, (2) specifies procedures for obtaining authorization to use pen registers, and (3) prescribes the procedure law enforcement officers must follow to obtain stored communications and records relating to communications services.

The Communications Assistance for Law Enforcement Act (CALEA) of 1994 governs the use of cellular telephones through regulations passed by the FCC. Regulations allow

government agents to (1) determine the general location of a cell phone user by identifying which cellular antenna was used by the communications company to transmit the beginning and end of any call under surveillance, (2) identify all callers on a conference call and monitor such conversations even after the target of the inquiry is no longer part of the conversation, and (3) determine if suspects are making use of such cell phone features as call forwarding and call waiting.

The Foreign Intelligence Surveillance Act (FISA) of 1978 regulates the collection of foreign intelligence information. It covers electronic eavesdropping and wiretapping, physical entries by government agents, and pen/trap orders. It created the Foreign Intelligence Surveillance Court (FISC), which issues warrants after some type of a hearing and after finding probable cause that four conditions have been met.

USING ELECTRONIC DEVICES FROM A PUBLIC PLACE

The Court has held that using a technological device to explore details of a home that would have been unknowable without physical intrusion is a search and therefore needs a search warrant (*Kyllo v. United States*, 533 U.S. 27 [2001]). In this case, Kyllo was suspected of growing marijuana in his house. From across the street and without entry into the home, the police used a thermal imaging device to examine the heat radiating from Kyllo's house. The whole procedure took only a few minutes. Results showed that the roof over the garage and a side wall of the house were relatively hot compared to the rest of the house and substantially hotter than neighboring homes. Based on this information, utility bills, and tips from informants, the officers obtained a warrant to search Kyllo's home. The search yielded more than 100 marijuana plants.

Kyllo v. United States (2001)

Tried and convicted, Kyllo appealed, saying the use of a thermal imaging device aimed at a private home, even if it was from a public street, for the purpose of detecting amounts of heat constituted a search and required a warrant. The Court agreed, saying in its decision, "We think that obtaining by sense-enhancing technology any information regarding the interior of the home that could not otherwise have been obtained without physical intrusion into a constitutionally protected area constitutes a search." In sum, the Court held that there is a limit to electronic surveillance even if it does not directly intrude into individual privacy. The limit here was drawn where the government uses a device that was not in general public use to explore details of a private home that would previously have been unknowable without physical intrusion. Read the Case Brief to learn more about this case.

ELECTRONIC TRACKING DEVICES THAT DO NOT INTERCEPT COMMUNICATION

Some electronic devices gather information (such as a suspect's location) but do not necessarily intercept communication. These devices do not come under Title III coverage, nor are they governed strictly by the concept of a reasonable expectation of privacy under the Fourth Amendment. Pen registers and electronic beepers (tracking devices in public places) are two examples.

Pen Registers

pen registers
devices that record the numbers dialed from a particular telephone.

Smith v. Maryland (1979)

The Fourth Amendment does not require that the police obtain judicial authorization before using **pen registers**, which record the numbers dialed from a particular telephone. In *Smith v. Maryland*, 442 U.S. 735 (1979), the Court held that not every use of an electronic device to gather information is governed by the Constitution. Pen registers gather information but do not intercept communication, so they do not come under the Fourth Amendment.

The Court gave two reasons for this decision. First, it is doubtful that telephone users in general have any expectation of privacy regarding the numbers they dial, because they typically know that the telephone company has facilities for recording all phone numbers dialed and in fact records them routinely for billing purposes. Second, even if Smith did harbor some subjective expectation of privacy, this expectation is not one that society is prepared to recognize as reasonable. When Smith voluntarily conveyed numerical information to the phone company and "exposed" that information to its equipment in the normal course of business, he assumed the risk that the company would reveal the information to the police.

United States v. New York Telephone Company (1977)

The Court has held that the police may obtain a court order to require a telephone company to assist in installing the pen register (*United States v. New York Telephone Company*, 434 U.S. 159 [1977]). Note, however, that the ECPA requires law enforcement agencies to obtain a court order (instead of a wiretap order) and specifies the procedure to be followed for obtaining that order.

In sum, the Fourth Amendment does not require the police to obtain judicial authorization before using pen registers, but federal law requires it and sets the procedure for obtaining it.

Tracking Devices

United States v. Knotts (1983)

United States v. Karo (1984)

The use of tracking devices (in this case a beeper) to keep track of a person traveling on public roads does not constitute a search, because a person has no reasonable expectation of privacy when traveling on a public thoroughfare (*United States v. Knotts*, 460 U.S. 276 [1983]). In a subsequent case decided the following year, the Court said that the warrantless monitoring of a beeper (which was installed by the police in an ether can and later delivered to the defendants) after the device had been unwittingly taken into a private residence violated the Fourth Amendment rights of the residents and others (*United States v. Karo*, 468 U.S. 705 [1984]).

Table 15.1 State Electronic Surveillance Laws

State	Cite	Includes Photo/Video	Includes Cell Phones?	Specifically Mentions "Electronic" or "Computer"?	Party Consent
Alabama	Ala. Code §13A-11-30	Yes—Ala. Code § 13A-11-32	Yes	Yes	One
Alaska	§42.20.310	Yes, if contain nudity—Alaska Stat. § 11.61.123.	Yes	Yes	One
Arizona	Ariz. Rev. Stat. Ann. §13-3005	Yes	Yes	Yes	One
Arkansas	Ark. Code §5-60-120 Ark. Code §5-16-101	Yes—Ark. Code §5-16-101	Yes	Yes	One
California	Cal. Penal Code §631, 632	Yes—Cal. Penal Code §647	Yes	Yes	All
Colorado	Colo Rev. Stat. §18-9-303	No	Yes	Yes	One
Connecticut	Conn. Gen. Stat. §52-570d:	No	Yes	Yes	All
Delaware	Del. Code Ann. tit. 11, §2402(c)(4)	Yes—Del. Code Ann. tit. 11, § 1335(2), (6)	Yes	Yes—"trespass by other means of communicating privately"	One
DC	D.C. Code Ann. § 23-541; §23-542	Yes—"intercepting device" means any electronic, mechanical, or other device or apparatus that can be used to intercept a wire or oral communication (§ 23-541).	Yes	Yes	One
Florida	Fla. Stat. ch. 934.03	Yes	Yes	Yes	All
Georgia	Ga. Code Ann. §16-11-62	Yes	Yes	Yes	One
Guam	GCA §70.35	Yes	Yes	Yes	One
Hawaii	Haw. Rev. Stat. §803-42	Yes	Yes	Yes	One
Idaho	Idaho Code §18-6702	Yes	Yes	Yes	One
Illinois	720 ILCS 5/14-2	Yes—720 ILCS 5/14-2	Yes	Yes	All
Indiana	Ind. Code Ann. §35-33.5-1-5	Yes	Yes	Yes	One
Iowa	Iowa Code §727.8	Yes	Yes	Yes—"communication of any kind"	One
Kansas	Kan. Stat. Ann. §21-6101	Yes	Yes	Yes	One
Kentucky	Ky. Rev. Stat. Ann. §526.010	Yes—"record . . . oral communications . . . by means of any electronic, mechanical or other device"	Yes - Ky. Atty Gen. Op. 84-310	Yes	One
Louisiana	La. Rev. Stat. §15:1303	Yes—see La. Rev. Stat. § 14:283	Yes	Yes	One
Maine	Me. Rev. Stat. Ann. tit. 15, §709	Yes—see Me. Rev. Stat. Ann. tit. 17-A, §511.	Yes	Yes	One
Maryland	Md. Code Ann., Courts and Judicial Proceedings §10-402	Yes	Yes	Yes—§ 10-410.	All
Massachusetts	Mass. Ann. Laws ch. 272, §99	Yes, when sound is involved	Yes	No	All
Michigan	Mich. Comp. Laws §750.539c	Yes—see 750.539d	Yes	Yes	All
Minnesota	Minn. Stat. §626A.02	Yes	Yes	Yes—626A.02	One
Mississippi	Miss. Code Ann.§41-29-501 to -537	Yes—see Miss. Code Ann. § 97-29-63	Yes	Yes—"other communications"	One
Missouri	Mo. Rev. Stat. §542.402	Yes, if partial nudity; see Mo. Rev. Stat. § 565.253.	Yes	Yes	One
Montana	Mont. Code Ann. §45-8-213	Yes	Yes	Yes—"electronic mail"	All

(continued)

Table 15.1 State Electronic Surveillance Laws *(continued)*

State	Cite	Includes Photo/Video	Includes Cell Phones?	Specifically Mentions "Electronic" or "Computer"?	Party Consent
Nebraska	Neb. Rev. Stat. §86-290	Yes—see Neb. Rev. Stat. § 86-276	Yes	Yes	One
Nevada	Nev. Rev. Stat. Ann. §200.620	Yes—see Nev. Rev. Stat. Ann. § 200.610.	Yes—"wireless methods"	Yes	All by court decision
New Hampshire	N. H. Rev. Stat. Ann. §570-A:2	Yes—NH Rev Stat §644:9	Yes	Yes	All
New Jersey	N.J. Stat. §2A:156A-3	Yes	Yes	Yes	One
New Mexico	N.M. Stat. Ann. §30-12-1	No	Yes—"using any apparatus to do or cause to be done any of the acts mentioned"	No	One
New York	N.Y. Penal Law §250.00, 250.05	Yes—see Gen. Bus. Law 395-b	Yes	Yes	One
North Carolina	N.C. Gen. Stat. §15A-287; §14-155.	Yes—see N.C. Gen. Stat. § 15A-286.	Yes	Yes - § 15A-287	One
North Dakota	N.D. Cent. Code §12.1-15-02	Yes—intercepting an oral communication "by use of any electronic, mechanical, or other device"	Yes—"by use of any electronic, mechanical, or other device"	No	One
Ohio	Ohio Rev. Code Ann. §2933.52	Yes—see Ohio Rev. Code § 2933.51	Yes	Yes	One
Oklahoma	13 Okl. St. § 176.2 et seq.	Yes-where an oral communication is recorded "through the use of any electronic, mechanical or other device"	Yes	Yes	One
Oregon	Or. Rev. Stat. §165.540, 165.543 §133.005; 163.700	Yes—Ore. Rev. Stat. § 163.700	Yes	Yes	One
Pennsylvania	18 Pa. Cons. Stat. §5703	Yes	Yes	Yes	All
Puerto Rico	P.R. Penal Code Art. 182	Yes	Yes	Yes	
Rhode Island	R.I. Gen. Laws §11-35-21, §12-5.1	Yes—See R.I. Gen Laws § 12-5.1	Yes	Yes	One
South Carolina	S.C. Code Ann. § 17-30-20	Yes—under "peeping tom" provision	Yes	Yes	One
South Dakota	S.D. Codified Laws § 23A-35A-20	Yes—S.D. Codified Laws § 22-21-1	Yes	Yes	One
Tennessee	Tenn. Code Ann. § 39-13-601	Yes—§ 39-13-605	Yes—§ 39-13-604	Yes	One
Texas	Texas Penal Code § 16.02	Yes	Yes	Yes	One
Utah	Utah Code Ann. § 77-23a-4	Yes—§ 76-9-402	Yes	Yes	One
Vermont	Vermont has passed no law specifically addressing interception of communications; however, the Vermont Supreme Court has held that an individual has a heightened expectation of privacy in the home and warrantless recording or electronic monitoring of communications in a person's home is an unlawful invasion of privacy.				
Virgin Islands	V.I. Code § 4102	Yes—any electronic means of recording of a private oral conversation	Yes	Yes	1
Virginia	Va. Code Ann. § 19.2-62	Yes	Yes	Yes	1
Washington	Wash. Rev. Code § 9.73.030	Yes—any means of recording of a private conversation	Yes	Yes	All
West Virginia	W. Va. Code § 62-1D-3	Yes	Yes	Yes	One
Wisconsin	Wis. Stat. § 968.31	Yes	Yes	Yes	One
Wyoming	Wyo. Stat. § 7-3-701	Yes	Yes	Yes	One
TOTALS		**44**	**44**	**50**	**40 = One party** **12 = All parties**

Source: National Council of State Legislatures (NCSL), http://www.ncsl.org/issues-research/telecom/electronic-surveillance-laws.aspx.

In a recent significant case, however, the Court held that attaching a GPS device to a motor vehicle and using that device to monitor the vehicle's movements constitutes a search under the Fourth Amendment (*United States v. Jones*, __ U.S. __ [2012]). In this case, government agents obtained a search warrant allowing them to install a GPS device in a vehicle that was registered in the name of the wife of the defendant, Antoine Jones. The warrant authorized the installation of the device within ten days after issuance and in the District of Columbia. The device was installed instead on the eleventh day and in the state of Maryland. Using this device, government agents tracked the vehicle's movements for twenty-eight days. With the information gathered, the agents obtained the indictment of Jones and others on drug trafficking conspiracy charges. The trial court suppressed the GPS data that was obtained while the vehicle was parked at Jones's residence but held the other data admissible because they were obtained when the vehicle was on public streets where the court said Jones did not have any reasonable expectation of privacy. The appeals court reversed, holding that the admission of some of the evidence obtained from a GPS device without a warrant (because the installation took place one day after the authorized time period) was an unreasonable search and seizure and in violation of the Fourth Amendment.

On appeal, the Court held that the evidence was not admissible, saying that what the officers did constituted a search under the Fourth Amendment and therefore needed a warrant. The Court said that the physical intrusion on an "effect" (referring to the motor vehicle) for the purpose of obtaining information constituted a search. Significantly, the Court's opinion concluded that it was not necessary in this case to use the reasonable expectation of privacy test, laid out in *Katz v. United States* (389 U.S. 347 [1967]), because the old common-law trespass to property test (the standard used before *Katz*) is still alive and is a supplement to the *Katz* test instead of being replaced by it, as many scholars had believed. The attachment of a GPS device to the motor vehicle without a warrant constituted trespass and violated the Fourth Amendment.

United States v. Jones (2012)

MYTH vs. REALITY

MYTH Police may install a tracking device on a vehicle any time it is in public, because there is no reasonable expectation of privacy in a public area.

FACT Police may not install a tracking device on a vehicle without a search warrant, as a vehicle is an "effect" protected by the Fourth Amendment from police trespass.

CASE BRIEF *United States v. Jones* (2012)

The Leading Case on the Use of a GPS Tracking Device

Facts: Government agents suspected Antoine Jones of drug trafficking. They applied for and obtained a search warrant to install a GPS tracking device on the vehicle of Jones's wife, which Jones was using. The warrant issued by the court specified that the GPS device be installed within ten days and in the District of Columbia. For some reason, the agents installed the GPS one day after the expiration of the authorization and in the state of Maryland.

The agents tracked the movements of Jones through this device for twenty-eight days. In the process, they obtained enough information to indict Jones and others on drug trafficking conspiracy charges. During trial, the trial court suppressed some of the information on the

ground that it was obtained while the vehicle was parked at Jones's residence. But the trial court admitted information obtained while the vehicle was in a public place. The trial court concluded that Jones had no reasonable expectation of privacy as to the data obtained while the vehicle was in a public place. Jones and companions were convicted. The Circuit Court of Appeals for the District of Columbia held that the warrantless use of a GPS tracking device violated the Fourth Amendment. The case reached the Court on appeal.

Issue: *Does the warrantless installation and use of a GPS tracking device on a motor vehicle to monitor its movements on public streets violate the Fourth Amendment?* Yes.

Decision: The decision of the District of Columbia Circuit Court of Appeals is affirmed.

Holding: The attachment of the GPS device to the vehicle and use of the device to monitor the vehicle's movements, constitutes a search under the Fourth Amendment. Evidence obtained from such warrantless search is not admissible as evidence in court.

Case Significance: This case is significant because it clarifies the law on the installation and use of tracking devices on motor vehicles, a common practice in law enforcement. In two earlier cases, the Court issued opinions that seemed clear-cut and straightforward. In *United States v. Knotts* (460 U.S. 276 [1983]), the Court held that the use of a tracking device to keep track of a person's whereabouts while traveling on public roads did not constitute a search and therefore did not need a warrant. A year later, in *United States v. Karo* (468 U.S. 705 [1984]), the Court said that evidence obtained from the warrantless monitoring of a tracker (installed by the police in an ether can and later delivered to the defendants without their knowledge) when the tracker was taken inside a private residence was not admissible because it violated defendant's Fourth Amendment right against unreasonable searches and seizures. The message conveyed by the Court in these two cases was that tracking devices could be used to monitor the movements of a suspect in a public place, but not in a private residence.

In *Jones*, the Court excluded the evidence obtained as a result of the installation of a GPS device in a motor vehicle. The Court did not focus on the use of the device in a public or private place, as was the concern in the two earlier cases. Instead, the Court focused on the warrantless installation of the device on the motor vehicle, saying that such installation needed a warrant. It said that the Fourth Amendment protects "the rights of the people to be secure in their persons, houses, papers, and effects, against unreasonable searches and seizures." What was involved in Jones was "effects," not persons, houses, or papers. The Court concluded that the agents' warrantless intrusion on an effect in an effort to obtain information constituted a search and needed a warrant.

This case is significant for two reasons: First, it is one of the few cases where the Fourth Amendment is applied by the Court to an effect instead of to persons, houses, or papers. Second, the Court said that the comparatively recent (1967) standard of reasonable expectation of privacy that was developed in the case of *Katz v. United States* (389 U.S. 347 [1967]) is not the only standard to be used to determine whether a person's Fourth Amendment rights have been breached. The Court said that the *Katz* test did not do away with the common-law trespass test. That is the test the Court applied in *Jones*. This is significant because after *Katz* and prior to *Jones*, some scholars had believed that the common-law trespass test was abandoned in *Katz* and replaced by the right to privacy test. The Court debunked this view and said that both tests are alive and well. In the *Jones* case, the warrantless installation of a GPS device may not have violated Jones's right to privacy, but it trespassed on an effect that belonged to Jones and his wife.

Excerpts from the Opinion: It is important to be clear about what occurred in this case: the government physically occupied private property for the purpose of obtaining information. We have no doubt that such a physical intrusion would have been considered a "search" within the meaning of the Fourth Amendment were it adopted.

The text of the Fourth Amendment reflects its close connection to property, since otherwise it would have referred simply to "the right of the people to be secure against unreasonable searches and seizures"; the phrase "in their persons, houses, papers, and effects" would have been superfluous. Consistent with this understanding, our Fourth Amendment jurisprudence was tied to common-law trespass, at least until the latter half of the 20th century. . . . Thus, in *Olmstead v. United States*, 277 U.S. 438 (1928), we held that wiretaps attached to telephone wires on the public streets did not constitute a Fourth Amendment search because "there was no entry of the houses or offices of the defendants."

Our later case, of course, have deviated from that exclusively property-based approach. In *Katz v. United States*, 489 U.S. 347 (1967), we said that "the Fourth Amendment protects people, not places," and found a violation in attachment of an eavesdropping device to a public telephone booth. Our later cases have applied the analysis of Justice Harlan's concurrence in that case, which said that a violation occurs when government officers violate a person's "reasonable expectation of privacy."

Cameras to Monitor Tracking and Other Offenders

Many cities in the United States today use automatic ticketing technology for law enforcement. In some instances, this technology involves photographing vehicle drivers, such as those running traffic red lights or not paying toll fees; in others, it involves photographing only the license plates of the offending vehicles. Tickets are mailed to the registered owners. One news item puts the issue of red-light cameras this way: "At the heart of the debate is this question: Do they save lives by reducing accidents or are they primarily a way for cities to raise money in an era of lagging tax revenue?"[9] The same source says that "according to the Insurance Institute for Highway Safety, red-light cameras are used in about 555 communities around the United States."[10] As of June 2015, twenty-four states have at least one red-light camera, while ten states prohibit them.

This form of law enforcement surveillance has spread to nontraffic situations. As another news item put it: "Go for dinner or a drink in Tampa's most popular entertainment district, and cameras mounted above the congested streets may scan your face for a match against a photo database of runaways and felons." It adds, "If the cameras find a probable match, you could be explaining yourself to a police officer within minutes." More and more places across the country are experimenting with these technological tools for law enforcement purposes.[11]

The extent of this form of electronic surveillance was recently summarized by *The Economist*, an international newsmagazine, as follows:

> Closed-circuit television cameras (CCTV) with infrared night vision peer down at citizens from street corners, and in banks, airports, and shopping malls. Every time someone clocks on a web page, makes a phone call, uses a credit card, or checks in with a micro chipped pass at work, that person leaves a data trail that can later be tracked. Every day, billions of bits of such personal data are stored, sifted, analyzed, cross-referenced with other information and, in many cases, used to build up profiles to predict possible future behavior.[12]

The constitutionality of these forms of surveillance has not been addressed by the Court, but cases will likely reach the lower courts soon. The issue raised will be a possible violation of the right to privacy rather than a Fourth Amendment violation, although that will also be raised.

It is fitting that this discussion of electronic surveillance in law enforcement end with a statement from Valeri Caproni, general counsel of the FBI, in her testimony before the House Judiciary Committee, Subcommittee on Crime, Terrorism, and Homeland Security, on February 17, 2011. She said:

> The government's consideration of its electronic surveillance challenges must account for the complexity and variety of today's merging communications services and technologies. The complexity and variety creates a range of opportunities and challenges for law enforcement. On the one hand, increased communications affords law enforcement potential access to more information relevant to preventing and solving crime. On the other hand, the pace of technological change means that law enforcement must update or develop new electronic surveillance techniques on a far more frequent basis, as existing tools will become obsolete quicker than ever before. In this setting, federal law enforcement faces new challenges on an ongoing basis. At the same time, state and local law enforcement agents, which traditionally have fewer technical resources necessary to perform lawful electronic surveillance, increasingly need to rely upon the federal government to serve as a central source of expertise.

HIGHLIGHT ＞ Do You Approve of Police Using Tiny Cameras to Record Their Interactions with the Public?

The use by the police of tiny cameras in day-to-day patrol work is seen in some quarters as a desirable prospect for the future of policing. A tiny camera is worn by the police and records what happens, among other things, in an encounter between the police and the public. Recording what the police do has been used by members of the public for a long time, but until the coming of tiny cameras, the police had not really gone into routinely recording what they do when they deal with the public because of the cost involved. Cameras, however, have gotten smaller, cheaper, and can store a lot of data. While a camera costs around $5,700, it is still considered cost-effective compared to the millions of dollars a department might spend in liability lawsuits.

Moreover, it is likely an effective control on possible officer misbehavior.

One police chief says, "There is no doubt in my mind that this is the wave of the future in policing. If we've got a way to actually record the events as they unfold, what better evidence is there for us to bring forward?" Once the picture is recorded, it is transmitted by the camera company to a secure site where nobody can tamper with it. It becomes a permanent and reliable record.[13] Critics maintain, however, that this practice raises privacy concerns and can be misused. What do you think?

Source: Based on "Tiny Cameras Seen as Future in Police Work," *USA Today*, February 16, 2010, p. 3A.

THE WAR ON TERROR

The tragic events of September 11, 2001, have left a deep and lasting effect on law enforcement. The war on terror and national security are primarily the responsibility of the federal government, but law enforcement officers on the state and local levels are also involved. One observer notes that "the problem of terrorism brings the need for preemptive, offensive policing to a new level. If law enforcement simply responds, it will have little impact on the prevention of terrorism. . . . If state and local agencies shift to offensive thinking and action . . . police contact with potential terrorists will increase."[14] As the threat of terrorism continues, local and state law enforcement agencies have become more involved with national law enforcement agencies to ensure that future attacks are minimized, if not completely prevented. Thus far those efforts have succeeded.

What is terrorism? There is no generally accepted international law definition, but the FBI defines it as "the unlawful use of force and violence against persons or property to intimidate or coerce a government, the civilian population or any segment thereof, in the furtherance of political or social objectives."[15] Even before the events of 9/11, the United States had legislation that punished terrorists and blunted the effects of terrorism. Among the earliest laws is FISA, passed in 1978, which authorized wiretaps in the interest of foreign intelligence. A more significant law is the Antiterrorism and Effective Death Penalty Act (AEDPA) of 1996, passed as a response to the Oklahoma bombing and the 1993 bombing of the World Trade Center in New York. The AEDPA authorizes the Secretary of State to identify and label an organization as terrorist if it meets certain criteria. It also seeks to prevent financial contributions to terrorist organizations and makes it difficult for a criminal alien to apply for a waiver of deportation. Two other major laws have been passed by the Congress of the United States since 9/11. These are the USA PATRIOT Act and the law creating the Department of Homeland Security.

The USA PATRIOT Act

Six weeks after the tragic events of 9/11, Congress passed a 342-page law proposed by the Bush administration just eight days after the destruction of the World Trade Center buildings. It became effective on February 1, 2002. The comprehensive law is titled the Uniting and Strengthening America by Providing Appropriate Tools Required to Intercept and Obstruct Terrorism Act of 2001. It is, however, more popularly known by its acronym, the **USA PATRIOT Act**. The law has more than 1,000 antiterrorism provisions that are subdivided into ten titles. First passed in 2001, the USA PATRIOT Act has since undergone many renewals and amendments.

Many provisions of the original USA PATRIOT Act of 2001 expired on December 31, 2005. Before its expiration, however, Congress extended the act to February 3, 2006, and then extended it again to March 10, 2006. After intense negotiations and a series of compromises with Congress, President George W. Bush signed the new USA PATRIOT Act on March 9, 2006. On May 26, 2011, President Barack Obama signed a four-year extension of three key provisions of the act involving roving wiretaps, searches of business records, and conducting surveillance of individuals suspected of terrorist-related activities not linked to terrorist groups. The USA PATRIOT Act was not renewed by Congress in June 2015, but at the time of this writing Congress was working on the creation of a new statutory scheme to replace the USA PATRIOT Act.

In general, the USA PATRIOT Act increases the surveillance power of the government in four areas[16]:

1. *Record searches*. It expands the government's ability to look at records on an individual's activity being held by third parties.
2. *Secret searches*. It expands the government's ability to search private property without notice to the owner.
3. *Intelligence searches*. It expands a narrow exception to the Fourth Amendment that has been created for the collection of foreign intelligence information.
4. *"Trap and trace" searches*. It expands another Fourth Amendment exception for spying that collects "addressing" information about the origin and destination of communication, as opposed to the content."

Summary of the Current USA PATRIOT Act Following is a brief outline and summary of the provisions of the current USA PATRIOT Act, taken from the U.S. Department of Justice website. It provides a quick glimpse at what the law contains.[17] The legislation specifies the ways whereby the war on terror is conducted, as follows:

1. The Patriot Act allows for investigators to use the tools that were already available to investigate organized crime and drug trafficking.

   - Allows law enforcement to use surveillance against more crimes of terror.
   - Allows federal agents to follow sophisticated terrorists trained to evade detection.
   - Allows law enforcement to conduct investigations without tipping off terrorists.
   - Allows federal agents to ask a court for an order to obtain business records in national security terrorism cases.

2. The Patriot Act facilitated information sharing and cooperation among government agencies so that they can better "connect the dots."

USA PATRIOT Act
acronym for the 2001 antiterrorism law, Uniting and Strengthening America by Providing Appropriate Tools Required to Intercept and Obstruct Terrorism Act of 2001, and subsequent amendments.

3. The Patriot Act updated the law to reflect new technologies and new threats.
4. The Patriot Act increased the penalties for those who commit terrorist crimes.

   ◆ Prohibits the harboring of terrorists.
   ◆ Enhanced the maximum penalties for various crimes likely to be committed by terrorists.
   ◆ Enhanced a number of conspiracy penalties.
   ◆ Punishes terrorist attacks on mass transit systems.
   ◆ Punishes bioterrorists.
   ◆ Eliminates the statutes of limitations for certain terrorism-related crimes and lengthens them for other terrorist-related crimes.

   The government publication concludes by saying: "The government's success in preventing another catastrophic attack on the American homeland since September 11, 2001, would have been much more difficult, if not impossible, without the USA Patriot Act."

The USA PATRIOT Act and subsequent amendments embody some of the more controversial and far-reaching laws ever passed by the U.S. Congress. They have the potential to modify current Court decisions on the Fourth Amendment, particularly those involving foreigners, nonresidents, and enemy combatants. Despite modifications and changes to the original law, challenges in court to the USA PATRIOT Act will continue in forthcoming years because some groups believe that the provisions of the law give too much power to the government at the expense of Fourth Amendment rights and the right to privacy.

The Department of Homeland Security

Department of Homeland Security
consolidated twenty-two federal agencies; its purpose is to secure the homeland from terrorist attacks.

The **Department of Homeland Security** was created by law in 2002 as another response to the events of September 11, 2001. Before that, there were twenty-two federal agencies that took care of security in the United States. Its overall purpose is to "mobilize and organize our nation to secure the homeland from terrorist attacks."[18] Its responsibilities are[19]:

◆ Prevent terrorism and enhance security
◆ Enforce and administer immigration laws
◆ Ensure resilience to disasters
◆ Secure and manage U.S. borders
◆ Safeguard and secure cyberspace
◆ Create a unified and integrated Department

The Homeland Security Act creates a cabinet-level position and brings together twenty-two federal agencies with widely varying histories and missions. (See Figure 15.1.) Among them are the Coast Guard, the Secret Service, the federal security guards in airports, and the Customs and Border Protection agency. It includes many of the organizations under which the powers of the USA PATRIOT Act are exercised. As of 2012, it had more than 240,000 employees and a budget of more than $40 billion. It aims to "improve security along and within the nation's borders, strengthen the ability of federal, state and local authorities to respond to an attack, better focus research into

Section 213. Authority for Delaying Notice of the Execution of a Warrant

This is more popularly known as the "sneak-and-peak" provision of the USA PATRIOT Act.

Section 3103a of title 18, United States Code, is amended–
(1) by inserting '(a) IN GENERAL ' before 'In addition'; and (2) by adding at the end the following:
'(b) DELAY– With respect to the issuance of any warrant or court order under this section, or any other rule of law, to search for and seize any property or material that constitutes evidence of a criminal offense in violation of the laws of the United States, any notice required, or that may be required, to be given may be delayed if
'(1) the court finds reasonable cause to believe that providing immediate notification of the execution of the warrant may have an adverse result (as defined in section 2705);
'(2) the warrant prohibits the seizure of any tangible property, any wire or electronic communication (as defined in section 2510), or, except as expressly provided in chapter 121, any stored wire or electronic information, except where the court finds reasonable necessity for the seizure; and
'(3) the warrant provides for the giving of such notice within a reasonable period of its execution, which period may thereafter be extended by the court for good cause shown.'

Section 214. Pen Register and Trap and Trace Authority under FISA

This is more popularly known as the "Trap-and-Trace" provision of the USA PATRIOT Act.

(a) APPLICATIONS AND ORDERS- Section 402 of the Foreign Intelligence Surveillance Act of 1978 (50 U.S.C. 1842) is amended–
(1) in subsection (a)(1), by striking 'for any investigation to gather foreign intelligence information or information concerning international terrorism' and inserting 'for any investigation to obtain foreign intelligence information not concerning a United States person or to protect against international terrorism or clandestine intelligence activities, provided that such investigation of a United States person is not conducted solely upon the basis of activities protected by the first amendment to the Constitution';

(2) by amending subsection (c)(2) to read as follows:
'(2) a certification by the applicant that the information likely to be obtained is foreign intelligence information not concerning a United States person or is relevant to an ongoing investigation to protect against international terrorism or clandestine intelligence activities, provided that such investigation of a United States person is not conducted solely upon the basis of activities protected by the first amendment to the Constitution.';
(3) by striking subsection (c)(3); and
(4) by amending subsection (d)(2)(A) to read as follows:
'(A) shall specify–
'(i) the identity, if known, of the person who is the subject of the investigation;
'(ii) the identity, if known, of the person to whom is leased or in whose name is listed the telephone line or other facility to which the pen register or trap and trace device is to be attached or applied;
'(iii) the attributes of the communications to which the order applies, such as the number or other identifier, and, if known, the location of the telephone line or other facility to which the pen register or trap and trace device is to be attached or applied and, in the case of a trap and trace device, the geographic limits of the trap and trace order.'.
(b) AUTHORIZATION DURING EMERGENCIES- Section 403 of the Foreign Intelligence Surveillance Act of 1978 (50 U.S.C. 1843) is amended--
(1) in subsection (a), by striking 'foreign intelligence information or information concerning international terrorism' and inserting 'foreign intelligence information not concerning a United States person or information to protect against international terrorism or clandestine intelligence activities, provided that such investigation of a United States person is not conducted solely upon the basis of activities protected by the first amendment to the Constitution'; and
(2) in subsection (b)(1), by striking 'foreign intelligence information or information concerning international terrorism' and inserting 'foreign intelligence information not concerning a United States person or information to protect against international terrorism or clandestine intelligence activities, provided that such investigation of a United States person is not conducted solely upon the basis of activities protected by the first amendment to the Constitution'.

nuclear, chemical and biological threats, and more rigorously assess intelligence about terrorists."[20]

The top priority of the Department of Homeland Security is "to prevent further terrorist attacks within the United States." But the department also plays the leading role in mitigating the aftermath of natural disasters and coordinating efforts to alleviate their impact. Thus, it played a big role, with mixed results, in coordinating the government's response to the Hurricane Katrina disaster in 2005.

Terrorism and the Police

Neither the USA PATRIOT Act nor the law creating the Department of Homeland Security defines the role of the police and local law enforcement agencies in the fight against terrorism. This reinforces the perception that terrorism is mainly viewed by legislatures and policy makers as a concern of national law enforcement agencies and not of local police departments. Nonetheless, various antiterrorism efforts are taking place on the local level. In his book *Homeland Security for Policing*, Willard M. Oliver of Sam Houston State University discusses the role of the police in homeland security. He observes: "In the aftermath of September 11th, there has been a near consensus that state and local police will play a role in homeland security, but that role has also been ill-defined.[21] He devotes the rest of the book to identifying the various strategic, operational, and tactical roles of state and local police agencies in homeland security. He concludes his book by saying: "A homeland security strategy for police should drive police operations and ultimately police tactics. It is imperative that police tactics evolve and change to meet the demands. Policing must learn to prevent future terrorist attacks by applying intelligence gathering to its standard operating procedures."[22]

Community Oriented Policing Services (COPS)
federal–local law enforcement program that promotes local police efforts to fight terrorism.

An example of federal-local law enforcement collaboration in connection with terrorism is **Community Oriented Policing Services (COPS)**. This program was in place prior to 9/11 and has many functions, but since 9/11 COPS has helped local law enforcement agencies strengthen their efforts against terrorism. According to an article by Glenn Rose, "When the Police Becomes the Arm of Homeland Security," it does this "by improving data and intelligence collection and processing, capitalizing on technology advancements, encouraging communication with other public agencies, and helping local agencies to respond to citizen fear and prepare to assist potential victims." Some local law enforcement departments are now mandated, by state law, ordinance, or agency policy, to actively participate in the effort of federal agencies to prevent terrorism and curtail illegal immigration. For example, the article notes that the police in Phoenix, Arizona, are reportedly required to "aggressively question people about their immigration status if they are pulled over on a minor traffic violation." The policy helps make the police become "the right hand of the Department of Homeland Security since they would turn over people to Customs Officers if they cannot produce proof that they are in the U.S. legally." The police in border cities in Arizona have also participated in law enforcement sweeps as part of the federal government's effort to curtail illegal immigration and minimize terrorism.[23]

FIGURE 15.1 U.S. Department of Homeland Security Organizational Chart

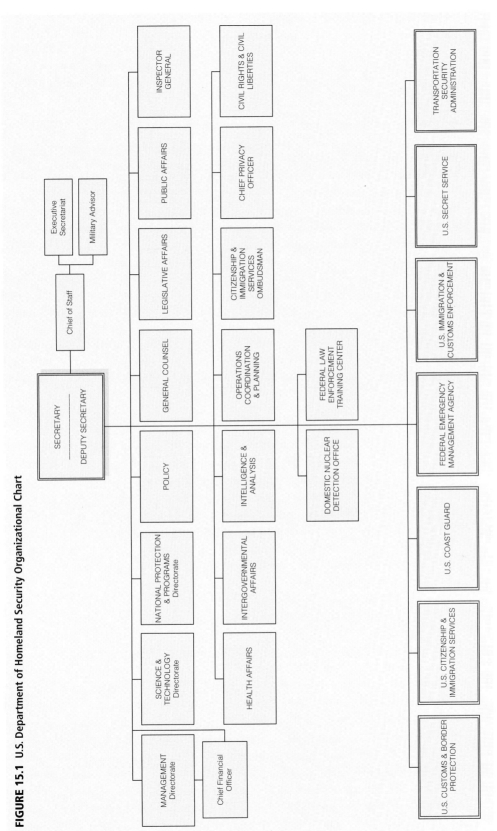

Source: http://www.dhs.gov/xlibrary/assets/dhs-orgchart.pdf

Legal Issues in the War on Terror

The broad sweep of the various laws, administrative rules, practices, and regulations aimed at curtailing terrorism has predictably spawned challenges that have found their way into U.S. courts. Issues that have generated legal challenges include those that follow:

◆ Does the military have the power to indefinitely detain persons suspected of terrorism even if they are U.S. citizens?
◆ Who is an enemy combatant?
◆ Are terror suspects who are also U.S. citizens to be treated as enemy combatants or as common criminals?
◆ Can deportation hearings for terror suspects be held behind closed doors?
◆ Can U.S. citizens in military prisons be blocked from their access to lawyers or federal courts after designating them "enemy combatants"?
◆ Can visa holders be held in detention in an effort to track down potential terrorists?
◆ Can immigration officers focus selectively on nationals from certain countries for closer immigration scrutiny?

Hamdi v. Rumsfeld (2004)

On June 28, 2004, the U.S. Supreme Court decided three cases involving terrorism and its aftermath. In the first case, *Hamdi v. Rumsfeld*, 542 U.S. 507 (2004), the Court held that due process requires that a U.S. citizen who is detained for allegedly fighting against the United States in Afghanistan as an enemy combatant should be given a meaningful opportunity to contest the factual basis for his detention before a neutral decision maker. In this case, Yaser Esam Hamdi, a U.S. citizen of Saudi descent, was released and deported to Saudi Arabia after renouncing his citizenship by prior agreement after his case was decided by the Court.

Rasul v. Bush (2004)

In the second case, *Rasul v. Bush*, 542 U.S. 466 (2004), the Court held that courts in the United States have the power to hear cases challenging the legality of the detention of foreign nationals captured abroad in connection with the fighting in Afghanistan and their detention in the Guantánamo Bay Detention Center, in Cuba.

Rumsfeld v. Padilla (2004)

In the third case, *Rumsfeld v. Padilla*, 542 U.S. 426 (2004), the Court held that it lacked jurisdiction in a petition filed by a detainee, a U.S. citizen, because the U.S. secretary of state, against whom the petition was brought, was not the immediate custodian of the detainee and therefore was not the person against whom the habeas should be filed. In this case, Jose Padilla, a U.S. citizen, was held in a navy detention center in South Carolina as an enemy combatant.

Hamdan v. Rumsfeld (2006)

A fourth case, decided by the Court in 2006, held that the president of the United States does not have the power to establish military tribunals without authority from Congress. The Court added that the procedures set up by the Bush administration failed to meet the standards of the U.S. Military Code of Justice and the Geneva Conventions for prisoners of war (*Hamdan v. Rumsfeld*, 548 U.S. 557 [2006]). The Court also held that Article 3 of the Third Geneva Convention was violated by the United States.

Munaf v. Geren (2008)

On June 12, 2008, the Court decided two cases that constituted legal setbacks to the government's war on terror. In the first case, the Court rejected the government's argument that U.S. federal courts lack jurisdiction over the detainees' habeas petitions (*Munaf v. Geren*, 553 U.S. 674 [2008]). This case involved two U.S. citizens, Shawqi Omar and Mohammad Munaf, who traveled to Iraq and allegedly took part in violence against the U.S. forces there. They were captured and placed in the custody of the U.S. military. The government had argued that U.S. federal courts had no jurisdiction over the habeas petitions filed by their families because Omar and Munaf were, in effect, prisoners of the multinational force in Iraq and not of the U.S. government. The Court concluded that the provisions of the U.S. habeas statute applied to persons held in custody as long as such custody was "under the color of the authority of the United States." The fact that custody was technically under the multinational force in Iraq did not matter because that force was under the authority and command of the United States.

In the second and more significant case, the Court ruled that prisoners at the Guantánamo Bay Detention Center, in Cuba, have a constitutional right to challenge their detention in federal court, even though they are not U.S. citizens. The Court held unconstitutional a provision of the Military Commissions Act, passed by the government in 2006, that deprived federal courts of jurisdiction to "hear habeas corpus petitioners from the detainees seeking to challenge their designation as enemy combatants" (*Boumedienne v. Bush*, 553 U.S. 723 [2008]). The Court held that the procedure provided by U.S. law "falls short of being a constitutionally adequate substitute" because

Boumedienne v. Bush (2008)

HIGHLIGHT ⟩ U.S. Law Enforcement and Narcoterrorism

In 1983, the then-president of Peru, Fernando Belaúnde Terry, first used the term *narcoterrorism*. He was referring to "the attempts of narcotics traffickers to influence the policies of a government or a society through violence and intimidation, and to hinder the enforcement of the law and the administration of justice by the systemic threat or use of such violence." *Narcoterrorism* is currently used to refer to the activities of "known terrorist organizations that engage in drug trafficking activity to fund their operations and gain recruits and expertise." The term is also used to refer the activities of terrorists in their violent reaction to the war on drugs by the United States government.*

In a testimony before the U.S. Representatives Subcommittee on Terrorism, Nonproliferation and Trade on October 12, 2011, Vanda Felbab-Brown, an expert on the subject, addresses the relationship between drug trade and criminal and belligerent groups in Afghanistan, Mexico, Columbia, and West Africa. In this testimony, Felbab-Brown said:

> The priority for the United States and the international community needs to be to combat the most disruptive and dangerous networks of organized crime and belligerency: those with the greatest links or potential links to international terrorist groups with global reach and those that are most rapacious and predatory to the society and equitable state and most concentrate rents from illicit economies to a narrow clique of people.†

In her testimony Felbab-Brown cautioned, however, that indiscriminate and hasty application of law enforcement can generate undesirable outcomes, which include:

> First, the weakest criminal groups can be eliminated through such an approach with law enforcement inadvertently increasing the efficiency, lethality, and coercive and corruption power of the remaining criminal groups operating in the region, and, second, such an application of law enforcement without prioritization can indeed push criminal groups into an alliance with terrorist groups—the opposite of what should be the purpose of law enforcement and especially outside policy intervention.

Thus, she cautioned the United States against "rushing to assistance whenever organized crime reaches visibility." Instead, she said the United States "needs to engage in law enforcement, anti-organized crime, counternarcotics, and counterterrorism assistance with extreme caution." She concluded with two proposals: "First, international assistance should be carefully calibrated to the absorptive capacity of the partner country" and "second, the international policy package needs to include a focus on broad state-building and on fostering good governance."‡

* "Narcoterrorism," Wikipedia, http://en.wikipedia.org/wiki/Narcoterrorism.

† "Narcoterrorism and the Long Reach of U.S. Law Enforcement." Testimony before the U.S. House of Representatives Subcommittee on Terrorism, Nonproliferation and Trade, by Vanda Felbab-Brown, author of *Shooting Up: Counterinsurgency and the War on Drugs.*

‡ Ibid.

it did not satisfy the "fundamental procedural protections of habeas corpus." This case is significant because at the time it was decided there were 200 habeas petitions awaiting disposition in federal district courts that had been filed by detainees at the Guantánamo Bay Detention Center.

In sum, the major decisions of the Court involving the war on terror and the war in Iraq have gone against the federal government, in effect saying that the provisions of the Constitution and federal laws apply to combatants, whether they be U.S. citizens or foreign nationals, who are involved in the war on terror.

Prospects

The United States has passed laws and crafted administrative regulations that form the core of the country's immediate responses to the terrorist attacks of September 11, 2001. As the laws summarized previously show, they are comprehensive, complex, and controversial. More laws and administrative regulations will be issued as the country experiences further terrorist threats or attacks and pursues the war on terror. Predictably, government responses have raised and will continue to raise constitutional and legal issues that the courts will have to resolve. Judicial decisions thus far have been mixed, indicating that although the courts are willing to give the government expanded power because of national security risks, some limits must be drawn, particularly if they affect citizens instead of foreign nationals. More cases will find their way to the Court, which has the task of striking a balance between national security and constitutional rights. Given the current composition of the Court and the compelling need for national security, it will not be surprising if the government prevails in many of the forthcoming 9/11 legal battles.

SUMMARY

- The old concept of electronic surveillance held that it violated the Fourth Amendment only if it involved trespass to property. The new concept holds that electronic surveillance is unconstitutional if it violates a reasonable expectation of privacy. Under the new concept, there is no need for trespass.
- Four federal laws govern electronic surveillance: Title III of the Omnibus Crime Control and Safe Streets Act of 1968, ECPA, CALEA, and FISA.
- The use of pen registers does not violate the Fourth Amendment, but the warrantless installation of a GPS on a motor vehicle to monitor its movements constitutes unreasonable search and seizure.

- Terrorism is defined as "the unlawful use of force and violence against persons or property to intimidate or coerce a government, the civilian population or any segment thereof, in the furtherance of political or social objectives."
- The USA PATRIOT Act (a series of laws passed by Congress) has greatly expanded the authority of federal, state, and local law enforcement to conduct searches and seizures, all aimed at enhancing the war on terror.
- The Department of Homeland Security brings together twenty-two federal agencies and is the main agency tasked with securing the United States from terrorist attacks.
- Federal laws do not clearly define the role of the police in the war on terror, but collaborative

activities are on-going between federal and local agencies.

◆ Many new legal issues have arisen related to terrorism and are being addressed by the courts.

REVIEW QUESTIONS

1. Distinguish between the old and the new concepts of electronic surveillance. In your opinion, which concept best respects individual privacy?
2. What does the case of *Katz v. United States* (1967) say, and why is this case important?
3. Give a summary of the following laws: Title III of the Omnibus Crime Control and Safe Streets Act of 1968, FISA, ECPA, CALEA, and FISA.
4. Under Title III of the Omnibus Crime Control and Safe Streets Act of 1968, law enforcement authorities cannot tap or intercept wire communications or use electronic devices to intercept private conversations, except in two situations. What are those situations? Discuss each.
5. How has the Foreign Intelligence Surveillance Act (FISA) of 1978, as amended, greatly expanded the authority of the government to gather surveillance intelligence?
6. Is your use of a cell phone protected by the Fourth Amendment? Is the use of cell phones similar to or different from your use of landline telephones under the Fourth Amendment? Explain your answer.
7. Give some of the main provisions of the USA PATRIOT Act. How has it expanded the authority of law enforcement agencies to search and seize?
8. Discuss how local police departments and federal law enforcement have cooperated and collaborated in the war on terror. How can those efforts be further improved?
9. Should government agents be allowed to tap the telephones of suspected terrorists without a warrant? Justify your answer based on the Fourth Amendment and the right to privacy.
10. What collaborative efforts, if any, are ongoing in your community between the local police and federal law enforcement on the war on terror? If you are not aware of any such efforts, visit your local police department for information.

TEST YOUR UNDERSTANDING

1. Fred lives in a rural area near Denver, Colorado. The police suspect he is a drug dealer. One day, when Fred's car was in a repair shop, the police attached an electronic beeper to it. They monitored the beeper for a few days and through it obtained information that Fred traveled many miles each day to a certain suspicious location; in addition, they obtained information from a reliable informant that Fred had suspicious cans and barrels in his home garage. Acting on this information, the police obtained a warrant to search Fred's house and garage. The judge issues the warrant. Was this issuance of a search warrant valid? Justify your answer.
2. Joe is an American who obtained his citizenship two years ago. He was recently caught fighting against U.S. forces in Iraq. He says that he is not a member of al-Qaeda but sympathizes with the cause of the Afghanistan people and is fighting to terminate U.S. presence in that country. He was brought to the Guantánamo Bay Detention Center and has been detained there for the past six months. Questions: Is Joe entitled to access to U.S. civilian courts, or is his case to be tried and resolved in military courts? Can Joe be detained indefinitely under army custody, assuming indefinite detention of enemy combatants is allowed under U.S. military law? Is Joe entitled to a civilian lawyer during trial like any other U.S. citizen who is tried for a serious crime? Finally, are his rights the same as or different from rights given to non-Americans captured in Afghanistan while fighting against U.S. military forces?
3. Paul is a police officer in Buffalo, New York, who suspects that one of his neighbors is in contact with foreign agents abroad and may be plotting to attack U.S. cities. Paul goes to the court to ask permission to wiretap his neighbor's home, but the court refuses authorization, saying that there is no probable cause to believe a crime has taken place. Paul later befriends the live-in girlfriend of the neighbor in question, and she gives Paul permission to wiretap their landline telephone. With the help of other police officers, Paul wiretaps the neighbor-suspect's home based on the consent given and, in fact, obtains

incriminating evidence. You are a judge in the court where a lawsuit has been brought for allegedly violating the neighbor-suspect's rights. Who wins this lawsuit and why? Answer based on federal and state law.

RECOMMENDED READINGS

Willard M. Oliver. *Homeland Security for Policing* (Upper Saddle River, NJ: Pearson Prentice Hall, 2007).

Richard H. Ward, Kathleen L. Kiernan, and Daniel Mabrey. *Homeland Security: An Introduction* (Cincinnati, OH: Anderson Publishing, 2006).

National Conference of State Legislatures. "Electronic Surveillance Laws," *http://www.ncsl .org/programs/lis/cip/surveillance.htm*.

Kam C. Wong. *The U.S.A Patriot Act: A Policy of Alienation*. Michigan Journal of Race & Law 2006/10/01, vol. 12.

NOTES

1. Robert A. Fiatal, "The Electronic Communications and Privacy Act: Addressing Today's Technology" (Part I), *FBI Law Enforcement Bulletin*, February 1988, pp. 25–30; Robert A. Fiatal, "The Electronic Communications and Privacy Act: Addressing Today's Technology" (Part II), *FBI Law Enforcement Bulletin*, March 1988, pp. 26–30; Robert A. Fiatal, "The Electronic Communications and Privacy Act: Addressing Today's Technology" (Part III), *FBI Law Enforcement Bulletin*, April 1988, pp. 24–30.
2. Ibid., Part I, p. 25.
3. The Stanford Student Computer and Network Privacy Project, "Electronic Communications Privacy Act (ECPA)," http://www.stanford .edu/group/privacyproject/legal/Ecpa.html.
4. Ibid.
5. Communications Assistance for Law Enforcement Act of 1994, HR 4922, 103d Cong., 2d sess.
6. *Time Magazine*, February 12, 2000, p. 8.
7. Ibid.
8. Richard H. Ward, Kathleen L. Kiernan, and Daniel Mabrey, *Homeland Security: An Introduction* (Cincinnati, OH: Anderson Publishing Company, 2006), pp. 254–255.
9. *USA Today*, April 9, 2012, p. 3A.
10. Ibid.
11. *Houston Chronicle*, October 26, 2002, p. 14A; and *USA Today*, February 25, 2008, p. 6A.
12. "Learning to Live with Big Brother," *The Economist*, September 29, 2007, p. 62.
13. Source: *USA Today*, February 16, 2010, p. 3A.
14. Jonathan R. White, *Terrorism and Homeland Security*, 5th ed. (Mason, OH: Thomson/ Wadsworth, 2006), p. 279.
15. 18 U.S.C. Section 2331(1), as noted in Willard M. Oliver, *Home Security for Policing* (Upper Saddle River, NJ: Pearson Prentice Hall, 2007), p. 107.
16. American Civil Liberties Union, "Surveillance Under the USA PATRIOT Act: What Is the USA PATRIOT Act?" December 10, 2010, http:// www.aclu.org/national-security/surveillance- under-usa-patriot-act.
17. U.S. Department of Justice, "The USA PATRIOT Act: Preserving Life & Liberty," http://www .justice.gov/archive/11/highlights.htm.
18. U.S. Department of Homeland Security, "Strategic Plan—Securing Our Homeland," http://www.dhs.gov/xabout/strategicplan/.
19. U.S. Department of Homeland Security: "What We Do: Mission and Responsibilities," http:// www.dhs.gov/xabout/responsibilities.shtm.
20. Richard W. Stevenson, "Signing Homeland Security Bill, Bush Appoints Ridge as Secretary," *New York Times*, November 26, 2002.
21. Willard M. Oliver, *Homeland Security Policing* (Upper Saddle River, NJ: Pearson Prentice Hall, 2007), p. 131.
22. Ibid., p. 208.
23. Glenn Rose, "When the Police Becomes the Arm of *Homeland Security*," *Philippine News*, April 2–8, 2008, p. A2.

Appendix A

Thirty Suggestions on How to Be an Effective Witness

Note: This appendix is based on the work of John Scott Blonien, senior assistant attorney general of the state of Washington, with additions and modifications by the authors.

As a witness, you have an important job to do. In order for the court to make a correct decision and for justice to be served, the evidence in a case must be presented by all the parties in a truthful manner. Otherwise, the administration of justice is tainted and flawed.

All witnesses are required to take an oath "to tell the truth, the whole truth and nothing but the truth." There are two ways, however, to tell the truth. One is ineffectively—in a halting, stumbling, hesitant manner—which makes the court and the jury doubt your testimony. The other is effectively—in a confident, straightforward, and candid manner—which makes you a more credible and useful witness.

Here is a list of thirty suggestions to help you become a more effective witness. Go over this list before testifying.

1. **Be prompt.** Never keep the court and the jury waiting.
2. **Dress properly and be neat.** Do not wear gaudy or "loud" clothing or dark glasses. If your work requires a uniform, ask your attorney whether wearing a uniform while testifying is appropriate.
3. **When taking the oath, stand upright, pay attention, and say "I do" clearly.**
4. **Be serious.** Avoid laughing, giggling, or talking about the case in the hallway or restrooms of the courthouse.
5. **Be sincere and candid; do not bluff.** It is better to admit a mistake than to try to bluff your way through.
6. **Testify from memory, but do not try to memorize what you are going to say.** If you do that, your testimony will sound rehearsed and will not be as believable. You are allowed to consult the notes you made concerning the event about which you are testifying. Ordinarily, however, these notes are also available to the opposing attorney and will probably be referred to during cross-examination. Remember your notes well.
7. **Prior to your testimony, try to picture the scene, the objects there, the distances, and what happened.** This will make your recollection more

accurate. If the question is about distances or time, and your answer is only an estimate, be sure to say so.

8. **Speak clearly and loudly.** The person farthest away in the courtroom should be able to hear you. Remember to glance at the judge and the jury and to talk to them honestly and openly, as you would speak to a friend or neighbor. Direct your answers mostly to the jury rather than to the opposing lawyer, your own lawyer, or the judge.

9. **Listen carefully to the questions asked.** Do not appear too eager to respond. Pause briefly before answering, and then give a well-considered answer.

10. **Never try to answer a question you do not understand.** If you do not understand a question, politely ask the person posing the question to repeat it.

11. **Explain your answer, if necessary.** Do not be afraid to politely ask the judge to allow you to explain your answer, particularly if the question cannot be answered truthfully with a simple "yes" or "no."

12. **Answer simply and directly, and answer only the question asked.** Do not volunteer information not actually sought by the questioner.

13. **Keep your answer short and to the point.** Avoid long narration.

14. **If you feel you did not answer the question correctly, make your correction immediately.** If your answer was not clear, clarify it.

15. **If you can, give categorical, definite answers.** Avoid saying, "I think," "I believe," or "In my opinion." If you do not know, say so. If asked about details that a person is not likely to remember, it is best simply to say, "I do not remember." Do not bluff, guess, or speculate.

16. **Do not give conclusions or opinions, unless asked.** In a courtroom, only expert witnesses are usually allowed to give conclusions or opinions. The court and jury are interested only in the facts, not in an opinion or conclusion. For example, "X's death was caused by stab wounds" is stating an opinion. On the other hand, saying that you saw Y stab X is stating a fact, assuming that was what you saw happen.

17. **Avoid saying, "That is all of the conversation," or "Nothing else happened."** Instead say, "That is all I recall," or "That is all I remember happening." It is possible that after some thought you might remember something else.

18. **Be polite and courteous.** This suggestion applies even if the attorney questioning you is aggressive or rude. Do not be cocky or antagonistic, or else you will lose credibility with the judge and jury.

19. **Remember that you are sworn to tell the truth; tell it.** Admit every material truth even if it is not to the advantage of your side. Do not stop to figure out whether your answer will help or hurt your cause. Just answer the questions truthfully and to the best of your recollection.

20. **Be aware that you are likely to be asked about earlier statements you made, if any, related to the case.** This would include any statements you may have made in an affidavit, deposition, or earlier testimony. Listen carefully to what is being read or repeated, and give a truthful answer.

21. **Do not be afraid to admit that you made an earlier statement.** As much as possible, your answer should be consistent with your previous statement. However, if there are discrepancies between your earlier statement and your current testimony, admit them and, if you can, explain them.

22. **Try not to appear nervous.** Avoid mannerisms (such as touching your nose or eyeglasses, wiping your eyebrow, or covering your mouth), which convey the impression that you are scared or are not telling the truth.

23. **Never lose your temper or show irritation.** The opposing attorney may try to agitate or aggravate you on cross-examination, in hopes that you will lose your temper and say things that will hurt your cause. Keep your cool at all times.

24. **If you do not want to answer a question, do not ask the court whether you must answer it.** This might make the judge or jury think you have something to hide. If the court wants you to answer the question, do so.

25. **Do not look at the attorney for your side or at the judge for help.** If the question is improper, the attorney for your side will probably object to it or have your answer stricken from the record after it is given. Give the attorney for your side an opportunity to react to or object to the question asked. Pause before giving an answer.

26. **Do not argue with the opposing attorney.** It is the job of the lawyer for your side to do that.

27. **Do not nod your head for a "yes" or "no" answer.** Speak clearly so that the court reporter or a recording device can hear or pick up your answer.

28. **Do not be intimidated by questions about whether you have conferred with your lawyer.** The opposing attorney might ask you the following question: "Have you talked to anybody about this case?" If you say, "No," the jury will know that is probably not true, because good attorneys try to talk to a witness before he or she takes the stand. If you say, "Yes," the defense lawyer might imply that you have been told what to say. Be honest and say that you have talked with whomever you have talked with—an attorney, the victim, other witnesses—and that you simply told them what the facts were. Suppose the opposing lawyer asks, in a loud and mocking voice, "Do you mean to tell this honorable court that you discussed your testimony in this case with the district attorney?" If you did, simply answer, "Yes." Remember, there is nothing wrong with your discussing the facts of the case with your attorney; that is expected. What is wrong is your lawyer telling you what to say.

29. **Avoid any discussion of any kind with a juror or potential juror in or out of the courthouse.** Do not discuss the case with anyone at the courthouse other than your attorney, particularly if somebody is listening.

30. **When you leave the witness stand after testifying, act confident.** Do not smile, appear downcast, or exude an air of triumph.

The Constitution of the United States

WE THE PEOPLE OF THE UNITED STATES, IN ORDER TO FORM A MORE PERFECT UNION, ESTABLISH JUSTICE, INSURE DOMESTIC TRANQUILITY, PROVIDE FOR THE COMMON DEFENCE, PROMOTE THE GENERAL WELFARE, AND SECURE THE BLESSINGS OF LIBERTY TO OURSELVES AND OUR POSTERITY, DO ORDAIN AND ESTABLISH THIS CONSTITUTION FOR THE UNITED STATES OF AMERICA.

ARTICLE I

SECTION 1. All legislative Powers herein granted shall be vested in a Congress of the United States, which shall consist of a Senate and House of Representatives.

SECTION 2. The House of Representatives shall be composed of Members chosen every second Year by the People of the several States, and the Electors in each State shall have the Qualifications requisite for Electors of the most numerous Branch of the State Legislature.

No Person shall be a Representative who shall not have attained to the Age of twenty five Years, and been seven Years a Citizen of the United States, and who shall not, when elected, be an Inhabitant of that State in which he shall be chosen.

Representatives and direct Taxes shall be apportioned among the several States which may be included within this Union, according to their respective Numbers, which shall be determined by adding to the whole Number of free Persons, including those bound to Service for a Term of Years, and excluding Indians not taxed, three fifths of all other Persons. The actual Enumeration shall be made within three Years after the first Meeting of the Congress of the United States, and within every subsequent Term of ten Years, in such Manner as they shall by Law direct. The Number of Representatives shall not exceed one for every thirty Thousand, but each State shall have at Least one Representative; and until such enumeration shall be made, the State of New Hampshire shall be entitled to chuse three, Massachusetts eight, Rhode-Island and Providence Plantations one, Connecticut five, New-York six, New Jersey four, Pennsylvania eight, Delaware one, Maryland six, Virginia ten, North Carolina five, South Carolina five, and Georgia three.

When vacancies happen in the Representation from any State, the Executive Authority thereof shall issue Writs of Election to fill such Vacancies.

The House of Representatives shall chuse their Speaker and other Officers; and shall have the sole Power of Impeachment.

SECTION 3. The Senate of the United States shall be composed of two Senators from each State, chosen by the Legislature thereof, for six Years; and each Senator shall have one Vote.

Immediately after they shall be assembled in Consequence of the first Election, they shall be divided as equally as may be into three Classes. The Seats of the Senators of the first Class shall be vacated at the Expiration of the second Year, of the second Class at the Expiration of the fourth Year, and of the third Class at the Expiration of the sixth Year, so that one third may be chosen every second Year; and if Vacancies happen by Resignation, or otherwise, during the Recess of the Legislature of any State, the Executive thereof may make temporary Appointments until the next Meeting of the Legislature, which shall then fill such Vacancies.

No person shall be a Senator who shall not have attained to the Age of thirty Years, and been nine Years a Citizen of the United States, and who shall not, when elected, be an Inhabitant of that State for which he shall be chosen.

The Vice President of the United States shall be President of the Senate, but shall have no Vote, unless they be equally divided.

The Senate shall chuse their other Officers, and also a President pro tempore, in the Absence of the Vice President, or when he shall exercise the Office of President of the United States.

The Senate shall have the sole Power to try all Impeachments. When sitting for that Purpose, they shall be on Oath or Affirmation. When the President of the United States is tried, the Chief Justice shall preside: And no Person shall be convicted without the Concurrence of two thirds of the Members present. Judgment in Cases of Impeachment shall not extend further than to removal from Office, and disqualification to hold and enjoy any Office of honor, Trust or Profit under the United States: but the Party convicted shall nevertheless be liable and subject to Indictment, Trial, Judgment and Punishment, according to law.

SECTION 4. The Times, Places and Manner of holding Elections for Senators and Representatives, shall be prescribed in each State by the Legislature thereof; but the Congress may at any time by Law make or alter such Regulations, except as to the Places of chusing Senators.

The Congress shall assemble at least once in every Year, and such Meeting shall be on the first Monday in December, unless they shall by Law appoint a different Day.

SECTION 5. Each House shall be the Judge of the Elections, Returns and Qualifications of its own Members, and a Majority of each shall constitute a Quorum to do Business; but a smaller Number may adjourn from day to day, and may be authorized to compel the Attendance of absent Members, in such Manner, and under such Penalties as each House may provide.

Each House may determine the Rules of its Proceedings, punish its Members for disorderly Behaviour, and, with the Concurrence of two thirds, expel a Member.

Each House shall keep a journal of its Proceedings, and from time to time publish the same, excepting such Parts as may in their Judgment require Secrecy; and the Yeas and Nays of the Members of either House on any question shall, at the Desire of one fifth of those Present, be entered on the Journal.

Neither House, during the Session of Congress, shall, without the Consent of the other, adjourn for more than three days, nor to any other Place than that in which the two Houses shall be sitting.

SECTION 6. The Senators and Representatives shall receive a Compensation for their Services, to be ascertained by Law, and paid out of the Treasury of the United States. They shall in all Cases, except Treason, Felony and Breach of the Peace, be privileged from Arrest during their Attendance at the Session of their respective Houses, and in going to and returning from the same; and for any Speech or Debate in either House, they shall not be questioned in any other Place.

No Senator or Representative shall, during the Time for which he was elected, be appointed to any civil Office under the Authority of the United States, which shall have been created, or the Emoluments whereof shall have been encreased during such time; and no Person holding any Office under the United States, shall be a Member of either House during his Continuance in Office.

SECTION 7. All Bills for raising Revenue shall originate in the House of Representatives; but the Senate may propose or concur with Amendments as on other Bills.

Every Bill which shall have passed the House of Representatives and the Senate, shall, before it become a Law, be presented to the President of the United States; If he approve he shall sign it, but if not he shall return it, with his Objections to that House in which it shall have originated, who shall enter the Objections at large on their Journal, and proceed to reconsider it. If after such Reconsideration two thirds of that House shall agree to pass the Bill, it shall be sent, together with the Objections, to the other House, by which it shall likewise be reconsidered, and if approved by two thirds of that House, it shall become a Law. But in all such Cases the Votes of both Houses shall be determined by yeas and Nays, and the Names of the Persons voting for and against the Bill shall be entered on the Journal of each House respectively. If any Bill shall not be returned by the President within ten Days (Sundays excepted) after it shall have been presented to him, the Same shall be a Law, in like Manner as if he had signed it, unless the Congress by their Adjournment prevent its Return, in which Case it shall not be a Law.

Every Order, Resolution, or Vote to which the Concurrence of the Senate and House of Representatives may be necessary (except on a question of Adjournment) shall be presented to the President of the United States; and before the Same shall take Effect, shall be approved by him, or being disapproved by him, shall be repassed by two thirds of the Senate and House of Representatives, according to the Rules and Limitations prescribed in the Case of a Bill.

SECTION 8. The Congress shall have Power To lay and collect Taxes, Duties, Imposts and Excises, to pay the Debts and provide for the common Defence and general Welfare of the United States; but all Duties, Imposts and Excises shall be uniform throughout the United States.

To borrow Money on the Credit of the United States;

To regulate Commerce with foreign Nations, and among the several States, and with the Indian Tribes;

To establish an uniform Rule of Naturalization, and uniform Laws on the subject of Bankruptcies throughout the United States;

To coin Money, regulate the Value thereof, and of foreign Coin, and fix the Standard of Weights and Measures;

To provide for the Punishment of counterfeiting the Securities and current Coin of the United States;

To establish Post Offices and post Roads;

To promote the Progress of Science and useful Arts, by securing for limited Times to Authors and Inventors the exclusive Right to their respective Writings and Discoveries;

To constitute Tribunals inferior to the supreme Court;

To define and punish Piracies and Felonies committed on the high Seas, and Offences against the Law of Nations;

To declare War, grant letters of Marque and Reprisal, and make rules concerning Captures on Land and Water;

To raise and support Armies, but no Appropriation of Money to that Use shall be for a longer Term than two Years;

To provide and maintain a Navy;

To make rules for the Government and Regulation of the land and naval Forces;

To provide for calling forth the Militia to execute the Laws of the Union, suppress Insurrections and repel Invasions;

To provide for organizing, arming, and disciplining, the Militia, and for governing such Part of them as may be employed in the Service of the United States, reserving to the States respectively, the Appointment of the Officers, and the Authority of training the Militia according to the discipline prescribed by Congress;

To exercise exclusive Legislation in all Cases whatsoever, over such District (not exceeding ten Miles square) as may, by Cession of particular States, and the Acceptance of Congress, become the Seat of the Government of the United States, and to exercise like Authority over all Places purchased by the Consent of the Legislature of the State in which the Same shall be, for the Erection of Forts, Magazines, Arsenals, dock-Yards, and other needful Buildings;—And

To make all Laws which shall be necessary and proper for carrying into Execution the foregoing Powers, and all other Powers vested by this Constitution in the Government of the United States, or in any Department or Officer thereof.

SECTION 9. The Migration or Importation of such Persons as any of the States now existing shall think proper to admit, shall not be prohibited by the Congress prior to the Year one thousand eight hundred and eight, but a Tax or duty may be imposed on such Importation, not exceeding ten dollars for each Person.

The Privilege of the Writ of Habeas Corpus shall not be suspended, unless when in Cases of Rebellion or Invasion the public Safety may require it.

No Bill of Attainder or ex post facto Law shall be passed.

No Capitation, or other direct, Tax shall be laid, unless in Proportion to the Census or Enumeration herein before directed to be taken.

No Tax or Duty shall be laid on Articles exported from any State.

No Preference shall be given by any Regulation of Commerce or Revenue to the Ports of one State over those of another; nor shall Vessels bound to, or from, one State, be obliged to enter, clear, or pay Duties in another.

No money shall be drawn from the Treasury, but in Consequence of Appropriations made by Law; and a regular Statement and Account of the Receipts and Expenditures of all public Money shall be published from time to time.

No Title of Nobility shall be granted by the United States: And no Person holding any Office of Profit or Trust under them, shall, without the Consent of the Congress, accept of any present, Emolument, Office, or Title, of any kind whatever, from any King, Prince, or foreign State.

SECTION 10. No State shall enter into any Treaty, Alliance, or Confederation; grant Letters of Marque and Reprisal; coin Money; emit Bills of Credit; make any Thing but gold and silver Coin a Tender in Payment of Debts; pass any Bill of Attainder, ex post facto Law, or Law impairing the Obligation of Contracts, or grant any Title of Nobility.

No State shall, without the Consent of the Congress, lay any Imposts or Duties on Imports or Exports, except what may be absolutely necessary for executing its inspection Laws; and the net Produce of all Duties and Imposts, laid by any State on Imports or Exports, shall be for the Use of the Treasury of the United States; and all such Laws shall be subject to the Revision and Controul of the Congress.

No State shall, without the Consent of Congress, lay any Duty of Tonnage, keep Troops, or Ships of War in time of Peace, enter into any Agreement or Compact with another State, or with a foreign Power, or engage in War, unless actually invaded, or in such imminent Danger as will not admit of delay.

ARTICLE II

SECTION 1. The executive Power shall be vested in a President of the United States of America. He shall hold his Office during the Term of four Years, and, together with the Vice President, chosen for the same Term, be elected, as follows.

Each State shall appoint, in such Manner as the Legislature thereof may direct, a Number of Electors, equal to the whole Number of Senators and Representatives to which the State may be entitled in the Congress: but no Senator or Representative, or Person holding an Office of Trust or Profit under the United States, shall be appointed an Elector.

The Electors shall meet in their respective States, and vote by Ballot for two Persons, of whom one at least shall not be an Inhabitant of the same State with themselves. And they shall make a List of all the Persons voted for, and of the Number of Votes for each; which List they shall sign and certify, and transmit sealed to the Seat of the Government of the United States, directed to the President of the Senate. The President of the Senate shall, in the Presence of the Senate and House of Representatives, open all the Certificates, and the Votes shall then be counted. The Person having the greatest Number of Votes shall be the President, if such Number be a Majority of the whole Number of Electors appointed; and if there be more than one who have such Majority, and have an equal Number of Votes, then the House of Representatives shall immediately chuse by Ballot one of them for President; and if no Person have a Majority, then from the five highest on the List the said House shall in like Manner chuse the President. But in chusing the President, the Votes shall be taken by States, the Representation from each State having one Vote; A quorum for this Purpose shall consist of a Member or Members from two thirds of the States, and a Majority of all the States shall be necessary to a Choice. In every Case, after the Choice of the President, the Person having the greatest Number of Votes of the Electors shall be the Vice President. But if there should remain two or more who have equal Votes, the Senate shall chuse from them by Ballot the Vice President.

The Congress may determine the Time of chusing the Electors, and the Day on which they shall give their Votes; which Day shall be the same throughout the United States.

No Person except a natural born Citizen, or a Citizen of the United States, at the time of the Adoption of this Constitution, shall be eligible to the Office of President; neither shall any Person be eligible to that Office who shall not have attained to the Age of thirty five Years, and been fourteen Years a Resident within the United States.

In Case of the Removal of the President from Office, or of his Death, Resignation, or Inability to discharge the Powers and Duties of the said Office, the Same shall devolve on the Vice President, and the Congress may by Law provide for the Case of Removal, Death, Resignation or Inability, both of the President and Vice President, declaring what Officer shall then act as President, and such Officer shall act accordingly, until the Disability be removed, or a President shall be elected.

The President shall, at stated Times, receive for his Services, a Compensation, which shall neither be increased nor diminished during the Period for which he shall have been elected, and he shall not receive within that Period any other Emolument from the United States, or any of them.

Before he enter on the Execution of his Office, he shall take the following Oath or Affirmation:—"I do solemnly swear (or affirm) that I will faithfully execute the Office of President of the United States, and will to the best of my Ability, preserve, protect and defend the Constitution of the United States."

SECTION 2. The President shall be Commander in Chief of the Army and Navy of the United States, and of the Militia of the several States, when called into the actual Service of the United States; he may require the Opinion, in writing, of the principal Officer in each of the executive Departments, upon any Subject relating to the Duties of their respective Offices, and he shall have Power to grant Reprieves and Pardons for Offenses against the United States, except in Cases of Impeachment.

He shall have Power, by and with the Advice and Consent of the Senate, to make Treaties, provided two thirds of the Senators present concur; and he shall nominate, and by and with the Advice and Consent of the Senate, shall appoint Ambassadors, other public Ministers and Consuls, Judges of the supreme Court, and all other Officers of the United States, whose Appointments are not herein otherwise provided for, and which shall be established by Law: but the Congress may by Law vest the Appointment of such inferior Officers, as they think proper, in the President alone, in the Courts of Law, or in the Heads of Departments.

The President shall have Power to fill up all Vacancies that may happen during the Recess of the Senate, by granting Commissions which shall expire at the End of their next Session.

SECTION 3. He shall from time to time give to the Congress Information of the State of the Union, and recommend to their Consideration such Measures as he shall judge necessary and expedient; he may, on extraordinary Occasions, convene both Houses, or either of them, and in Case of Disagreement between them, with Respect to the Time of Adjournment, he may adjourn them to such Time as he shall think proper; he shall receive Ambassadors and other public Ministers; he shall take Care that the Laws be faithfully executed, and shall Commission all the Officers of the United States.

SECTION 4. The President, Vice President and all civil Officers of the United States, shall be removed from Office on Impeachment for, and Conviction of, Treason, Bribery, or other high Crimes and Misdemeanors.

ARTICLE III

SECTION 1. The judicial Power of the United States shall be vested in one supreme Court, and in such inferior Courts as the Congress may from time to time ordain and establish. The Judges, both of the supreme and inferior Courts, shall hold their Offices during good Behaviour, and shall, at stated Times, receive for their Services a Compensation, which shall not be diminished during their Continuance in Office.

SECTION 2. The judicial Power shall extend to all Cases, in Law and Equity, arising under this Constitution, the Laws of the United States, and Treaties made, or which shall be made, under their Authority;—to all Cases affecting Ambassadors, other public Ministers and Consuls;—to all Cases of admiralty and maritime Jurisdiction;—to Controversies to which the United States shall be a Party;—to Controversies between two or more States;—between a State and Citizens of another State;—between Citizens of different States;—between Citizens of the same State claiming Lands under Grants of different States, and between a State, or the Citizens thereof, and foreign States, Citizens or Subjects.

In all Cases affecting Ambassadors, other public Ministers and Consuls, and those in which a State shall be Party, the supreme Court shall have original Jurisdiction. In all the other Cases before mentioned, the supreme Court shall have appellate Jurisdiction, both as to Law and Fact, with such Exceptions, and under such Regulations as the Congress shall make.

The Trial of all Crimes, except in Cases of Impeachment, shall be by Jury; and such Trial shall be held in the State where the said Crimes shall have been committed; but when not committed within any State, the Trial shall be at such Place or Places as the Congress may by Law have directed.

SECTION 3. Treason against the United States shall consist only in levying War against them, or in adhering to their Enemies, giving them Aid and Comfort. No Person shall be convicted of Treason unless on the Testimony of two Witnesses to the same overt Act, or on Confession in open Court. The Congress shall have Power to declare the Punishment of Treason, but no Attainder of Treason shall work Corruption of Blood, or Forfeiture except during the Life of the Person attainted.

ARTICLE IV

SECTION 1. Full Faith and Credit shall be given in each State to the public Acts, Records, and judicial Proceedings of every other State. And the Congress may by general Laws prescribe the Manner in which such Acts, Records and Proceedings shall be proved, and the Effect thereof.

SECTION 2. The Citizens of each State shall be entitled to all Privileges and Immunities of Citizens in the several States.

A Person charged in any State with Treason, Felony, or other Crime, who shall flee from Justice, and be found in another State, shall on Demand of the executive Authority of the State from which he fled, be delivered up, to be removed to the State having Jurisdiction of the Crime.

No person held to Service or Labour in one State, under the Laws thereof, escaping into another, shall, in Consequence of any Law or Regulation therein, be discharged from such Service or Labour, but shall be delivered up on Claim of the Party to whom such Service or Labour may be due.

SECTION 3. New States may be admitted by the Congress into this Union; but no new State shall be formed or erected within the Jurisdiction of any other State; nor any State be formed by the Junction of two or more States, or Parts of States, without the Consent of the Legislatures of the States concerned as well as of the Congress.

The Congress shall have Power to dispose of and make all needful Rules and Regulations respecting the Territory or other Property belonging to the United States; and nothing in this Constitution shall be so construed as to Prejudice any Claims of the United States, or of any particular State.

SECTION 4. The United States shall guarantee to every State in this Union a Republican Form of Government, and shall protect each of them against Invasion; and on Application of the Legislature, or of the Executive (when the Legislature cannot be convened) against domestic Violence.

ARTICLE V

The Congress, whenever two thirds of both Houses shall deem it necessary, shall propose Amendments to this Constitution, or, on the Application of the Legislatures of two thirds of the several States, shall call a Convention for proposing Amendments, which, in either Case, shall be valid to all Intents and Purposes, as Part of this Constitution, when ratified by the Legislatures of three fourths of the several States, or by Conventions in three fourths thereof, as the one or the other Mode of Ratification may be proposed by the Congress; Provided that no Amendment which may be made prior to the Year One thousand eight hundred and eight shall in any Manner affect the first and fourth Clauses in the Ninth Section of the first Article; and that no State, without its Consent, shall be deprived of its equal Suffrage in the Senate.

ARTICLE VI

All Debts contracted and Engagements entered into, before the Adoption of this Constitution, shall be as valid against the United States under this Constitution, as under the Confederation. This Constitution, and the Laws of the United States which shall be made in Pursuance thereof; and all Treaties made, or which shall be made, under the Authority of the United States, shall be the supreme Law of the Land; and the Judges in every State shall be bound thereby, any Thing in the Constitution or Laws of any State to the Contrary notwithstanding.

The Senators and Representatives before mentioned, and the Members of the several State Legislatures, and all executive and judicial Officers, both of the United States and of the several States, shall be bound by Oath or Affirmation, to support this Constitution; but no religious Test shall ever be required as a Qualification to any Office or public Trust under the United States.

ARTICLE VII

The Ratification of the Conventions of nine States, shall be sufficient for the Establishment of this Constitution between the States so ratifying the Same.

Done in Convention by the Unanimous Consent of the States present the Seventeenth Day of September in the Year of our Lord one thousand seven hundred and Eighty seven and of the Independence of the United States of America the Twelfth In witness whereof We have hereunto subscribed our Names,

AMENDMENTS TO THE CONSTITUTION
(The first ten Amendments were ratified December 15, 1791, and form what is known as the "Bill of Rights.")

AMENDMENT 1
Congress shall make no law respecting an establishment of religion, or prohibiting the free exercise thereof; or abridging the freedom of speech, or of the press; or the right of the people peaceably to assemble, and to petition the Government for a redress of grievances.

AMENDMENT 2
A well-regulated Militia, being necessary to the security of a free State, the right of the people to keep and bear Arms, shall not be infringed.

AMENDMENT 3
No Soldier shall, in time of peace be quartered in any house, without the consent of the Owner, nor in time of war, but in a manner to be prescribed by law.

AMENDMENT 4
The right of the people to be secure in their persons, houses, papers, and effects, against unreasonable searches and seizures, shall not be violated, and no Warrants shall issue, but upon probable cause, supported by Oath or

affirmation, and particularly describing the place to be searched, and the persons or things to be seized.

AMENDMENT 5

No person shall be held to answer for a capital, or otherwise infamous crime, unless on a presentment or indictment of a Grand Jury, except in cases arising in the land or naval forces, or in the Militia, when in actual service in time of War or public danger; nor shall any person be subject for the same offence to be twice put in jeopardy of life or limb; nor shall be compelled in any criminal case to be a witness against himself, nor be deprived of life, liberty, or property, without due process of law; nor shall private property be taken for public use without just compensation.

AMENDMENT 6

In all criminal prosecutions, the accused shall enjoy the right to a speedy and public trial, by an impartial jury of the State and district wherein the crime shall have been committed, which district shall have been previously ascertained by law, and to be informed of the nature and cause of the accusation; to be confronted with the witnesses against him; to have compulsory process for obtaining witnesses in his favor, and to have the Assistance of Counsel for his defence.

AMENDMENT 7

In Suits at common law, where the value in controversy shall exceed twenty dollars, the right of trial by jury shall be preserved, and no fact tried by a jury, shall be otherwise re-examined in any Court of the United States, than according to the rules of the common law.

AMENDMENT 8

Excessive bail shall not be required, nor excessive fines imposed, nor cruel and unusual punishments inflicted.

AMENDMENT 9

The enumeration in the Constitution, of certain rights, shall not be construed to deny or disparage others retained by the people.

AMENDMENT 10

The powers not delegated to the United States by the Constitution, nor prohibited by it to the States, are reserved to the States respectively, or to the people.

AMENDMENT 11

(Ratified February 7, 1795)

The Judicial power of the United States shall not be construed to extend to any suit in law or equity, commenced or prosecuted against one of the United States by Citizens of another State, or by Citizens or Subjects of any Foreign State.

AMENDMENT 12

(Ratified July 27, 1804)

The Electors shall meet in their respective states and vote by ballot for President and Vice President, one of whom, at least, shall not be an inhabitant of the same state with themselves; they shall name in their ballots the person voted for as President, and in distinct ballots the person voted for as Vice President, and they shall make distinct lists of all persons voted for as President, and of all persons voted for as Vice President, and of the number of votes for each, which lists they shall sign and certify, and transmit sealed to the seat of the Government of the United States, directed to the President of the Senate;—The President of the Senate shall, in the presence of the Senate and House of Representatives, open all the certificates and the votes shall then be counted;—The person having the greatest number of votes for President, shall be the President, if such number be a majority of the whole number of Electors appointed; and if no person have such majority, then from the persons having the highest numbers not exceeding three on the list of those voted for as President, the House of Representatives shall choose immediately, by ballot, the President. But in choosing the President, the votes shall be taken by States, the representation from each State having one vote; a quorum for this purpose shall consist of a member or members from two-thirds of the states, and a majority of all the states shall be necessary to a choice. And if the House of Representatives shall not choose a President whenever the right of choice shall devolve upon them, before the fourth day of March next following, then the Vice President shall act as President, as in case of the death or other constitutional disability of the President.—The person having the greatest number of votes as Vice President, shall be the Vice President, if such number be a majority of the whole number of Electors appointed, and if no person have a majority, then from the two highest numbers on the list, the Senate shall choose the Vice President; a quorum for the purpose shall consist of two-thirds of the whole number of Senators, and a majority of the whole number shall be necessary to a choice. But no person constitutionally ineligible to the office of President shall be eligible to that of Vice President of the United States.

AMENDMENT 13

(Ratified December 6, 1865)

SECTION 1. Neither slavery nor involuntary servitude, except as a punishment for crime whereof the party shall have been duly convicted, shall exist within the United States, or any place subject to their jurisdiction.

SECTION 2. Congress shall have power to enforce this article by appropriate legislation.

AMENDMENT 14

(Ratified July 9, 1868)

SECTION 1. All persons born or naturalized in the United States, and subject to the jurisdiction thereof, are citizens of the United States and of the State wherein they reside. No State shall make or enforce any law which shall abridge the privileges or immunities of citizens of the United States; nor shall any State deprive any person of life, liberty, or property, without due process of law; nor deny any person within its jurisdiction the equal protection of the laws.

SECTION 2. Representatives shall be apportioned among the several States according to their respective numbers, counting the whole number of persons in each State, excluding Indians not taxed. But when the right to vote at any election for the choice of Electors for President and Vice President of the United States, Representatives in Congress, the Executive and Judicial officers of a State, or the members of the Legislature thereof, is denied to any of the male inhabitants of such State, being twenty-one years of age, and citizens of the United States, or in any way abridged, except for participation in rebellion, or other crime, the basis of representation therein shall be reduced in the proportion which the number of such male citizens shall bear to the whole number of male citizens twenty-one years of age in such State.

SECTION 3. No person shall be a Senator or Representative in Congress, or elector of President and Vice President, or hold any office, civil or military, under the United States, or under any State, who, having previously taken an oath, as a member of Congress, or as an officer of the United States, or as a member of any State legislature, or as an executive or judicial officer of any State, to support the Constitution of the United States, shall have engaged in insurrection or rebellion against the same, or given aid or comfort to the enemies thereof. But Congress may by a vote of two-thirds of each House, remove such disability.

SECTION 4. The validity of the public debt of the United States, authorized by law, including debts incurred for payment of pensions and bounties for services in suppressing insurrection or rebellion, shall not be questioned. But neither the United States nor any State shall assume or pay any debt or obligation incurred in aid of insurrection or rebellion against the United States, or any claim for the loss or emancipation of any slave; but all such debts, obligations and claims shall be held illegal and void.

SECTION 5. The Congress shall have power to enforce, by appropriate legislation, the provisions of this article.

AMENDMENT 15

(Ratified February 3, 1870)

SECTION 1. The right of citizens of the United States to vote shall not be denied or abridged by the United States or by any State on account of race, color, or previous condition of servitude.

SECTION 2. The Congress shall have power to enforce this article by appropriate legislation.

AMENDMENT 16

(Ratified February 3, 1913)

The Congress shall have power to lay and collect taxes on incomes, from whatever sources derived, without apportionment among the several States, and without regard to any census or enumeration.

AMENDMENT 17

(Ratified April 8, 1913)

The Senate of the United States shall be composed of two Senators from each State, elected by the people thereof, for six years; and each Senator shall have one vote. The electors in each State shall have the qualifications requisite for electors of the most numerous branch of the State legislatures. When vacancies happen in the representation of any State in the Senate, the executive authority of such State shall issue writs of election to fill such vacancies: *Provided*, That the legislature of any State may empower the Executive thereof to make temporary appointments until the people fill the vacancies by election as the Legislature may direct.

This amendment shall not be so construed as to affect the election or term of any Senator chosen before it becomes valid as part of the Constitution.

AMENDMENT 18

(Ratified January 16, 1919. Repealed December 5, 1933, by Amendment 21)

SECTION 1. After one year from the ratification of this article the manufacture, sale, or transportation of intoxicating liquors within, the importation thereof into, or the exportation thereof from the United States and all territory subject to the jurisdiction thereof for beverage purposes is hereby prohibited.

SECTION 2. The Congress and the several States shall have concurrent power to enforce this article by appropriate legislation.

SECTION 3. This article shall be inoperative unless it shall have been ratified as an amendment to the Constitution by the Legislatures of the several States, as provided in the Constitution, within seven years from the date of the submission hereof to the States by the Congress.

AMENDMENT 19

(Ratified August 18, 1920)

The right of citizens of the United States to vote shall not be denied or abridged by the United States or by any State on account of sex.

Congress shall have power to enforce this article by appropriate legislation.

AMENDMENT 20

(Ratified January 23, 1933)

SECTION 1. The terms of the President and the Vice President shall end at noon on the 20th day of January, and the terms of Senators and Representatives at noon on the 3d day of January, of the years in which such terms would have ended if this article had not been ratified; and the terms of their successors shall then begin.

SECTION 2. The Congress shall assemble at least once in every year, and such meeting shall begin at noon on the 3d day of January, unless they shall by law appoint a different day.

SECTION 3. If, at the time fixed for the beginning of the term of the President, the President elect shall have died, the Vice President elect shall become President. If a President shall not have been chosen before the time fixed for the beginning of his term, or if the President elect shall have failed to qualify, then the Vice President elect shall act as President until a President shall have qualified; and the Congress may by law provide for the case wherein neither a President elect nor a Vice President shall have qualified, declaring who shall then act as President, or the manner in which one who is to act shall be selected, and such person shall act accordingly until a President or Vice President shall have qualified.

SECTION 4. The Congress may by law provide for the case of the death of any of the persons from whom the House of Representatives may choose a President whenever the right of choice shall have devolved upon them, and for the case of the death of any of the persons from whom the Senate may choose a Vice President whenever the right of choice shall have devolved upon them.

SECTION 5. Sections 1 and 2 shall take effect on the 15th day of October following the ratification of this article.

SECTION 6. This article shall be inoperative unless it shall have been ratified as an amendment to the Constitution by the legislatures of three-fourths of the several States within seven years from the date of its submission.

AMENDMENT 21

(Ratified December 5, 1933)

SECTION 1. The eighteenth article of amendment to the Constitution of the United States is hereby repealed.

SECTION 2. The transportation or importation into any State, Territory, or possession of the United States for delivery or use therein of intoxicating liquors, in violation of the laws thereof, is hereby prohibited.

SECTION 3. This article shall be inoperative unless it shall have been ratified as an amendment to the Constitution by conventions in the several States, as provided in the Constitution, within seven years from the date of the submission hereof to the States by the Congress.

AMENDMENT 22

(Ratified February 27, 1951)

SECTION 1. No person shall be elected to the office of the President more than twice, and no person who has held the office of President, or acted as President, for more than two years of a term to which some other person was elected President shall be elected to the office of President more than once. But this Article shall not apply to any person holding the office of President when this Article was proposed by Congress, and shall not prevent any person who may be holding the office of President, or acting as President, during the term within which this Article becomes operative from holding the office of President or acting as President during the remainder of such term.

SECTION 2. This article shall be inoperative unless it shall have been ratified as an amendment to the Constitution by the Legislatures of three-fourths of the several States within seven years from the date of its submission to the States by the Congress.

AMENDMENT 23

(Ratified March 29, 1961)

SECTION 1. The District constituting the seat of Government of the United States shall appoint in such manner as Congress may direct:

A number of electors of President and Vice President equal to the whole number of Senators and Representatives in Congress to which the District would be entitled if it were a State, but in no event more than the least populous State; they shall be in addition to those appointed by the States, but they shall be considered, for the purposes of the election of President and Vice President, to be electors appointed by a State; and they shall meet in the District and perform such duties as provided by the twelfth article of amendment.

SECTION 2. The Congress shall have power to enforce this article by appropriate legislation.

AMENDMENT 24

(Ratified January 23, 1964)

SECTION 1. The right of citizens of the United States to vote in any primary or other election for President or Vice President, for electors for President or Vice President, or for Senator or Representative in Congress, shall not be denied or abridged by the United States or any State by reason of failure to pay poll tax or any other tax.

SECTION 2. Congress shall have power to enforce this article by appropriate legislation.

AMENDMENT 25

(Ratified February 10, 1967)

SECTION 1. In case of the removal of the President from office or of his death or resignation, the Vice President shall become President.

SECTION 2. Whenever there is a vacancy in the office of the Vice President, the President shall nominate a Vice President who shall take office upon confirmation by a majority vote of both Houses of Congress.

SECTION 3. Whenever the President transmits to the President pro tempore of the Senate and the Speaker of the House of Representatives his written declaration that he is unable to discharge the powers and duties of his office, and until he transmits to them a written declaration to the contrary, such powers and duties shall be discharged by the Vice President as Acting President.

SECTION 4. Whenever the Vice President and a majority of either the principal officers of the executive departments or of such other body as Congress may by law provide, transmit to the President pro tempore of the Senate and the Speaker of the House of Representatives their written declaration that the President is unable to discharge the powers and duties of his office, the Vice President shall immediately assume the powers and duties of the office as Acting President.

Thereafter, when the President transmits to the President pro tempore of the Senate and the Speaker of the House of Representatives his written declaration that no inability exists, he shall resume the powers and duties of his office unless the Vice President and a majority of either the principal officers of the executive department or of such other body as Congress may by law provide, transmit within four days to the President pro tempore of the Senate and the Speaker of the House of Representatives their written declaration that the President is unable to discharge the powers and duties of his office. Thereupon Congress shall decide the issue, assembling within forty-eight hours for that purpose if not in session. If the Congress, within twenty-one days after receipt of the latter written declaration, or, if Congress is not in session within twenty-one days after Congress is required to assemble, determines by two-thirds vote of both houses that the President is unable to discharge the powers and duties of his office, the Vice President shall continue to discharge the same as Acting President; otherwise, the President shall resume the powers and duties of his office.

AMENDMENT 26

(Ratified July 1, 1971)

SECTION 1. The right of citizens of the United States, who are eighteen years of age or older, to vote shall not be denied or abridged by the United States or by any state on account of age.

SECTION 2. The Congress shall have power to enforce this article by appropriate legislation.

AMENDMENT 27

(Ratified May 7, 1992)

No law varying the compensation for the services of the Senators and Representatives shall take effect, until an election of Representatives shall have intervened.

Appendix C

The Top Twenty Cases in Criminal Procedure (A Subjective List Created by Two Professors)

1. *Katz v. United States* (reasonable expectation of privacy)
2. *Illinois v. Gates* (probable cause)
3. *Mapp v. Ohio* (exclusionary rule)
4. *Terry v. Ohio* (stop and frisk)
5. *Minnesota v. Dickerson* (stop and frisk)
6. *Chimel v. California* (arrest)
7. *United States v. Robinson* (arrest)
8. *Wilson v. Arkansas* (knock and announce rule)
9. *Payton v. New York* (arrest warrants)
10. *Oliver v. United States* (open fields)
11. *Schneckloth v. Bustamonte* (consent searches)
12. *Georgia v. Randolph* (consent searches)
13. *Carroll v. United States* (motor vehicle searches)
14. *United States v. Ross* (motor vehicle searches)
15. *New York v. Belton* (search incident to arrest in vehicles)
16. *Whren v. United States* (pretext stops)
17. *Miranda v. Arizona* (*Miranda* warnings)
18. *Schmerber v. California* (intrusive searches)
19. *United States v. Wade* (pretrial identification procedures)
20. *Tennessee v. Garner* (use of deadly force)

Glossary

abandonment: The giving up of a thing or item without limitation as to any particular person or purpose.

acting under color of law: Officer using power possessed by virtue of law.

acting within the scope of authority: When the officer is discharging the duties generally assigned.

actual seizure: The taking of a person into custody with the use of hands, force or firearms.

administrative searches: Searches conducted by government investigators to determine whether there are violations of government rules and regulations.

admission: Person admits to something related to the act but may not have committed it.

affirmation: The decision of the lower court is upheld on appeal.

Alford plea: A plea in which the defendant claims innocence yet pleads guilty for other reasons.

anticipatory search warrant: A warrant obtained based on probable cause and on an expectation that seizable items will be found at a certain place.

apparent authority principle: Appears to have authority but, in reality, does not.

arraignment: The appearance of an accused in court where he or she is informed of the charges and asked to plead.

arrest: The taking of a person into custody against his or her will for the purpose of criminal prosecution or interrogation.

arrest warrant: Writ issued by a duly authorized person that instructs a law enforcement officer to bring the person to a magistrate or judge in connection with an offense with which he or she has been charged.

assault: The attempt or threat to inflict bodily harm on another person.

bail: The security required by the court and given by the accused to ensure the accused's attendance in court at a specified time.

battery: The intentional infliction of harmful or offensive bodily contact.

bench warrant: A process issued by the court for the attachment or arrest of a person.

bifurcated procedure: A trial procedure where the guilt–innocence stage and the sentencing stage are separate.

bifurcated trial: The trial has two stages: The guilt or innocence stage and the punishment stage.

bill of indictment: A written accusation of a crime submitted to the grand jury by the prosecutor.

Bill of Rights: The first ten amendments to the U.S. Constitution.

blanket exceptions: Exceptions that apply to a certain type of case regardless of circumstances.

blended sentencing: Sentences given to juveniles that combine juvenile and adult sentences.

booking: Making an entry in the police blotter or arrest book indicating the suspect's name, the time of arrest, and the offense involved.

***Brady* rule:** The prosecutor has a duty to disclose evidence favorable to a defendant.

brain fingerprinting: Assesses a suspect's response to stimuli in the form of words or pictures presented on a computer monitor.

capias: A warrant issued by the court for an officer to take a defendant into custody.

case-by-case incorporation: Examines the facts of a specific case to determine whether there is an injustice so serious as to justify extending the provisions of the Bill of Rights to this particular case.

case citation: Indicates where a case may be found in legal publications.

case law: Law promulgated in cases decided by the courts.

challenge for cause: A challenge for the dismissal of a juror based on causes specified by law.

Chimel **rule:** A rule that allows police officers after an arrest to search the arrestee's "area of immediate control."

citation: An order issued by a court or law enforcement officer requiring the person to appear in court at a specified date to answer certain charges.

citizen's arrest: An arrest made by a citizen or nonlaw enforcement personnel without a warrant.

clearly established constitutional right: A right so established that a reasonable police officer would have known his or her act was unlawful.

collateral derivative evidence: Evidence of a secondary nature that is related to the case but not directly a part of it.

common law: Law generally derived from ancient usages and customs or from judgments and decrees of courts recognizing, affirming, and enforcing them.

Communications Assistance for Law Enforcement Act (CALEA) of 1994: Enacted to keep up with advances in telecommunications technology.

communicative self-incrimination: That which explicitly or implicitly relates a factual assertion or discloses information.

Community Oriented Policing Services (COPS): Federal-local law enforcement program that promotes local police efforts to fight terrorism.

community service: Places an offender in unpaid position with nonprofit or tax-supported agencies to perform a specified service.

complaint: A charge made before a proper law enforcement or judicial officer alleging the commission of a criminal offense.

concurrent sentence: Sentences served at the same time.

confession: Person says he or she committed the act.

consecutive sentence: Sentences served one after the other.

constructive seizure: Occurs without any physical touching, grabbing, holding, or use of force when the individual peacefully submits to the officer's will and control.

contemporaneous search: The search must occur at the time as, or very close in time and place to, the arrest.

court-appointed counsel: A defense lawyer appointed by the court for a defendant who is too poor to pay.

criminal procedure: The process followed by the police and the courts in the apprehension and punishment of criminals.

curtilage: The area to which extends the intimate activity associated with the "sanctity of a man's home, and the privacies of life."

custodial interrogation: An interrogation that takes place while a suspect is in custody.

custody: When the suspect is under arrest or deprived of freedom in a significant way.

Daubert **doctrine:** Allows the admission in court of expert testimony pertaining to scientific, technical, or other specialized knowledge that will assist the trier of fact to understand the evidence or to determine a fact in issue.

deadly force: Force that, when used, poses a high risk of death or serious injury to its human target.

deep pockets theory: Officers generally have limited financial resources, but the city, county, or municipality has deeper pockets of funds.

deliberate indifference: No fixed definition; generally a higher form of negligence than "mere indifference," but lower than "conduct that shocks the conscience."

Department of Homeland Security: Consolidated twenty-two federal agencies; its purpose is to secure the homeland from terrorist attacks.

deprived of freedom in a significant way: When a person's freedom of movement is limited by the police and a reasonable person in the same circumstances would feel he or she was in custody.

determinate sentence: A sentence that specifies the period of incarceration based on guidelines.

discovery: The procedure used in a case to obtain information from the other party.

discretionary act: An act that involves personal deliberation, decision, and judgment.

DNA testing: Compares a suspect's DNA with DNA recovered during the investigation.

double jeopardy: Being punished more than once for the same offense.

drug courier profile: A set of identifiers developed by law enforcement agencies describing the types of individuals who are likely to transport drugs.

dual court system: The United States has two court systems: one for federal cases and another for state cases.

dual sovereignty: Federal and state governments are both considered sovereign.

due process clause: Fundamental fairness.

Edwards **rule:** Once a suspect invokes the right to remain silent, he or she cannot be questioned again for the same offense unless he or she initiates further communication, exchanges, or conversation with the police.

Electronic Communications and Privacy Act (ECPA) of 1986: Amends and supplements the provisions of Title III.

electronic monitoring: An offender is placed on an electronic monitor that constantly tracks his or her location.

electronic surveillance: The use of electronic devices to monitor a person's activities or location.

en banc: As one body.

exclusionary rule: States that evidence obtained by the government in violation of the Fourth Amendment guarantee against unreasonable search and seizure is not admissible in a criminal prosecution to prove guilt.

Exculpatory evidence: Evidence that tends to show the defendant did not commit the crime charged.

exigent circumstances: Emergency circumstances that make obtaining a warrant impractical, useless, dangerous, or unnecessary, and that justify warrantless arrests or entries into homes or premises.

Extended border search: A search conducted some distance away from the border. Such searches are generally upheld by courts upon a showing of reasonable suspicion.

facial recognition technology: A way of identifying suspects by comparing driver's license photos with pictures of convicts in a high-tech analysis of chin widths and nose sizes.

factory surveys: Surprise visits to factories by officials to determine if employees are illegal aliens.

false arrest: When the officer makes an illegal arrest.

false imprisonment: When a person is placed in confinement without any valid reason.

felony: A crime usually punishable by death or imprisonment in a prison for more than one year.

fine: Monetary punishment.

fishing expedition: An act to see if some type of usable evidence can be found on the suspect.

Foreign Intelligence Surveillance Act (FISA) of 1978: Sets the procedure for foreign intelligence surveillance.

forfeiture: Taking away the property of an offender without compensation.

frisk: A pat-down for weapons.

fruit of the poisonous tree doctrine: Once the primary evidence is shown to have been unlawfully obtained, any secondary evidence derived from it is also inadmissible.

Frye **doctrine:** For scientific evidence to be admissible at trial, the procedures used must be sufficiently established to have gained general acceptance in the particular field to which they belong.

functional equivalent of an interrogation: Instances in which no questions are actually asked by the police but in which the circumstances are so conducive to making a statement or confession that the courts consider them to be the equivalent of interrogation.

general on-the-scene questioning: Questioning at the scene of the crime.

good faith: When an officer "acts in the honest belief that the action taken or the decision was appropriate under the circumstances."

good faith exception: Evidence obtained by the police is admissible even if there was an error or mistake, as long as the error or mistake was not committed by the police, or, if committed by the police, it was honest and reasonable.

grand jury: A jury that usually determines whether a person should be charged with an offense.

habeas corpus: A writ directed to a person detaining another commanding that person to produce the body of a person who is imprisoned or detained in court and explain why detention should be continued.

harmless error: The evidence erroneously admitted by the trial court did not contribute to the conviction and there is other evidence to support the verdict.

harmless error rule: A rule stating that an error made by the trial court in admitting illegally obtained evidence does not lead to a reversal of the conviction if the error is determined to be harmless. The prosecution has the burden of proving that the error is in fact harmless.

hung jury: A jury that cannot agree to convict or acquit an accused.

immunity: The person granted immunity will not be prosecuted in a criminal case.

inadvertence: The officer must have no prior knowledge that the evidence was present in the place; the discovery must be purely accidental.

incorporation controversy: Issue of whether the Bill of Rights protects the public only against violations of rights by federal officials or whether it also protects against violations of rights by state officials.

indemnification: Compensation for incurred hurt, loss, or damage.

independent source exception: Evidence obtained is admissible if the police can prove that it was obtained from an independent source not connected with the illegal search or seizure.

indeterminate sentence: A sentence that gives wide discretion to the sentencing authority.

indictment: A written accusation of a crime filed by the grand jury.

indigent defendant: A defendant who is too poor to hire a lawyer.

inevitable discovery exception: Evidence is admissible if the police can prove that they would inevitably have discovered the evidence anyway by lawful means.

information: A criminal charge filed by the prosecutor without the intervention of a grand jury.

intelligent waiver: One given by a suspect who knows what he or she is doing.

intensive probation: The probationer is supervised more closely than in regular probation.

intentional tort: Occurs when there is an intention on the part of the officer to bring some physical harm or mental coercion upon another person.

intermediate sanction: A sanction that is less severe and less costly than prison, but more restrictive than traditional probation.

interrogation: When the police ask questions that tend to incriminate or create the functional equivalent of an interrogation.

John Doe warrant: Issued when the person to be arrested is well described in the warrant, but not identified by name.

judge-made rule: A rule crafted by judges, not provided for in the Constitution.

judicial precedent: Decisions of courts have value as precedent for future cases similarly circumstanced.

judicial review: The power of courts to declare law or acts unconstitutional.

jurisdiction: The power of a court to try a case.

jury of peers: A jury that is not consciously restricted to a particular group.

jury nullification: When a jury decides a case contrary to the weight of the evidence presented during trial.

***Kirby* rule:** A person who has not been formally charged with an offense is not entitled to a lawyer during a lineup.

level of proof: The degree of certainty required by the law for an act by government agents to be legal.

lineup: A police identification procedure where the suspect is shown to a victim or witness for purposes of identification.

mandatory sentences: Sentences that must be imposed by the judge or jury; no deviation is allowed.

man of reasonable caution: Refers to the average man or woman on the street. It does not refer to a person with training in the law.

***Miranda* rule:** Evidence obtained by the police during custodial interrogations cannot be used in court during trial unless the defendant was first informed of the right not to incriminate oneself and the right to a lawyer.

***Miranda* warnings:** The warnings about the right against self-incrimination and the right to counsel that must be given to a person who is under custodial interrogation.

Mirandized: A term used by law enforcement officers to indicate that the suspect has been given the *Miranda* warnings.

misdemeanor: A crime usually punishable with jail time or other nonprison penalties.

monetary penalty: A sum of money exacted by an administrative agency for the doing of or failure to perform some act.

motion: A request made orally or in writing, asking the judge for a legal ruling on a something related to a case.

motion for a directed verdict of acquittal: A motion filed by the defense seeking acquittal of the accused before the prosecution failed to introduce sufficient evidence to convict the defendant.

motion for a mistrial: A motion filed seeking for the trial to be declared invalid before it is completed alleging improper conduct.

municipal custom: A persistent widespread practice that is so common or well settled as to constitute municipal policy.

municipal policy: A statement, ordinance, regulation, or decision that is officially adopted and promulgated by governmental authorities.

negligence tort: A tort that occurs when there is a breach of a common law or statutory duty to act reasonably toward those who may foreseeably be harmed by one's conduct.

neutral and detached magistrate: A magistrate who is not aligned with the government.

new approach to prisoners' rights: Prisoners have the same rights as people in the free world, except those rights that can be denied them for justified reasons.

new concept of electronic surveillance: Electronic surveillance is unconstitutional if it violates a reasonable expectation of privacy.

nolle prosequi motion: A motion seeking dismissal of charges.

nolo contendere plea: A plea of "no contest."

nondeadly force: Force that, when used, is not likely to result in serious bodily injury or death.

nonunanimous verdict: A verdict by a jury that is not the result of a unanimous vote.

official immunity: A defense in state tort cases if an act is discretionary, done in good faith, and the officer was acting within the scope of authority.

old approach to prisoners' rights: Prisoners had only a few rights because they are incarcerated.

old concept of electronic surveillance: Electronic surveillance was unconstitutional only if there was a trespass.

Open fields doctrine: All areas and outside of the curtilage. Areas inside the curtilage are protected by the Fourth Amendment; areas outside the curtilage are not.

open view: Applies to instances when the officer is out in open space but sees an item within an enclosed area.

original jurisdiction: The case is brought to the Court directly instead of on appeal.

parole: The prisoner is released before the end of his or her prison term, but subject to supervision by a parole officer.

Pen register: A device that records the phone numbers called from a phone.

peremptory challenge: The dismissal of a prospective juror for reasons that need not be stated.

petty offense: For purposes of a jury trial, it is an offense whose maximum penalty is six months or less.

photographic identification: A form of suspect identification where a victim or witness is shown photographs to try to identify the suspect.

physical self-incrimination: Involves real or physical evidence.

Plain odor doctrine: Related to the plain view doctrine, this doctrine states that officers may seize items when the odor emanating from the item indicate contraband (such as marijuana, which has a distinctive odor) is present.

plain touch doctrine: If an officer feels what he or she believes is a weapon, contraband, or evidence, the officer may expand the search or seize the object.

plain view doctrine: Items that are within the sight of an officer who is legally in the place from which the view is made may properly be seized without a warrant as long as such items are immediately recognizable as subject to seizure.

plea: An accused's response in court to the indictment or information.

plea bargain: Defendant agrees to plead guilty in exchange for a lower charge, a lower sentence, or other considerations.

positive school of criminology: Advocates that the penalty should "fit the offender" instead of the offense.

Posse comitatus: The authority of a sheriff or other law enforcement official, to conscript a citizen to assist the law enforcement officer in the apprehension of a felon. The authority existed at common law and was authorized under federal law in 1878.

preliminary hearing: A hearing held before a judge or magistrate within a reasonably short time after arrest.

presumptive sentences: A specified sentence is set by law, but may be increased or decreased depending on the presence of aggravating or mitigating circumstances.

pretextual stop: A valid stop that is used as a pretext to search a vehicle.

probable cause defense: A reasonable good faith belief in the legality of the action taken.

Preventive detention: The jailing of persons in order to prevent them from committing further offenses.

prima facie case: A case that is strong enough to prevail if it is not contradicted by the opposing party.

privilege of a witness: Any witness, other than an accused on the witness stand, has the privilege to refuse to disclose any information that may tend to incriminate him or her.

privilege of the accused: The privilege not to testify during trial.

probable cause: More than bare suspicion; it exists when the facts and circumstances within the officers' knowledge and of which they had reasonably trustworthy information are sufficient in themselves to warrant a man of reasonable caution in the belief that an offense has been or is being committed.

probation: A convicted offender is allowed to remain free in the community, subject to court-imposed conditions and under the supervision of a probation officer.

procedural due process: The legal process that is to be followed, depending upon the type of proceeding involved.

protective sweep: The police look at rooms or places in the house other than where the arrest takes place.

public duty doctrine: Government functions are owed to the general public but not to specific individuals, thus there is generally no liability for failing to protect a member of the public.

public safety exception: Responses to questions by the police without the *Miranda* warnings are admissible if the questions are reasonably prompted by concerns for public safety.

punitive force: Force that is used to punish rather than to accomplish lawful results.

purged taint exception: Evidence obtained is admissible if the defendant's subsequent voluntary act dissipates the taint of the initial illegality.

qualified immunity defense: An officer is not civilly liable unless he or she violated a clearly established statutory or constitutional right of which a reasonable person would have known.

racial profiling: Any police-initiated action that relies on race, ethnicity, or the national origin of an individual instead of on individual acts or behavior.

reasonable expectation of privacy: Exists when a person exhibits an actual expectation of privacy, and the expectation is one that society is prepared to recognize as reasonable.

reasonable force: Force that a prudent and cautious person would use if exposed to similar circumstances.

reasonable suspicion: That "Quantum of knowledge sufficient to induce an ordinarily prudent and cautious man under similar circumstances to believe criminal activity is at hand." Not defined with precision by the Court, but is a less demanding standard than probable cause.

rebuttal evidence: Evidence presented to destroy the credibility of witnesses or any evidence presented by the other side in a case.

release on recognizance (ROR): The release of a person without monetary bail.

restitution: A victim is restored to his or her original situation prior to the loss or injury.

retained counsel: An attorney chosen and paid by the accused.

reversal: The decision of the lower court is overthrown on appeal.

reverse-and-remand decision: The lower court's decision is reversed but the lower court can hear further arguments and give another decision in the case.

right to privacy: The right to be let alone.

rule of four: At least four justices must agree for the Court to consider the case on its merits.

rule of law: No person is above the law.

search: The exploration or examination of an individual's home, premises, or person to discover things or items that may be used by the government as evidence in a criminal proceeding.

search warrant: A written order, issued by a magistrate, directing a peace officer to search for property connected with a crime and bring it before the court.

Section 1983 case: A lawsuit filed under federal law that seeks damages from a police officer, supervisor, and/or department.

seizure: The taking of a person into custody.

selective incorporation: Only those rights considered fundamental should be applied to the states.

sentencing: The formal pronouncement of punishment following conviction in a criminal prosecution.

sentencing disparity: Different sentences given for similar crimes committed under similar circumstances.

sentencing guidelines: Guidelines that provide structure for judges by specifying the sentencing range that should be imposed for offenses.

sequestration: An order by the court keeping the jurors together during trial or deliberation and not allowing them to go home at night or weekends.

serious offense: For purposes of a jury trial, one for which more than six months imprisonment is authorized.

shock probation: An offender serves time in prison, after which he or she is discharged and placed on probation.

showup: One-on-one confrontation between a suspect and a witness to crime.

silver platter doctrine: Permitted federal courts to admit evidence illegally seized by state law enforcement officer and handed over to federal officers for use in federal cases.

sobriety checkpoints: A form of roadblock in which the police stop every vehicle for the purpose of controlling drunk driving.

special conditions: Conditions to meet the special needs of an offender.

special needs exception: An exception to the requirements of a warrant and probable cause under the Fourth Amendment; it allows warrantless searches and searches on less-than-probable cause in cases where there are needs to be met other than those of law enforcement, such as the supervision of high school students, probationers, and parolees.

special relationship: If a duty is owed to a particular person rather than to the general public, then a police officer or agency that breaches that duty can be held liable.

standing: A legal concept that determines whether a person can legally file a lawsuit or submit a petition to the court.

Standing mute: When a person charged with a crime refuses to enter a plea. In such circumstances, the judge will enter a plea of "not guilty" on the defendant's behalf, thereby forcing the prosecution to prove guilt beyond a reasonable doubt.

stare decisis: To abide by or adhere to, decided cases.

stationhouse detention: Detention takes place at the police station and is used for obtaining fingerprints, photographs, conducting police lineups, or securing identification or other types of evidence.

statutory law: Law passed by legislatures.

stop: Detaining a person briefly so the officer can ask questions.

substantive due process: There are aspects of a person's life that cannot be regulated by the government because they are so basic and private to the individual.

summons: A writ directed to the sheriff or other officer requiring the officer to notify a person that he or she must appear in court on a day named and answer the complaint.

telephonic warrant: Issued after a telephonic communication between the issuing judge and the officer.

testimonial self-incrimination: That which explicitly or implicitly relates a factual assertion or discloses information.

Title III of the Omnibus Crime Control and Safe Streets Act of 1968: Government agents cannot tap or intercept wire communications except if a court order has authorized the wiretap, or if consent is given by one of the parties.

tort: A civil wrong in which the action of one person causes injury to the person or property of another, in violation of a legal duty imposed by law.

total incorporation: All the rights in the Bill of Rights should be held as applying to the States.

total incorporation plus: In addition to applying all the provisions of the Bill of Rights to the States, other rights ought to be added, such as the right to clean air, clean water, and a clean environment.

transactional immunity: Full immunity, meaning the witness can no longer be prosecuted for any offense arising out of that act or transaction.

under color of law: When the officer uses power possessed by virtue of law and made possible only because the officer is clothed with the authority of the state.

USA PATRIOT Act: Acronym for the 2001 antiterrorism law, Uniting and Strengthening America by Providing Appropriate Tools Required to Intercept and Obstruct Terrorism Act of 2001, and subsequent amendments.

use and derivative use immunity: Partial immunity, meaning the witness can still be prosecuted on the basis of evidence other than his or her testimony, if the prosecutor has such independent evidence.

use-of-force continuum: Description of an escalating series of actions an officer may appropriately use, from no force to deadly force.

vehicle impoundment: Takes place when the police take control of a vehicle for law enforcement reasons.

vehicle inventory: The police list the personal effects and properties they find in the vehicle.

venire: A group of prospective jurors assembled according to procedures established by law.

venue: The place where a case is to be tried.

verdict: The pronouncement of defendant's guilt or innocence. A third pronouncement relating to mental health can occur in some states.

voir dire: A process in which prospective jurors are questioned to determine whether there are grounds for challenge.

voluntary statement: A statement given without coercion and of the suspect's own free will.

voluntary waiver: A waiver that is not the result of any threat, force, or coercion.

volunteered statement: One given by the suspect without interrogation.

***Wade-Gilbert* rule:** After being formally charged with a crime, a suspect in a lineup or other confrontation is entitled to have a lawyer present.

waiver: An intentional giving up of a known right or remedy.

wrongful death: When death occurs as a result of an officer's unlawful action or inaction.

Case Index

Subject Index

service of, 164
types of, 158
Assault, 447
Attorney General's Task Force on Violent Crime, 113

Bail, 40–41
Bail bond agents, 41
Battery, 447
Baze, Ralph, 416
Baze v. Rees, 416, 417–418
Belongings, 140
Bench warrants, 36, 158
Berkemer v. McCarty, 335, 336–337, 344
Bifurcated procedure, 60
Bifurcated trial, 414
Bill Blackwood Law Enforcement Management Institute of
    Texas (LEMIT), 306
Bill of indictment, 44
Bill of Rights, 362, 369, 389
    criminal procedure and, 34
    definition, 14
Binding over decision, 42
BJS. *See* Bureau of Justice Statistics (BJS)
Black's Law Dictionary, 291
Blackstone, Sir William, 369
Blanket exceptions, 174
Blended sentencing, 411
Blinded lineup, 307
Blood alcohol concentration (BAC), 319
Body cavity searches, 283
Booking, 38
Boot camps, 425
Border searches
    characteristics of, 282–283
    detention of alimentary canal smugglers, 284
    disassembling the gas tank, 284
    extent of government power in, 284–285
    factory surveys of aliens, 285
    motor vehicle inventory searches, 254–255
    searching vehicles away from the border, 284–285
    stopping vehicles at fixed checkpoints, 285
    strip, body cavity, and x-ray searches, 283
    summary of case law on, 285
    temporary detention of aliens believed to be illegal and, 283
Bowling, Thomas, 416
Brady rule
    on disclosure of evidence to the accused, 389
Brain fingerprinting, 321–322
Breathalyzer tests, 232, 319–320
Bright-line rule, 154
Brutality, 329
Bureau of Justice Statistics (BJS), 381
Burger, Warren E., 112
Buses, 221–222
Bush, George W., 481

CALEA. *See* Communications Assistance for Law
    Enforcement Act (CALEA) of 1994
Cameras
    to monitor tracking and other offenders, 479
Capias, 46, 165
Caproni, Valeri, 479

Case briefs, elements of, 27–29
Case-by-case incorporation, 23
Case citation, 25–26
Case law, 18
Cases
    on consent given by a co-occupant of a shared dwelling,
        204–205
    on exclusionary rule, 94–95
    on the good faith exception, 103
    on motor vehicle searches, 244
    on open fields doctrine, 277–278
    on plain view doctrine doctrine, 268–269
    on reasonable suspicion, 82–83
    on searches, 204–205
    on a search incident to an arrest, 204–205
    on stop and frisk, 120–121
    on the sufficiency of allegations for probable cause, 76–77
Cases illustrating the pre-*Miranda* voluntariness test, 328–330
    coercion and brutality-confession not valid, 329
    confession not voluntary-confession not valid, 329–330
    deception-confession not valid, 329
    suspect denied counsel at the police station-confession not
        valid, 330
CEDs. *See* Conducted energy devices (CEDs)
Cell phones, 218–219
Challenges for cause, 52, 373
Chimel rule, 205
"Christian burial" speech, 348
CIA, 318
Citations, 35–36, 165
Citizen's arrests, 178
City or county as defendant, 456–457
Civil lawsuits
    against the police, 450
Civil liability
    under federal law, 436–446
    under state tort law, 446–453
Civil liability under federal law, 436–446
    acting under color of law, 438
    defenses in Section 1983 cases, 439–446
    requirements for a Section 1983 lawsuit to succeed,
        437–439
    Section 1983, 437
    violation of a right, 438–439
Civil liability under state tort law, 446–453
    federal (Section 1983) and state tort cases compared, 453
    official immunity is a defense in state tort cases,
        452–453
    other sources of police, 451–452
    state tort cases, 446–451
Civil rights case. *See* Section 1983 cases
Claims of ineffective counsel
    in death penalty cases, 385–387
    during plea bargaining, 387
Class A misdemeanor, 405
Clearly established constitutional right, 442
Closed packages, 247–248
Closely related rule, 80–81
Closing arguments, 55–56
CODIS. *See* Combined DNA Index System (CODIS)
Coercion, 329
    mental (psychological), 328
    physical, 328

Motor vehicle searches. *See also* Motor vehicle inventory searches
    abandoned vehicles, 256
    accident cases, 257
    general rule, 240
    importance of state laws and department policies in, 258
    leading case on, 244
    objective reasonableness rule in, 244–245
    other issues, 251–255
    passenger compartment of, 170
    that are not contemporaneous, 251–252
    use of electronic devices to monitor vehicles, 253–254
    vehicle as subject of crime, 256
    warrantless, 245–251
    weapons in, 143
Motor vehicle stops
    application of stop and frisk, 141–143
    arrest for a nonjailable offense from, 234
    arrest if probable cause develops, 233
    arrests of vehicle passengers, 237
    based on race alone, 126
    based on racial profiling, 125
    Breathalyzer test requirement, 232
    general rule, 229–230
    importance of state laws and department policies in, 258
    locate and examine the VIN, 231–232
    Miranda warnings and, 231
    motor vehicle if probable cause is established, 233
    motor vehicle passengers' belongings, 233–234
    order driver and passengers to get out of the vehicle and, 230–231
    passengers seized in, 236
    as pretexts for vehicle searches, 234–236
    producing required documents and, 231
    roadblocks and, 237–240
    search based on consent, 234
    and searches with consent and freedom to leave, 236
    search passenger compartment, 170, 232
    search passengers' belongings, 233–234
    search vehicle if probable cause is established, 233
    what police can do after, 230–234
Mug-shot identification. *See* Photographic identifications
Munaf, Mohammad, 486–487
Municipal custom, 457. *See also* Municipal policy
Municipal policy, 457. *See also* Municipal custom

Narcoterrorism, 487
National Academy of Sciences, 315, 318
National DNA database, 315–316
National Institute of Justice, 181, 308, 312, 316
National Legal Aid & Defender Association, 381
Nazi war crimes, 394
Negligence tort, 448–451
Negligent lawyer, 385
Neil v. Biggers, 298, 301–302
Neutral and detached magistrate, 163, 198
New approach to prisoners' rights, 419
New concept of electronic surveillance, 466–467
New Jersey Supreme Court, 307, 308
News media, 398–399
New York Criminal Procedure, Article 140, § 140.50, 119
New York Police Department, 329
Nichols, Terry, 12, 13

Nolle prosequi motion, 44
Nolo contendere plea, 46
Noncriminal proceedings, 109
Nondeadly force, 447
    deadly force *vs.*, 180
    use of, 180
Nonjailable offenses, 177–178, 234
Nontestimonial self-incrimination
    vs. testimonial self-incrimination, 392–393
Nonunanimous verdicts
    defined, 371
    vs. unanimous verdicts, 371–372
Noriega, Manuel, 13

Obama, Barack, 481
Objective reasonableness rule, 244–245
Off-duty officers, 222
Office of Technology Assessment, 319
Officer misconduct, 91
Official immunity, 452. *See also* Partial immunity; Qualified immunity
    acting within the scope of authority, 453
    as a defense in state tort cases, 452–453
    defined, 452
    discretionary act, 453
    good faith, 453
Oklahoma bombing, 480
Old approach to prisoners' rights, 419
Old concept of electronic surveillance, 465–466
Oliver, Willard M., 484
Omar, Shawqi, 486–487
Omnibus Crime Control and Safe Streets Act of 1968, 469, 471
Open fields doctrine
    areas not included in, 272–279
    broader meaning of, 276
    definition, 272
    leading case on, 277–278
    plain view and, 279
    sense-enhancement technology and, 278
Open view, 270
Operation Cease-Fire, 131
Oral confessions, 357–358
Oral statements, 195
Ordinary citizens, information given by, 78
Original juridiction, 5

Padilla, Jose, 486
Parens patriae, 408
Parole, 420
    revocation hearings, 110
Parolees
    searches of, 212–213
    without suspicion, 131–132
Partial disclosure, 397
Partial immunity, 452. *See also* Official immunity
Pen registers, 474
Pepper spray, 181
Peremptory challenges, 52, 373
Petty offenses, 176
    defined, 373
    vs. serious offenses, 372–373
Photo array identification. *See* Photographic identifications
Photographic identifications, 290, 303–305

RANK / CASE	HOLDING	VOTE AND MAJORITY OPINION WRITER	CHAPTER IN THE BOOK	PAGE
15. *Illinois v. Gates,* 462 U.S. 213 (1983)	A warrant may be issued on the basis of an affidavit that is entirely hearsay (such as when a police officer swears to facts reported to him or her by the crime victim, witnesses, or police informants). However, the affidavit must show by a totality of the circumstances that there is a fair probability that contraband or evidence of a crime will be found in a particular place.	6 to 3 Justice Rehnquist	3	71
16. *Whren v. United States,* 517 U.S. 806 (1996)	The temporary detention of a motorist that is supported by probable cause to believe that the motorist has committed a traffic violation is valid even if the actual motivation of the law enforcement officer is to determine if the motorist has drugs.	9 to 0 Justice Scalia	8	234
17. *Tennessee v. Garner,* 411 U.S. 1 (1985)	It is constitutionally reasonable for a police officer to use deadly force when the officer has probable cause to believe that the suspect poses a threat or serious physical harm, either to the officer or to others.	6 to 3 Justice White	6	182
18. *New York v. Belton,* 453 U.S. 454 (1981)	The police may examine the contents of any container found in the passenger compartment of a car, as long as it may reasonably be thought to contain something that might pose a danger to the officer or hold evidence in support of the offense for which the suspect has been arrested.	6 to 3 Justice Stewart	8	246
19.[†] *Brady v. Maryland,* 373 U.S. 83 (1963)	Due process is violated when the prosecution suppresses evidence favorable to an accused upon request where the evidence is material either to guilt or to punishment. This applies whether the prosecution acted in bad faith or in good faith in suppressing the evidence.	7 to 2 Justice Douglas	Not applicable	

Note: The selections and ranking are likely controversial. They are subjective choices, made by the author after consultation with several colleagues. Comments, disagreements, and suggestions are welcome and will be considered in preparing the next edition.

[*]*Not discussed in this text. A Sentencing case.*

[†]*Not discussed in this text. A Rights of the Accused case.*

THE
CRIMINAL JUSTICE
SYSTEM

CRIME

CONVICTION

REFUSAL TO INDICT

GRAND JURY

CHARGES DISMISSED

FELONIES

GATHER INFORMATION

PRELIMINARY HEARNING

ARRAIGNMENT

TRIAL

REDUCTION OF CHARGE

PLEA BARGAIN

MISDEMEANORS

PRELIMINARY HEARNING

CHARGES DISMISSED

REPORTED AND OBSERVED CRIME

UNRESOLVED CRIME OR NO ARREST

INVESTIGATION

CHARGES DROPPED OR DISMISSED

BAIL OR DETENTION HEARING

ARRAIGNMENT

TRIAL

RELEASED WITHOUT PROSECUTION

ARREST

CHARGES DROPPED OR DISMISSED

INITIAL APPEARANCE

RELEASED WITHOUT PROSECUTION

CHARGES FILED

PLEA BARGAIN

ENTRY INTO THE SYSTEM   PROSECUTION AND PRETRIAL SERVICES   ADJUDICATION